The Belgian Essays

The Pensionnat Heger in the later nineteenth century. *Le Soir*, Brussels.

The Belgian Essays

Charlotte Brontë and Emily Brontë

Edited and translated by Sue Lonoff

A Critical Edition

YALE UNIVERSITY PRESS   NEW HAVEN AND LONDON

Designed by Rebecca Gibb.
Set in Times Roman type by The Composing Room of Michigan, Inc., Grand Rapids,
Michigan
Printed in the United States of America by BookCrafters, Inc., Chelsea, Michigan

Library of Congress Cataloging-in-Publication Data
Brontë, Charlotte, 1816–1855.
The Belgian essays / Charlotte Brontë and Emily Brontë:
edited and translated by Sue Lonoff.
p.   cm.
Includes bibliographical references and index.
ISBN 0-300-06489-6 (cloth : alk. paper)
1. Brontë, Charlotte, 1816–1855—Translations into English.
2. Brontë, Emily, 1818–1848—Translations into English. 3. College
prose, French—Translation into English. I. Brontë, Emily,
1818–1848. II. Lonoff de Cuevas, Sue. III. Title.
PR4165.E54B76   1996
844'.708—dc20
                                                                                    95-48323
                                                                                    CIP

A catalogue record for this book is available from the British Library.

10   9   8   7   6   5   4   3   2   1

For John

Contents

Devoirs (Essays) of 1843

Illustrations

Preface

It's in all the Brontë biographies. On February 15, 1842, at the ages of twenty-five and twenty-three, Charlotte and Emily Brontë became students at the Pensionnat Heger in Brussels. For the next nine months they worked unrelentingly, until their aunt's death took them back to Haworth. In January, Charlotte went to Brussels for a second year, ostensibly to teach while she continued her studies, actually to be near Constantin Heger, the professor she would later call her "master" and the husband of the pensionnat's directrice. She left again on New Year's Day of 1844, never to return to the Continent. But memories of her foreign venture stayed with her. Over time she would fix on them, heighten them, build on them, and finally rewrite them in her novels.

Yet despite the hundreds of published descriptions of the Pensionnat Heger and the life the sisters led there, this remains a chapter with many pages missing. Only three years later, in 1847, the Brontës emerged as major Victorian authors. How did those months in Brussels conduce to that emergence? Beyond the often-analyzed effects of Charlotte's passion, could there have been a writer's connection?

"They wanted learning. They came for learning. They would learn," Elizabeth Gaskell wrote later.[1] The most direct proofs of that learning are their *devoirs,* the essays that they wrote in response to Constantin Heger's instructions. "Homework" is one translation of *devoir,* and if the Brontës had been ordinary schoolgirls set to doing grammar drills and pattern-book assignments, their homework might have vanished with no loss. But they came to the pensionnat as prolific writers with years of juvenilia behind them. They encountered a professor who also broke the mold, a man whose energy to teach matched theirs to learn. So despite the evident restrictions—composing under orders and in a foreign language—they wrote some extraordinary essays.

Heger soon recognized their talent; already in the habit of saving student samples, he preserved a number of their devoirs. Charlotte too tended to preserve what she had written, so much of her Brussels work returned with her to Haworth, where it stayed until after her death. Both collections gradually thinned out. Heger gave manuscripts to eager friends and students;[2] Charlotte's, which became her husband's property, were bought by a dealer who scattered them.[3] Still, by the early 1980s thirty compositions were on record—nine by Emily, the rest by Charlotte—together with second drafts, fragments, and dictations that often have a bearing on the texts.[4]

This material remains little known and less examined. Twelve of Charlotte's devoirs have been published, four of them solely in translation; this count includes the two that Gaskell printed in 1857. Emily's devoirs are more accessible; eight have been printed, two bilingually, the rest in French or in English translation. Of the published versions by either sister, only seven include evidence of Heger's responses, though in manuscript the pages may be thick with them. Scholarly studies are similarly spotty, perhaps two dozen articles or chapters over the past century,[5] and of all the biographies written since Gaskell's, only the most recent, Juliet Barker's, examines the devoirs as an integral part of the sisters' experience in Brussels.[6]

Why have these texts received so little attention, unlike the least scrap of their fiction, poems, and letters?[7] Perhaps because, as literature, they seem so insignificant, so foreign to the Brontës' English writings. Perhaps because their language makes them marginal. Perhaps because the manuscripts look so unpromising: mold-flecked pages, often scored with corrections, now gathered in archives on two continents. Typically, the Brontës wrote on paper from their notebooks, which they ruled and sometimes bound with cotton thread. The author's name went at the top left, the date at top right; a centered title followed, with a double line beneath it, and then the composition in a clear and careful script, a receptor for far less tidy comments. Even now, rebound in leather or preserved in mats and folders, they retain an inescapable identity as homework, themes written by two students learning French.

But readers of the devoirs should not be misled by their format or their obvious objectives. Examining them closely leads to recognition— these writings were pivotal for both the Brontë sisters—and to unpredictable discoveries. Little enough remains in any case by Emily: the poems, the single novel, the diary papers, fragments. Even if she wrote reluctantly and sparely, nine essays make a difference to the record. Charlotte's devoirs tell a more complex story. They offer vital clues to her growth as a writer, evidence and signals of transition. They give evidence, as well, of her exposure to new concepts, to critical analysis, to literature. Her two terms in Brussels engendered major changes in the ways she thought about composing. The devoirs exemplify some of those changes. Others would germinate years later in Haworth, coming to fruition in the plots of her novels, as well as in their style and form and language.

At the pensionnat, the Brontës kept to themselves. As English Protestants, provincial and overaged, they would have been outsiders in any case. For the purposes of learning, they could manage to comply; Charlotte even found herself submitting happily. But their more profound response to this new culture was entrenchment: in work, in their beliefs, and in their difference. Nevertheless, it is crucial to remember that they did not live or work in a vacuum. Insular they may have been, but never inattentive. As children they had learned to soak up information and recycle it into their plays. Their fantasies were fed by facts, political, historical, religious, literary, geographic. Living in Brussels and studying under Heger exposed them to new authors, new conditions for writing, and a teacher who urged them to experiment. Charlotte took to Heger's system, thriving intellectually even when her optimism soured. Emily did not, but she accepted necessity and wrote her resistance as well as her ideas into the papers he assigned.

It follows that the devoirs are rarely simple documents, even when they look brief and obvious. They refer to sources in French and English, some apparent, others little known or subtle. They link to other Brontë writings, earlier and later, again in ways both plain and less detectable. Connections emerge too among the devoirs themselves, especially when their sources are traced and identified, and when they are read as related sets or as pairs responding to the same assignment. Heger's comments interject questions and suggestions as well as immediate revisions; they often prompt Charlotte to read and think further, with results that emerge in later essays.

In sum, the devoirs are a network of resources for anyone concerned with the Brontës. But to be explored, they must be accurately published, translated, and set within their multiple contexts. In this volume, I have tried to do those things.

My first aim was to make all the known texts available, in complete and readable transcriptions. Uncorrected devoirs posed few legibility problems since, aside from two rough drafts by Charlotte, they are compositions written to be read by a foreigner, not minuscule juvenilia manuscripts. But those that Heger laced and interlaced with corrections could not be transcribed legibly without some compromises; manuscript notes explain the changes. In a few cases, they are so overwritten that I also provide an unmarked version. Accurate transcription was also complicated by Heger's handwriting, his unexplained abbreviations, his intricate insertions, and his marking symbols—an array of lines, slashes, and carets. But whatever the problems entailed in reproduction, to decipher what he wrote is to gain access to the dialogue between an exceptional teacher and his students and to see how all three went about their work. Charlotte's *dictées* further illuminate that process; they too are reprinted here whenever they are clearly a source for her devoirs or Emily's.

My second aim, accurate translation of the devoirs, posed literary rather than technical questions. These are essays written in far from perfect French by authors who, in English, are extraordinary stylists. To what extent should their roughness be preserved? In Emily's case, a literal translation can make the sense of the original clearer because she often stuck to English rather than French syntax and thought of English rather than French idioms. In Charlotte's case, the question is tougher. More advanced in French, more attuned to its cadences, and keener to show

Heger what she was learning, she struggled to make her devoirs eloquent. Strict translation safeguards the record of her struggles and reveals her striking progress over time. It also enables English readers to understand the purposes of Heger's interventions. But ambition sometimes led her into awkward constructions that would not only jar if they were literally translated but might also belie what she intended. To try second-guessing her intentions, however, by putting her French into Brontëan English could lead to distortion—and parody. My solution was to do modern versions that stay as close to the originals as possible without emphasizing the errors. They can be checked against the typescripts in French that appear on facing pages.

The third and final aim of this edition, to set the devoirs in their multiple contexts, entailed more decisions than the others. Which contexts, in the first place, should be explicated? The site, rooms, furniture, and garden of the pensionnat have been described by dozens of Brontë biographers, from Gaskell through Rebecca Fraser. Accounts of Heger's dramatic personality and its effects on one susceptible student have multiplied since Charlotte wrote *Villette*. But if attention has been lavished on the man and the setting, much less has been paid to the kinds of instruction the Brontës received as Heger's students or to the influence, immediate and long-term, that he exerted over them as writers. Gaskell's interview with him remains the primary account, but she met him fourteen years after Charlotte's departure, a fact that should prompt at least tentative questions about the exactness of his memories. Further accounts of the Brontës and the Hegers have been given by younger and later students, but few connections have been drawn between these memoirs and the essays the sisters produced. The books Heger consulted for his lectures and dictées are a more specific source of information; Enid Duthie and David H. Musselwhite have checked into some of them, but many more remain to be traced. Then (as I have said) there are the clues within the devoirs, relationships among texts, and the retrospective hints that Charlotte's four novels provide. Finally, these writings have to be considered in the context of the sisters' lives and works.

Deciding where and how to present this information was a further editorial issue. A chronology, notes, and comments on each devoir—or, in four cases, on corresponding pairs—were basic requirements for a scholarly edition of texts as little studied as these. In coming to decisions I was guided by two images. The first one was of readers asking, Why do the devoirs matter? How did writing them affect the two Brontës? What stories lie behind them? And what about Heger? In answer, I wrote the introduction. The second image was of a scholar-archaeologist, excavating in libraries rather than digs, who would not only have to piece the fragments together but also explain what the evidence signified and how it might amplify a reader's understanding of individual devoirs and their ambience. That image guided me in the construction of the comments. The more exhaustive apparatus of scholarship has been relegated to the back of the book, where it appears in notes and an appendix.

Gaps remain in the record, inevitably. Heger's library is gone, as are his notes (if he kept them), and so are any notes and dictées of Emily's. Two of Charlotte's devoirs known earlier in this century, "L'Ingratitude" and "Lettre d'un Missionaire, Sierre-Leone, Afrique," have disappeared. And the number of devoirs on record almost certainly falls short of the number they produced. According to the dates on the manuscripts, for instance, a month elapsed between Charlotte's first and second devoirs; then, within the space of two weeks, she did three more. A creative writer might compose in fits and starts, but in a well-regulated school like the pensionnat, assignments would have fallen due more steadily.

Perhaps other devoirs will surface if the known texts attract more attention. This edition is a step in that direction.

Acknowledgments

This edition was begun at the suggestion of Juliet R. W. Barker, whose help has continued through the years. It was prepared with the assistance of Anna Marshall Shields and Sabine Mourlon-Beernaert, who helped me to decipher, transcribe, edit, and proofread the devoirs. Shelley Salamensky and Monique Tyc also assisted in the editing. Grants from the Derek Bok Center, Harvard University, made this assistance possible and James D. Wilkinson, the center's director, provided additional help.

The Hegers' great-great-great grandson, François Fierens, gave me generous access to his family's archives and to material not previously published. I am indebted as well to the books and correspondence of Christine Alexander and Enid Duthie; to Linda Simon, for her advice on the introduction; to Janet Larson, for her research leads; to Anne Anninger, for providing definitions of the Brontë sisters' lettering; to Timothy Boyd, for information on classical allusions; to Janet Gezari, for her helpful review of the manuscript; and to Jane Sellars for her encouragement.

I gratefully acknowledge permission to reproduce the devoirs from the Brotherton Collection, Leeds University Library (and to Christopher Sheppard for his help); the Brontë Parsonage Museum (and to Kathryn White, Ann Dinsdale and Sally Johnson for their help); the British

Library; François Fierens; the Friends Historical Library of Swarthmore College; the Huntington Library; the Henry W. and Albert A. Berg Collection, The New York Public Library, Astor, Lenox and Tilden Foundations; the Parrish Collection, Princeton University Library; the Robert H. Taylor Collection, Princeton University Library; the John Rylands University Library of Manchester; and the Harry Ransom Humanities Research Center, the University of Texas at Austin. The collections of the Widener, Andover, and Houghton Libraries at Harvard made it possible to read many sources in editions available to Heger. I am also grateful to librarians at the Bibliothèque Royale Albert Ier, Brussels, and to Ruth Rogers and Marilyn Hatch, Special Collections, Margaret Clapp Library, Wellesley College.

The editing and production of this book was made possible by Ellen Graham, Jonathan Brent, Cynthia Wells, Lawrence Kenney, Rebecca Gibb, and Susan Abel of the Yale University Press and by Sarah St. Onge, an extraordinary manuscript editor. Transcription of the devoirs in WordPerfect 5.1 was facilitated by that company's support staff, which spent patient hours answering my questions.

Finally, this edition owes its existence to John de Cuevas, who revised translations and read and reread the manuscript with exhaustless patience.

L'instituteur doit activer la pensée de son élève, développer son intelligence, rectifier son jugement, le munir de bons principes, et le mettre à même des précieux matériaux qui lui fournissent les annales de l'esprit humain; c'est ensuite à l'élève à bâtir l'edifice. Au sortir de ses classes, un bon élève a appris à apprendre; le professeur a développé les forces de son intelligence en les exerçant et en les dirigeant; c'est maintenant à lui de les appliquer.

The instructor must activate the thinking of his student, develop his intelligence, rectify his judgment, arm him with good principles, and set before him those precious materials that provide him with the record of the human spirit; after that, it is up to the student to build the edifice. On leaving his classes, a good student has learned how to learn; the professor has developed the powers of his intelligence in exercising and directing them; it is now up to him to apply them.

—from the prospectus of the Athénée Royal (1844)

Introduction

The Two Sisters

In 1839 Charlotte Brontë wrote "The Last of Angria," announcing her intention to abandon the fervid plots and settings of her youthful romances. Though post-Angrian material continued to trickle out through the end of 1840, she ended the saga after that year or destroyed whatever she attempted. When she resumed writing in 1846 or began once again to retain her manuscripts, her work was of a different order: far more realistic, limited, and local—distinctive in its style, but not inflated.

It has been argued, with justice, that Charlotte's best work transposes the romantic intensity of the juvenilia to a context that is psychologically and factually credible.[1] Nonetheless, a gap remains. The novels stand apart from her earlier stories, and they are unquestionably better. How did she effect the transformation? What happened to the writer in that interval?

If I specify "writer," it is because the normal question—what happened to *her*—has been answered. Two months short of her twenty-sixth birthday, hungry for experience and possibly for romance, Charlotte encountered thirty-two-year-old Constantin Georges Romain Heger. At first he struck her as absurdly temperamental, a domineering, dark-browed little man. But his potent intelligence and passion for literature aroused her even as she mocked him. Respect turned into homage and then into obsession. She had to return for a second year in Brussels, though she seems to have denied the kind of feeling that prompted her, at least while she remained within the pensionnat. But Zoë Parent-Heger (five years older than her husband) evidently understood the situation and took discreet measures to control it. Charlotte found herself increasingly cut off from her professor, kept at a distance from the unsuspecting husband by the wife she would resent for a lifetime. Her bitter isolation was further reinforced by her contempt for Catholics and Belgians. After months of indecision and deepening depression, she resolved to go home to Haworth Parsonage. More agony followed; she passed two years in which, she said, her happiness and peace of mind abandoned her. She suffered from confinement, from a fear of going blind, from family problems, from emotional privation. Ultimately, she came to terms with her experience and sublimated feeling into fiction. That, at least, is the prevailing explanation.[2]

But redirected passion and hard-won maturity fall short as explanations for the radical changes in Charlotte's methods, style, focus, and authority. The question of the gap remains: what happened to her writing, if she did not give it up or destroy it? The answer, for the months she spent in Brussels at any rate, is that she continued to write but in a new form, the form of the essay or devoir.

A sketch of her background as a writer and student may explain why this shift in genre mattered. In the thirteen years of writing that preceded her first trip, Charlotte Brontë had produced at least 103 prose manuscripts and another 180 poetry manuscripts.[3] She had taught herself how to describe, how to narrate, and how to develop character and dialogue. So although her early tales are uneven, they constitute a rigorous apprenticeship. Her formal education had been patchy: ten dismal months at the Clergy Daughters School at Cowan Bridge when she was eight and nine;[4] then, when she was fourteen, the first of three half-years at Miss Wooler's school at Roe Head. Like her siblings, however, she had read everything that came her way, sat listening while her aunt and father spoke of current events, and transposed what she learned into her fiction. With a freedom accorded few grown women of the period, she had pursued whatever held her interest: politics, history, the classics, myth and literature, geography, the lives of famous men.[5] More traditionally, she grew up on the Bible.

Her attraction to things French was apparent a dozen years before she made plans to go to Brussels. French characters began to appear in her fiction as early as 1829.[6] In 1830, when she was fourteen, she translated the first book of *The Henriade*, by Voltaire.[7] Exactly four months later, she changed the name of the Glass Town (capital and center of the children's juvenilia) to a compound French and Greek word: "Verreopolis." Heger told Gaskell that the Brontës knew no French, but Charlotte's friend Ellen Nussey contradicts him, and so does the fact that she won the French prize at the end of her second term at Roe Head.[8] Before Charlotte went there she knew "a little French," and at the school "[s]he soon began to make a good figure in French lessons." That knowledge helped her "when afterwards she was engaged in translation or dictation."[9] She also used French (faultily) in writing to Ellen and in many of her juvenilia narratives.[10] In her stories, she associates the language with Paris, and Paris with glamour and high culture. She links it too with worldliness; the characters who linger there are often disillusioned or corrupted. She never visited the city of her fantasies. A Paris school was far beyond the Brontës' narrow means and, very possibly, beyond her father's tolerance. But in settling for Brussels and the Pensionnat Heger, she began to trade illusion for reality.

Her position as a student, in itself, gave rise to changes beyond the obvious shifts in place and language. For the first time, she would show nearly everything she wrote to an audience outside the family circle. In Haworth, she had hypothesized an audience: subscribers to the magazines that she and Branwell edited, the readers she addressed within her fictions. But when she tried to reach beyond her fantasy audience—she sought advice from Southey and then Hartley Coleridge—she met with condescension and discouragement.[11] In Brussels, her reader was neither a projection nor a stranger who would toss her work aside. Heger was a teacher she could ardently respect: "*the only master I have ever had.*"[12]

Of course, her Yorkshire readers were not all imaginary. She wrote letters to her family and friends, and at Roe Head School she probably wrote themes.[13] But those writings were in one sphere, the world in which she moved and worked, while Glass Town and then Angria formed a separate sphere, or "world below," the children's own term for their creation. That disjunction became dangerous. The Angrian saga was absorbingly private, its references a maze no untrained reader could negotiate. It functioned as a refuge from reality, an opiate, impeding her progress as a novelist. Increasingly, she sensed the limitations of a fiction that was overheated, tortuous, and implausible. But the habits formed through all those years of writing overpowered her whenever she tried, alone, to break them.

In Brussels, the barriers started crumbling. At night she still got caught up in her Angrian visions, especially in her lonely second term. But the devoirs represented a more public mode of writing in a language that released the hold of habit. She had to think in French, or do accurate translations, and make her thoughts accessible and clear. Composing on demand necessitated further changes. To write the kind of devoir that would satisfy Heger, she had to fuse creative and expository methods, to invent yet still accede to formal discipline.

Lawrence Dessner speculates, rightly, that Charlotte's months in Belgium were "a time of crucial intellectual and artistic growth."[14] In part, that growth resulted from exposure to new sources: the extracts Heger read aloud and lectured on; the works she consulted before she wrote her devoirs; more broadly, her excursions into Brussels and the countryside and life within that smaller world, the pensionnat. In part, it resulted from Heger's efforts to make her a more reflective writer. The change from unself-conscious to premeditated writing, together with the shift into a language not her own, led to more than occasional awkwardness. Still, she was taking firm if clumsy steps away from the solipsistic universe of Angria.

This motive for studying abroad, however, had to be kept from her family. Maria Branwell never would have funded the trip if she had realized she was furthering her niece's ambition to become a professional writer. Charlotte's stated purpose was to add to her accomplishments so that she and her two younger sisters could establish a school of their own.

From the time she started planning her Belgian venture, she had Emily in mind as her companion. Anne, the youngest sibling, was to have her turn later, if their plans for a school worked out. Charlotte's success in persuading her reclusive sibling was probably furthered by Emily's own vision of running a school close to home with her sisters—and enjoying the income it would bring them. She spells out that vision in the diary paper she wrote six months before their journey: "I guess that at the time appointed for the opening of this paper [four years from July 30, 1841]—we (i.e.) Charlotte, Anne, and I—shall be all merrily seated in our own sitting-room in some pleasant and flourishing seminary having just gathered in for the midsummer holydays our debts will be paid off, and we shall have cash in hand to a considerable amount. papa, Aunt and Branwell will either have been—or be coming—to visit us—it will be a fine warm summery[?] evening. very different from this bleak lookout. . . ."[15] She may also have gone, at least in part, to please Charlotte, who thought of the trip as a reward for her sister and who might not have been allowed to realize her own dreams if a member of the family had not joined her.[16]

Heger's long- and short-term influence on Emily is much less clear than his influence on Charlotte, not only because the evidence is meager, but because her writing seems so independent. In her diary paper of 1845, the only account she left of those months, she simply notes that she and Charlotte went to Brussels and that they returned "in consequence of Aunt's death."[17] It is Charlotte who, as usual, speaks for her sister, here, in a memoir she wrote in 1850. Emily, she says, failed miserably when she first attempted formal schooling (at Roe Head),

> and it was some years before the experiment of sending her
> from home was again ventured on. After the age of twenty, hav-
> ing meantime studied alone with diligence and perseverance,
> she went with me to an establishment on the Continent: the
> same suffering and conflict ensued, heightened by the strong re-
> coil of her upright, heretic and English spirit from the gentle
> Jesuitry of the foreign and Romish system. Once more she
> seemed sinking, but this time she rallied through the mere force
> of resolution: with inward remorse and shame she looked back
> on her former failure, and resolved to conquer in this second
> ordeal. She did conquer: but the victory cost her dear. She was

never happy till she carried her hard-won knowledge back to the remote English village. . . .[18]

Charlotte edits out her part in the experiment by using the passive phrase "was . . . ventured on." Still, her account accords with everything now known about Emily's character.

Unlike Charlotte, Emily never wanted wings that would carry her away from Haworth; she never would have gone to Brussels hoping to find "connections far more improving, polished, and cultivated, than any [she] had yet known."[19] She had no desire to give up her juvenilia, the Gondal cycle she and Anne shared. In fact, she drafted Gondal poems in Belgium.[20]

It is tempting to read "Self-Interrogation," the last of the three, as a personal reflection:

> "The vanished day? It leaves a sense
> Of labour hardly done;
> Of little, gained with vast expense,—
> A sense of grief alone!"

But the lines are in quotation, and their speaker is imaged as an aging soldier, reproached by time and conscience, who has "little learnt to bear" his defeat.[21] Later references to fighting could be metaphorical but seem to point to Gondal's civil wars. And even if she did project her mood into her speaker, Emily was no defeated warrior. Whatever her attitude toward Heger and his teaching, she had not left home to squander her time. Once committed, she drove herself relentlessly. She learned passable French and the rudiments of German, she gained skill in drawing,[22] and, studying under Heger's brother-in-law, "the best professor [of music] in Belgium,"[23] she rapidly improved as a pianist.

The Brontës' industry and progress delighted the Hegers who, from the first, had approved the sisters' purpose in seeking instruction abroad. They themselves had been drawn together by a mutual dedication to teaching,[24] and they remained professionals who shared responsibilities, the wife managing the school and its expenses, the husband teaching there and at the Athénée Royal (the high school for boys across the way). If, despite this sharing, Constantin Heger held basically conservative views about women's roles, he recognized that people placed as the Brontës were would need an education to maintain themselves. He later told Gaskell how he and his wife had warmed to "the simple earnest tone" of Charlotte's letter of inquiry: "These are the daughters of an English pastor, of moderate means, anxious to learn with an ulterior view of instructing others, and to whom the risk of additional expense is of great consequence. Let us name a specific sum, within which all expenses shall be included."[25] These themes emerge again in the letter he sent to Patrick Brontë after Aunt Branwell's death: "In a year each of your daughters would have been quite prepared for any eventuality of the future; each of them while receiving instruction was at the same time acquiring the science of teaching."[26]

Heger almost certainly continued to believe that he was preparing and encouraging the Brontës to become successful teachers in England. In the meantime, they were gifted and assiduous students, a credit to the school and to his methods. "With such pupils we have had but little to do," he declared to Patrick Brontë in seeking their return, "their advancement is your work more than ours. We have not had to teach them the value of time and instruction; they had learnt all that in their paternal home, and we, on our part, have had only the feeble merit of directing their efforts and providing suitable aliment for the praiseworthy activity for which your daughters are indebted to your example and teaching."[27] This declaration is more telling as a sample of his prose than as a comment on his merits or their father's. Charlotte and Emily had formed their own work habits, and Heger's apparently modest disclaimer belies the complexity of his intervention and the power he exerted in the classroom.

The Professor and His System

By all accounts, Constantin Heger was an unforgettable teacher. According to one obituary notice, he had "a precious gift, a sort of intellectual magnetism, by virtue of which he entered the mind of a student, exciting its curiosity [and] keeping it incessantly alert. . . ."[28] Even for students immune to that gift, he was a force that could not be disregarded, a teacher who blended sensitivity with discipline, histrionics and high-handedness with unaffected kindness, and openness with judgment and authority. For much of his life, he held a full-time post at the Athénée Royal, where he specialized in rhetoric and literature and, by his own choice, taught the youngest class of boys. He also taught classes to the girls at his wife's pensionnat, gave dramatic readings to her whole school on some evenings, and spent others doing charitable work. (In his Prize Day speech of 1834 at the Athénée, he had noted that "the number of children attending school in Belgium is *one* out of *eleven* inhabitants." He later gave free evening classes to laborers and the poor).[29] When the Brontës arrived, the Hegers had three daughters, and Zoë Heger was visibly pregnant with the son she gave birth to six weeks later. She had a fourth daughter toward the end of Charlotte's last term and a second son three years later. Heger was devoted to his wife, his growing family, his religion, and his profession.

Although his schedule left him little time for private lessons, he believed in personal commitment to his students—to all of them, not just the special cases. As he told the abbé Richardson, who came to him for help, a teacher should be guided by two precepts: "His first requirement was perfect self-sacrifice . . . 'un dévou absolu' were his words. . . . For him the foundation, and the essential requirements for success [in the classroom] were order and discipline . . . obtained not by fear, but by patience and unfailing watchfulness. . . . His next precept was to study the pupils, to know each one of them, to neglect none, and above all never to allow an aversion towards any [to enter one's heart]."[30] According to Frederika Macdonald, who studied at the pensionnat in 1859, he excelled "in calling out one's best faculties; in stimulating one's natural gifts; in lifting one above satisfaction with mediocrity; in fastening one's attention on models of perfection; in inspiring one with a sense of reverence and love for them. . . ."[31]

These reminiscences accord with Gaskell's interview and subsequent description of his methods. First, in keeping with his policies, he studied his new English pupils. What he saw convinced him that they could learn French without the usual drilling in grammar and vocabulary. (Charlotte's early notebooks include such exercises, but probably another teacher gave them.) After consulting with his wife, he decided to teach them by a "new plan." Actually, the method was one he had "occasionally" employed with his older French and Belgian students, though not with pupils learning the language. It entailed reading them "some of the master-pieces of the most celebrated French authors." Then he would move from the whole to the parts, pointing out the author's strengths and weaknesses. The field might be literature, religion, or history, the extract a portrait, poem, or narrative. He would indicate aspects of its style and technique and then direct the sisters to write a composition that would "[reproduce] their own thoughts in a somewhat similar manner."[32] As they improved, he advanced to "synthetical teaching," presenting and contrasting several accounts of the same event or individual. He would prompt them to trace the differences back to the perspectives and characters of the various authors. "And from these conflicting characters," Gaskell concludes, "he would require them to sift and collect the elements of truth, and try to unite them into a perfect whole."[33]

At least one of Charlotte's notebooks supports this explanation.[34] It contains copies of the extracts Heger dictated, and for several of those dictées there are corresponding devoirs. For example, he dictated Chateaubriand's "Evening Prayer on Board a Ship"; she wrote a devoir, "Evening Prayer in a Camp." He dictated a passage from Chateaubriand's *The Martyrs*; she wrote about the Protestant Anne Askew's martyrdom. He dictated Michaud's "Capture of Jerusalem by the Crusaders" and Hugo's "Mirabeau on the Tribune"; she wrote about Peter, the hermit-crusader, and modeled her methods after Hugo's.

But the devoirs of both sisters suggest that Heger did not always give assignments of this kind. Some were much simpler: compose an invitation and have the recipient turn it down. Others were more structured: he would dictate an outline of *la matière*, or content, and leave them to fill in the details. In one case, Millevoye's "The Fall of the Leaves," he apparently asked Charlotte to consider how the poem produced its effects on the reader.

In his interview with Gaskell, Heger gives the impression that he devised assignments for the Brontës exclusively. That too is less than fully accurate, for even if he meant to give them special attention, Heger was a very busy teacher. As Charlotte told Ellen three months after arriving, the "few private lessons" he had "vouchsafed to give" them were to be considered "a great favour."[35] It seems likely that she transcribed some, perhaps most, of her dictées in a class with other students; that she and

Emily (when her French improved enough) did assignments normally required of the others; and that when Heger gave them private lessons, he recycled at least some of his readings and lectures from his more advanced classes at the pensionnat or Athénée.[36] Translations of English excerpts into French he probably assigned to Charlotte alone, since no one else was equipped to do them, but they would not entail much preparation time.

Both the Gaskell interview and the devoirs make it clear that Heger set the terms of each assignment, with the exception of Charlotte's "Jane" fragment and perhaps a few texts from her second year. Even when his instructions are not extant, they can sometimes be conjectured from the devoirs. In the first term, they seem to have been quite specific; later, when Charlotte was teaching and studying, he probably gave her more latitude. But even when he supervised their writing projects closely, he recognized their need for self-expression. As he said to Gaskell, "it is necessary . . . before sitting down to write on a subject, to have thoughts and feelings about it. I cannot tell on what subject your heart and mind have been excited. I must leave that to you."[37]

To this system, the sisters responded so differently that they almost seem to have encountered two professors: Charlotte's master and Emily's autocrat. Charlotte took to the discipline that Heger imposed. She welcomed his mentorship because it suited her to read and write responsively. As she told Ellen Nussey in an often-quoted passage, "I was twenty-six years old a week or two since—and at that ripe time of life I am a schoolgirl—a complete school-girl and on the whole very happy in that capacity It felt very strange at first to submit to authority instead of exercising it—to obey orders instead of giving them—but I like that state of things—I returned to it with the same avidity that a cow that has long been kept on dry hay returns to fresh grass. . . ."[38] But to believe that she submitted as calmly as a cow is to misunderstand her motives and his methods. If a few early pieces stick closely to his models—"The Sick Young Girl" is the obvious example—the rest display initiative and, despite some shaky French, a rhetoric that marks them as her own. And she would only have consented to obey a teacher who earned her respect and confidence.

Heger gained both for a number of reasons, none of them especially romantic. Despite a mercurial, choleric disposition, he was a thorough professional. He could emote like an Angrian hero, bursting into tears when his students behaved stupidly or lighting up with pleasure as he read some lofty passage.[39] But his moods were signs of his commitment to his work and a factor in his "intellectual magnetism." Charlotte initially made fun of his behavior: "sometimes he borrows the lineaments of an insane Tom-cat—sometimes those of a delirious Hyena—occasionally—but very seldom he discards these perilous attractions and assumes an air not above one hundred degrees removed from what you would call mild & gentleman-like."[40] Yet as Lucy Snowe's development in *Villette* suggests, Charlotte came to treasure her teacher's liberating influence. She herself was constantly divided between opposites: reason and imagination, self-restraint and ardor, duty and rebellion, humility and boldness. Heger unself-consciously united mind and heart and demanded that his students do the same. He commended the proofs of feeling in her essays—he faulted one of Emily's for lacking filial sentiment—but he also kept after her to discipline her writing, to control the tone, the metaphors, and the structure.

Years later, Heger claimed that the sisters "hardly ever" kept to the subject he set them.[41] But the evidence suggests that Charlotte meant to follow orders, though her interests sometimes carried her off course. In any case, her work became a forum for her views, a means of demonstrating culture and intelligence. In one four-page devoir, "The Immensity of God," she alludes to Milton, quotes from the eighth psalm, remarks on advances in the science of optics, and briefly cites Huygens's views on distant stars and light waves. In her longest essay, "Athens Saved by Poetry," she draws on Plutarch, Homer, Euripides, and Sophocles as she develops a dramatic confrontation between a Spartan general and a poet. She had gone abroad determined to increase her accomplishments. Under Heger, she acquired new motives: to impress him by her industry, champion her religion, and write better essays than the natives. (As one of her classmates commented later, "she mixed in moral reflections, where we related only the facts . . .").[42]

Perhaps she was also spurred by rivalry with Emily, although that is difficult to prove.[43] In Heger's view, Charlotte was completely unselfish in catering to her sister's demands. But she had maneuvered Emily into going, and if she subsequently made herself compliant, doing so was proof that she could manage her less proficient sibling as well as the routines. As she says in her May letter to Nussey, she takes to Heger's regimen with bovine "avidity," whereas Emily works "like a horse." She finds Heger amusing and quite bearable, whereas Emily and Heger "don't draw well together at all." She has the grounding in French and the temperament to get through the course of instruction. Emily, less prepared and far more prone to homesickness, is coping, but with enormous effort.[44] Heger would nonetheless tell Gaskell that Emily had the greater genius, and Charlotte concurred in his estimate. "I should say Ellis will not be seen in his full strength till he is seen as an essayist," she wrote as Currer Bell in 1848.[45] Ellis's only essays are the devoirs, which Heger, not Charlotte, preserved.

Emily's thoughts about the texts she was producing are missing from the record, as usual, but clashes with Heger could have been predicted by anyone aware of her character. For her, independence and freedom of will were primary conditions of existence. Heger proposed to have her learn by "catching the echo" of another author's style. She found that plan repugnant and said so. More strictly, she "said she saw no good to be derived from it; and that, by adopting it, they should lose all originality of thought and expression."[46] Heger, Gaskell adds, "had no time" to argue, and perhaps no patience for objections from a woman who could barely speak his language.

The friction between them was not minor. Heger believed that imitation was central to all forms of learning. Like Emily's, his conviction was rooted in ontology, his sense of the nature of being. The child, he said later, first learns virtue and morality by seeking the approval of its parents; to emulate the work and behavior of those who are superior comes naturally to humankind, "created in the image of God and for God." Emulation could become harmful if overdone. Properly directed and nurtured, however, it would be the student's "surest and wisest" guide.[47] These ideas (taken from Heger's second Prize Day speech, which Charlotte heard in 1843 with so much pleasure) intimate the basis of his differences with Emily. Motherless at three and profoundly unconventional, in both her religion and her indifference to approval, she could hardly have "drawn well" with a man whose tenets were so deeply communal and orthodox.

In practice, his plan gave her more freedom than it promised. "Harold" and probably "The Cat" and "The Butterfly" are essays that echo or respond to other writings, yet all three are distinctively Emily's; Heger did not try to rein her in. Once she submitted a devoir, however, it was subject to another form of his control: corrections that could become so intrusive that they virtually took over her pages. Charlotte welcomed these signs of Heger's attention. Emily almost certainly did not.

Still, she never stopped working, and she made dramatic progress. If in fact she arrived knowing scarcely any French, her achievement within four months was staggering. Charlotte would claim in 1850 that "on [Emily's] mind time and experience alone could work: to the influence of other intellects, it was not amenable."[48] It may not have been amenable to Heger's, but she made her way through his French and German readings and wrote telling essays in response to his assignments, even the constricting ones. She kept to her own ways, nevertheless, by writing on English themes whenever she could and, less overtly, by adhering to the order of English rather than French sentences. Charlotte, after her earliest devoirs, seemed to be thinking in the new language. Emily sought equivalents and translated.

Heger's impressions of this singular pupil have been quoted many times since Gaskell printed them. He admired her "head for logic" and capacity to argue but felt that these formidable gifts were impaired by her "stubborn tenacity of will." He added, "She should have been a man—a great navigator" or a historian. Instead, she was a woman taking his classes, her shyness no mask for the convictions that made her "obtuse to all reasoning where her own wishes, or her own sense of right, was concerned."[49] Heger wanted to be tolerant, unlike the Brontës, but his sense of right was as powerful as theirs, and by any kind of logic that prevailed in his world, Emily should have conceded. Yet despite the irritation he must sometimes have felt, he remained a fair and even a generous teacher, praising her devoirs and praising her in the letter he wrote to Patrick Brontë.

With Charlotte, of course, he encountered no such problems. Long before she was aware of her passion for the man, she was fervently responsive to the mentor.

Teaching by Precept

Heger was exceptionally thoughtful about the processes of learning and composing. Impetuous in performance, he based his practice nonetheless on theories, plans, and precepts that he codified. Gaskell draws on some of his ideas when she describes his methods of teaching; for example, he believed in studying the framework or construction of a piece, in his terms, *la charpente*.[50] More pragmatic rules and hints—the need to stick to the point, for example—can be gathered from his comments on the devoirs.

Although Charlotte does not say so, Heger also liked to express his views epigrammatically. As Frederika Macdonald recalls, "he held in reserve a store of . . . really luminous phrases, that he would use as little Lanterns. . . ."[51] Her memoir of her own two years at the pensionnat includes half-a-dozen examples. In print, those maxims seem preachy and didactic, mementos of a system long outdated. But considered in conjunction with Charlotte's past experience, they offer provocative clues to the influence that he exerted over her writing.

First, "before entering upon the study of any noble or high order of thoughts," Heger ordered his students to shed their vulgar interests, as one would leave one's shoes outside a mosque. He instructed them in methods of "putting off the shoes"—preparing individually for meditative study—and he began his lessons by summoning one pupil to stand and recite the invocation:

> Spirit of Wisdom, guide us:
> Spirit of Truthfulness, teach us:
> Spirit of Charity, invigorate us:
> Spirit of Prudence, preserve us:
> Spirit of Strength, defend us:
> Spirit of Justice, enlighten us:
> Comforting spirit, soothe us.[52]

There is no way of knowing whether this litany introduced any of the Brontës' classes (though Macdonald implies that Heger's routines were long established by her time, seventeen years later). But whether or not he invoked these guardian spirits, he would have promoted the concept of the sanctuary, thereby conferring a professor's blessing on a practice the sisters had grown up with. It is important, however, to discriminate between his "sacred space" and the Brontës' "world below." Heger had no sealed compartments in his system. His students were to contemplate, to take in great ideas, and then return enriched to daily life. More practically, they were to turn to their desks and put what they had learned into their devoirs. Writing thus became a means of integration, not a medium of secrecy and separateness.

Heger's second principle, according to Macdonald, was "[t]hat one must give one's soul as many forms as possible. *Il faut donner à son âme toutes les formes possibles.*"[53] Again, the words sanction Charlotte Brontë's convictions. She had written her stories under various guises— Arthur Florian Wellesley, Captain Tree, Charles Townshend—and populated them with evolving characters. Determined also "to cultivate her tastes" rather than just equip herself to earn a living, she had (in Mary Taylor's words) "picked up every scrap of information concerning painting, sculpture, poetry, music, etc., as if it were gold."[54] But living in Haworth was scarcely conducive to the growth of an eclectic sensibility.

In contrast, Heger's program was broad and comprehensive. Believing "that every sort of literature and literary style has its merits, *except the literature that is not literary and the style that is bad,*"[55] he provided a range of readings on natural phenomena, animals, social customs, heroes, traits, religious and historical events. He lectured not only on standard authors from the seventeenth through the nineteenth centuries but also, and unusually, on the French Romantics, whose works were still coming out.[56] He also had his students write devoirs in several modes: descriptive, epistolary, meditative, analytic.

It is easy now to smile at Heger's fuzzy terminology and sweeping use of "*style,*" "*soul,*" and "*literature.*" But a theory deficient in elements of grandeur would never have satisfied a Brontë. "I believe," Charlotte wrote about "The Fall of the Leaves," "that all true poetry is but the faithful imprint of something that happens or has happened in the poet's soul." Heger concurred: "very good quite right." But he added, "Poet or not . . . study form," advice that would prove indispensable.

His third maxim, as Macdonald recalls it, prescribed the proper use of imagery: "One must never employ, nor tolerate the employment of, a literary image as *an argument.* The purpose of a literary image is to illuminate as a vision, and to interpret as a parable. An image that does not serve both these purposes is a fault in style."[57] His response to Charlotte's Millevoye essay suggests what he meant by "interpret" and "illuminate." He agrees with her that genius is a gift from heaven; work alone cannot create a poet. But then he turns to "force" and "machinery." He asks her to "imagine two men of equal strength," the first "without a lever," who "will lift 1,000 pounds," the other "with a lever" who "will uproot a plane tree" by employing the same amount of effort. Shifting from mechanics to the arts, he compares uncultivated genius to a painter ignorant of color and perspective, a Demosthenes whose stammering prompts hisses, a singing soul whose outlet is a rough and raucous voice, a "sublime musician" with an "untuned piano," and finally, a diamond "without the lapidary." These analogies, following one after the other, develop and illustrate his point. In effect, as he progresses the boundaries blur, so that the metaphors constitute the message. Yet at the same time they accompany an argument: "Without study, no *art*."

Whatever the apparent ambiguity between Heger's theory of the image and his practice, the principle struck a chord in Charlotte. She was aware of her own inclination to substitute imagery for argument. In a fragment that she left untitled and unfinished, a letter that begins "My dear Jane," the narrator, groping to express a thought, declares, "I see everything through the colored glass of simile." "I see everything" has been canceled, however, and revision had been added in the margin: "as you well know, I have the bad habit of seeing everything [through the colored glass]. . . ."[58] The change hints at the customary split in Charlotte's thinking. Though she sometimes felt guilty about the way she visualized, she remained reluctant to curb her "bad habit," and "My dear Jane" continues with just the kind of simile that Heger could attack "as an argument": "And this idea appears before me like a bird, who comes from a distant land of charity and mildness and who, alighting on the branch of a vine that I imagine being close to me but is not, folds its brilliant wings and looks at me with an eye that seems to say, 'Have pity on your friend Jane. She is better and sweeter than you. . . .'"

The fragment becomes increasingly disordered, and she abandons it eighteen lines later. But she never lost the impulse to vivify concepts "through the colored glass of simile." In her books, ideas take the forms of animals and people; they come to her protagonists as visions or as voices. Consider the passage in *The Professor,* the novel she deliberately stripped of ornament, in which hypochondria, like a demon lover, sings and whispers to the captive William Crimsworth (ch. 23); or consider how Lucy Snowe envisions Human Justice in the devoir Paul Emanuel compels her to write (ch. 35). These passages, however, abide by Heger's rule in that they illustrate an argument the speaker has implied or communicate a state of mind through parable.

More broadly, Heger's lessons on imagery catalyzed a newly elaborate use of metaphor. As Alexander says, Charlotte had grown up with "A Visual Imagination."[59] Her ability to visualize approached hallucination, as she herself notes in journal entries. She did not just conceive of her Angrian characters. They appeared before her, she heard their conversations, and her feet "trod the . . . shores" of their kingdom.[60]

But until she went to Brussels, her tropes were rarely intricate. At nineteen, she refers to her fantasy kingdom as "the ark which for me floats alone on the face of this world's desolate and boundless deluge."[61] In telling Ellen Nussey of her project for a school, she alludes to the "chicken" that may either "come out . . . full-fledged" or "turn addle and die before it cheeps."[62] But the metaphoric language in the juvenilia is more apt to be derivative and brief. Flames dart from the earth or circle "like fiery snakes"; a corpse is "all untouched by the wasting finger of decay."[63] Descriptions abound. She sketches clothes, countenances, scenery and buildings, the movements and expressions of her characters. But her very aptitude for literal depiction may have limited her interest in analogy. Why conceive of something her protagonist was "like" when a portrait could be taken directly? "[Lady Zenobia's] head was bare, her tall person was enveloped in the tattered remnants of a dark velvet mantle. Her dishevelled hair hung in wild elf-locks over her face, neck and shoulders, almost concealing her features, which were emaciated and pale as death."[64] Even when her imagery pertains to mind and character, it lacks psychological complexity: "The Duke of Zamorna's conscience— a vessel of a thousand tons burthen—brought up a cargo of blood to his face, his nostrils opened—his head was as high, his chest as full & his attitude, standing by the table, as bold as if, from the ramparts of Gazemba, he was watching Arundel's Horsemen scouring the Wilderness."[65]

The one exception is the famous poem she wrote at Roe Head late in 1835. Cut off from the conditions that fostered creativity and fearful that her kingdom was receding from her grasp, she invoked the power of metaphor to summon it back and revive her capacity for visions:

> We wove a web in childhood
>   A web of sunny air
> We dug a spring in infancy
> Of water pure and fair
>
> We sowed in youth a mustard seed
> We cut an almond rod
> We are now grown up to riper age
> Are they withered in the sod. . . .[66]

This poem aside, she was far from using metaphor to animate abstractions and intensify description. She had yet to learn how tropes could work complexly and symbolically.

In Brussels, she began to absorb those lessons and grasp the potential of the image. Heger taught by example and lecture (on Hugo's "Mirabeau on the Tribune," for instance), as well as by his comments on her devoirs, and she began to respond. In "Athens Saved by Poetry," Cassandra reveals herself, "white, stiff, petrified, as if her veins were filled with ice in place of blood; all disheveled, her locks in disarray, streaming at the mercy of the wind; her white shoulders gleaming beneath her wild hair, like the moon through clouds." This passage echoes the one on Zenobia, but simile and a more compressed, inverted syntax advance it beyond representation.

For the first time, Charlotte was writing in a genre that forced her to be clear about abstractions. Heger's assignments made her think like a critic about an author's style, the effect of a passage, and the motives and perspective that prompted it. She also had to imitate style and substance, to write texts that echoed what she studied. In the juvenilia, she had attempted parodies and modeled her romances after Byron's. But her approach had not been reflective; character and action were paramount. For her devoirs, she could still compose episodes and portraits, but she also had to think about concepts. They came to her as images, and so she described them: Vice as a woman with a garland of flowers and a serpent peeking out from the petals; Reason as a bird that becomes a mocking ape as it exposes the narrator's hypocrisy.[67] Perhaps she had thought imagistically since childhood, but Heger helped her define what she was doing. He guided and legitimated impulse.

Heger's fourth maxim, according to Macdonald, was "that one must never neglect the warning one's ear gives one of a *fault* in style; and never trust one's ear exclusively about the merits of a literary style."[68] To develop his students' ears he often read aloud to them, uniting an actor's range and power with a pedagogue's desire to mold and stimulate.[69] "He was a magnificent reader," one of them remembered, "—you saw, you felt, you laughed, you cried, you grew hot, you grew cold, you joyed, you mourned, you went through a riot of emotion, exactly in proportion as he wished."[70]

Though the Brontës may not have responded so effusively, listening was a key part of their training. As Gaskell writes, "they were to catch the spirit and rhythm [of French] rather from the ear and the heart . . . than by over-careful and anxious study of its grammatical rules."[71] The method could produce its own anxieties. Forbidden for some weeks to use a grammar book or dictionary, Charlotte made elementary errors. In the long run, however, Heger's aural training improved her style in French and in English.

Of course, as a child she had never lacked a rich and diverse oral culture. Every Sunday the Brontë children heard their father's sermons. When the papers came, he read the news aloud. Tabitha Ackroyd, the servant, told them stories, and Branwell sometimes read to the girls as they sewed, perhaps as Robert Moore in *Shirley* reads to Caroline Helstone.[72] Their own early tales began as "Plays" that they acted out or narrated. And all their sagas were collaborative efforts. Charlotte and Branwell maintained Angria together, discussing their plans or keeping current through their letters, while Emily and Anne kept developing Gondal until Emily died (at thirty).

But no one knows how much of the writing they shared orally or how much critical judgment they exercised. Judging from the evidence of the juvenilia, Charlotte's ear was poorly attuned to faults of style, or she got so carried away by her visions that she could not be bothered to correct them. Ampersands and dashes string her clauses together; adjectives and adverbs proliferate. Even now, when the manuscripts appear in print with punctuation edited for clarity, reading the stories aloud smoothly is difficult because of their undisciplined syntax. Although she attempted to control her last novelettes, dramatic improvement in style and sound came only in the novels after Brussels.

How much of the improvement can be credited to Heger, how much to her exposure to French literature and language, and how much to maturity and discipline? Probably these factors are interconnected and mutually reinforcing. To judge by Charlotte's devoirs, the study of French increased her awareness of word order, stress, and the ebb and flow of clauses in a sentence. Gropingly at first, but with increasing fluency, she tried for effects of her own. Heger provided a conceptual framework, criteria for assessing tone and nuance. He also showed her how her work sounded by reading it (and Emily's) aloud to other students.[73]

These lessons traveled with her to Haworth. When she "accidentally lighted" on Emily's poems, she assessed their merits partly by their sound: "To my ear, they had also a peculiar music—wild, melancholy, and elevating."[74] When the three "Bells" were writing their novels, they consulted each other in the evenings. "Once or twice a week," Charlotte told Elizabeth Gaskell, "each read to the others what she had written, and heard what they had to say about it."[75] Charlotte rarely felt the need to alter her work as a result of these conferences. But by then, she was choosing and arranging words with care and weighing their effect on an audience.

Heger's fifth rule was directed to the struggling writer: "One must not fight with a difficult sentence; but take it for a walk with one; or sleep with the thought of it present in one's mind; and let the difficulty arrange itself whilst one looks on."[76] Like his maxim on the sanctuary, this one reinforces an idea long familiar to the Brontës. As an adolescent, Charlotte looked on, or inward, while her characters enacted their dramas. She wrote with her eyes nearly closed, in a state of trance, trusting her visions to inspire her. But again, there is a critical difference between her approach and Heger's. His rule was not to be construed as an endorsement of uncontrolled, unconscious invention. It was a method of getting around the frustration that could leave a writer blocked. Here as elsewhere his advice was functional, not because he disavowed intuition, but because he distinguished between "gifts" like creativity and faculties that people could develop.

Although Charlotte would continue to rely on inspiration, her subsequent method of invoking it recalls this maxim. Asked by Gaskell about Lucy Snowe's drugged vision, she replied by explaining the "process" she followed whenever she "had to describe anything which had not fallen within her own experience": she would think "intently on it for many and many a night before falling asleep" until, perhaps weeks later, "she wakened up in the morning with all clear before her. . . ."[77]

Heger's sixth and final maxim—"One should not read, before sitting down to write, a great stylist with a marked manner of his own; unless this manner happens to resemble one's own"[78]—seems less applicable to her. Other authors' styles did not rub off on Charlotte, despite her responsive sensibility. But the emphasis on manner and the training he provided probably had long-range consequences. Ultimately, she would forge a personal style as distinct as any writer's in English.[79]

The effects of Heger's precepts on Emily Brontë are less traceable but easy to surmise. Maxims, by definition, codify ideas. Emily detested codification. She could teach herself what she needed to know about the concept of the sanctuary, imagery, and style. Besides, her writing was already distinctive—beyond the range of Heger's "little Lanterns." As for giving her soul "as many forms as possible," her retort can be imagined from the answer she gave to the girls who teased her about her appearance: "I wish to be as God made me."[80] Still, as Heger's pupil she was bound to do her homework and submit her devoirs to his scrutiny. Like Charlotte, she had to take account of his corrections, whatever her opinion of his precepts.

Teaching through Practice

Unlike much of the evidence for Heger's principles, the proofs of his practice come directly from the manuscripts the Brontës submitted or transcribed. His markings do not just offer text-specific comments. They open a window on his methods, his attitude, and his relations with each sister. Even unmarked devoirs can yield clues to his influence when set within the context of his precepts and instructions or analyzed as units in a sequence.

Of the extant essays that they wrote to be read by him (a count excluding Charlotte's notes and fragments), ten are clean copies, eight have been corrected lightly, and nine bear signs of heavy intervention. There are also four revised drafts, two with his corrections and two, mailed to Gaskell, in his handwriting. This count only hints at the procedures Heger expected his students to follow. As Macdonald says, "The pupil was supposed to write in her own note-book a rough copy of the composition, leaving a wide margin for corrections. The fair copy of the exercise given Monsieur Héger was also to have a wide margin. In the ordinary course when the corrected exercise was returned the pupil was held to verify the remarks made, and to re-write the composition, for her own benefit only, with the improvements suggested."[81] Presumably, then, some of the surviving clean copies are revisions of drafts that Heger corrected. (In one case, "The Death of Moses," there was certainly a marked draft, since Gaskell saw it in Brussels.) And the stages of revision can be complex. Charlotte occasionally wrote her own corrections on the copy Heger handed back to her, and Heger himself returned to several of the manuscripts, marking them more thoroughly the second time. Sometimes his pencil moved lightly through their pages, merely underscoring faulty words or elements. At other times, his pen was persistently in motion: he drew wavy lines and straight lines, crossed words out, revised phrasing, used the margins to pose questions and express his admiration, and appended observations at the end.

Heger may have thought that Emily had more genius, but Charlotte got the bulk of his attention. The comments throughout her pages are more numerous, and further remarks follow three of her devoirs, as opposed to two brief end comments on Emily's. The kind of attention he gave them also differs. On Emily's pages it takes two forms: he praises what he likes and revises French that is either faulty or limited. While this procedure lets her know what needs fixing, it does little to engage her in the work. On Charlotte's pages too he corrects by rewriting, but he makes much more effort to involve her. When the reasons for correction are not self-evident, he lets her know why he objects. By framing his objections as inquiries or glosses, he prompts her to weigh the effects she has pro-

duced and the assumptions that underlie her statements. Thus his comments—assenting, chiding, asking—form a dialogue responsive to the
text and to its author.

Predictably, the commonest notations alert both sisters to errors.
Verbs in the imperfect tense are changed to the past; particle and gender
flaws are rectified; punctuation (never Charlotte's forte) is adjusted; un-
idiomatic phrasing is crossed out or overwritten. He gets after "bar-
barisms," English words that they insert where they do not know the
French ones.[82] When Charlotte has vocabulary problems, he either tells
her to look up the meaning or adds the word or phrase she should have
chosen: "discours" ("speech" or "address") in place of "sermons"; "convoqua" ("convoked") in place of "appella" ("called") where she writes
of summoning a counsel.[83]

But even on this technical level, Heger does not merely tighten nuts
and bolts. He corrects to gain precision, to bring details into focus, and to
clarify vision and concepts. In Charlotte's "Palace of Death," for example, where she says that War's arm seems "assez fort pour brandiller la
lance d'un Achille" ("strong enough to wave about the lance of an
Achilles"), he hints at the distinction between "brandiller" (to "swing"
or "shake") and "brandir" (to "brandish" or "flourish"). Where she observes, "Death smiled," he asks "How?" And when Ambition tells Death
that her empire will soon be filled—"bientôt votre empire sera rempli"—
he replaces "sera rempli" with "regorgera" ("will be glutted"), which is
both more precise and more evocative. Through such notation, he guided
Charlotte toward a new and necessary critical awareness.

Of course she was conscious of her talent. She excelled at illustration,
and not in words alone, since she had painted, sketched, and reproduced
engravings. But the sheer extravagance of items in the juvenilia works
against selection and emphasis. Often, she combines striking details with
clichés or submerges them in protracted dialogues. At the pensionnat,
confronted with more formal writing projects, she put the old word-
painting skills to use: "It was the eve of a battle; one might have said that
the glorious orb [of the setting sun] presaged the carnage of the morrow,
so enflamed did its disk appear, so lit up the west seemed from its fires.
The broken columns, the ancient vaults, the hieroglyphs engraved on the
temple walls were covered with a ruby tint. The moon, pale and serene,

rose in the east; everywhere the sky was clear and in the midst of the desert, the pyramids arose from the sea of sand, like vast rocks of granite that neither tempest nor hurricane could dislodge." After these lines from "Evening Prayer in a Camp," she intended to portray a band of Protestant soldiers who gather to pray within the pagan ruins before braving the next day's bloody combat. But the setting overwhelms its subject; the sunset takes precedence over the account it was meant to introduce and illuminate; "all this, I know better how to feel than to paint," the narrator concludes apologetically.

Heger's "tr bon" beside the sunset passage acknowledges Charlotte's skill at description. But he must have been aware, as she was, that the rest of the devoir goes downhill. He recasts her awkward ending: "all this, I have felt profoundly and can paint but feebly today." More important, within the week he turned her attention to selectivity and contrast. At the end of her next devoir, "The Nest," he added "Advice" that opens with a salient question: "What importance should be given to the details, in developing a subject?" His answer assumes that rules of composition apply equally to literature and art:

> *Remorselessly* sacrifice everything that does not contribute to clarity, verisimilitude, and effect.
>
> Accentuate everything that sets the main idea in relief, so that the impression be colorful, picturesque. It's sufficient that the rest be *in its proper place, but in half-tone.* This is what gives to style, as to painting, its unity, perspective, and *effect.*

He also assumes that these neoclassic principles apply to work from other literary movements, for he next directs her to a poem by the French Romantic Lamartine: "we will analyze it together, *from the point of view of the details.*"

The lesson seems to have taken. In "The Immensity of God," the devoir she wrote in response to Lamartine's poem, her setting leads seamlessly into its subject. Subsequently she introduces details not only as illuminating shafts within her narratives but also to accentuate ideas: "Napoleon was born in Corsica and died on St. Helena; between the two islands there is but a vast continent and the immense ocean. He was born a notary's son and died a captive; between the two states there is but the career of a triumphant soldier, but a hundred fields of battle, but a throne, a sea of blood and a Golgotha. Truly his life is a rainbow; the two extreme ends touch the earth, the intervening arc spans the skies."[84]

Heger's responses alone do not explain the evolution in Charlotte's methods. Exposure to the work of the French Romantics, increasing facility in the new language, and a climate that fostered experimentation could all have worked together to promote it. But certainly he encouraged her development by praising what he liked. His expressions of approval in her margins—"Bon," "tr. bon," or simply "B"—can be classified under several headings. They appear next to phrases in felicitous French; they acknowledge noble sentiments, tellingly expressed; most often, they commend striking images and details, the strokes that bring a narrative to life.

Intervention, in itself, was a means of releasing her from habits that the juvenilia had inculcated. In Haworth, she had had little motive to edit or to keep digressions from burgeoning. She made some revisions in her early poems and stories, cutting words or occasionally whole lines, and in her final stories she made even stronger efforts to rein in her imagination. But words were her outlet and her refuge. The trancelike state released her from conscious mediation and a self that was small and plain and powerless.

Heger unwittingly broke the hold of habit by limiting her scope, imposing new constraints, and making her look sharply at her writing. She had to ground each devoir in sources beyond the self: the readings, his instructions, her researches. Because she had a different aim and project every time, she could not indulge in labyrinthine plotting. If she wandered or lost track of her aims, her text would lose the unity he valued.[85]

She did not relinquish Angria entirely. She extols her childhood hero, Wellington, in one devoir and signs another "Howard," her pseudonym for Haworth. She also retains the Romantic hyperbole that she would only hold in check much later: ". . . it took no more than an old oak with a mossy trunk, and with twisted branches, than a bubbling spring bordered with wild flowers, than the ivy-covered ruins of a tower bristling with brambles and thorns, to throw me into the most exquisite transports of the soul."[86] But then, she was writing for a man who liked theatrics.

She also chose narrators who made such excess plausible—here, an impetuous young artist.

Heger never stopped alerting her to matters of "form" and "art," to unity, economy, placement, proportion, consistency of tone, and plausibility. When in "Peter the Hermit" she suspends a description to talk about "natures" with "indomitable ardor," he chides, "You have begun to speak of Peter . . . get to the point."[87] When in "The Death of Napoleon" she starts to digress from a comparison between his exile and Prometheus's, he draws lines through her wandering sentences and adds "vulture of Prometheus" in the margin. The draft he mailed to Gaskell amplifies this hint: "Perhaps there [Napoleon] too felt, gnawing at his flank, those insatiable vultures of whom the fable speaks. . . ."

Dessner claims that Heger's approach anticipates that of the New Critics.[88] Like them, he read texts closely and examined construction, but he also worked within a critical tradition that placed the creator in the foreground. Buffon, in his speech on style, defines the crucial bond between an author's mind and spirit and his writing: "To write well is to think well, sense well, and express well, all at once—to have at the same time wit, soul, and taste."[89] And Heger, who introduced the Brontës to Buffon's work,[90] made this principle a basis of his method. To develop his students' minds and tastes he exposed them to wide and various readings. As M. H. Spielmann says, Heger's system required them "to analyse (always 'analyse') concisely not the work only but the author's intention, his emotion, manner, and so forth, and especially their own thoughts, emotions and impressions, and to seek out the principles involved."[91] He believed too that instruction must be personal; if a teacher wanted to improve a student's work, he would have to appeal to that student's sensibility, the matrix from which the work arose.

For the emotionally vulnerable Charlotte, this blurring of the boundaries became treacherous. She might see that when his comments were addressed to the writer, they pointed to issues in the writing; she might even understand that his copious revisions—like his loading her with books and their discussions in his study—were signs of his professional commitment; yet they drew her in as powerfully as love notes.

How accountable is Heger for stoking her passion? Certainly he made no overtures to Charlotte that anyone could label improper. The teacher-pupil poems that she wrote three years later bear witness to a taskmaster who rarely offered praise and a student who thrived on severity.[92] In fact, he often commented warmly, though never in the language of romance. His inscription on the copy of the Prize Day speech that he gave her—"to Miss Charlotte Brontë, [from] her master and friend"[93]— further indicates his view of their relations.

Nonetheless, Heger had experience of the world and the will to connect with his students. As a youthful secretary in Paris, he had ghost-written letters to his employer's mistress.[94] And his later correspondence with another former student suggests that his efforts to reach out in empathy could shade into something more flirtatious: "I only have to think of you to see you. I often give myself the pleasure when my duties are over, when the light fades. . . . I sit down, smoking my cigar, and with a hearty will I evoke your image—and you come . . . you, with that little air, affectionate undoubtedly, but independent and resolute . . . in fact, just as I knew you, my dear L——, and as I have esteemed and loved you."[95] He responded to the devoirs of the hungry Charlotte with an amplitude he rarely matched with Emily. Aware of the disparity, how could she not have been tempted to believe he found her special?

Emily was in no such danger. A fiercely autonomous thinker, wholly unused to any supervision, she could hardly have enjoyed preparing work for a professor whose practice was to write all over it. Still, her devoirs offer circumstantial evidence that she did not resist entirely. First and most important, she wrote them. Whatever it cost her to submit to his methods, she did his assignments. She probably argued or took liberties with them and exercised what Heger called "her strong, imperious will."[96] Over time, however, she may have come to realize that her early objection was groundless; no curriculum could make her "lose all originality of thought and expression." Even when he gave restrictive instructions, she reacted as only she could.

In one of her most formulaic essays, for example, a teacher declines to attend a pupil's musical soiree. Heger set the format, invitation and refusal. Emily decided on the extras: ". . . I have heard that you are to play a piece on this occasion, and forgive me if I advise you (out of pure friendship) to choose a time when everyone is occupied with something other than music, for I fear that your performance will be a little too remarkable."[97] Devoirs like this one might be disconcerting, but they were never dull. (Years later, another English student asked Heger why he had retained the Brontës' devoirs. He replied, "because I saw the genius in them.")[98]

The aptitude for charting her own course through assignments made Emily a poor candidate for training. Unlike Charlotte, she already wrote concisely and logically; no one had to discipline *her* use of imagery or teach her to stick the point. Deliberately or not, she also stuck to topics on which she either knew as much as he did or could offer as valid an opinion. French was the one area in which she needed help. There, Heger could and did correct her. But that she welcomed a professor's intervention, as Charlotte did, seems more than unlikely.

Again, the marked devoirs are the only extant evidence; they point to trouble. "Portrait: King Harold before the Battle of Hastings" exists in two versions, the one she wrote that June and Heger's "copy" for Gaskell. By stripping Emily's version of his corrections, I have added a third—in effect, the draft she gave him. Examined successively, these versions reveal a triple-layered process of revision. Heger seems to have begun making changes on a first round. Then he went back and added others, sometimes canceling the first layer and sometimes supplementing it. Finally, for Gaskell, he applied the polish that he thought the essay ought to have. Emily did not live to see that version, but already, in the one she would have gotten back, her spare unvarnished prose is being coated. She refers to those who are gathered on the "champ," the ordinary word for field. Heger qualifies her noun in pencil: "there on that field of battle." Then in ink he converts "field" to "plain where soon must be decided the fate of a kingdom." Later, envisioning Harold with his courtiers, she writes "that his body is a true prisoner." Heger cuts "true" and "body" (which he may have found indelicate) and substitutes his own phrase for hers: "in a word that he is no more than a prisoner in his crown and royal purple."

Some of Heger's changes do rectify her French. Others add substance to terse statements. When she writes that the touch of death's hand "is, to the hero, what the stroke that gave him liberty was to the slave," Heger amplifies her analogy: the swordstroke that brings death is but the liberating tap of the rod with which the master frees the slave. But in a devoir of only 540 words, the mass of correction alone is overwhelming. He does not just revise; he takes over.

He is just as high-handed with Charlotte. Near the end of her devoir "The Death of Napoleon," she compares "the glory of Wellington" to "one of the ancient oaks that shades the mansion of his fathers": "It grows slowly; it needs time not only to spread its large branches but to sink deep roots, roots that will twist themselves around the solid foundations of the island whose Savior and Defender he has been." Heger does not tamper with the sense of the comparison, not even when she says that Napoleon's fame will wither overnight, like Jonah's vine. But in his version he adds his own touches to her metaphor: "The oak grows slowly; it needs time to spread its gnarled branches toward the sky and to sink into the soil those deep roots that will entangle themselves in the solid foundations of the land. But then, the centuries'-old tree, steadfast as the rock where it has its base, will brave both the weather's ills [faux du temps] and the winds' & tempests' efforts." His additions enhance the analogy; "temps," which can mean both "weather" and "time," recalls an earlier reference to the fickle English mob and Wellington's unshakable integrity. But they also prolong a eulogy that carries the narrator away from Napoleon and alters the whole thrust of the essay.

How did Charlotte take his high-handedness? As she herself realized, she was ready, even ravenous, to learn from a powerful mentor. With the blurring of distinctions between mentor and love object—clearly abetted by Heger's mode of teaching—any form of notice became positive. Here it may have been especially welcome, since Wellington was her other idol. But in any case, she would have acquiesced. As she declares in a retrospective poem, "Obedience was my heart's free choice / Whatere his word severe."[99]

Still, the choices she was making as a writer depended less on acquiescence or romance than on a new self-consciousness about her work. To trace the growth of that awareness more closely and to see why her devoirs were so pivotal, I want now to turn to the topic that produced the most sustained master-pupil dialogue.

Genius

Genius had fascinated Charlotte Brontë from the time she began inventing plays and stories, and from the first she took the concept personally. She and her siblings called themselves the Four Genii who ruled the developing Glass Town. As Genius Talii she determined her characters' destinies, creating, destroying, and reviving them. Though the Genii vanished from the saga in a few years, she never lost interest in the powers of genius or gave up hope that she had been endowed with them. She thought of genius as an overwhelming force, mysterious yet living, almost tangible. Its presence was manifest in great men and great works of art; its powers were instinctual, not studied. Romantic doctrine almost certainly influenced her thinking: like Coleridge, she distinguished between genius and mere talent; like Wordsworth, she exalted spontaneity. Thus her observation in "The Fall of the Leaves" that poetry expresses what happens in the poet's soul—provided the poet is a genius.

Heger was seven years older than Charlotte, but his standards, shaped in part by his classical training, allied him with an earlier generation. Impassioned and individualistic in the classroom, he had obvious affinities with the French Romantics whose works he admired and taught. He also looked for signs of ardor in his students' compositions and urged them to express what they felt. But his methods—emulation, the following of models, going by the rules, attention to form—were neoclassic rather than Romantic. Or perhaps, like many critics at the turn of the century, he wanted to synthesize those strains.

Inspiration and control, and their relationship to genius, become issues in at least five of Charlotte's devoirs. "Peter the Hermit," an essay from her first term, raises them briefly yet suggestively. She wrote it in response to Heger's instructions to imitate a "portrait" by Hugo.[100] But as Duthie says, she does not treat her hero or his rhetoric as Hugo treated Mirabeau the orator; instead, she "show[s] her passionate and romantic admiration for the quality of genius in itself."[101] The historical Peter was small and plain, as undistinguished physically as Charlotte. Yet the chronicles report him persuading kings and soldiers because he had the power of the word, the force of eloquence, and faith that he was serving as God's messenger. She calls him a man of "indomitable ardor." The French "indomptable" can also mean "unruly" or, in the case of animals, "untamable," and she notes that Peter was undoubtedly "troubled by stormy passions" in his youth. But after years as a warrior and more years as a monk, "inspiration" was "brought to birth . . . in his soul." In a section she omits from the draft Gaskell published, she creates a tableau of the field before the battle, with the meager little man in his poor gray habit surrounded by the towering multitudes. Yet Peter does not seem to see anything around him because, she says, his eyes are raised to "God and the angels": "His genius has already mastered that whole army and at this moment he masters himself."

Heger has corrected both drafts of the devoir, concentrating mainly on her faulty, heavy prose and on lapses from narrative unity. Yet while he cuts her allusion to "God and the angels," he does not question her attitude toward genius or her basic attitude toward faith. Charlotte seems to have acted on her own in deleting the sentence on mastery and genius, perhaps because it no longer fit her narrative once she cut the tableau of the battlefield. But both she and Heger would come back to that subject, Heger indirectly through the readings he assigned and Charlotte forthrightly in most of the devoirs she wrote during her second year abroad.

Her analysis of Millevoye's "Fall of the Leaves" shows the impact of Heger's lessons on her belief in the prerogatives and mysteries of genius. Initially, she planned to consider the poem's effects and speculate on its development. She probably also meant to show Heger that she understood the principles of composition, both through her comments on the poem he had assigned and through her own focused discussion. Accordingly, she starts with the impressions the poem evokes and then pursues their causes through a series of questions: Did Millevoye work with conscious intention? Did he prepare his canvas, trace the rough outlines, seek and collect images and details, and then balance and adjust all the parts so that they would form a unified whole? "Is that the method all great poets follow?" At this point, conviction rebels against order and Millevoye fades into the background. Conceding the value of this method for the novice or the second-rate talent that is only fit to imitate, she scorns it as the basis for a masterpiece. Lyric poetry, though possibly not tragedy or epic, springs by inspiration from the soul of the poet. Genius, awakened by passionate feelings, need not search for details or think about unity; "inspiration takes the place of reflection," and the heart, "filled with a single idea," intuitively seizes on the form.

Heger praises a number of these statements; he agrees that inspiration is paramount. But when she writes, "the man of genius produces, without work," he immediately intervenes to check her. Genius may be exempt from ordinary methods, but not from effort, study, and experience. In a page of observations he refutes her assertion, often turning her own metaphors against her. For example, when she deprecates mechanical invention, he asks her whether a lever is worth nothing, possibly recalling that in "Peter the Hermit" she compares the mind of genius to a lever.

Implicit in Heger's refutation is his sense of the person he addresses: on the one hand, a bright, enthusiastic student who still requires training and correction; on the other, a writer of exceptional talent who has compelled him to take issue. By then, he must have known that she longed to be a poet, that when she spoke of genius and the force of inspiration she was thinking of herself as well as Millevoye. Though he could hardly have believed she would realize her ambition, his final words allow her to keep hoping. If she is destined to become a poet, the study of form will make her powerful. If not, it will give her a just appreciation of poetry's "merit and . . . charms."

These considerations must have been on her mind when she began her next devoir, "The Death of Napoleon," for she takes up her subject by asking how an ordinary person should approach the man of towering genius. Does the person "without distinguished talent" have the right to express views on Napoleon's life and death? Her answer is a loaded affirmative: "one cannot deprive mediocrity of the right to judge genius, but it does not follow that her judgment will always be sound." The balanced dispositions of conventional people render them unfit to judge the excesses of genius: "Mediocrity can see the faults of Genius . . . but she is too cold, too limited, too egotistical to understand its struggles, its suffering, its sacrifices; she is envious too, and so its very virtues appear to her under a false and tarnished light." The section ends with a caveat: "Let her then approach [Napoleon's tomb] with respect," neither bowing down nor hurling insults, and "preserving her independent though inferior dignity of being. . . ."

This preamble—which fills fifty-two lines of manuscript and represents nearly a quarter of the devoir—has been excised from the final version. Thematically and structurally, the cut improves the essay, which focuses without it on Napoleon Bonaparte and not on Charlotte's attitude toward genius. Yet as a clue to the tensions that were building in her life and work, the opening is not at all superfluous. Though the tone is initially objective, even humble, it soon becomes judgmental and reproving. Though the narrator first speaks as an ordinary person, she soon begins denouncing conventional people and, at least implicitly, allying herself with passionate, misunderstood genius. But perhaps the strangest shift occurs near the end of the essay, when she contrasts Bonaparte with Wellington. There she ascribes the duke's greatness—that which makes him Napoleon's superior—to many of the qualities linked here with mediocrity: self-control, balance, disdain for passionate excess, and resistance to the claims of all but conscience. Neither Charlotte nor Heger perceived this contradiction, although Heger has scored her pages heavily. But then, perhaps they were not prepared to view the essay as a devoir à clef.

Later readers may detect Charlotte Brontë's self-doubt behind the narrator's façade of self-confidence. Is *she* to remain an ordinary person whose refuge will lie in maintaining her dignity and staying "independent though inferior"? Or will her genius be realized and respected? Acknowledgment of any kind had grown much scarcer by May 1843, when she wrote "The Death of Napoleon."[102] Zoë Heger, "always cool & always reasoning,"[103] was leaving her in virtual isolation. Worse, as she reported in a letter to Emily, Madame was trying to turn Heger away from her, either from misjudgment and ignorance of her character or from an instinctual "aversion."[104]

Significantly, at the beginning of this devoir the "ordinary person" is masculine in gender, a "simple particulier" who shows the proper humility in approaching his exalted subject. But when the narrator alludes to the enemy of genius—a chilly, hidebound, and envious creature—her subject shifts from the masculine "person" to a feminine noun, "Mediocrité." In French, such shifts are a function of grammar rather than personal animus. But Charlotte was an Englishwoman coping with an anger that could only be voiced through her writing. Later still, when the nar-

rator returns from this digression, she retains the feminine pronoun—
"let her take care"—though logically the subject should be "the common
person" or the neutral but more inclusive "we."

Yet in this section, as so often happens in the devoirs, the personal
emerges obliquely. It can be discerned by those who know of Charlotte's
suffering, but it does not undermine her inquiry. It is further controlled
by the dialogic patterning—the questions, the movement from one side
to the other—which erects a securely logical structure over feelings of uncertainty and turbulence. This method of disclosing tension while veiling
it marks a step away from her Angrian romances toward the more controlled realism of her novels.

Genius goes unmentioned in "Athens Saved by Poetry," the devoir
she wrote after the lonely summer holiday. But she creates a virtual genius in the "indefinably superior" Athenian who sings to save the city
from destruction. Another of her physically undersized heroes, he has an
advantage over his captors because he is cultivated, self-possessed,
gifted, and able to use his resources. In a departure from her earlier protagonists, the poet creates through emulation; recalling Orpheus, who
charmed the wild beasts, he resolves to charm the brutish Spartans. The
song he composes is inspired by Greek legends, his legacy from childhood
and his homeland. But the text does not deliver the fairy-tale ending that
its title seems to promise. In a cynical finale, criticized by Heger, the poet
discovers that artistry and resolution cannot rouse the insensible. He can
save himself, though, and he does.

Again, Charlotte's situation seeps into her devoir, but it is distanced
and objectified. In contrast, her letters portray a self-chained captive,
aware that she should rescue herself by leaving Brussels but unable to
forgo the chance of getting through to Heger. By then, her devoirs were
her only medium.

In the last of the essays that deals with genius, "Letter from a Poor
Painter to a Great Lord," she invents a subject much closer to home, a
talented painter who has gone abroad to study and is trying to solicit a patron. Often his aspirations correspond to Charlotte's, but the characteri-
zation establishes distinctions between the young man and his creator.
The "I" of her "Letter" is self-confident, impetuous, defiant, and extreme
in thought and action. He refuses to beg for the great lord's patronage,

claiming that he knows the man's character well enough to recognize his preference for plain facts. He takes two pages to explain why he solicits this patron, rather than another, and spends the next nine on the history of his life and the discovery and pursuit of his vocation. His quest is in the high Romantic mode. He has wandered through the forests of his native country and traveled to Venice, Rome, and Florence. Though poor and sternly disciplined by hardship, he has obtained an education. Most important, he is certain that his soul contains "a few grains of that pure gold which is called Genius."

But the writer who endows her persona with such confidence has also been absorbing Heger's precepts. Her painter distinguishes between the gift of genius and the training that is his responsibility. He distinguishes too between following the vulgar herd—trying to imitate the ways of mediocrity—and striving to emulate the methods of great artists. In several passages marked "G" (for "Good") by Heger, he speaks of the passion and sense of vocation that have enabled him to overcome adversity. After four years of study, he has gained what he desired: "an intimate knowledge of all the technical mysteries of Painting, a taste cultivated in accord with the rules of art." Now, he is ready to use his genius for the benefit of others.[105]

In short, as she develops this series of devoirs, Charlotte progresses from naive enthusiasm to a much more thoughtful attitude toward genius. While she still maintains that genius is inspired and inspiring, she speaks with growing frequency of qualifying factors: study, self-discipline, technique, deliberate choices. Heger prompted many of the qualifications. Her life, then and later, reinforced them.

The Limits of Instruction

Charlotte Brontë could modify her attitude toward genius, but she could not modify her feelings for Heger or alter the increasingly one-sided bond that kept her chained to an illusion. Heger continued to attend to her devoirs; otherwise, as 1843 wore on, she had to get by with glimpses of her idol and the hope of exchanging a few words with him. Still, she refused to acknowledge his detachment; instead, she focused her rage on his wife.

Patricia Beer has said in reference to Charlotte's passion, "If M.

Heger had not existed, she would have had to invent him."[106] In effect she did invent him or, at least, reconstruct him as the master she was yearning to have. Paradoxically, the extent of her invention has been hidden by the fiction she spun from her experience. No one who knew Heger (including his son Paul) could mistake the source of *Villette*'s Paul Emanuel.[107] But Charlotte captured the extravagant professor and banished the bourgeois head of household. She also dropped aspects of his teaching from Emanuel, his penchant for maxims, for example. More important, *Villette* brings out his personal traits and flaws but leaves his teaching practices uncriticized. From the first, Heger struck her as "a man of power as to mind";[108] the lasting force of that conviction precluded any questions about it.

Surviving texts—devoirs, dictées, letters, Prize Day speeches—indicate four practices of Heger's that Charlotte would have mocked or protested in anyone but her professor. He edited imperiously, not just student essays, but also the prose of major authors; he reveled in sentiment; he based his teaching on sexist assumptions; and he weighted the readings toward Catholicism. But having determined to regard him as her master, she either ignored these imperfections, accepted them, or found productive ways to cope with them.

Apparently, she knew that Heger censored the texts he read his students. In *Villette,* Lucy Snowe reports that M. Paul "[took] care always to expunge, with the severest hand, whatever passage, phrase, or word, could be deemed unsuited to an audience of 'jeune filles'"; she even praises his ability to fill the gaps by "improvis[ing] whole paragraphs, no less vigorous than irreproachable. . . ." These substitutions, she suggests, are the price to be paid for the luxury of hearing "current literature."[109] Heger exercised a similar control in preparing passages to dictate. His dictée from Chateaubriand's *The Martyrs* omits the line, "Cymodoce in the arms of Hierocles!"—a change that tames the sexual implications of the previous line, "Cymodoce in a place of infamy!"[110] But he could be just as imperious in altering innocuous extracts. In "Evening Prayer on Board a Ship," another dictée from Chateaubriand, he made more than a dozen changes. It is possible that Charlotte mistranscribed a few words or that Heger dictated this part of *The Genius of Christianity* from memory. Even so, a narrator standing on a ship's deck would not have witnessed sea monsters "astonished" at the sailors' chants and then "plunging to the depth of their caverns."

Strictures were looser in the nineteenth century, and Heger was accustomed to making adjustments in any composition before him. Nonetheless, Charlotte's acceptance of this practice suggests that she suspended her critical judgment or let his standards govern her own. Presumably she grew used to this process and, in the long term, even followed his example. As Nancy Armstrong has argued, when Charlotte wrote the preface to *Wuthering Heights* (and edited Emily's poems after her death) she was packaging her sister's work for a market of Victorian readers.[111] Heger too was packaging literature of value, making it safe or enlivening it for readers not quite ready to accept it in its primal state.

His literary tastes have been hailed by Enid Duthie and others as advanced for his period. Certainly, he introduced the Brontës to the French Romantics: Bernardin de Saint-Pierre, Chateaubriand, Nodier, Lamartine, Hugo, Alfred de Musset. But his assignments were not always at that level:

> Oh why have I no mother?
> Why, unlike that bird, am I alone?
> Its nest sways gently in the branches of the elm.
> > Nothing on earth do I own.
> > I had not even a cradle,
> For I was a child found
> Before the church of the village, on a stone.[112]

This verse from Soumet's poem "The Poor Girl" is not an anomalous dictée. Heger, who distributed bonbons from his pockets, had a frankly sentimental streak. It comes out in a number of his revisions and the comment he appends to a "Letter" of Emily's: "No token of remembrance for papa?" With it went a taste for melodrama. In revising Charlotte's devoirs, he often makes her heavy French more graceful, but he also converts it into prose that an impassioned speaker could declaim.

Again, Charlotte seems to have submitted. At most, she demurs by not incorporating all of the revisions he suggests. But she had come to Brussels with a taste for high-flown language that she was not quite ready to curb, and with Heger she did not have to curb it. Ironically, he cured her of that taste without meaning to, by failing to answer the letters she wrote him in 1843–45. When she finally and bitterly accepted his indifference—"At last I looked up and saw I prayed to a stone"[113]—she lost her appetite for grandiosity. She may always have objected to his sentimental dictées, but her only known response would come years later, in *Shirley*, where Caroline Helstone rejects the insipid "little poems" that Hortense Moore makes her read.[114]

Charlotte's acquiescence cannot be detached from her attitude toward gender and power. Though she had taken the initiative of going to Brussels and had negotiated funding for the trip through her aunt, she continued to concede to masculine authority, as she had within her juvenilia manuscripts and in her claims about their authorship.[115] She wrote those narratives under male pseudonyms: Wellesley, Tree, Douro, Townshend. Even when she signed her name, she used "C. Brontë" oftener than "Charlotte." At the pensionnat she was writing essays, not romances, and putting her name on every devoir. But she was not yet ready to compose from an explicitly feminine perspective or define her voice as a woman's. "Athens Saved by Poetry" includes a woman speaker—two, since Electra's tale incorporates Cassandra's—but she remains a victim whose role in the narrative is orchestrated by a male poet. Elsewhere, Charlotte's narrators are either male or neutral, insofar as she could keep their voices genderless. The "I" of "The Nest," for example, might be feminine, a stroller in the woods who discovers eggs that hatch, but Charlotte includes no adjectives to mark the speaker's gender; in contrast, "the Atheist" in the same devoir is clearly marked as male. When she does choose women as her subjects, as in "Sacrifice of an Indian Widow" and "Anne Askew," they do not control the discourse; a narrator observes and describes them.

Nonetheless, each time Charlotte turned in an essay, she was asserting her ideas. Respecting and even requiring Heger's dominance, she still resolved to show him what a woman could do and win his recognition of her talent.

Heger's own attitude toward gender relations was advanced for his time but hardly radical. He believed in education for women and men, but women's education was to serve different purposes. As he wrote to a later student, Margaret Mossman, "It is not desirable for a woman to be a blue-stocking, but she must be educated. Without education she can neither supervise her children's studies nor share her husband's ideas. Education is a bond between husband and wife—ignorance is a barrier."[116] He emphasizes similar aims in a Prize Day speech of 1837, almost certainly delivered at the pensionnat. Girls, he says, need to complete their education, to use the faculties God has given them, to maintain regular habits of work, and to accept their defined role within the family. They are also to obey their masters and their parents, especially the mother who has taught them to love "duty, order, and work."[117]

These ideas inform his selection of assignments. Some, like the ones he described to Gaskell, could have been given as readily to male students; others seem tilted toward women. In outlining "The Siege of Oudenarde," for instance, he highlights the women's participation and the threatened execution of the leader's children. Charlotte writes a response sure to please him: the general's wife is worthy of her soldier husband, and the "ladies" of Oudenarde act with an ardor reminiscent of Greek and Roman matrons. In contrast, Emily's matching devoir asserts her defiance of the norms: "Even the women, that class condemned by the laws of society to be a heavy burden in any situation of action and danger, on that occasion cast aside their degrading privileges, and took a distinguished part. . . ."

But if Charlotte still needed to believe she had a master, she did not remain uncritical later. In her reconstruction of Heger as Emanuel, she flays his sexism relentlessly. Paul's seating of Lucy in the corner of an art exhibit, where she is to stare at four paintings of a woman's life,[118] is not unlike Heger's sending Charlotte off to write about some of his more insipid dictées. It would take her another ten years, however, to liberate the voice of dissent.

Meanwhile, at the pensionnat she would have observed that his theory did not dominate his practice. In the Hegers' marriage, both members made decisions; it was evidently a partnership. Zoë Heger worked with visible competence, running the household and the school. In fact, aside from genius, she had what Charlotte wanted: independent means, a companionate marriage, sexual fulfillment, and Heger.[119] Indirectly, Heger's own situation may have influenced his attitude toward Charlotte. Whatever his opinion of bluestockings, he would have perceived that she was not apt to marry, that her livelihood depended on her learning, and that if she longed to become a writer he could do her no good by dissuading her. Instead, he and his wife both attempted to prepare her for a vocation like their own. In this respect, his single fault may have been obtuseness, his own resistance to perceiving the intensity of her emotional attachment.

In *Villette,* Charlotte portrays Madame Beck as the one who keeps Emanuel in thrall to Catholic priests. In fact, Heger was more apt than his wife to have designed the "course of instruction, based on Religion" that the pensionnat's circular advertised.[120] A "profoundly and openly religious" man,[121] he allegedly resigned from the Athénée in protest when the state threatened to make religious instruction noncompulsory.[122] His own teaching was decisively Catholic. A poetry anthology with many of the poems he taught (which he gave Charlotte to take back to Haworth) bears the imprimatur of the archbishop of Paris.[123] Of the twenty excerpts in her notebook of dictées, six introduce some aspect of religion—evening prayer, morning prayer, the death of a martyr, the capture of Jerusalem, divinely inspired hope, the virtual divinity of kings— and three more are written by clerics.[124] Heger also concentrated on works by the Romantics, but only by those who were religiously correct. Rousseau does not appear in his agenda.

Beyond the curriculum, however, he made no attempt to press his beliefs on the Brontës. In the words of an obituary notice, he was "without narrowness or intolerance, having respect for sincere convictions and inquiries made in good faith. . . ."[125] That respect is demonstrated in his marking of their devoirs. In "Evening Prayer" especially, he tones down Charlotte's prejudice without inflicting views of his own. *Villette* and Charlotte's letters offer further tribute to the broad-mindedness that went with his religion,[126] a quality the Brontës did not share.

But then, nothing in their background could have prepared them for the pensionnat's Catholic and continental ambience. Daughters of an anti-Catholic Anglican clergyman, confirmed in insularity before they left Yorkshire, they had formed their notions of life abroad through literature, journals, and juvenilia fantasies. "The difference in Country & religion makes a broad line of demarcation between us & all the rest,"[127]

Charlotte wrote in her first letter home. They responded to that difference by drawing the line tighter. Their own religion gave them the equipment.

Gaskell writes that Charlotte and Emily were "national" whenever they had the opportunity and Protestant always, "to the backbone."[128] Charlotte's work supports these observations: religion plays a major role in nine or ten devoirs and a minor one in half-a-dozen others. In contrast, Emily alludes to religion in only three of her nine surviving devoirs— "King Harold before the Battle of Hastings," "Filial Love," and "The Butterfly"—in terms that seem nondenominational. This disparity reflects long-standing differences. Whereas Emily considered religion a matter between herself and God, Charlotte's concern with religion and ethics repeatedly emerges in her writings. A series of letters to Ellen Nussey documents an early crisis of faith, and throughout the juvenilia there are references to Scripture.[129] "She was nourished on the Bible," Heger said to Gaskell,[130] and in Brussels she relied on it for arguments, evidence, illustrations, models, and analogies.

But the paucity of Emily's religious references does not preclude their importance. In Brussels, religion became for both sisters a means of self-expression, a connection with home, and a language in which they felt confident. Emily's allusions also hint at the tenets she absorbed from Wesleyan Methodism. The conclusion of her essay on the cat, for instance—"undoubtedly [cats] remember always that they owe all their misery and all their evil qualities to the great ancestor of humankind"— has an antecedent in the preaching of John Wesley: "In the living part of the creation were seen the most deplorable effects of Adam's apostasy. The whole animated creation . . . was thereby 'made subject' to such 'vanity' as the inanimate creatures could not be. They were subject to that fell monster, death. . . . They were made subject to its forerunner, pain. . . . How many millions of creatures in the sea, in the air, and on every part of the earth, can now no otherwise preserve their own lives than by taking away the lives of others ? . . ."[131] Wesley also preached that there would be a new creation, an idea whose importance to "The Butterfly" has been partly explored by J. Hillis Miller but remains to be investigated further.[132] In these ways and others, Emily's Belgian essays drew her back to earlier teachings. She may not have appreciated Heger or his orders, but she wrote her convictions into her devoirs and perhaps defined them in doing so.

If Emily's work exhibits traces of Wesleyan and possibly Calvinist doctrine, Charlotte's is more orthodoxly Anglican. Elizabeth Rigby, who attacked *Jane Eyre* as "pre-eminently an anti-Christian composition,"[133] would have found little to censure in Charlotte's devoirs, whose pieties befit the clergyman's daughter rather than the pioneering rebel. Occasionally her faith invigorates her imagery: Anne Askew "stretches herself willingly on the bed of torture . . . closing her eyes, as if she were going to sleep"; Moses climbs Mount Nebo with a ray of divinity lighting up his "bald brow and . . . white hair." Oftener, it leads her into biblical quotations and platitudes.

And yet her motives for proclaiming faith in Brussels are similar to those that make *Jane Eyre* seem "anti-Christian": disgust at "humbug" and contempt for zealots who manipulate others through their dogma.[134] In her novels, such convictions lead her undervalued heroines to acts of self-assertion and defiance. At the pensionnat, they led a defensive Charlotte Brontë to do her most reverential writing. Professing faith was tantamount to guarding her identity. The Bible was her bulwark and her weapon. It also gave her a perceptible advantage over the other students and teachers, since Catholics did not study it as she had. She learned quickly that by using her knowledge, she could earn Heger's respect.

In her "Death of Moses," for example, she shows him what an Englishwoman raised on Scripture can do with a celebrated subject. As she probably knew from the books Heger lent her, Moses had become a topic for many religious Romantics. Hugo wrote about his cradle on the Nile, Lamartine wrote of his climb up Mount Sinai, Chateaubriand wrote of his destruction of the tablets, and Vigny wrote of his encounter with God on the summit of Mount Nebo.[135] While Charlotte's devoir may allude to one or more of these texts,[136] its primary source is the Bible. She sweeps through Deuteronomy, 1 and 2 Kings, and Luke, culling names and episodes for her panorama of the patriarch's last hours.

Since there are no marks on the surviving version—Gaskell saw another, which did have corrections—Heger's approval can only be assumed from the fact that he kept two copies and exhibited one to illustrate what the Bible meant to Charlotte. Elsewhere (as I have noted) he made some attempt to moderate her displays of prejudice. When she wrote of an Egyptian idol "whose brutal image seemed to be the symbol of its worshipers' ignorance," he underlined and then reworked the passage: "[it seemed] to have remained standing only to indicate what the beliefs of the world were, before the coming of J.C."[137] By and large, though, he encouraged her interest in religion, indirectly through his own dedication to his faith and directly through his lectures and assignments. Of course, their creeds clashed, but his exceptional tolerance encouraged her to override the differences; he could write "*Good*" beside a passage whose theology or politics defied his own convictions.

In Charlotte's view, the differences were also offset by their underlying kindred sensibilities. They had in common a belief in moral engagement, in the use of one's faculties, in literature. They shared a love of nature that was sensory and spiritual. The storm, the sunset, and the night sky impressed them—as they impressed the religious Romantics—as natural phenomena to be observed in detail and as symbols of God's transcendent power.[138]

Later, she would write exceptional passages about the disclosure of such empathy. "I was conscious of rapport between you and myself," Paul Emanuel declares to Lucy Snowe, "You are patient, and I am choleric; you are quiet and pale, and I am tanned and fiery; you are a strict Protestant, and I am a sort of lay Jesuit: but we are alike—there is affinity. . . . [I] believe that you were born under my star."[139] But in Brussels, the rapport between master and student sometimes worked against her progress as a writer. She could not have had a better mentor than Heger when his critical faculties were active. But his weakness for exalted moral statements, for sentimental scenes and lush descriptions, fed her own inclinations toward hyperbole and preaching. And Heger was not the one to curb them. With a curious disregard for his own principles, he often made her phrasing more florid by his editing and so inadvertently signaled his approval of the style she knew she had to give up.

She would only abandon it when she accepted the end of her relationship with Heger. Then, illusions gone and anger surging, she mutinied against his kind of prose. She also launched the reconstruction of Heger that her final novel would complete. William Crimsworth of *The Profes-*

sor—cool, self-possessed, and in control of his emotions—has little in common with Emanuel. But he is an ideal master for Frances Evans Henri, whom he teaches with an empathy that strongly suggests wish fulfillment on the part of his author. "To me," says Crimsworth, "it was not difficult to discover how I could best foster my pupil, cherish her starved feelings and induce the outward manifestation of that inward vigour which sunless drought and blighting blast had hitherto forbidden to expand. Constancy of Attention—a kindness as mute as watchful, always standing by her, cloaked in the rough garb of austerity and making its real nature known only by a rare glance of interest, or a cordial and gentle word; real respect masked with seeming imperiousness, directing, urging her actions—yet helping her too and that with devoted care."[140]

In his own fashion, Heger fostered his pupil, at least until Zoë Heger noticed that she was a woman transgressing the boundaries between the academic and the personal. That his methods of teaching encouraged such transgression was, of course, peripheral to the problem his wife faced as the head of a school that could be put out of business if rumors of misconduct got started. Charlotte had no recourse in Brussels. In her fiction, however, she would wipe out those boundaries, making the mentoring relationship the seedbed of romance and of personal fulfillment.

After Brussels

What long-range effects did Heger's teaching have? How did the experience of writing devoirs influence the Brontë sisters later? Again, the answers are much clearer for Charlotte than for Emily, though Emily's absolute silence on the pensionnat has not kept scholars from guessing. David E. Musselwhite, the most intrepid, argues that Brussels made her later writing possible. He asks, "what enabled Emily Brontë not only to break out of the stranglehold of Haworth and its insistence on her 'femininity,' but also to soar beyond the manic-depressive and essentially adolescent world of the Gondal poems and write some of the great mystical poems of the language and what some would argue to be its greatest novel?" The answer for him is "Héger's impact."[141] He bases this conjecture on a Lacanian reading of her childhood;[142] on the assumption that her devoirs represent a "dramatic and qualitative" break from Gondal;

on the claim that in Heger she found "a second 'Symbolic Father,'" very different from her own;[143] and, as his spelling of that father's name suggests, on research that is less than thorough.

The contradictions between Musselwhite's claims and the evidence should be apparent. There is simply not enough of the Gondal saga extant to determine whether Emily broke away from it, or brought themes from Gondal stories into her devoirs, or, like her sister, chose to make distinctions between private and public modes of writing. The dates on her poems make it plain, however, that death and inhumanity haunted her imagination years before she went to Brussels. Heger's conduct may have been paternalistic, but there is not a clue that Emily welcomed his attention, and there are many that he left her with the Hobson's choice of following his orders, whatever her own wishes, or resisting through the devoirs she submitted. The texts that resulted are indeed uninhibited, but Heger's role in freeing them is questionable. Emily is more likely to have said what she meant to say, whatever constraints he put her under.

These objections voiced, Musselwhite makes several points that might be pursued more seriously. What he refers to as "the sustained, almost vindictive misanthropy" of her devoirs does carry over into *Wuthering Heights*.[144] But so does the promise of a new order with which "The Butterfly" concludes. The "search for the origins of Heathcliff" should probably encompass Hugo's essay on Mirabeau and the three contrasting passages on Cromwell that Heger read to the Brontës.[145] But to say that Heathcliff is "modelled on" those two revolutionaries goes too far.[146] More broadly, whatever Emily thought of her venture, it did take her out of her environment and language, force her to consider French and German literature, and make her, however reluctantly, aware of a culture that differed from her own.

One apparent result is that her devoirs place their subjects in difficult or alien settings. The child whose health declines among foreigners, the king whose territory is threatened by invasion, and the brother returning from self-imposed exile recognize their separateness yet call for reconnection to a relative, to roots, or to their kind. Her experience of exile and knowledge of its costs may also have informed the poems on Gondal's civil wars that she wrote after 1842.

Against these facts, Charlotte Brontë's efforts to represent her sister as a rustic genius look increasingly like a reconstruction guided by her own literary purposes. The conversion was not willfully self-interested and may not even have been conscious. If anything, as Armstrong argues, it was to make Emily's writing acceptable to the English reading public of the 1850s. But the Emily of Charlotte's notices and memoir, the Emily whose mind was "not amenable" to "the influence of other intellects," is not the student who rose to the challenge of writing devoirs at the pensionnat.

For Heger and his readings did influence her. At the very least, they pressured her into producing, and once she undertook his assignments, she did not do them halfway. "The Palace of Death," for example, is a set piece outlined by Heger and based on a children's fable—hardly a project that allowed Emily the freedom her sister claimed she needed. Still, she keeps to Heger's plot (on Death's choice of a vice-regent) and concludes as he ordered, with the triumph of Intemperance. But she adds a collaborator, Civilization, and an argument about the corruption of humanity as far-reaching as it is terse. Charlotte's corresponding "Palace of Death," though studded with biblical and literary references, lacks the intellectual cogency of Emily's and its allegorical complexity.

That Emily could comply and still express her own views hints that she and Heger were getting along better or at least had reached a viable arrangement. He may still have found her exceptionally stubborn, but her talent, in music as well as composition, evoked his unstinting admiration. (Nearly a year after her departure, he inscribed a copy of his current Prize Day speech to her "in token of sincere affection.")[147] More important, she was making it clear to him—and Charlotte—that she could work effectively under compulsion, whatever her initial resistance.

This discovery is not coincidental to the genesis of *Wuthering Heights* four years later. Emily had written well over a hundred poems when Charlotte "accidentally lighted on" her notebook and talked her into publication.[148] But no novel existed for Charlotte to promote, so far as anybody knows, and before it could be written, something had to spur Emily into production. According to Charlotte, the catalyst was the experience of publishing their poetry: "Ill-success failed to crush us: the mere effort to succeed had given a wonderful zest to existence; it must be pursued. We each set to work on a prose tale. . . ."[149] Again, as in the passage "it was some years before the experiment of sending [Emily] from home was again ventured on,"[150] she omits the agent from her sentence. To whose existence did publishing give zest? Did the three sisters agree on this pursuit, or did the most ambitious one take charge? The next sentence glides over these questions, leaving the reader to assume that all three were committed to seeing their work in print.

But the rest of the record on Emily contests the assumption Charlotte's passage sets up. She was angry when Charlotte came across her poems, furious when Charlotte disclosed to William Smith that "Ellis Bell" was actually Emily Brontë, scornful of public opinion in any case, and resolutely private in her ways. It seems likelier, then, that if she gave her consent and undertook a novel in conjunction with her sisters, they used some other method of persuasion. The motive most commonly proposed is Emily's sympathy with her sisters' unhappiness. In the autumn of 1846, Charlotte was still recovering from Heger, Anne perhaps from the death of William Weightman, their father was still weak from a cataract operation, and all of them had to cope with Branwell. Writing may have given all three sisters a haven, but Emily could have stuck to Gondal.

Charlotte, however, had discovered from Brussels how to bring Emily around. As she had fired up her sisters with the prospect of their own school, so she could fire them up with thoughts of publishing. As she had chosen Emily for her foreign venture, so she could choose Ellis (or her poetry) to spearhead the Bells' adventure into print. Even if Emily expressed reservations, Charlotte had seen that her sister would produce—and produce no common text—if she were kept to it. Charlotte later told Gaskell that the sisters had "retained the old habit . . . begun in their aunt's life-time, of putting away their work at nine o'clock," so that they could talk about stories in progress and read aloud what they had written.[151] But if, before Brussels, they had read to each other, they were reading now with the additional motive of preparing work for a larger audience. Emily had had that experience. Reluctantly or not, she had heard her devoirs read aloud, made into public discourse at the pensionnat.

In Brussels, she also got a grounding in German and perhaps a lasting taste for German literature that subtly influenced her writing. As Stevie Davies observes, "She had visited Brussels when the influence of the German school was in full flood in the French-speaking countries of Europe."[152] Romer Wilson, Ruth MacKay, and other critics connect the plot of *Wuthering Heights* to a story Emily allegedly read at the pensionnat, E. T. A. Hoffman's "Das Majorat" ("The Entail").[153] Closer to home was "The Poems and Ballads of Schiller," a yearlong series of translations that appeared in *Blackwood's* between September 1842 and August 1843. Since it began the month before Elizabeth Branwell died, the early numbers would have been in the house by the time the sisters returned. Gérin points out that Emily must have seen them, since she replaced her aunt as the member of the family who read political and other news to Patrick Brontë each day.[154] Charlotte too must have read these translations (by Bulwer-Lytton, though he is unnamed) and possibly made copies of her favorites. A few months later, back in Brussels, she did her own translations of Schiller into French; all five of those poems were featured in *Blackwood's* between September and December.[155]

As always, it is easier to trace the effects of Charlotte's education on her later work. What she absorbed comes to the foreground in her novels, converted yet often recognizable; thus Jane Eyre translates Schiller at Moor House.[156] But what Emily took in became so thoroughly her own that unless her words echo a source familiar to her, a line of Byron's or Cowper's or Milton's, tracing becomes at best conjectural. It is similarly hard to know what she recycles from her juvenilia into her devoirs and from them into her adult work. Only "Letter from one brother to another" clearly demonstrates such continuity.[157]

Nonetheless, I would risk some speculation. Catherine Earnshaw is lured from the Heights by the promise of the Grange's social advantages, not wholly unlike Charlotte, who hoped to find in Belgium "connections far more improving, polished, and cultivated, than any [she] had yet known." Whatever Charlotte gained there, her misery afterward may have reminded Emily again that civilization brings destruction in its wake, as she says in "The Palace of Death."

But if civilizing first divides Catherine from Heathcliff, teaching—a concomitant of civilization—brings her daughter and Hareton together. Their relationship begins in hostility: young Catherine mocks his efforts to teach himself to read, and he retaliates by burning the books. But on Lockwood's final visit, he finds them absorbed in their literacy project and each other. Although Catherine takes the lead in instruction and courtship, Hareton holds his own in acquiescing, so that they never fall into the roles of dominating master and subordinate. Emily's version of the teacher-pupil enterprise thus counters her sister's and rewrites it. An echo of Heger may also be latent in the dialogue connected to the lessons. "He is not *envious* but *emulous* of your attainments," Nelly explains to the scornful Catherine before she is ready to help Hareton.[158] Emulation is the method that Heger recommended and practiced with the Brontës.

The influence of Brussels and Heger on Charlotte's work is too massive to sum up in a few pages. She seems to have pieced every scrap of her experience into the fabric of her fiction. Characters, episodes, methods of instruction, allusions to her readings and to cultural events gave her matter for all four of her novels. The pensionnat itself emerges in two of them with a fidelity to atmosphere and detail that witnesses and researchers confirm. Over time, she would prove equally faithful to the personal myth that she embroidered on this fabric—of the cold, scheming, and unscrupulous directress, the English younger woman who is almost a victim, and the master-lover who rescues her.

Zoë Heger later told her daughter Louise that when she saw Charlotte off on the packet boat, Charlotte flung back the words "Je me vengerai!"—"I will be revenged!"[159] Apparently the Hegers never read *The Professor,* whose Zoraïde Reuter they might have found even more offensive than *Villette*'s Modeste Beck. But to anyone aware of Charlotte's originals, *Villette* (which they did read) was sufficiently vengeful, a vilification of the woman whose sole fault had been to see what Charlotte hid from herself. Nonetheless, when English tourists came to the pensionnat, they were seldom turned away, and Constantin Heger, with typical tolerance, preserved the Brontës' manuscripts and welcomed Mrs. Gaskell, although his wife did not join him. Still, it was Zoë Heger who saved Charlotte's correspondence, perhaps as insurance against any charges that her husband had complied in that self-constructed romance.[160]

Charlotte's four famous letters to Heger, written in the two years that followed her departure, can be read as adjuncts to her devoirs. In them she continues to practice her French. She tells him that she memorizes half a page each day "from a book written in familiar style," so that when they meet again, as they must, she will not "remain dumb" before him.[161]

But the voice of the letters is not moderate or neutral. With increasing anguish, she pleads for his attention and for news of his health and his family. Suffering and deprivation break down the control she had struggled to acquire in Brussels, and the personal emerges unmediated: "Monsieur, the poor have not need of much to sustain them—they ask only for the crumbs that fall from the rich men's table. But if they are refused the crumbs they die of hunger. Nor do I, either, need much affection from those I love. I should not know what to do with a friendship entire and complete—I am not used to it. But you showed me of yore a *little* interest, when I was your pupil in Brussels, and I hold on to the maintenance of that *little* interest—I hold on to it as I would hold on to life.[162] Aware that her morbidity can only put him off, she is nonetheless powerless to curb it:

> . . . I tell you frankly that I have tried meanwhile to forget you. . . . I have done everything; I have sought occupation; I have denied myself absolutely the pleasure of speaking about you—even to Emily; but I have been able to conquer neither my regrets nor my impatience. That, indeed, is humiliating—to be unable to control one's own thoughts, to be the slave of a regret, of a memory, the slave of a fixed and dominant idea which lords it over the mind. Why cannot I have just as much friendship for you, as you for me—neither more nor less? Then should I be so tranquil, so free—I could keep silence then for ten years without an effort.[163]

Confronted with an obsession so intense, Heger chose not to reply. Charlotte was left to undergo a bitter and protracted convalescence. But of course she did not remain silent. Already, by the time she wrote this passage, she had come across Emily's verses. Within two months, she would be contacting publishers about a book of poems by the Bells.

As painful as this aftermath was, it had the effect of transmuting the lessons she had learned under Heger at the pensionnat. She no longer submitted to his dictates without question. Instead, she took from his teaching what she needed for her own mature style and methods.

Her very conception of a personal voice metamorphosed in response to her experience. She had gained a new consciousness of literary style, not only from reading in a foreign language, but also from coming to realize its centrality to Heger's thinking and teaching. In this, he was at one with his colleagues at the Athénée, as a passage by his friend A. Baron makes evident: "I understand by style the process personal to each writer, not only for expressing, but for finding and arranging his ideas. Style depends, not on the nature of the subject, but on the temperament, the heart, the mind, the taste of the writer, the whole necessarily modified by the influence of the era and country. That is the true meaning of Buffon's saying, the style is the man. Style is what one calls in the arts *the manner, the doing,* that which gives the painter or the sculptor his cachet, that which distinguishes him from others and constitutes his originality. . . ." Heger's lectures imply this definition, though he may not have gone along with Baron's conclusion, "The first ambition of the writer should therefore be to have a style of his own." He aimed to make the Brontës proficient in French through imitation and analysis of other authors' styles. If later they chose to move beyond apprenticeship, his method would have laid the foundation.[164]

Still, he must have persuaded Charlotte that style manifests the writer's special genius, for when she returned to writing after Brussels, she established both a voice and a style of her own. She went through a frustrating period of latency, cocooned in longing, misery, and shame. But she emerged with a new and distinctive way of writing, characterized by traits that Margot Peters has classified: emphatic adverbs, syntactic inversion, and a pervasive use of antithesis—in sentence structure, language, form, and plot.[165] Heger did not instruct her in her style, but he put her on the road to discovery.

The manuscripts of her adult novels suggest another outcome of her Brussels experience: she changed from a writer who counted on genius to one who had learned about discipline. Those holograph copies do not look, or read, like texts conceived on impulse. As a group they differ sharply from the juvenilia manuscripts, whose fine print flows across the page, uncensored. All are penned in script that is eminently legible. All contain revisions of various kinds, ranging from replacement of a single word or phrase through deletions or additions of long passages.[166] These signs of attention connect them with the devoirs she prepared and revised for Heger. It is true that only the publisher's copies of *Jane Eyre* (1847),

Shirley (1849), and *Villette* (1853) are extant, but Gaskell, who saw early drafts, attests to Brontë's concern for the truth and precision of her phrasing; a similar concern is apparent in fragments that date from the years after Brussels.[167]

Nostalgia for the older, more spontaneous methods is apparent in an episode from *Shirley*. Shirley, Brontë writes, might be reading by moonlight from a book that "set her brain astir, furnished her mind with pictures." Closing the book, she would walk through the parlor, feeling "[a] still, deep, inborn delight," a feeling "not to be reached or ravished by human agency, because by no human agency bestowed: the pure gift of God to His creature, the free dower of Nature to her child":

> This joy gives her experience of a genii-life. Buoyant . . . her eye
> seeks, and her soul possesses, the vision of life as she wishes it.
> No—not as she wishes it: she has not time to wish; the swift
> glory spreads out, sweeping and kindling, and multiplies its
> splendours faster than Thought can effect combinations, faster
> than Aspiration can utter her longings. Shirley says nothing
> while the trance is upon her—she is quite mute; but if Mrs.
> Pryor speaks to her now, she goes out quietly and continues her
> walk up-stairs in the dim gallery.
>
> If Shirley were not an indolent, a reckless, an ignorant being,
> she would take a pen at such moments; or at least while the rec-
> ollection of such moments was yet fresh on her spirit: she would
> seize, she would fix the apparition, tell the vision revealed . . .
> and thus possess what she was enabled to create.[168]

Charlotte's own "genii-life" remained a source of creativity, the basis of her power as a novelist. But she did not write her novels in a passive state of trance, although portions of them came to her as visions. The need for control was constantly with her as she struggled toward felicitous expression.

Gaskell has described Charlotte's method of writing, how she guided thought and vision into language:

> One set of words was the truthful mirror of her thoughts; no
> others, however apparently identical in meaning, would do. . . .

She would wait patiently searching for th⟨
presented itself to her. . . . She never wrote ⟨
until she clearly understood what she wanted ⟨
erately chosen the words, and arranged them in ⟨.
der. . . . She wrote on . . . bits of paper in a minute h⟨
each against a piece of board. . . . Her finished manus⟨
were copied from these pencil scraps, in clear, legible, de⟨
traced writing, almost as easy to read as print.[169]

Gaskell claims that Charlotte rarely changed a word or a phrase, though sometimes she might delete a sentence. But Margaret Smith, who has examined all four manuscripts, questions the truth of this assertion.[170] And Charlotte herself effectively refutes it in a letter to W. S. Williams: "I can work indefatigably at the correction of a work before it leaves my hands," she tells him, "but when once I have looked on it as completed and submitted to the inspection of others, it becomes next to impossible to alter or amend."[171]

Despite this declaration, she made a major change in response to Williams's warning about the French in *Shirley*.[172] Conceding that some readers might consider it pretentious, she removed the French text of Shirley's devoir and substituted one in English. "The First Blue-Stocking" ("La Première Femme Savante") is Shirley's version of the myth of creation.[173] Her Eva—a passionate but undirected woman—marries a heaven-sent seraph "named Genius" who keeps her from succumbing to the "Father of Lies" and helps her to achieve immortality. Charlotte also changed the chapter heading, replacing "Le Cheval dompté," the manuscript caption, with the title of the new English devoir. As a conversation later in the chapter explains, "Le Cheval dompté" is a piece by Jacques-Bénigne Bossuet; in fact, it is one of the extracts that Heger dictated to his students. The phrase is not precisely translatable; the closest equivalent is "The Tamed Horse," though "tamed" implies too much subordination. But *dompté* itself is well-defined within the passage, as Bossuet contrasts the horse who lacks control with one who has learned to know his master: "His ardor has changed to force, or rather, since the force was in some way in that ardor, it is regulated. Notice: it is not destroyed, it is regulated."[174]

ext, both the devoir and Bossuet's title prefigure the conclu-
of the novel: spirited Shirley is to marry Louis Moore, the only master she chooses to submit to. But both signify beyond the novel's boundaries, pointing toward a resolution of conflicts that haunted Charlotte's
thinking and writing. She wanted to reconcile genius with humanity, to
find a means of synthesizing ardor and restraint, the flash of inspiration
and reflection. Heger left her with a word that represented one solution
to the pull between these opposites. *Dompté*—which, like *indompté,* recurs throughout her Brussels work—became, for her, a symbol of productive regulation, of control that leaves the energy of genius unimpaired
while directing it precisely and truthfully. She discerned this synthesis in
Thackeray's writing; it was one of her reasons for admiring him. Thackeray, she said, was a Titan of an author, but his energy was "sane . . . deliberate . . . thoughtful": "Thackeray is never borne away by his own ar-
dour—he has it under control. His genius obeys him—it is his servant, it
works no fantastic changes at its own wild will, it must still achieve the
task which reason and sense assign it, and none other."[175]

"The First Blue-Stocking" suggests another legacy of Charlotte's
years in Brussels. In writing it, she reverts to the exalted rhetoric of her
later devoirs: the poet's song in "Athens Saved by Poetry," for instance,
or parts of "The Death of Moses." By having Moore recite it to Shirley,
she also recreates Heger's practice of reading outstanding work aloud.
But here, the recitation is more complex. Charlotte's actual devoirs could
not deal with sexuality; accounts of love and passion were out of bounds
in Brussels. But when as an adult she returned to this genre, she literally
married sexual desire and intellectual empowerment. This devoir inscribes Shirley's past in her present and so enables her to resume and develop her relationship with her former tutor. And it is not an exception.

Paul Emanuel compels Lucy Snowe to produce a devoir for two ex-
aminers; the result is the satire on human justice that he reads over her
shoulder.[176] William Crimsworth first becomes aware of Frances's merits from the devoir she writes about King Alfred. As he unrolls the manuscript to give it back, "her depression beam[s] as a cloud might, behind
which the sun is burning." He directs her attention to her work's "numerous faults" with the warning that perfecting her English will take
years. But once he has noted and explained her errors and shown her

"how the words or phrases ought to have been written," the dialogue becomes more encouraging: "As to the substance of your devoir . . . it has surprised me; I perused it with pleasure because I saw in it some proofs of taste and fancy. Taste and fancy are not the highest gifts of the human mind but such as they are you possess them. . . . You may then take courage; cultivate the faculties that God and Nature have bestowed on you. . . ." Frances responds with a transfigured countenance and a smile in her eyes, "almost triumphant," which tells him, "I am glad you have been forced to discover so much of my nature; you need not so carefully moderate your language. Do you think I am myself a stranger to myself? What you tell me in terms so qualified, I have known fully from a child."[177]

In all four of Charlotte's novels, the heroines receive the recognition their creator longed for. Each of them elicits the affection of a man without surrendering her values or identity. And the catalyst of love and admiration, in all but one case, is student writing. *Jane Eyre* is the only book that lacks a devoir, and there Jane's paintings fill a comparable purpose. Rochester makes her fetch them when they first converse at Thornfield and quickly finds the three that are outstanding. Their dialogue reveals his understanding of the artist, his acuity, and the interest he would hide from her.[178]

In some ways, these inner texts are throwbacks. Jane's pictures recall the supernatural landscapes of Charlotte's pre-Angrian stories. Shirley's devoir is grandiloquent: "I claim as mine the lost atom of life: I take to myself the spark of soul—burning, heretofore, forgotten!"[179] Lucy's "beldame" is as indifferent to justice as any scheming libertine in Angria. But the adult texts do not display the sexual imbalance, the assumption that men dominate and women submit, which is fundamental to the juvenilia. In these examples, or rather through their agency, imbalances begin to be rectified. They are clearly wrought by female minds and female hands, and their existence is proof that the character who wrote them is intelligent and feeling. In every case, the man to whom they are offered constrains the emotions they arouse. Ultimately, though, he will challenge rule and custom, accepting the creator as a person of exceptional endowments and a woman he can love.

When Charlotte was working under her professor, the boundaries between intellectual and amorous passion dissolved. Perhaps they were never to solidify again. But over time something else formed: a writer's connection of enormous importance for her novels. The devoirs are the instruments of this connection and texts that in themselves repay close reading.

A Chronology of Charlotte and Emily Brontë's Belgian Experience

Charlotte was born in 1816 and Emily in 1818, the third and fifth of the Rev. Patrick Brontë and Maria Brontë's six children. In 1820 the family settled in the parsonage of Haworth in Yorkshire, a county that the girls never left until they traveled to Brussels in 1842. After Maria Brontë died in 1821, her sister Elizabeth Branwell arrived from Cornwall, to look after the children and household. More deaths followed: sent to the Clergy Daughters' School in 1824, the two oldest girls contracted tuberculosis and died the following May and June. Charlotte and Emily also went to the school but were sent home when the second sister's health failed. From 1829 until well into their twenties, the four surviving siblings had an outlet unsuspected by their father and aunt: fantasy kingdoms that they created and chronicled in stories and poems. Emily and Anne eventually split off to develop the kingdom of Gondal, leaving Charlotte and Branwell with the kingdom of Angria. The siblings' formal education was conducted at home until 1831–32, when Charlotte went to Miss Wooler's school at Roe Head, where she met her lifelong friends Ellen Nussey and Mary Taylor. She returned to teach at Roe Head in 1835, bringing Emily with her as a student, but Emily became so intensely homesick that she left after three months. Charlotte later accepted two positions as a governess but hated the work and the confinement. Like Branwell, she dreamed of becoming a great writer; unlike him, she would realize her dream. Her more public and immediate ambition was to open a school close to home with her sisters and prepare herself by studying abroad.

1841

July 19   CB letter to Ellen Nussey, alluding to the sisters' project for establishing a school, with capital to be lent by Aunt Branwell.

August 7   CB letter to Nussey, alluding to Mary and Martha Taylor's travels on the Continent and her own longing to go abroad: "Such a strong wish for wings . . . such an urgent thirst to see—to know—to learn. . . ." She describes the gift they sent her from Brussels, "one of the most splendid capitals of Europe."

September 29   CB letter to Aunt Elizabeth Branwell, outlining her project and asking for a loan of fifty or a hundred pounds. She explains why she should go to school abroad for six months before undertaking a school of her own and gives reasons for choosing Brussels rather than Paris or some other town in France: it is cheaper; it has fine educational facilities; Martha Taylor is currently at school there (at the Château de Koekelberg). She proposes to go with EB.

November 2   CB letter to Nussey, indicating Aunt Branwell's consent. She has turned down a proposal to run Miss Wooler's old school: "a fire was kindled in my very heart which I could not quench—I so longed to increase my attainments to become something better than I am. . . ." She reports that Mary Taylor is pouring oil on the fire, and she has "fixed on Emily" to go with her.

November 7   CB letter to EB, confirming their plans and proposing "to seek employment abroad" after their six months in Brussels; she does not intend to come home for a year.

December 9(?)   CB letter to Nussey, reporting that she has "heard of a less expensive establishment" than the Château de Koekelberg: "Brussels is still my promised land, but there is the wilderness of Time and Space to cross before I reach it."

1842

January 20 CB letter to Nussey, indicating that she and EB "expect to leave England in less than three weeks." They now plan to go to Lille, rather than Brussels, because Patrick Brontë has received a poor report of the French schools in Brussels from his contact, Mrs. Jenkins (wife of the chaplain to the British embassy).

late January Mrs. Jenkins writes to recommend the Pensionnat Heger and puts Charlotte in touch with Mme Heger (Zoë Heger-Parent); satisfied with her responses, the Brontës shift back to Brussels.

February 8–14 CB and EB leave Haworth for the Continent, accompanied by their father and Mary and Joe Taylor. They spend three days in London, departing by packet boat for Ostend on Saturday, February 12. Arriving at midnight after a rough crossing, they spend Sunday and Sunday night in Ostend. On Monday they travel to Brussels by stagecoach, staying overnight at the Hôtel d'Hollande. The Taylors leave them in the morning.

February 15 Mr. and Mrs. Jenkins arrive to conduct the Brontës to the Pensionnat Heger at 32, rue d'Isabelle and present them to Mme Heger. Patrick Brontë remains in Brussels for several days but does not meet Constantin Heger.

March(?) First of several CB *cahiers,* or exercise books, with translations (English and French).[1] Other CB cahiers contain grammar exercises and literary extracts.

March 16 CB devoir "L'Ingratitude" (missing).

n.d. CB devoir "Lettre d'un Missionaire, Sierra-Leone, Afrique" (missing).

March 26 CB letter to Nussey on the back of Mary Taylor's letter to her, expressing satisfaction with the school.

March 28 Mme Heger gives birth to her fourth child (first son).

April 17 CB devoir "Sacrifice d'une veuve Indienne."

April 18 CB devoir "La jeune Fille malade."

April 26 CB devoir "La Prière du Soir dans un camp."

April 30 CB devoir "Le Nid."

May 4 Heger's commentary added to "Le Nid."

May(?) CB letter to Nussey, expressing her delight with her present life:

"I think I am never unhappy. . . . My time, constantly occupied, passes too rapidly." She gives her impressions of the school and the Belgians, along with her first assessment of Heger: "he is professor of Rhetoric a man of power as to mind but very choleric & irritable in temperament. . . ." Emily, who is working "like a horse," does not get along with Heger. She herself cries when he is "very ferocious . . . & that sets all things straight." He has given them a "few private lessons."

May(?)   CB devoir "L'Immensité de Dieu."

May 15   EB devoir "Le Chat."

May(?)   CB fragment "Plaidoyer pour les chats" and "Les deux chiens."

n.d.   EB devoir "Le Siège d'Oudenarde" and CB devoir "Le siège d'Oudenarde."

June 2   CB devoir "Anne Askew: Imitation"

June   EB devoir "Portrait: Le Roi Harold avant la Bataille de Hastings." Heger's version, "Portrait: Harold la veille de la Bataille de Hastings," also dated "Juin [18]42," is clearly a later revision.

June 23   CB devoir "Portrait: Pierre l'Ermite" (first version).

July   CB letter to Nussey, reporting Mme Heger's proposal that the sisters remain six more months. She offers to employ Charlotte as an English teacher and Emily as a part-time music teacher in exchange for board and lessons in French and German. "Monsieur & Madame Heger begin to recognize the valuable points of [Emily's] character under her singularities." The letter communicates CB's further impressions of Brussels, including her contempt for the Catholic faith and the Belgian character. Still, she is happy and well occupied.

July   Arrival at the pensionnat of Dr. Thomas Wheelwright's five daughters as day boarders. The oldest, Laetitia, will become CB's lifelong friend.

July 16   EB devoir "Lettre (Madame)."

July 21   CB devoir "Lettre d'invitation à un Ecclésiastique."

July 26   EB devoir "Lettre (Ma chère Maman)."

July 31   CB devoir "Imitation: Portrait de Pierre L'Hermite" (second version).

August 4   CB sketches a river scene; two days later, she draws a tree and cottage. Other landscapes by CB and one by EB suggest that they are making expeditions to the country to draw from nature.[2]

August 5   EB devoirs "L'Amour Filial" and "Lettre d'un frère à un frère."

August 11   EB devoir "Le Papillon" and CB devoir "La Chenille."

August 15   Beginning of "les grandes vacances" (end of term). Over the vacation, the three youngest Wheelwright girls begin piano lessons with Emily.

August 24(?)   CB devoir "Le But de la Vie."

Summer or autumn   CB visits the triennial exhibition of paintings at the Brussels Salon.[3]

September 24   Mary Taylor writes to Nussey that the sisters "are well; not only in health but in mind & hope. They are content with their present position & even gay. . . ." She approves of their remaining, even though one "at least" could earn more money in Bradford.

October 6   CB devoir "La Justice humaine."

October 12   Martha Taylor dies of cholera at Koekelberg. CB arrives there the following morning and attends the funeral service on the fourteenth.

October 16   CB devoir "Le Palais de la Mort."

October 18   EB devoir "Le Palais de la Mort."

October 30   CB and EB walk with Mary Taylor to the Protestant cemetery where Martha is buried and spend the evening with Mary's cousins.

November 2   The sisters learn that Aunt Branwell is gravely ill. They decide to return home immediately.

November 3   A letter from home arrives informing them that Aunt Branwell died on October 29.

November 5   Heger writes a letter to Patrick Brontë, praising the progress that the sisters have made, indicating the affection he and his wife have for them, and urging their father to let them return for a year so that they can finish their studies. That accomplished, the Hegers would be prepared to offer at least one of them a teaching position.

November 6   The sisters return to England by steam packet from Antwerp, CB carrying Heger's letter. They arrive in Haworth on November 8.

November 15   Letter from CB to Nussey, noting that she has received an affectionate letter from Mme Heger.

November or December   Mme Heger writes CB a "kind and affection-ate" letter.[4]

November–December   Domestic arrangements at Haworth are reorga-nized. EB determines to keep house for their father, and Anne finds Bran-well a job as a tutor, leaving CB free to return to Brussels, as she wishes.

1843

January 14(?)   Letter from CB to Nussey, announcing her impending departure for Brussels "the last week in this month."

January 27   Prompted by "an irresistible impulse,"[5] CB leaves for Brus-sels. She goes directly from London to the packet boat for Ostend, stays overnight in Ostend the night of the twenty-eighth, and takes the train to Brussels the next day. At "7 Sunday evening" she arrives at the pension-nat, where Mme Heger welcomes her "with great kindness."

January 29   She returns as "Mlle Charlotte," teacher of English. She is to instruct students in the First Class (for which a new schoolroom has been built) and give occasional lessons to M. Heger and his brother-in-law, M. Chapelle. She is also to study German and continue her studies in literature. Her salary is set at sixteen pounds a year, out of which she is to pay for her German lessons and her laundry.

January 30   Letter to Nussey, describing her journey and reception. First allusion to Miss (Mary) Dixon, a cousin of Mary Taylor's, who has called. The Dixons, like the Wheelwrights, are living in Brussels.

February   CB translates Belmontet's "Les Orphelins" into English. Be-tween February and May, working in three languages (English, French, German), she translates poems by Barbier, Scott, Schiller, and Byron, as well as selections in prose.

February 16   Mary Taylor writes Nussey that Charlotte "seems *content* at least but [I] fear her sister's absence [will?] have a bad effect. When people have so little amusement they cannot afford to lose *any.*"

March 6   Letter to Nussey, describing her life in Brussels. "I am not too much overloaded with occupation and besides teaching English I have time to improve myself in German." First hint of her low spirits and her isolation at the school, though she still speaks well of both Hegers. They have invited her to use their sitting room, but she hesitates to intrude on the family. M. Heger makes progress in English. He has taken her to "The Carnival." She feels sorry for Mary Taylor, who "has nobody to be so good to her as Mr Heger is to me—to lend her books to converse with her sometimes &c."

Winter or spring   Letter to Mary Dixon, arranging a visit in which CB will sit for a portrait. She cannot go on Thursday because Mme Heger is taking her out "with herself and Mr Heger." She can go on Friday but must be back in time to give M. Heger his English lesson. During this period she visits the Wheelwrights and the Dixons frequently.

March 30   Devoir "La Chute des Feuilles."

April(?)   Letter to Nussey, complaining of the bitter cold in February and most of March. She wishes Nussey were there, but with reservations: "there are privations & humiliations to submit to—there is monotony and uniformity of life—and above all there is a constant sense of solitude in the midst of numbers—the Protestant the Foreigner is a solitary being whether as teacher or pupil. . . ." However, she is still "thankful" for her position. She replies indignantly to gossip back at home that she is seeking a husband in Brussels: "I never exchange a word with any other man than Monsieur Heger and seldom indeed with him. . . ."

May 1   Letter to Branwell, revealing the change in her attitude—"I grow exceedingly misanthropic and sour"—and her continuing contempt for nearly everyone at the pensionnat. First hint of her distrust of Mme Heger. Allusion to M. Heger as the "black Swan," the sole exception to the falseness and coldness in the house. But she has little contact with him, except for his occasionally "loading" her with books. Her recurrence at night to "the world below," her fantasy kingdom of Angria. In a postscript to Anne, she announces Heger's gift of "a little German Testament," which surprises her.

May 22(?)   Letter from EB to Nussey, suggesting that Nussey spend half a year in Brussels and then bring CB home, "otherwise she might vegetate there till the age of Methusaleh [*sic*] for mere lack of courage to face the voyage."

May 29   Letter to EB, asking for money (which she could draw from Aunt Branwell's legacy) and reporting, with bitterness, on the other teachers, one of them "the regular spy of Mme Heger." She ridicules a pupil in the English classes of which she is now in full charge. The Hegers "rarely" talk to her, and she is "convinced" that Mme Heger does not like her. She cites Madame's influence over her husband, his lecture to her on "*bienveillance*" (goodwill), her concern for the loss of his "goodwill," and her loneliness.

n.d.   Fragment "Letter (Ma chère Jane)."

May 31   Devoir "La Mort de Napoléon." Heger's version, "Sur la mort de Napoléon," also dated May 31, is clearly a later revision.

June 2   Incomplete letter to her father, acknowledging her pleasure in hearing about home: "I had begun to get low-spirited at not receiving any news. . . ."

June 5   Letter in German, probably an exercise, indicating a more positive attitude toward Mme Heger and describing a walk in the country with another teacher and three pupils; she catches cold, the first indication of decline in her physical health.

early or mid-June   Mary Dixon leaves Brussels, increasing CB's sense of isolation.

late June(?)   Letter to Nussey,[6] indicating depression, ill health, and "a very desolate heart." She reports the drastic change in Mme Heger's attitude; Madame takes no notice of her, even on school holidays, when CB is entirely alone. CB says she suspects the reason but does not reveal it, nor does she make any plans to leave.

July 3   CB sends EB a copy of *Les Psaumes de David Mis en Vers Français.* "Paris" precedes the date in the inscription, which reads: "I send you this nice little book . . . as it will enable you to polish up your French. I shall never be satisfied until you are able to read Racine, Corneille, and Moliere sufficiently well to thoroughly appreciate all their thousand beauties." She adds that she will return "D.V. [God willing] by the 20th."[7]

July   Notes on "La Mort de Moïse."

July(?)   Devoir "La Mort de Moïse."

August 6   Letter to Nussey, speaking of her "low spirits" and her dread of the coming long vacation, when she will be left virtually alone in the deserted school for five weeks. Though she longs to go home, she expresses her resolution to stay until she acquires German.

August 15   Beginning of "Les Grandes Vacances." Heger delivers the

Prize Day address at the Athénée Royal. He presents Charlotte with a gift, an edition of the works of Bernardin de St. Pierre. Later, he gives her a printed copy of his speech. That evening, there are two concerts; CB probably attends the one with a German choir in the Parc de Bruxelles.[8]

September 2   Letter to EB, discussing her excursions into Brussels and the countryside and her confession to a priest the day before at the Cathedral of Ste. Gudule.

September(?)   CB takes a few lessons in arithmetic with Heger.[9]

September 13   Heger signs a copy of his Prize Day speech for Emily, "in token of sincere affection."[10]

October 1   Letter to EB, indicating that she is homesick and unhappy but still resolved to remain. Her glimpse of Queen Victoria, who pleased the Belgians on her visit.

October 6   Devoir "Athènes sauvée par la Poësie" (first version).

October 13   Letter to Nussey, expressing her sense of desolation since the departure of Mary Dixon and the Wheelwrights from Brussels. She has gone to Mme Heger and given notice. Madame would have released her at once, but M. Heger intervened and induced her to remain. She discusses her ambivalence.

October 14   Entry in her schoolbook. She is cold and "tired of being amongst foreigners it is a dreary life especially as there is only one person in this house worthy of being liked—also another, who seems a rosy sugar plum but I know her to be coloured chalk."

October 15   Letter to Mary Dixon, reiterating her loneliness and weariness of the Belgians yet saying she may stay until spring. Mary Taylor (now teaching in Germany) has written and offered "to share her lessons" with Charlotte, who "of course" declines to "take advantage of this goodness."[11]

October 17   Devoir "Lettre d'un pauvre Peintre à un grand Seigneur."

November 15   Mme Heger gives birth to her fifth child (a daughter).

December 10   Concert by the Société de la Grande Harmonie, attended by the royal family and probably by CB.[12]

December 17   Expecting CB's departure in a fortnight, a teacher at the pensionnat, Mlle Sophie, gives her "a little box as a souvenir"[13] and writes her an affectionate note.

December 19   Letter to EB: "I have taken my determination." Persuaded at last by Mary Taylor, she has told Mme Heger of her departure. She plans to be at home the day after New Year's.

December 22   Devoir: "Athènes sauvée par la Poësie" (second version).

December 25   CB dines with Mr. and Mrs. Jenkins and other members of the English colony.

December 29   Heger gives CB a diploma, testifying to her qualifications as a teacher of French and sealed with the seal of the Athénée Royal.

1844

January 1   CB leaves Brussels. That morning, Heger gives her an anthology of French poetry.[14] Mme Heger travels with her to Ostend, where CB boards the packet boat, which leaves the next morning for England.

January 23   In a letter, CB tells Nussey how greatly she suffered before leaving Brussels: "I think however long I live I shall never forget what the parting with Monsr Heger cost me—It grieved me so much to grieve him who has been so true and kind and disinterested a friend." She adds that he offered to have her take one of his daughters to Haworth as a pupil (she refused) and that she was surprised to see how much her Belgian students regretted her departure.

July 24   CB's first letter to Heger.

October 24   CB's second letter to Heger.

1845

January 8   CB's third letter to Heger.

November 18   CB's fourth and final letter to Heger; with it she probably mailed her last known drawing, "Ashburnham Church On the Valley-Land."[15]

Editorial Method

The French transcripts follow the devoir manuscripts as closely as possible. The spelling, grammar, and punctuation are the authors'; only paragraph indentations have been standardized. Signs that could not be reproduced because of space constraints and computer limitations are listed in the Editorial Notes. The English transcripts correspond to the French but occasionally streamline Heger's notations for the purpose of making his aims clearer; for instance, when Heger underlines grammatical errors that do not carry over or words that translate into idiomatic English, I omit corrections and underlines from the translations. I also normalize punctuation, but not in uncorrected versions of devoirs that Heger will repunctuate. Where his punctuation cannot be distinguished from the Brontës', attributions are listed in the Editorial Notes. And because it was not always possible to make the English versions equal in length to the French, I have added spaces to the translated versions to coordinate paragraphs on facing pages.

Both Charlotte and Emily write in a well-practiced italic hand. Emily's letters are spikier than Charlotte's, and she does her titles in the same lettering; the rare exceptions are cited below. Charlotte is more experimental. For the body of her devoirs she uses her italic hand, but often she prints proper nouns in upright letters in roman or midway between script and printing, identified below as "CB's proper-noun print." For her titles she may use slanted roman letters or a double-line roman, sometimes with a more ornate or Gothic first letter. Her most decorative title, "Le But de la Vie," is in a print that resembles a sixteenth-century French lettering called "la batarde" (fig. 5). Although her models cannot be determined, in the nineteenth-century Renaissance and medieval types were widely imitated, and quite possibly the Brontës came across examples in the books they read in Haworth. (I am grateful to Anne Anninger, Philip Hofer Curator of Prints and Manuscripts at Harvard's Houghton Library, for supplying this information.)

When Charlotte writes drafts that she will not show Heger, her writing remains legible but much less polished; it is cited below as "CB's rough-draft script."

Several features of the manuscripts are not indicated in the typescript. I list the most common ones here.

1. Charlotte puts a double, not a single, underline below the name and date of each devoir.

2. Heger often uses a wavy underline (w.u.) to show that he wants changes that are not strictly necessary. Straight underlines presumably point to errors in grammar and vocabulary. Sometimes, the distinction between the two kinds of corrections breaks down; when it does, the word is marked "w.u.?" here.

3. Heger uses wavy vertical lines in the margins with a "B" or "Bon" to indicate outstanding passages; in the reproductions of the devoirs here, those lines are straight.

4. His slashes often slice diagonally through a whole word. Like his additions to the sisters' words, they may extend below and above the line.

5. He may write on top of his pupils' words, indicated on the page by a perpendicular line through one or more letters or, when legible, by one letter over another. The size of the overwriting varies enormously throughout the devoirs. Such corrections that would not show up in print are indicated in the Editorial Notes by the overwrite sign >, as in "H's *du > de*."

6. In referring to Heger's double underlining, I use the abbreviation "d.u."

7. In devoirs that Heger has corrected, vertical or diagonal strokes that run through more than one line of text indicate his deletions.

Symbols

CB	Charlotte Brontë
EB	Emily Brontë
H	Constantin Heger
italics	Heger's comments and corrections
bold	the second and dominant layer of Heger's corrections; indicates that he went through the MS twice, in pencil and ink or in two inks.
\the	deletion; a slash usually applies to the whole word when it occurs in the middle
I the	overwriting; one or two vertical lines through a letter or word indicate that Heger superimposed on it the letter(s) or word printed above it
=====	double underline; indicates that Heger drew at least two lines beneath the word or letter and sometimes three or four (as cited in the Editorial Notes)
	in dictées, indicates that Heger's word or phrase does not appear in any known published version of the text.

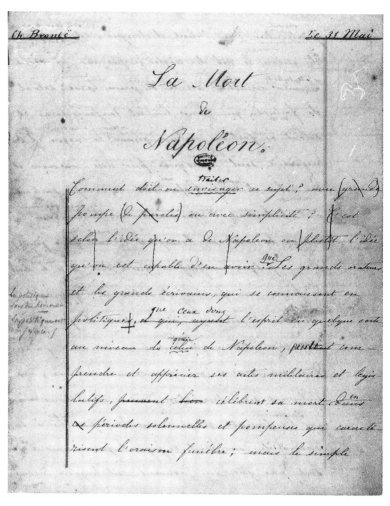

First page of Charlotte Brontë's "The Death of Napoleon." The Brontë Society.

Devoirs of 1842

<u>Charlotte Brontë</u>   <u>17 April 1842</u>

Sacrifice

of an Indian Widow

===

                                 it   *it*
Hindustan is rich, ~~she~~ is powerful, but despite her wealth and power she

5   is enslaved.   What good are her diamonds and her gold, while she

remains subject to the despotism of an arrogant and cruel Hierarchy?,

Are all the mines of Golconda worth a single ray from that star of

Bethlehem which the Magi saw of old in the East?

Such thoughts came to my mind, on the evening of a day when I had

10 been a spectator at one of those horrible sacrifices that have stained every

page of the history of Hindustan with blood.

I was alone — the window of my room was open, the sun's last rays

shone through the large leaves and brilliant flowers of some Indian plants

that encircled the trellis.

15 A perfect silence reigned throughout the house, and in the garden,

only the evening breeze whispered from time to time in the branches of

a palm, and stirred the delicate tendrils of some flowers springing up
                        edge
along the <u>margin</u> of a fountain.   That breeze was light, but in its soft
                                                             barbaric
murmurs, I seemed again to hear the cries, the shouts of the^ crowd that

20 I had seen that morning.

Neither the ordinance of Lord Bentinck nor the efforts of the

authorities had sufficed to hinder the sacrifice.   The widow herself

resisted all the entreaties of those who wished to save her life; all the

preparations were made by her parents and that very day, the tragedy had

25 been enacted.
                                                   at two o'clock
I went to the place to witness the heartrending spectacle^   The

procession left the house of the deceased.   There it was not the sad and

silent train, which, in European countries, accompanies the dead man to

Sacrifice

d'une veuve Indienne

———

L'Indoustan est riche, ~~elle~~ *il* est puissantè mais malgré ses richeses et son   L'Inde

pouvoir e*il*le est eclave. À quoi bon sont ses diamants et son or, tandis   Anglaise   5

qu'elle est sou<u>mise</u> au despotisme d'une Hiérarchie arrogante et cruelle?,

Toutes les mines de Golunde valent-elles un seul rayon de cette étoile de

Bethléem qu'autrefois les Mages ~~voyaient~~ *virent* en Orient?

De telles pensées me vinrent dans l'esprit, le soir d'un jour que

j'avais été spectateur d'un de ces sacrifices horribles qui ont souilli d*é*e   10

sang chaque page de l'histoire d*l'*eIndoustan.

J'étais seul — la fenêtre de ma chambre était ouverte, les derniers

rayons du soleil brillaient à travers les larges feuilles, et les fleurs

éclatantes, de quelques plantes indiennes dont le treillis était entouré.

Un silence parfait régnait partout dans la maison, et dans le jardin,   15

seulement la brise du soir soufflait de temps en temps dans les branches

d'un palmier, et remuait les tendrons delicats de quelques fleurs naissant

sur la <u>marge</u> *bord* d'une fontaine Cette brise était legére, mais dans ses doux

murmures, il me semblait entendre encore les cris, les hurlements de

cette foule ^ *barbare* que j'avais vue le matin.   20

Ni l'ordonnance de Lord Bentinck, ni les efforts des autorités

n'avaient suffi à*pr pour* empêcher le sacrifice. La veuve elle-même r<u>ésistait</u>

à tou<u>*t*es</u> les instances de ceux qui voulaient lui sauver la vie; tous les

préparatifs <u>étaient faits pa</u>r ses parents et ce jour même, la tragédie <u>avait</u>

<u>été</u> achevée.   25

Je me suis rendu <u>au lieu</u> pour être temoin de ce spectacle déchirant^ *à deux*

heures

Le cortége sortit de la maison du défunt; ce n'était pas là, le train triste

et silencieux, qui, dans les pays européens, accompagne le mort à son

his burial; it was the turbulent troupe of pagan savages who celebrate,
with frantic gestures and dreadful cries, the orgies of the Demon they
take to be God. The procession was preceded by an orchestra. The dull
sound of the Gong, the shrill chords of the fifes, the clang of the
cymbals, and the rolling of the drums together made a deafening uproar.

Four Brahmins carried the body in their midst. The center of this
tableau, the principal figures offered a strange contrast to all who
surrounded them. One did not see the body; it was covered with a kind
of mortuary cloth, whose folds outlined the rigid contours of the man
who was laid out beneath them. The widow was a woman twenty-three
to twenty-four years old; despite an excess of flesh, she still possessed
beauty and freshness. She was dressed in a white robe, diamonds
glittered in her hair, and pearl ornaments adorned her arms and her
brown neck; her aspect expressed resignation and firmness. Near her
there appeared a young person of sixteen, the daughter of the deceased
by a first wife; from her cries and her sobs, one would have thought her
the victim rather than the other. From time to time the widow offered
her consolation.

The procession halted forty measures from the sea; the widow sat on
the ground; her parents and the Brahmins set about constructing the pyre.
They drove four stakes into the ground, from eight feet to six feet apart.
They filled the enclosure with dried herbs and wood. While they were
making these preparations, the widow repeated prayers that a Brahmin
read from a book; she was offered some fruits; she placed her hand on
them and at the same time someone announced that all was ready. She
rose and advanced toward the pyre with a firm step; then I observed that
the blood had left her face and that although still resolute, she was very
pale.

I thought she was going to renounce the sacrifice; I hoped so; but no,
either pride or religion sustained her to the end. She sat down close to

enterrement; c'était la troupe turbulente de païens sauvages, qui célébrent

avec des gestes frénétiques et des cris épouvantables, les orgies du

était
Démon qu'il croit être Dieu. Le cortége fut précédé par un orchestre.

Le son sourd du Gong, les accords aigus des fifres, le bruit des

cymbales, et les roulements des tambours faisaient ensemble un vacarme

étourdissant

Quatre Brahmes portaient le corps au milieu — Le centre de ce

avec
tableau, les figures principales offraient un étrange contraste à tout ce qui

les entourait. On ne voyait pas le corps, il était couvert d'une espèce de

drap mortuaire, dont les plis dessinaient les lignes rigides de ce qui était

étendu là dessous. La veuve était une femme agée de vingt trois à vingt

quatre ans; malgré un excès d'embonpoint, elle possédait encore de la

beauté et de la fraîcheur. Elle était vêtue d'une robe blanche, des dia-

mants brillaient dans ses cheveux, et des ornements de perles décoraient

ses bras et son cou brun; son aspect exprimait la résignation et la fer-

meté. Près d'elle parut une jeune personne de seize ans, fille du défunt

par une première femme, à ses cris, et à ses sanglots on l'aurait crue la

ait
victime plutôt que l'autre. De temps en temps la veuve lui offrit des

consolations.

Le cortége s'arrêta à quarante toises de la mer, la veuve s'assit par

er
terre, ses parents et les Brahmes se mettaient à construire le bûcher. Ils

enfoncèrent en terre quatre pieux, de huits pieds, à six pieds de distance

— ils remplirent l'enceinte d'herbes sèches et de bois. Pendant qu'ils

faisaient ces préparatifs, la veuve répetait des prières qu'un Brahme lisait

dans un livre; on lui présenta des fruits elle y posa sa main et en même

temps on annonça que tout était prêt. Elle se léva, s'avança vers le

bûcher d'une marche ferme, alors je remarquai que le sang avait quitté

son visage et quoique toujours resolue, elle était très pâle.

Je crus qu'elle allait renoncer au sacrifice, je l'esperai, mais non, ou

la
l'orgueil, ou la religion la soutint jusqu'au fin, elle s'assit près du

the corpse, which had already been laid on the pyre. Then she turned her head to bid the world an eternal farewell.

Never in my life will I forget that moment; her eyes sought the sun, the azure sky — I thought I saw in their gaze an agonizing struggle between bodily weakness and spiritual power.

But already the flame was set to the pyre, and already thick clouds of smoke were beginning to envelop the pile. I caught a glimpse of some convulsive movements from the widow at the first approaches of fire, but soon all was in flame; at the same time the crowd uttered horrible cries of triumph; those cries mingled with the clanging noise of instruments. In some instants the sacrifice was consummated; then the procession disbanded and the Brahmins, remaining alone, collected the ashes of the victim.

From tumult followed calm; in the feeble lamentations of the wind I seemed to hear a voice deploring the fate of that unhappy woman.

=====

cadavre, qu'on avait déjà étendu sur le bûcher — alors elle retourna sa
tête pour dire au monde un éternel adieu.

60

Jamais de ma vie je n'oublierai ce moment, ses yeux cherchèrent le
soleil, le ciel azuré — je crus voir dans leur regard une lutte agonisante
entre la faiblesse du corps et la puissance de l'esprit.

Mais déjà le feu était mis au bûcher, et déjà les nuages épaisses de
fumée commençait à envelopper le pile — j'entrevoyais quelques mouvements convulsifs de la veuve aux premières atteintes du feu, mais bientôt
tout était en flammes; en même temps la foule poussa des cris horribles
de triomphe, ces cris furent mêlés au bruit éclatant des instruments — en
quelques instants le sacrifice était consommé; alors le cortége se sépara,
et les Brahmes restant seuls, recueillirent les cendres de la victime.

65

70

Au tumulte succéda le calme, dans les plaintes faibles du vent il me
semblait entendre une voix que déplorait le sort de cette malheureuse
femme.

Comments

Charlotte Brontë wrote of widow burning at three stages of her life. The first time, she was eighteen and immersed in her Angrian saga. An evil spell leaves Zamorna, the hero, close to death, and when his wife tries to help, he taunts her: "[W]hat do you say to a suttee? . . . When I am dead, erect a pile on the shores of the Calabar; let me be carried there in state. I shall be laid on the timber. Then you, Mary, will ascend, take my head on your knee, greet my cold and bloodless lips with a few of those burning kisses—no need to apply the torches, we shall of ourselves kindle into a burst of flames so vivid that, when the inhabitants of Verdopolis look out from their casements eastward, the glow of the setting, not the rising, sun will be seen on the oriental skyline. Hah! Queen of Angria, how would you like that?[1]

The third time, she was thirty-one and more than halfway through *Jane Eyre*. Rochester, in many ways Zamorna's successor, is singing to Jane at her request:

> My love has sworn, with sealing kiss,
> With me to live—to die . . .

These lines from the final verse—in fact a poem by Charlotte—launch Jane's defense against his lovemaking. She asks him what he means by "such a pagan idea," assuring him that *she* does not intend to perish with him: "I had as good a right to die when my time came as he had: but I should bide that time, and not be hurried away in a suttee."[2]

This intervening devoir takes the humor out of burning. Constrained by limited facility in French and probably aware that Heger would mark her text, Charlotte narrates with a missionary earnestness, combining Christian outrage at pagan barbarism with a keen eye and ear for its effects.

Why did she choose to write of widow burning? No instructions accompany the essay; no dictée in her notebook corresponds to it. But all her other devoirs respond to assignments, so Heger may have set instructions orally. At some point, though perhaps not as early as April, he read her "The Death of Joan of Arc," a poem by Casimir Delavigne.[3] It too indicts a power-hungry clerisy and rages at the burning of a woman. Delavigne goes even further than Charlotte in detailing the agony of immolation. His image of Joan's "half-consumed arm," now ironically "disarmed" by the environing flame,[4] may have led Charlotte to recall accounts of sati[5] that she had read years earlier in Haworth. Even without Delavigne's lines as stimulus, she was reading poems about other female victims; her next devoir would be based on at least one of them. And the consciousness of living among foreigners was strong in her. She wrote, as does her narrator, in alien territory, gazing from her window at the garden of the pensionnat, one of two Protestants surrounded by Catholics who struck her as benighted, if not heathen.

Throughout the Brontës' childhood, reports of widow sacrifice had circulated widely. Most were printed first in Indian newspapers or in Baptist missionary journals and then reprinted in England. *Blackwood's* carried at least one account within the time the Brontë children were consulting it.[6] Another source that Patrick Brontë might have brought home was *The Cottage Magazine* put out by John Buckworth, his former vicar at Dewsbury.[7] In juvenilia manuscripts of 1829 and 1830, Charlotte refers to Bentinck and Golconda,[8] and while those brief allusions do not prove that she kept well informed, details here suggest that she knew the regulations on sati that prevailed until 1829.

For example, she seems to know that the widow had to go to her death voluntarily; a Hindu decree of 1813 had made forced immolation illegal. The same instructions banned sati in cases where the woman was under sixteen, the age of this victim's grieving stepdaughter. In consequence, magistrates attended the ceremonies, both to ensure that no coercion was employed and to rescue the widow if she reconsidered, since the family or the crowd might bar escape. Missionaries too made a practice of attending. If they could not influence or rescue the victim, at least they could bear witness, as Brontë's speaker does, "with the hope [as one wrote later] that case after case will not always be brought to public notice without some good effect being produced."[9] Bentinck's ordinance of December 4, 1829, put an official end to sati by declaring its abettors "guilty of culpable homicide."[10] This devoir thus appears to be anachronistic, except that, as its speaker says, official abolition did not halt widow sacrifice completely.

Wherever Charlotte Brontë got her information, her essay adopts the perspective and the patterns of colonial eyewitness narratives. Her speaker is more sensitive to sounds than most real witnesses but otherwise provides the kind of details they provided—on the noisy procession, the digging of the pit, the widow's posture on the pyre, and so forth. Though she does not refer to her reporter's gender, the endings of her adjectives mark him as a man, as does his freedom in going to the site. This too is characteristic. As the critic Lata Mani has observed, these accounts were almost all produced by European men and "organized around four moments: the narrator hastening to the spot on receiving information that a burning is about to occur; the monitoring of the widow's demeanor and the attempts to dissuade her; details of the practices that precede the burning; the setting alight of the pyre and the death of the widow."[11] Each of these moments is represented here, with a few deviations. Charlotte's narrator does not simply rush to the site; he follows the cortege as it advances. Nor does he attempt to stop the widow; since earlier entreaties by others have failed, he watches and records what he observes. He reserves his most elaborate descriptions for the widow; they too conform to type in accenting her youthfulness, her beauty, and the fear that pales her cheek.

But in one crucial aspect, Charlotte's widow differs from the conventional victim. She does not figure solely as an object, either of coercion or of the bystander's gaze. She is a subject who chooses, perseveres, consoles, and struggles at the end to conquer weakness. Though the narrator hopes she will reverse her decision, she remains fixed in her obedience to a faith that extols a woman's suicide as saintliness.[12] Charlotte strengthens this reading, though perhaps unconsciously, by using the feminine pronoun for Hindustan, a noun that is masculine in French. My translation retains "she" to emphasize the parallel: as Hindustan remains the slavish victim of male despots, implicitly too blind to see the light that streams from Bethlehem, so the widow fails to grasp the horror of self-sacrifice and dies a willing victim to her creed.

The voluntary martyrdom of women, a subject that pervades the juvenilia, was one to which Charlotte compulsively returned. Less than two months later, she wrote about Anne Askew, a sixteenth-century Protestant tortured to death for refusing to become a Catholic. In fact, although that devoir leaves Askew in a dungeon, she was subsequently burnt alive before a crowd of spectators. Perhaps, since her decision was religiously correct, Charlotte chose to focus on temptation and resistance, rather than on the spectacle of dying.

Still, both devoirs pose the question: what is it worth to survive? Though her answers would only become clear in *Jane Eyre,* which makes complex and intricate allusions to sati,[13] her search for them was clearly under way.

Charlotte Brontë   April 18th 1842

The Sick Young
Girl

===

Sleep is the friend of the fortunate, it seeks the bed of roses, but it rarely   *alas!*
^approaches the bed of thorns; to me it is almost unknown.

I have lain awake the whole night; pain bending over my bed has been my sole companion; how long the hours have seemed to me!

Now that the sun has risen I see its rays with a dull and troubled
                                                              garlands
eye. But a little bird that has built its nest in the ivy which surrounds my window starts to sing. He sings of this lovely summer morning, of the dew that fills the chalice of each flower, of the fresh wind that wafts their scent aloft.

Why can I not sing like that bird? Why am I not free like him? Now he spreads his wings, he rises, he soars on high; he is going to sing closer to the gates of heaven. My thought follows him across the vast fields of the air.

When my parents embrace me, I weep because I can do nothing to answer their tenderness. My more fortunate brothers and sisters can prove their affection by their devotedness; the children of peasants can work for their parents; as for me − I bring happiness to no one.

Oh if I could sleep! In the realm of dreams I would again perhaps
                                    It is but there
find freedom, the joys that I have lost. It is there alone that I can recall the life of my childhood.

Nonetheless, I fear to see the image of death in my dreams. I have sometimes had frightful thoughts about it while I slept; a phantom has glided into my chamber, it has spoken in my ear and has told me that my
                                          the cold stone
days on earth have nearly run out, and that the portal of the grave was

La jeune Fille
malade

Le sommeil est l'ami des heureux, il cherche le lit de roses, mais il   *obs.*[?]
    rarement   *hélas!*   *m'*
s'approche ^ du lit d'épines; pour mòi il est presqu' inconnu.   5

J'ai veillé toute la nuit; la douleur penchée sur ma couche a été ma

seule compagne: que les heures m'ont paru longues!

Maintenant que le soleil se lève je vois ses rayons d'un oeil morne

et troublé: mais un petit oiseau qui a bâti son nid dans la lierre qui
   tapisse   ÷
entoure ma fenêtre, commence à chanter; il chante de ce beau matin   10
                                                       le
d'été, de la rosée qui remplit le calice de chaque fleur, du vent frais qui

emporte leurs parfums.

Pourquoi ne puis-je pas chanter comme cet oiseau? pourquoi ne suis

je pas libre comme lui? Maintenant il déploie ses ailes, il part, il   ‖

s'élance en haut, il va chanter plus près des portes du ciel. Ma pensée   15

le suit à travers les vastes champs de l'air.

Quand mes parents m'embrassent, je pleure parceque je ne ⎪ puis rien

faire pour repondre à leur tendresse⎪. Mes frères et mes soeurs plus

heureux peuvent témoigner leur affection par leur dévouement, les

enfants du paysan peuvent travailler pour leurs parents, moi — je ne fais   20

le bonheur de personne. *es*[?]

O si je pouvais dormir! dans la région des songes — je retrouverais
                         Ce n'   *que*
peut-être la liberté, les joies que j'ai perdues. C'est là seùl que je puis

me rappeller la vie de mon enfance.

Cependant je crains de voir l'image de la mort dans mes songes, j'ai   25
                                                           f
eu quelquefois d'affreuses pensées pendant que je dormais, un phantôme

s'est glissé dans ma chambre il m'a parlé à l'oreille et m'a dit que mes
                                          la froide pierre
jours étaient presque écoulés sur la terre, et que le portail du tombeau

half-open
opening to receive me. Life for me is painful and full of suffering, but

am I not still too young to die?

    I have suffered long, I am weary of suffering. Oh God, have pity on

me! Jesus thy son healed the young daughter of Jairus; may he also heal

me. Christ grant my prayer!

    God heard the lament of the poor invalid. He restored her to health

and life. One morning when the sun was scarcely risen, she was seen on

the mountain. Her face was still pale, but happiness and gratitude
were sparkling
sparkled in her gaze.

s'entrouv.

s'^ouvrait pour me recevoir. La vie est pour moi pénible et pleine de

souffrances, mais, ne suis-je pas encore trop jeune pour mourir?

J'ai souffert long-temps, je suis lasse de souffrir — O Dieu ayez pitié

de moi! Jesus <u>ton</u> fils, a guéri la jeune fille de Jairus qu'il me guérisse

aussi. Christ exaucez ma prière!

Dieu écouta la plainte de la pauvre malade, il lui rendit la santé et la

vie. Un matin lorsque le soleil était à peine levé on la rencontra sur la

montagne, son visage était encore pâle, mais le bonheur et la reconnais-
[?]

aient
sance brillèrent dans ses regards.

[First entry in Charlotte Brontë's notebook of dictations.]

The Poor Girl

I fled from painful slumber
Unattended by any happy dreams
I walked upon the mountain
Ahead of the sun's first beams.
  Awakening with nature
The young bird on the hawthorn bloom was cheeping
Its mother brought it nourishment
My eyes were wet with weeping.

Oh why have I no mother?
Why, unlike that bird, am I alone?
Its nest sways gently in the branches of the elm.
  Nothing on earth do I own.
  I had not even a cradle,
For I was a child found
Before the church of the village, on a stone.

  Exiled far from my parents,
I know not of their caresses and sweet care.
  And the children of the valley
Never call me their sister;
  In the games they play at twilight, I don't share.
Ne'er beneath the leafy roof of his cottage
Does the joyful ploughman ask me to take ease.
  From afar, I see his family,
  Around the rustling branches,
Beseeching goodnight kisses on their knees.

La Pauvre Fille

J'ai fui ce pénible sommeil

Qu'aucun songe heureux n'accompagne

J'ai devancé sur la montagne

Les premiers rayons du soleil   5

     S'éveillant avec la nature

Le jeune oiseau chantait sur l'aubépine en fleur

Sa mère lui portait la douce nourriture

Mes yeux se sont mouillés de pleurs.

O! pourquoi n'ai-je pas de mère?   10

Pourquoi ne suis-je pas semblable au jeune oiseau

Dont le nid se balance aux branches de l'ormeau?

     Rien ne m'appartient sur la terre,

     Je n'eus pas même de berceau,

Et je suis un enfant trouvé sur une pierre   15

     Devant l'église du hameau

          ts
     Loin de mes parens exilée,

De leurs embrassements j'ignore la douceur,

     Et les enfants de la vallée

Ne m'appellent jamais leur soeur. +   20

Jamais sous son toit de feuillée

Le joyeux laboureur ne m'invite à m'asseoir;

     Et de loin, je vois sa famille

     Autour du sarment qui pétille,

Chercher sur les genoux, les caresses du soir.   25

    + Je ne partage pas les jeux de la veillée

Toward the chapel, host to all,

I weeping turn and go;

It's the only resting spot

30   Where I am no stranger here below,

The only one ahead of me that closes not.

Often I gaze upon the stone

Where my bitter sorrows started;

There I seek the trace of tears

35   That perhaps my mother shed, ere she departed.

Often too, my wandering steps

Cross the graveyard, a refuge there to gain.

But for me all graves are indifferent,

The poor girl has no parent

40   In the coffin's realm, as on the earthly plane.

I have wept for fourteen springs,

Far from the arms that bereft me

Return, my mother, I wait for you

At the stone where once you left me.

45   Alas, it was not long the girl awaited.

In grief she died; her prayer remained unsated.

It is said that an unknown woman

Appeared in the village one day, face concealed.

They led her to the humble burying-ground,

50   But amid the grasses and the heath so thick congealed,

The place of the grave could not be found.

[Alexander Soumet]

Vers la chapelle hospitalière,

En pleurant, j'adresse mes pas;

C'est La seule demeure ici-bas

Où je ne suis point etrangère   30

La seule devant moi, qui ne se ferme pas.

Souvent je contemple la pierre

Où commencèrent mes douleurs;

J'y cherche la trace des pleurs

Qu'en m'y laissant, peut-être y répandit ma mère.   35

Souvent aussi, mes pas errants,

Parcourent des tombeaux l'asile solitaire,

Mais pour moi, les tombeaux sont tous indifférents,

La pauvre fille est sans parents

Au milieu des ce^rcueils, ainsi que sur la terre   40

J'ai pleuré quatorze printemps

Loin des bras qui m'ont repoussée;

Reviens, ma mère, je t'attends

Sur la pierre où tu m'as laissé

La pauvre fille, Hélas n'attendit pas long-temps.   45

Plaintive, elle mourait, en priant pour sa mère;

On dit qu'une femme étrangère

Un jour, le front voilé, parut dans le hameau

On conduisit ses pas vers l'humble cimetière,

Mais parmi les gazons, et l'épaisse bruyère   50

On ne put découvrir la place du tombeau.

[Alexandre Soumet]

Comments

I was twenty-six years old a week or two since—and at that ripe time of life I am a schoolgirl—a complete school-girl and on the whole very happy in that capacity It felt very strange at first to submit to authority instead of exercising it—to obey orders instead of giving them—but I like that state of things.

—Letter to Ellen Nussey, May [5] 1842[1]

This devoir, dated three days prior to her birthday, may be Charlotte's most submissive schoolgirl exercise. Her main source is "The Poor Girl" ("La Pauvre Fille"), the first dictée she transcribed in a notebook of twenty-one selections. Its author, Alexandre Soumet, had been a famous pre-Romantic dramatist,[2] and though his reputation faded after 1830, teachers continued to assign "The Poor Girl" (1814) throughout the nineteenth century.[3] Presumably, Heger instructed his students to base their essays on Soumet's lyric, which may have been one of several poems about mistreated maidens that he read to them.[4] Charlotte complied in a devoir that imitates its plaintive evocation of suffering.

Her version, however, conspicuously alters the motive of the speaker's grief and pain. No trace remains of the social issue, the victimization of an innocent child who suffers for the sins of the mother. Other themes and details carry over to the devoir—troubled sleep, the singing bird, family love, exclusion—but illness replaces illegitimacy, and a higher rather than a lower status separates this narrator from peasants. Charlotte's speaker ends where Soumet's begins, on the mountain with the day ahead of her, and since, unlike the absent mother, God responds in time, she is spared the early death that claims the outcast.

Charlotte also demonstrates scholarly diligence by bringing in additional sources. Heger's margin comment at line 28 identifies a second French poem that she drew on, "The Young Captive," by André Chénier. Its narrator, imprisoned and innocent, protests in words that the invalid echoes: "And though the present hour has griefs and cares / I would not die so soon."[5] Three lines later, she refers to the biblical daughter of Jairus (Jesus brought the twelve-year-old girl back from the dead when her parents had given her up).[6] An earlier allusion to the bird at heaven's gate may be a tacit borrowing from Shakespeare. The image occurs in Sonnet 29 and, with chaliced flowers, in *Cymbelline*.[7]

Of course, by the early nineteenth century, bird flight was a common trope for freedom. Romantic poets used it, and so does Chénier, in a phrase that anticipates line 16 of the devoir:

> Hope ever gives me wings.
> As when, escaped the cruel fowler's snare,
> More light, more joyful in the fields of air
> Philomel soars and sings.[8]

Perhaps most important, Charlotte Brontë used it when she thought about studying abroad. Writing Ellen Nussey in 1841, she speaks of "such a vehement impatience of restraint & steady work, such a strong wish for wings. . . ."[9]

It seems strange to link this text with the fulfillment of that longing. Its prose is stiff, its speaker limply passive. Soumet's young girl walks, observes, seeks refuge, and implores her mother; Charlotte's lies in bed and prays for rescue. She does not name her malaise, which Enid Duthie suggests is "largely a neurosis caused by loneliness."[10] But pallor, pain, and sleepless nights are common signs of illness, and Charlotte, with two older sisters dead of consumption, Maria at twelve and Elizabeth at eleven, might have assumed that disease-related lethargy required no further explanation.

In any case, she was given an elegiac lyric (or perhaps two, counting Chénier's) as her model. She did not respond with a dirge. She chose to write recovery into her devoir and refute the whispering phantom of depression. God saves the sick young girl, and Heger commends Charlotte on the paragraph that tells of her revival. Otherwise he corrects the essay lightly, underlining some but not all of the errors and heightening its sentimentality. (He may already have heightened the poem's sentimentality by tacking on its final verse. All of the authorized published editions end with the poor girl's entreaty.)

Whatever Brontë thought of his comments or of Soumet's poem, she makes no further reference to either until 1849. But her letter of May 1842 and a later poem imply that she had started to care about impressing Heger. She was also grateful for her own rejuvenation, after two dreary jobs as a governess: "Hitherto both Emily and I have had good health, and therefore we have been able to work well."[11]

The postscript to her experience of these poems emerges seven years later, in *Shirley*. Hortense Moore, teaching French to Caroline Helstone, assigns her "a volume of short fugitive pieces," but Caroline sneers at all the "little poems," except for Chénier's "The Young Captive." Later she recites it for Hortense's brother Robert, the man she secretly loves. Charlotte Brontë comments in a footnote: "Caroline had never seen Millevoye's 'Jeune Malade' [presumably a reference to "The Fall of the Leaves"],[12] otherwise she would have known that there is a better poem in the French language than Chénier's 'Captive;' a poem worthy to have been written in English,—an inartificial, genuine, impressive strain. To how many other samples of French verse can the same epithets be applied with truth?"[13]

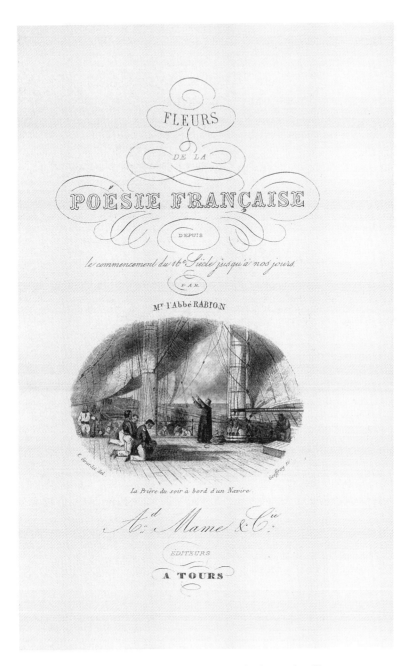

FLEURS

DE LA

POÉSIE FRANÇAISE

DEPUIS

le commencement du 16ᵉ Siècle jusqu'à nos jours.

PAR

Mr l'Abbé RABION.

La Prière du soir à bord d'un Navire.

Aᵈ Mame & Cⁱᵉ

ÉDITEURS

A TOURS

Title page from an anthology Heger used in his classes that illustrates "Evening Prayer on Board a Ship"; he later gave Charlotte this book. Harvard College Library.

Evening Prayer

in a Camp

=====

scarcely
The desert sun, whose heat we could then endure, was approaching the

why long?   end of its long course; its last rays gleamed amid the ruins of an
troop
Egyptian temple where a band of soldiers were assembled to say their

evening prayer.
a
It was the eve of battle; one might have said that the glorious orb
good
very good   presaged the carnage of the morrow, so inflamed did its disk appear,
ablaze
and so lit up the west seemed from its fires. The broken columns, the
sculpted
ancient vaults, the hieroglyphs engraved on the temple walls were

covered with a ruby tint. The moon, pale and serene, rose in the east;

everywhere the sky was clear, and in the middle of the desert, the
towered above
pyramids arose from the sea of sand, like vast rocks of granite that

neither tempest nor hurricane could dislodge.

The scene was imposing, and it seemed to me to attest to the influ-
ose
ence of religion. The soldiers assembled in the temple were inhabitants
located
of a country far from the banks of the Nile; they came from the Scottish
they
Highlands, and belonged to General Abercrombie's brigade.
soldiers
I felt profoundly touched when all those hardy warriors, going down
an old man
on their knees, listened to the prayer recited by a veteran who seemed

to be the patriarch of the clan. It was the Paternoster — the Lord's

Prayer. How touching was the devotion of those men who, in a foreign
G
land, faithful to the simple and stern forms of the Christian faith, asked

for God's aid in the name of his son! How they went to the soul, those
image very
good,
rendition   divine and sacred words, pronounced in the desolate sanctuary of an
mediocre   *have remained standing only to indicate*
idol whose brutal image seemed to be the symbol of its worshipers'
what the beliefs of the world were, before the coming of J.C.
ignorance.

La Prière du Soir

dans un camp

═══════

à peine
Le soleil du désert, dont nous pouvions alors soutenir la chaleur,
du
approchait au terme de sa longue carrière; ses derniers rayons apparais-   *pourquoi*   5
troupe   *longue?*
saient entre les ruines d'un temple égyptien où une /bande\ de soldats

s'étaient assemblés pour dire leur prière du soir.
        d'une   *bon*
    C'était la veille de bataille, on eût dit que l'orbe glorieux présageait

le carnage du lendemain, tant son disque paraissait enflammé, et tant   *tr bon*
        embrasé
l'occident semblait s'allumer de ses feux. Les colonnes brisées, les   10
            sculptés
voûtes antiques, les hiéroglyphes gravés sur les murs du temple étaient
                                                            à
couverts d'une teinte de rubis; la lune pâle et sereine se lévait dans

l'orient, partout le ciel était pur et au milieu du désert, les pyramides
se dressaient au-dessus
s'élèvaient / de la mer de sable, comme de vastes rochers de granit que
                        vent
ni l'orage, ni l'ouragan ne peut ébranler.   15

    La scène était imposante! et elle me semblait attester l'influence| de
        C
la religion. Les soldats assemblés dans le temple étaient les habitants
    situé
d'un pays loin des rivages du Nil: ils venaient des Montagnes d'Ecosse,
ils
et appartenait à la brigade de général Abercrombie.
                                        soldats
    Je me sentis profondément touché lorsque tous ces hardis guerriers   20
                                        vieillard
se mettant à genoux, ecoutèrent la prière, récitée par un vétéran qui
                                    a   *u*
semblait la patriarche du clan. C'était le Pater Noster — la prière de

notre Seigneur. Qu'elle était touchante la dévotion de ces hommes qui,
                                                                            B
dans un pays étranger, fidèles aux formes simples et sévères du culte
                                    à
chrétien,— demandaient du secours de Dieu au nom de son fils! comme   25
                                                                        image très
ils allaient à l'âme ces mots divins et sacrés prononcés dans l'asile desolé   *bonne*
                    n'être restée debout que pour   *médiocremt.*
d'une idole dont l'image brutale semblait le symbole de l'ignorance de   *rendue*
remarquer ce qu'étaient les croyances du monde, avant la venue de J.C.
ses adorateurs!

That abasement before the One who decides the fate of battles, that

powerful influence of the religion which ~~had~~ changed the pagan temple

into a Christian church, that muffled noise of the English camp sounding
those ~~pagan~~ [?] moving silhouettes
afar across the vast plain; the forms of Arabs and of Bedouins, those

descendants of Ishmael who, mounted on their light chargers, galloped

here and there in the distance; the twilight rapidly approaching, the stars

that were beginning to pierce the heaven's deep blue, those somber and
that troop   *soldiers*
solitary ruins in the middle of the desert, the band of Christian ~~heroes~~
that
gathered there, the lone solemn voice that made itself heard in the silence

— the consciousness that tomorrow morning the sun must rise on a battle-

field, and that tomorrow evening it must set on a Golgotha, a field of
I have felt profoundly and can paint but feebly today.
blood — all this, I know better how to feel than to paint!

Cette humiliation devant celui qui décide le sort des batailles, cette

influence puissante de la religion qui ~~avait~~ chang*éait* le temple païen d*en*àns

une église chrétienne, ce bruit sourd du camp Anglais s'étendant *au* de loin

       les silhouettes ~~*payens*~~ [?] *mobiles*
sur la vaste plaine; les formes des Arabes et des Bedouins, ces descen-

dans d'Ishmaël qui montés sur leurs legers coursiers gallopaient ça et là

dans le lointain; le crépuscule approchant rapidement, les étoiles qui

commençaient à percer le bleu foncé du ciel, ces ruines sombres et soli-

      cette troupe   *soldats*   *cette*
taires au milieu du desert, la bande de ~~heros~~ chrétiens y réunie, là seule

voix solennelle qui se faisait entendre dans le silence — la conscience que

demain matin le soleil devait se lever sur un champ de bataille, et que

demain-soir il devait se coucher sur un Golgotha, un champ de sang,—

     j'ai profondément   *et ce*   *je ne peux* [?] *peindre que bien*
voilà ce que je sais mieux sentir que peindre   *faiblement aujourd'hui.* |

Evening Prayer
On Board a Ship

The Sun's orb, whose glare my eyes could then endure, ready to plunge
into the glittering waves, appeared through the rigging of the vessel, and
still shed light upon those boundless spaces.

One might have said, from the swaying of the stern, that the radiant
star at every moment changed its horizon. The masts, the stays, and the
yards of the ship were covered with a rosy tint; a few clouds wandered
aimlessly in the east, where the moon rose slowly; the rest of the sky
was clear; and at the northern horizon, forming a glorious triangle with
the day star and that of the night, a waterspout glistening with the colors
of a prism arose from the sea like a crystal column, supporting the vault
of heaven.

He was much to be pitied, who could not recognize the beauty of
God in this glorious spectacle! Tears involuntarily gushed from my eyes
when all my companions, doffing their tarred hats, began in their rough
voices to sing their simple hymns to Our Lady of Deliverance, patroness
of sailors. How touching was the prayer of those men who, on a fragile
plank in the middle of the ocean, contemplated a sun setting on the
waves! How it struck the soul, that poor sailor's invocation to the
mother of sorrows!

That abasement before the One who sends storms and calm; that
awareness of our paltriness before the Infinite; those chants prolonged
afar over slumbering waves; the monsters of the deep, astonished at these
unknown accents, plunging to the depth of their caverns; night
approaching with its hidden dangers; the wonder of our vessel amid so
many wonders, a religious crew seized with admiration and awe; an
august priest in prayer; God hovering over the abyss, one hand detaining

Prière du Soir
à bord d'u[n] vaisseau

Le globe du Soleil, dont mes yeux pouvaient alors soutenir l'eclat, prêt
à se plonger dans les vagues étincelantes, apparaissait entre les cordages
du vaisseau, et versait encore le jour, dans des espaces sans bornes.   5

   On eût dit par le balancement de la poupe, que l'astre radieux chan-
geait à chaque instant d'horizon. Les mâts, les haubans, et les vergues
du navire étaient couverts d'une teinte de rose, quelques nuages erraient
sans ordre dans l'orient, où la lune montait avec lenteur; le reste du ciel
était pur; et à l'horizon du nord, formant un glorieux triangle avec l'astre   10
du jour et celui de la nuit, une trombe chargée des couleurs du prisme,
s'élevait de la mer comme un colonne de cristal, supportant la voûte du ciel.

   Il eût été bien à plaindre, celui qui dans ce beau spectacle n'eut pas
reconnu la beauté de Dieu! Des larmes coulèrent malgré moi de mes
paupières, lorsque tous mes compagnons, ôtant leurs chapeaux   15
goudronnés, vinrent à entonner de leurs voix rauques leurs simples
cantiques à notre dame de bon secours, patronne des mariniers. Qu'elle
était touchante la prière de ces hommes, qui, sur une planche fragile, au
milieu de l'ocean contemplaient un soleil couchant sur les flots! Comme
elle allait à l'âme cette invocation du pauvre mâtelot à la mère de   20
douleur!

   Cette humiliation devant celui qui envoie les orages et le calme; cette
conscience de notre petitesse à la vue de l'Infini, ces chants étendant au
loin sur les vagues endormies; les monstres marins, etonnés de ces
accents inconnus, se precipitant au fond de leurs goufres; la nuit   25
s'approchant avec ses embûches; la merveille de notre vaisseau au milieu
de tant de merveilles, un équipage religieux saisi d'admiration et de
crainte; un prêtre auguste en prière; Dieu penché sur l'abyme, d'une

the sun at the gates of the west, the other raising the moon at the opposite horizon, and lending an attentive ear, across the immensity, to the feeble voice of His creature. All this, no one would know how to paint and the whole heart of mankind scarce suffices to take in.

Chateaubriand

main retenant le soleil aux portes de l'occident de l'autre élevant la lune à l'horizon opposé, et prêtant à travers l'immensité une oreille attentive à faible voix de sa créature. Voilà ce qu'on ne saurait peindre et ce que tout le coeur de l'homme suffit à peine pour contenir.

30

Chateaubriand

Comments

The instructions for this devoir are not hard to guess. Heger dictated a passage to his students, probably as part of a lesson on Chateaubriand, and asked them to write an imitation. Again, Charlotte seems to have been happy to comply. Her devoir imitates the style of the dictée as well as its form, theme, and details. Yet she also makes the composition her own by shifting the site from the ocean to the desert, exchanging the sailors for soldiers from the Highlands, and transforming the religious ambience to one that is biblical and Protestant. Her men are Christian heroes, their reverence at sunset the prelude to a bloody scene of battle. Beyond these clear similarities and differences, the devoir offers evidence of complex interaction, not only between Heger and his conscientious student, but also between them and their sources.

"Evening Prayer on Board a Ship" is Heger's title for his excerpt from the *Genius of Christianity* (*Génie du Christianisme*, 1802). In this seminal Romantic text, Chateaubriand argues that of all religions Christianity is "the most poetic, the most humane, the most favorable to liberty, to the arts, and to letters."[1] He argues further that it can and must inspire contemporary writers and artists. To show how nature's wonders make God's existence manifest, he recalls "two views of nature, one from the sea, the other from the land,"[2] which he observed on his voyage to America. Heger's excerpt opens in the middle of the seascape and continues to its end.[3]

He has not merely excerpted the passage, however. Discrepancies between the source and his dictée recur throughout Brontë's transcription.[4] She may be responsible for minor variations. Hearing words pronounced by a native speaker, she could have mistaken singular for plural forms and omitted capital letters. But none of the words reprinted here in shaded letters appear in any extant version of the text, and by 1842 the authorized edition was widely available in Brussels. So Heger almost certainly chose to take liberties, alluding to sea monsters that Chateaubriand could not have seen and elaborating features of the vessel, the sunset, and its humbling effect on the observer.

What difference might these alterations make for Charlotte Brontë? Little, with respect to this devoir. Her description of the temple, which Heger praises, incorporates two of his changes. He substitutes "column" for "pillar" of water (12), and she envisions broken stone columns (10); his sun tints the masts and sails a rosy pink (8), and hers turns the temple ruby red (12). But embellished or unmodified, Chateaubriand's narrative communicates beliefs that Charlotte shared. She did not need to be converted to religion, or to a romantic vision of nature, or to the idea that they connected. What she did require was guidance from a teacher she could trust, a man whose passion for the written word matched hers.

Heger's lesson would have reawakened memories of Glass Town and the writing she and Branwell did together. Branwell at age twelve put out two tiny volumes of poems by his alter ego, "Young Soult the Ryhmer," with "NOTES = AND COMMENTARYS BY: MONSEIUR DE LA CHATEUBRIAND Author of Travles in Greece the Holy land &c. . . ."[5] The travel book he cites was in the library at Ponden House, just across the moors from Haworth, and whether he read it through or merely scanned it, he would have shared his findings with his sister.[6] Three years later, when Charlotte was sixteen, a series of articles in *Blackwood's* (a major influence on the juvenilia) informed English readers that Chateaubriand was the greatest French writer of the age.[7] The second article compares him with Scott, whom she idolized, and quotes long extracts from *The Genius*.[8] Again, it is not clear that she read those articles; it is clear, however, that she knew about Chateaubriand and that her hopes for more authentic information were being fulfilled. As for the liberties Heger took with sources, she and her siblings had always borrowed freely, so that even if she did become aware of her teacher's license, she would have been unlikely to object.

But she had also gone abroad to liberate her writing from a style she perceived as overheated. Heger's alterations do not conduce to coolness; he tends to heighten drama and sentiment. Yet even though Charlotte made fun of his excesses,[9] she seems to have accepted and provisionally adopted his literary preferences and standards.

Her desire for his approval may be hinted, as well, in the devoir's subtler debt to Chateaubriand. *The Genius of Christianity* influenced a generation's attitude toward ruins. Earlier Romantics had perceived their picturesqueness; Chateaubriand discerned their metaphysics (summed up here in a modern critic's paraphrase): "ruins show us the fragility of human existence, they teach us the precariousness of nations, they reveal time's irremediable flight."[10] Charlotte's temple illustrates that lesson. Her choice of an Egyptian locale could also indicate that she had read beyond the given passage; elsewhere in his text Chateaubriand alludes to the desert and the Sphinx.[11] Then there was the book that Branwell cited, *Travels in Greece, Palestine, Egypt, and Barbary,* which juxtaposes the endurance of the pyramids with the impermanence of nations.[12]

But however far she went in accommodating Heger, her patriotism and faith remained inflexible. Through General Abercrombie and his Highland brigade, she affirms her fundamental loyalties. Again, her source was probably Branwell.[13] He managed most of the juvenilia battles, and, since the siblings composed in tandem, Charlotte was obliged to keep up. The spelling too points to a juvenilia origin. A doctor in Verdopolis is called John Abercrombie, after a real Scottish physician,[14] and a sketch she drew in Brussels of a man in Highland dress is similarly labeled "Abercrombie" (fig. 7). Here, though, she was thinking of Sir Ralph Abercromby (1734–1801), the general who reformed the British army in the latter eighteenth century. Abercromby waged his last campaign in Alexandria, supported by two battalions of Highlanders, the Forty-second and the Twenty-eighth. The devoir does not name their opponent, though Charlotte would have known they fought the French. Abercromby's troops won the battle, but he himself was hit by a musket ball and died aboard ship a week later.[15] Charlotte's allusion to "a Golgotha, a field of blood" (39–40) is therefore doubly resonant: it maintains the motif of presentiment and demonstrates her knowledge of scripture.[16]

Her other biblical allusion, to "descendants of Ishmael" (33), reconfirms her faith and insularity. Ishmael was Abraham's son by Hagar, his wife's Egyptian handmaiden, and so not only a racial hybrid, lower in status than legitimate Isaac, but also an outcast from the chosen people.[17] A more specifically Protestant bias is latent in her portrait of the warriors (20). Chateaubriand's sailors, implicitly Catholic, intone canticles and pray to the Virgin; Charlotte's more austere and conscientious soldiers recite the Lord's Prayer and call on Jesus. There is nothing latent in the prejudice she brings to her description of the heathen idol's worshipers; but at that point, Heger intervenes. He tells her she has poorly expressed her "image," a word that could refer to the literal rendition or to her idea of the scene. In either case, he does not scold her for intolerance. He directs his comments to the essay, not to the beliefs of its writer. Nevertheless, in revising her sentence he significantly moderates its prejudice.

Charlotte's reaction to Heger's message can only be inferred from later writings. In the devoirs that follow, she continues to scorn beliefs and customs that are not Anglo-Protestant. But respect for his broadmindedness seems to have been part of her increasing admiration and attachment. More than ten years later, in creating Paul Emanuel, she makes religious tolerance endemic in his character. Toward the end of *Villette*, Lucy Snowe confronts him over their religious differences. She confesses her abhorrence of Catholic ritual and her preference for pure, simple forms of worship. Emanuel responds in Charlotte Brontë's language, but the outlook he communicates is Heger's: "Whatever say priests or controversialists . . . God is good, and loves all the sincere. Believe, then, what you can; believe it as you can."[18]

Heger has marked up this essay extensively, using both pen and pencil. Though he may have gone into similar detail on drafts of prior devoirs that are no longer extant, his effort seems to indicate a deepening relationship—from Charlotte's perspective, if not his.

Charlotte Brontë   [draft before correction]   <u>April 30th 1842</u>

The Nest

When I was young, I loved to walk in a certain lane of a certain wood,
either because it was deserted or because I found there the always first violets

5 of the year.

I recall a little discovery that I made in that lane, on a day in April

18 ...... no matter what year. The weather was mild; spring was begin-

ning to scatter the flowers and the buds with which it hides the traces

of winter.

10 Amid the light foliage of an acacia I saw a Nest, and in the nest a

bird, of what kind I do not know; I saw only its head and its eye, large,

moist, and brilliant with which it seemed to follow my every movement.

The picture was framed by a garland of tender green leaves and by

flowers, white as snow. I approached; the bird moved off and I caught

15 sight of two eggs, pure as two pearls half hidden in the nest. I extended

my hand as if to take them; the bird fluttered its wings, but it did not

fly away; it sought to defend its treasure by making efforts to pierce

me with its little beak. I let myself be vanquished in the combat.

It seems to me that I speak of a trifle, of a bird's nest, but it's

20 because I did not know how to express the thoughts to which this simple

object gave birth in my mind. In continuing my walk I reflected on the

causes that had excited such courage in the heart of a creature ordinar-

ily so timid and so fearful. I reflected on the paternal goodness that

appears in all the works of God, on the infinite benevolence that has

25 furnished the means for the preservation of His creatures. Very common

reflections, very worn, but that will always be true.

Le Nid

Quand j'étais jeune, j'aimais beaucoup à me promener dans une certaine

allée d'un certain bois, soit parcequ'il était solitaire soit parceque j'y
toujours
trouvais les première violettes de l'année.   5

Je me rappelle une pétite découverte que je faisais dans cette allée,

un jour du mois d'Avril 18...... n'importe quelle année — Il faisait

un temps doux, le printemps commençait à répandre les fleurs et les

bourgeons dont il cache les traces de l'hiver.

Parmi la feuillage léger d'un acacia je vit un Nid, et dans le nid un   10

oiseau, je ne sais pas de quelle espèce, je ne vit que sa tête et son oeil

large, humide et brillant dont il semblait guetter tous mes mouvements.

Le tableau était encadré d'une guirlande de feuilles vert tendre et de

fleurs, blanches comme la neige. Je m'approchais; l'oiseau se rémuait

et j'entrevit deux oeufs, pures comme deux perles demi cachés dans le   15

nid; je tendis la main comme pour les prendre, l'oiseau tremoussait des

ailes mais il ne s'envola pas, il chercha à défendre son trésor en faisant

des efforts pour me percer avec son petit bec. Je me laissai vaincre dans

le combat.

Il me semble que je parle d'une bagatelle, d'un nid d'oiseau, mais   20

c'est parceque je n'ai pas su exprimer les pensées que cet objet simple

faisait naître dans mon esprit. En continuant ma promenade je réflé-

chissais sur les causes qui avaient excité tant de courage dans le coeur

d'une créature ordinairement si timide et si craintive. Je réfléchissais

sur la bonté paternelle qui parait dans tous les oeuvres de Dieu, sur la   25

bienveillance infinie qui a pourvu des moyens pour la conservation de

ses créatures. Reflexions très communes, très usées mais qui seront

toujours vraies.

I often revisited that nest. At the end of fifteen days I found no more eggs; the young birds had been escaped from their prison and at every moment they demanded the food that it was their mother's pleasure to bring them. Often in watching the tireless care of that bird for her little ones, I said to myself, miracles have not ceased, one still sees on earth the presence of God in His works. The nest of a bird is but a line, but a word in the vast volume that Nature offers for the instruction of the whole human race, and of which each page is filled with the proofs of God's existence.

If the Atheist wished to study this volume, he would soon find a remedy for the canker of skepticism that gnaws at his heart. It is said that there are no more wonders on earth because God no longer finds a tabernacle in the cloud or in the column of fire; but if one looked closely at the lowliest flower, the puniest insect, one would see in the delicate petals, in the gauzy wings, the traces of the same divine hand that engraved the stern law of the Hebrews on tablets of stone, of the same all-powerful hand that gave the mountains their foundations and the seas their bounds.

———

Je revisitais souvent ce nid, au bout de quinze jours je ne trouvais
plus d'oeufs, les jeunes oiseaux avait eut échappés de leur prison et
à chaque instant ils demandaient la nourriture que leur mère se plaisait
de leur porter. Souvent en regardant les soins infatigables de cet oiseau
pour ses petits, je disais en moi-même, les miracles ne sont pas cessé,
on voit encore sur la terre, la présence de Dieu dans ses oeuvres. Le
nid d'un oiseau n'est qu'une ligne, qu'un mot dans le vaste volume que
la Nature offre pour l'instruction de toute la race humaine, et dont
chaque page est rempli des preuves de l'existence de Dieu.

Si l'Athée voulait étudier ce v[olume], il trouverait bientôt un reméde
pour ce chancre de scepticisme qui lui ronge le coeur. On dit qu'il
n'y a plus de merveilles sur la terre parceque Dieu ne trouve plus un
tabernacle dans le nuage ou dans la colonne de feu, mais si on regardait
bien la moindre fleur, la plus chétif insecte on verrait dans les pétales
delicats dans les ailes de gaze, des traces de la même main divine qui
grava sur les tables de pierre la loi sévère des Hébreux, de la même main
tout-puissante qui donna aux montagnes leurs fondements et aux mers
leurs bornes

Charlotte Brontë   April 30th 1842

The Nest

═══════

When I was young, I loved to walk in a certain lane of a certain wood,
                                                                always
either because it was deserted or because I found there the first violets

5   of the year.

I recall a little discovery that I made in that lane, on a day in April
    what   *the*   *the air was warm*
18 ...... no matter what year? The weather was mild; spring was begin-
    open   *and tinge with crimson [the] shivering [buds]*, which
ning to scatter the flowers and the buds with which it hides the traces
hide themselves in [winter].
of winter.
           tender and light
10   **G**   Amid the light foliage of an acacia I saw a Nest, and in the nest a

bird, of what kind I do not know; I saw only its head and its eye, large,
           that
    G   moist, and brilliant with which it seemed to follow my every movement.
                 pale
    G   The picture was framed by a garland of tender-green leaves and by
              frightened
flowers, white as snow. I approached; the bird moved off and I caught
            and
15   **G**   sight of two eggs, pure as two pearls half hidden in the nest. I extended
    half-opening its gasping beak   *beat*
my hand as if to take them; the bird fluttered its wings, but it did not
           its resistance, feeble but intrepid,
fly away; it sought to defend its treasure; by making efforts to pierce
halted my movement and conquered my cupidity.
me with its little beak. I let myself be vanquished in the combat.

It seems to me that I speak of a trifle,: of a bird's nest,! but it's
    that   *the whole world of ideas and feelings*   *so*
20   because I did not know how to express the thoughts to which this simple
        aroused
object gave birth in my mind. In continuing my walk, I reflected on the
        kindled
causes that had excited such courage in the heart of a creature ordinar-

ily so timid and so fearful... I reflected on the paternal goodness that
shines
appears in all the works of God, on the infinite benevolence that has
           of effectively [preserving] all
25   furnished the means for the preservation of His creatures. Very common

reflections, very worn, but that will always be true.

Charlotte Brontë   April 30th 1842

Le Nid

Quand j'étais jeune, j'aimais beaucoup à me promener dans une certaine

allée d'un certain bois, soit parcequ'il était solitaire soit parceque j'y
                                        toujours
trouvais les première violettes de l'année.   5

                                                        fis
        Je me rappelle une pétite découverte que je faisais dans cette allée,

                                        q
un jour du mois d'Avril 18...... n'importe quelle *l*'année? — Il faisait
l'air était tiède   *entr'ouvrir   et à empourprer*
un temps doux, le printemps commençait à répandre les fleurs et les
        frileux, qui se cachent ———
bourgeons dont il cache les traces de l'hiver.
                e tendre et léger   *s*
        Parmi la feuillage léger d'un acacia je vit un Nid, et dans le nid un   *B*   10

                                                        s
oiseau, je ne sais pas de quelle espèce, je ne vit que sa tête et son oeil

                                qui
large, humide et brillant dont il semblait guetter tous mes mouvements.   *B*
                                                pâle
Le tableau était encadré d'une guirlande de feuilles vert-tendre et de   *B*

                                                effrayé
fleurs, blanches comme la neige. Je m'approchais; l'oiseau se rémuait
                s   *et*
et j'entrevit deux oeufs, purs comme deux perles demi cachés dans le   *B*   15
                                entr'ouvrant un bec hâletant   agita—┐*s*
nid; je tendis la main comme pour les prendre, l'oiseau tremoussait des
                        [p]oint   *sa*
ailes mais il ne s'envola pas:, il cherchait à défendre son trésor en
résistance, faible mais intrépide, arrêta mon mouvement et vainquit ma convoitise.
faisant des\efforts pour me percer\avec son petit\bec. Je me laissai

vaincre dans le combat.

        Il ~~me~~ semble que je parle d'une bagatelle,: d'\un nid d'oiseau,*!* ~~mais~~   20
                tout le monde d'idées et de sentiments   si
c'est ~~parceque~~ je n'ai pas su exprimer les pensées que cet objet simple
        souleva
faisait naître dans mon esprit. En continuant ma promenade, je réflé-
                                allumé
chissais sur les causes qui avaient excité tant de courage dans le coeur

d'une créature ordinairement si timide et si craintive... Je réfléchis~~sais~~
                        éclate
sur la bonté paternelle qui parait dans tous les oeuvres de Dieu, sur la   25
                                efficaces [?]   *toutes*
bienveillance infinie qui a pourvu des moyens ~~pour~~ la conservation de

ses créatures. Reflexions très communes, très usées mais qui seront

toujours vraies.

I often ~~re~~visited that nest. At the end of fifteen days I found no
_{but} _{who had} **narrow demanded**
more eggs; the young birds ~~had been~~ escaped from their ˇprison ~~and~~ ˇat

every moment ~~they demanded~~ the food that it was their mother's pleasure

to bring them. Often in watching the tireless care of that bird for her
Everywhere, always
little ones, I said to myself, miracles have not ceased; one ~~still~~ sees on
God [*presen*]*t*
earth ~~the~~ presence ~~of God~~ in His works. The nest of a bird is but a line,
opens to
~~but~~ a word in the vast volume that Nature offers for the instruction of the
abounds in ⌐
whole human race, and of which each page is filled with the proofs of

God's existence.

If the Atheist wished to study this volume, he would soon find ~~a~~
You say
remedy for the canker of skepticism that gnaws at his heart. It is said
appears in
that there are no more wonders on earth because God no longer finds a
of *a*
tabernacle ~~in~~ the cloud*s* or in the column of fire; but ~~if one~~ looked
you will *those*
~~closely~~ at the lowliest flower, the puniest insect; one would see in the
those *wonders*
the traces delicate petals, in the gauzy wings, the traces of the ~~same~~ divine hand
.... of the
hand? that engraved the stern law of the Hebrews on tablets of stone, of the

same all-powerful hand that gave the mountains their foundations and

the seas their bounds.

———

Advice: — *What importance should be given to details, in developing a*
subject? —

Remorselessly sacrifice everything that does not contribute to clarity,
verisimilitude, and effect.

Accentuate everything that sets the main idea in relief, so that the
impression be colorful, picturesque. It's sufficient that the rest be in its proper
place, but in half-tone. *That is what gives to style, as to painting, unity,*
perspective, and effect.

Read Harmony XIV of Lamartine, The Infinite: *we will analyze it*
together, from the point of view of the details.

May 4 C. Heger

Je ~~revisitai~~s souvent ce nid,: au bout de quinze jours je ne trouvai~~s~~
mais de   *qui* *s'étaient*   *étroite*
plus d'oeufs,: l~~è~~s jeunes oiseaux ~~avait eut~~ échappés de leur˘ prison ~~et~~   30
demandaient   *à*
˘à chaque instant ~~ils demandaient~~ la nourriture que leur mère se plaisait
à
~~de~~ leur porter. Souvent en regardant les soins infatigables de cet oiseau

pour ses petits, je disais en moi-même, les miracles ne sont pas cess~~és~~ | ,:
Partout, toujours   *Dieu*   *t*
˘on voit ~~encore~~ sur la terre, ~~la~~ présen~~c~~e ~~de Dieu~~ dans ses oeuvres. Le

nid d'un oiseau n'est qu'une ligne, ~~qu~~'un mot dans le vaste volume que   35
           ouvre à
la Nature offre pour l'instruction de toute la race humaine, et dont
            abonde en
chaque page est remplie | des preuves de l'existence de Dieu.

Si l'Athée voulait étudier ce v[olume], il trouverait bientôt ~~un~~ reméde
      à   *u*   *Tu*   *s*
~~pour~~ c~~e~~ *ce* chancre d~~e~~ scepticisme qui lui ronge le coeur. O~~n~~ di~~t~~ qu'il
                                          se montre   *dans*
n'y a plus de merveilles sur la terre parceque Dieu ne trouve plus˘un   40
         d   *une*   *e*
tabernacle ~~dans~~ le nuage*s* ou dans l~~a~~ colonne de feu; mais ~~si~~ ~~on~~ regard~~ait~~
                            tu   *s*   *c*
~~bien~~ la moindre fleur, la plus chétif insecte; o~~n~~ verrai~~t~~, dans l~~e~~s pétales
    c   *les merveilles*
délicats dans l~~e~~s ailes de gaze, des traces de la ~~même~~ main divine qui   *des traces*
                                                            .... de la main?
grava sur les tables de pierre la loi sévère des Hébreux, de la même main

tout-puissant~~e~~, qui donna aux montagnes leurs fondements et aux mers   45

leurs bornes . |

Conseil: — *quelle importance faut-il donner aux détails, dans le développement*

    d'un sujet? —

    Sacrifiez impitoyablem^t. *tout ce qui ne contribue pas à la clarté, à la*

vraisemblance et à l'effet.   50

    accusez fortement tout ce qui donne du relief à la pensée principale; que

l'expression soit alors colorée, pittoresque; Il suffit que le reste soit à sa place,

mais dans la demi-teinte. *c'est ce qui donne au style, comme à la peinture,*

l'unité la perspective, et l'effet.

    Lisez la XIV harmonie de Lamartine: L'infini; *nous l'analyserons*   55

ensemble, du point de vue des détails

    4 mai   *C. Heger*

Comments

That night, on going to bed . . . I feasted . . . on the spectacle of ideal drawings, which I saw in the dark, all the work of my own hands: . . . sweet paintings . . . of wrens' nests enclosing pearl-like eggs, wreathed about with young ivy sprays.

—*Jane Eyre*[1]

This devoir follows by only four days the one that Charlotte based on a passage from *The Genius of Christianity*. Heger took that passage from the section "Existence of God proved by the wonders of nature,"[2] so the sequence may not be coincidental. He could have made the title the theme of his next assignment, asking his students to draw on their experience, or she could have chosen to echo the message implicit in his lectures on Chateaubriand. Clearly, she remains in her submissive mode. Nothing in the devoir's conventional pieties anticipates the protest of her novels.

The French here is much rougher than that of "Evening Prayer," and Heger has reworked it so extensively, using a pencil and later a pen, that making out the sense becomes a challenge. Nonetheless, the master-pupil dialogue progresses, through and because of these problems. Heger does not merely correct Charlotte's errors or smooth her awkward constructions. He continually replaces and supplements lackluster adjectives and verbs. Though he writes "B[on]" next to picture-making phrases, his revisions imply the imprecision of her details and, in the passage on the bird's resistance (17–18), the implausibility of pecking.

Charlotte was writing about April on an April day, during her first spring away from Yorkshire. The pensionnat garden had its own lanes and alleys, and the Hegers arranged expeditions to the countryside for their students and teachers. But the Brontës had learned to draw by copying from magazines and popular engravings, and this "picture" resembles such models. Distanced in time and space from Brussels, the episode becomes increasingly generic. Acacia and violets aside, her bird could have hatched its eggs in any wood.

What accounts for the decline from "Evening Prayer"? Was its imaginary Egypt more real to her, or is there a prosaic explanation? In a letter of early May, she reports that Heger had forbidden her the use of a dictionary or a grammar. Though his rule applied to translating, not to composition,[3] the absence of a plural adjective with violets ("first" in English, "premières" in French), together with the number of faulty verb forms (like the third person "vit" when she means to say "I saw"), suggests that she worked without a reference book. The English word "April" in her header (1) also suggests that she lacked the time or motive to edit. Possibly she cared more about the message than the details that convey it.

If so, Heger's comment—"Advice," not "Criticism"—reminds her of their interdependence. He tells her how to improve her technique; more important, he offers to work with her. He speaks of composition in painterly terms, of unity, emphasis, proportion, and coloring. His words reflect a neoclassical tradition which assumes that literature and painting correspond and that both try to render nature truthfully. But in the nineteenth century, *impression* and *picturesque* were also key terms for the Romantics, and if Heger's rhetoric evokes an older theory, his practice connects him with his era. Here, as in the other devoirs he revises, he encourages striking and colorful effects and images that generate emotion.

The natural theology that Charlotte articulates may also be connected to her schoolwork. When Lawrence Jay Dessner published this devoir, he said that "her theology might seem out of date when one considers intellectual life in Europe in 1842."[4] But Heger was teaching Chateaubriand and Lamartine, both of whom saw nature as divinely ordained. Chateaubriand devotes four chapters of *Genius* to religious ornithology. "The admirable wisdom of Providence is nowhere more conspicuous than in the nests of birds,"[5] he begins chapter 6. He gives details on nest building, the nestling, and the mother's care, always as evidence for the larger arguments that God is responsible for nature's marvels and that atheism is not tenable. No proof exists that Heger spoke about this chapter or that Charlotte read and used it as a source; the trope of nature as a volume was a commonplace, like little birds as signs of God's benevolence. Still, the chapter ends by conflating three elements that figure in her devoirs of this period—Egypt, inscription, and the verb *ronger* (to eat away, gnaw, or erode): "Time has eroded the inscriptions of the kings of Memphis from their funereal pyramids; yet it has not been able to efface a single letter of the history that the Egyptian ibis bears engraved on its eggshell."[6]

Charlotte's own history of biblical study is inscribed in her devoir's closing lines. The Mosaic allusions and scriptural cadences announce that her own faith is unshakable. In a later devoir, "The Death of Moses," she recurs to the column and cloud; there, they become details in an argument for literal belief in the Bible. If her orthodoxy seems surprising, her circumstances help to explain it. Although she wanted to break out as a writer, she refused to loosen the armor of faith that kept her secure among strangers.

She did read Lamartine's Harmony "The Infinite" and probably discussed it with Heger. Then she tried again to develop an essay that would move from illustration to reflection.

Charlotte Brontë, unfinished pencil drawing of a picturesque landscape, probably done in Brussels in 1842. Harry Ransom Humanities Research Center, University of Texas at Austin.

[Charlotte Brontë]

The Immensity of God

Yesterday evening, at sunset, I went walking in the fields. Little by little, night approached without my being aware of it. At first I amused myself by looking at the rich variety of colors that tinted the west. As they grew pale and faded, a few stars appeared successively in the sky, and soon the whole firmament blazed with a thousand fires. The azure of space borrowed a new luster from the pure atmosphere of the season and from the rays of all the luminaries crossing it. The Milky Way was of a dazzling whiteness; finally, as if to complete the tableau, the moon arose, majestic and surrounded by clouds, as Milton represents her. She showed nature under a new aspect; the shadows of the painting seemed more delicate, the ~~lights~~ highlights more artistically arranged than when the sun shone on it.

While I contemplated the path of the moon, pursuing her course among the stars, there occurred to me a thought that has often disquieted men of a serious and reflective nature. David himself alludes to it when he says, "When I consider the heavens, the work of thy fingers, the moon and the stars which thou hast ordained, I ask: 'What is man, that thou art mindful of him; and the son of man, that thou visitest him?'" Similarly, when I contemplated that infinite multitude of stars, or (to speak as a philosopher) of suns that lighted my way, when I expanded the idea, and imagined another firmament, strewn with suns and worlds beyond the one that we see, and all these worlds lighted by the luminaries of another firmament, still further away; while I pursued this thought, I could not keep myself from reflecting on my own insignificance, contrasted with the immensity of the works of God.

If the sun which lights this part of the universe were annihilated, along with the entire planetary system of which it is the center, that

L'Immensité de Dieu

Hier au soir, au coucher du soleil je me promenais dans les champs. Peu

à peu la nuit s'approchait sans que je m'en aperçusse. D'abord je

m'amusais à regarder la riche variété des couleurs dont l'occident ~~fut~~ était

teint; à mesure qu'elles palissaient et s'éteignaient quelques étoiles   5

paraissaient successivement dans le ciel et bientôt tout le firmament

brillait de mille feux. L'azur de l'espace empruntait un nouvel éclat de

l'atmosphère pure de la saison et des rayons de tous ces luminaires qui

le traversaient. La voie lactée était d'une blancheur éblouissante; enfin,

comme pour achever le tableau, la lune se lèva, majestueuse, et entourée   10

de nuages comme Milton la represente; elle montra la nature sous un

nouvel aspect; les ombres de la peinture paraissaient plus delicates, les

~~lumières~~ clairs plus artistement disposées que lorsque le soleil y brillait.

Tandis que je contemplais la marche de la lune, poursuivant son

cours parmi les astres, il me vint dans l'esprit une pensée qui a souvent   15

servi à inquieter ~~des~~ les hommes d'un caractère sérieux et rêveur. David

lui-même y fait allusion quand il dit "Lorsque je regarde les cieux,

l'ouvrage de tes doigts, la lune et les étoiles que tu as agencées, je dis:

'Qu'est-ce que l'homme mortel, que tu te souviennes de lui; et que le fils

de l'homme, que tu le visites?" De même lorsque je contemplais cette   20

multitude infinie d'astres, ou (pour parler en philosophe) de soleils qui

m'éclairaient, lorsque j'élargissais l'idée, et imaginais un autre firma-

ment, parsemés de soleils et de mondes au-dessus de celui que nous

voyons, et tous ces mondes éclairés par les luminaires d'un autre firma-

ment, encore plus loin; tandis que je poursuivais cette pensée je ne   25

pouvais pas m'empecher de réfléchir sur ma propre insignifiance con-

trastée avec l'immensité des oeuvres de Dieu.

Si le soleil qui éclaire cette partie de l'univers était annéanti, ainsi

would be no more, in respect to all creation, than if a grain of sand were
removed from the shore. The space they occupy and is so tiny in comparison
with the great Whole that their disappearance would scarcely leave a gap.
One would perceive no empty space if one could survey the entire universe in a single glance. ~~By the aid of the telescope we [?]~~ And there
may exist beings who have this capability; man himself, someday, may
attain it. By the aid of the telescope, we see many stars that we could
not see with the naked eye, and as the science of optics improves, these
discoveries will increase. Huygens is carried away by this idea, so far
as to believe that there are stars so distant from the earth that their rays,
always in movement from their creation to the present, have not yet
arrived at our sphere. Beyond all doubt, the universe has fixed limits
but, when we consider that it is the work of an infinite power, ordered
by an infinite goodness and possessing unlimited space to exercise its
functions, how can our imagination set its bounds?

que tout le système de planètes dont il est le centre, ce ne serait à l'égard
de toute la creation que comme si on otait un grain de sable de la grève;
l'espace qu'ils occupent ẻt si petitẻ en comparaison avec le grand Tout

> est

qui leur disparition y laisseront à peine une lacune: on ne s'apercevrait
pas du vide si on pouvait parcourir tout l'univers d'un seul coup d'oeil –
~~Par l'aide du téléscope nous [?]~~ et il peut exister des êtres qui ont cette
capabilité, l'homme-même, plus tard, peut y atteindre. Par l'aide du
téléscope nous voyons plusieurs étoiles qu'il nous était impossible de voir
de l'oeil seul, et à mesure qu'on perfectionne l'optique ces découvertes
ṡẻṙò s'augmenteront.— Huygenius se laisse entrainer par cette idée
jusqu'à croire qu'il y a des étoiles tellement eloignées de la terre, que
leurs rayons toujours en mouvement depuis leur création jusqu'à present
ne sont pas encore arrivés à notre sphère. Il n'y a pas de doute que
l'univers ait des limites fixes mais, lorsque nous considérons que c'est
l'ouvrage d'un pouvoir infini, reglé par une bonté infinie et possedant
unẻ espace illimité pour exercer ses fonctions, comment notre imagination peut-elle y mettre des bornes?

30

35

40

45

Comments

... It is in the unclouded night-sky, where His worlds wheel their silent course, that we read clearest His infinitude, His omnipotence, His omnipresence. I had risen to my knees to pray for Mr. Rochester. Looking up, I, with tear-dimmed eyes, saw the mighty milky-way. Remembering what it was—what countless systems there swept space like a soft trace of light—I felt the might and strength of God.

—Jane Eyre[1]

Read the XIVth Harmony of Lamartine: *The Infinite*. We will analyze it together. . . .

—C. Heger, May 4

Charlotte Brontë wrote this essay in a notebook, omitting her name and the date. Because the pages were removed and rebound, its position in the sequence of her devoirs can no longer be confirmed.[2] But whether she composed it in May or later, internal and contextual evidence connects it to Heger's advice. Almost certainly, she read "The Infinite" and Lamartine's "Commentary" on it. Then she tried to assimilate their content while retaining a perspective of her own.

The poem Heger cites is the fourth, not the fourteenth, in Alphonse de Lamartine's *Harmonies poétiques et religieuses* (Poetic and religious harmonies), second series (1830); its full title is "L'Infini dans les cieux" (The infinite in the heavens). Lamartine sets this long (216-line) meditation on a starry summer night. Its speaker lets his thoughts "[f]loat like a sea where the moon is cradled," as he contemplates the heavens and the vistas they illuminate. Raising his eyes, he thinks of "suns without number" and the planets that they guide, "revolving in those immensities." He thinks too of man, an "Atom" in the scale of infinity: ". . . how he must say to himself, What am I?/Oh! what am I, Lord!"[3]

Encountering that question, Charlotte must have recognized its origins in Psalm 8, a psalm of David, for her *devoir* reproduces the passage almost verbatim from the King James version. Lamartine says elsewhere that he wanted these poems to resemble "modern psalms, like those David had written with his tears,"[4] so her replacement follows his intention. She also tends to follow the movement of "The Infinite" from the speaker's vision to a broader meditation, though the tableau of the sunset and night sky are her own, as is the allusion to Milton.[5]

But Lamartine's question sets the poem on a course from which Charlotte's *devoir* diverges. His speaker grows oppressed by his reflections on mortality and rescues himself by recalling God's concern for all forms of creation. In contrast, she shifts from a religious to a scientific perspective. No source has yet emerged for her reference to Huygens, the seventeenth-century founder of the theory of light waves;[6] perhaps she learned his name in a discussion with Heger, who also gave lessons in arithmetic.[7] Primarily, however, she took her cues from Lamartine, who comments on his own poem in these words: "When one thinks that Herschell's telescope has already counted more than five million stars; that each of these stars is a world greater and more important than this earthly globe; that these five million worlds are only the borders of that creation; that, if we were to arrive at the furthest remove, we would perceive from there other gulfs of infinite space, filled with other worlds incalculable, and that this voyage would last myriads of centuries, without our ever being able to arrive at the limits between nothingness and God. . . . "[8]

What should be made of Charlotte's borrowings? Read without

awareness of its sources, this devoir attests to her astonishing progress; read with that awareness, it is derivative. Even the sand grains come from Lamartine.[9] Moreover, its indebtedness is complex. Two of Lamartine's objectives for his Harmonies—to show how the natural universe manifests God's wonders and to draw inspiration from "the bards of Israel"—reflect the influence of Chateaubriand, whose work he greatly admired.[10] His title echoes *Harmonies of Nature,* a collection by Bernardin de Saint-Pierre, whom Charlotte cites years later in *Shirley.*[11] Bernardin made the word *reflets* famous; Lamartine brings it into "The Infinite," and Charlotte brings it into her novel.[12] So even if she had studied only Lamartine, she would indirectly have drawn on two more authors. But of course she knew of the others through Heger, who gave her two volumes of Bernardin later,[13] and perhaps through independent reading.

Heger too leaves traces of his presence. His "Advice" on "The Nest" uses painterly language, and she portrays the moon here as a consummate artist, skillfully disposing lights and shadows (11–13). More broadly, he believed that scientific knowledge inevitably led to greater faith. As he said in one of his Prize Day speeches, "Thus each step, along the scientific way, is a step toward God; thus the further upstream one moves on science's great river, the more one sees that heaven is its source."[14] As he said in the other, emulation was essential to the process of acquiring any knowledge.

Charlotte was used to appropriating. For the juvenilia, the children borrowed recklessly, imitating everything from dialogue to graphics. The differences in Brussels were that Heger set the terms, that in a foreign language she was not at her ease, and that student work exacted far more discipline. Charlotte could obey, and she could imitate; the challenge was to harmonize what she took from others with her own ideas and modes of expression.

"The Immensity of God" takes on that challenge. It compacts Lamartine's ideas into three paragraphs. Its descriptions of the night sky show increasing control of the nuances of poetic French. Charlotte did not always know the French equivalents for images and concepts that she wanted to communicate: *artistically, ordained, gap, naked eye.* But she got Heger's message about using details to set her main idea in relief. If the shift from a Miltonic moon to optics is surprising, the essay does not swerve from its subject. It is also, despite the speaker's claim of insignificance, unswerving in its sense of possibility. *Bounds* ends this devoir, as it ended "The Nest," but here the punctuation is a question mark. Under the protection of her faith and her professor, she saw no limitations ahead.

Emily J. Brontë   May 15th 1842

The Cat .

═══════

I can say with sincerity that I like cats; also I can give very good reasons
why those who despise them are wrong.

A cat is an animal who has more human feelings than almost any
other being.   We cannot sustain a comparison with the dog, it is
infinitely too good; but the cat, although it differs in some physical
points, is extremely like us in disposition.

There may be people, in truth, who would say that this resemblance
extends only to the most wicked men; that it is limited to their excessive
hypocrisy, cruelty, and ingratitude; detestable vices in our race and
equally odious in that of cats.

Without disputing the limits that those individuals set on our affinity,
I answer that if hypocrisy, cruelty, and ingratitude are exclusively the
domain of the wicked, that class comprises everyone.   Our education
develops one of those qualities in great perfection; the others flourish
without nurture, and far from condemning them, we regard all three with
great complacency.   A cat, in its own interest, sometimes hides its
misanthropy under the guise of amiable gentleness; instead of tearing
what it desires from its master's hand, it approaches with a caressing air,
rubs its pretty little head against him, and advances a paw whose touch
is soft as down.   When it has gained its end, it resumes its character of
Timon; and that artfulness in it is called hypocrisy.   In ourselves, we
give it another name, politeness, and he who did not use it to hide his
real feelings would soon be driven from society.

"But," says some delicate lady, who has murdered a half-dozen

Le Chat .

Je puis dire avec sincérité, que j'aime les chats; aussi je sais rendre des très bonnes raisons, pourquoi ceux qui les haïssent, ont tort.

Un chat est un animal qui a plus des sentiments humains que presque tout autre être. Nous ne pouvons soutenir une comparaison avec le chien, il est infiniment trop bon: màïs mais le chat, encore qu'il diffère en quelques points physiques, est extrêmement semblable à nous en disposition

Il peut être des gens, en vérité, qui diraient que cette ressemblance ne lui approche qu'aux hommes les plus méchants; qu'elle est bornée à son excès d'hypocrisie, de cruauté, et d'ingratitude; vices détestables dans notre race et également odieux en celle des chats.

Sans disputer les limites que ces individus mettent à notre affinité, je reponds, que si l'hypocrisie, le cruauté et l'ingratitude sont exclusivement la propriété des méchants, cette classe renferme tout le monde; notre éducation développe une de ces qualités en grande perfection, les autres fleurissent sans soins, et loin de les condamner, nous regardons tous les trois, avec beaucoup de complaisance. Un chat, pour son intérêt propre cache quelquefois sa misanthropie sous une apparence de douceur très aimable; au lieu d'arracher ce qu'il désire de la main de son maitre il s'approche d'un air caressant, frotte sa jolie petite tête contre lui, et avance une patte dont la touche est douce comme le duvet. Lorsqu'il est venu à bout, il reprend son caractère de Timon, et cette finesse est nommée l'hypocrisie en lui, en nous mêmes, nous lui donnons un autre nom, c'est la politesse et celui qui ne l'employait pas pour déguiser ses vrais sentiments serait bientôt chassé de société.

"Mais," dit quelque dame délicate, qui a meurtri une demi-douzaine

lapdogs through pure affection, "the cat is such a cruel beast, he is not content to kill his prey, he torments it before its death; you cannot make that accusation against us." More or less, Madame. Your husband, for example, likes hunting very much, but foxes being rare on his land, he would not have the means to pursue this amusement often, if he did not manage his supplies thus: once he has run an animal to its last breath, he snatches it from the jaws of the hounds and saves it to suffer the same infliction two or three more times, ending finally in death. You yourself avoid a bloody spectacle because it wounds your weak nerves. But I have seen you embrace your child in transports, when he came to show you a beautiful butterfly crushed between his cruel little fingers; and at that moment, I really wanted to have a cat, with the tail of a half-devoured rat hanging from its mouth, to present as the image, the true copy, of your angel. You could not refuse to kiss him, and if he scratched us both in revenge, so much the better. Little boys are rather liable to acknowledge their friends' caresses in that way, and the resemblance would be more perfect. The ingratitude of cats is another name for penetration. They know how to value our favors at their true price, because they guess the motives that prompt us to grant them, and if those motives might sometimes be good, undoubtedly they remember always that they owe all their misery and all their evil qualities to the great ancestor of humankind. For assuredly, the cat was not wicked in Paradise.

de bichons par pure affection, "le chat est une bête si cruelle, il ne se contente pas de tuer sa proie, il la tourmente avant sa mort; vous ne pouvez faire cette accusation contre nous." A peu près Madame — monsieur votre mari, par exemple, aime beaucoup la chasse; mais les renards étant rares dans sa terre, il n'aurait pas le moyen de prendre cette amusement souvent, s'il ne manageait point ses materiaux ainsi, lorsqu'il a couru un animal à son dernier soupir, il le tire des gueules des chiens, et le reserve pour souffrir encore deux ou trois fois la même infliction, terminant finalement en la mort. Vous évitez vous-même un spectacle sanglant, parce qu'il blesse vos faibles nerfs; mais j'ai vous vue embrasser avec transport votre enfant, quand il venait vous montrer un beau papillon écrasé entre ses cruels petits doigts; et, à ce moment, j'ai voulu bien avoir un chat, avec la queue d'un rat demi-englouti, pendant de sa bouche, à présenter comme l'image, la vraie copie, de votre ange; vous ne pourriez refuser de le baiser, et s'il nous égratignait tous deux en revanche, tant mieux, les petits garcons sont assez liables à reconnaître ainsi, les caresses de leurs amis, et la ressemblance serait plus parfaite. L'ingratitude des chats est un autre nom pour la pénétration. Ils savent estimer nos faveurs à leur juste prix, parce qu'ils dévinent les motifs qui nous poussent de leur donner, et si ces motifs puissent quelquefois être bons, sans doute ils se souviennent toujours, qu'ils doivent toutes leurs misères et toutes leurs mauvaises qualités au grand aïeul du genre humain. Car, assurément, le chat n'était pas méchant en Paradis

[Two extracts from one of Charlotte Brontë's notebooks]

Plea for Cats

The cause of cats is, I admit, sirs, harder to defend. In general one has
a poor opinion of their character, and their claws have made them many
enemies. But still justice should be done. If cats are wicked, we are not
very good.

Laura! my hat! my walking stick! my gloves! I have to go out.

I walked three hours, then I slept nine

Come with me, presently; — no, impossible now

The Two Dogs

A good husband's indulgence toward his wife. Among other presents,
a puppy that he brings her. Detail what it symbolizes; his kindness. The
caresses and attention of which Bijou is the object; how he deserved
them; here describe his little talents. Tell how he grows ugly in growing
up; how his limbs enlarge. The signs he shows of being a big sheepdog.
Madam's disgust for him; the rebuffs he suffers, the caresses with which
he confronts this ill treatment. Clumsy, for that is what she calls him
now, banished to the yard; his degradation; detail his privations, the
change in food and company. Philosophic reflections to be put in
Clumsy's mouth; he can no longer be delicate; his ugliness has cost him
dear; destiny is fickle for everyone; wisdom and courage. Grounds for
consolation — a pretty poodle given to Madame by her husband. Describe
the delicacy of all parts of her body. Zephyrette, a well-bred dog,
placed above all animals of her kind; her agility, playfulness — good
heart.

The summer spent in the country; people of the house asleep; two
robbers letting themselves in through the garden. Paint their advance —
with the dread that crime inspires; the fear that the night, the moonlight,

Plaidoyer pour les chats

La cause des chats est, je l'avoue, messieurs, plus difficile à defendre.

On a généralement mauvaise opinion de leur caractère, et leurs griffes

leur ont fait beaucoup d'ennemis; mais il faudrait aussi se rendre justice.

Si les chats sont méchants, nous ne sommes pas très bons.   5

Laure! mon chapeau! ma canne! mes gants! je dois sortir

J'ai marché trois heures puis j'en ai dormi neuf

Viens avec moi, tantôt; — non, maintenant impossible

Les deux chiens

Complaisance d'un bon mari pour sa femme. entre autres présents jeune   10

chien qu'il lui apporte; detailler de quoi - il est le symbole; sa gentil-

lesse; les caresses et les soins dont Bijou est l'objet; comment il les

méritait, décrire ici ses petits talents; dire comment il enlaidit en

grandissant; ses membres qui grossissent. indices qu'il offre d'un gros

chien de troupeau; dégout de madame pour lui, rebuts qu'il en éprouve   15

caresses qu'il oppose à ces mauvais traitements.   Pataud c'est ainsi

qu'elle le nomme maintenant, chassé à la cour; sa dégradation; détailler

ses privations le changement de nourriture et de compagnie; reflexions

philosophiques ¢òħ qu'on mettra dans la bouche de Pataud; il ne doit plus

être delicat; sa laideur lui coûte cher; le destin est inconstant pour tout 20

le monde; sagesse et courage. motifs de consolation — jolie bar[b]ette

donnée à Madame par monsieur; décrire la finesse de toutes les parties

de son corps — Zéphyrette chienne accomplie mise au-dessus de tous les

animaux de son espèce, légèreté espièglerie - bon coeur.

L'été passé à la campagne; sommeil des gens de la maison; deux   25

voleurs s'introduisant par le jardin; peindre leur marche — dans la crainte

qu'inspire le crime; effroi que la nuit, le clair de lune, le bruit des

the sound of the leaves excites in them; paint Clumsy's attention and the whole attitude and actions of a dog who hears a noise; his fury. Here you will describe the combat that takes place between the dog and the robbers, one of them armed with a knife; the victory going to Clumsy despite his wounds. Awakening, alarm, arrival of everyone and of Zephyrette. Describe the spectacle of the battlefield, the men, and the dying animal; caresses given to the burglars by Zephyrette. At that sight

the master's regret over his conduct toward Clumsy and the preference given to the thankless Zephryette; the repentence he expresses; caresses and last breath of the dying Clumsy. Moral on the scheming flatterer and the man of merit.

feuilles excitent en eux; peindre l'attention de Pataud et toute l'attitude et les actions d'un chien qui entend du bruit, sa fureur Ici on décrira le combat qui s'engage entre les chiens et les voleurs, dont l'un est armé d'un glaive; victoire restant à Pataud malgré ses blessures; réveille, alarme, arrivée de tout le monde et de Zephyrette; décrire le spectacle du champ de bataille, les hommes, et l'animal mourant caresses faites par Zephyrette aux voleurs; à cette vue regret du maître sur sa conduite envers Pataud et la préférence donnée à l'ingrate Zephyrette, repentir qu'il exprime; caresses et dernier soupir de Pataud expirant, moral sur le flatteur intriguant et l'homme de mérite

30

35

Comments

This is the first of Emily Brontë's devoirs or at least the earliest survivor (she probably wrote others, long since lost, in the four months that she had been in Brussels). But whatever its place in the series of her devoirs, "The Cat" is a singular essay. If, as Charlotte alleges, Emily came to Belgium with only a rudimentary knowledge of French, she made all but incredible progress.[1] She also learned while keeping compliance to a minimum, unlike her more submissive sibling. Manifest in almost every line here is resistance: to conventional notions about animals and humans, to the expectations of her sentimental teacher, and to the very language she was using.

Emily entrenches her essay in Englishness, and not just through its fox-hunting landowner. She looks for French equivalents of English words—"par pure affection," "lorsqu'il a couru un animal," "a son dernier soupir," and so forth—rather than for corresponding idioms. Her spelling tends to be more accurate than Charlotte's, and she is less likely to leave out accents, perhaps because she used a dictionary. But she ignores or even defies French sentence order, as if accommodation would change what she was thinking or alter the process of her mind.

How much autonomy did Heger's lessons give her? In his interview with Gaskell, he declared that he always left the choice of subject to his students. But the point of choice came after he presented a text or model, lectured, and provided instructions. Those instructions might be loose or rigorous. Their range is suggested by the two excerpts I have taken from one of Charlotte's notebooks.[2] "Plea for Cats" seems to be Charlotte's attempt to launch a devoir on the same topic; "The Two Dogs" seems to be a transcript of Heger's instructions for a corresponding devoir. In the first case, the title implies his assignment: defend cats against those who dislike them. Heger could have prefaced the assignment with a reading (one possibility is cited below), but the sisters would have had considerable latitude in structuring and writing their essays. In contrast, "The Two Dogs" would have locked the writer into a format as well as an attitude. It is not atypical; Heger often dictated *matière* for his students to develop.[3] But neither sister seems to have worked with this outline, which Emily—the owner of a large fierce mastiff, Keeper—could only have regarded with contempt.[4] If she reacted, she did so surreptitiously, by ruthlessly mocking the respectable ambience that "The Two Dogs" implicitly endorses. (Five years later, in *The Professor,* Charlotte gave the name Zéphyrine to a teacher "more distinguished in appearance and deportment" than her colleagues "but in character, a genuine Parisian coquette, perfidious, mercenary and dry-hearted.")[5]

Syntax and vocabulary errors conceded, Emily's views emerge with startling clarity. She makes no attempt to mouth traditional pieties or engage in the give and take of dialogue. She inserts a protest from a "delicate lady," but the answer cuts off further exchange. She argues through examples that display her scorn of orthodoxies, social as well as pietistic. Her approach, in the words of the critic John Hewish, is "characteristically sardonic . . . the first statement in prose of her romantic misanthropy, pessimism, and dislike of convention."[6]

There are, however, precedents for some of her ideas, as well as traditions to which they are not foreign. John Wesley preached that animals shared in Adam's fall and expulsion from paradise, and Emily's conclusion echoes that tenet, which she could have learned in childhood from her Aunt Branwell (who, like her mother, had been raised as a Methodist) or from local evangelicals.[7] She also seems aware of the conventions of satire, and perhaps of the seventeenth-century character.[8]

More immediately, the essay may respond to a French text such as Buffon's *Natural History*. One of Charlotte's notebooks includes a dictée from the opening of his chapter on the horse,[9] and if Heger gave his students one Buffon passage, he might have gone back for another. These lines, from a late-eighteenth-century translation, begin the chapter Buffon calls "Le chat":

> The cat is an unfaithful domestic, and kept only from the necessity we find of opposing him to other domestics still more incommodious, and which cannot be hunted; for we value not those people, who, being fond of all brutes, foolishly keep cats for their amusement. Though these animals, when young, are frolicksome and beautiful, they possess, at the same time, an innate malice, and perverse dispositions, which increase as they grow up, and which education learns them to conceal, but not to subdue. From determined robbers, the best education can only convert them into flattering thieves; for they have the same address, subtlety, and desire of plunder. . . . They easily assume the habits of society, but never acquire its manners; for they have only the appearance of attachment or friendship. This disingenuity of character is betrayed by the obliquity of their movements, and the duplicity of their eyes. They never look their best benefactor in the face; but, either from distrust or falseness, they approach him by windings, in order to procure caresses, in which they have no other pleasure than what arises from flattering those who bestow them. Very different from that faithful animal the dog, whose sentiments totally centre in the person and happiness of his master, the cat appears to have no feelings which are not interested, to have no affection that is not conditional, and to carry on no intercourse with men, but with the view of turning it to his own advantage. By these dispositions, the cat has a greater relation to man than to the dog, in whom there is not the smallest mark of insincerity or injustice.[10]

No direct proof exists that Heger taught this passage or that Emily knew of its existence. Still, the corresponding details mount up: duplicity, cruelty, self-interested flattery, and perhaps most tellingly, the temperament that makes cats resemble humans rather than dogs. Also manifest in Emily's pages is resistance to attitudes like Buffon's. He disdains people foolish enough to care for a creature so ineducable; she defends her liking for cats on the grounds of their intractability. His anthropomorphism implicitly confirms the chain of being that sets people above animals. Hers not only challenges the primacy of humans, it exposes their beastliness and folly.

In short, this is writing that transgresses codes of syntax, politeness, hierarchy, family sentiment, and discourse appropriate to young ladies. Heger's response to it can only be guessed, since no corrections appear on her pages. Pretty clearly, however, he made no attempt to muffle the voice that spoke so trenchantly and plainly.

Emily J. Brontë

The Siege of Oudenarde

Outside the walls of Oudenarde was camped an army of 30,000 Ghents; within, the garrison was weak in numbers but strong in that spirit of noble dedication which equally inspires the true patriot and the martyr. Even the women, that class condemned by the laws of society to be a heavy burden in any situation of action and danger, on that occasion cast aside their degrading privileges, and took a distinguished part in the work of defense. Still there was one heart, among those men so brave and faithful, one traitor's soul low enough to weigh a handful of gold in the balance against the independence of his country. That wretch found the means to seize the two sons of Commander Lalaing, and he delivered them to the enemy at a moment when its patience was starting to run out and its energy to weaken. The Ghents, joyful at this prize, led the children within sight of their father and announced that either the town must surrender at once, or the boys would die. It rested with Lalaing to pronounce their sentence; his refusal would be the signal for their death. The commander regarded his sons, whose eyes, filled with tears, implored his help. At their side he saw the soldiers armed with glaives who would end their days. For a moment he hesitated; nature wrestled strongly with honor; his breast swelled with a terrible emotion. But finally the patriot subdued the father; he turned to face the Ghents: "Take," said he, "the life of these poor children. I cannot weigh it against the liberty of my country, and as for their souls, I entrust them to God. My sentence is pronounced."

The enemy, struck by this response, recoiled from a useless crime. A short time after, help arrived and Oudenarde was saved.

most vaunted
In this act, the Flemish general appears as great as the ~~greatest~~ heroes

Le Siège d'Oudenarde.

Dehors les murs d'Oudenarde campait une armée de 30 000 Ghentois, en

dedans la garnison était faible en nombre mais forte dans cet esprit de

noble devouement qui inspire également le vrai patriote et le martyre.   5

Même les femmes, cette classe condamnée par les lois de la société,

d'être un lourd fardeau en tout cas d'action et de danger, sur cette

occasion, mettaient à côté leurs privilèges dégradants, et prenaient une

part distinguée dans les travaux de défense. Cependant il y avait un

coeur, parmi ces hommes si braves et fidĕles, un ame de traître, assez   10

basse pour peser une poignée d'or dans la balance contre l'indépendance

de son pays; cet miserable trouvait de moyens à s'emparer des deux fils

du commandant Lalaing, et les liverait à l'ennemi au moment où son

patience commencait à s'épuiser et son énergie à s'affaibler.   Les

Ghentois joyeux de cette prise amenaient les enfants à la vue de leur père   15

et annoncaient que, ou la ville capitulerait toute-suite, ou les garcons

mouriraient, il restait avec Lalaing à prononcer leur sentence, son refus

serait le signal de leur mort. Le commandant regardait ses fils dont les

yeux pleins de larmes implorait son secours, à leurs côtés il voyait les

soldats armés des glaives qui devraient finir leurs jours; un moment il   20

hesitait, la nature luttait fortement avec l'honneur — son sein gonflait

d'une emotion terrible, mais enfin le patriote subjugait le père, il se

tournait vers les Ghentois; "prenez, dit il "la vie de ces pauvres enfants,

je ne puis ^pas^ la balancer contre la liberté de ma patrie, et pour leurs ames

je les confie à Dieu. Mon sentence est prononcé."   25

L'ennemi frappé de cette reponse, reculait devant un crime inutile.

Peu de temps après des secours arrivaient et Oudenarde était sauvée.

Dans ce trait le général flamand apparait aussi grand que les þ

that history has preserved for our admiration, ~~and~~ the men who could leap with Martius Curtius into a living tomb are more numerous than those who, like Lalaing, could sacrifice the tenderest affections of the heart for the love of their country⸻

30

héros les plus ~~grands~~ ^{vantés} que l'histoire a conservit pour notre admiration, ~~et~~

les hommes qui pourraient sauter avec Martius Curtius dans une tombe   30

vivante sont plus nombreux que ceux qui pourraient sacrifier les comme

Lalaing les plus tendres affections du leur coeur pour l'amour de leur

patrie_____

The Siege of Oudenarde

had
The general of the Ghentish army has just summoned the town of Oude-

narde; he offered its inhabitants the terms of peace. He promised to

respect their rights and to restrain the license of his troups, he desired
of their town
only that they give him the key to the gates ^ and that they recognize him

as their conqueror. But the courage of the citizens of Oudenarde was not

yet weakened, nor their forces exhausted by the long siege they had

endured. Their commanding officer, Simon de Lalaing, was a brave and

loyal man, and he communicated heroism and steadfastness to all around
continue
him. Hence he refused to accept the Ghents' offers and prepared to offer
the   offered
a resolute and indomitable resistance that he had so far^ to the beseigers'

efforts.

The garrison under his orders was small in number but devoted; the
men
inhabitants of the town shared their leader's sentiments; the women

shared them equally, and Madame Lalaing especially showed herself
being the wife
worthy of her husband of a soldier. Under her auspices all the ladies of

Oudenarde, animated by an ardor like that which a common danger

formerly inspired in Greek and Roman matrons, took part in the work of
Thus
defense.^ The town thus defended seemed impregnable; all the efforts of

the Ghents were useless; but at last, as they recognized that force could

not succeed, they decided to employ stratagem. A traitor (perhaps the

only one in the town of Oudenarde) surrendered the two sons of the

Count of Lalaing to them. The count was summoned to a meeting; his

two sons were brought before him; he was informed that if he still

refused to yield, his children would be sacrificed to the sword. The

count saw them surrounded by rude and savage Ghents. He saw their

terror, their tears, their hands joined and raised to him as if to entreat

Le siège d'Oudenarde

Le général de l'armée Ghentoise ~~vient~~ ᵛᵉⁿᵃⁱᵗ de sommer la ville d'Oudenarde,

il offrait aux habitants des conditions de paix — il promettait de respecter

leurs droits et de reprimer la licence de ses troupes, seulement il voulait

qu'on lui donnût les clefs des portes ^ ᵈᵉ ˡᵉᵘʳ ᵛⁱˡˡᵉ et qu'on lui reconnût pour ˡᵉ leur

vainqueur. Mais le courage des habitants d'Oudenarde n'était pas encore

affaibli ni leurs forces epuisées par le long siège qu'ils avaient soutenu

— leur comandant Simon de Lalaing était un homme brave et fidèle et il

communiquait de l'heroisme et de la fidèlité à touks ceux qui l'environ-

naient — il refusa donc d'accepter les offres des Ghentois et se prepara

de ~~faire une~~ ᶜᵒⁿᵗⁱⁿᵘᵉʳ ˡᵃ résistance resolue et indomptable que jusqu'ici il leur avait^ ᵒᶠᶠᵉʳᵗᵃ

aux efforts des assiégeants

La garnison sous ses ordres était peu nombreuse mais devouée, les

habitants ʰᵒᵐᵐᵉˢ de la ville partageaient les sentiments de leur chef — les femmes

les partageaient également et surtout se\mon Madame de Lalaing se mon-

trait digne de son\mari ᵈ'êᵗʳᵉ ˡᵃ ᶠᵉᵐᵐᵉ d'un soldat. Sous ses auspices toutes les dames

d'Oudenarde animées d'une ardeur semblable à celle qu'un danger

commun inspirait autrefois aux matrones grecques et romaines, prirent

part aux travaux de défense. La ville défendu\ainsi ᴬⁱⁿˢⁱ semblait imprenable,

tous les efforts des Ghentois étaient inutiles, mais enfin ꜱꞮ comme ils

s'~~apercevaient~~ ᶜᵘʳᵉⁿᵗ que la force ne pouvait pas y reussir; ils s'avisèrent

d'employer le stratagème — Un traître (le seul peutêtre dans la ville

d'Oudenarde) leur livra les deux fils du Comte de Lalaing — On appelait

le comte à une conférence, on amena ses deux fils à sa vue on l'avertit

que s'il refusa encore de céder ses enfants serait immolés par le glaive.

Le comte les ~~voyait~~ ᵛⁱᵗ entourés des Ghentois rudes et farouches, il ~~voyait~~ ᵛⁱᵗ

leur frayeur, leurs larmes, leurs mains joints et levées vers lui comme

deliver

him to ~~save~~ them. He even heard their feeble cries from afar, and the
30   words, "Father, father, come and help us!" ~~The~~ A frightful struggle
rent his heart; for some moments he said not a word. He covered his
eyes with his hands and pressed his brow against the battlements; before
long he stood upright. His face was pale, and his lips livid. He replied
in a voice firm and resonant, ~~"Ghent~~ "Let my children die, God will
35   take them to his breast; for myself I have only one duty to fulfill, it is to
remain faithful to my country. Ghents, I am not vanquished, begone!"

The enemy recoiled from a useless crime, the allies of Oudenarde
sent help in time to release Lalaing from his perious position, and the
40   town was saved. Ancient history does not present us with a nobler
example of dedication than that which Simon Lalaing offers us here.
had opened
Marcus Curtius, hurling himself into the gaping pit that ~~opened~~ in the
middle of the forum, was not impelled by a courage more sublime than
the commander of Oudenarde, sacrificing his feelings as a father to his
45   principles as a patriot.

pour le supplier à les ~~sauver~~ delivrer — même il entendit de loin leurs cris faibles — et les mots "mon père, mon père venez nous aider." ~~Les~~ Un combat affreux déchirait son coeur pendant quelques instants il ne disait pas mot — il couvrit les yeux de ses mains et appuya son front sur les crénaux de la muraille bientôt il se réleva — sa figure était pâle, et ses lèvres livides — il repondit d'une voix ferme et sonore ~~"Ghent~~ "Que mes enfants meurent Dieu les recevra dans son sein, pour moi je n'ai qu'un devoir à remplir, c'est de rester fidèle à ma patrie — Ghentois je ne suis pas vaincue, eloignez-vous"

L'ennemi recula devant un crime inutile les alliés d'Oudenarde envoyèrent des secours à temps de degager Lalaing de sa position perilleuse, et la ville fut sauvée. L'histoire ancienne ne nous présente pas un plus noble ~~exp~~ exemple de dévouement que celui que nous offre ici Simon Lalaing — Marcus Curtius s'elançant dans le gouffre béant qui ~~s'ouvrit~~ s'était ouvert au milieu du Forum n'était pas animé d'un courage plus sublime que le commandant d'Oudenarde sacrifiant ses sentiments comme père à ses principes comme patriote.

30

35

40

45

Comments

Mystery surrounds these devoirs. Neither one is dated, though the level of the French and the numerous corrections in Charlotte's manuscript suggest that they are early productions. Few historians would recognize their subject, a fifteenth-century siege that lasted less than two weeks, or the regional hero who, at least in Heger's version, surpassed Rome's Marcus Curtius in bravery. Nobody knows how the essays traveled from the pensionnat to a collector with no other Brontë manuscripts and then to a college library in Swarthmore, Pennsylvania.[1] Their origins, however, can be partly reconstructed: Heger gave instructions, probably in class, and the Brontë sisters dutifully responded. From evidence still extant, his motives and his sources can also be inferred.

Within a list of subjects that Heger was to teach at the Athénée Royal in 1842, there is this notation under "History": "some account of the great men of antiquity and of those who made Belgium renowned."[2] Belgium had become a nation only twelve years prior to the Brontës' arrival, but Heger could have drawn on regional histories and then compared local with classical heroes. Once prepared, he could also have adapted the boys' lessons to an audience of girls at the pensionnat.

These devoirs support such conjectures. Both configure topics in a similar pattern: the setting of the siege, the women's contribution, the treachery, the tempting of the father, his response, and the closing Marcus Curtius allusion. This patterning suggests that Heger outlined the material and asked his students to fill in the details, as he did when he dictated the *matière* for the essays on the palace of Death. Here, though, the subject comes from history, not legend. There was a siege of Oudenarde in 1452, and Simon de Lalaing led the resistance.

Oudenarde (or Audenarde) is in East Flanders, about thirty-eight miles from Brussels; in that era, it was part of Brabant. The town of Ghent, then as now part of Flanders, is some seventeen miles from Oudenarde. Since 1384, Flanders had been under control of the dukes of Burgundy. In 1430 Philip the Good, the reigning duke, was chosen by the Brabançons to be their ruler, and in 1440 he took Bruges. Thus until 1477, when Philip's son, Charles the Bold, was killed in battle, the Burgundians governed all the regions that would later be unified as Belgium. Most citizens welcomed Philip's leadership. Under his rule the cloth industry flourished, shipping ports expanded, and prosperity spread. But Ghent, which had maintained a separate constitution and took pride in its status as an independent city, revolted against Burgundy in 1450, and when in the spring of 1452 Ghentish soldiers threatened to attack the town of Oudenarde, Philip sent Lalaing to the rescue.

Lalaing was the younger son of a nobleman as well as a Knight of the Golden Fleece, an order Philip had created. A seasoned warrior, he had fought in Cypress, in Paris against Joan of Arc, in England and Scotland, and throughout the continent before being sent to Oudenarde.[3] He arrived there with his wife and ménage—sixty lancers and two hundred archers, by one account[4]—and started preparing for a siege. The Ghents set out for Oudenarde on April 14; Lalaing held them off until April 27, when they were defeated in a battle beyond the walls by allies whom Philip had dispatched.

Heger did not have to read late-medieval chronicles to get this information on Oudenarde. In the 1820s Guillaume de Barante issued his *Histoire des ducs de Bourgogne*. A classic of Romantic historiography,[5] it was reprinted in Brussels in 1838 and again in 1839–40. Barante believed in bringing out the story of events, and from the seven columns he wrote about this siege, Heger could have culled half-a-dozen episodes. The

Ghents, for example, shot arrows across the walls with messages attached in French and English that "reminded" Lalaing of the money he had been paid to deliver the town to their forces.[6] Had Heger been teaching the boys at the Athénée, he might also have expounded on the general's countertactics, such as placing vats of water in the streets to douse the Ghents' red-hot cannonballs.[7]

But, as Heger must have realized, he was teaching young women with a negligible interest in warfare. It was nonetheless his duty to give future wives and mothers some grounding in events within their area, to make them familiar with great men close to home as well as with the heroes of antiquity. So he looked for details that would hold their attention, and then he dramatized the story further.

According to Barante and other published chronicles, "The lord of Lalaing had left two children in Hainaut. The Ghents looked for two boys of the same size and almost the same appearance; they led them to the rampart and cried from afar to the captain and his wife, who was there bringing stones to the wall, that they had just seized the children on a journey to Hainaut, and that they were going to put them to death if the town did not surrender. They counted on the mother's fondness and the knight's weakness. But Lalaing aimed the cannons' muzzles at that very spot, and ordered his men to fire harder."[8] Another account adds that he staked out his banner with the motto "Let all perish, save honor!"[9] but no version extant departs from Barante on the matter of the substitute children. The plot that Heger outlined for his students was history converted to fiction.

The Brontë sisters worked with it in characteristic ways, Emily rendering the details tersely, with the logic that Heger would later remark on,[10] Charlotte paying less attention to form and more to human interest and imagery. Emily goes swiftly through her narrative, detouring only to scorn the social code that disables the women it privileges. Charlotte amplifies the spectacle of anguish; she lingers on the children pleading for deliverance and the father struggling to control himself. Emily's siege progresses through a series of antitheses: the vast Ghentish army and the few inside the walls, a traitor weighing gold against the town's independence, Lalaing's human nature contending against honor, and the foe's retreat preceding the arrival of new allies. Her Lalaing decrees a sentence that will lead to separation of the sire from his sons and the boys' souls from their bodies. In contrast, Charlotte's siege is a communal enterprise, with Lalaing as the leader, his wife a worthy helpmate, and all but the traitor contributing. Implicitly, her version approves the hierarchies that this structure of community imposes. Her Lalaing envisions God receiving the boys and himself remaining loyal to his country, his duty to the fatherland outranking on principle the passion of a father for his children. Emily's version, spare though it is, implies a different vision of loyalty, one in which valiant individuals join forces and a commander sacrifices ruthlessly to guard the independence of his homeland.

It is tempting to read Emily's insistence on liberty into her approach to French. Though her spelling is actually better than her sister's, her syntax remains staunchly English. Of course, inexperience alone might account for the number of lines that appear to be transliterated and for the style that one modern Belgian reader terms oral (*parlé*) rather than written.[11] Whatever the reasons, she seems unconcerned with nuance, whereas Charlotte clearly struggles to make her French fluent and to better her phrasing through revision. The sheer number of corrections, all in Charlotte's handwriting, suggests that she drafted her devoir as she thought it out and then rechecked its phrasing and grammar.

Neither sister pays more than cursory attention to the Marcus Curtius legend.[12] Charlotte makes an earlier allusion to antiquity, comparing Oudenarde's women to Greek and Roman matrons, but she has little to say about the hero whose bravery is fatal. (In 362 B.C. a chasm opened in the center of the Forum; seers declared that it would continue to gape until Rome's most valued possession was thrown into it. Understanding that nothing was worth more than a brave citizen, the noble Marcus Curtius leaped into the pit, which immediately closed on him.)[13] Perhaps the desire to finish writing accounts for her conciseness; perhaps Roman heroism interested her less than the drama of a father in conflict. In any case, Emily and Charlotte react when the domestic and the military intersect, when women become unconventionally useful, and when courage takes the form of self-mastery.

Anne Askew

Imitation   *of Eudorus* /

=====

In the reign of Mary, Queen of England, a young woman named Anne
Askew was to be put to the torture because she did not want to renounce
the Protestant religion and profess the Catholic faith.

The fatal day has arrived. In the evening she must suffer her
punishment, and already the sun has set. Anne is all alone in her cell;
she is seated on a pallet; her eyes are lowered; she is mute and still, like
an image carved in marble. Through the iron grate that closes the
window, the moon can be seen. Its disk is cut in sections by the black
bars, but a few rays penetrate the darkness and glow upon the form of
the young captive.

Anne is motionless, voiceless, her tongue is frozen in her mouth.
Nonetheless her soul cries out — she feels the sting of death in her heart,
and she prays as Jesus Christ prayed in the garden of Gethsemane, "O
my Father, if it be possible, let this cup pass from me!"

A bell sounds. The noise of steps and voices is heard, the prison
door opens and the torturer enters, followed by his satellites. Anne lifts
her eyes for a moment. Then she turns her head as if she wanted to seek
some refuge, some defense. But there is no longer any refuge for her on
earth, and the somber vault of her prison hides the heavens from her.

The torturer begins his preparations. His satellites, obeying his
orders conveyed more by signs than words, set up the instrument of
torture. Next, approaching the victim, they remove her veil and cut off
her long blond locks; soon the dark, dank paving-stone is all bestrewn
with ringlets of gold. Anne does not resist; just like a lamb, mute before
the shearer, she does not open her mouth. Her arms are bound with

Anne Askew

Imitation   *de Eudore* /

Sous le règne de Marie, reine d'Angleterre, une jeune fille nommée Anne Askew allait être menée au supplice, parce qu'elle ne voulait pas renoncer à la religion protestante et professer la croyance catholique.

Le jour fatal est arrivé, le soir elle doit subir sa punition et le soleil s'est déjà couché. Anne est toute seule dans sa cellule, elle est assise sur une paillasse, ses yeux sont baissés, elle est muette et immobile comme un image taillée en marbre. À travers la grille, dont la fenêtre est fermée, on voit la lune, son disque est entrecoupé par les barres noires, mais quelque rayons pénétrent l'obscurité et reluisent sur la forme de la jeune captive.

Anne est sans mouvement, sans voix sa langue est glacée dans sa bouche — cependant son âme crie — elle sent l'aiguillon de la mort dans son coeur et elle prie comme pria Jesus Christ dans le jardin de Gethsémané "Mon Père que cette coupe passe loin de moi s'il est possible!"

Une cloche sonne, on entend le bruit de pas et ^ de voix, la porte du prison s'ouvre et le bourreau entre, suivi de ses satellites. Anne lève les yeux pour un instant, puis elle tourne la tête comme si elle voulait chercher quelque asile, quelque defense, mais il n'y a plus d'asile pour elle sur la terre, et la voûte sombre de sa prison lui cache les cieux.

Le bourreau commence ses préparations, ses satellites, obéissant à ses ordres communiqués par des signes plutôt que par des paroles, dressent l'instrument de torture, alors ils s'approchent de la victime la dépouillent de sa voile, et lui coupent ses longs cheveux blonds, bientôt le pavé noir et humide est tout jonché des boucles dorées. Anne ne résiste pas, de même qu'un agneau, muet devant celui que le tond, elle

ropes and she is stretched upon the <u>rack</u>. The torturer bends over to
begin his job.

At this horrible crisis, even as the muscles in his arms were bulging
from the force he was readying for his first effort, the door of the prison
opened, and a man entered in haste. It was the secretary of Gardiner,
Bishop of Winchester and Chancellor of England. He brusquely shoved
the torturer aside, unknotted the ropes with which Anne was bound, and
said to her, "Anne Askew, I come from the palace. Milord the Bishop
has interceded for you. He has obtained your pardon. Here is the letter
that he sends you. Read it."

At first, Anne did not hear him; her mind was too distraught by the
horrors with which she found herself surrounded, and she did not com-
prehend that someone was speaking to her. But little by little she
regained consciousness, she roused herself, and she opened the letter,
which was conceived in these words:

"The queen takes pity on your youth and inexperience. She wants
to grant you the favor of your life. Only renounce the heretical dogmas
by which you have been led astray, confess your errors, reenter the
bosom of the holy Catholic church, and riches, honors, life, will be your
recompense.

                                        Stephen Gardiner"

"My God, my God!" Anne cried out in a rending voice, "do not forsake
me. They tempt me as they tempted Cranmer in his final hour."

"And you must yield as Cranmer yielded," retorted the secretary.

"And die as he died, soiled by apostasy," said she, "because your
church did not keep the oath it swore to Cranmer and it will not keep the
one it swears to me."

"Cranmer was an old man, hardened in heresy; he well deserved his
fate. But you are young; you still have time to expiate your crimes.
Think of all the horrors of the death that you must undergo if you refuse

n'ouvre pas la bouche; on lui serre les bras avec des cordes et l'étend sur le <u>rack</u> — le bourreau se courbe pour commencer sa besogne. À cette crise horrible pendant que les muscles de son bras étaient tout enflés de la force qu'il se préparait de mettre à son premier effort, la porte du prison s'ouvrit, et un homme entra à la hâte, c'était le secrétaire de Gardiner, évêque de Winchester et chancelier d'Angleterre. Il écarta brusquement le bourreau, il dénoua les cordes dont Anne était liée, et lui dit "Anne Askew j'arrive du palais — monseigneur l'évêque a intercédé pour vous, il a obtenu votre pardon voici la lettre qu'il vous envoye — lisez."

D'abord Anne ne l'entendit pas, son esprit était tout égaré par les horreurs dont elle se trouvait entourée, elle ne comprit pas qu' on lui adressait la parole, mais peu à peu elle reprit connaissance, elle se releva, elle ouvrit la lettre, elle était conçue en ces mots

"La reine a pitié de votre jeunesse et de votre inexpérience, elle veut vous faire grâce de votre vie — rénoncez seulement aux dogmes hérétiques, dont vous vous étes egarée, confessez vos erreurs, rentrez dans le sein de la sainte église catholique et les richesses, les honneurs, la vie, sera votre recompense

Etienne Gardiner

Mon Dieu, mon Dieu!" s'écria-t Anne d'une voix déchirante "ne m'abandonnez pas, on me tente comme on tenta Cranmer à sa dernière heure"

"Et vous devez céder comme Cranmer ceda" repartit le sécrétaire

"Et mourir comme il mourut, souillée d'apostasie" disait elle "car votre église n'a pas gardé le serment qu'elle jura à Cranmer et elle ne gardera pas ce qu'elle jure à moi"

"Cranmer était un vieillard endurci dans l'hérésie, il a bien mérité son sort, mais vous êtes jeune, vous avez encore le temps d'expier vos forfaits. Pensez à toutes les horreurs de la mort que vous devez subir si vous refusez de signer la formule de renonciation. Je dois bientôt vous

to sign the formula of renunciation. I must soon leave you, and when
I close the door of this dungeon you will remain alone with the torturer.
He will seize you; he will stretch you again on that bed, which is no bed
of roses; these thick walls will conceal your agony and smother your
groans. All this night will be, for you, a night of mortal suffering
because the torture for which you are destined is as slow as it is sharp.
Do not hesitate. Here is a pen; there are witnesses. Sign and live."

A horrible temptation seized the young woman's heart. She lost sight
of the glorious hope of her religion. The tempting spirit said to her,
"You are going to die for an illusion; all religion is futile. If there was
a God in heaven would he thus abandon his people to the barbarous
hands of their enemies? There is neither heaven nor hell. After death,
there is nothing but Annihilation. Live then for as long as you can. You
are young and fair, and life offers you so many joys! Sign."

The scrutinizing gaze of the secretary reads these thoughts in her
countenance; he draws a table toward her; he places before her the
formula of renunciation. Silence reigns in the prison. Anne takes the
pen, she leans over the paper, she has already begun tracing the first
letters of her name, when an inner voice seems to say to her:

"Whosoever shall deny me before men, him will I also deny before
my Father which is in heaven. And fear not them which take the life
from the body, but are not able to kill the soul: but rather fear him which
is able to destroy both soul and body in Gehenna." And Anne Askew
lets the pen drop. She stretches herself willingly on the bed of torture.
And closing her eyes, as if she were going to sleep, she says,

"I am Protestant."

quitter, et quand je ferme la porte de ce cachot vous resterez seule avec

le bourreau, il s'emparera de vous, il vous étendra encore sur cette 60

couche qui n'est pas une couche de roses — ces murs épais cacheront vos

angoisses et étoufferont vos gémissements; toute cette nuit sera pour vous

une nuit de douleur mortelle car le supplice qu'on vous destine est aussi

lent qu'il est aigu; n'hesitez pas, voici une plume, voilà des témoins,

signez et vivez." 65

Une tentation horrible s'empara du coeur de la jeune fille elle perdit

de vue l'espoir glorieux de sa religion, l'esprit tentateur lui disait "vous

allez mourir pour une illusion, toute religion est vaine, s'il était un Dieu

dans le ciel abandonnerait-il ainsi son peuple aux mains barbares de leurs
                                                                        ses

ennemis? Il n'y a ni ciel ni enfer — après la mort il n'y a que l'Anéan- 70

tissement — vivez donc aussi long-temps que vous pourrez Vous étes

jeune et belle et la vie vous offre tant de joies! — signez."

Le regard scrutateur du sécrétaire lit ces pensées sur sa figure il lui

approche une table il place devant elle la formule de la renonciation — le

silence régne dans le prison, Anne prend la plume, elle se penche sur le 75

papier déjà elle commence à tracer les premiers lettres de son nom,

lorsque une voix intérieure semble lui dire

"Quiconque me reniera devant les hommes je le rénierai aussi devant

mon père qui est aux cieux, ne craignez donc point ceux qui ôtent la vie

du corps et qui ne peuvent faire mourir l'âme — mais craignez plutôt 80

celui qui peut perdre et l'âme et le corps dans la Géhenne," et Anne

Askew laisse tomber la plume — elle s'étend volontairement sur le lit de

supplice — et fermant les yeux, comme si elle s'endorme, elle dit

"Je suis protestante."

Eudorus

Christian Conduct

Fourth Century

In the reign of Galerius a Christian named Eudorus, betrothed to the young Cymodoce, was to be thrown to the lions. On the eve of the fatal day, he was taking his final meal with his comrades, destined as he was to martyrdom.

In the midst of this affecting spectacle, a slave was seen approaching in haste: he forced his way through the crowd, inquired for Eudorus, and placed in his hands a letter from the judge. Eudorus unrolled the missive; it was couched in these words:

"Festus the Judge, to Eudorus the Christian, greeting.

"Cymodoce is condemned to the abodes of infamy. Hierocles is there awaiting her. I entreat you, by the esteem with which you have inspired me, to sacrifice to the gods: come and reclaim your spouse: I swear to deliver her to you pure, and worthy of you."

Eudorus swooned; all crowded around him; the soldiers near him seized the letter; the people demanded it; a tribune read it in a loud voice; the bishops stood mute in consternation; the whole assembly was tumult and disorder. Eudorus recovered his senses, and the soldiers were already at his knees, saying to him:

"Companion, sacrifice to the gods! Here are our eagles in default of an altar."

And they presented him a cup full of wine for the libation. A horrible temptation seized the soul of Eudorus. Cymodoce in a place of infamy! [Cymodoce in the arms of Hierocles!] The bosom of the martyr heaved with emotion; the bandages burst from his wounds, and his blood flowed in streams from his body. The people, seized with pity, fell

Eudore

Moeurs Chretiennes

IV Siècle

Sous le règne de Galérius, un Chrétien nommé Eudore, fiancé à la jeune Cymodocée, allait être livré aux bêtes féroces. La veille du jour fatal, il prenait le dernier repas avec ses frères destinés comme lui au martyre

Au milieu de cette scène touchante, on voit accourir un esclave, il perce la foule, il demande Eudore, il lui remet une lettre de la part du juge.

Eudore déroule la lettre, elle était conçue en ces mots;

Festus juge, à Eudore chretien, salut. Cymodocée est condamnée aux lieux infâmes Hiéroclès l'y attend, je t'en supplie, par l'estime que tu m'as inspiré, sacrifie aux dieux, viens redemander ton épouse, je jure de te la rendre pure et digne de toi.

Eudore s'évanouit, on s'empresse autour de lui; les soldats qui l'environnent, se saississent de la lettre, le peuple la réclame un tribun en fit la lecture à haute voix.

Les évêques restent muets et consternés, l'assemblé s'agite en tumulte. Eudore revient à la lumière, les soldats étaient à ses genoux et lui disaient "Compagnon sacrifiez! voila nos aigles au defauts d'autels." Et ils lui présentait la coupe pleine de vin pour la libation; une tentation horrible s'empara du coeur d'Eudore. Cymodocée aux lieux infâmes! [. . .] la poitrine du martyr se soulève, l'appareil de ses plaies se brise et le sang coule en abondance. Le peuple, saisi de pitié, tombe lui même aux genoux, et répéte avec les soldats "Sacrifiez! sacrifiez!" Alors Eudore d'une voix sourde,

"Où sont les aigles?" Les soldats frappent leurs boucliers en signe de triomphe, et se hâtent d'apporter les enseignes. Eudore se lève, le

themselves at his knees, and repeated with the soldiers:

30   "Sacrifice! Sacrifice!"

"Where are the eagles?" said Eudorus, in a hollow voice.

The soldiers struck their bucklers together in token of triumph, and hastened to bring the banners. Eudorus arose; the centurions supported him; he advanced to the foot of the eagles; silence reigned in the crowd.

35 Eudorus took the cup; the bishops veiled their faces in their robes, and the confessors uttered a cry: at this cry, the cup fell from the hands of Eudorus, he overthrew the eagles, and turning toward the martyrs, exclaimed:

        "I am a Christian!"

        [François-Réné de] Chateaubriand

centurions le soutiennent, il s'avance aux pieds des aigles, le silence

règne parmi la foule; Eudore prend la coupe, les évêques se voilent la

tête de leurs robes, les confesseurs poussent un cri, à ce cri, la coupe

tombe des mains d'Eudore — il renverse les aigles, et se tournant vers les

martyrs il dit

"Je suis Chrétien"

Chateaubriand

Comments

Late in May 1842, Heger dictated a passage from Chateaubriand's *Martyrs* to his students. They were then, presumably, to write an imitation, drawing on memories of a comparable episode or of another persecuted victim. Charlotte Brontë responded with an essay on a woman who died for her faith in 1546, a martyr in the Protestant tradition.

Without prior knowledge of Anne Askew and her era, she could not have ventured on the project. Whatever the dungeon and the maiden owe to fairy tale, both had been described in Tudor chronicles.[1] History, however, is as malleable in the devoir as it is throughout *The Martyrs*. Like Chateaubriand, Charlotte had a vision to convey and an objective beyond historiography. He was trying to prove what he had argued in *Genius,* that Christianity surpassed Greece and Rome as a source and inspiration of literature. She was trying, once again, to confirm the strength of Protestant devotion under pressure.

For the first time, an assignment of Heger's gave her license to write dramatic narrative. Eudorus and Cymodoce die holy deaths, but they live with the intensity of her Angrians. She had vowed to discontinue her juvenilia romances and the fictions she considered self-indulgent. But Anne Askew's temptations were religious, not erotic, and her plight lured

Charlotte back into the Gothic mode. In choosing a subject so English and Protestant, she also strengthened the "line of demarcation" she perceived between herself and the Catholics of the pensionnat.[2] Withdrawn and shy of speaking, she deflected her prejudice to Catholics dead three hundred years.

In structure, "Anne Askew" closely imitates "Eudorus," Heger's title for the excerpt from *The Martyrs.* The opening sentences, the death threats, the letters, the temptations, and the final lines coordinate. Dictée and devoir combine narrative with dialogue, and both exploit the drama of religious persecution. But Chateaubriand develops his tableau as a crowd scene,[3] whereas Charlotte stages hers in gloom and shadow, replacing the clamor of Chateaubriand's arena with a silence that Anne's torturers disrupt.

A less apparent transformation also takes place: historic fact, allegedly the basis of both episodes, glides without a ripple into fiction. Of course, Chateaubriand did not profess to mirror history in the Christian epic he created. Rather, he attempted to increase the human interest by researching the ambience and context. He steeped himself in writings of the early church fathers; he toured Rome, Greece, Constantinople, Jerusalem, the ruins of Carthage, and Spain; he sketched and made extensive notes from sources. For seven years he labored over *The Martyrs,* which was promptly assailed for its inaccuracies.[4] Charlotte had at most several days to do her writing, and she had brought no history books with her. Where did she get her information?

The two examinations and martyrdom of Anne Askew (1521?–1546) are recounted, in Askew's own words, in John Foxe's *Actes and Monuments,* more commonly called *The Book of Martyrs.* Throughout the nineteenth century, the Religious Tract Society published editions of this famous martyrology. When Charlotte was fifteen, it also published Askew's history in its series on British Reformers. Another account of Askew's life appears in George Ballard's *Memoirs of Several Ladies of Great Britain* (1752); it too circulated in England. And a twenty-line reference to Anne Askew appears in William Mavor's *Universal History,* the series that Charlotte recommended to Ellen Nussey in 1834.[5] She may not have been exposed to any of these texts; of Mavor's, she wrote, "[Read it] if you *can I* never did."[6] But clearly, she had access to some account of Askew's life, at Haworth or Miss Wooler's school at Roe Head. She must also have recalled her studies, formal or informal, of the early English Reformation. They enabled her to set Anne Askew in context and allude to persecutors with real counterparts: Stephen Gardiner (1490?–1555), Thomas Cranmer (1489–1556), and the anonymous torturer.

That she worked from memory, rather than sourcebooks, is apparent from the errors that stud her brief narrative. Henry VIII was on the throne, not Mary Tudor; Askew's martyrdom preceded Cranmer's by ten years; though Gardiner and his party were behind the persecution, Wriosthesley was the chancellor who offered her pardon; he himself racked her, taking over from the jailer; and Askew not only survived the night of racking but also wrote it up in detail afterward.

Did Heger suspect that Charlotte strayed from the facts? Was he impressed with the drama she constructed? Or did his comments focus on her grammar? There are no answers, since the draft has not been marked, and without more clues to the sources Charlotte drew on, it is risky to attack her for distorting them. She may only have been told about Askew's martyrdom, or she may have skimmed through Foxe ten years earlier. Nonetheless, the gender issues that her narrative raises make the risk of speculation worth taking.

Her Anne Askew resembles the juvenilia women who are always at the mercy of male tempters. Beautiful and innocent, helpless and imprisoned, she has only the power of refusal. Though she uses that power to choose death over retraction, she dies a willing victim, not a rebel.[7] At first she cannot speak; fear makes her voiceless. Recovering, she cries for God's assistance. When the secretary and an evil spirit prompt her, she picks up the pen to trace her signature but stops because another voice addresses her. Allegedly interior, its words come from St. Matthew, as do two of her previous sentences. Finally, she affirms her Protestant identity; the voice is hers, the phrasing Chateaubriand's.

In limiting Anne's power over destiny and language, Charlotte disconnects her from the real Anne Askew, a woman who would not be kept from speaking. Tied to the stake and facing death by public burning, she corrected the preacher when he misquoted the Bible and so forcefully exhorted the three men who died with her that they "set apart all kind of fear."[8] Throughout her ordeal she kept producing documents: point-by-point accounts of her two examinations, letters, confessions, prayers, descriptions of her tortures, and a ballad that she "made and sang" in Newgate.[9] Confident and capable, she parried men's words with her own arguments and used scripture as a weapon of resistance; when she kept silent, she was being politic: "Then [Bonner, the bishop of London] asked me, why I had so few words? And I answered, 'God hath given me the gift of knowledge, but not of utterance: and Solomon saith, That a woman of few words is the gift of God'" [Prov. xix.14]."[10]

Charlotte keeps a few authentic details. The historical Askew too was young and beautiful, a martyr in her twenty-fifth year. But unlike the shrinking virgin of the devoir, she was married and the mother of two children. She came from a noble Lincolnshire family; her father had forced her to marry. She submitted and then immersed herself in biblical studies that eventually convinced her to turn Protestant. When her husband, led by priests, drove her out of the house, she moved to London and took back her maiden name. There, her independence and her manifest scholarship made her a target for Tudor conservatives, who claimed that only clergy had the right to interpret and communicate the meaning of scripture. Anne Askew had friends at court and well-connected relatives. She might have saved herself without recanting her beliefs by responding more submissively when questioned. Instead, she chose resistance, textual and oral. She bested men by quoting from the Bible.

No hint of this biography appears in Charlotte's devoir, which draws on a different narrative tradition, one that D. A. Miller terms the "feminine carceral."[11] Biblical quotations aside, this golden-haired victim belongs with her jailers in the kind of Gothic novel that flourished in the late eighteenth century. Like Emily and Anne, whose Gondal poems abound in dungeon scenes, the adolescent Charlotte had been drawn to Gothic fiction. Within the three months prior to writing this essay, she had read "The Young Captive," Chénier's poem about a maiden facing death (line 13 echoes its title.)[12] Her portrayal of a shorn and fainting Askew seems predictable enough at this period.

And yet in her own devoirs she was making use of scripture, proving to Heger that despite imperfect French she knew it better than any Catholic schoolgirl. Submissive she might be, but not in matters of religion, where, like Askew, she relied on the Bible.[13] As a writer too she might have found a precedent in Askew, whose pen kept flowing through torture and confinement and who, though she talked about her weakness as a woman, found the means to get her statements into print.

What accounts for Charlotte's authorial choices? Perhaps she had read about Anne Askew years earlier, at an age when the drama of martyrdom, but not the drier details of the inquiry, impressed her.[14] Possibly she started to reinvent the character while she was a schoolgirl at Miss Wooler's. Ellen Nussey has alluded to the tales she told her classmates, and this narrative may have been one of them. Whatever its genesis, the devoir suggests that Charlotte, then about a year older than her martyr, was not yet ready to create a woman speaking with a power defiantly her own.

Portrait

King Harold before the Battle of Hastings

———

Among all those gathered that evening, on the field, which, on the
morrow, would be the scene of so great a catastrophe, one could easily
distinguish the king, not by his finery and his retinue, but by his countenance and his bearing.

He walked a little distanced from the camp, upon a height that gave
him an ample view of the plain where his army extended like an ocean
on all sides, as far as the horizon, which glowed with the enemy's fires.

When he turned his gaze toward that latter spectacle, when he saw
the sky reddened by that hostile light, when he considered that it was on
his land that the usurpers reposed and that it was his forests that provided
their flames, then, turning his eyes on the countryside below, when he
contemplated the long lines of his troops, which he knew to be as brave
as they were numerous, as faithful as they were brave, when he thought
of the power and of the justice of his cause, a sublime expression lit up
his face, his soul fortified itself with the strongest exploits and, burning
with a noble ardor, armed with an unshakable dauntlessness, he could not
imagine defeat.

At that moment, the spirit of Harold gathered within itself the
energy, the power, and the hopes of the nation. Then, he was no more
a king; he was a hero. The situation had trans[f]ormed him; for in peace
he would doubtless have been, like almost all other princes seated on a
tranquil throne, a nothing, a wretch entombed within his palace, sunk in
pleasures, deceived by flatterers, knowing, provided he be not wholly
imbecile, that of all his people he is the least free; that he is a creature
who dares not act, who scarcely dares to think for itself. That all those

Portrait

Le Roi Harold avant la Bataille de Hastings

———

Parmi tous ceux réunis ce soir, sur le champ, qui, demain, serait la scène
d'un catastrophe si grande, on pouvait facilement distinguer le roi, non   5
par sa parure et sa suite, mais par sa figure et son maintien.

Il se promenait un peu éloigné du camp, sur une éminence, qui lui
donnait une ample vue de la plaine où son armée s'étendait comme
un océan de tous côtés, jusqu'à l'horizon, qui reluisait des feux de
l'ennemi.   10

Quand il portait ses regards vers ce dernier spectacle, quand il voyait
le ciel rougi de cette lumière hostile, quand il songeait que c'était sur sa
terre que les usurpateurs se reposaient et que c'étaient ses forêts qui four-
nissaient leurs flammes, puis, tournant les yeux sur la campagne en bas,
quand il contemplait les longues lignes de ses troupes qu'il savait être   15
aussi braves que nombreuses, aussi fidèles que braves, quand il pensait
de sa puissance et de la justice de sa cause, une expression sublime illuminait son visage, son âme se fortifiait aux exploits les plus grands et,
brulant d'une noble ardeur, armé d'une intrépidité inébranlable, il ne
pouvait imaginer la defaite.   20

À ce moment, l'esprit de Harold réunissait dans lui-même l'énergie,
le pouvoir, et les espérances de la nation. Alors, il n'était plus un roi,
il était un héros. La situation lui avait transormé, car en paix il aurait
été sans doute, comme presque tous les autres princes assis sur un tranquille trône, un rien, un misérable enseveli dans son palais, abîmé en   25
plaisirs, trompé de flatteurs, sachant, pourvu qu'il ne soit pas tout à fait
imbécille, que de tout son peuple il est le moins libre; qu'il est une créature qui n'ose pas agir, qui n'ose guère penser par elle-même. Que tous

who surround him try to entangle his soul in a labyrinth of follies and
vices; that it is the universal interest to blind his eyes, so that his hand
cannot move without being directed by a minister, and so that his body
is a true prisoner, having his kingdom for prison and his subjects for
guards.

Harold, on the field of battle, without palace, without ministers,
without courtiers, without pomp, without luxury, having only the sky of
his country above him for a roof, and that land beneath his feet, which
he holds from his ancestors, and which he will only abandon with his life
— Harold, surround by that crowd of devoted hearts, the representatives
of millions more, all entrusting to him their safety, their liberty, and
their existence as a people — what a difference! As visible to men as to
his Creator, the soul divine shines in his eyes; a multitude of human
passions awake there at the same time, but they are exalted, sanctified,
almost deified. That courage has no rashness, that pride has no arrogance, that indigation has no injustice, that assurance has no presumption. He is inwardly convinced that a mortal power will not fell him.
The hand of Death, alone, can bear the victory away from his arms, and
Harold is ready to succumb before it, because the touch of that hand is,
to the hero, what the stroke that gave him liberty was to the slave.

ceux qui l'environnent tachent d'embrouiller son âme dans une labyrinthe
de folies et de vices, que c'est l'intérêt universel d'aveugler ses yeux, 30
que sa main ne peut pas mouvoir sans être dirigée par un ministre, et
que son corps est un vrai prisonnier, ayant son royaume pour prison et
ses sujets pour gardes.

Harold, sur le champ de bataille, sans palais, sans ministres, sans
courtisans, sans faste, sans luxe, n'ayant que le ciel de sa patrie au- 35
dessus de lui pour toit, et cette terre sous ses pieds, qu'il tient de ses
ancêtres, et qu'il n'abandonnera qu'avec la vie — Harold entouré de cette
foule de coeurs dévoués, les réprésentatifs de millions plus, tous confiant
à lui leur sureté, leur liberté et leur existence comme un peuple — quelle
différence! Aussi visible aux hommes qu'à son Créateur, l'âme divine 40
brille dans ses yeux, une multitude de passions humaines y éveillent en
même temps, mais elles sont exaltées, sanctifiées, presque déifiées. Ce
courage n'a pas de témerité, cette fierté n'a pas d'arrogance, cette
indignation n'a pas d'injustice, cette assurance n'a pas de présomption.
Il est intérieurement convaincu qu'une pouvoir mortel ne l'abattra — La 45
main de la Mort, seule, peut emporter la victoire de ses armes, et Harold
est prêt à succomber devant elle, parceque la touche de cette main est au
héros, comme le coup qui lui rendait la liberté, était à l'esclave.

Portrait

King Harold before the Battle of Hastings

———

those men   *there in that* ⌐ *of battle*
Among all those gathered that evening, on the | field, which, on the
must be will   ⌊ *plain where soon must*
5   morrow, would be the scene of so great a catastrophe, one could easily
be decided the fate of a kingdom
distinguish the king, not by his finery and his retinue, but by his coun-

tenance and his bearing.
far
He walked a little distanced from the camp, upon a height that gave

G }   him an ample view of the plain where his army extended like an ocean

10   on all sides, as far as the horizon, which glowed with the enemy's fires.
the fires of the enemy camp
When he turned his gaze toward that latter spectacle, when he saw

the sky reddened by that hostile light, when he considered that it was on
his own territory   *fed the fires*
his land that the usurpers reposed and that it was his forests that provided
of their camps. **When** *lowering*   *valley*
their flames, ~~then~~, turning his eyes on the ~~countryside below, when~~ he

15   contemplated the long lines of his troops, which he knew to be as brave

as they were numerous, as faithful as they were brave, when he thought

of his power and of the justice of his cause, a sublime expression lit up
pale
his face, his soul fortified itself with | the strongest exploits and, burning

with a noble ardor, armed with an unshakable dauntlessness, he could

20   not imagine defeat.; *it is then that* ⌐
his   *in* [him] *all*
(At that moment, the spirit of) Harold gathered within ~~itself~~ the
all   *of a*
energy, the power, and the hopes ~~of the~~ nation. Then, he was no more
complete
a king; he was a hero. The situation had transformed him. For in peace
of his era ~~vegetating~~ *indifferent*
he would doubtless have been, like almost all other princes seated /on
and peaceful on his **he would have been**   [ed] *slave confined*
25   a tranquil/ throne, a nothing, a wretch entombed within his palace,
his   *were*
sunk in pleasures, deceived by flatterers, knowing, provided he be not
the man the   , ⌐*the most in-*
wholly imbecile, that of all his people he is ~~the~~ least free; that he is a
capable of acting — — *and* — — — — — — — *and of* [thinking]   *him*
creature who dares not act, who scarcely dares to think for itself. That

Portrait

Le Roi Harold avant la Bataille de Hastings

---

    ces hommes   *là dans cette*   *de bataille*   ~~devait être~~
Parmi tous ceux réunis ce soir, sur le ⌈champ, qui, demain, serait la
                              ⌊*plaine où devait se décider bientôt*
scène d'un catastrophe si grande, on pouvait facilement distinguer le roi,   5
le sort d'un royaume
non par sa parure et sa suite, mais par sa figure et son maintien.
              loin
    Il se promenait un peu éloigné du camp, sur une éminence, qui lui

donnait une ample vue de la plaine où son armée s'étendait comme   ⎰ *B*

un océan de tous côtés, jusqu'à l'horizon, qui reluisait des feux de

l'ennemi.   10
                      les feux du camp ennemi
    Quand il portait ses regards vers ce dernier spectacle, quand il voyait
                                            son
le ciel rougi de cette lumière hostile, quand il songeait que c'était sur sa
territoire, à lui,   *alimentaient*
terre que les usurpateurs se reposaient et que c'étaient ses forêts qui four-
les feux de leurs bivouacs. Quand abaissant   *vallée*   *de*
nissaient leurs flammes, ~~puis~~, tournant les yeux sur la ~~campagne en bas~~,

~~quand~~ il contemplait les longues lignes de ses troupes qu'il savait être   15

aussi braves que nombreuses, aussi fidèles que braves, quand il pensait
à   *à*
de sa puissance et de la justice de sa cause, une expression sublime illu-
     pâle
minait son visage, son âme se fortifiait aux exploits les plus grands et,

brulant d'une noble ardeur, armé d'une intrépidité inébranlable, il ne

pouvait imaginer la defaite.; *c'est qu'alors*   20
     ⌈*en*   *son*   *en*   *toute*
    (À ce moment, l'esprit de) Harold réunissait dans lui-même l'énergie,
       toutes   *d'une*
le pouvoir, et les espérances ~~de la~~ nation. Alors, il n'était plus un roi,
                               l'   *f* [?]   ~~complèt~~
il était un héros. La situation lui avait transormé, car en paix il aurait
                            de son époque ~~végétant~~ *indifferent et*
été sans doute, comme presque tous les autres princes assis /sur un tran-
paisible sur son   *il eut été*   *esclave confiné*
quille/ trône, un rien, un misérable enseveli dans son palais, abîmé en   25
            par ses   *fût*
plaisirs, trompé de flatteurs, sachant,, pourvu qu'il ne soit pas tout à fait
                       l'homme le   ⌈*le plus incapable*
imbécile, que de tout son peuple il est le moins libre.; qu'il est une créa-
d'agir— et — — — — — — — — *et de*   *lui*
ture qui n'ose par agir, qui n'ose guère penser par elle-même. Que tous

all those who surround him try to entangle his soul in a labyrinth of

30 follies and vices; that it is the universal interest to blind his eyes, so that
he cannot make a move, without a minister   ing it;   in a word
his hand cannot move without being directed by a minister, and so that
he is no more than a   in his crown and royal purple
his body is a true prisoner, having his kingdom for prison and his
courtiers
subjects for guards.

But Harold, on the field of battle, without palace, without ministers,

above him

35 without courtiers, without pomp, without luxury, having only the sky of

vG   *that land*

his country above him for a roof, and that land beneath his feet, which

he holds from his ancestors, and which he will only abandon with his

life; Harold, surrounded by that crowd of devoted hearts, the represen-
who have entrusted in
tatives of millions more, all entrusting to him their safety, their liberty,

Harold is no longer

40 and their existence as a people — what a difference! As visible to men
[just] a man he is transfigured   of a people wholly united beams

his soul is   *his*
exalted and
as to his Creator, the soul divine shines in his eyes; a multitude of
                            egoistic until that hour
human passions awake there at the same time, but they are exalted, sanc-
His   more   his
tified, almost deified. That courage has no rashness, that pride has no
more   his   more anger   his   more
arrogance, that indignation has no injustice, that assurance has no pre-
human

45 sumption. He is inwardly convinced that a mortal power will not fell
and in [?]   tear
him. The hand of Death, alone, can bear the victory away from his
but Death [?]
arms, and Harold is ready to succumb before it, because the touch of that

hand is, to the hero, what the stroke that gave him liberty was to the

slave.

---

on the field of battle

50 *The stroke of the sword that kills a hero It is the stroke of the rod with which*
                                                        but
the master taps his slave to free him. —

                    d'égarer   *en*
ceux qui l'environnent tachent d'~~embrouiller~~ son âme dans uǹe labyrinthe
                    de ceux qui l'entourent est
de folies et de vices; que ~~c'est~~ l'intérêt universel d'aveugler ses yeux,   30
          qu'il ne peut mouvoir, sans qu'un ministre ne la   ;   en un mot
que sa main ne peut pàs *se* mouvoir sans être dirigéè ~~par un ministre~~,
          'il   qu'il n'est, dans son ~~roy~~ sa couronne et la pourpre royale, qu'un
~~et~~ que ~~son corps~~ est un ~~vrai~~ prisonnier˘, ayant son royaume pour prison
          courtisans
et ses˘sujets pour gardes.

Mais Harold, sur le champ de bataille, sans palais, sans ministres, sans
                    au-dessus de lui
courtisans, sans faste, sans luxe, n'ayant˘ que le ciel de sa patrie ~~au-~~   35   *tB*
                              cette terre
~~dessus de lui pour toit~~, et ~~cette terre~~ sous ses pieds,˘qu'il tient de ses

ancêtres, et qu'il n'abandonnera qu'avec la vie˙; Harold, entouré ~~de cette~~
                                             qui lui ont con[?]
~~foule~~ de coeurs dévoués, ~~les réprésentatifs de millions plus~~, toùs confié-

~~ant à lui~~ leur sureté, leur liberté et leur existence ~~comme un peuple —~~   *son âme*
              Harold n'est n'a plus un d'homme c'est Il est transfiguré   *s'exalte et*
quelle différence! Aussi visible aux hommes qu'à son Créateur, l'âme   40
          d'un peuple tout unis rayonne   [?]   ses   égoïstes
djvine˘brille dans ses yeux, ~~une multitude de~~ passions humaines y éveil-
jusqu'à cette heure
lent en même temps, mais elles sont exaltées, sanctifiées, presque déi-
          Son   plus   sa   plus
fiées. | C̀è courage n'a pas de témerité, ~~cette~~ fierté ~~n'a pas~~ d'arrogance,
son   plus de colere-   son   plus
~~cette~~ indignation ~~n'a pas~~ d'~~injustice~~, ~~cette~~ assurance ~~n'a pas~~ de présomp-
                              humain
tion. Il est intérieurement convaincu qu'une pouvoir mortel ne l'abattra   45
          et en [?]   arracher   à
— ~~La main de~~ La Mort, seule˘, peut emporter la victoire de ses armes,
mais la Mort [?] seul
~~et~~ Harold est prêt à succomber devant elle, parceque la touche de cette

main est au héros, comme le coup qui lui rendait la liberté, était à

l'esclave.

—————————

                    sur le champ de bataille
Le coup de l'épée qui tue un héros Ç'est le coup de baguette dont le maître   50
                    N   que
frappait son esclave pour l'affranchir.—

Portrait

Harold on the Eve of the Battle of Hastings

———

Among all those men gathered there, on that plain, where the fate
of a kingdom must soon be decided, one could easily distinguish the
king, not by his finery and his retinue, but by his countenance and his
bearing.

He walked far from the camp, to a height that gave him an ample
view of the plain where, like an ocean, his army extended on all sides as
far as the horizon, which the enemy's fires illuminated. When he considered that it was on his own territory that the usurpers reposed; that it
was his forests that fed the fires of their bivouacs; when, lowering his
eyes to the valley, he contemplated the long lines of his troops, which he
knew to be as brave as they were numerous, as faithful as they were
brave, when he weighed in his mind both the power and the justice of his
cause, a sublime expression lit up his pale face, and he could not imagine
defeat.

It was then that Harold reunited in himself all the energy, all the
hopes, of a nation. Harold was no more a man, but a King.

In times of peace, he would doubtless have been, like all the other
princes seated on a tranquil throne, a luxurious slave, confined in his
palace, sunk in pleasures, deceived by his flatterers, knowing, unless he
be a complete imbecile, that, of all his people, he is the man least free;
that he can neither act, nor scarcely think for himself; that all those who
surround him try to lead him astray; that never can he move without
being directed by a minister, and that his body is a royal prisoner, having
his kingdom for prison and his subjects for guards.

But on the field of battle, without palace, without ministers,

Portrait

Harold la veille de la Bataille de Hastings

———

Parmi tous ces hommes réunis là, dans cette plaine, où devait se décider bientôt le sort d'une royaume, on eut facilem^t· distingué le roi, non par sa parure et sa suite, mais à sa figure et à son maintien.

Il se promenait loin du camp, sur une éminence qui lui donnait une ample vue de la plaine, où comme un océan, s'étendait de tous côtés, son armée, jusqu'à l'horizon, qu'illuminaient les feux de l'ennemi —. Quand il songeait que c'était sur son territoire à lui, que les usurpateurs reposaient; que c'était ses forêts qui alimentaient les feux de leurs bivouacs; quand abaissant les yeux sur la vallée, il contemplait les longues lignes de ses troupes, qu'il savait être aussi braves que nombreuses, aussi fidèles que braves, quand il pesait dans son esprit, et sa puissance et la justice de sa cause, une expression sublime illuminait son pâle visage, et il ne pouvait imaginer la défaite. —

C'est qu'alors Harold réunissait en lui toute l'énergie toutes les espérances d'une nation. Harold n'était plus un homme, mais un Roi.

En temps de paix, il eût été sans doute, comme tous les autres princes assis sur un trône tranquille, un luxueux esclave, confiné dans son palais, abîmé dans les plaisirs, trompé par ses flatteurs, sachant, pour ce qu'il ne soit pas tout à fait imbécile, que, de tout son peuple, il est l'homme le moins libre; qu'il ne peut ni agir, ni guère penser par lui-même; que tous ceux qui l'environnent tâchent d'égarer; que jamais ne peut se mouvoir sans être dirigée par un ministre, et que son corps est un royal prisonnier, ayant son royaume pour prison, et ses sujets pour gardes.

Mais sur le champ de bataille, sans palais, sans ministres, sans

without courtiers, without pomp, without luxury, Harold, having only the sky of his country above him, for a roof, and that land, beneath his feet, that land which he holds from his ancestors and which he will only abandon with his life; Harold, surrounded by devoted hearts, who have entrusted in him their safety, their liberty, their existence — what a difference! Harold is no more a man; his passions bubble up, they become exalted, but shedding their egotism, they are purified; they are sanctified: his courage has no more rashness; his pride has no more arrogance — his assurance is without presumption; his indigation is without injustice.

Let the enemy come! still the victory is Harold's. He feels that all must retreat, fall, before him . . . . . But Death? . . . — to him who fights in defense of his native soil, the stroke of death is the stroke given to the slave, to liberate him and set him free.

courtisans, sans faste, sans luxe, Harold, n'ayant que le ciel de sa patrie
au-dessus de lui, pour toit, et cette terre, sous ses pieds, cette terre qu'il
tient de ses ancêtres et qu'il n'abandonnera qu'avec la vie; Harold
entouré de coeurs dévoués, qui lui ont confié leur sûreté, leur liberté,
leur existence, — Quelle différence! Harold n'est plus un homme; ses
passions bouillonnent, s'exaltent, mais dépouillant ce qu'elles ont d'égoiste, elles s'épurent; elles sont sanctifiées: son courage n'a plus de
témérité; sa fierté n'a plus d'arrogance — son assurance est sans présomption; son indignation est sans injustice.

Qu'ils viennent, les ennemis! et la victoire est à Harold. — Il sent
que tout doit reculer, tomber, devant lui . . . . . Mais la Mort? . . . — à
qui combat pour la défense du sol natal, le coup de mort, c'est le coup
donné à l'esclave, pour l'affranchir et le rendre libre.

Mirabeau

on the Tribune

―――――

When the sovereign orator, taken with some sudden thought, mounted the tribune; when this man found himself face to face with his people; when he was on his feet and walking on the envious Assembly, like the man-god on the waters, without being engulfed by them; when his sardonic and luminous gaze, fixed from the height of that tribune on the men and on the ideas of his time, seemed to measure the littleness of the men by the greatness of the ideas, then he was no longer calumniated, nor hooted, nor insulted. In vain might his enemies act, in vain might they talk, in vain might they pile up against him; the first breath from his mouth, as he opened it to speak, made the whole heap crumble. When this man was on the tribune exercising his genius, his countenance became radiant and all faded before it. [*]

Mirabeau on the tribune! All contemporaries are unanimous on this point now, it is something magnificent. There he is really himself, himself all complete and all-powerful. There, no more table, no more paper, no more writing desk bristling with pens, no more solitary chamber, no more silence and meditation; but marble you can pound, a staircase you can climb on the run, a tribune, cage of sorts for this kind of wild beast, where you can come and go, walk, stop, breathe, pant, cross your arms, clench your fists, paint your words with a gesture, and light up an idea with a glance; a mass of men you can stare at; a grand tumult, magnificent accompaniment for a grand voice; a crowd that hates the orator, the Assembly, enveloped in a crowd that loves him, the people; around him all these intelligences, all these souls, all these passions, all these mediocrities, all these ambitions, all these diverse

Mirabeau

à la Tribune

Quand l'orateur souverain, pris d'une subite pensée, montait à la tribune, quand cet homme se trouvait face à face avec son peuple, quand il était là debout et marchant sur l'envieuse assemblée, comme l'homme-Dieu sur la mer, sans être englouti par elle, quand son regard sardonique et lumineux, fixé, du haut, de cette tribune, sur les hommes, et sur les idées de son temps, avait l'air de mesurer la petitesse des hommes sur la grandeur des idées, alors il n'était plus ni calomnié, ni hué, ni injurié; ses ennemis avaient beau faire, avaient beau dire, avaient beau amoncelé contre lui, le premier souffle de sa bouche, ouverte pour parler, faisait crouler tous ces entassements. Quand cet homme était à la tribune dans la fonction de son génie, sa figure devenait splendide et tout s'évanouissait devant elle. [*] Mirabeau à la tribune! tous les contemporains sont unanimes sur ce point maintenant, c'est quelque chose de magnifique. Là il est bien lui, lui tout entier, lui tout puissant. Là, plus de table, plus de papier, plus d'écritoire hérissée de plumes, plus de cabinet solitaire, plus de silence et de méditation; mais un marbre qu'on peut frapper, un escalier qu'on peut monter en courant une tribune, espèce de cage de cette sorte de bête fauve où l'on peut aller et venir, marcher, s'arrêter, souffler, haleter, croiser ses bras, crisper ses poings peindre sa parole avec son geste, et illuminer une idée avec un coup d'oeil; un tas d'hommes qu'on peut regarder fixement; un grand tumulte, magnifique accompagnement pour une grande voix; une foule qui hait l'orateur, l'assemblée, enveloppée d'une foule qui l'aime, le peuple; autour de lui, toutes ces intelligences, toutes ces âmes, toutes ces passions, toutes ces médiocrités, toutes ces ambitions, toutes ces natures diverses et qu'il

natures which he knows, and from which he can draw the sound he wants, as from the keys of an immense harpsichord; above him the vault

of the hall of the Constituent Assembly, toward which he often raises his eyes as if to seek his thoughts there, for monarchies are overthrown by the ideas that fall from such a vault on such a head. Oh, how at home he is there, that man, on his terrain! How firm and sure his footing there! How great this genius, which diminished itself in books, becomes

in speech! How happily the tribune changes the conditions of production for that thought! After Mirabeau writer, Mirabeau orator, — what a transfiguration!

Everything about him was potent. His abrupt and sudden gesture was full of empire. At the tribune he had a colossal movement of the

shoulders; like the elephant who carries his armed turret in battle, so he carried his thought. His voice, even when he only hurled a word from his bench, had a formidable and revolutionary tone that could be singled out in the Assembly, like the roar of the lion in the menagerie. His locks, when he shook his head, were something like a mane. His brow

set all in motion, like Jupiter's; his hands sometimes seemed to mold the marble of the tribune. His whole face, his whole attitude, his whole person, was swollen with a full-blooded pride that had its grandeur. His head had a grandiose and glaring ugliness, whose effect was at moments electric and terrible.

Victor Hugo

connait, et desquelles il peut tirer le son qu'il veut, comme les touches d'un immense clavecin; au-dessus de lui, la voûte de la salle de l'assemblée constituante, vers laquelle ses yeux se lèvent souvent comme pour y chercher des pensées, car on renverse les monarchies avec les idées qui tombent d'une pareille voûte sur un pareille tête. Oh! qu'il est bien là sur son terrain, cet homme! qu'il y a bien le pied ferme et sûr! que ce génie qui s'amoindrissait dans les livres est grand dans un discours! comme la tribune change heureusement les conditions de la production pour cette pensée! Après Mirabeau écrivain, Mirabeau orateur, quelle transfiguration!

Tout en lui était puissant. Son geste brusque et saccadé était plein d'empire. À la tribune, il avait un colossal mouvement d'épaules: comme l'éléphant qui porte sa tour armée en guerre, lui, il portait sa pensée. Sa voix, lors même qu'il ne jetait qu'un mot de son banc, avait un accent formidable et révolutionnaire qu'on démêlait dans l'assemblée comme le rugissement du lion dans la ménagerie. Sa chevelure, quand il secouait la tête avait quelque chose d'une crinière. Son sourcil remuait tout, comme celui de Jupiter, ses mains quelquefois semblaient pétrir le marbre de la tribune: Tout son visage, toute son attitude, toute sa personne était bouffie d'un orgueil pléthorique qui avait sa grandeur. Sa tête avait une laideur grandiose et fulgurante dont l'effet, par moment, était électrique et terrible.

Victor Hugo

Comments

English history and Heger's lesson are recognizable sources for this de-voir, but neither one accounts for its King Harold. Emily's reflective and solitary leader, exalted from his status as a pampered princeling, bears little relation to the harried Anglo-Saxon whose defeat by William launched the Norman Conquest. Nineteen days before the fight that left him dead on the field, the historical Harold crushed an uprising by his brother and the king of Norway. He knew that his kingdom was precari-ously held together, threatened from within and without. However he might count on his loyal troops at Hastings, he could expect no easy reign.[1]

Emily's Harold may have sprung from an imagination primed on the battles of her Gondals. Her poems hint at a king cut down in civil war-fare,[2] although in the absence of surviving manuscripts the details may never be known. In contrast, much is known about the devoir's Belgian origins, since Heger told Gaskell why Emily had written it and even mailed her a copy. The more his statements are examined, however, the more problematic they become.

When Gaskell interviewed him in 1856, Heger explained that in the summer of 1842 he had given the Brontë sisters a lesson on "Victor

Hugo's celebrated portrait of Mirabeau" to initiate a writing assignment.[3] In a follow-up letter he added, "in my lesson I limited myself to that which concerns *Mirabeau the orator,* that is to say paragraph VI. It was after analyzing that piece, considered particularly from the point of view of the background, of the arrangement, of what one might call *the structure* [*la charpente*], that the two enclosed portraits were done."[4] What, precisely, did he enclose?

Almost certainly, the packet contained two copies he had made for Gaskell at her request: "On the Death of Napoleon," his version of Charlotte's "The Death of Napoleon" (May 31, 1843); and "Portrait: Harold on the Eve of the Battle of Hastings," his version of Emily's "Portrait: King Harold before the Battle of Hastings" (June 1842). From Heger's description and internal evidence, it is clear that both devoirs respond to "Sur Mirabeau," though Gaskell did not view them as a pair. Instead, she linked Emily's devoir on Harold to Charlotte's "Imitation: Portrait of Peter the Hermit" (July 31, 1842), a devoir Heger apparently showed her in Brussels and perhaps gave her to take home.[5] Wherever and whenever she received that manuscript, she printed it in her *Life of Charlotte Brontë,* citing Emily's "companion portrait" with the comment, "It appears to me that her *devoir* is superior to Charlotte's in power and in imagination, and fully equal to it in language."[6] Of course, she did not see the draft as Emily wrote it; she judged by the version Heger sent her.

But as even a glimpse at the typescripts reveals, Heger massively revised his "copy." (A man who could make a dozen changes in a dictée of two paragraphs by Chateaubriand would hardly scruple at refining the text of a twenty-three-year-old English novice.) In fact, he made corrections in three layers. He went through Emily's draft with a pen; then he went back with a pencil;[7] later, in preparing the copy for Gaskell (or an antecedent version of 1842), he again changed Emily's words and his own.

Emily wrote on fabric to which paper had been glued; the resulting sheet was folded and ruled to make four pages, the outer ones of cloth, the inner ones of paper. On the cloth side her writing remains visible but faded; Heger's, especially on page 4, has paled into near illegibility. Even on the paper side (pages 2 and 3), his circles, lines, crossouts, and roundabout corrections make deciphering the manuscript a challenge. But whatever the risk of missing or misreading words, getting at the text is a requisite for anyone who wants to know not only what Emily wrote and he adjusted but also what she took from the experience.

The process of composing began, as Heger said, with his lecture on Victor Hugo's "portrait." His account, or Gaskell's, implies a private lesson. But the piece he describes, "Mirabeau on the Tribune," appears in a notebook of Charlotte's dictées, exercises she took down in class. His recall of details fourteen years later also suggests that he gave this lesson more than once, and not for the Brontës alone. The topic would have had a personal appeal for him, since he excelled at oratory rather than at writing, and the piece itself seems made to be declaimed.

Hugo's "Mirabeau" consists of seven parts, not "paragraphs," and fills thirty pages in print. For his dictée, Heger joined a passage from part 3 to a longer passage from part 6. (An asterisk indicates the juncture in the version here. In Charlotte's, a shift in style is the only hint; the literary language becomes less formal, and the past tense switches to present.) Heger told Gaskell that in giving his lesson, "he had pointed out to them the fault in Victor Hugo's style as being exaggeration in conception, and, at the same time, he had made them notice the extreme beauty of his 'nuances' of expression."[8] He lectured too on the background or foundation,[9] which may have entailed a brief biography.

Honoré Gabriel de Riqueti, comte de Mirabeau (1749–91), rose with the French Revolution. Before it began, he was a profligate and wastrel whose family despaired of reforming him. Hugo focuses obsessively on contrast: Mirabeau's transformation from a wretch into a hero, his internal contradictions, and the drastic swings in his reputation. To Hugo he was the consummate symbol of the people of 1789; "scorned," "defamed," "ill educated," held too long in nonage, subject to his father's will as they had been to royalty's, "he was in everything like the ardent years in which he shone."[10]

This figure has little in common with the Harold defeated at Hastings. Mirabeau thrived by attacking the monarchy; Harold died trying to keep his crown. Mirabeau seized his power in the Assembly; Harold was driven into combat. Mirabeau's death in bed, from natural causes, left him a hero in his time; Harold's, on the field, left England open to a conquest that abased its people and its language. Still, in Hugo's version of Mirabeau's life, there were seeds that Emily could transplant: the image of a leader looking out on multitudes, a life of extremes that could be rendered dramatically, the principle of holding one's own ground. Harold, like Mirabeau, could symbolize a nation and, envisioning his charge, become transfigured. In these respects her portrait might be influenced by Hugo's and so comply with Heger's instructions.

But in Emily's soil, the seeds grow her way. For example, in Hugo, transformation occurs when Mirabeau shifts from writing to speaking; more broadly, it entails the metamorphosis of Mirabeau into a public figure. Emily takes no interest in public recognition. Her Harold undergoes his transformation in solitude. Even when she places him among his troops, they are the backdrop, not the source of exaltation. She also turns away from the historical record, after a curt identification of the battle site and coming catastrophe. Her Harold is not the attacked, ambitious ruler who could never have risked lapsing into idleness. Rather, she constructs a prince who reaches his peak in the moment of potentiality.

This vision of heroism differs radically from Hugo's, her sister's, and presumably Heger's. They assume that greatness is connected to accomplishment. Heroes in their terms (given currency by Carlyle)[11] are people of genius who seize or create the moment for altering history. Hugo claims that Mirabeau died at the right time, before the Revolution could topple him.[12] Emily too conceives of death as fortunate; it can free Harold, if not quite at his summit, then before he can descend into new slavery. But she keeps her hero poised in the space of revelation. Potential, not action, transforms him.[13]

Heger probably knew little about Anglo-Saxon England, but as a staunch republican, he would have warmed to the contrast between a free man and one bound either as a slave or king. He praised her devoir's pictorial details: Harold gazing across to the horizon, Harold stripped of trappings on the field. He must also have realized that despite her stubbornness, she tried to respond to the model he had given her, to imitate Hugo's parallel constructions and syntactically coordinated lists. And because he was so heavily invested in his metier, he could not resist improving her efforts.

The French of her devoir is flawed and often awkward, but Heger has gone beyond correcting it. He overlays the voice of Emily Brontë with the voice of a trained rhetorician. He alters and finally eliminates her metaphors, replacing them with his own or Hugo's. In his version, Harold's soul is not tangled in a labyrinth; courtiers lead him astray. And Harold no longer stands with his soul in his eyes, his passions made pure in the sight of his creator; his egotism boils away. (Hugo's "Mirabeau" alludes more than once to stifled passions that finally bubble out.)[14]

If Heger made his "copy" exclusively for Gaskell, Emily of course would not have seen it. His motive then would have been to show off her genius, and the success of his own teaching methods, while silently correcting her worst errors. There is, however, another possibility, that "Harold on the Eve" is based on a variant that Heger prepared in 1842. He read outstanding devoirs aloud in the classroom, and on Prize Day, which came at the end of the school year, he singled out the best to read in public. In performance, his version, like the dictée from Hugo, would project; it would build to a crescendo. And Emily would have been in the audience or rudely and conspicuously absent.

No record exists of her reaction—to a public reading, to his heavy corrections, or to undergoing the process of his teaching—except in Charlotte's comment, "Emily and he don't draw well together at all."[15] But its absence and the incomplete state of printed versions of the text[16] have not kept scholars from conjecturing. John Hewish, who saw the draft in Emily's handwriting, says that Heger's comment on her "final simile" is "a clue to their failure to 'draw well together.'"[17] The manuscript provides more clues than one. Any person as fiercely independent as Emily would have had a hard time dealing with the quantity, much less the kinds, of change that he imposed. But outright resistance would not necessarily sabotage the learning experience.

Even critics who dislike this devoir—Muriel Spark calls it "in many ways absurd"[18]—recognize precursors of *Wuthering Heights* in its hero and its attitude toward death. David Musselwhite, its most attentive reader, considers both "Harold" and Hugo's portrait crucial in Emily's development. Musselwhite did not see the draft with Heger's markings. If he had, he might have been less likely to argue that "thanks to the eruption into her life of a teacher of authority and genius who recognized her real strength, Emily could disengage herself from the taboos of her family and society and enter again into the sovereign possession of her own true being."[19] But in other ways, he makes persuasive connections among

Hugo's Mirabeau, Emily's Heathcliff, and the structure of *Wuthering Heights*.[20]

One message of her uncorrected draft is that under the pressure of unsought circumstance, "a nothing" can achieve greatness. Emily did not choose to subject herself to Heger, nor did she produce great essays under his tutelage. But she did continue to produce. It remains to be shown how "the conditions of production," a phrase that occurs in the Mirabeau dictée,[21] affected the writer she became.

Portrait

Peter the Hermit.

From time to time, there appear on earth certain men destined to be the instruments of great change, moral or political, in their epoch. Sometimes it is a conquerer, an Alexander or an Attila, who passes like a *very G.* hurricane and purifies the moral atmosphere as the storm purifies the physical atmosphere. Sometimes, it is a revolutionary, a Cromwell or

makes reparation   for
a Robespierre who <u>avenges</u> through a king the vices of a whole dynasty.

Sometimes it is a religious enthusiast like Mahomet or Peter the Hermit,

with his only lever that of thought
who raises up entire nations | by dint of exciting the profoundest sen-

timents of the human heart. \ *uproots them, transplants them into a new*

climate.

If one reflects on the history of Peter the Hermit | one will recognize that he is worthy of being placed in the first rank of remarkable men. |

He was a gentleman from Picardy in France; why *then* did he not pass his

passed theirs   at table and the hunt,
life as other gentlemen, his contemporaries, ^ in eating, drinking, and
in his bed
sleeping, without worrying about Saladin or about the Saracens? Is it not
because   does not
that there exists in certain natures an indomitable <u>ardor</u> that ~~will not~~
permit
~~suffer~~ them to remain inactive, that forces them to bestir themselves so

as to exercise the powerful faculties which, even asleep, are ready like

G Sampson to break the bonds that hold them back?

Peter chose the profession of arms. If his ardor had been of the kind that arises from robust health and steady nerves, he would have been always a brave soldier and nothing more; but his ardor was that of the soul, its flame was pure and it rose up to heaven. Undoubtedly Peter's

extreme
youth was troubled by stormy passions; powerful natures are powerful in everything, they know not tepidity either in good or in evil; so

Portrait

Pierre l'Ermite.

═══════

De temps en temps, il parait sur la terre des hommes destinés à être les

instruments de grands changements, moraux ou politiques, dans leur   5

siècle. Quelquefois c'est un conquérant, un Alexandre ou un Attila qui

passe comme un ouragan et purifie l'atmosphère morale comme l'orage   *tr B.*

purifie l'atmosphère physique — quelquefois, c'est un révolutionnaire, un

                  fait expier par

Cromwell ou un Robespierre qui <u>ven</u>ge sur un roi les vices de toute une

dynastie; quelquefois c'est un enthousiaste religieux comme Mahomète   10

         avec le seul levier de la pensée

ou Pierre l'Ermite, qui˅ soulève des nations entières | à force d'exciter

les sentiments les plus profonds du coeur humain\ *les déracine les trans-*

plante dans un climat nouveau. /

    Si l'on réfléchit sur l'histoire du Pierre l'Ermite | on reconnaitra qu'il

est digne d'être mis au premier rang des hommes remarquables |. Il était   15

                     s   ont passé <u>les leurs</u>   *à table et*

gentilhomme de Picardie en France, pourquoi *donc* n'a-t-il passé sa vie

comme les autres gentilhommes ses contemporains ^ en mangeant, en

à la chasse dans son lit

buvant et en dormant, sans s'inquiéter de Saladin ou des⌣ses Sarrasins?

      parce,

N'est-ce pas/qu'il y a dans certaines natures, une <u>ardeur</u> indomptable qui

    leur permet pas de

ne ~~les souffrira pas de~~ rester inactives, qui les force de se remuer afin |╫   20

d'exercer les facultés puissantes qui, même en dormant sont prêtes

comme Sampson à briser les noeuds qui les retiennent.   *B*

         des

    Pierre prit la profession d'armes, si son ardeur avait été de cette

espèce qui provient d'une robuste santé et des bons nerfs, il aurait été   [?]

toujours un brave militaire et rien de plus; mais son ardeur était celle de   25

l'âme, sa flamme était pure et elle s'élevait vers le ciel. Sans doute la

                       par

jeunesse de Pierre était troublée de passions orageuses; les natures puis-

    extrèmes

santes sont puissantes en tout, elles ne connaissent pas la tiédeur ni dans

at first
Peter searched avidly for the glory that withers and the pleasures that
deceive, but very soon he made the discovery that what he pursued was

could
but an illusion which he ~~was~~ never ~~able~~ to attain. Therefore he retraced

compare

his steps, he recommenced the voyage of his life, but this time he

avoided the broad road that leads to perdition and took the narrow road

cast off
that leads to life. Since the way was long and difficult, he s~~t~~ri~~pp~~ed

himself òf the helmet and the weapons of a soldier and donned the

simple habit of a monk.

monast
To the military life succeeded the <u>hermetic</u> life, because extremes
in   *the sincerity of repentance*   *brings with it*
meet; ~~and~~ the sincere man ~~who experiences true~~ repentance, ~~seeks always~~
the rigor of the [penitence]
~~to expiate great crimes~~ by great penitence.

But Peter had in himself a principle that kept him from remaining

long inactive; his ideas, whatever the subject might be, could not be

confined; it was not enough for him that he himself was religious, that

he himself was convinced of the reality of Christianity; all of Europe, all

of Asia must share his conviction and profess its faith in the Cross. Piety

elevated by Genius and nourished by Solitude brought to birth a kind of

cell
inspiration in his soul, and when he left his <u>cave</u> and reappeared in the

world, he bore like Moses the imprint of Divinity on his countenance |

G   and everyone recognized in him the true apostle of the cross.

Mahomet had never moved the soft nations of the East as Peter then

. It required
that eloquence
and of a fire   force of the eloquence that persuaded kings to sell their kingdoms so as
force almost
miraculous   to procure weapons and soldiers to aid Peter in the holy war that he

moved the austere people of the West. We can scarcely conceive the

wanted to raise against the infidels.

Peter's power was not in any way a physical power, for Nature, or

to put it better, God, is impartial in the distribution of his gifts; on one

of his children he bestows grace, beauty, bodily perfection; on another,

short
spirit, moral grandeur. Hence Peter was a ~~little~~ man, of a displeasing

d'abord
le bien ni dans le mal; Pierre donc cherchait avidement la gloire qui se

fit
flétrit et les plaisirs qui trompent, mais il faisait bientôt la découverte que   30

pourrait
ce qu'il poursuivait n'était qu'une illusion à laquelle il ne ~~pouvait~~ jamais   ‖

atteindre | _ il retourna donc sur ses pas, il recommença | le voyage de   *comparais.*

la vie, mais cette fois il évita le chemin spacieux qui méne à la perdition

et il prit le chemin étroit qui méne à la vie: puisque le trajet était long et

il jetta   les
difficile, il se ~~dépourvut~~ du *le* casque et *des* armes du soldat et se vêtit   35

de l'habit simple du moine.

monast
À la vie militaire succéda la vie <u>érémétique</u>, car les extrêmes se   .

chez   la sincerité du repentir
touchent; et l'homme sincère ~~qui éprouve le véritable~~ repentir, ~~cherche~~
amène avec lui la rigueur de la [penitence]
~~toujours à expier de grands forfaits~~ par de grandes pénitences.

Mais Pierre avait en lui un principe qui l'empêchait de rester long-   40

temps inactif, ses idées sur qu<u>el</u> sujet qu'il soit ne pouvaient pas être bor-   · /

fut
nées, il ne lui suffisait pas que lui-même était religieux, que lui-même   · /

fut
était convaincu de la réalité de Christianisme, il fallait que toute   · /

l'Europe, que toute l'Asie partageât sa conviction et professât la croyance

fit
de la Croix. La Piété élevée par la Génie et nourrie par la Solitude faisait   .   45

sa cellule
naître une espèce d'inspiration dans son âme, et lorsqu'il quitta son <u>antre</u>   /

et reparut dans le monde, il portait comme Moïse l'empreinte de la

Divinité sur son front | et tout réconnurent en lui le véritable apôtre de   *B*

la croix

Mahométe n'avait jamais remué les molles nations de l'Orient comme   50

alors Pierre rémuait les peuples austères de l'Occident Nous pouvons à   . *Il faillait*
cette éloquence
peine concevoir la force de cette éloquence qui persuadait aux rois de   *et d'une ~~fougue à~~*
force presque
vendre leurs royaumes afin de procurer des armes et des soldats pour   *miraculeuse*

aider à Pierre dans la guerre sainte qu'il voulait livrer aux <u>infidelles</u>.   [?]

La puissance de Pierre n'était nullement une puissance physique, car   55

la Nature, ou pour mieux dire, Dieu, est impartial dans la distribution de

ses dons; il accorde à l'un de ses enfants la grâce, la beauté les per-

fections corporelles, à l'autre, l'esprit, la grandeur morale; Pierre donc

physiognomy; but he had that courage, that constancy, that enthusiasm, that energy of feeling which crushes all opposition and makes the will of

very G

indeed

a single man become the law of an entire nation.

Imagination delights in painting the image of the Cenobite amid the armed Crusaders. The canvas is large, for one would not know how to represent such a subject in miniature. In it one sees a vast plain covered with an innumerable multitude of all the peoples of the West: free, enslaved, small and large. A hundred flags float in the air; on one side is the flag of Spain, on the other that of Austria; here the lion of the sea, there the fleur de lis. Everywhere the standard of the Temple unfurls its crimson folds and everywhere appear the fierce Templars, dressed in their long white robes and bearing the red cross on their shoulders. The setting is in the Holy Land, and that mountain which you see, covered with a dark and ancient forest, is Lebanon with all its cedars; that river which reflects on its surface the innumerable tents of the Crusaders is the Jordan; that town whose towers shine in the light of a setting sun is Jerusalem; and that grand dome, which rises above the other buildings, is the roof of the Temple.

But why are all those warriors leaning on their lances? Why do some of them incline their heads as if to listen, and why do the others raise their eyes as if to worship? Look at the center of the canvas; there one sees a pyramidal group; those two big strong men, whose gigantic forms and stern and powerful countenances impose respect, are the leaders of the army, Godfrey and Tancred. But who is the one who appears at the center? There is nothing imposing, nothing magnificent in that form; but there is something quite remarkable.

He is a scrawny little man, a poor hermit, dressed in a poor gray habit; without weapons, without plumes, without helmet. What force then inspires him so that he remains standing there, alone, although

était un ~~petit~~ *petit* homme d'une physionomie peu agréable; mais il avait ce

courage, cette constance, cet enthousiasme, cette energie de sentiment qui   60

écrase toute opposition et qui fait que la volonté d'un seul homme de-   *tr B*

vienne˘la *bien* loi de toute une nation.

L'imagination se plait à peindre l'image du Cenobite au milieu des

croisés armés. Le tableau est grand, car on ne saurait representer un tel

sujet en miniature. On y voit une vaste plaine couverte d'une multitude   65

innombrable de tous les peuples de l'occident, libres, esclaves, petits et

grands. Cent drapeaux flottent dans l'air, de l'un côté est le drapeau de

l'Espagne, de l'autre de\l'autre celui d'Autriche, ici le lion de la mer, là,

la fleur de lis — partout l'étendard du Temple déroule ses plis cramoisis

et partout paraissent les fiers templiers vêtus de leurs longs manteaux   70

blancs et portant la croix rouge sur leurs épaules. La scène est en la

Terre sainte, et cette montagne que vous voyez, couverte d'une forêt

noire et ancienne est Lebanon avec tous ses cédres cette rivière qui

réfléchit à sa surface les tentes innombrables des croisés est le Jourdain,

cette ville dont les tours brillent à la lumière d'un soleil qui se couche est   75

Jerusalem, et ce grande dôme qui s'élève au-dessus des autres batiments

est le toit du Temple.

Mais pourquoi tous ces guerriers s'appuyent-ils sur leurs lances?

Pourquoi quelques-uns inclinent-ils la tête comme pour écouter, et pour-

quoi les autres lèvent-ils les yeux comme pour adorer? Regardez au   80

centre du tableau; là on voit un groupe pyramidal; ces deux hommes

grands et forts, dont les formes gigantesques, les figures graves et

puissantes, imposent du respect sont les chefs de l'armée Godfroi et

Tancréde; mais qui est celui qui parait au milieu? Il n'y a rien d'im-

posant, rien de magnifique dans cette forme, mais il y a quelque chose   85

de bien remarquable.

C'est un homme petit, amaigri, un pauvre ermite, vêtu d'un pauvre

habit gris; sans armes, sans plumes, sans casque. Quelle force donc

surrounded by a multitude? A multitude that he seems neither to see, nor
to hear, because | his eyes are upraised, are fixed on heaven; their expres-
sion seems to say, "I see God and the angels, and I have lost sight of the
90   earth."

It is the cenobite; it is Peter. His genius has already mastered that
whole army and at this moment he masters himself. | That poor gray
habit is for him like the mantle of the prophet Elijah; it envelops him
with inspiration. He reads into the future; he sees Jerusalem delivered,
95   the holy sepulchre free; he sees the silver crescent torn away from the
Temple, and the Oriflamme and Red Cross established in its place. Not
only does he see these marvels, but he makes all those who surround him
see them. He has put hope and courage in the hearts of all these soldiers.
The battle will be fought tomorrow morning, but the victory is decided
100   that evening. Peter has promised, and the Crusaders trust his word, as
the Israelites trusted that of Moses and of Joshua.

l'inspire qu'il reste là debout, seul, quoiqu'è entouré d'une multitude? Une multitude qu'il ne semble ni voir, ni entendre, car | ses yeux sont levés, sont fixés vers le ciel, leur expression semble dire "Je vois Dieu et les anges et j'ai perdu de vue la terre."

C'est le cenobite, c'est Pierre. Son génie a déjà maîtrisé toute cette armée et dans ce moment il maîtrise lui-même: | ce pauvre habit gris, est pour lui comme le manteau du prophète Elijah, il l'enveloppe d'inspiration. Il lit dans l'avenir; il voit Jerusalem delivré, le saint sepulchre libre; Il voit le croissant argenté arraché du Temple, et l'Oriflamme et la Croix rouge établies à sa place; non seulement il voit ces merveilles mais il les fait voir à tous ceux qui l'entourent; il a mis l'espérance et le courage dans les coeurs de tous ses soldats; la bataille sera livrée demain matin mais la victoire est decidée ce soir. Pierre à promis et les croisés se fient à sa parole comme les Israëlites se fiaient à celle de Moïse et de Josua

Imitation

Portrait of Peter the Hermit

=====

From time to time, there appear on earth certain men, (destined to be
predestined
the) instruments of great change, moral or political, ~~in~~ ~~their~~ ~~epoch~~.

Sometimes it is a conquerer, an Alexander or an Attila, who passes like

a hurricane and purifies the moral atmosphere as the storm purifies the

physical atmosphere. Sometimes, it is a revolutionary, a Cromwell or
faults and the
a Robespierre who avenges through a king the⌣vices of a whole dynasty.

Sometimes it is a religious enthusiast like Mahomet or Peter the Hermit,

who, with his only lever that of thought, raises up entire nations, uproots

them, and transplants them into a new climate, (populating Asia with the

inhabitants of Europe). Peter the Hermit was a gentleman from Picardy

~~in~~ ~~France~~; why then did he not pass his life as other gentlemen, his

contemporaries, passed theirs, at table, at the hunt, in his bed, without
his
worrying about Saladin or about the Saracens? Is it not because there
a hotbed of activity
exists in certain natures an indomitable ardor that does not permit them

to remain inactive, that forces them to bestir themselves so as to exercise

the powerful faculties which, even asleep, are ready like Sampson to

break the bonds that hold them back?

If he had had only that vulgar
Peter chose the profession of arms. If his⌣ardor │ had been of the

kind that arises from robust health ~~and~~ ~~steady~~ ~~nerves~~, he would have

been always a brave soldier and nothing more; but his ardor was that of
It is true that at first
the soul, its flame was pure and it rose up to heaven. Undoubtedly

Peter's youth was troubled by stormy passions; powerful natures are

extreme in everything, they know nòt tepidity neither in good nor in evil;

so at first so Peter searched avidly for the glory that withers and the

Marginal notes:

5 *Why that suppression?*

10

This detail only fits Peter.

unnecessary when you write
15 *in French*

You have begun to speak of Peter, you have entered into the subject, get to
20 *the point.*

25

Charlotte Brontë   Le 31 Juillet 1842

Imitation

Portrait de Pierre l'Hermite.

———

De temps en temps, il parait sur la terre des hommes, (destinés à être les)

     prédestinés

instruments˘ de grands changements, moraux ou politiques, ~~dans leur~~   *pourquoi*   5
     cette
~~siècle~~. Quelquefois c'est un conquérant, un Alexandre ou un Attila, qui   *suppression?*

passe comme un ouragan, et purifie l'atmosphère moralè comme l'orage

purifie l'atmosphère physique; quelquefois, c'est un révolutionnaire, un

                    fautes et les

Cromwell ou un Robespierre qui fait expier par un roi les ˘vices de toute

une dynastie; quelquefois c'est un enthousiaste réligieux comme   10

Mahomèt ou Pierre l'Ermite, qui, avec le seul levier de la pensée soulève

des nations entières, les déracine et les transplante dans des climats   *Ce détail ne*
convient qu'à
nouveaux, (peuplant l'Asie avec les habitants de l'Europe).   Pierre   *Pierre /*

l'Ermite était gentilhomme de Picardie ~~en France~~; pourquoi donc n'a-t-il   *inutile quand* 15
vous écrivez
passé sa vie comme les autres gentilshommes ses contemporains ont passé   *en français.*

la leur, à table, à la chasse dans son lit, sans s'inquiéter de Saladin ou
     ses
des˘ Sarrasins? N'est-ce pas, parcequ'il y a dans certaines natures, unè
foyer d'activité
ardeur indomptable qui ne leur permet pas de rester inactives| qui les   *Vous avez*
   à   *commmencé à*
force |de se remuer afin d'exercer les|facultés puissantes, qui, même en   *parler de*   20
Pierre, vous êtes
dormant sont prêtes comme Sampson à briser les noeuds |qui les   *entreé dans le*
sujet, marchez
retiennent?   *au but. —*

        s'il n'avait eu que cette   *vulgaire*

Pierre prit la profession des armes, si son˘ ardeur | avait été de cette
                                 c'eut

espèce ˘qui provient d'une robuste santé ~~et des bons nerfs~~, il aurait été

toujòurs un brave militaire et rien de plus; mais son ardeur était celle de   25
                        Il est vrai que ~~d'abord~~
l'âme sa flamme était pure et elle s'élevait vers le ciel. Sans doute la
    fut
jeunesse de Pierre était troublée par passions orageuses; les natures puis-

santes sont extrêmes en tout, elles ne connaissent pàs la tièdeur ni dans

le bien ni dans le mal; Pierre donc chercha d'abord avidément la gloire

he realized

pleasures that deceive, but very soon ~~he made~~ the discovery that what

he pursued was but ~~an~~ illusion ~~which he could never attain~~. Therefore he

needless, when you have said
30 *illusion.*

retraced his steps, he recommenced the voyage of his life, but this time

he avoided the broad road that leads to perdition and he took the narrow

As

road that leads to life. ~~Since~~ the way was long and difficult, he cast off

the helmet and the weapons of a soldier and donned the simple habit of

a monk. To the military life succeeded the monastic life, because ex-

with the ~~sincere man~~   *necessarily*   *in train*
35 tremes meet and^the sincerity of repentance brings with it the rigor of

the penitence. — *Thus Peter converted into a monk;*

he

But ~~Peter~~ had in himself a principle that kept him from remaining

long inactive; his ideas, whatever the subject might be, could not be

confined; it was not enough for him that he himself was religious, that

40 he himself was convinced of the reality of Christianity; all of Europe, all

of Asia must share his conviction and profess its faith in the Cross.

fervent —————   *exalted his*
Piety elevated by Genius and nourished by Solitude brought to birth a

soul to
kind of inspiration ~~in his soul~~, and when he quitted his cell and reap-

peared in the world, he bore like Moses the imprint of Divinity on his

45 countenance, and everyone recognized in him the ~~true~~ apostle of the cross.

Mahomet had not ~~ever~~ moved the soft nations of the East as Peter

then moved the austere people of the West. That eloquence must have

since it [persuad]ed
had an almost miraculous force which could persuade kings to sell their

to get   *offer*
kingdoms so as to procure weapons and soldiers to aid Peter in the holy

50 war that he wanted to raise against the infidels.

the hermit's
Peter's power was not in any way a physical power, for Nature, or

to put it better, God, is impartial in the distribution of his gifts; he

bestows on one of his ~~children~~ grace, beauty, bodily perfection, on

another spirit, moral grandeur. Hence, Peter was a short man, of a

55 displeasing physiognomy; but he had that courage, that constancy, that

enthusiasm, that energy of feeling which crushes all opposition and

makes the will of a single man become the law of an entire nation.

qui se flétrit et les plaisirs qui trompent, mais ~~il fit~~ *il s'aperçut* bientôt la découverte   30

que ce qu'il poursuivait n'était qu'une illusion ~~à laquelle il ne pourrait~~   *inutile, quand*
vous avez dit
~~jamais atteindre~~; il retourna donc sur ses pas, il recommença le voyage   *illusion.*

de la vie, mais cette fois il évita le chemin spacieux qui méne à la perdi-

tion et il prit le chemin étroit qui méne à la vie: ~~puisque~~ *comme* le trajet était

long et difficile, il jeta le casque et les armes du soldat, et se vêtit de   35

l'habit simple du moine. À la vie militaire succéda la vie monastique,
~~chez l'hom~~me ~~sincère~~   *nécessairemt à sa suite*
car, les extrêmes se touchent ^la sincerité du repentir amène ~~avec lui~~

la rigueur de la penitence.— *Voila donc Pierre devenu moine*;
il
Mais ~~Pierre~~ avait en lui un principe qui l'empêchait de rester long-
que se fut
temps inactif, ses idées, sur quel sujet qu'il soit ne pouvaient pas être   40

bornées; il ne lui suffisait pas que lui-même fût religieux, que lui-même

fût convaincu de la réalité de Christianisme, il fallait que toute l'Europe,

que toute l'Asie partageât sa conviction et professât la croyance de la
fervente   *exalta son*
Croix. La Piété élevée par le Génie et nourrie par la Solitude fît naître
âme jusqu'à l'
une espèce d'inspiration ~~dans son âme~~, et lorsqu'il quitta sa cellule et   45

reparut dans le monde, il portait comme Moïse l'empreinte de la Divinité
s
sur son front et tout réconnurent en lui le ~~'véritable~~ apôtre de la croix

Mahométe n'avait ~~jamais~~ remué les molles nations de l'Orient comme

alors Pierre rémua les peuples austères de l'Occident: il fallait que cette
puis qu'elle   *aie*
eloquence fût d'une force presque miraculeuse qui pouvait persuader aux   50
pour avoir
rois de vendre leurs royaumes afin de procurer des armes et des soldats
à offrir
pour aider à Pierre dans la guerre sainte qu'il voulait livrer aux infidèles.
l'hermite
La puissance de Pierre n'était nullement une puissance physique,

car la Nature, ou pour mieux dire, Dieu, est impartial dans la distribu-

tion de ses dons; il accorde à l'un de ses ~~enfants~~ la grâce, la beauté, les   55

perfections corporelles, à l'autre, l'esprit, la grandeur morale. Pierre

donc était un homme, petit, d'une physionomie peu agréable; mais il

avait ce courage, cette constance, cet enthousiasme, cette energie de

sentiment qui écrase toute opposition et qui fait que la volonté d'un seul

^{correct} To form a[^] idea of the influence which^{^ that man} exercised on the ~~characters~~ ^{*events*}

and the ideas of his time, he must be represented in the midst of the army

of crusaders, in his double role of prophet and warrior; the poor hermit

the humble
dressed in a poor gray habit is there, ~~more powerful than a king; he is~~

an avid   ;
surrounded by a multitude,/ ~~a multitude~~ that sees him only, and as for

him,/ he sees only heaven; his upraised eyes/ seem to say: "I see God

and/ the angels, and I have lost sight of the/ earth!"

but that   frock
~~In that moment~~ the poor gray ~~habit~~ is for him like the mantle of the

Peter
prophet Elijah; it envelops him with inspiration. ~~He~~ reads into the

he sees
future; he sees Jerusalem delivered;, the holy sepulchre free; ~~he sees~~ the

on it   re
silver crescent torn away from the Temple, and the Oriflamme and Red

are   Peter
Cross established in its place. Not only does he see these marvels, but

revived
he makes all those who surround him see them. He has put hope and

all those bodies exhausted by fatigue and privation   not
courage in[˘] the hearts of all these soldiers. The battle will *not* be fought

until
tomorrow ~~morning~~, but the victory is decided, that evening. Peter has

promised/ and the Crusaders trust his ~~promise~~ word, as the Israelites

trusted that of Moses and of Joshua./

homme devienne *t* la loi de toute une nation.

Pour former une^ *se* idée de l'influence qu'exerçait^ *cet homme* sur les ~~caractères~~ *juste* *choses*

et les idées de son temps, il faut se le representer au milieu de l'armée

des croisés, dans son double rôle de prophète et du guerrier; le pauvre

ermite vêtu du pauvre habit gris est là ~~plus puissant qu'un roi~~; ~~il est~~ *de l'humble*

entouré ~~d'une~~ multitude, / ~~une multitude~~ qui ne voit que lui, tandisque *de la* *avide;/*

lui, il ne voit que le ciel; ces yeux lévés/ semblent dire: "Je vois Dieu

et les/ anges et j'ai perdu de vue la terre/!"

~~Dans ce moment~~ le pauvre ~~habit~~ gris est pour lui comme le manteau *mais ce* *froc*

d'Elijah; il l'enveloppe d'inspiration: ~~il~~ lit dans l'avenir; il voit Jérusalem *Pierre*

delivré;¨ le saint sepulchre libre; ~~il voit~~ le croissant argenté arraché du *il voit* *en*

Temple, et l'Oriflamme et la Croix rouge établies à sa place; non seule- *ro* *sont* *s*

ment il voit ces merveilles, mais il les fait voir à tous ceux qui l'entour- *Pierre*

ent, il a mis l'espérance et le courage dans¨ les coeurs de tous ces *ravivé* *tous ces corps épuisés de fatigues et de*

soldats;— la bataille ne sera livrée¨demain ~~matin~~, mais la victoire est *privations* *ne* *que*

décidée, ce soir. Pierre a promis/ et les croisés se fient à sa ~~promesse~~

parole, comme les Israëlites se fiaient à celle de Moïse et de Josuà./ *e*

The Capture of Jerusalem
by the Crusaders

. . . The imagination turns with dread from these scenes of desolation, and can scarcely, amidst the carnage, contemplate the touching image of the Christians of Jerusalem, whose chains the Crusaders had just broken. Scarcely had the city been taken, when they were seen flocking to meet the conquerors; they shared with them the provisions that they had been able to steal from the Saracens; and all together thanked the God who had made the arms of the soldiers of the cross triumphant.

Peter the Hermit, who, five years before, had promised to arm the West for the deliverance of the Christians of Jerusalem, must indeed have enjoyed the spectacle of their gratitude and joy. The faithful of the holy city, amid the crowd of Crusaders, seemed only to seek and to see the pious cenobite, who had visited them in their sufferings, and whose promises had all just been realized.

They pressed in a crowd around the venerable hermit. It was to him that they addressed their songs of praise. It was he whom they proclaimed their liberator. They related to him the evils they had suffered during his absence; they could scarcely believe what was happening before their eyes, and in their enthusiasm, they expressed astonishment that God should have employed only a single man to raise up so many nations, and to effect such prodigies.

[Joseph-François] Michau[d]

Prise de Jerusalem
par les croisés

. . . L'Imagination se détourne avec effroi de ses scènes de désolation et peut à peine au milieu du carnage, contempler l'image touchante des chrétiens de Jérusalem dont les croisés venaient de briser les fers. À peine la ville venait-elle d'être conquise, qu'on les vit accourir au-devant des vainqueurs; ils partageaient avec eux les vivres qu'ils avaient pu dérober aux Sarrasins tous remerciaient ensemble le Dieu qui avait fait triompher les armes des soldats de la croix.

L'ermite Pierre qui cinq ans auparavant avait promis d'armer l'Occident pour la délivrance des Chrétiens de Jérusalem, dût jouir alors du spectacle de leur reconnaissance et de leur joie. Les fidèles de la ville sainte au milieu de la foule des croisés semblaient ne chercher, ne voir que le cenobite pieux, qui les avait visités dans leurs souffrances et dont toutes les promesses venaient d'être accomplies.

Ils se pressaient en foule autour de l'ermite vénérable c'est à lui qu'ils s'adressaient leurs cantiques; C'est lui qu'ils proclamaient leur libérateur, ils lui racontaient les maux qu'ils avaient soufferts pendant son absence; ils pouvaient à peine croire à ce qui se passait sous leurs yeux, et dans leur enthousiasme, ils s'étonnaient que Dieu se fut servi d'un seul homme pour soulever tant de nations pour opérer tant de prodiges.

Michaut

5

10

15

20

Comments

When Elizabeth Gaskell interviewed Heger in Brussels, he still owned at least six of Charlotte's devoirs.[1] He had given others away as souvenirs, and presumably he made her a gift of this one, in the version dated July 31 (the June draft had gone home with Charlotte).[2] Whether he and Gaskell chose "Peter" together or he selected it before her arrival, it was a good essay for her purposes. By printing the devoir with his explanation, she could illustrate his methods of teaching and commenting—in her words, "give a proof of his success."[3] She could draw comparisons to Emily's "Harold," also written to imitate Hugo's "On Mirabeau," and then invite her readers to measure Charlotte's progress by reproducing the devoir on Napoleon that Charlotte composed ten months later.

But the sequence is not quite as neat as Gaskell makes it, or perhaps as Heger led her to conclude. Like "Mirabeau," "Peter the Hermit" describes a leader with a turbulent past who rouses people through the power of language and finds himself in finding a cause. Like "Harold," "Peter" portrays that leader on the evening before a famous battle. As Emily seizes on the moment of transfiguration, so Charlotte's first draft catches Peter at the moment where he masters himself.

But Charlotte's devoir alludes to more than "Mirabeau" and brings

134

in more than one of Heger's lessons. It draws on Joseph Michaud's *History of the Crusades,* probably on Carlyle's *On Heroes,* and inevitably on the Bible. Gaskell did not know about the dictée from Michaud, the obvious source of Charlotte's subject, and she says that Heger had the sisters study Carlyle only after "they had made further progress."[4] But Heger might have forgotten a few details, fourteen years and hundreds of students later, and, in any case, ambitious Charlotte Brontë would have wanted to do more than he required.

It is not hard to see why Peter the Hermit appealed to a woman less than five feet tall who struck other students as looking "insignificant" and skinny, "maigrelette."[5] Meager and ill-favored, "without fortune or renown," Peter single-handedly launched the First Crusade through "the force of his character and his genius," or so Michaud alleges in 1808, on the basis of earlier chronicles.[6] Later historians who have sifted fact from legend come up with a somewhat different story. Peter's preaching did inspire an army of peasants, a section of which he led to Constantinople, but the Turks destroyed his troops in 1096, three years before the Siege of Jerusalem, and after that he took his orders from the princes, even trying at one point to escape.[7] Michaud includes much of this material, but, like the legend makers, he glorifies Peter, and Charlotte, less interested in fact than in heroism, uncritically draws on his account. In addition to the "raising up" of nations, an image that occurs at the end of the dictée, "noble family of Picardy," "ignoble and vulgar exterior," "[b]orn with a restless, active spirit," "profession of arms," and "ardent mind" all appear in Michaud, as does a description of the cenobite becoming exalted in solitude.[8]

Whether Heger added these details in class or Charlotte borrowed the book to find them, her apotheosis of Peter goes even further than Michaud's. Wherever she can, she works in biblical allusions—to Samson, the Sermon on the Mount, Elijah, Moses—that reinforce Peter's claims to glory. She seems not to have considered that in drafting such a portrait, she might be guilty of the kind of hagiography she hated when Catholics were responsible. Every evening, students who boarded at the pensionnat heard a "pious lecture" based on legends of the saints. In Gaskell's words, they were "Charlotte's night-mare."[9] Yet Charlotte herself became carried away when she thought about Jerusalem delivered.

But even in childhood, biblical cities had sparked her imagination. (The imaginary canvas in version one, with its "multitude" and Lebanon and Jordan in the background, may owe something to the John Martin engravings that hung on the parsonage walls.)[10] Her fascination with martyrs and missionaries also informs her account of Peter, who combines in one small person the lone man with a cause and the charismatic leader of legions. She had given up romances of the Angrian kind, but the romance of religion, with Peter as its hero, was a licit and tenable replacement.

By bracketing him with Mohammed near the opening, Charlotte foreshadows the conclusion of her essay, where the crescent, symbol of Muslim ascendancy, yields to the Christian cross. She is obviously trying for a formal introduction—Emily, in contrast, plunges into "Harold"— and establishing parameters for heroism. In this, Charlotte probably echoes Carlyle, whose theories about great men she could have encountered on her own or in one of Heger's lectures. Carlyle, of course, did not originate the notion that men of genius sway the course of history. But in his influential study, *On Heroes, Hero-Worship, and the Heroic in History,* he classifies leaders as she starts to do here. In Lecture II, "The Hero as Prophet," he too cites the example of Mohammed, and in Lecture VI, "The Hero as King," one of his examples is Napoleon. Carlyle gave his six lectures in May 1840 and published them in 1841. Charlotte may not have read the book in England, but if she had come across a review of it, she would have known its thesis and framework.[11] And so when Heger asked the Brontës to read Carlyle (on Cromwell, the other subject of Lecture VI) she might for once have been ahead of him.

Her desire to show Heger what she was learning is apparent in several small touches. Hugo says in his opening section that the family's name for Mirabeau was "The Hurricane"; Charlotte begins with a metaphor of tempest. Mirabeau was ugly, his face pitted with smallpox scars, but in speaking, he was "something magnificent"; her Peter has "nothing magnificent" in his form, and yet he is "something quite remarkable."[12]

But perhaps more meaningful to Charlotte than these details was the lesson of Peter's career. He was born, she says, with irrepressible energy and faculties that demanded exercise. He was also born into a rank and a milieu that hampered his use of those faculties. His ardor carried him through wrong choices and a period of isolated penance, but he only achieved greatness when divine inspiration and a mission empowered his eloquence. Then his genius brought him mastery over others and, with the final addition of self-mastery, enabled him to fulfill his promise.

Detaching this plot from its historical particulars makes Charlotte's investment in it clearer. She knew what it was to live with frustrated energies and talent that demanded an outlet. She too had aspirations: to write, to make a difference, to rouse her readers' feelings, to be recognized. The image of Peter, eyes fixed on the heavens while thousands surrounding him attend to his words, is crucial, one suspects, to her fantasies.

But her ambition motivated efforts that got beyond her control. Yielding to fervor, she forgot Heger's warning: "*Remorselessly* sacrifice everything that does not contribute to clarity, verisimilitude, and effect."[13] Emily Brontë needed no prompting from Heger to stick to the point. Her devoir keeps strictly to Harold in his territory, building toward the moment that transforms him. In contrast, Charlotte promises a portrait of a great man and delivers a religious encomium. She opens with a sweep through history and then shifts bumpily to Peter. She implies that she will focus on his greatness as a leader but detours to his troubled soul and then, in draft one, to her imaginary canvas. She never shows Peter the orator in action, as Hugo so lavishly shows Mirabeau.

Heger responds to both drafts of the devoir, as he probably did in other cases where the manuscripts have not survived. He seems to have gone quickly through the June version, revising imagery and details in the first half and indicating passages to cut. In the July version Charlotte follows his suggestions, exchanging her words for his and cutting canceled passages, but she herself initiates few changes. He goes through that draft more thoroughly, adding marginal comments and corrections, some to lines he left alone earlier. Grammar aside, his revisions trim excess, especially religious excess, and refine the details of her phrasing. In effect, he extends the lesson on "Mirabeau" in which he pointed out that the fault of Hugo's style was "exaggeration in conception" and the beauty, "his 'nuances' of expression."[14] He also tries to hold her to her subject, though his promptings are not always consistent. In one round, he praises her allusion to Samson; in the next, he strikes it out. In June he leaves her conclusion alone; in July he reworks it. Nor does he always recognize the signs of her diligence and enterprise.

When she paints her imaginary canvas in version one, "the image of the Cenobite amid the armed crusaders," she is not just writing picturesque prose with a subtext. She is echoing a passage by Michaud. Heger did not dictate the lines in which Peter stands on the Mount of Olives, exhorting the troops and promising them victory at the next day's siege of Jerusalem.[15] But Charlotte could assume he had read them, so that though she abandons Hugo's genre of portrait, she does not abandon Heger's lessons. If he had asked for another kind of devoir, he might even have praised her description. Instead he puts two pencil strokes through its opening,[16] and she deletes two picture-making paragraphs in version two.

If Charlotte had been more like Emily, she might have held her ground and kept her tableau. If she had been more like Lucy Snow in *Villette,* she might at least have argued for her vision. But Lucy was a fiction, more than ten years in the future. For the Charlotte Brontë of 1842, as for the speaker of a poem she wrote later, "Obedience was [the] heart's free choice."[17] She followed Heger's orders in revising her devoir, and, again, she wrote a happy ending.

Letter .

Madam,

Tomorrow, there will be a small musical party at our house, to which
I am directed to invite you. The execution of that order gives me great
pleasure, because I can assure you that the pieces are well chosen, that
most of the musicians are skillful, and therefore, that you will spend
some pleasant hours here.

Beyond the pleasure of seeing you, your friends expect from your
hands a [contribution] to the evening's amusements. Thus I hope that
you will not refuse to come, since that would be a deprivation, both for
you and for them.

I am, Madam,

your respectful student

Reply.

Dear Miss,

It would have been, in truth, a great pleasure for me had I been able
to accept your invitation; but in a life like mine, our inclination cannot
always be followed, and unfortunately the day of your party is, of all the
days of my week, the busiest. Thus I find myself obliged to give up the
pleasure of seeing my friends and of contributing whatever I could to
their amusement.

But when I suffer a disappointment, I ordinarily seek some compensa-
tion in return; and at present, I console myself with the thought that if I
am denied the opportunity to exhibit my small talent, at least, I will not

Lettre .

Madame,

Demain, il y aura chez nous une petite soirée musicale, à laquelle je
suis dirigée à vous inviter. L'exécution de cet ordre me donne beaucoup   5
de plaisir, parceque je puis vous assurer que les morceaux sont bien
choisis, que la plupart des musiciens sont habiles, et par conséquence,
que vous y passiez quelques heures agréables.

Outre le plaisir de vous voir, vos amis attendent à vos mains une [?]
aux amusements de la soirée, ainsi j'espère que vous ne refusiez pas d'y   10
venir, puisqu'il serait une privation, et pour vous-même, et pour eux.

> Je suis, Madame,
> votre élève respecteuse

Réponse.

Mademoiselle,   15

Il aurait été, en verité, un grand plaisir pour moi si j'avais pu
accepter votre invitation; mais dans une vie comme la mienne, il ne faut
pas toujours suivre notre inclination et malheureusement, le jour de votre
soirée, est, de tous les jours de ma semaine, le plus occupé: ainsi je me
trouve obligée à renoncer au bonheur de voir mes amis et de contribuer   20
ce que je pusse à leur amusement.

Mais lorsque j'éprouve des contre-temps je cherche ordinairement
quelque dédommagement en revanche, et à présent, je me console avec
l'idée que si je suis privée de l'opportunité d'exhiber mon petit talent, au

undergo the mortification of witnessing the poor results of my work with you; because I have heard that you are to play a piece on this occasion, and forgive me if I advise you (out of pure friendship) to choose a time when everyone is occupied with something other than music, for I fear that your performance will be a little too remarkable.

Still, I would not want to discourage you. Good day, and good luck with all my heart.

———

moins, je n'aurais pas la mortification d'être témoin du mauvais succès 25
de mon travail à l'égard de vous; parceque j'ai ouï dire que vous deviez
jouer un morceau sur cette occasion, et pardonnez moi si je vous conseille (c'est par pure amitié) de choisir le temps quand tout le monde sont
occupé d'autre chose que la musique, car je crains que votre exécution
ne soit un peu trop remarquable. 30

Cependant je ne voudrais vous décourager, bon jour, et bon succès
de tout mon coeur ___

———

Letter

of invitation to a Clergyman

====

Dear Sir,

          pastor
  In fulfilling your duties as a priest[?], have you never found yourself obliged to write a letter to a rich miser, to entreat him to contribute to a charitable fund? If you have found yourself in this circumstance you may very well imagine my feelings in addressing you at this moment.

  "But," you say, "I am not a miser." Yes, sir, you are, and so much
         always
so that until now it has˘ been alw impossible for me to wrest from you the least part of that treasure you guard with such vigilance. That treasure, sir, is not money; it is time. I beseech you, be generous for once. Next Thursday I am giving a small party at home, and I entreat you to honor it with your presence. Be sure that in granting me a few hours of your so precious time, you will turn it to better account than by remaining at home, or perhaps even by visiting the poor of your parish. I need not tell you how much the presence of a pious and respectable clergyman in a society contributes to curbing all vain and idle remarks, nor how much the conversation of a learned man adds to the pleasure and profit of the gathering. Neither need I tell you that my friends share my feelings toward you, and that if you come your arrival will be a pleasure for all, whereas if you do not come your absence will be for all a disappointment.

    Begging to remain, Sir, yours sincerely,

      &c. . . . . .

Lettre

d'invitation à un Ecclésiastique

======

Monsieur
                                    pasteur
En remplissant vos devoirs comme prêtre[?] vous êtes vous jamais   5

trouve dans la necessité d'écrire une lettre à un riche avare pour lui prier

de contribuer à un fonds charitable? Si une telle circonstance vous est

arrivée, vous pouvez très bien concevoir quels sont mes sentiments en

vous adressant dans ce moment.

"Cependant" dites-vous "Je ne suis pas avare." Oui monsieur vous   10
                                    toujours
l'étes et à un tel point que jusqu'ici il m'a^été tou impossible de vous

dérober la moindre partie de ce trésor que vous gardez avec tant de vigi-

lance: ce trésor monsieur, ce n'est pas l'argent, c'est le temps. Je vous

en supplie soyez généreux pour une seule fois; Jeudi prochain je donne

une petite soirée chez moi et je vous prie de vouloir bien l'honorer de   15

votre présence; soyez sûr qu'en m'accordant quelques heures de ce temps

si précieux q vous le mettrez plus à profit qu'en restant chez vous, ou

peutêtre même en visitant les pauvres de votre paroisse. Je n'ai pas

besoin de vous dire combien la présence d'un ecclésiastique pieux et

respectable dans une Société, contribue à réprimer tous propos vains et   20

inutiles, ni combien la conversation d'un homme instruit ajoute aux

agréments et aux avantages de la réunion. Je n'ai pas non plus besoin de

vous dire que mes amis partage mes sentiments à votre égard, et que si

vous venez votre arrivée sera un plaisir pour tous, au contraire si vous

ne venez pas votre absence sera pour tout un désappointement.   25

Je vous prie Monsieur d'accepter les assurances de mon estime et de

mon affection inalterable

&c. . . . . . .

======

Reply

You know, Sir, that whenever one wishes to take a step of any kind, there are always two personages to consult, Inclination and Duty. Now, when I received your kind invitation, I first consulted Inclination. "Go," said she, "you will have a great deal of pleasure, you will spend a charming evening, you will enjoy the society and the conversation of those whom you like and who like you." I was on the point of yielding when Duty spoke: "But you cannot go," said he. "You have already promised to visit such and such persons, to fulfill such and such obligations; in accepting this invitation you will break your promise; do you think that your time is your own? No. It is an asset that belongs to your parishioners, and of which you are only the guardian. You must be thrifty with it, even miserly. Take your pen, thank your friend and tell him that you cannot come." Thus, Sir, I have obeyed that strict monitor; and if I do not beg you to pardon me, it is because I am convinced that in obeying him I only do what I have to do.

Farewell &c. . . . . .

======

Vous savez Monsieur que lorsqu'on veut faire une démarche quel- 30
conque, il y a toujours deux personnages à consulter, l'Inclination et le
Devoir. Or, quand j'ai reçu votre bonne invitation j'ai consulté d'abord
l'Inclination "Allez" dit-elle "vous aurez beaucoup de plaisir vous pas-
serez une charmante soirée, vous jouirez de la société et de la conversation de ceux que vous aimez et qui vous aiment." J'étais sur le point de 35
céder lorsque le Devoir prit la parole "Mais vous ne pouvez-pas aller
dit-il Vous avez déjà promis de visiter telles et telles personnes de
remplir telles et telles obligations; en acceptant cette invitation vous man-
querez à votre parole: pensez vous que votre temps êtes à vous? Non
c'est un bien qui appartient à vos paroissiens et dont vous n'êtes que le 40
gardien; vous devez en être économe, avare même: prenez votre plume,
remerciez votre ami et dites lui que vous ne pouvez pas venir." Ainsi
Monsieur j'ai obéi à ce moniteur sévère − et si je ne vous prie pas de me
pardonner c'est parceque je suis convaincu qu'en lui obéissant je ne fais
que ce que je dois faire 45

Adieu &c......

Comments

The probable instructions for this pair of matching devoirs—compose an invitation to a party, then have the recipient decline it—do not leave much room for self-expression. Still, both sisters used what there was.

Emily was making rapid progress as a pianist and was soon to study under Heger's brother-in-law, M. Chapelle, a teacher at the Royal Conservatory.[1] Perhaps in exchange, the Hegers asked her to give piano lessons to younger girls whose parents requested that option; Emily reluctantly complied. As Laetitia Wheelwright reported years later, "She taught my three youngest sisters music for 4 months, to my annoyance, as she would only take them in play hours so as not to curtail her own school hours. . . ."[2] Her impatience with inferior performance and her resistance to polite social formulas are visible throughout this devoir, whose brevity may be a further sign of her defiance.

Like Emily, the pupil who extends the invitation writes under orders. She addresses her married, adult teacher with respect, but she also keeps her blandishments minimal. At this musical soiree, the participants perform; conversation is not cited as an option. The flattery quotient is low, compared to Charlotte's, and the economics of inducement differ as well. Where Charlotte's petitioner entreats a miser by holding out the hope of mutual profit, Emily's expects her guest to make a contribution in return for having been invited. The extraordinary twist in the penultimate paragraph is somehow typical of Emily. Whether she intended its tactlessness and humor will probably remain a moot question. But as Edward Chitham comments, she "seems to be taking no pains to commend herself personally" to Heger.[3]

In contrast, Charlotte's letter ingratiates self-consciously. The form of the assignment, request and response, suits her proclivity for dialogue. In both sections, she elaborates on the format, adding questions and answers within the invitation and personification in the answer. Never slow to voice her Protestant principles, she writes in the guise of a male parishioner—insistent, self-abasing, and long-winded. The clergyman's response sustains the economic metaphor and complicates the gender issues further: Inclination, feminine in French, yields to Duty, imperative and masculine.

But Charlotte did not invent these personages in response to the assignment Heger gave her. They lingered in her memory from Roe Head. At fifteen, she had written to her new friend, Ellen Nussey, "I am extremely obliged to your Sister for her kind invitation. . . . But we are often compelled to bend our inclinations to our duty (as Miss Wooler observed the other day)."[4]

Both devoirs pose problems for the translator. Emily's does not always make full sense in French because its syntax is so anglicized. Charlotte's does not because her urge toward complex French constructions sometimes outstrips her control. For her, each assignment becomes an invitation to reach, however awkwardly, beyond her limitations to gain the treasure of her master's comments.

Letter

My dear Mama,

It seems to me a very long time since I have seen you, and a long
time, even, that I have not heard from you. If you were ill, they would
have written me; I am not afraid of that, but I am afraid that you think
less often of your daughter in her absence. Lately, I am saddened by
very little things, and at this thought above all, I cannot help crying.
They say that my health is frail, and they have made me keep to my
room and give up my studies and my companions. It is perhaps for this
reason that I am^{so} sad, because it is very tiresome to be confined the
whole day in a solitary chamber where I have nothing to do, from
morning until night, but to daydream and to listen, from time to time, to
the joyous cries of the other children, who play and laugh without
thinking of me.

I long to be at home once again, and to see the house and the people
that I love so much. At least if you could come here, I believe that your
presence alone would cure me.

Come then, dear Mama, and forgive this letter; it speaks only of me,
but I myself would speak to you of many other things.

Your devoted daughter,

Lettre

Ma chère Maman,

   Il me semble bien longtemps depuis que je vous aie vue, et long-
temps même, que je n'aie pas reçu de vos nouvelles. Si vous étiez   5
malade, on m'écrirait; je ne crains pas cela, mais je crains que vous
songiez moins souvent de votre fille dans son absence; dernierement,
je suis attristé par de très petites choses, et à cette idée surtout, je ne
puis m'empêcher de pleurer. On dit que ma santé est faible, et on m'a
fait garder ma chambre et quitter mes études et mes compagnes; c'est   10
                                              si
peut-être pour cette raison que je suis^ triste, parce qu'il est bien ennuyeux d'être enfermée toute la journée dans un appartement solitaire, où
je n'ai rien à faire, du matin jusqu'au soir, que de rêver et d'écouter,
de temps en temps, les cris joyeux des autres enfants, qui jouent et rient
sans songer de moi.   15

   Il me tarde d'être chez nous encore une fois, et de voir la maison
et les personnes que j'aime tant. Au moins si vous pouviez venir ici,
je crois que votre seule présence me guerirait.—

   Venez donc, chère Maman, et pardonnez cette lettre; elle ne parle
que de moi, mais moi, je vous parlerais de bien d'autres choses.   20

                              Votre fille devouée,

Emily Brontë   July 26th 1842

Letter

My dear Mama,

                    that It is a   *very*
It seems to me a ~~very~~ long time since I have seen you, and a long
          also   since
time even, that I have not heard from you. If you were ill, they would
                    that reassures me a little
have written me; I am not afraid of that, but I am afraid that you think
                    absent   *Here, in my exile, it takes only*
less often of your daughter in her absence. Lately, I am saddened by
          to make me sad; and ~~when it occurs to me~~ at the idea that I could be forgotten
very little things, and at this thought above all, I cannot help crying.
                    to me here
They say that my health is frail; ~~and~~ they have made me keep to my
                                                    also
room and give up | my studies and my companions. It is perhaps for this
                    so
reason, that I am sad,: ~~because~~ it is very tiresome to be confined the
          alone, isolated   *there is*   *except*
whole day in a solitary chamber where | ~~I have~~ nothing to do | , from
          to
morning ~~until~~ night, ~~but to~~ daydream and ~~to~~ listen, from time to time,

to the joyous cries of the other children, who play, and laugh without

thinking of me.
                    go   *all*
I long to be at home, once again, and to see *again* the house and the
          those
people that I love ~~so much~~. *If* At least ~~if~~ you could come here, I believe
                              restore happiness and health.
that your presence alone would cure me.
                              if in   I
Come then, dear Mama; and forgive this letter, it speaks only of me,
come; I have to
~~but~~ I ~~myself~~ would speak to you of many other things.

                              Your devoted daughter,

No token of remembrance for papa? —
                              C. Heger
          that's a mistake.

Good (margin line 12)
Good (margin line 16)

Emily Brontë   <u>26 Juillet 1842</u>

Lettre

Ma chère Maman,

           qu' Il y a p   *trop*
    Il ~~me semble bien~~ longtemps <u>de</u>puis que je vous ai<u>t</u> vue, et long-
     aussi   *n'ai*
temps <u>même</u>, que je n'aie pàs reçu de vos nouvelles. Si vous étiez   5
               cela me rassure un peu ⌐
malade, on m'écrirait; je ne crains pas cela, | mais je crains que vous
                   à   *te*   *il me faut ici,*
songiez moins souvent <u>de</u> votre fille dàhs sòh | absencè; dèrhièrèmènt,
dans mon exil,   *que de*   *pr m'attrister.— et ~~quand me vient~~ à*
je <u>suis</u> <u>attristé par de très petites</u> choses, | et <u>à cette idée</u> surtout, je ne
l'idée qu'on m'oublie   *me ici*
puis m'empêcher de pleurer. On dit que ma santé est faible; ~~et~~ on m'a

fait garder ma chambre et quitter | mes études et mes compagnes; c'est   10
    aussi   *si*
peut-être pour cette raison, que je suis triste,: ~~parce qu~~'il est bien ennu-
                     ⌐*seule, isolée*
yeux d'être enfermée toute la journée|<u>dans un appartement solitaire,</u> où
    à ne   *sinon*
| ~~je n~~'ai rien à faire |, du matin ~~jusqu~~'au soir, ~~que de~~ rêver et ~~d~~'écouter,   *Bon*

de temps en temps, les cris joyeux des autres enfants, qui jouent, et rient
       à
sans songer <u>de</u> moi.   15
         de rentrer
    Il me tarde d'être chez nous, <u>encore une fois</u>, èt de *re*voir la maison
    tous ceux   *Bon*
et l<u>es</u> p<u>erson</u>nes que j'aime ~~tant~~. *Si* Au moins Sì vous pouviez venir ici,
                              rendrait joie et santé.
je crois que votre seule présence mè guerirait.—
                     si dans   *je*
    Venez donc, chère Maman; et pardonnez cette lettre\~~elle~~ ne par<u>le</u>
     venez; j'ai à ⌐
que de moi, ~~mais moi~~, je vous parlerais de bien d'autres choses.   20

                             Votre fille <u>devouée</u>,

Aucune marque de souvenir pr papa —
                              C. Heger
          <u>*c'est une faute*</u>.

Comments

Emily Brontë wrote three successive devoirs on relationships among family members; this is the first and the shortest. It is also the only text from Brussels or Haworth that brings a daughter into contact with her mother, if only to reveal the space between them.

When Emily was three years old, her own mother died, after seven months of lying close to death. Patrick Brontë withdrew in grief, emerging as a concerned but hard-pressed parent to his six children. Although Maria, the eldest, tried to act as a mother and Aunt Branwell came from Penzance to supervise the household, Emily learned autonomy early.

Her letter writer complains of languishing in solitude (perhaps, as Margaret Homans says, in quarantine).[1] She herself found solitude essential. But sequestered in the pensionnat, cut off from Haworth and the moors, she must have suffered agonies of homesickness.[2] Her health held up, however; she did not become an invalid; stoic resolution kept her going. The weak and plaintive child of the devoir is a construct, achieved despite the limits of the author's French.

Emily may have been writing to order, rather than using her letter as a medium for a more personal appeal. Poems about suffering female innocents seem to have been staples of Heger's teaching; Charlotte wrote

"The Sick Young Girl" on April 18 in response to "The Poor Girl," which he dictated. But the interval of three months suggests that the sisters were not fulfilling the same assignment—unless Heger waited until Emily had learned sufficient French to respond to Soumet's verses.

Or she may have been drawing on her Gondal saga, in which, according to Fanny Ratchford, adversity separates children from their parents or leaves them to imprisonment and suffering.[3] In her other extant writings, however, she shows contempt for characters who lack the resources to sustain themselves, whether they are children or adults.

Absence is very much the theme of the devoir. The letter writer suffers from loss of health and homesickness; she dreads being out of others' thoughts. The mother she addresses is both literally distant and missing as an individual separate from the daughter, who focuses almost exclusively on her own illness, deprivation, and desires. All the other references to people are generic—"they," "my companions," "other children," "persons"—and as Heger notes, there is no sign of a father.

He has corrected her short page extensively, perhaps an indication of his interest in her progress, or in family sentiment, or both. His changes make her language more idiomatic but sacrifice its childlike directness.

Five years later, on her own territory, Emily created young Linton Heathcliff, another self-absorbed and fretful invalid. Though by then she must have given little conscious thought to devoirs, perhaps their traces did not fade entirely.[4]

Filial Love

"Honor thy father and thy mother if thou wouldst live." It is by such
a commandment that God gives us knowledge of the baseness of our
race, of how it appears in His sight. To fulfill the gentlest, the holiest
of all duties man must be threatened; it is through fear that the maniac
must be forced to sanctify himself. In this commandment is hidden a
more bitter reproach than any open accusation could contain, a charge
against us of absolute blindness or of infernal ingratitude.

Parents love their children; this is a principle of nature. The doe
does not fear the dogs when her little one is in danger; the bird dies on
its nest. This instinct is a particle of the divine spirit we share with
every animal that exists. Has God not put a similar feeling into the heart
of the child? Truly there is something of the kind, yet still the voice of
thunder cries out, "Honor your parents or you will die!" Now, that
commandment is not given, that threat is not added, for nothing. There
may be men who scorn their happiness, their duty, and their God to such
a point that the spark of heavenly fire dies out in their breast, leaving
them a moral chaos without light and without order, a hideous transfiguration of the image in which they were created.

These monsters, the virtuous soul does well to shun with horror. It
is a just instinct; we must shun them, but do not curse them. Why add
our malediction to God's? Rather pity, rather lament their condition.
For they have never given a thought to what their parents have done for
them. For the memory of their youth has never recalled ^to them^ the hopes and
affection of the father they disobey; and the long hours of patient suffer-

L'Amour Filial

"Tu honoreras ton père et ta mère si tu veux vivre". C'est par un tel
commandement que Dieu nous donne une connaissance de la bassesse de
notre race, de ce qu'elle paraît à ses yeux; pour remplir le plus doux, le   5
plus saint de tous les devoirs il lui faut une menace; c'est par peur qu'il
faut forcer la maniaque à bénir elle-même. Dans cette commandement
est caché un reproche plus amer qu'aucune accusation ouverte ne puisse
renfermer, une charge contre nous, d'aveuglement entier ou d'ingratitude
infernale.   10

  Les parents aiment leurs enfants, c'est un principe de la nature; la
daine ne craint pas les chiens lorsque son petit est en danger, l'oiseau
meurt sur son nid; cet instinct est une particule de l'âme divine que nous
partageons avec tout animal qui existe, et Dieu n-a-t-il pas mis dans le
coeur de l'enfant un pareil sentiment? Quelque chose vraiment il y a et   15
cependant la voix tonnante leur crie: "Honorez vos parents ou vous
mourerez!" Or, ce commandement n'est pas donné, cette menace n'est
pas ajoutée pour rien: il peut être des hommes qui méprisent leur bonheur, leur devoir et leur Dieu à ce point que l'étincelle de feu céleste
s'éteint dans leur sein, et les laisse un chaos moral sans lumière et sans   20
ordre, une transfiguration hidieuse de l'image dans laquelle ils étaient
créés.

  Ces monstres, l'âme verteuse est portée d'éviter avec horreur. C'est
un instinct juste, nous devons les éviter, mais ne les maudissez pas. pourquoi ajouter notre malediction à celle de Dieu? Plutôt plaignez, plutôt   25
pleurez leur condition. C'est qu'ils n'aient jamais pensé de ce que leurs
parents ont fait pour eux. C'est que la mémoire de leurs jeunes ans
                                                                    leur
ne'^a jamais rappelé les espérances et l'affection de ce père qu'ils

ing, the cares, the tears, the untiring devotion of the mother whom they kill by the cruelest of deaths, turning to poison the limitless love that should be the sustenance of her unhappy old age.

³⁰ The hour will come when conscience will awake; then there will be a terrible retribution. What mediator will plead then for the criminal? It is God who accuses him. What power will save the wretch? It is God who condemns him. He has rejected happiness in mortal life to assure himself of torment in eternal life.

³⁵ Let angels and men weep for his fate — he was their brother.

désobeissent; et les longues heures de patiente souffrance, les soins, les larmes la dévotion infatigable de cette mère qu'ils tuent par la plus cruelle des morts, tournant en poison l'amour illimité qui doit être la nourriture de sa malheureuse viellesse.

L'heure viendra quand la conscience s'evleillera, alors il aura une rétribution terrible; quel médiateur plaidera alors pour le criminel? C'est Dieu qui l'accuse; Quelle puissance sauvera le miserable? c'est Dieu qui le condamne. Il a rejeté le bonheur dans la vie mortelle pour s'assurer du tourment dans la vie éternelle.

Que les anges et les hommes pleurent son sort — il était leur frère.

―――――――

Comments

Shut from his Maker's smile
The accursed man shall be
Compassion reigns a little while
Revenge eternally—

—Emily Brontë[1]

On August 5, ten days before the long vacation and ten days after "My dear Mother," Emily finished "Filial Love" and "Letter from one brother to another." No instructions accompany these devoirs, and nothing in Charlotte's notebooks corresponds to this one, although she did write an earlier essay entitled "Ingratitude," now missing. Emily could have been fulfilling a series of linked assignments on the family, but these pieces do not form an easy triptych. The first half of "The Butterfly," submitted six days later, is closer to "Filial Love" in mood and imagery, and factors that have nothing to do with the topic could account for the dates of their production. As the end of term neared, Emily might have realized that she still owed Heger second drafts of old papers and produced them in a flurry of activity.[2]

Whatever Heger called for, Emily's response could hardly have been what he expected. As her starting point, she takes the Fifth Commandment: "Honor thy father and thy mother: that thy days may be long upon the land which the Lord thy God giveth thee."[3] Her paraphrase, however, replaces the incentive of the King James version with a threat. An exegesis follows, as grim as any Calvinist sermon that could have marked her childhood.

How might she have come to her position? Tom Winnifrith proposes several possible sources for the young Brontës' views of eternal punishment: Patrick Brontë, Carus Wilson, Henry Nussey, and Edward Robinson, whose library contained an "impressive array of Evangelical sermons."[4] Any one of these men might also have preached or written of children's relations to their parents. Certainly, the parallels between this devoir and Calvin's sermon on the Fifth Commandment suggest that at some point Emily heard judgments on filial ingratitude that stayed with her: "Now it is quite a detestable thing, as well as contrary to nature, for a child not to acknowledge those through whom he came into the world, those who have fed and clothed him. Therefore when a child disowns his father and his mother, he is a monster. Everyone will look upon him with disgust. And why? [Because] without God speaking a word, without our having any holy Scripture, or anyone preaching to us, nature already shows us that a child's duty toward his father and mother is one which cannot be broken."[5]

There is also a suggestion of Wesleyan theology in the two questions at the end of the devoir, which correspond in form to a biblical passage that underlies the Doctrine of Justification: "Who shall lay any thing to the charge of God's elect? It is God that justifieth. Who is he that condemneth? It is Christ . . . who also maketh intercession for us."[6] But if Emily's language echoes the text Wesley drew on, her purpose, unlike his, is to accuse. Her wretches reverse the order of creation, casting themselves from light into darkness[7] and behaving with maniacal unreason. In short, whatever her debt to such doctrines, she also redefines them to make them congruent with a harsher personal theology.

Inflexible judgments of the human condition are characteristic of her devoirs. But the ending of this one is uncharacteristic in its fracturing of narrative consistency. Unlike Charlotte, Emily usually pursues her topics with undeviating logic. The rhetorical patterns are clear and consistent: effect follows cause, examples illustrate ideas, and conclusions reflect back on openings. So a daughter starts by speaking of a mother's long absence and ends by imploring her to come; a king experiences moments of insight and, as a result, becomes heroic. This devoir progresses reasonably enough from an issue (filial love corrupted in humans), to an outcome (monsters of ingratitude), and then to a further issue (how should we regard them?) and its outgrowth (God will take charge; pity them). But when "they" gives way to "him" in the penultimate paragraph, or even with the anguished mother in the line above, the narrative abruptly turns personal. The object of her questions is no generic outcast: he is an unsalvageable brother.

Has she heard something new about Branwell? Has she recalled some character from Gondal? In "Lines," a poem she wrote in 1839, the speaker wonders whether an "iron man," known from childhood and since turned criminal, has become "So lost that not a gleam may come / No vision of his mother's face." After a single glance at him, however, the speaker gives up hope for his redemption.[8] Janet Gezari conjectures that this poem transposes news of Branwell to a Gondal episode;[9] perhaps a similar transposition occurs at the end of "Filial Love," but the clues are much too slim to be reliable.

First page of Emily Brontë's "Letter from one brother to another." Harry Ransom Humanities Research Center, University of Texas at Austin..

Emily J. Brontë.   [draft before correction]   August 5th 1842

Letter

from one brother to another

===============

My brother,

A letter received from me will be for you as a letter received from the tomb. Ten long years, ten years of suffering, of work and of change have gone by since we departed from our father's house, angry with each other and vowing an eternal separation. Those years have dissipated many hopes, in my case they have brought many griefs, but amidst it all, I kept hidden in my heart that vow, born of anger and fed by pride.

I have crossed the ocean, I have traveled in a number of countries, I have been the poorest of the poor, ill among strangers, without the power to offer the work of my hands in exchange for the bread that I was eating. Also, I have delighted in riches and all the pleasures that they can provide for their possessor; but always alone, always friendless, enough to flatter me, but no one to love me.

Nonetheless I never dreamed of being reconciled with you; I did not wish to enjoy again that erstwhile harmony of souls which formed the happiness of our childhood, or if the thought came to me sometimes I chased it away as an unworthy and degrading weakness.

At length my body and my spirit were weary of wandering; my bark was tossed by storms, I longed to come into port. I formed the resolution to end my days where they were begun and I directed my course toward the land and the house so long abandoned.

Yesterday at evening I arrived at the old gates of the park; it was a night of storm and pouring rain but through the darkness I distinguished from afar the light of the windows, which cast long rays

Lettre

d'un frère à un frère

=========

Mon frère,

Une lettre reçue de moi sera pour vous comme une lettre reçue du   5

tombeau. Dix longs ans, dix ans de souffrance, de travail et de change-

ment se sont passés depuis nous partîmes de la maison de notre père,

irrites l'un contre l'autre et vouant une séparation éternelle. Ces ans

ont dissipé bien des espérances à mon egard ils ont apporté bien

des douleurs, mais au milieu de tout, je conservais caché dans mon coeur   10

ce voeu, né de la colère et nourri de l'orgeuil.

J'ai traversé l'océan, j'ai voyagé dans plusieurs pays, j'ai été le plus

pauvre des pauvres, malade parmi des étrangers, sans le pouvoir d'offrir

le travail de mes mains en échange pour le pain que je mangeais. Aussi,

j'ai joui des richesses et de tous les plaisirs qu'elles puissent fournir au   15

possesseur; mais toujours seul, toujours sans ami, assez de me flatter,

mais personne de m'aimer.

Cependant je ne songeais jamais de me réconcilier avec vous; je ne

désirais pas de gouter encore cette ancienne concorde d'âmes qui formait

le bonheur de notre enfance, ou si la pensée me venait quelquefois je   20

la chassai bientôt comme une faiblesse indigne et dégradante.

Enfin mon corps et mon esprit étaient fatigués d'errer; ma barque

était ébranlée des tempêtes, il me tardait d'être au port. Je formai la

résolution de finir mes jours où ils s'étaient commencés et je dirigai

mon cours vers la terre et la maison si longtemps abandonnées.   25

Hier au soir je suis arrivé aux vieilles portes du parc; c'était une nuit

orageuse et versante de pluie mais à travers l'obscurité je distinguais

de loin la lumière des fenêtres qui lançait de longs rayons á entre les

between the branches of the trees and guided me to the door. I entered
all was tranquil within. I traversed the hall, the corridor, the ante-
chambers, without encountering anyone and found myself finally in the
library, our own retreat, the place consacrated to so many memories that
a century of estrangement could not efface. While I contemplated by the
uncertain light of the fire the paintings on the walls, the rows of books
underneath, and all the familiar objects that surrounded me, something
stirred in the room. It was a large dog that arose from a corner and
approached to examine the stranger; he did not find a stranger. He
recognized me, and he attested his recognition by the most expressive
caresses; but I pushed him away, because he was yours.

Forgive, Edward, this last act of the tyrant who had so long usurped
the place of nature in my breast; an instant later I was on my knees
praying and crying and abjuring my enmity forever; I went to bed happy,
I awake h̶a̶p̶p̶y̶ sad; perhaps that my repentence comes too late, perhaps
that your heart is hardened more than mine. But in the past my brother
was always the last to become angry and the first to forget an injury.
Edward, come assure me that your nature has not changed — do not write
but come.

rameaux des arbres et me guidait à la porte. J'y entrai tout était

tranquille en-dedans je traversai la salle, le corridor, les antichambres, 30

sans recontrer aucune personne et me trouvai enfin dans la bibliothèque

notre propre retraite, le lieu consacré à tant de souvenirs qu'un siècle

d'éloignement ne pût effacer. Pendant je contemplais par la lumière

douteuse du feu, les tableaux sur les murs, les rangs de livres au dessous

et tous les objets familiers qui m'entourait, quelquechose se remuait 35

dans la chambre c'était un grand chien qui s'éleva d'un coin et s'appro-

chait pour examiner l'étranger, il ne trouva pas un étranger; il m're-

conn~~aissait~~nut et il témoigna sa reconnaissance par des caresses les plus

expressives; mais moi, je le repoussai, parcequ'il était le votre.

Pardonnez, Edouard, à ce dernier acte du tyran qui avait usurpé si 40

longtemps la place de la nature dans mon sein; l'instant après je fut à

genoux priant et pleurant et abjurant mon inimitie pour jamais je me

couchai heureux, je me éveille ~~heureux~~ triste; peutêtre que mon repentir

vienne trop tard; peutêtre que votre coeur soit plus endurci que le mien.

mais mon frère était autrefois toujours le dernier à se fâcher et le premier 45

à oublier une injure. Edouard viens m'assurer que votre nature n'est pas

changé — n'ecris pas mais viens

Emily J. Brontë.   August 5th 1842

— fault
⁓ revise
Letter

from one brother to another

===========

My brother,

come from
A letter (received) from me will be for you as a letter received from
beyond the grave
the tomb. Ten long years, ten years of suffering, of work and of change
slowly slipped away[?]   left
have gone by since we departed from our father's house, angry with each
mutually   hatred   extinguished in me
other and vowing an eternal separation. Those years have dissipated
and
many hopes, (in my case) they have brought *me* many griefs, but amidst

it all, I kept hidden in my heart that vow, born of anger and fed by

pride.
many
I have crossed the ocean, I have traveled in a number of countries,

I have been the poorest of the poor, ill among strangers, without the

power to offer the work of my hands in exchange for the bread that I was
Sometimes
eating. Also, I have delighted │in riches and all the pleasures that they
buy
can provide for their possessor│; but always alone, always friendless,

(enough to flatter me), but no one to love me.

Nonetheless I never dreamed of being reconciled with you; I did not
that tender and calm
wish to enjoy again that erstwhile harmony of souls (which formed the)
that
happiness of our childhood, or if the thought came to me sometimes I

chased it away as an unworthy and degrading weakness.
being
At length my body and my spirit ~~were~~ weary of wandering; my bark
so many
(~~was~~) tossed by storms, I longed to come into port. I formed the reso-
had   wished to see again—
lution to end my days where they were begun and (I directed my course
┌─────────┐ *of my birth   family*
toward) the land and the house so long abandoned.

Yesterday ~~at~~ evening I arrived at the old gates of the park; it
on
was a night of storm and pouring rain; but through the darkness I dis-
projecting   pale
tinguished from afar the light of the windows, which cast long rays

Emily J. Brontë.   5 Août 1842

− *faute*
⌣ *à changer*   Lettre

                          d'un frère à un frère

                          ════════

Mon frère,
                                                          venue d'
    Une lettre (reçue) de moi sera pour vous comme une lettre reçue du   5
outre tombe   *nées*   *nées*
tombeau. Dix longs ans, dix ans de souffrance, de travail et de change-
              lentement écoulées[?]   *avons quitté*
ment se sont passés depuis nous partîmes de la maison de notre père,
                          nous   *haine*   *ées*
irrites l'un contre l'autre et vouant une séparation éternelle. Ces ans
              éteint en moi   *et*
ont dissipé bien des espérances (à mon égard) ils m'ont apporté bien

des douleurs, mais au milieu de tout, je conservais caché dans mon coeur   10

ce voeu, né de la colère et nourri de l'orgeuil.
                                  maints
    J'ai traversé l'océan, j'ai voyagé dans plusieurs pays, j'ai été le plus

pauvre des pauvres, malade parmi des étrangers, sans le pouvoir d'offrir
                                  du   *Parfois*
le travail de mes mains en échange pour le pain que je mangeais. Aussi,
                                  qui s'achètent
j'ai joui des richesses et de tous les plaisirs qu'elles puissent fournir au   15

possesseur; mais toujours seul, toujours sans ami, (assez de me flatter),
              pour
mais personne de m'aimer.
                              à
    Cependant je ne songeais jamais de me réconcilier avec vous; je ne
                                          ce doux et
désirais pas de goûter encore cette ancienne concorde d'âmes (qui formait
calme   *cette*
le) bonheur de notre enfance, ou si la pensée me venait quelquefois je   20

la chassais bientôt comme une faiblesse indigne et dégradante.
                              ant
    Enfin mon corps et mon esprit étaient fatigués d'errer; ma barque
              tant de
(était) ébranlée des tempêtes, il me tardait d'être au port. Je formai la
                              avaient   *voulus*
résolution de finir mes jours où ils s'étaient commencés et (je dirigai
revoir ————————   *natale*   *paternelle*
mon cours vers) la terre et la maison si longtemps abandonnées.   25
                                          par
    Hier au soir je suis arrivé aux vieilles portes du parc; c'était une nuit

orageuse et versante de pluie mais à travers l'obscurité; je distinguais
                              projetant   *pâles*
de loin la lumière des fenêtres qui lançait de longs rayons entre les

between the branches of the trees; and *the door was half-open;* guided me to the door. I entered;
silent
all was tranquil within.   I traversed the hall, the corridor, the ante-

chambers, without encountering anyone and found myself finally in the
common   *in the past, and then revived in me a thousand*
library, our own retreat, the place consacrated to so many memories that

a century of estrangement could not efface. While I contemplated by the *in*
hearth
uncertain light of the fire the paintings on the walls, the rows of books

underneath, and all the familiar objects that surrounded me, something
dark
stirred in the room. It was a large dog that arose from a corner and

approached to examine the stranger; (he did not find a stranger.) He
it to me
recognized me, and he attested his recognition (by the most expressive

caresses(; but I pushed him away, because he was yours.
and cruel victory of the wicked growth which
Forgive, Edward, this last act of the tyrant who had so long usurped
had silenced   *heart*
the place of nature in my breast; an instant later I was on my knees
why?
praying and crying and abjuring my enmity forever; I went to bed happy,
awoke   *has been   tardy*
I awake happy sad; perhaps that my repentence comes too late; perhaps

that your heart is hardened more than mine. But in the past my brother
deny wrongs
was always the last to become angry and the first to forget an injury.

Edward, come assure me that your nature has not changed — do not write

but come.

la porte était entreouverte;

rameaux des arbres; et me guidait à la porte. J'y entrai; tout était
silencieux   *l'*
tranquille en-dedans je traversai ~~la salle~~, le corridor, les antichambres,   30

sans recontrer ~~aucune~~ personne et me trouvai enfin dans la bibliothèque
commune   *autrefois, et alors se ravivèrent en moi mille*
notre propre retraite, le lieu consacré à tant de souvenirs qu'un siècle
n'a   *à*
d'éloignement ne pût effacer.   Pendant je contemplais par la lumière
foyer   *ées*
douteuse du feu, les tableaux sur les murs, les rangs de livres au dessous
ent
et tous les objets familiers qui m'entourait, quelquechose se remuait   35
se   *obscur*
dans la chambre ~~c'était~~ un grand chien qui s'éleva d'un coin et s'appro-

me le
chait pour examiner l'étranger, (il ne trouva pas un étranger;) il m're-
connaissaitnut et il témoigna sa reconnaissance par des caresses les ~~plus~~

~~expressives~~; mais moi, je le repoussai, parcequ'il était le vôtre.
e   et cruelle victoire du mauvais déve-
Pardonnez, Edouard, à ce dernier acte du tyran qui avait usurpé si   40
loppement qui avait fait taire   cœur   j'étais
longtemps là place de la nature dans mon sein; l'instant après ~~je fut~~ à

genoux priant et pleurant et abjurant mon inimitie pour jamais; je me
pourquoi?   ~~se~~   ai
couchai heureux, je me'éveille heureux triste; peutêtre ~~que~~ mon repentir   C.
a-t-il   est-il
vienne trop tardé; peutêtre ~~que~~ votre coeur soit plus endurci que le mien. H
                                                                             e
mais mon frère était autrefois toujours le dernier à se fâcher et le premier g   45
nier   torts   tq   e
à oublier une injure. Edouard viens m'assurer que votre nature n'est pas   r

changée — n'ecris pas mais viens

Comments

Though storms untold his mind have tossed,
He cannot utterly have lost
Remembrance of his early home—. . .
                                    —Emily Brontë[1]

As I spoke, I observed a large dog . . . raise its ears as if about to bark, and
then smoothing them back, announce by a wag of the tail that some one approached whom it did not consider a stranger.
                          —Nellie Dean, in *Wuthering Heights*[2]

Most of Emily Brontë's devoirs seem dissociated from her writings in
English. The exception is this letter, which evokes two themes that engaged the Brontës from the nursery through adulthood: brothers, once
close, who have quarreled and parted and the exile's return to his home.

The prototype for brothers first emerges in "The Islanders," a "play"
the Brontë children began in 1827,[3] when Emily was nine. The children's
Marquis of Douro (Arthur Wellesley) and Lord Charles Wellesley are
fictional versions of Wellington's two sons. As the cycle evolved into "The

Glass Town" and then "Angria," the brothers diverged in personality and power, Douro/Zamorna becoming a ruler and seducer, Charles a writer and cynic. By the time Charlotte wrote "The Spell" in 1834, Charles had been banished from Zamorna's Wellesley House, presumably because of his prying.[4]

In the same year Branwell's manuscript, "The Wool Is Rising," alludes to another pair of disaffected brothers, the sons of Alexander Percy, earl of Northangerland, who disowns them as soon as they are born. The Percy twins are forced into an early alliance and together establish a small wool-combing business, but when Edward, the elder, succeeds as a merchant he tyrannizes over the younger William, whom he keeps as an ill-paid clerk. William manages to get an army commission, goes abroad, prospers, and then returns home, where animosity between the siblings lingers.[5] In Charlotte's later story, "The Duke of Zamorna" (1838), William's bitterness pours out: "I always affected indifference to [Edward's] savage, hard, calculating barbarity, and I always will affect indifference to it to my dying day. But if there be a power superior to humanity, that power has witnessed feelings wringing my heart in silence which will never find voice in words."[6]

Charlotte's attachment to the brothers plot survived her resolution to leave Angria behind. She recycled it twice in the 1840s, retaining the names Edward and William for the eponymous brothers of *Ashworth* (1840–41) and the Crimsworth brothers of *The Professor* (1846).

Emily did not share the attachment. Even before the first appearance of the Percy twins, probably as early as 1832, she and Anne had broken away to develop plays and stories of their own. In the surviving poems about Gondal there are clear allusions to departure and exile and hints of familial conflict and betrayal, but no direct accounts of sibling rivalry. Fannie Ratchford claims that "fraternal strife had a place in Emily and Anne's Gondal play and Gondal poems,"[7] but the evidence remains inconclusive. Only one extant poem names a brother, and the speaker, R. Gleneden, could be either male or female.[8] Civil wars between the Republicans and Royalists—political rather than personal conflict—occasion the divisions in the couplet Ratchford quotes from the last poem Emily composed:

When kindred strive—God help the weak!
A brother's ruth 'tis vain to seek.[9]

Even less tenable as proof are the references to "Edward" in the poem first printed as "A Death-Scene." That name does not appear in the original text. It was substituted for Emily's "Elbë" when she and Charlotte edited the poem for publication.[10]

Ratchford is probably right, though, in claiming that Emily and Anne remained aware of the plots their older brother and sister were devising. And in alien Brussels, Emily may have taken comfort in returning to the old family cycle. Her letter writer's tale of estrangement and wandering recalls the hardships William Percy suffered; more pointedly, she names his brother Edward. Here, however, Edward seems the gentler of the siblings, the one least likely to hold grudges. His position at the time of his brother's homecoming is not entirely clear. Whether he too has stayed away throughout the interval, whether the dog's presence signifies his master's, whether the writer slips out and where he goes to bed—these are questions that the devoir ignores. The gaps in narrative logic could result from Emily's lack of interest in contingent detail and limited control over her medium, or they could result from her assumption that the context, long familiar to all four Brontës, required no further explanation.

Beyond asking why the wanderer goes to bed happy, Heger ignores the ambiguities. Ostensibly, he concentrates on grammar flaws and awkwardness (in manuscript, distinguished by straight and wavy underlining); he also fills in missing punctuation. But clearly, his revisions go beyond polishing. They nudge the text toward sentiment and melodrama, substituting pathos for plain speaking. Of course, he had no notion of the sources Emily was tapping or the ambience of Haworth and the parsonage. Allusions to a stormy night, a view through lighted windows, a library that memory hallows, and a dog would not resonate for him as they would for a generation primed on *Wuthering Heights*.

The letter writer's character alone, though undeveloped, would mark this as Emily's devoir. Like Heathcliff, he goes abruptly into an exile that is self-imposed and fueled by pride and anger; he returns hardened in his grievances. Those grievances, when acted out, collapse abruptly; between extremes there is no middle way. As soon as the desire to reconcile seizes him, he subjugates his pride and writes a supplicating letter that halts at the threshold of a new, or conceivably new, era in fraternal relations.

It is tempting to read this appeal in the context of Emily's relations with Branwell. Long before she left for Brussels, her beloved older brother had degenerated into a drinker and an addict. By August news from home had probably reached her that Branwell had been fired from his job as a railroad clerk and implicated in the theft of funds. Perhaps she felt angry, even personally aggrieved at his spineless and dishonorable conduct; perhaps older, stronger feelings about family loyalty compelled her to reconcile with him. But too much speculation has already entered into the dissection of Emily Brontë's character. It is safer to surmise that "Letter from one brother . . ." is a link in a lifelong chain of writings.

[Devoir]

The Butterfly.

In one of those moods that everyone falls into sometimes, when the
world of the imagination suffers a winter that blights its vegetation; when
the light of life seems to go out and existence becomes a barren desert
where we wander, exposed to all the tempests that blow under heaven,
without hope of rest or shelter — in one of these black humors, I was
walking one evening at the edge of a forest. It was summer; the sun was
still shining high in the west and the air resounded with the songs of
birds. All appeared happy, but for me, it was only an appearance. I sat
at the foot of an old oak, among whose branches the nightingale had just
begun its vespers. "Poor fool," I said to myself, "is it to guide the
bullet to your breast or the child to your brood that you sing so loud and
clear?   Silence that untimely tune, perch yourself on your nest;
tomorrow, perhaps, it will be empty." But why address myself to you
alone? All creation is equally mad. Behold those flies playing above the
brook; the swallows and fish diminish their number every minute. These
will become, in their turn, the prey of some tyrant of the air or water;
and man for his amusement or his needs will kill their murderers.
Nature is an inexplicable problem; it exists on a principle of destruction.
Every being must be the tireless instrument of death to others, or itself
must cease to live, yet nonetheless we celebrate the day of our birth, and
we praise God for having entered such a world.

During my soliloquy I picked a flower at my side; it was fair and
freshly opened, but an ugly caterpillar had hidden itself among the petals
and already they were shriveling and fading. "Sad image of the earth
and its inhabitants!" I exclaimed. "This worm lives only to injure the

[Devoir]
Le Papillon.

=====

Dans une de ces dispositions de l'âme où chacun se trouve quelquefois,
lorsque le monde de l'imagination souffre un hiver qui fletrit toute sa   5
végétation; lorsque la lumière de la vie semble s'éteindre et l'existence
devient un désert stérile où nous errons, exposés à toutes les tempêtes qui
soufflent sous le ciel, sans espérance ni de repos ni d'abri — dans une de
ces humeurs noires, je me promenais un soir sur les confines d'une forêt,
c'était en été; le soleil brillait encore haut dans l'occident et l'air reten-   10
tissait des chants d'oiseaux: tout paraissait heureux, mais pour moi, ce
n'était qu'une apparence. Je m'assis au pied d'un vieux chêne, parmi les
rameaux duquel, le rossignol venait de commencer ses vêpres. "Pauvre
fou, je me dis, "est-ce pour guider la balle à ton sein ou l'enfant à tes
petits que tu chantes si haut et si clair? Tais cette mélodie malàpropos,   15
blottis toi sur ton nid; demain, peutêtre, il sera vide". Mais pourquoi
m'adresser à toi seul? la création entière est également insensée. Voila
ces mouches jouant au-dessus du ruisseau des hirondelles et des poissons
en diminuent le nombre chaque minute: ceux-ci deviendront, en leur
tour, la proie de quelque tyran de l'air ou de l'eau; et l'homme pour son   20
amusement ou pour ses besoins, tuera leurs meurtriers. La nature est un
problème inexplicable, elle existe sur un principe de destruction; il faut
que tout être soit l'instrument infatigable de mort aux autres, ou qu'il
cesse de vivre lui-même; et cependant, nous célébrons le jour de notre
naissance, et nous louons Dieu d'avoir entré un tel monde. Pendant mon   25
soliloque je cueillis une fleur à mes côtés, elle était belle et fraîchement
épanouie mais une laide chenille s'était cachée parmi les pétales et déjà
elles se ridaient et se fanaient. "Triste image de la terre et de ses

plant that protects it. Why was it created, and why was man created? He torments, he kills, he devours; he suffers, dies, is devoured — there you have his whole story. It is true that there is a heaven for the saint, but the saint leaves enough misery here below to sadden him even before the throne of God.

I threw the flower to earth. At that moment the universe appeared to me a vast machine constructed only to produce evil. I almost doubted the goodness of God, in not annihilating man on the day he first sinned. "The world should have been destroyed," I said, "crushed as I crush this reptile which has done nothing in its life but render all that it touches as disgusting as itself." I had scarcely removed my foot from the poor insect when, like a censoring angel sent from heaven, there came fluttering through the trees a butterfly with large wings of lustrous gold and purple. It shone but a moment before my eyes; then, rising among the leaves, it vanished into the height of the azure vault. I was mute, but an inner voice said to me, "Let not the creature judge his Creator; here is a symbol of the world to come. As the ugly caterpillar is the origin of the splendid butterfly, so this globe is the embryo of a new heaven and a new earth whose poorest beauty will infinitely exceed your mortal imagination. And when you see the magnificent result of that which seems so base to you now, how you will scorn your blind presumption, in accusing Omniscience for not having made nature perish in her infancy.

God is the god of justice and mercy; then surely, every grief that he inflicts on his creatures, be they human or animal, rational or irrational, every suffering of our unhappy nature is only a seed of that divine harvest which will be gathered when, Sin having spent its last drop of venom, Death having launched its final shaft, both will perish on the pyre of a universe in flames and leave their ancient victims to an eternal empire of happiness and glory.

habitants!" récriai-je, "ce ver ne vit que de nuire à la plante qui le protège: pourquoi était-il créé – et pourquoi l'homme était il créé? Il tourment il tue, il dévore; il souffre, se meurt, est dévoré – voila toute son histoire. C'est vrai qu'il y a un ciel pour le saint mais le saint laisse assez de misère ici bas de l'attrister même devant le trône de Dieu.

Je jetai la fleur à terre; en ce moment l'univers me paraissait une vaste machine construite seulement pour produire le mal: je doutais presque de la bonté de Dieu, dans ce qu'il n'anéantit pas l'homme sur le jour du premier péché. "Le monde aurai dû être detruit," je dis, "ecrasé comme j'ecrase ce reptile qui n'a rien fait pendant sa vie que rendre tout ce qu'il touche aussi dégoutant que lui-même". Je n'eus guère ôté mon pied du pauvre insecte lorsque, comme un ange censeur envoyé du ciel, voltigeait à travers les arbres un papillon aux grandes ailes de luisant or et de poupre: il ne brillait qu'un moment devant mes yeux, puis, remontant parmi les feuilles, il s'evanouit dans la hauteur de la voute azurée. Je fus muette, mais une voix interieure me dit "Que la créature ne juge pas son Créateur, voila un symbole du monde à venir – comme la laide chenille est l'origine du splendide papillon, ainsi ce globe est l'embrion d'un nouveau ciel et d'une nouvelle terre dont la beauté la plus pauvre excédera infiniment ton imagination mortelle et quand tu verras le resultat magnifique de ce qui te semble maintenant si basse combien mépriseras tu ta présomption aveugle, en accusant Omniscience qu'elle n'avait pas fait périr la nature dans son enfance.

Dieu est le dieu de justice et de miséricorde; puis assurément, chaque peine qu'il inflige sur ses créatures, soient elles - humaines ou animales, raisonables ou irraisonables, chaque souffrance de notre malheureuse nature n'est qu'une semence de cette moisson divine qui sera recueillie quand Le péché ayant dépensé sa dernière goutte de venin, La Mort ayant lancé son dernier trait tous deux expireront sur le bucher d'un univers en flammes et laisseront leurs anciennes victimes à un empire éternel de bonheur et de gloire –

Charlotte Brontë

[Devoir]

The Caterpillar

═══════

Works produced by the same agent nearly always show a certain analogy

5   to one another: poems written by the same author, pictures painted by the

same master resemble one another in design and conception, and the

greatest work of all, the Universe, which in its entirety and in its

thousand details is the production of a single agent, shows throughout a

resemblance, a harmony so perfect that the lowest things often serve to

10   remind us of the loftiest.

One of God's principal works is man, created in His image, set a

little lower than the angels. One of God's lesser works, is it not the

worm — the caterpillar, which slowly creeps among the plants and passes

its life nibbling their leaves?

15   But here there is no resemblance, there is only opposition. What

connection exists between the poor caterpillar and man, noble and

intelligent?

Let us reflect a bit. The caterpillar lives a crass, material life; it

eats, it creeps today; it ate, it crept yesterday; it will eat, it will creep

20   tomorrow. Thus it lives during an entire season, the lovely season of

spring. Then it begins to spin; it hangs from a branch; it forms its

                                     in it
cocoon; it envelops itself. This is its coffin; now it is dead. The chry-

salis falls to earth; soon it is covered by a heap of dead leaves, or rather,

since it is spring, by withered flowers fallen from the fruit trees. For a

25   month it rests there, w̶i̶t̶h̶o̶u̶t̶ deprived of light, of movement, of life.

And after? The heat of summer begins. The insect enclosed within the

chrysalis feels its influence. The principle of life revives; it stirs in its

[Devoir]

La Chenille

Les oeuvres produites par le même agent, presentent presque toujours
une certaine analogie les unes avec les autres: les poèmes écrits par le   5
même auteur; les tableaux peints par le même maître se ressemblent en
dessein et en idée, et la plus grande oeuvre de toutes, l'Univers, qui dans
son entier et dans ses mille détails est la production d'un seul agent
montre partout une ressemblance une harmonie tellement parfaite, que les
choses les plus basses servent souvent à nous rappeler les choses les plus   10
élevées.

Une des oeuvres principales de Dieu est l'homme créé dans son
image, mis un peu plus bas que les anges, une des moindres oeuvres de
Dieu, n'est-ce pas le ver − la chenille., qui rampe lentement parmi les
plantes et qui passe sa vie en rongeant leurs feuilles?   15

Mais ici il n'y a pas de ressemblance, il n'y a que d'opposition, quel
rapport existe entre la pauvre chenille et l'homme noble et intelligent?

Réfléchissons un peu; la chenille passe une vie grossière, matérielle,
elle mange, elle rampe aujourd'hui; elle a mangé, elle a rampé hier; elle
mangera, elle rampera demain; ainsi elle vit pendant toute une saison, la   20
belle saison du printemps; alors elle commence à filer; elle se suspend
d'une branche; elle forme sa coque, elle s'enveloppe, c'est son cercueil,
maintenant elle est morte. La chrysalide tombe à terre, bientôt elle est
couverte d'un amas de feuilles mortes, ou plutôt, puisque c'est le printemps, des fleurs fanées, tombées des arbres fruitiers; pendant un mois   25
elle y reste s̶a̶n̶s̶ privée de lumière de mouvement, de vie. Et après? Les
chaleurs de l'été commence; l'insecte renfermé dans la chrysalide ressent
leur influence; le principe de la vie est ranimé, il se remue dans son

tomb. Finally it bursts the coffin; it escapes. What do we see now? It is not the caterpillar that leaves the chrysalis and that, delivering itself to the summer breeze, flies lightly in the air. The breeze carries it to the branches of a tree; it rests there an instant. Its vibrant wings gleam in the sunlight with a hummingbird's colors; among the leaves that surround it, it resembles a radiant flower. What then is this creature, so beautiful, so delicate? It is the caterpillar transformed into a butterfly. It has quitted its material life; it has launched itself into an entirely spiritual life. It no longer eats nor creeps. That which was sister to the worm is now companion to the flowers and birds.

Let us consider the life of man. He fancies himself intelligent, he fancies himself noble. He boasts of the results of his perseverance, his creative faculty, his inventions and discoveries. But if he should measure the things he knows against those of which he is ignorant, if he should compare what for him is possible with what for him is absolutely impossible, then he would find that boasting of his inventions, of his understanding is as if (according to a man equally remarkable for his talents and his humility) as if a child who gathered shells scattered on the ocean shore believed he was securing the treasures hidden in its bosom.

But if man is not great he is good; there is faith, there is charity on earth. Yes, every man has his moments of goodness, but his everyday life is a caterpillar's life. Here below he creeps; worldly cares overwhelm him. The needs of his body disturb the aspirations of his soul. The life of a virtuous man is no more than a continual struggle of nature against religion. As for the vicious man, he seems to enjoy a calmer life because he delivers himself without resistance to the temptations that obsess him.

Finally man dies; he is enclosed in a coffin, his grave is dug, he is interred there. It is a resting place even darker and more humid than that of the chrysalis beneath the dead leaves. After death, does any hope

tombeau enfin il crève le cercueil, il s'échappe. Que voit-on maintenant,? ce n'est pas la chenille qui sort de la chrysalide et qui se livrant à la brise de l'été vole légèrement dans l'air. La brise le porte sur les branches d'un arbre, il s'y repose un instant, ses ailes vibrantes brillent au soleil des couleurs du colibri, parmi les feuilles qui l'entourent, il ressemble à une fleur resplendissante. Quelle est donc cette créature si belle, si delicate? C'est la chenille transformée en papillon: elle a quitté sa vie matérielle, elle s'est élancée dans une vie entièrement spirituelle elle ne mange ni ne rampe plus; elle qui était soeur du ver est maintenant compagne des fleurs et des oiseaux.

Pensons à la vie de l'homme: il se croit intelligent, il se croit noble; il se vante des resultats de sa persévérance; de sa faculté créatrice, de ses inventions de ses découvertes; mais qu'il mésure les choses qu'il sait avec les choses qu'il ignore; qu'il compare ce qui pour lui est possible avec ce qui pour lui est absolument impossible, alors il trouverait que vanter de ses inventions, de ses connaissances c'est comme si (selon le sentiment d'un homme également remarquable pour ses talents et pour son humilité) comme si un enfant qui ramassait les coquilles épandues sur le rivage de l'ocean pensât qu'il s'emparait des trésors cachés dans son sein.

Mais si l'homme n'est pas grand il est bon il y a de la piété, de la charité sur la terre; oui tout homme a ses moments de bonté, mais sa vie ordinaire est la vie de la chenille; ici-bas il rampe; les soucis terrestres l'accablent; les besoins de son corps troublent les aspirations de son âme, la vie de l'homme vertueux n'est qu'une lutte continuelle de la nature contre la religion; quant à l'homme vicieux il semble jouir d'une vie plus calme parcequ'il se livre sans résistance aux tentations qui l'obsédent

Enfin l'homme meurt on le renferme dans le cercueil, on creuse le tombeau, on l'y enterre; c'est une demeure obscure et humide, encore plus que celle de la chrysalide sous les feuilles mortes Après la mort

remain for man? Does his corpse not become the prey of worms? Does corruption not change his flesh to dust? Does his whole material body not undergo the most absolute annihilation? Why then does man enter the world? Is it only to suffer and die? Faith speaks; listen to her voice:

The body is sown in corruption, it will be raised in incorruption; it is sown in dishonor, it will be raised in glory; it is sown in weakness, it will be raised in power; it is sown an animal body, it will be raised a spiritual body. In a moment, in the twinkling of an eye, at the sound of the last trump we shall all be changed, for the trumpet shall sound and the dead will arise incorruptible. Then shall be brought to pass the saying that is written, death is swallowed up forever.

reste-il pour l'homme aucune espérance? Son cadavre ne devient-il pas

la proie des vers? La corruption ne change-t-elle pas sa chair en boue? 60

Tout son corps matériel ne subit-elle pas l'anéantissement le plus absolu?

Pourquoi donc l'homme entre-t-il dans le monde? est-ce pour souffrir et

pour mourir? La Foi parle écoutez sa voix:

Le corps est semé corruptible, il ressuscitera incorruptible; il est

semé méprisable, il ressuscitera glorieux; il est semé infirme il ressus- 65

citera plein de force; il est semé corps animal, il ressuscitera corps

spirituel. En un moment, en un clin d'oeil au son de la dernière trom-

pette nous serons tous changé, car la trompette sonnera et les morts

réssuciteront incorruptibles. Alors cette parole de l'écriture sera accom-

plie, la mort est engloutie pour toujours. 70

Comments

These manuscripts are both dated August 11, just four days before the end of term. They are clean copies, devoid of Heger's markings, and both are preceded by a page with the single word "Devoir" in embellished letters. Charlotte often printed titles in a modified Gothic ("La Chenille" appears in the same print on the next page), but Emily wrote titles in her usual neat and slanting script, so in this case she did something extra. Perhaps she prepared this copy for Heger to keep in his file of student samples. If so, the early tensions between them must have eased, a hypothesis borne out by Charlotte's letter on the Hegers' rising estimate of her sister's character.[1] Or perhaps she simply got invested in her essay, whatever her attitude toward schoolwork and the teacher who forced her to communicate in French. (Charlotte, in contrast, welcomed any opportunity to write for her professor and advance her transformation from a halting to an eloquent French essayist.)

What motivated Emily's investment? Almost certainly, not the opportunity to write on a subject of her choice. The correspondences between the two devoirs testify to Heger's supervision; theme and topic never matched so closely when he let the Brontës pick for themselves.[2] Still, they vary more than the devoirs that expand on an outline he dictated.[3] So perhaps after lecturing on one or more extracts, he asked the sisters to write of metamorphosis, apply its lessons to humanity, and end with an appropriate moral. That is what their devoirs most obviously do, though why this topic should have galvanized Emily Brontë remains to be guessed.

Earlier studies hint at several answers: she was making an intensely personal statement; she was working out a "mystic's eschatology"; she was crystallizing visions of destruction and creation that were seminal to her later writing.[4] Clearly her speaker's mood portends the bitterness that breaks out in her later poems and novel:

> And why should we be glad at all?
> The leaf is hardly green,
> Before a token of its fall
> Is on the surface seen![5]

Its transformation also links the devoir back to Wordsworth: out of tune with nature, an isolated self finds relief through a moment's revelation.[6]

But to seek incentives only in the author's psyche or within the context of an English tradition is to disregard what was most immediate in Emily's and Charlotte's lives. Few critics have looked at the conditions of production or positioned this devoir in relation to the others. One clear lesson to be drawn from comparison is that Emily once again constructs an argument by working through a series of antitheses; in its oppositional patterning, this essay is consistent with "Harold" and "The Siege of Oudenarde." Her topic, metamorphosis, prescribes the basic contrast between the ugly worm and the luminescent butterfly; it also implies a connection between these forms that Emily chooses not to emphasize. Charlotte illustrates the stages of the insect's transformation, mixing metaphor with naturalistic details. She also shows a penchant for triadic patterning: yesterday, today, and tomorrow; caterpillar, chrysalis, and butterfly. But Emily obliterates the metamorphic process; her speaker crushes the insect underfoot, and the butterfly wings past an instant later. Before and after this decisive moment, contrasts shape and sequence the discourse: the winter of imagination and the summer evening; the speaker's bleak consciousness and nature's fecund ignorance; seeming and reality; bloom and spoilage; creature and creator; old and new world. Although a chain of being is implicit in her narrative, she stresses antagonism rather than linkage, and the suffering that "seeds" the coming harvest.

Further oppositions emerge from examining the devoir in its context. Like the two she submitted six days earlier, "Filial Love" and "Letter from one brother to another," it opens with a speaker devoid of illusions who caustically reflects on humanity and nature. But in the second paragraph the bitterness abruptly gives way to a visionary faith: though the nature of nature is that "every being must be the tireless instrument of death to others," the butterfly heralds a God who is somehow going to validate this suffering and destruction. To many modern readers, the shift seems unconvincing. John Hewish, for example, wonders if the "pious coda" was written to satisfy Heger.[7] But a survey of the models Heger could have provided suggests that, on the contrary, Emily Brontë was defining her position against his.

No direct precedent appears in Charlotte's copybooks, but three of the authors whose texts Heger excerpted—Buffon, Lamartine, and Chateaubriand—allude to insects elsewhere in the volumes he consulted. Bernardin de Saint-Pierre, whose books he gave her later, also wrote frequently of insects.[8] To Buffon, the eighteenth-century naturalist, they were an inferior life form that nonetheless made God's wisdom manifest: "How infinitely great must that Eternal Mind be who framed all with such amazing skill:—who sees with a single glance the operation and mechanism of the whole, from the minute anatomy of the ant, to those innumerable worlds, those vast and splendid orbs that gild the unbounded expanse of the universe!"[9] To Lamartine, a seminal Romantic, the world of insects appeared less mechanistic; nonetheless he viewed it as a microcosm that revealed God's loving fecundity:

> There, near the beehives,
> The spider spins her wonders,
> The serpent hisses, and the ant
> Leads toward conquests of sand
> Its innumerable legions
> That a sleepy lizard crushes![10]

To Chateaubriand also, insect life attested to the wonders of divine creation. He claimed that the coexistence of its phases supported the biblical version of earth's origins and refuted theory based on fossil evidence: "What, in fact, can be more probable than that the Author of Nature originally produced both venerable forests and young plantations and that the animals were created, some full of days, others adorned with the graces of infancy. The oaks, on springing from the fruitful soil, doubtless bore at once the aged crows and the new progeny of doves. *Worm, chrysalis, and butterfly—the insect crawled upon the grass, suspended its golden egg in the forest, or fluttered aloft in the air.*"[11] If proof existed that the Brontës knew this passage, then Emily's conflation of the crushed worm with the butterfly and Charlotte's allusion to pupation would clearly be responses to the text their teacher gave them. But even in its absence, the consensus in these sources suggests a rationale for both their devoirs.

At the Pensionnat Heger, religious and secular instruction were to form a seamless whole. These passages would have been teachable because they combined the idealism of natural theology (or *Naturphilosophie,* its Germanic counterpart) with the contemplation of nature.[12] But for Englishwomen raised in a Protestant tradition, who walked the moors in all weathers, using their eyes and ears, its rosiness would not just sentimentalize creation; it would falsify nature as they knew it.[13] Charlotte's solution, judging by her devoir, was to hold to the ideals but shun the sentiment. Emily, however, could not readily bypass the struggle for existence in the forest. Like many evangelical and dissenting Christians, she held to a harsher mythos of creation: with the expulsion of Adam from paradise, the animal kingdom fell too.

That Emily conceived of animals as fallen is strongly hinted in "The Cat." Dogs might remain superior to humans, but Adam, "the great ancestor of humankind," had nonetheless brought evil to all forms of life. As J. Hillis Miller first observed, her vision of the forest's chain of endless cruelty "matches the traditional Christian description of the state of nature . . . after the fall. . . ." Miller points out that this vision is "strikingly like" Wesley's in his sermon "The General Deliverance":[14]

> . . . [W]hat savage fierceness, what unrelenting cruelty, are invariably observed in thousands of creatures, yea, are inseparable from their natures. Is it only the lion, the tiger, the wolf,

among the inhabitants of the forest and plains; the shark and a few more voracious monsters among the inhabitants of the waters; or the eagle among birds; that tears the flesh, sucks the blood, and crushes the bones of their helpless fellow-creatures? Nay, the harmless fly, the laborious ant, the painted butterfly, are treated in the same merciless manner even by the innocent songsters of the grove! . . .

. . . Yea, such at present is the miserable constitution of the world, to such "vanity" is it now "subjected," that an immense majority of creatures . . . can no otherwise preserve their own lives than by destroying their fellow-creatures.

Wesley adds that man outstrips the animals in cruelty, since he torments other creatures "of his free choice; and perhaps continues their lingering pain till . . . death signs their release."[15]

But he does not conclude with a vision of destruction, any more than do the Brontës. Alluding to Revelation 21 (like Emily) and to I Corinthians 15 (like Charlotte), he speaks of a new heaven and a new earth in which the "brute creation" will achieve an unimaginable beauty, freedom, and affection: "when God has 'renewed the face of the earth,' and their corruptible body has put on incorruption, they shall enjoy happiness suited to their state, without alloy, without interruption, and without end."[16]

Emily could have arrived at her convictions with no direct knowledge of Wesley's. But certainly, she had been exposed to his teachings through Elizabeth Branwell, brought up a Wesleyan Methodist, and through Patrick Brontë, an Anglican whose views were strongly influenced by Methodism.[17] Two other fundamental Wesleyan tenets, Justification and the New Birth, may also have a bearing on her devoir. Justification entails divine forgiveness, bestowed not because the sinner has earned it, but because God grants it as a supernatural act of grace. New Birth refers to the individual's awakening from spiritual death to a new life in God and is often, though not always, instantaneous. Wesley figures it in terms of the senses: the "eyes of [the believer's] understanding are opened," and his spirit begins to hear and feel.[18]

When the narrator of "The Butterfly" stamps the worm underfoot, she descends to the nadir of belief. She takes it on herself to criticize the universe, "a vast machine constructed only to produce evil," and to replace God's decision with her own: "The world should have been destroyed." Her arrogant judgment marks her as a creature as fallen as the ones she has condemned. Yet the butterfly, "like a censoring angel sent from heaven," enlightens the speaker in rebuking her. It does not flash before her in reward for right conduct, but as an unearned sign of grace and mercy. In that moment, her understanding alters. Her old voice falls silent, and an inner voice teaches her to read creation with a new awareness and scorn the blindness of her past presumption.

This Wesleyan analysis does not do away with the problem that the ending imposes. If thematically the butterfly augurs a new earth and heaven, linguistically it augurs deconstruction. The language that proclaims the speaker's transformed understanding is less precise and vigorous, less visually arresting, than the language that images the forest. As Margaret Homans says, "In the negative part . . . the energy of her pessimism is her own";[19] that energy evaporates when her voice yields to the voice of religious instruction. Emily might profess belief in an ultimately merciful deity, but here as elsewhere she writes most effectively of merciless, unpitying behavior.[20] Still, this apocalyptic ending seems to counteract the pleading conclusion of "Letter from one brother" and the harshness of "Filial Love." If Emily were trying to work through something personal—say, recent news that Branwell had once again disgraced himself—this devoir would signal a victory.

Charlotte's essay displays none of these tensions; through a series of balanced questions and comparisons, it reaches a conventional moral. Her vision of salvation is, as always, staunchly biblical. The words from I Corinthians that end her devoir also appear in the Book of Common Prayer and so by implication connect it to Anglican rather than Methodist theology. Man's pride may be misplaced, and his accomplishments inflated; still, she does not question his position in the chain of being or hint that all creation is "insensée"—mad or senseless. Where Emily discloses a cycle of destruction, she portrays a cycle of life.

In effect, she responds to Heger's lesson by producing one of her own. The basis of that lesson is the metamorphic process, or rather, her romantic version of it. Appetite becomes a key to her discourse, a means of merging faith with realism. Her caterpillar creeps along, consuming and gorging, a counterpart to mankind in its gross sensuality; if it did not keep eating, however, it would never survive to spin its chrysalis. Delivered from its coffin, it lives without an appetite and so becomes a symbol of the spiritual within this world, as well as a symbol of the next one. Of course, to preach this lesson she must ignore the final phase, the sexual reproduction of the "spiritual" butterfly that leads to the next round of worms. Realism prompts her to replace "dead leaves" with the "withered [spring] flowers" that fall upon the chrysalis, but realism ends where it would call God's design, or her own design, into question.

For if piety appears to motivate her efforts, her less apparent interest is in rhetoric itself: in producing a fluent and harmonious text that will manifest her increasing command of structure, syntax, imagery, and language.[21] Hints that she writes for a professor of rhetoric are implicit in her opening (a classical exordium), the caterpillar section (a classical exemplum), and the measured voice of her narrator. Emily's narrative seems strikingly personal; it asks to be read as a confession. But Charlotte's avoids any personal reference; she assumes the voice of a self-assured lecturer discoursing on life and the hereafter.

Unusually, and in accord with Heger's promptings, she pursues her theme without digressing, as Heger kept urging her to do.[22] He had also advised her to consider the construction of her devoirs in painterly terms,[23] and here she makes the classical assumption that poetry and painting are analogous. But the arts figure too as Romantic examples, in that they reveal the unique signature of the "agent" (or genius) who created them. The universe similarly manifests its authorship in its "design" and its "myriad details," an assumption that Heger would have shared.

These efforts result in a controlled but much less memorable essay than Emily's "Butterfly." Still, as her final composition of the term, it attests to the progress she has made. Its theme may be banal, but in a French critic's words, "the expression is rich, supple and poetic."[24] And if one of her aims was to impress her professor, its provenance suggests that she succeeded: this is one of two devoirs by Charlotte Brontë that still belong to Heger's descendants.

Le But de la Vie

Le soir d'un jour d'automne une
jeune étudiant se trouvait seul dans
son appartement : il était assis à une
table, il appuyait sa tête sur sa main,
son corps était courbé, ses yeux étaient
fixés sur les pages d'un livre, tout son
aspect indiquait une grande préoccupation.
Le silence régnait dans la chambre, on
n'entendait que le bruissement du vent
qui soufflait de temps en temps dans les
feuilles desséchées d'un arbre près de la
fenêtre : bientôt la cloche sonna dans

First page of Charlotte Brontë's "The Aim of Life." Berg Collection, New York Public Library.

The Aim of Life

On the evening of an autumn day a young student found himself alone in his apartment. He was seated at a table; he leaned his head on his hand, his body was bent over, his eyes were fixed on the pages of a book; his whole demeanor indicated a great preoccupation. Silence reigned in the chamber. Only the rustling of the wind could be heard, which blew
stirred
from time to time in the dry leaves of a tree near the window. Before long, the bell tolled in the church of his college; this dull and lingering sound disturbed his thoughts. He raised his head, he looked around like
through
a man who has just awakened. The sun had already set, and the shades
twinkled
of twilight brought the first stars. A painful feeling furrowed the student's brow; he closed his book, he hurled it away, and rising with an impetuous movement, he paced with long strides through the chamber.

"Once again," he thought, "I deceive myself; once again the hours slip away without my noticing their passage. What have I done since the morning? I have studied, I have studied hard; hence I have not wasted my time. My companions, my professors will applaud me. They will say, there's the young scholar, the toiler, the man of learning! How fine
at
it is to abstain thus in the spring of life from worldly pleasures and devote oneself to study, to Science! Fine! Ah, if those people knew my heart as I myself know it, they would sooner say cowardly. What aversion have I conquered? What stern but necessary duty have I fulfilled today? None. It is my taste to study; it is my natural inclination to live in retirement. I have an antipathy to the noise, the movement, the gaiety of the world — and why? Is it the loftiness of my character that keeps me from finding happiness in the whirl of pleasures?

Le But de la Vie

Le soir d'un jour d'automne un jeune étudiant se trouvait seul dans son

appartement: il etait assis à une table, il appuyait sa tête sur sa main, son

corps était courbé, ses yeux étaient fixés sur les pages d'un livre, tout   5

son aspect indiquait une grande préoccupation. Le silence régnait dans

la chambre, on n'entendait que le bruissement du vent qui soufflait de
                                           agitait
temps en temps dàns les feuilles dessechées d'un arbre près de la fenêtre:

bientôt la cloche sonna dans l'eglise de son collège; ce bruit sourd et

traînant troubla ses pensées, il leva la tête, il regarda autour de lui   10

comme un homme qui vient de s'éveiller; déjà le soleil s'était couché,
à travers   *scintillaient*
èt les ombres du crépuscule amenait les premières étoiles. Un sentiment

pénible contracta le front de l'étudiant, il ferma son livre, il le jeta loin

de lui, et se levant d'un mouvement impetueux, il se promena à longs pas

dans la chambre.   15

"Encore une fois" disait-il en soi-même "je me trompe, encore une

fois les heures s'ecoulent sans que je m'aperçois de leur progrés. Qu'ai

je fait depuis le matin? j'ai étudié, j'ai bien étudié, donc je n'ai pas

perdu mon temps, mes compagnons, mes professeurs m'applaudiront, ils

diront voilà le jeune savant, le travailleur, l'homme instruit! Que c'est   20
                              au
beau de s'abstenir ainsi dàns le printemps de sa vie des plaisirs du monde

de se dévouer à l'étude, à la Science! Beau! ah si ces gens connaissaient

mon coeur comme je le connais moi même, ils diraient plutôt lâche!

Quelle aversion ai-je vaincue? quel devoir sévère mais nécessaire ai-je

rempli aujourd'hui?   Aucun; c'est mon goût d'étudier, c'est mon   25

penchant naturel de vivre dans la retraite: j'ai une antipathie pour le bruit

le mouvement, la gaieté du monde – et pourquoi? est-ce l'élévation de

mon caractère qui m'empêche de trouver le bonheur dans le tourbillon

Or is it lack of vivacity, of spirit that renders me incapable of seeking it there? Be silent, Self-love, and let reply the dry, cold, stern voice of Conscience.

I flee the world because I do not have the qualities needed to shine in it. Vivacity, grace, and liveliness I lack. The taciturn man is always a burden on society. In solitude no one reproaches him for his faults, no one is bored by his presence. His books are companions who speak to him without expecting a reply; hence he loves solitude because he is at ease in it, a base and contemptible motive that comes from selfishness and indolence. They say that such and such a young man has wasted his youth in frivolous pursuits; I too have wasted mine. Here I am, a quarter of the way through my life; what have I done? Concience, reply again; it is you I want to listen to now, too often I have heeded only self-love.

I have lived the life that pleased me most. I have yielded to the natural inclinations of my soul; I have let the defects of my disposition grow without fighting energetically against their growth. They call me a thinker, an observer; often when I think, I feel that I must practice; often when I observe, I feel that I must act. Must I continue to live this way? That's impossible. I am now past twenty, I have acquired some knowledge, now it's a question of using it. Hitherto, I have lived for myself; henceforth, I must live for others. Hitherto, my light work has always found a reward, the sweet reward of the approval of those whom I respect; henceforth, I must resign myself to hard work without reward. Hitherto, I have sought only instruction; henceforth, I must seek patience, energy, and mastery over myself. Hitherto, I have borne only the burden of my own faults; henceforth, I must take on the overwhelming burden of others' faults, and I must not succumb beneath that weight, I must not see myself as a martyr. I must support it firmly, saying that

des plaisirs? ou est-ce le manque de vivacité, d'esprit qui me rend incapable de l'y chercher? Tais-toi Amour-propre et laisse répondre la voix sèche, froide, sévère de la Conscience.

Je fuis le monde parceque je n'ai pas les qualités necessaires pour y briller; la vivacité, la grâce, l'enjouement me manque l'homme taciturne est toujours à charge à la société, dans la solitude personne ne lui réproche ses défauts, personne n'est ennuyée de sa presence; Ses livres sont des compagnons qui lui parlent sans s'attendre à une reponse, il aime donc la solitude parcequ'il s'y trouve à son aise, motif bas et méprisable qui vient de l'egoïsme et de la paresse. On dit tel et tel jeune homme a dissipé sa jeunesse dans des poursuites frivoles, moi j'ai dissipé la mienne aussi; me voilà au quart de ma vie, qu'ai-je fait? Conscience reponds encore, c'est toi que je veux écouter maintenant, trop souvent je n'ai écouté que l'amour-propre.

J'ai vecu la vie qui me plaisait le plus j'ai cédé aux inclinations naturelles de mon âme, j'ai laissé augmenter les défauts de ma disposition sans lutter avec energie contre leur accroissement; on m'appelle penseur, observateur, souvent lorsque je pense je sens que je dois pratiquer, lorsque j'observe je sens que je dois agir. Dois-je continuer de vivre ainsi? C'est impossible — J'ai maintenant plus que vingt ans, j'ai acquis quelques connaissances, à présent il s'agit de les utiliser. Jusqu'ici j'ai vécu pour moi-même, désormais je dois vivre pour les autres; jusqu'ici mon travail léger a toujours trouvé une récompense, la récompense si douce de l'approbation de ceux que je respecte, désormais je dois me resigner à un travail dur sans récompense; jusqu'ici je n'ai cherché que l'instruction, désormais je dois chercher la patience, l'énergie, l'empire sur moi-même; jusqu'ici je n'ai porté le fardeau que de mes propres défauts, désormais je dois me charger du fardeau accablant des défauts des autres, et je ne dois pas succomber sous ce poids, je ne dois pas me regarder comme martyr, je dois le soutenir avec

it is my share of the common ~~failings~~ ^{sufferings} of the whole human race. I am

no more to be pitied than the rest of the world. And where will I find

that firmness; who will give me that energy? Ah! Those are questions

60   that betray a faint spirit. It is within my duty to seek them out. Religion

and Reason alone can give them to me. And perhaps if I walk resolutely

in the path that Duty shows me, however sad, however painful it appears

to me now, perhaps those difficulties will be smoothed away, and the

task that seems impracticable to me now will become almost easy. If I

65   must be convinced by discouragements, by ill success, that I am not

capable of doing what is expected of me, then what remains for me?

Inactive and impotent despair? No; the ancients have shown us through

the beautiful allegory of the Phoenix that true greatness is tested by

afflictions, that it rises more glorious from its ashes; and if I am not

70   capable of the energy that mines fresh vigor from adversity, at least I can

suffer it patiently, without abasing myself through useless complaint.

The weakest creature must be capable of that passive courage which

suffers in silence and which relies, in the tempest, on the hope of a better

life.

fermeté, en disant c'est mon partage des d̶é̶f̶a̶u̶t̶s̶ douleurs communes à tout le   60

genre humain; je ne suis plus à plaindre que le reste du monde; et où

trouverai-je cette fermeté, qui me donnera cette energie? Ah! voilà des

questions qui trahissent l'esprit faible — c'est dans mon devoir que je dois

les chercher — c'est la Religion et la Raison seule qui peuvent me les

donner. Et peut-être si je marche resolument dans le chemin que le   65

Devoir me montre, tout triste, tout pénible qu'il me parait maintenant,

peutêtre ces difficultés s'aplaniront, et la tâche, qui, maintenant me

semble impracticable, deviendra presque facile. Si je dois être convaincu

par des découragements, par des mauvais succés que je ne suis pas

capable de faire ce que l'on attend de moi, alors que me reste? Le des-   70

espoir inactif et impotent? Non, les anciens nous ont montré par la belle

allégorie du Phénix que la véritable grandeur est à l'épreuve des

afflictions qu'elle naît plus glorieuse de sa cendre, et si je ne suis pas

capable de cette énergie qui puise une nouvelle vigueur de l'adversité, du

moins je puis la souffrir patiemment, sans m'avilir par des plaintes   75

inutiles; l'être le plus faible doit être capable de ce courage passif, qui

se tait dans la douleur, et qui s'appuie dans la tempête sur l'espérance

d'une meilleure vie

Comments

It is tempting but risky to read Charlotte Brontë's devoirs for clues to her emotions. "The Aim of Life" particularly demonstrates the risks, since the omission of the year from the manuscript leaves questions about its context open. Did she write it in August 1842, when Emily remained with her in Brussels? Or is it a product of the following August when, isolated and increasingly despondent, she tried to brace her courage by writing?

The argument seems to link this devoir to Charlotte's second summer at the pensionnat. Its narrator's resolution to resist self-centered solitude and reach out to others, despite disinclination, echo statements in her letters of that period.[1] His impulse to confess also seems to anticipate the one that drove Charlotte to the priest at Ste Gudule on September 1, 1843. However, self-conflict and self-mastery are themes that recur throughout her writing; they are clearly present in "Peter the Hermit," a devoir from June of her first year. That summer, she could also have been grappling with the prospect of a change in her status: both Hegers wanted her to stay on as a teacher of English. Teaching would offset the cost of her lessons and help her prepare for the career she had chosen, but it would also force her to become less cloistered and sacrifice privacy for service.

A more immediate challenge to her privacy appears in the manuscript itself. On the outside of its back page is the name "Sarah Anne," written in a child's careful script. Almost certainly, the writer was Sarah Anne Wheelwright, the fourth of five daughters of Dr. Thomas Wheelwright, who, with her sisters, began classes at the pensionnat in July 1842.[2] Because the family was resident in Brussels, the children were usually day students, but for several weeks that summer or autumn they may have boarded while their parents took a trip up the Rhine.[3] Charlotte, who had taken to the girls from the outset, looked after them and helped them with their studies; the signature of the nearly eight-year-old Sarah Anne might therefore be a witness to her care. Then again, Charlotte remained friendly with the Wheelwrights and visited them often after Emily's departure,[4] so Sarah Anne could have signed the page the next year—though probably not as late as August 24, since according to Charlotte, "in the latter part of August" the Wheelwrights moved away from Brussels.[5]

If the content leaves the date of the text indeterminate, the level of her French points to 1842, rather than 1843. The devoir opens smoothly but becomes less fluent as the internal dialogue progresses. She also makes a couple of basic errors—"soi-même" for "lui-même," "plus que vingt" for "plus de vingt"—that someone who had lived among French speakers for two years would not be likely to make.[6] Her other devoir written from a student's perspective, "Letter from a Poor Painter to a Great Lord" (October 17, 1843), shows far more facility with language.

The manuscript itself offers clues to its production, yet they too are far from conclusive. Charlotte penned the title in elaborate letters, which she uses nowhere else.[7] The hand-ruled pages have been sewn together and assembled as a little book. These features may mark it as a special offering: perhaps to show Heger before he went on holiday; perhaps to greet him after his return. If this were an 1843 text, the offering could have been reciprocal: he gave her a book of poems on August 15, the day on which the school term ended, and later, a copy of the speech he delivered that day at the Athénée Royal.[8] But even during the first August, Charlotte could have wanted him to recognize the efforts she was making.

What this evidence may demonstrate most is the problem of reading biographically. Nonetheless, the traces of her life that are inscribed here can help provide a context for analysis. The muffled bell, for instance, suggests the sound that reached the Brontë sisters as they studied at the pensionnat.[9] The allusion to pacing goes back much further, to passages in Charlotte's juvenilia: "A figure came towards the window & then paced back again & was almost lost in the shadow of the opposite end—again it appeared drawing near slowly—as slowly it withdrew to the dusk of the distance—To & fro it paced with the same measured step down the whole length of the large old parlour. . . ."[10] This figure is Elizabeth Hastings, but Charlotte and her sisters paced the same way.[11]

All along, the speaker conforms to a type of confined and questing Brontë character. Like William Crimsworth, he is narrowly righteous; like Jane Eyre, he apostrophizes reason and religion; like Lucy Snowe, he spends years as a recluse but is drawn to a more active life of service. Most obviously personal, to readers familiar with letters from Charlotte's adolescence and her fiction, are the conflict between inclination and duty; the angry frustration that he seeks to master; and the conscience that flays its possessor. The differences here are that the student is fighting intellectual, rather than creative, inclinations; that the battle is structured as a formal dialogue,[12] written to be read and corrected by a teacher; and that once again she makes the speaker male.

Charlotte puts the student's age as past twenty. She herself was past twenty-five yet still unable or unwilling to cast a woman in the narrator's role. Of course, within her culture, the title alone would imply a masculine perspective. Women were not supposed to aspire to a life beyond the private sphere. The academic milieu, emphasis on reasoning, and prospect of giving service in the world would also have been indices of maleness. Even the student's self-absorption would have had gender implications. His egoism does not take the form of vanity; he does not seek love and admiration—quite the opposite. He vows to survive without anyone's approval and overcome frailty through stoicism. Still, he is obsessed with his effect on those around them, as he imagines them to be. "They," in other words, are the objects of his own projections, rather than independent subjects.

Paradoxically, Charlotte frames his resolution in language that connects it to feminine behavior. The last two lines closely parallel a passage from a book used at Miss Wooler's and many other schools as a guide to womens' education and conduct, Hester Chapone's *Letters on the Improvement of the Mind*: "The same degree of active courage is not to be expected in woman as in man; and, not belonging to her nature, it is not agreeable in her: but passive courage—patience, and fortitude under sufferings—presence of mind, and calm resignation in danger—are surely desirable in every rational creature. . . ."[13] In effect, then, her student conflates genders, like Crimsworth—and remains as self-involved.

The allegory near the end of the devoir suggests a further link to *The Professor*. That novel was her phoenix, the first book to arise from the ashes of her Brussels experience. It is hardly a glorious production, but it attests to her tenacity, her hope, and her rejection of passivity and silence.

<u>Charlotte Brontë</u>   [draft before correction]   <u>October 6th</u>

Human Justice

In all ages, moralists ancient and modern have given sermons on the imperfections of the human race. According to these people, all gold

5   here on earth is mixed with lead; perfection is beyond man's reach; the best institutes of the wisest legislators have their faults. Sometimes one tires of hearing these dry dictums so often repeated, yet the moralists are right. It's easy to make fun of their axioms but it's difficult to refute them. What is there for example more lofty than the abstract idea of

10   justice? But the thing, as it is administered among men, is subject to many an abuse.

Let us take the case of one indicted, of a man accused of a crime; true Justice demands that conviction precede punishment, but human Justice finds that a mere suspicion suffices to authorize the

15   imposition of severe penalties. The accused undergoes a long imprisonment before being called before the tribunal that must decide his fate; the man perhaps innocent is associated with wretches hardened by vice. If, unfortunately, he has already shown some tendencies to learn quickly the lessons of vice, where will he find masters who will know better how

20   to develop those tendencies and bring them to perfection? If on the contrary, his soul is yet pure, what sufferings can be compared to those that the good man endures, surrounded by vicious and wretched creatures whose condition he cannot improve?

But at last, the indicted man is summoned to appear before his judge;

25   his trial is conducted; the cleverest lawyer in the kingdom is entrusted with the office of accuser; the king's prosecutor sets for him the false traps of the law. He puts into play against him all the arts, all the tricks of his trade; he tries to embarrass him, to intimidate him. Some-

La Justice humaine

De tout temps les moralistes anciens et modernes ont fait des sermons sur les imperfections du genre humain. Selon ces gens, tout or ici-bas est melé de plomb; la perfection est hors de la portée de l'homme; les meilleurs instituts des plus sages legislateurs ont leurs défauts. Quelquefois on s'impatiente d'entendre si souvent répéter ces dictums secs, cependant les moralistes ont raison; c'est facile de se moquer de leurs axiomes mais c'est dificile de les réfuter. Qu'y-a-t-il par exemple de plus élévé que l'idée abstraite de la justice? mais la chose, comme on l'administre parmi les hommes, est sujette à bien des abus.

Prenons le cas d'un prevenu d'un homme accusé de crime; la véritable Justice exige que la conviction précéde la punition, mais la Justice humaine trouve que le seul soupçon suffit pour autoriser l'imposition des peines sévères. Le prévenu subit un long emprisonnement avant d'être appelé devant le tribunal qui doit décider son sort; l'homme peut-être innocent est associé avec des miserables endurcis par le vice: si, malheureusement, il a déjà montré des dispositions pour apprendre vite les leçons de vice, où trouvera-t-il des maîtres qui sauront mieux developper ces dispositions et les conduire à la perfection? Si au contraire, son âme est encore pure, quelles souffrances peuvent être comparées à celles qu'éprouve l'homme de bien, entouré des êtres vicieux et malheureux dont il ne peut pas améliorer la condition?

Mais enfin, le prévenu est sommé de comparaître devant son juge; on lui fait son procés; l'avocat le plus habile du royaume est chargé de l'office d'accusateur: le procureur du roi tend pour lui les pièges trompeurs, de la loi: il met en jeu contre lui tous les arts, toutes les ruses de son métier; il tâche de l'embarrasser, de l'intimider. Quelquefois en

times in so acting, the prosecutor is the friend of justice; he removes
the mask of vice, and in showing its features as they are, he condemns
him to the punishment due him. But sometimes in this way he is the
enemy of virtue; those harsh epithets, those bitter invectives, that
declamation so full of strength is so much filth, flung upon the white
robe of innocence.

According to allegory, that filth always falls away and leaves the
garments stainless; but in reality, innocence sometimes yields to the
attacks of injustice; she succumbs to them and lets herself be covered by
the black mud that is flung on her. Still, out of five accused men, three
are ordinarily acquitted; is Justice then just after all? Yes, she is just in
the eyes of the world, she well fulfills her public duties; but follow the
accused man when he leaves the tribunal; accompany him home, to that
household from which he was torn some months before. Perhaps he is
a poor man, and during his absence hunger, thirst, misery, three sinister
guests, have visited his family. He finds his wife and his children
changed; they are paler, sadder; but with his return joy is rekindled in
their hearts. Hope accompanies him, and his presence seems to banish
suffering. The father of the family counsels courage, patience: "I will
work hard," says he, "and so my children will no longer be hungry, and
my wife will no longer be sad." He leaves his house to look for work;
the search is longer than he expected to find it; he realizes that for him
everything has changed, that he is a leper. The law has recognized his
innocence, but a false accusation has sullied its whiteness, and human
justice thrusts him aside. Thus rejected from the halls of virtue, vice
offers him asylum. Perhaps he again resists its attractions, but perhaps
too he yields to them; then on whom does the weight of his crime fall?
Must he alone bear all of it? Or should the Pharisees whose contempt
thrust him into despair bear a part?

———

agissant ainsi, le procureur est l'ami de la justice, il ôte le masque de vice, et en montrant ses traits tels qu'ils sont, il le condamne à la punition qui lui est dûe; mais quelquefois ainsi il est l'ennemi de la vertu, ces epithètes âpres, ces invectives amères, cette déclamation si pleine de force est autant de fange, jetée sur la robe blanche de l'innocence.

Selon l'allegorie cette fange tombe toujours, et laisse les vêtements sans tâche, mais selon la realité l'innocence céde quelquefois aux attaques de l'injustice; elle y succombe et se laisse couvrir de la boue noire qu'on jette sur elle. Cependant sur cinq prévenus, trois sont ordinairement acquittés; la Justice donc est juste après tout? Oui elle est juste aux yeux du monde, elle remplit bien ses devoirs publics; mais suivez le prévenu lorsqu'il quitte le tribunal; accompagnez-le chez lui, à cette maison d'où il était arraché il y a quelques mois, peut être c'est un homme pauvre et pendant son absence la faim, le soif, la misère, trois hôtes sinistres, ont visité sa famille; il trouve sa femme et ses enfants changés, ils sont plus pâles, plus tristes, mais à son retour la joie se rallume dans leurs coeurs; l'espérance l'accompagne et sa présence semble bannir la souffrance. Le père de famille conseille le courage, la patience; "je travaillerai" dit il "et alors mes enfants n'auront plus faim, et ma femme ne sera plus triste" Il quitte sa maison pour chercher le travail, la recherche est plus longue qu'il ne s'était attendu de le trouver; il s'aperçoit que pour lui tout est changé, qu'il est lepre. La loi a reconnu son innocence mais une fausse accusation en a souillé la blancheur et la justice humaine le repousse. Renvoyé ainsi des demeures de la vertu, le vice lui ouvre ses asiles; peut être il resiste encore à ses attraits, mais peut-être aussi il y céde; alors sur qui retombe le poids de son crime? Est-ce lui seul qui doit tout soutenir?_ ou les pharisiens dont le mépris l'a poussé au désespoir doivent-ils se charger d'une partie?

Human Justice

In all ages, moralists ancient and modern have given ~~sermons~~ *discourses* on the

imperfections of the human race. According to these ~~people~~ *persons*, all gold
                                                                    is alloyed
here on earth ~~is mixed~~ with lead; perfection is beyond man's reach; the
              ions   *some*
best ~~institutes~~ of the wisest legislators have ~~their~~ faults. Sometimes
                                          axioms
one tires of hearing these dry ~~dictums~~ so often repeated, yet the moralists
                                 It is   *in opinions   it is*
are right. ~~It's~~ easy to make fun of their axioms but ~~it's~~ difficult to refute

them. What is there, for example, more lofty than the abstract idea of
                                   its administration
justice? But ~~the thing~~, ~~as it is~~ ~~administered~~ among men, is subject to

many an abuse.
    Let us say a few words about those   *by way of example*
    ~~Let us take the case of one~~ indicted, ^~~of a man men accused of a~~
                                             judgment
~~crime~~; true Justice demands that ~~conviction~~ precede punishment, but

human Justice finds that a mere suspicion suffices to authorize the
                                           infliction
~~imposition~~ of severe penalties. The accused undergoes a long imprison-

ment before being called before the tribunal that must decide his fate; the

man perhaps innocent is associated with wretches hardened by vice. If,
                                                      contrary to virtue
unfortunately, he has already shown some tendencies ~~to learn quickly~~
                                                      ~~crime~~   *know*
~~the lessons of vice~~, where will he find masters who will know better how

to develop those tendencies and ~~bring them to perfection~~? If on the con-

trary, his soul is yet pure, what sufferings can be compared to those that

the good man endures, surrounded by vicious and wretched creatures
      faults he cannot correct and whose
whose^ condition he cannot improve?.

    But at last, the indicted man is summoned to appear before his judge;

his trial is conducted; the cleverest lawyer in the kingdom is entrusted

with the office of accuser; the king's prosecutor sets for him ~~the~~ false
                                                              stratagems
traps ; ~~of the law~~. He puts into play against him all the ~~arts~~, all the
that the adept ~~lawyer~~ accuser knows so well to set for the defense attorney ignorant
tricks of *the* h~~is~~ trade; he tries to embarrass him, to intimidate him. Some-

Marginal annotations (left margin):

*Ce [for it],
when the
aux[?] pre-
cedes. — Il
when the aux[?]
follows./
G*

obj[?]

objon[?]

[?]

Charlotte Brontë   Le 6 Octobre

La Justice humaine

                                      discours
De tout temps les moralistes anciens et modernes ont fait des ~~sermons~~
                                     personnages
sur les imperfections du genre humain. Selon ces ~~gens~~, tout or ici-bas
a un alliage
~~est mêlé~~ de plomb; la perfection est hors de la portée de l'homme; les   5
                           des
meilleurs institut~~i~~ons des plus sages législateurs ont ~~leurs~~ défauts. Quel-
                                        axiomes
quefois on s'impatiente d'entendre si souvent répéter ces ~~dictums~~ secs,   *Ce, quand*
              Il   *l'aux*[?] *pré-*
cependant les moralistes ont raison; ~~c'est~~ facile de se moquer de leurs *cède. — Il*
~~ja~~ opinions   *il*   *quand l'aux*[?]
axiomes mais ~~c'est~~ difficile de les réfuter. Qu'y-a-t-il, par exemple, de   *suit./*
                                  son administration   { *B*
plus élevé que l'idée abstraite de la justice? mais ~~la chose, comme on~~
                                                          10
~~l'administre~~ parmi les hommes, est sujette à bien des abus.
      Disons quelques mots des   pour exemple
      ~~Prenons le cas d'un~~ prévenus^ ~~des un hommes accusés de crime~~; la
                         le jugement
véritable Justice exige que ~~la conviction~~ précède la punition, mais la Jus-
                                        infliction
tice humaine trouve que le seul soupçon suffit pour autoriser l'~~imposition~~

des peines sévères. Le prévenu subit un long emprisonnement avant   15

d'être appelé devant le tribunal qui doit décider de son sort; l'homme
                                    à
peut-être innocent est associé ~~avec~~ des misérables endurcis par le vice: *obj*[?]
                                            contraires à la
si, malheureusement, il a déjà montré des dispositions ~~pour apprendre~~
vertu   ~~crime~~   *sachent*
~~vite les leçons de vice~~, où trouvera-t-il des maîtres qui sauront mieux dé- *objon*[?]

velopper ces dispositions et les ~~conduire à la perfection~~? Si au contraire, 20

son âme est encore pure, quelles souffrances peuvent être comparées à
                                        d'
celles qu'éprouve l'homme de bien, entouré ~~des~~ êtres vicieux et mal-   *à*
                      ni corriger les défauts. ni⌋   ⌊____⌋   [?]
heureux dont il ne peut^pas améliorer la condition?.

     Mais enfin, le prévenu est sommé de comparaître devant son juge;

on lui fait son procés; l'avocat le plus habile du royaume est chargé de   25

l'office d'accusateur: le procureur du roi tend pour lui les ~~pièges~~ tromp-
                                    artifices   *u*
eurs ⸝ ⸝de la loi: il met en jeu contre lui tous les ~~arts~~, toutes les ruses d~~e~~
      que l'~~avocat~~ accusateur habile sait si bien tendre pour le défenseur ignorant
son métier; il tâche de l'embarrasser, de l'intimider. Quelquefois en

G
Good } 30

public minister　　　　　　　　　　　　*tears*
times in so acting, the prosecutor is the friend of justice; he removes
　　from　　　　　　　the
the mask of vice, and in showing its features as they are, he condemns

him to the punishment due him. But sometimes in this way he is the

enemy of virtue; those harsh epithets, those bitter invectives, that

are　　　　　　*opprobrium*
Good　declamation so full of strength is so much filth, flung upon the white

robe of innocence.

35　　According to allegory, that filth always falls away and leaves the

garments stainless; but in reality, innocence sometimes yields to the

attacks of injustice; she succumbs to them and lets herself be covered by

the black mud that is flung on her. Still, out of five accused men, three

are ordinarily acquitted; is Justice then just after all? Yes, she is just in

Good }
40　the eyes of the world, she well fulfills her public duties; but follow the

accused man when he leaves the tribunal; accompany him home, to that

household from which he was torn some months before. Perhaps he is

good }　a poor man, and during his absence hunger, thirst, misery, three sinister

guests, have visited his family. He finds his wife and his children
　　　　　　　　　　　　　　　　it is true
45　changed; they are paler, sadder; ~~but~~ with his return joy is rekindled in
　　　　　　　　　　returns with him
their hearts. Hope accompanies him, and his presence seems to banish
　I will work, says　　　　*who*　　　*and*　*am going to*
suffering. The father of the family counsels courage, patience: "I ~~will~~
　very　*wife,*　*and*　　*the*
work hard," says he, ~~"and so my~~ children will longer be hungry, and ~~my~~
you
~~wife~~ will no longer be sad." He leaves his house to look for work; the

50　search is longer than he expected to find it; he realizes that for him
Good

everything has changed, that he is a leper. The law has recognized his

innocence, but a false accusation has sullied its whiteness, and human
　(unclear)
justice thrusts him aside. Thus rejected from the halls of virtue, vice

offers him asylum. Perhaps he again resists its attractions, but perhaps

55　too he yields to them; & then on whom does the weight of his crime fall?
　　　　　　　　　else
Must he alone bear all of it? Or should the Pharisees whose contempt

thrust him into despair bear a part?　　of the burden
　　　　　　　　　　　　　　of what?

ministère public   _arache_   _au_

agissant ainsi, le procureur est l'ami de la justice, il ôte le masque de   { B
           les   _Bon_

vice, et en montrant ses traits tels qu'ils sont, il le condamne à la   30

punition qui lui est dûe; mais quelquefois ainsi il est l'ennemi de la

vertu, ces épithètes âpres, ces invectives amères, cette déclamation si
             sont   d'opprobre

pleine de force est autant de fange, jetée sur la robe blanche de l'inno-   _Bon_

cence.

Selon l'allégorie cette fange tombe toujours, et laisse les vêtements   35

sans tâche, mais selon la réalité l'innocence céde quelquefois aux attaques

de l'injustice; elle y succombe et se laisse couvrir de la boue noire qu'on

jette sur elle. Cependant sur cinq prévenus, trois sont ordinairement

acquittés; la Justice donc est juste après tout? oui elle est juste aux yeux   { _Bon_

du monde, elle remplit bien ses devoirs publics; mais suivez le prévenu   40

lorsqu'il quitte le tribunal; accompagnez-le chez lui, à cette maison d'où
      fut

il était arraché il y a quelques mois, peut être c'est un homme pauvre et
                          a

pendant son absence la faim, le soif, la misère, trois hôtes sinistres, ont   { _bon_

visite sa famille; il trouve sa femme et ses enfants changés, ils sont plus
                      il est vrai

pâles, plus tristes, mais à son retour la joie se rallume dans leurs coeurs;   45
        revient avec lui   _Je travaillerai dit_

l'espérance l'accompagne et sa présence semble bannir la souffrance. Le
         qui   _et_   _vais bien_   _femme,_

père de famille conseille le courage, la patience; "je travaillerai" dit il
   _et_   _les_   _tu ne_

"et alors mes enfants n'auront plus faim, et ma femme ne seras plus triste"

Il quitte sa maison pour chercher le travail, la recherche est plus longue   _Bon_
                                 a

qu'il ne s'était attendu de le trouver; il s'aperçoit que pour lui tout est   50

changé, qu'il est lepre. La loi a reconnu son innocence mais une fausse
                                   (peu clair)

accusation en a souillé la blancheur et la justice humaine le repousse.

Renvoyé ainsi des demeures de la vertu, le vice lui ouvre ses asiles; peut

être il resiste encore à ses attraits, mais peut-être aussi il y cède; & alors

sur qui retombe le poids de son crime? Est-ce lui seul qui doit tout sou-   55
      bien

tenir?_ ou les pharisiens dont le mépris l'a poussé au désespoir doivent-

ils se charger d'une partie? du fardeau
            de quoi?

Comments

An idea once seized, I fell to work. "Human Justice" rushed before me in novel guise, a red, random beldame with arms akimbo. I saw her in her house, the den of confusion: servants called to her for orders or help which she did not give; beggars stood at her door waiting and starving unnoticed; a swarm of children, sick and quarrelsome, crawled round her feet and yelled in her ears appeals for notice, sympathy, cure, redress. The honest woman cared for none of these things. She had a warm seat of her own by the fire, she had her own solace in a short black pipe, and a bottle of Mrs. Sweeny's soothing syrup; she smoked and she sipped and she enjoyed her paradise, and whenever a cry of the suffering souls about her pierced her ears too keenly—my jolly dame seized the poker or the hearth-brush: if the offender was weak, wronged, and sickly, she effectually settled him; if he was strong, lively, and violent, she only menaced, then plunged her hand in her deep pouch, and flung a liberal shower of sugar-plums.

—Lucy Snowe, *Villette*[1]

Ten years separate Charlotte Brontë's devoir from the "sketch" that she has Lucy "[scratch] hurriedly on paper" to satisfy Paul Emanuel's colleagues.[2] Only their titles seem to link these compositions, whose differences affirm their author's striking transformation from a pupil bent on earning her professor's approval to a woman writing her fourth novel, her way. Suggestive comparisons can nonetheless be drawn between the real and the fictional essays. The devoir manuscript exemplifies her methods of composing and revising at the pensionnat. *Villette* reconstitutes those methods in recalling them and so points up the changes in her attitude toward devoirs—and, more broadly, toward the self engaged in writing.

The date on "La Justice humaine" identifies it as an essay from the start of the fall term. (Although she omits the year, its flawed French and its brevity both argue for 1842; by the next fall, her devoirs were much longer.) In contrast, Lucy writes her "Human Justice" in May, for reasons intrinsic in *Villette*'s plot: since Paul is to sail for Guadeloupe in August, the romance between them must develop earlier. Charlotte also makes Lucy's an impromptu composition, evoked in a traumatic confrontation. Paul has put his protégée's talent on exhibit, first by showing one of her devoirs to his associates and then by subjecting her to their examination when they charge that he himself composed her work. Under pressure, Lucy can do nothing; the theme, "Human Justice," which Rochemorte dictates, strikes her as a "[b]lank, cold abstraction." She only breaks through her nervousness and anger when she realizes that these were the two men who pursued her on the night of her arrival in Villette: "'Pious mentors!' thought I. 'Pure guides for youth! If "Human Justice" were what she ought be. . . .'"[3]

Charlotte's devoir may also have begun with instructions to write on the theme of human justice, but the rest of the context is pure fiction. Heger would not have forced a struggling, timid foreigner to show off work so manifestly fault-ridden. When he did exhibit the Brontë sisters' devoirs, he read them aloud or fixed them up. His schedule, always heavy, also makes it more than doubtful that he singled her out for this assignment; more probably, he gave it to the class. One of Charlotte's notebooks contains two successive dictées that trace the practical effects of abstract concepts: "Slander," by Massillon, and "On Truth," by Frayssinous.[4] Possibly he introduced "Justice" in this context, or he could simply have instructed his students to humanize that lofty abstraction.

Whatever its genesis, Charlotte's composition is hardly as spontaneous as Lucy's. Even if she seized on an immediate idea, the legal terms probably required some research, and she knew she would have to give

Heger a draft that he would mark and return for her revisions.[5] Few of the Brontës' devoirs have survived with all the interim stages in evidence, but the manuscript of this one attests to at least four levels of writing and response.[6] Charlotte wrote the text in her tidy devoir hand, using a brown ink. Heger made a few light marks in pencil, mainly underlines, and much more extensive notations in a rusty ink (reproduced here in bold type). Charlotte then responded with corrections and additions, crossing out the words he questioned with neat slash marks and adding substitutions in a more condensed script. She also seems to have initiated changes unprompted by Heger's corrections.

What can be deduced from this process? Evidently, that Heger liked the essay. His "Goods" convey approval of her principles and images, although he keeps alerting her to inapt phrasing and imprecision in her use of terms. Perhaps because it clashes with the image of stained innocence, he underscores "that he is a leper"; Charlotte's response is to delete the clause. Elsewhere, she responds by finding idiomatic substitutes. She also expands two explanations. Heger himself does not rewrite as much as usual; however, in the section where the father returns home, he tinkers with the dialogue to make it more overt in its display of family sentiment and courage.

Charlotte's own courage extends only to questioning a system that is manifestly unjust. In form, this "Human Justice" takes no risks. It opens by repeating the clichés of the moralists; then it narrows down to the argument and case in point. There is no rebellion in its moral indignation or its imagery of innocence defiled.

Whether, in the fall of 1852, she retrieved "Human Justice" from the pile she brought from Brussels will remain an unanswerable question.[7] She may not have needed that token of her past when she set about composing Lucy's "show-trial."[8] She could have thought instead about the justice she received when her master failed to answer her letters. Perhaps too her naïveté in writing him so candidly struck her now as bitterly ironic. Whatever her motives, in inventing Lucy's devoir she entirely subverted her old tenets. Lucy's "Human Justice" has no proper introduction, no reasoning through cause and effect to reach conclusions. It bypasses the high tone and the trappings of the moralist for coarsely appropriate realism. Significantly too, it changes gender.

In 1842 Charlotte's narrator is implicitly male and middle class. The subjects of her discourse—suspect, lawyers, judge, and cellmates—move in spheres that the Victorians recognized as masculine: the courtroom, the prison, and the workplace. Virtue and innocence, feminine nouns in French, are powerless compared to (masculine) vice. Against its temptations, the home provides scant shelter; the wife of the acquitted man is grouped with his children as an object he may or may not rescue. Justice, another feminine noun, is as dubious a refuge as the home. Its decree of acquittal carries no weight in a masculine world composed of Pharisees.

In 1852 Charlotte shifts the site of power to a beldame in a paradise of squalor. Oblivious to children, charity, and household, possessor of a deep pouch as well as a poker, she puffs her pipe and guzzles whiskey while claimants groan and grovel.[9] Lucy (whose ambivalence, rebellion, and androgyny have all been widely discussed by modern critics)[10] is a fit creator of this creature who undermines the ideals of justice and the feminine. She cannot gratify Paul when he puts her on display as a paragon of intellect and learning; after he hurries her away from the schoolroom, where she sat copying an intricate engraving, she reacts by losing her voice. But memory and a rush of moral outrage combine to release her from her temporary impotence. Rather than the voice, the loaded pen becomes her weapon, replacing the copyist's pencil.

Lucy recalls this scene from the perspective of a more mature woman looking back. Analogously, Charlotte Brontë represents Lucy from her own adult perspective on Brussels. As Lucy's improvised "sketch" supersedes the derivative copy she was making in her classroom, so the "Human Justice" Charlotte sketches in *Villette* supersedes her old, deferential devoir. Thus the text that Lucy leaves with her readers, uncorrected—she withdraws before Paul or his colleagues can comment—symbolically recasts Charlotte's actual devoir and her earlier authorial persona.

The Palace of Death

═══════

Theme

In times past, when death had something to do; her sole minister was old
age, but before long . . . and death had so much business then that she
wanted to appoint a prime minister . . . . Assembly in her palace; all the
purveyors of Death are seen arriving; each one justifies his claim; her
majesty death appears extremely perplexed when the door opens and a
beauty . . . . description of Intemperance . . . . Death chooses her as
viceroy and dismisses the assembly saying.

═══════

In times past, when the earth was young, Death had little occupation; she already existed, if one can speak of her existence who lets
herself be seen and felt only in replacing life by nothingness; but her
empire was still weak, because the vigor and vitality of the young sphere
that God had just launched in space resisted that cold influence which
wanted to freeze everything.

good thought

In that epoch /, man was a noble savage, submitting to no law, save
the law of nature; subject to no sovereign, save his God. Methuselah and
Enoch, Abraham and Jacob, were but Asiatic shepherds, who roved over
the plains of Mesopotamia, pitching their tents wherever there was pas-
turage for their camels. War, ambition, excess were for them unknown,
and when death wanted to summon them to her realm, the only minister
of whom she could avail herself was old age. But finally the golden age
ran out; to the first patriarchs there succeeded a race of ambitious men,
who, abandoning pastoral life, leaving the plains and the deserts, built
themselves cities where luxury and consequently vice soon found a habitation. At that time Death perceived that her barren empire was starting

objon the original state is not a wild state. noble savage.

Good

Then

in

Le Palais de la Mort

─────

Matière

Autrefois lorsque la mort avait quelque chose à faire; son unique ministre

etait la vieillesse, mais bientôt . . . et la mort eut tant d'affaires alors   5

qu'elle voulut prendre un premier ministre . . . . Assemblée dans son

palais; on voit arriver tous les pourvoyeurs de la Mort; chacun fait valoir

son titre; sa majesté la mort parait fort embarrassée lorsque la porte

s'ouvre et une beauté . . . . description de l'Intempérance . . . . La Mort

la choisit pour vice-roi et congédie l'assemblée en disant.   10

─────

Autrefois, lorsque la terre était jeune, la Mort avait peu d'occupa-

tion: elle existait déjà, si on peut <u>parler de</u> l'existence de celle qui se   *pensée*
bonne

laisse voir et sentir seulement en remplaçant la vie par le néant, mais son   [?]

empire était encore faible car la vigueur et la vitalité de la jeune sphère

que Dieu venait de lancer dans l'espace, resistaient à cette influence   15

froide qui voulait tout glacer.   *obj<u>on</u>*
                                          obj<u>on</u>

À cette époque /, l'homme était un <u>noble sauvage</u>, soumis à nulle loi,   *l'état primitif*
n'est pas l'état

excepté la loi de la nature; assujetti à nul souverain, excepté son Dieu.   *sauvage.*
noble sauvage
Mathusalem et Enoch, Abrahame et Jacob n'étaient que des bergers asia-

la

tiques, qui rôdaient dans les plaines de Mésopotamie, en dressant leurs   20

de temps à *es*   *s*   *s*

tentes partout où il y avait du pâturage pour leurs chameaux. La guerre,

à

l'ambition l'<u>excè</u>s étaient pour eux inconnus, et lorsque la mort voulut   (,)

put

les appeler dans son royaume, le seul ministre dont elle po<u>uvait</u> se servir

fut

était la vieillesse. Mais enfin le siècle d'or s'écoula, aux premiers patri-

arches succéda une race d'hommes ambitieux, qui, abandonnant la vie   25

pastorale, quittant les plaines et les déserts, se bâtirent des villes où le   *Bon*

Alors

luxe et par conséquent le vice trouvèrent bientôt <u>une habitation</u>. À ce

en

to be populous, that each day new inhabitants entered it.   Old age

look up the
meaning of
this word.

complained; <u>he</u> did not want to be in charge of all the young people and
all

each

^the children that some plague or massacre consigned to him every day.

why?

At last Death found herself obliged to choose a prime minister; as soon

the

as she announced her intention, several candidates solicited ~~her~~ prefer-

ence.

one decides
a thing; one
decides [re-
flexive] to...

convoked

Before deciding ~~about it~~, she called a council in her palace.   This

edifice resembled the one that the caprice of a Northern sovereign had

constructed on the banks of the Dan Neva.   Neither marble, nor stone,

nor precious wood, nor gilding, were to be seen there.   Winter had been

very good
idea

the architect, and he had drawn its materials from the bosom of an icy

chandelier

sea.   No candlestick shone there, but a pale and bluish moonlight made

visible domes, columns, and vaults carved in ice.   The counselors of Death

were ranked in order before her throne.   Perhaps it was light reflected

tin
[mirroring]

from the cold walls that imparted to their tints a certain deathly pallor,

and it was undoubtedly the importance of the question they were going

to decide that made them keep a singularly profound silence.   Never had

been seen a more sage assembly; the statues that populate a church are

neither more motionless, nor less talkative.

Death entered and sat upon her throne; she arrived noiselessly; it was

had

as if a shadow passed across the crowd.   A large veil concealed her fea-

tures and her form, but, when she raised her scepter to signal the candi-

to let pass the hand and

dates to approach, the folds of the veil half-opened to reveal ˇthe arm of

a skeleton.

you do well
to make her
the first —
Why ~~the first~~?

an

First to put herself forward was Ambition, imposing woman with a

broad forehead and eyes aglitter with burning fire, but her whole aspect

and all her movements lacked calm and dignity.

~~reaper~~

"Mighty Sovereign," said she, "I am a faithful laborer in these fields;

wherever I have sown seeds in the earth, it offers a rich harvest to your

là,

temps la Mort s'aperçut que son empire désert commençait à se peupler,

que chaque jour il y entrait de nouveaux habitants. La vieillesse se

de tous
plaignit, il ne voulut pas se charger de toutes les jeunes gens et les   30

chaque   *cherchez le*
enfants que quelque peste ou quelque massacre lui consignait tous les   *sens de ce mot.*

jours; enfin la Mort se trouva dans la necessité de choisir un premier   *pourquoi?*

ministre; aussitôt qu'elle annonça son intention, plusieurs candidats

l
briguèrent sa préférence.

convoqua   *on décide*
    Avant d'y décider elle appela un conseil dans son palais. Cet edifice   *une chose*   35
                                                          on se décide à...

ressemblait à celui que le caprice d'un souverain du Nord fit construire

de la
sur les rives du Dah Néva. On n'y voyait ni marbre, ni pierre ni bois

précieux, ni dorure; l'Hiver en avait été l'architecte et il avait tiré ses   *idée*
lustre - lampe   *très bonne*
matériaux du sein d'une mer glaciale: nul chandelier n'y brillait, mais un

clair de lune pâle et bleuâtre faisait voir des dômes, des colomnes et des   40
                                                             obj.[?]

voûtes taillis en glace Les conseillers de la Mort étaient rangés en ordre

devant son trône; c'était peut-être le reflet des murs froids qui commu-

niquait à leur teinte une certaine pâleur mortelle et c'était sans doute   *étain*

l'importance de la question qu'ils allaient décider qui les faisait garde un

silence singulièrement profond: jamais on n'a vu une assemblée plus   45

sage; les statues qui peuplent une église ne sont ni plus immobiles, ni

moins causeuses.

    La Mort entra et s'assit sur son trône; elle arriva sans bruit; c'était

eût   é
comme si une ombre passait à travers la foule; un grand voile cachait ses

traits et sa forme, mais, lorsqu'elle leva son sceptre pour faire signe aux   50

pr. laisser passer une main et
candidats de s'approcher, les plis du voile s'entreouvrirent et on vit ˇ un

bras de squelette.

une   *vous faites*
    Premièrement se présenta l'Ambition, femme auguste au front large,   *Bien / de la*
                                                       placer la 1re —
aux yeux étincelants d'un feu ardent, mais tout son aspect et tous ses   *Pourquoi la 1re?*

mouvements manquaient de calme et de dignité.   55

moissonneur
    "Souveraine puissante" dit-elle, "Je suis un fidèle laboureur dans ces

champs; partout où j'ai ensemencé la terre, elle offre une riche moisson

scythe; once my influence has slipped into a man's heart, he no longer

regards the life of his fellow creatures as a precious thing that he must

not touch; all the affections, friendship, love, flee at my approach; ~~and~~

look up the
meaning of
this word

discord, hatred, envy, conspiracy, treason follow me." As she pro-

nounced these words, a long train of sinister phantoms glid wearing

masks, daggers, and black cloaks glided across the room. They seemed

to pass through the vitreous wall and, in vanishing, left traces of blood

in their steps. "Those are my children," said ambition. "If today you

choose me as minister, tomorrow I will send them among ~~all~~ the peoples

glutted
of the earth, and very soon your empire will be filled with inhabitants."

Death did not answer. She raised her scepter a second time and a

Why an
Amazon?

new candidate was introduced. It was a form of Amazon, garbed like

Thalestris in a scarlet robe, short and tucked up; she bore a bow in her

hand and a quiver over her shoulder; she led on a leash two huge dogs,

ferocious as two wolves; the features of this woman resembled those of

brandish
wave about }

look up
this word

a man; her bearing was proud and bold; her muscular arm appeared

strong enough to wave about the lance of an Achilles. "I am War!" said

she. "I come from a battlefield; my garments are still stained with the

made
blood I have seen flow. Who can serve you more faithfully than I, oh

Death? Who has led more victims to your feet? When I unleash Mas-

on
sacre and Carnage ~~after~~ the human race (and she pointed to the fierce

G

beasts she held on the leash) the moans of widows and cries of orphans

announce your victory."
How? that was worth a word. ed

Death smiled, War's speech seem~~ing~~ to please her; she was going to

there entered
make her choice, when the door opened and ^ a third candidate entered,

a young, fair, and richly dressed woman. She had an air so gay, a step

had
so jaunty, coloring so vivid, that at first sight one would have said that

Health herself had entered the palace of Death. But upon examining her

closely, one realized that joy delirium rather than joy shone in her eyes,

à votre faux; aussitôt que mon influence s'est glissée dans le coeur d'un homme, il ne regarde plus la vie de ses semblables comme une chose précieuse à laquelle il ne doit pas toucher; toutes les affections, l'amitié, l'amour, s'enfuient à mon approche; èt la discorde, la haine, l'envie, la conspiration, la trahison me suivent." Tandis qu'elle prononçait ces mots, un long train de fantômes sinistres ğlïšš portant le masque, le poignard et le manteau noir glissaient à travers la salle; ils semblèrent passer par la muraille vitreuse et en disparaissant, ils laissèrent des traces de sang sur leurs pas. "Ce sont mes enfants" dit l'ambition "Si aujourd'hui vous me choisissez pour ministre, demain je les enverrai parmi tòùs

regorgera
les peuples de la terre, et bientôt votre empire sera rempli d'habitants."

La Mort ne répondit pas, elle leva son sceptre une seconde fois et un

fut
nouveau candidat était introduit C'était une forme d'Amazone, vêtue comme Thalestre en robe écarlate, courte et retroussée, elle portait un arc à la main et un carquois sur l'épaule; elle menait en laisse deux grands chiens féroces comme deux loups; les traits de cette femme ressemblaient à ceux d'un homme, son maintien était fier et hardi; son bras musculeux paraissait assez fort pour brandiller la lance d'un Achille. "Je suis la Guerre!" dit-elle "J'arrive d'un champš de bataille, mes vête-

fait
ments sont encore teints du sang que j'ai vu couler. Qui peut te servir plus fidèlement que moi, ô Mort? qui a mené plus de victimes à tes

sur
pieds?, quand je lâche après le genre humain le Massacre et le Carnage, (et elle montra les bêtes féroces qu'elle tenait en laisse) les plaintes des veuves et les cris des orphelins annoncent ta victoire."

Comment? cela méritait un mot.)
La Mort sourit, leš discours de la Guerre semblant lui plaire, elle

son   *il entra*
allait décider sa choix, lorsque la porte s'ouvrit et^ un troisième candidat èhtrà; une femme jeune, belle, et richement vêtue: elle avait l'air si gai, la démarche si legère, les couleurs si vives, qu'au premier abord on

eût
aurait dit que la Santé elle-même s'était introduite dans le palais de la

e
Mort. Mais lorsqu'on l'examina de près on s'aperçut que là jòïè délire

cherchez le sens de ce mot. [?]
—

Pourquoi une amazone

{brandir
{brandiller

cherchez ce mot, [?]

B

60

65

70

75

80

85

complexion

look up
[?]

Good

90

95

that fever colored her <u>tint</u>, and that disorder characterized her whole attire. Her disheveled head was crowned with a garland of flowers; those flowers seemed fresh and fair, but among the petals, twisted in the stems, one saw a serpent glitter.

Intemperance (for thus was this enchantress named) stepped proudly before Ambition and War. "I claim my right," said she. "For one victim that my rivals have sacrificed on the altars of Death, I can easily count a hundred."

<u>Death</u> arose. "My sister," said she, "you alone are worthy of being <u>Death</u>'s viceroy. War and Ambition are but your children; all the demons that destroy man are born of you, and it is from your intoxicating cup that the human race drinks the deadly poison of its days.

<hr>

plutôt que la joie brillait dans ses yeux, que le fièvre colorait <u>sa</u> teinte, *son teint* *cherchez* [?]

que le désordre caractèrisait toute sa mise; sa tête échevelée était

couronnée d'une guirlande de fleurs; ces fleurs paraissaient fraîches et *Bon* 90

belles, mais entre les pétales, entortillé dans les tiges on voyait luire un

serpent.

L'Intempérance (car c'était ainsi que s'appellait cette enchanteresse

pass<u>ait</u> fièrement devant l'Ambition et la Guerre. "Je réclame mon

droit" dit-elle "Pour une victime que mes rivales ont sacrifiée sur les 95

autels de la Mort, je puis bien compter cent *en* ".

La <u>Mor</u>t se leva, "Ma soeur" dit-elle; "toi seule es digne d'être la

vice-reine de la <u>Mor</u>t − La Guerre et l'Ambition ne sont que tes enfants;

tous les démons qui perdent l'homme naissent de toi, et c'est dans ta

coupe enivrante que le genre humain boit le poison mortel de ses jours. 100

Theme. The Palace of Death.

───────────

Theme

In times past, when . . . . Death had something to do; her sole minister was then Old Age, but before long . . . . . . and Death had so much business then that she wanted to appoint a prime minister.

Assembly in her palace; all the purveyors of Death are seen arriving; each one justifies his claim; her majesty Death seeming extremely per-
when the door opens
plexed ^ and a beauty . . . . . description of Intemperance . . . . Death chooses her as viceroy and dismisses the assembly saying . . . .

The Palace of Death.

───────────

In times past, when men were few in number, Death lived frugally and husbanded her means. Her sole minister then was old age, who guarded the gate of her palace and from time to time admitted a solitary victim to appease the hunger of her mistress. This abstinence was soon recompensed; her majesty's prey increased prodigiously and Old Age began to find that she had too much to do.

It was at this time that Death decided to change her way of living, to appoint new agents, and to take a prime minister.

On the day set for the nomination, the silence of the somber palace was broken by the arrival of candidates from all quarters; the vaults, the chambers, and the galleries resounded with the noise of steps that came and went, as if the bones that lay strewn about the pavement had suddenly come back to life; and Death, looking down from the height of her throne, smiled hideously to see what multitudes hastened to serve her. Among the first arrivals were Wrath and Vengeance, who hurried to

Good

Matière. Le palais de la Mort.

Matière

========

Autrefois, lorsque . . . . La Mort avait quelquechose à faire; son unique

ministre était alors la Vieillesse, mais bientôt . . . . . . et La Mort avait

tant d'affaires alors qu'elle voulut prendre un premier ministre.   5

    Assemblée dans son palais; on voit arriver tous les pourvoyeurs de

la Mort; chacun fait valoir son titre; sa majesté La Mort paraissait fort
         lorsque la porte s'ouvre
embarrassée ⌃ et une beauté . . . . . description de l'Intempérance . . . .

La Mort la choisit pour vice-roi et congédie l'assemblée en disant . . . .

Le Palais de la Mort.   10

========

    Autrefois, lorsque les hommes étaient un petit nombre, la Mort vivait

frugalement et ménageait ses moyens; son unique ministre était alors la

vieillesse, qui gardait la porte de son palais et introduisait de temps en

temps une victime solitaire pour apaiser la faim de sa maitresse; cette
       fut
abstinence était bientôt récompensée; la proie de sa majesté s'augmentait   15

prodigieusement et la Vieillesse commençait à trouver qu'elle avait trop

à faire.

    Il était à cette époque que la Mort se décida à changer sa manière de

vivre, à appointer des agents nouveaux et à prendre un premier ministre.

    Le jour fixé pour la nomination le silence du sombre palais fut rompu   20

par l'arrivée des candidats de tous côtés, les voûtes, les chambres et les

galeries résonnaient du bruit des pas qui allaient et venaient, comme si

les ossements qui jonchaient leur pavé s'étaient subitement réanimés et   *Bon*

la Mort, regardant du haut de son trône, sourit hideusement de voir

quelles multitudes accouraient à lui servir. Parmi les premiers venus on   25

voyait la Colère et la Vengeance qui allèrent se mettre en face de sa

station themselves before her Majesty, loudly arguing about the justice of their particular rights. Envy and Treason took their positions behind in the shadow. Famine and Plague, attended by their companions Sloth and Avarice, secured very convenient places in the crowd and cast a scornful eye over the other guests. Nonetheless they were forced to give way when Ambition and Fanaticism appeared; the retinues of those two personages filled the council chamber, and they imperiously demanded an immediate audience.

"I doubt not," said the former, "that your majesty will be fair in her decision, but why waste time in vain disputes when a glance will suffice to determine the one who is alone worthy of the office in question? Who are all these pretenders who besiege your throne? What can they do in your service? The ablest among them is no more capable of governing your empire than is a soldier, with no quality other than his courage, of commanding an army. They know how to strike one victim here and another there; they know how to entrap feeble prey, the men on whom your mark has been visible since birth, and those are the limits of their usefulness; as for me, I will lead the elite of the race to your portals, those who are furthest from your power. I will harvest them in their flower and offer them to you as troops at the same stroke. Besides, I have so many means; it is not the sword alone that wins my victories; I have other agents, secret but powerful allies. Fanatacism himself is but an instrument that I shall employ for my profit."

On hearing these words, Fanaticism shook his savage head, and raising toward Death an eye burning with the fire of obsession, he began: "I know this blusterer will happily borrow my weapons and march under my banners, but is that any reason for that she should presume to compare herself with me? Not only will I be as powerful as she at overturning states and desolating realms, but I will enter into families; I will

Good

Majesté, en disputant hautement^sur^ la justice de leurs droits particuliers;

L'Envie et la Trahison prirent leurs stations derrière dans l'ombre; la

Famine et la Peste, assistées par leurs compagnes la Paresse et l'Avarice,

obtinrent des places très commodes parmi la foule et jetèrent un regarde   30

méprisant sur les autres hôtes; cependant elles se trouvèrent forcées à

céder quand l'Ambition et le Fanatisme paraissaient; les cortèges de ces

deux personnages emplissaient la salle de conseil et ils demandèrent im-

perieusement une audience prompte.

"Je ne doute pas," dit la première, "que votre majesté sera juste   35

dans sa décision mais à quoi bon consumer le temps en vaines

contestations quand un coup-d'oeil suffira à déterminer celle qui est seule

digne de l'office en question? Quels sont tous ces prétendants qui

assiégent votre trône? Que peuvent ils faire dans votre service? Le plus

habile parmi eux n'est pas plus capable de gouverner votre empire qu'un   40

soldat qui n'a d'autre qualité que son courage, de commander une armée.

Ils savent frapper une victime ici et une autre là; ils savent attrapper la   *Bon*

faible proie, les hommes sur lesquels votre signe est visible depuis leur

naissance, et cela est ^ce sont^ les limités de leur utilité; tandis que moi, je

menerai à vos portes l'élite de la race; ceux qui sont les plus éloignés de   45

votre pouvoir; je les moissonerai dans l^la^eur fleur et vous les offrirai par

troupes à la fois. Puis j'ai tant de moyens; il n'est pas le glaive seul qui

gagne mes victoires; j'ai d'autres agents, des alliés secrets mais puis-

sants; le Fanatisme lui-même n'est qu'un instrument que j'emploierai à

me servir."   50

En entendant ces mots le Fanatisme secoua sa tête sauvage et levant

vers la Mort un oeil brulant du feu de la manie il commenca: "Je su^a^is

que cette glorieuse sera aise d'emprunter mes armes et de marcher sous

mes enseignes, mais est cela une raison pour qu'elle présume à se comparer

avec moi? Non seulement suis je ^je serai^ puissant comme elle à renverser les   55

royaumes ^états^ et à désoler les royaumes, mais j'entrerai dans les familles

55 set the son against the father, the daughter against the mother; inspired^ by me

the faithful friend will become a mortal enemy, the wife will betray her

husband, the domestic his master. No sentiment can withstand me; I will

traverse the earth beneath heaven's ligh[?] banners and crowns will be as stones

beneath my feet. As for the other candidates, they are unworthy of

60 attention; Wrath is irreasonable barbarism; vengeance is partial; Famine can be

conquered by industry; Plague is capricious. Your prime minister must

be someone who is always close to men, who surrounds and possesses

them. Decide then between Ambition and me; we are the only ones be-

tween whom your choice can hesitate might."

65 Fanaticism fell silent, and her Majesty seemed to waver in doubt

between these two rivals when the door of the hall opened, and there

entered a person before whom everyone fell back in astonishment, for

she had a figure that seemed to glow with joy and health, her step was

as light as a zephyr, and Death herself appeared uneasy at her first

70 approach; however, she soon reassured herself. "You recognize me," the

stranger said to her; "I arrive later than the others, but I know that my

claim is certain. Some of my rivals are formidable, I admit, and I may

perhaps be surpassed by several in striking deeds that draw the admira-

tion of the mob, but I have a friend before whom this whole assembly

75 will be forced to succumb. Her name is Civilization: in a few years G. she

will come to dwell on this earth with us, and each century will amplify

her power. In the end, she will divert Ambition from your service; she

will put the brake of law on wrath; she will wrest the weapons from

Fanaticism's hands; she will chase confine Famine off among the savages. I

80 alone will grow and flourish under her reign; the power of all the others

will expire with their partisans; mine will exist even when I am dead.

If once I make acquaintance with the father, my influence will extend to

the son, and before men unite to banish me from their society, I will

have changed their entire nature and made the whole species an easier

par moi
j'opposerai le fils au père, la fille à la mère; inspirés^ l'ami fidèle de-
a
viendront un ennemi mortel, la femme trahira son mari, le domestique

son maître; nul sentiment ne peut me resister; je traverserai la terre sous
bannières
les lum[?] du ciel et les couronnes seront commes des pierres sous mes   60

pieds. Quant aux autres candidats ils ne sont pas dignes d'attention; la
barbarisme
Colère est irraisonnable; la vengeance est partiale; la Famine peut être

vaincue par l'industrie; la Peste est capricieuse. Votre premier ministre

doit être quelqu'un qui est toujours près des hommes, qui les entoure et

les possède; décidez donc entre l'Ambition et moi, nous sommes les seuls   65
puisse
sur lesquels votre choix peut hésiter."

Le Fanatisme se tut, et sa Majesté semblait balancer en doute entre

ces deux rivaux lorsque la porte de la salle s'ouvrit et il y entra une

personne devant laquelle tout le monde recula en étonnement car elle

avait une figure qui paraissait rayonner de joie et de santé, son pas était   70

leger comme un zephyr et la Mort elle-même semblait inquiete à sa pre-

mière approche; cependant elle se rassura bientôt: "Vous me connaissez,"

lui dit l'étrangère, "je viens plus tardè que les autres mais je sais que ma

cause est sûre. Quelqu'uns de mes rivaux sont formidables j'avoue et il

est possible que je sois surpassée par plusieurs en faits éclatants qui   75

attirent l'admiration du vulgaire, mais j'ai une amie devant laquelle toute

cette assemblée sera forcée à succomber; elle se nomme la Civilization:
B.
en quelques années elle viendra habiter cette terre avec nous et chaque

siècle augmentera son pouvoir. A la fin elle détournera l'Ambition de

votre service; elle jetera sur la colère le frein de la loi; elle arrachera les   80
confinera
armes des mains du Fanatisme; elle chassera la Famine parmi les sau-

vages: moi seule j'agrandirai et fleurirai sous son règne; la puissance de

tous les autres expirera avec leurs partisans; la mienne existera lorsque

même je suis morte. Si une fois je fais connaissance avec le père mon

influence s'étendra au fils et avant que les hommes s'unissent pour me   85

bannir de leur société j'aurai changé toute leur nature et rendue l'espèce

prey for your Majesty, so effectively, in fact, that Old Age will have almost a sinecure and your palace will be gorged with victims." "Say no more," said Death, descending from her throne and embracing Intemperance (for that was the stranger's name). "It is enough that I know you. For the others, I have lucrative and important offices; they will all be my ministers, but for you alone is reserved the honor of being my viceroy."

entière un plus facile proie à votre Majesté, si effectivement en effet, que
la Vieillesse aura presque une sinecure et votre palais sera gorgé de victimes." "Ne parlez plus," dit la Mort descendant de son trône et embras-
sant l'Intempérance (c'est ainsi que l'étrangère s'appelait) "il suffit que
je vous connais; pour les autres j'ai des offices lucratifs et importants,
ils seront tous mes ministres, mais à vous seule est reservé l'honneur
d'être mon vice-roi."

Comments

These devoirs provide direct evidence of Heger's mode of instruction: both sisters took down his topic outline, which they were then expected to develop. Probably they sat side by side in the classroom while Heger dictated in curt phrases.[1] They must have listened closely to get the terms right; perhaps they compared guidelines or conferred about their claimants.[2] Still, their responses take widely different tacks, not because they disregard the terms of the assignment, but because they remain such different writers.

Curiously, neither of the previous translators considered the role of the "Matière." Dorothy Cornish omitted the contents page from Charlotte's, published in 1952 in English only,[3] and in any case she could not have known about its counterpart, which only arrived in England two years later. Margaret Lane also left out the contents of Emily's when she read her translation of that text in 1954 on the BBC's Third Programme. Emily, she claimed, had made her "own choice" of subject, though perhaps Branwell's intemperance had impressed her.[4] A couple of Lane's listeners suggested English sources, including "The Court of Death," a fable by John Gay,[5] but it did not occur to them, or to Lane, that in a Brussels pensionnat the source of Emily's devoir might be French. Even when Lane's version was reprinted with the outline,[6] no attention was paid to its significance.

In 1967 J. M. Maxwell finally put the pieces together. Both sisters, he pointed out, had written devoirs based on Emily's "introductory material." He also cited a French source for her introduction: "La Mort" in Jean-Pierre Florian's *Fables* (1792). Florian's rhyming lines describe a gathering in hell for the purpose of choosing Death's prime minister; the contenders include Fever, Gout, War, Plague, a doctor, and finally Intemperance, whom she picks. Maxwell did not claim that this was Heger's "precise source," since it omits both Old Age and Ambition.[7] But he was unaware that Heger touched up his sources and sometimes took ideas from several.[8]

Heger had paternal and professional reasons for browsing through fable collections. He was then the father of four children under six (Marie Pauline, the oldest, had turned five in September) and, by all accounts, enjoyed the role of papa. He chose to teach the youngest class of boys at the Athénée, the level following primary school, and he had a reputation as a speaker who could spellbind students of all ages. Perhaps he found a volume in a local bookstore with a version of "La Mort" that included Old Age and set the gathering in a palace, unlike Florian's; or perhaps he supplemented Florian's version, which in other ways anticipates his. Florian's meter tends to jiggle and particulars are scanty, but Heger needed only an outline and a venue that older students would not find too childish. He apparently succeeded, since even the resistant Emily took to this assignment.

Several factors might explain her willingness. Death was a topic that could always lure her, even in a fairytale guise. Neither she nor Charlotte had outgrown their own mythologies; both remained engaged, if not submerged, in juvenilia. Charlotte was trying to get away from Angria, and Emily's grinding studies left her little time for Gondal, but the fable was a genre that could bridge the space between these homemade cycles and the classroom. Another genre, allegory, also links these devoirs to more familiar reading at the parsonage. Charlotte grew up on *Pilgrim's Progress* and later incorporated it, and allegory, into her four adult novels. Whether Emily read Bunyan too remains uncertain; her poems suggest the genre was well known to her.[9] Not least, the contents opened a channel for dissent. She could voice a satirist's contempt for vice and folly and give fantasy its own internal logic.

Nothing in her devoir is extrinsic to its arguments, and little derives from outside sources. The specters whose footsteps rattle in the chambers probably owe something to Gondal's court and dungeon scenes or to Gothic fiction read in adolescence.[10] Wrath, Sloth, and Avarice are among the seven deadly sins, while Famine, Plague, and Vengeance have biblical resonance. But these personifications are subordinate to more inventive evils. Nominally, Emily follows Heger's outline in making Intemperance the winner. But Intemperance remains unnamed until Death embraces her, a strategy congruent with insidious infiltration, and speaks as the confederate of Civilization, the evil Emily chooses to make paramount. Unlike Charlotte, she limits description of the claimants to animating touches; she elaborates instead on their methods, their rejoinders, and the scourging consequences of their actions. Parallel construction and imagery carry her ideas but never overwhelm them.

Charlotte's devoir, in contrast, keys into her penchant for representation and tableau. Her descriptions of the claimants recall methods she developed and practiced in her juvenilia.[11] They also presage Jane Eyre's barbed portraits of the company that gathers at Thornfield.[12] Characteristically, she pauses in the action to picture form, costume, and physiognomy. Whereas Emily's candidates define themselves in arguing, Charlotte's are defined before they enter into speech and, in speaking, launch additional description.

Into Heger's outline, Charlotte reads an opportunity to demonstrate what she has learned. Her opening allusions to existence and the "young sphere" recall the conflation of religion and astronomy in "The Immensity of God." "Noble savage" clearly refers to Rousseau, and the roster of patriarchs from Genesis that follows, like the later reference to laboring in the fields, reaffirms her knowledge of the Bible. Her classical allusions are less easy to pinpoint. She could have read the *Iliad* at the Ponden House library,[13] or Heger could have talked about Achilles. She could have read descriptions of the Amazon Thalestris or seen her featured in a painting. In either case, she expurgates some details: Thalestris, hoping for a daughter who would rule the earth, coerced Alexander into mating with her; she hunted with her left side naked to the breast and her robe knotted up above the knee.[14] The ice and its architect are Charlotte's invention, the palace an analogue to the Egyptian temple she describes in "Evening Prayer in a Camp." Her reference to the Neva (and deletion of "Dan") could come from a lesson in geography (the boys in Heger's classes, and so perhaps the girls, were taught "geographic nomenclature").[15] The veil that covers Death's skeletal arm may also have a classroom precedent: in one of her translations, "Un banquet Egyptien," the narrator raises the veil of an immobile guest to find "that the form it hid . . . was a skeleton!"[16]

Heger's classes also supplemented what she learned from Bunyan on the figurative uses of allegory. This dictée appears in two of her notebooks, the first time as a test with corrections: "There is in heaven a power divine, a constant companion of religion and virtue. . . . Although her eyes are blindfolded, her gaze penetrates the future; sometimes she holds budding flowers in her hand, sometimes a cup filled with an enchanting liqueur; nothing approaches the charm of her voice, or the grace of her smile; the closer one comes to the grave, the more she shows herself, pure and shining, to comforted mortals. Faith and Charity say to her, 'My sister.' Her name is . . . Hope."[17] In the absence of a date, its connection to "The Palace of Death" can only be provisional. But Intemperance's flowers, intoxicating cup, and sinister sisterhood with Death suggest that Charlotte deliberately echoes Heger's sentimental set piece, subverting it to meet his new demands.[18]

Even when these debts to other sources go unrecognized, most readers find her devoir inferior to Emily's, less powerfully argued and developed. But if power is defined by what it gains for its possessor, her devoir may be the more successful. Heger's responses to Emily's text are cosmetic rather than substantive. He strikes out a sentence (though it follows his instructions), awards her a couple of "Goods" for salient details, adjusts two verbs, and underlines her anglicisms. Fourteen years later, he told Gaskell that he rated Emily's genius more highly than Charlotte's.[19] But on this project she commands far less of his attention than her acquiescent sister.

Charlotte's text elicits abundant comments—on ideas, order, detail, grammar, word choice. Several take the form of questions and demands, both stimulants to further work and thinking. Why does Death require a prime minister? Why does Ambition come first? (Emily makes comparable statements and choices, but Heger says nothing about them.) He is rigorous in refining idiom and nuance, generous when he sees her struggling with ideas that her French is insufficient to convey. "Good thought," he writes next to a convoluted statement about the paradox of Death's existence.

Throughout her devoir, Charlotte confuses two nouns derived from *teindre,* "to color or dye": the masculine form, *teint,* connotes complexion or coloring; the feminine, *teinte,* tint or shade. Heger does not simply correct her confusion. Next to her description of the palace carved of ice (*glace*) he writes *tain,* a homonym from *étain,* "tin or tinfoil." When glass, also *glace* in French, is coated with tinfoil, it becomes a mirroring surface. French poetry is rich in mirror imagery, and Charlotte may again be demonstrating knowledge when she alludes to walls whose icy pallor is reflected in the company's complexions. Heger was her guide to that tradition; together they had analyzed a "Harmonie" by Lamartine in which the word *reflet* appears.[20] Here, then, *teint-teinte-tain* can be read as a signifier, not just of wordplay, but of intimate connection between this eager learner and her teacher.

Of course, their intimacy was her construct. Heger may have been flattered by her progress and attention, but nothing suggests that he had any aim in commenting beyond her educational development. And yet, if she compared the text that she got back with Emily's, she might well have concluded that he favored her. Emily personifies a Civilization that subjugates Death's cohorts in four lean clauses (77–79 [79–82F]). Charlotte moralizes on the movement into cities, where civilized refinements "soon [find] a habitation" (26–27). Hers are the lines that rate his "Goods." Possibly, Heger was tempering his treatment to the level and ambition of his students. Charlotte craved fluency in French, unlike her sister, and she benefited more from his responses. In any case, their contact was abruptly broken off by the news of Aunt Branwell's final illness.

For the Brontë sisters, October was a month of death. Their father's 28-year-old curate, William Weightman, had died on September 6 of cholera. Martha Taylor died as they were doing this assignment; her memorial service was its postscript. Aunt Branwell's death followed on October 29, putting an end to their semester abroad and to Emily's travels out of Yorkshire. But the comments on this devoir and its predecessors hint that, for Charlotte, a new writing life had opened. She had thirsted for connection with a master and a reader, for attention as a person and an author. Unconscious of the poison in the cup that lured her back, she returned as soon as family duties lightened.

Emily appears to have put this experience behind her and returned to the Gondals. However, both her saga and *Wuthering Heights* disclose more than cursory traces of her "Palace." In the year before her death, she was absorbed in depicting the effects of fanatical belief; civil wars between the Republicans and Royalists tear Gondal's families apart. As for Civilization as a minister of death, one has only to think of Catherine Earnshaw at the Grange and her rationale for turning from Heathcliff.

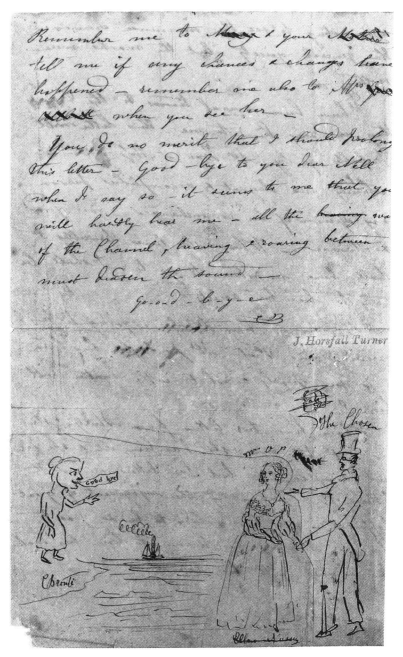

"Good-bye," Charlotte Brontë's cartoon from a letter of March 6, 1843.
Standing on the continent, she waves across the channel to Ellen Nussey,
who is with a suitor. The Brontë Society.

Devoirs of 1843

An Essay on Style
The Fall of the Leaves

————

What impression strikes one on reading the piece entitled "The Fall of
the Leaves"? It is not easy to shed light on this question in a single
answer, because one does not always feel the same impression. The first
time one reads it, the effect is vivid; the second time, and forever after,
sorrowful.

Why this difference, and how can so touching a lament produce a
feeling rather vivid than sorrowful? I do not quite know, but it seems to
me that the first time, one feels the joy of a miner who has just discovered a diamond of great price and that the second time, one surren-
renders to the sweet melancholy of someone who hears a plaintive air.
Whence comes this double impression? What is the source of this influence whose power is proved by the lively and varied emotions it excites
in us? To seek the cause of an effect so remarkable is to engage in
useful work, first, because it exerts the mind to reason and, next,
because it can lead us to a favorable end. The mechanic, seeing an in-
genious device, closely examines all its parts; he tries to delve into the
principles that regulated its construction. We too, when we behold a
perfect work of the mind, can we not conduct the same examination and,
in dissecting the details, attempt to discover the secret of their union?
It is through study that the mechanic learns how to invent, and by
employing similar means, can we not achieve a similar end? Yet, since
this latter result is not quite certain, let us not flatter ourselves too much
that we succeed, for fear of finding ourselves in the position of that
German student who believed he was learning to create, in learning to
dissect.

Devoir de Style
La Chute des Feuilles

━━━━━━

Quelle impression ressent-on à la lecture du morceau intitulé "la chute des feuilles?" Ce n'est pas facile d'éclaircir cette question en une seule réponse, parcequ'on ne ressent pas toujours la même impression. La prémière fois qu'on le lit on éprouve une impression vive; la seconde fois, et toujours après, une impression triste.

Pourquoi cette différence et comment une plainte si touchante peut-elle produire un sentiment plutôt vif que triste? Je ne sais pas trop bien mais il me semble que la première fois, on éprouve la joie d'un mineur qui vient de trouver un diamant de grand prix et que la seconde fois, on se livre à la douce melancholie de celui qui écoute un air plaintif. D'où vient cette double impression? Quelle est la source de cette influence dont la force est prouvée par les émotions vives et variées qu'elle excite chez nous? Rechercher la cause qui produit un effet si remarquable, c'est faire un travail utile, d'abord, parcequ'il exerce l'esprit au raisonnement et ensuite parcequ'il peut nous conduire à un but avantageux. Le mécanicien qui voit une oeuvre ingénieuse, en examine bien toutes les parties, il tâche d'approfondir les principes qui en ont réglé la construction; et nous, lorsque nous voyons un ouvrage parfait de l'esprit, ne pouvons nous pas faire le même examen et en disséquant les détails essayer de découvrir le secret de leur union? C'est par l'étude que le mécanicien apprend à inventer, et en employant un pareil moyen, ne pouvons nous pas atteindre à un pareil but? Pourtant, puisque ce dernier résultat n'est pas bien certain, ne nous flattons pas trop d'y réussir, de peur de nous trouver dans la position de cet étudiant allemand qui croyait apprendre à créer, en apprenant a disséquer.

What did Millevoye intend in writing "The Fall of the Leaves"? He

30

portents ⎤
signs ⎦
external

intended to express ~~in written words~~ what a man experiences who, still

in   symptoms   of the fatal germ devel-
young, senses w̲i̲t̲h̲i̲n̲ himself the p̲o̲r̲t̲e̲n̲t̲s̲ and s̲i̲g̲n̲s̲ of an impending and
oping in him
inevitable death. What means did he use to develop the idea that he had

conceived? Did he not first set himself to think about the period and

might
setting he ought to choose, so that the beginning may be the right prelude

why?⎦
35   to all that must follow? In choosing Autumn as the period, did he not

good
isn't it the
autumn wind too
that harvests
poets and leaves
grown yellow.

tell himself, "I choose it because it is the season consecrated to melan-

(2nd)   1st
choly, when the leaves fall, the flowers wither, the days grow short, and

the brief twilights usher in nights long and somber? In choosing a wood

for the setting, did he not recollect that it is in the woods that the ravages

40   of Autumn are the most visible? It is there that the earth veils herself in

leaves the trees have t̲h̲r̲o̲w̲n̲ ̲a̲w̲a̲y̲; that the last flowers appear pale and

languishing between the ivy and the humid moss carpeting the roots of

the west wind
sighs, the
south winds
moan roar
45 *howl rattle*
bellow.
CH

ancient trees; that the winds, the somber south winds, make heard

fixed
their most mournful s̲i̲g̲h̲s̲? Having thus prepared his canvas and traced
obscure[?]
the first r̲u̲d̲e̲ outlines of his sketch, has he not carefully searched out the

details, gathered together the images most apt to make his main idea

stand out? Has he not carefully weighed each thought, carefully con-

sidered each accessory, carefully measured and adjusted each part of the

in no way offended
great Whole so that their conjunction offered no o̲f̲f̲e̲n̲s̲e̲ against the
~~very idea~~   the art of writing
50   m̲a̲s̲t̲e̲r̲-̲p̲r̲i̲n̲c̲i̲p̲a̲l̲ of composition, the principal of Unity? Is that indeed

the process Millevoye followed? Is that the method all great poets

follow?

Dear children of Apollo, souls made of fire!
"Souls made of fire and children of the Sun?"
Dear children of Apollo, of fire, like their father!

Alas! I know not; those great minds alone must answer. But there is one

obscure
55   thing that I know well, because the a̲s̲s̲u̲r̲a̲n̲c̲e̲ of it depends on reason

rather than genius: it is that for novices in literature, for those who want

could
to imitate the great masters, this method is the only one that can guide
why?

Que s'est proposé Millevoye en écrivant la chute des feuilles? Il s'est

proposé d'exprimer ~~par des paroles écrites~~ ce qu'éprouve un homme,   30

en   *symptômes*   *de développer en*   } *presages*
qui, jeune encore, sent chez lui les présages et les signes ^ d'une mort   { *signes*
lui le germe fatal   *extérieurs*
prochaine et inevitable. De quels moyens s'est-il servis pour developper

l'idée qu'il avait conçue?   Ne s'est-il pas d'abord mis à penser quelle

fût
époque et quelle scène il fallait choisir afin que le commencement soit le

pourquoi?⌋
juste prelude de tout ce qui doit suivre? En choisissant l'Automne pour   35

époque ne s'est il pas dit "je le choisis parceque c'est la saison consacrée   *bon*
(No 2)   *No 1*   *n'est-ce pas*
à la melancholie, où les feuilles tombent, les fleurs se flétrissent, les   *aussi au[?] vent*
                                                                                 qui moisonne les
jours se raccourcissent et les crépuscules brefs annoncent des nuits   *hommes poètes et*
                                                                                 les feuilles
longues et sombres? En choisissant un bois pour scène ne s'est-il pas   *jaunies.*

rappelé que c'est dans les bois que les ravages de l'Automne sont les plus   40

visibles; c'est là que la terre se voile des feuilles que les arbres ont

jetées, que les dernières fleurs apparaissent pâles et languissantes entre

le lierre et la mousse humide tapissant les racines des vieux arbres, que   *le zéphir*
                                                                                 soupire, les
les vents, les sombres Autans, font entendre leurs plus mornes soupirs?   *autans se*
                      arrêté   *obscur[?]*   *plaignent*
Ayant ainsi préparé son canevas et tracé les premiers rudes contours de   *grondent*   45
                                                                                 hurlent râlent
son esquisse, n'a-t-il pas soigneusement cherché les détails, rassemblé les   *mugissent.*
                                                                                 CH
images, propres à faire ressortir son idée principale? N'a-t-il pas bien

pesé chaque pensée, bien considéré chaque accessoire, bien mesuré et

ajusté chaque partie du grand Tout de manière que leur réunion ne pre-
péchât en rien   ~~*l'idée même*~~   *l'art d'écrire*
sentât nul pèché contre le maître-principe de la composition, le principe   50

de l'Unité? Est-ce bien là le procédé que suivit Millevoye? Est-ce la

méthode que suivent tous les grands poètes?

> *Chers enfants d'Apollon, âmes faites de feu!*
> "Souls made of fire and children of the Sun?"
> *Chers enfants d'Apollon, de feu, comme leur père!*

Hélas! je ne sais ~~pas~~: c'est à ces grands esprits seuls de répondre, mais

obscur.
il y a une chose que je sais bien, parce que l'assurance en, depend plutôt   55

de la raison que du génie, c'est que pour les novices en littérature, pour

ceux qui veulent imiter les grands maîtres, cette méthode c'est la seule

them to any goal, however little eligible it may be. Perhaps in following

it they will never find anything but lead in their crucibles; but perhaps
                    if
too ⌃ the dormant spark of genius ignites during the process, a new light

60

will illumine their minds, the true secret of Alchemy will be revealed,
                              barbarism already noted
and their lead will be transmuted into gold.
                                                          very
        Nonetheless, though I dare not dogmatize about a subject so far
                                            compared to what?⌐
beyond my reach, I may be allowed to speculate a little. There is so

much verse and so few poems; one is so often bored by reading extrav-

65

aganzas that speak only of flowers, scents, birds, and rays of sunshine

or else of mad passions or absurd emotions that do not touch the reader's

feelings because they never stirred the writer's heart. One grows so

weary of all these insipidities, one is so entirely convinced that man
            to [*satisfy the needs of his soul something other*]
requires⌃something else to satisfy the needs of his soul than the aroma

70

of flowers or dreams of passion, that when one encounters what he

needs, sane and solid nourishment, true and vigorous feeling expressed

in simple and natural language, it's as if one heard the voice of a friend;
one
he discovers within himself the echo of each word. One tells oneself that

it is well worth the effort to seek the origin of sounds so grave and so

75

sweet.

        I believe that all true poetry is but the faithful imprint of something

very good ⌉

that happens or has happened in us in the poet's soul. To compose a

quite right⌋

great poem, an epic or a tragedy, undoubtedly, one needs a plan, erudi-

tion and reasoning. But to write a fugitive little poem like "The Fall of

80

the Leaves," does one need anything other than genius cooperating with

a feeling, an affection, or a passion of some kind? If, for example, the
                        that rules the spirit
feeling holding sway for the moment over the spirit is sorrow, could it

not be that genius whets the sorrow and that sorrow purifies the genius?

unclear

Together, are they not like a cut diamond for which language is but the

85

wax in which they stamp their imprint? I believe that genius, thus

very good
———

awakened, has no need to seek the details, that it scarcely pauses to

puisse
qui peut les conduire à un but tant soit peu éligible: peutêtre qu'en la
└*pourquoi?*
suivant ne trouveront-ils jamais que du plomb dans leurs creusets; peut-
            si
être aussi ʌ l'étincelle dormante du génie s'allume pendant l'opération,   60

une nouvelle lumière éclairera leurs esprits, le vrai secret de l'Alchimie
                        barbarisme déjà signalé.
se révélera et leur plomb se transmuera en or.
                                                fort┐
Cependant, quoique je n'ose pas dogmatiser sur un sujet tellement
                        *à quelle comparaison*ˆ
au-delà de ma portée, on me permettra d'y speculer un peu. Il y a tant

de vers et si peu de poèmes, on s'ennuie si souvent de la lecture   65

d'extravagances qui ne parlent que de fleurs de parfums, d'oiseaux, de

rayons de soleil, ou bien de passions insensées ou de sentiments outrés

qui ne touchent pas la sensibilité du lecteur parcequ'ils n'ont jamais ému

le coeur de l'écrivain; on est si fatigué de toutes ces insipidités, on est
                            pour
si bien persuadé que l'homme demandeˆ | autre chose | pour satisfaire aux   70
                                      └───────────
besoins de son âme que l'arome des fleurs ou les rêves de la folie, que

lorsqu'on rencontre ce qu'il lui faut une nourriture saine et solide, un

sentiment vrai et vigoureux exprimé dans un langage simple et naturel,
                                        on
c'est comme si on endendit une voix d'ami, il se trouve en soi l'echo de

chaque mot; on se dit qu'il vaut bien la peine de rechercher l'origine de   75

sons si graves et si doux

Je crois que toute poésie réelle n'est que l'empreinte fidèle de quel-   *très bon* ┐
                                                                                         │
que chose qui se passe ou qui s'est passé en nous dans l'âme du poète;   *très juste*┘

pour composer un grand poème, une epopée ou une tragédie, sans doute,

il faut un plan, de l'érudition et du raisonnement, mais, pour écrire un   80

petit poème fugitif tel que "La chute des feuilles", faut-il autre chose que

le génie, coopérant avec un sentiment, une affection ou une passion quel-
                                    qui domine l'âme
conque?   Si, par exemple, le sentiment possédant pour le moment

l'empire de l'esprit, est le chagrin, n'est-ce pas que le génie aiguise le   *peu clair*

chagrin et que le chagrin purifie le génie? ensemble, ne sont-ils comme   85

un diamant gravé pour qui le langage n'est que la cire où ils estampent   *très bon*
                                                                              ─────────
leur empreinte? Je crois que le génie, ainsi eveillé, n'a pas besoin de

reflect, that it does not think about unity. I believe that the details come

quite naturally without the poet's seeking them, that inspiration takes the

90   *excellent*   place of reflection. And as for unity, I believe there is no unity more

perfect than that which arises from a heart filled with a single idea. It

would be as impossible for the torrent, swollen with rain, driven by the

tempest, to turn from its impetuous course, as for a man stirred by

passion, shattered by grief, willingly to abandon his despair or his joy

95   and speak of things alien to them. The nature of genius resembles that

of instinct; its operation is both simple and marvelous. The man of

a possible procedure, but it will be with this product as

very weak [?]   genius produces, without work and as if in a single effort, results which

with all natural products. It is ingot gold — others will shape that gold; ~~it's the~~

the man without genius — however wise, however persevering he may be

~~wine-grower~~ *Virgil-Aeneas — Plautus-Molière — Daubenton-Buffon — etc.*

— cannot attain. The realm of genius is not limited to intelligence; it is

100   in the heart above all that this spiritual king has established his throne;

and it is in whetting sensitivity, in giving great intensity to the passions,

a keen impetus to the affections, that he announces his presence and

reveals his power. If Millevoye had been a cold, phlegmatic, and unfeel-

what matter that

ing man, no matter if he had had the instruction of a hundred academies,

105   the wisdom of a thousand philosophers; he would never have composed

"The Fall of the Leaves." The impression of grief, feeble in his thought,

would have been feebler still in his written words. But it is time that I

on the subject I want to discuss.

stopped, and I see that I have said nothing yet˘. I have only broached the

At the very outset of my theme I discovered in myself an idea,

first question of my theme. I have transgressed despite myself. At the

a conviction that would out — my conscience demanded it — and conscience must

110   start I had indeed the intention of following my plan without straying

be obeyed. I return now to my subject.

from it.

~~One can~~

observation

———

Work does not make the poet; man does not make his genius, he receives

it from heaven — that is ~~inconte~~ *incontestable.*

115   *Mechanics does not create* force; ~~but~~ *it regulates its use, it multiplies*

chercher des détails, qu'il ne s'arrête guère pour refléchir, qu'il ne pense

pas à l'unité: je crois que les détails viennent tout naturellement sans que

le poète les cherche, que l'inspiration tient la place de la réflexion et   90

quant à la unité, je pense qu'il n'y a pas d'unité plus parfaite que celle   *excellent*

qui resulte d'un coeur rempli d'une seule idée: il serait aussi impossible

pour le torrent, gonflé de pluies, lancé par la tempête, de détourner son

cours impétueux, que pour l'homme, ému de passion, brisé de douleur,

de quitter volontairement son chagrin ou sa joie et de parler des choses   95

qui leur sont étrangères.   La nature d̰e génie tient à celle d'instinct; son
                                                              (1)
opération est à la fois simple et merveilleuse; l'homme de génie produit,
                              (1) opérn. possible, mais il en sera de ce
san̰s travail et comme par un seul effort, des résultats auxquels l'homme   *très*
produit là comme de tous les produits naturels. — C'est l'or en barres—d'autres   *faible [?]*
sans génie quelque savant, quelque persévérant qu'il soit ne pourrait
le façonneront cet or, c'est du vigneron Virgile-Ennius — Plaute-Molière — &a
jamais atteindre. L'empire de génie ne se borne pas à l'intelligence; c'est   100
Daubenton-Buffon — &a
surtout dans le coeur que ce roi spirituel a établi son trône et c'est en

aiguisant la sensibilité, en donnant une grande vivacité aux passions, un

vif élan aux affections qu'il annonce sa présence et démontre sa force.

Si Millevoye avait été un homme froid, flegmatique, insensible,
  peu importe qu'il eût
n'importe, s'il avait possédé l'instruction de cent académies, la sagesse   105

de mille philosophes, il n'aurait jamais composé "La chute des feuilles".
                                                sa
L'impression de douleur, faible dans sḛs pensée, aurait été plus faible

encore dans ses paroles écrites.   Mais il est temps que je m'arrête et je
                              du sujet que je veux traiter.
m'aperçois que je n'ai encore rien dit /; je n'ai entamé que la première
tout au début de ma thèse, j'ai trouvé en moi une idée, une conviction qui voulait
question de ma thèse; j'ai pêché malgré moi, au commencement j'avais   110
se faire jour—. c'était une exigence de ma conscience—. et la conscience veut être
bien l'intention de suivre le cadre sans m'en écarter.
obéie— Je reviens maintenant à mon sujet. —.
On peut

observation

———

le <u>travail</u> ne fait pas le poëte; l'homme ne fait pas son génie, il le reçoit

du ciel—. c'est inconte incontestable. —

La mécanique ne crée pas la <u>force</u>; mais elle en régle l'emploi elle en   115

its effect a hundredfold.

Man knows not what <u>genius</u> is; it is a gift from Heaven, it is something di<u>vine</u>, says he. It is the same with <u>force</u>.

120
~~Put~~[?] But imagine two men of equal strength, one without a lever, the other with a lever.

—the first will lift 1,000 pounds, the second, in making the <u>same</u> effort, will uproot a plane tree.

Is the <u>lever</u> nothing?

       no   *either*
125
~~Nature~~ Without ~~the~~ <u>voice</u> ~~to~~ singer —doubtless; but no singer˘ without <u>craft</u>, without study, without <u>imitation</u>.

    ~~Witho the craft of singing no gen~~

Nature makes the painter. What would he be however without the study of pespective, the art of coloration, etc. How much would his paintings be worth, how long would they last?

130
Without study, no <u>art</u>. Without art no effect on humanity, because art epitomizes that which all the centuries bequeath to us, all that man has found <u>beautiful</u>, that which has had an effect on man, all that has he has found worth saving from oblivion —

wine—grape—
press
135
uncultivated
land—
vigorous
shoots—
bitter fruit

food for the
table, etc.
"For culinary
140 *art one does*
not improvise
a dinner but
without a
chef

Genius, without study ~~and~~ without art, without the knowledge of what has been done, is <u>force</u> without the lever; it is Demosthenes, a sublime orator, who stammers and gets himself hissed; it is the soul that sings within and which, to express its inner songs, has only a rude and uncultivated voice; it is the sublime musician, finally, who has only an untuned piano to make the world hear the dulcet melodies that he hears reverberating inwardly.

    Certainly
~~The cut[?] does not~~ the lapidary does not make the diamond, but without the lapidary the most beautiful diamond is a pebble.

<u>Poet</u> or <u>not</u>, then, study form. If a poet you will be more powerful & your works will live. If not, you will not create poetry, but you will savor its merit and its charms.

*centuple l*d*'effet.* —

   *l'homme ne sait pas ce que c'est que le g*é*nie, c'est un don du Ciel.*

*c'est quelque chose de d*i*vin, dit-il.- Il en est de même de la force;*

   ~~*Mettez*~~ [?] *Mais supposez deux hommes de même force l'un sans levier,*

l'autre avec un levier   120

   — *le 1*^{er} *soulèvera 1,000. livres, le second en faisant même effort,*

déracinera un platane —

   Le levier n'est-il rien? —
                                                      point de
   ~~*La nature*~~ *Sans* ~~*la*~~ *voix* ~~*au*~~ *chanteur — Sans doute — mais point de*
      aussi
chanteur˘ sans art, sans étude, sans imitation —.   125

   ~~*Sa*~~ ~~*l'art de chanter point de gen*~~

   La nature fait le peintre — que serait-il cependant sans l'étude de la

perspective, de l'art des couleurs —. *&a — Combien vaudraient combien*

dureraient ses tableaux —.

   Sans étude, point d'art. — *Sans art point d'effet sur les hommes, puisque*   130

l'art est ~~*le*~~ *résumé de ce que tous les siècles nous lèguent de tout ce que*

l'homme a trouvé beau, de ce qui a fait effet sur l'homme, de tout ce qu'il a

trouvé digne d'être sauvé de l'oubli —

   le génie, sans l'étude ~~*et*~~ *sans l'art, sans la connaissance de ce qui a été*   *vin—raisin—*
                                                                                                                                      pressoir
fait, c'est la force, sans le levier, c'est Démosthène sublime orateur, qui bégaie   135

                                                                                                                                      terre inculte—
et se fait siffler —. *c'est l'âme qui chante en-dedans, et qui n'a p*^{r}· *exprimer*   *jets vigoureux—*
                                                                                                                                      fruits âpres
ses chants intérieurs, qu'une voix rude et inculte; c'est le sublime musicien

                                                                                                                                      mets, &a
enfin qui n'a qu'un piano discord p^r *faire entendre au monde, les suaves*   *"Pour l'art*
                                                                                                                                      culinaire on
mélodies qu'il entend résonner en lui —.   *n'improvise pas*
      Certes   *un dîner*
   ~~*La tail*~~[?] ~~*ne*~~ *la lapidaire ne fait pas le diamant, mais sans le lapidaire*   *mais sans* 140
                                                                                                                                      cuisinier
le plus beau diamant est un caillou.

   *Po*ë*te ou non étudiez donc la forme — Po*ë*te vous serez plus puissant &*

*vos oeuvres vivront—Dans le cas contraire, vous ne ferez pas de po*ë*sie, mais*

vous en savourerez le mérite et les charmes —.

The Fall of the Leaves

With the leafy remains of our forest,

Autumn had littered the ground.

The copse was bare of mystery,

The nightingale's voice without sound.

Sad and deathbound at his dawning,

A sickly youth, pacing slow, appears;

One more time he wanders through

The woodland dear to his earliest years:

"Farewell, beloved forest . . . . I succumb;

Your mourning speaks to my ill-fated breath,

And in each leaf that falls

I see a harbinger of death.

Oracle of fate at Epidaurus,

You told me, 'Once more, as in the past,

The leaves of the forest will yellow before your eyes,

But for you, this time will be the last.

Eternal cypress wreathes you:

Paler than pale autumn,

Toward the tomb you even now incline.

Your withering youth passes

Before the meadow grasses,

Before the laden branches of the vine.'

And I die . . . . The somber west winds touched me,

Of their frigid breath I feel the sting.

And I have seen, like a vain deluding shadow,

The evanescence of my lovely spring.

Fall, fall to earth, leaf ephemeral!

5

10

15

20

25

The spirit in
these moments
of sadness
inclines toward
the happy
years of
childhood

an omen
mysterious
vague

picturesque -
marvelous[?]
calm of autumn

profoundly
moving

La chute des Feuilles

De la dépouille de nos bois,

L'automne avait jonché la terre:

Le bocage était sans mystère,

Le rossignol était sans voix.   5

Triste et mourant, à son aurore,

Un jeune malade, à pas lents,

Parcourait une fois encore   L'esprit dans ses
                                                  moments de tris-
Le bois cher à ses premiers ans: tesse s'incline
                                                  vers les beaux
"Bois, que j'aime! adieu . . . . je succombe;   années de la   10
                                                  jeunesse
"Votre deuil me prédit mon sort,

"Et dans chaque feuille qui tombe

Je vois un présage de mort."

Fatal oracle d'Épidaure,   présage
                                                  mystérieux vague
Tu m'as dit "Les feuilles des bois   15

"À tes yeux jauniront encore

"Mais, c'est pour la dernière fois.

"L'eternel cyprès t'environne: pitoresque -
                                                  merveilleux[?]
"Plus pâle que la pâle automne,   calme de
                                                  l'automne   20
"Tu t'inclines vers le tombeau.

"Ta jeunesse sera flétrie

"Avant l'herbe de la prairie,

"Avant les pampres du coteau"

Et je meurs . . . . De leur froide haleine   profondement
                                                  touchant
M'ont touché les sombres Autans: 25

Et j'ai vu comme un ombre vaine

S'évanouir mon beau printemps.

Tombe, tombe, feuille éphémère!

Veil from the eye this path of sorrow.

30 Hide from the despair of my mother

The place where I shall be tomorrow.

he no longer has But if along the lonely path,
faith in love —
for him it is My grief-torn beloved
like a dream

Comes weeping when daylight has fled,

35 Awaken with your soft noise, for an instant's consolation,

My shade from the realms of the dead!"

He speaks, he wanders off . . . . without returning!

The last leaf falling in the gloom

Signaled the youth's last day, departing.

40 Beneath the oak they hollowed out his tomb . . . .

bitter But his beloved did not come to see him,

Never visited the isolated stone.

With the sound of his steps alone

The shepherd of the valley

45 Disturbed the silence of that mausoleum.

[Charles-Hubert] Millevoye

Voile aux yeux ce triste chemin

Cache au desespoir de ma mère   30

La place où je serai demain.

Mais, vers la solitaire allée,   il ne se fie plus à
                                        l'amour — c'est
Si mon amante echevelée   pour lui comme
                                        un songe
Venait pleurer quand le jour fuit,

Eveille par ton leger bruit   35

Mon ombre un instant consolée!

Il dit, s'éloigne . . . . et sans retour!

La dernière feuille qui tombe

A signalé son dernier jour.

Sous le chêne on creusa sa tombe   40

Mais son amante ne vint pas   amère

Visiter la pierre isolée

Et le pâtre de la vallée

Troubla seul du bruit de ses pas

Le silence du mausolée   45

Millevoye

Comments

This is the first surviving devoir from Charlotte's second period in Brussels. She wrote it two months after her return and about nine months after she had transcribed "The Fall of the Leaves" in her notebook.[1] In the interval, she had made the transition from a pupil attending Heger's classes to a teacher giving classes of her own. She continued to study German and French literature and to submit compositions to Heger, but perhaps less frequently and with greater latitude now that her status had changed. She had also undertaken to improve Heger's English, and although the lessons may have stopped by mid-March, she had yet to feel isolated from him. He was still keeping her supplied with books and conversing with her "sometimes,"[2] though less often.

In the cold, raw months that followed her return, she completed a number of translations: passages from Scott and Byron into French, poems by Belmontet and Barbier into English, and ballads by Schiller into French.[3] One of those translations, from *The Lady of the Lake,* may have turned her interest back to this lyric. It is a "Coronach," or funeral song, for a Highland hero who dies young. Scott's anapestic lines seem far removed from Millevoye's, but Charlotte's French rendition brings them closer:

The Autumn winds rushing
    Waft the leaves that are serest,
But our flower was in flushing
    When blighting was nearest.[4]

Les vents sombres d'Automne
Ne détachent que des feuilles jaunes et séches [*sic*]
Mais notre fleur venait de s'épanouir
Quand le souffle de la Mort l'abattit.[5]

Because she did not date her translation, the connections can only be guessed. Did Scott's verses reevoke the elegy she first transcribed in 1842, or did some remark of Heger's draw her back to it? Does her *devoir* respond to an assignment he gave her, or did she independently undertake an exercise like those he had required the year before? Certainly, at this time she was thinking about poetry and about her future as a writer. She had come back from Haworth with samples of her work, poems and stories that she probably intended to show him and a copybook of poems she was revising. Translation also made her pay attention to workmanship, compelling her to analyze—"dissect," to use her metaphor—the passages that others had created.

Whatever her incentive for returning to "The Fall of the Leaves," she assumes that she is writing about a little masterpiece, an estimate still common in the early 1840s, some thirty years after its first publication as the winner of a noted competition, the Jeux Floraux. (Sainte-Beuve, writing in 1837, calls it the "pearl" of Millevoye's elegies, "the piece that everyone remembers. . . .")[6] If informed French taste had shifted to Lamartine and Hugo, and Millevoye had slipped to the rank of minor poet, Heger was neither out of date nor unconventional in asking his students to study it.

Charlotte begins by trying to describe the "impression" that the reader experiences. As she tackles this subject, her prose is stiff and formal; she tries out the language of a scholar. It becomes less constrained when she describes the woods in autumn, but her French does not flow until she reaches the questions that she wants, again, to open up with Heger: What is the source of the power that engenders art? What is the nature of genius?[7]

She had come to Brussels an entrenched Romantic. Grounded in Wordsworth, she preferred to think as he did that "poetry is the spontaneous overflow of powerful feelings," that its object is to carry truth "alive into the heart by passion," and that its words should be natural and simple, "language really used by men."[8] But Heger had impressed her with the value of analysis and the necessity of discipline. "Effect," not "impression," is the term he emphasized in previous comments about the craft of writing:

> *Remorselessly* sacrifice everything that does not contribute to clarity, verisimilitude, and effect.
>
> Accentuate everything that sets the main idea in relief. . . .
> It's sufficient that the rest be *in its proper place, but in half-tone.*
> That is what gives to style, as to painting, unity, perspective, and *effect.*[9]

Charlotte is probably recalling these strictures when she asks how Millevoye composed his elegy; portions of lines 44–50 (45–51F) paraphrase these comments on "The Nest." But the oppositions that she sets up there and later—between verse and poetry, novice work and masterwork, grand- and small-scale literature, plan and inspiration—suggest that she still finds these tenets uncongenial, however much she wants to please her teacher.

Heger's "observation" here acknowledges dichotomies, but only to challenge their exclusiveness: whatever the artist receives from God or nature, the gift must be developed and disciplined. He never implies, as she so often does, that passion is at odds with preparation. In his interlinear comments he also prompts her to examine the claims she makes dogmatically. "Why?" he asks, when she says that methodical study alone can lead beginners to their goal. When she fails to follow the principle of unity, abandoning the topic she had chosen to investigate, he gives her an excuse for digressing. An exigence of conscience has led her off the subject, and in this case the internal force supersedes the rules. In these ways and others, he addresses her concerns and prods her into thinking more flexibly.

At no point does he note that her defense of "The Fall of the Leaves" is based on a misconception. Millevoye's is not a "fugitive little poem" in which pure genius cooperates with feeling. The poet may have launched it in a fit of inspiration, but he put his early draft through a series of revisions, placed the poem first in a collection of his elegies, and headed the collection with an essay "On the Elegy" that traces the tradition of the genre.[10]

Legend ascribes to the poem the kind of origin that Charlotte would have found congenial: "On the day of Saint-Severin's fair, at Crécy [October 23, 1809], Millevoye had been invited to dine with a retired magistrate. The poet set out that morning for a stroll through the forest. The other guests awaited him vainly. He did not return until that night. On the morrow, peasants reported having seen him alone and making gestures. Some days later, Millevoye read the *Chute des feuilles.*"[11] Heger may not have been aware of the legend (this version was transcribed in 1897), but he would have known and recounted to his students other details that make Millevoye appealing: the poet exhibited unusual precocity; as a young adult, he developed a weak chest; he died at thirty-three in 1816— the year in which Charlotte was born.

Yet if his life appears romantic, his career firmly roots him within a neoclassical tradition. Millevoye was a student of the classics, an essayist, a satirist, a translator of Homer, and a poet proud of imitating others. He read the new Romantics and shared some of their beliefs, as his theory on the elegy suggests. But he was not awash in sorrow, nor was his heart a quarry for the little gems emotion could strike out of it. The elegy, he believed, came naturally to man and should remain temperate and simple: "Even in singing of happiness, it can keep its characteristic tinge of sadness. This mixture of opposing impressions adds to its effect. Above all it delights in the remembrance of what is no more. . . . For it, no object is inanimate; ruins are living, solitude is peopled, and the tomb ceases to be mute."[12]

Charlotte may have known nothing about Millevoye's theory, though her comment in the devoir on instruction and academies hints that she knew something of his background. Still, she immediately senses that "The Fall of the Leaves" gives rise to opposing impressions. Resisting their mixture, she divides them metonymically: one response replaces the other. She also resists or misses any signal that the elegy's effects are studied. "Oracle of fate at Epidaurus," for example, is both portent and classical allusion: Epidaurus, a city in ancient Greece with a temple sacred to Aesculapius, was visited by invalids who sought to learn their fate. Millevoye echoes the allusion with "mausoleum," the final word of the poem: Mausolos, governor of a kingdom near Epidaurus, built himself a monumental tomb.[13] That the image of a mausoleum might clash with the image of a grave beneath an oak in the forest seems not to have occurred to the poet and his readers, and certainly not to Charlotte Brontë. But then, she does not claim to be a learned academic, and Heger does not attempt to make her one. They speak of Art, the sources and results of creativity. They explicate through metaphor, not theory.

For both of them, poets are "[s]ouls made of fire," children of the god of light and prophecy. For both, "true poetry" emerges from the heart and finds an outlet in figurative language. Charlotte's own imagery earns frequent responses—expressions of approval, reservations, questions, and corrections that embellish or fine-tune. In his "observation," Heger picks up on her metaphors, so that they become a form of currency between the two, a medium of connection and exchange. For example, the diamond, cited first in line 12, becomes a figure for the processes of genius (85–86), and then, in Heger's end comment, a reminder that the artist needs technique to bring the gem out of the rock (140–41).

It seems, finally, beside the point to wonder at her judgment in taking "The Fall of the Leaves" and Millevoye as exemplars of genius. As a writer, she required "sane and solid nourishment"; she found it not so much in the voice of the poet as in Heger's voice, responding to hers.

Charlotte Brontë's sketch "Abercrombie." The Brontë Society.

[Charlotte Brontë] [no date]

[Letter]

My dear Jane

A long time ago I stopped writing to you because you never answered my letters, and finally I got tired of keeping up a correspondence of which I alone bore all the costs. I confess that I have been
have [found]
excessively angry at you. I find you so weak as to be incapable of doing what you know to be your duty. If now I take the first steps to renew
and last
our intimacy, it's because I want to make one lone attempt to emancipate
indolence
you from that shameful servitude in which your laziness confines you. Also I have no intention whatsoever of flattering you in this letter — rich, young, and beautiful as you are. You encounter enough flatterers in the salons where you slackly spend your life. As for me, I reserve the privilege of annoying you, of irritating you, of casting painful doubts in your mind about the usefulness of the life you lead

What do you do with your time? Listen while I trace the sketch of one of your days. It matters little whether you rise early or late, since if you rise at an early hour, it is never with the aim of doing something useful. In getting dressed you remain a long time before your mirror
it
because idleness having made you your mind sterile, has left you no pleasure beyond the contemplation of the graces of your body. You descend and you breakfast. In breakfasting, you pay too much attention to your appetite — your taste — because, no longer familiar with intellectual pleasures, you take refuge in bodi material pleasures. After break-
yet
fast, your conscience, half smothered but still not not altogether dead, utters its feeble cry. "Jane," it says, "Devote an hour to some reading or some serious occupation." You try; you cannot persevere, you do not have the strength. Light thoughts come fluttering around your mind;

[Lettre]

Ma chère Jane

Il y a longtemps que j'ai cessé de vous écrire parceque vous ne
répondiez jamais à mes lettres et à la fin je me suis lassée d'entretenir
une correspondance dont moi seule faisais tous les frais. J'avoue que j'ai
                                                                      ~~ai~~
été excessivement fachée contre vous — je vous trouvée si faible d'être   5
incapable de faire ce que vous savez être de votre devoir — si maintenant
je fais les premiers pas pour renouveler notre intimité c'est parceque je
                          et dernier
veux tenter un seul effort pour vous emanciper de cette honteuse servi-
                  l'indolence
tude où ~~votre paresse~~ vous retient — Aussi je n'ai nullement l'intention
de vous flatter dans cette lettre riche jeune et belle comme vous l'êtes —   10
vous trouvez assez de flatteurs dans les salons où vous passez mollement
votre vie — quant à moi je me reserve le privilége de vous irriter de vous
troubler de jeter dans votre esprit des doutes pénibles sur l'utilité de la
vie que vous menez

Que faites vous de votre temps? — écoutez je vais tracer le tableau   15
d'une de vos journées — Peu importe si vous vous levez tôt ou tard puisque si vous vous levez de bonne heure ce n'est jamais dans le but de
faire quelquechose d'utile — en vous habillant vous restez long-temps
devant votre miroir parceque la paresse ~~vous~~ ayant rendu votre esprit
            elle
sterile, ne vous a laissé d'autre plaisir que la contemplation des graces   20
de votre corps — vous descendez et vous déjeunez — en déjeunant vous
consultez trop votre appétit — votre gout — car ne connaissant plus les
jouissances intellectuelles vous vous refugiez dans les jouissances ~~corp~~
materielles Après le déjeuner — votre conscience à demie-étouffée mais
            encore
~~pas cependant~~ pas ^ tout - à fait morte, pousse son faible cri. "Jane"   25
dit-elle — "Consacrez une heure à quelque lecture ou quelque occupation
sérieuse — vous essayez — vous ne pouvez pas persévérer, vous n'avez

you let them enter; and the noble resolution to do well escapes. ~~It~~
has
~~does not find~~ ~~it was not shown hospitality in that slack soul and~~ You

waste ~~not[?]~~ the morning skimming through novels. In the afternoon you

30 go for a walk, you make some calls. In the evening you dress and go out

into society. That is how you live, you who must one day marry, and

who a little later must die —

I paused for an instant because several ~~because several~~ thoughts came
personal
into my mind, and I had to push them away, they were too ~~very~~ complex

35 [*] As you
well know I
have the bad
habit of seeing
everything

to disentangle in a letter. Now they have all departed; I know not what

abyss has engulfed them; and there remains with me but a single idea,

less severe and more tender: ~~I see everything~~ [*] through the colored
glass
~~field glass~~ of simile. And this idea appears before me like a bird, who

comes from a distant land of charity and mildness and who, resting on

40 the branch of a vine that I imagine being close to me but is not, folds
and
its brilliant wings, looks at me with an eye that seems to say, "Have pity

on your friend Jane. She is better and sweeter than you. Do you too not

love pleasure? Are you too never idle?"

slack
Ah yes — But my idleness is not the ~~heavy~~ indolence of Jane, it is a

45 heavy depression that drops upon my heart and crushes its faculties

the bird
changes into a
little monkey
who asks me
in a mocking
tone as he
~~hop~~ teeters on
a vinestock

But I want none of that tender tone. Fly away, bird ~~I want not~~

I have sworn to speak as a stoic — as a stern mentor — mocking — without

pity. "Are you not fond of pleasures" ~~says the bird, hopping up the~~

~~vinestock~~. The little demon pushes me to the limit: "I grow impatient

50 "Yes I love them, naughty sprite, I love them all — novels, walks
visits
— parties — ~~and with passion~~ —

~~Have you never read novels? says he in an insinuating manner~~
as for novels
"I have read some — or rather I have devoured them by the

thousands

pas la force — des pensées légères viennent voltiger autour de votre esprit

— vous les laissez entrer — et la noble resolution de bien faire s'échappe

'a
— ~~il ne trouve~~ ~~on ne lui a pas donné~~ l'hospitalité dans cette âme molle et   30

vous dissipez ~~pas~~ la matinée en parcourant des romans — l'après-midi

vous vous promenez — vous faites des visites — le soir vous vous habillez

et vous allez en société — voilà comment vous vivez vous qui devez un

jour vous marier — et qui un peu plus tard devez mourir —

    Je me suis arrêté un instant car plusieurs ~~car plusieurs~~ pensées me   35
                              propre
sont venues dans l'esprit — et j'ai du les repousser elles étaient trop ~~très~~

compliquées pour démêler dans une lettre à présent elle sont toutes   [*]Comme vous
                                savez bien j'ai
                           ne   la mauvaise
parties je ne sais quele abŷme les a englouties — et il me reste qu'une   habitude
                                le   de tout voir
seule idée, moins sévère et plus tendre — ~~je vois tout~~ [*] à travers ~~la~~
  vere
~~lunette~~ coloré de la comparaison — et cette idée me apparait comme un   40

oiseau — qui vient de loin d'une terre de charité et de douceur et qui se

reposant sur une branche de vigne que je me figure d'être près de moi
                                et
mais qui ne l'est pas — ploie ses ailes brillantes — me regarde d'un oeil

qui semble dire "ayez pitié de votre amie Jane. elle est meilleure et plus

douce que vous — est-ce que vous aussi vous n'aimez pas les plaisirs —?"   45

Vous aussi n'êtes vous jamais paresseuse—?"
                               molle
    Ah oui — mais ~~mai~~ paresse ce n'est pas la ~~lourd~~ indolence de Jane
                                ľ
c'est un lourd découragement qui me tombe sur le coeur et en écrase les

facultés

    Mais je ne veux pas de ce ton tendre — envole-toi oiseau ~~je ne veux~~   l'oiseau se 50
                                  transforme en
~~pas~~ j'ai fait serment de parler en stoique — en mentor sévère — moqueur   petit singe qui
                                  me demande
— impitoyable —. "N'aimez vous pas les plaisirs" ~~dit l'oiseau en sautant~~ d'un ton
                                  moqueur en ~~saut~~
~~sur la cep de vigne~~ — Le petit démon me pousse au bout "je m'impatiente se balançant sur
                                  un cep de vigne
    "Oui je les aime mechante fée — je les aime tous — romans prome-
                  visites
nades — soirées — ~~et avec passion~~ —   55

    ~~N'avez-vous jamais lu des romans? dit-il d'un ton insinuant~~
quant aux romans
    "J'en ai lus — ou plutôt j'en ai dévorés par miliers

55 ~~The monkey laughs; pushed to the limit I would like to slap him~~ monkey

~~and vine~~ I ~~bang my hand against a hard desk~~ monkey ~~and vine — disappear~~

I wish she
knew how
delicious
it is

I love walks too and I wish that Jane loved them as I do ~~and~~ after
or at work
8 - 3 - 4 hours passed in study — to go out of one's room — to quit one's

books - ~~one~~ & then to leave behind the cities with their filthy streets and

60 sad boulevards and go climbing in the dusky mountains and breathe
the virgin air that blows about their summits
~~an~~ air that seems to fill your veins with life and your soul with joy —
a[?]
I remember you made the remark to me that those walks in the

country lacked interest, that you find it more amusing to make calls; I

too make calls; one finds many acquaintances among the mountains. To

65 begin with there is a certain gray rock, a giant who dwells alone at the

bottom of a ravine, next a certain cataract whose voice awakens an eter-

nal echo in a vast desert of heath
by dint of breathing the
whose inhabi-
tant is com-
patriot of
the eagle.
70 and where
one reads that
royal affinity
in which his
~~gaze~~ eye
vivid and pier-
cing wholly
like that of
the sovereign
of the skies
75

I am not speaking of the flat country where ~~man living always in the~~
pestilent air   one
~~marshes~~ of the marshes degenerates into a kind of frog — cold, heavy,

phlegmatic. I speak of the mountainous country — read highlands — where
of
man is compatriot ~~with~~ the eagle — and where ~~a gaze of fire ro[?]~~ his

eye‑piercing and bold attests to his affinity with the king of the skies—

Having cast an eye over these last lines I find them both stupid and

false, and I truly beg your pardon for having written them. A fact: even
leads
though I consider the mountains as veritable steps in Jacob's ladder,

which us from the earth to heaven, I know that they are not always

angels whom one sees going up and down. And although I regard the
places   sad
plains as deserts ‸ ~~without interest and without joy~~, habitations of owls
from time to time
and, if you like, of croaking frogs, I know that one finds there ~~also~~
a   a   his
80 ~~some~~ men ~~(very few) but some~~) worthy through their talents and through
his independence   of
~~their~~ virtues of being ~~chiefs of the clans~~ native to ~~Glen Morven or~~ of
the peak
having been born on ~~the summits~~ of Ben Nevis or ~~Shihallion~~. I have

made honorable amends and I continue

~~Le singe rit, poussé au bout. je voudrais lui donner une tape singe et vigne~~

je ~~heurte la main contre un dur pupitre~~ singe ~~et vigne — se sont évanouis~~

J'aime aussi les promenades et je voudrais que Jane les aimées[?]
ou au travail
comme moi ~~et~~ après 8 - 3 - 4 heures passées à l'étude — de sortir de sa

Je voudrais 60
qu'elle savait
combien il
est délicieux

chambre — de quitter ses livres — ~~on~~ & puis de laisser loin les villes avec

leurs sales rues et tristes boulevards et d'aller gravir des montagnes
l'air vierge qui souffle autour de leurs sommets
brunes et respirer ~~un~~ air qui semble remplir vos veines de vie et votre

âme de joie —   65

un[?]
Je me rappelle que vous m'avez fait l'observation que ces prome-

nades à la campagne manquaient interêt que vous trouvez plus amusant

de faire des visites moi aussi je fais des visites on trouve beaucoup de

connaissances parmi les montagnes — d'abord il y a certain roc gris —

géant qui demeure seul au fond d'une ravine — puis certaine cataracte   70

dont la voix éveille un éternel echo dans un vaste desert de bruyère
à force de respirer
Je ne parle pas de la compagne platte où ~~l'homme vivant toujours~~
l'air empesté   l'on
~~dans des marais~~ des marais dégénère en un espèce de grenouille — froid,

dont l'habitant
est compatriote
de l'aigle. et où
on lit cette
affinité royale
dont ~~ses~~ ~~regards~~

lourd, flegmatique — je parle de la campagne montagneuse — lisez hauts-
de
pays — où l'homme est compatriote ~~avec~~ l'aigle — et où ~~un regard de feu~~

son oeil 75
vifs et perçant
tout semblable à
celui du
souverain des
airs

~~ro[?]~~ son oeil‸ perçant et hardi atteste son affinité avec le roi des airs —
es
Ayant jeté l'oeil sur ses derniers lignes je l'ai trouve à la fois stupides

et fausses et je vous demande bien pardon de les avoir écrites — un fait,
véritables degrés
bien que je considère les montagnes comme ~~veritables degres~~ de l'échelle
conduit
de Jacob — qui nous de la terre au ciel — je sais que ce ne sont pas   80

toujours des anges qu'on y voit monter et descendre — et bien que je
lieux
regarde les plaines comme des ‸ deserts ~~sans intérêt et sans joie~~ habita-
tristes
tions de hiboux et si vous voulez de grenouilles croassantes je sais qu'on
de temps en temps un
y trouve ~~aussi quel~~ques homme‸ ~~(bien peu) mais quelques uns)~~ digne‸ par
ses   son independance   de
leur talents et par ~~leur~~ ~~vertus~~ d'être ~~chefs des clans~~ natifs de ~~Glen~~   85
le pic
~~Morven ou~~ d'avoir été né sur ~~les sommets~~ de Ben Nevis ~~ou Shihallion~~

— J'ai fait l'amende honorable et je continue

Comments

It is a curious metaphysical fact that always in the evening when I am in the
great Dormitory alone . . . I always recur as fanatically as ever to the old
ideas the old faces & the old scenes in the world below

—Charlotte to Branwell Brontë, May 1, 1843[1]

"My dear Jane" is not literally a devoir. It is a manuscript that Charlotte
abandoned—undated, untitled, and unsigned. She did not begin by rul-
ing pages from her notebook or transcribe it in her usual devoir hand. She
wrote on unlined paper, adding only a left margin and apparently composing as she went.[2] Though the fifth page breaks off with the words "I
continue," no sequel has ever turned up. Still, she cared enough about the
fragment to preserve it with her devoirs and copybooks from Brussels.

The content disappoints any hope that she was saving a precursor of
Jane Eyre. Neither the recipient nor the writer of this letter anticipates
Charlotte's famous governess. But they do have predecessors in her later
juvenilia, that "world below" which drew her back compulsively. Her representation of this Jane tallies with descriptions of the Angrian character

Jane Moore, and the letter writer seems to be Elizabeth Hastings or a later variant of that character.

Christine Alexander traces Jane Moore back to an entry in Charlotte's Roe Head journal (ca. March 1837).[3] During that period she was "far from home" at school and unable to focus on her usual heroines because she felt depressed and lacked privacy.[4] Jane was Charlotte's creation entirely, not Branwell's, as Alexander also points out, and she may have gestated for weeks or months in Charlotte's thoughts before emerging as a protagonist. She becomes a major character in "Stancliffe's Hotel" (1838) and subsequently in "Henry Hastings" (1839).[5]

From the outset, Charlotte casts this youngest daughter of a merchant as a woman who lacks depth and intelligence. She is, however, "a superb animal"[6]: beautiful and proud, yet also docile. In the words of the Angrian nobleman Sir William Percy

> [Jane] is what the world calls exquisitely sweet-tempered—a sweet-temper in a beautiful face is a divine thing to gaze on—& she has a kind of simplicity about her—which disclaims affectation—She does not know human nature—she does not penetrate into the minds of those about her—She does not fix her heart fervently on some point which it would be destructive to take it from—She has none of that strong refinement of the senses which makes some temperaments thrill with undefined emotion at changes or chances in the skies or the earth, in a softness in the clouds, a trembling of moonlight in water—an old & vast tree—the tone of the passing wind at night—or any other little accident of nature which contains in it more botheration than sense—Well, & what of that?[7]

In "Henry Hastings," Jane's companion is the small, plain-featured Elizabeth Hastings, the sister of the title character. Elizabeth, whose brother is more dissolute than Branwell, earns a comfortable living as a teacher in Zamorna. "[S]he went to school at Paris—," Jane informs Sir William, "& she speaks French very well—." Jane suspects, however, that Elizabeth is happiest in "the moors & mountains" of her native Pendleton.[8] She has the capacity for feeling that Jane lacks and the moral strength missing in her brother; when Sir William begs her to become his mistress, she refuses even though she loves him.

Whether Elizabeth draws away from Jane or leaves the city later, as the cycle continues, are conjectures that no evidence corroborates. But it is clear that four years after writing "Henry Hastings," Charlotte was again away at school and isolated and again elaborating on her Angrians. This time, however, she ventured to write in French, a shift with consequences for her methods. She had grown up writing her stories spontaneously, often in a trancelike state. As the settings, episodes, and dialogue came to her, so she set them down, without a struggle. But devoir composition had accustomed her to thinking more about the words she set on paper. And in French the idioms came less readily; nuancing her thoughts required effort.

She seems to have begun with a plan for this letter: to have its writer upbraid Jane for her indolence and set her on a course of reform. For the first two paragraphs she sticks to that agenda, checking the flow of language only to refine her words: "indolence" for "laziness," "material" for "bodily." However, as she struggles to define Jane's slackness, a more extensive process of revision begins. She pauses after references to marriage and death that again imply the waste of a life passed thoughtlessly, and with the pause, prearrangement vanishes. Dropping her one-sided address to the absent Jane, together with her tacit pose of moral ascendancy, the writer digresses into a dialogue about her own subversive desires. As her imaginary questioners press her, the distinction between Jane's correspondent and Charlotte Brontë breaks down. It is Charlotte who perceives "through the colored glass of simile," Charlotte who suffers from crushing depression, and ultimately Charlotte who exempts one man from the charges she levels against lowlanders.

Confession does not rid her of her demons; the monkey disappears because her hand strikes the desk, not because she wills herself back to reality. Still, by defining and describing these encounters, she transforms her addictive "habit" into a writer's activity. She also complicates that writer's identity—which, for once, is manifestly feminine.

With the disappearance of the monkey and vine, the alleged correspondence resumes; but Jane becomes peripheral, an inexplicit "you," as a narrator with Charlotte's longings and biases replaces the letter-writing moralist. One evident longing was to walk in the mountains of a Scotland she knew only through her reading and through the imaginative reconstructions that she wrote into her juvenilia stories.[9] In an earlier devoir, "Evening Prayer in a Camp," she describes General Abercrombie's troop of Highland soldiers; but there she sets them in the deserts of Egypt rather than their native terrain. Here, she cites Glen Morven, Ben Nevis, and "Shihallion," names she could have come across in Scott's poems and novels or the magazines she read in adolescence.[10] She also sketches Abercrombie on the facing page, in Highland dress, with the mountains outlined in the background (fig. 7).[11] Her approach to these high places, by the gray rock and the cataract, probably required no invention. Haworth guidebooks still direct visitors to a nearby waterfall where two streams converge near a large stone shaped like a seat;[12] both streams and stone are smaller than the landmarks she envisions, but imagination could have enlarged them. Typically, these life-enhancing regions are set against the pestilent marshes of the flat country.

The targets of her contempt are obvious enough; almost from the time of her arrival, Charlotte scorned the Belgians. In 1842 she wrote to Ellen Nussey, "If the national character . . . is to be measured by the character of most of the girls in this school, it is a character singularly cold, selfish, animal and inferior."[13] The details of her mockery in this text, however, suggest it was written in her second year in Brussels, perhaps in the late spring or early summer. In her May 1, 1843, letter to Branwell, for example, she says about the "persons" in the pensionnat, "nobody ever gets into a passion here—such a thing is not known—the phlegm that thickens their blood is too gluey to boil. . . . The black Swan Mr. Heger is the sole veritable exception. . . ."[14] Aside from converting the swan into a clan chief (81), "My dear Jane" offers the same judgments. Its writer seems alienated, angry, and conflicted, but not about to fall into the "gulf of low spirits" that Charlotte envisions by September.[15] She can still make fun of her own austerity and try to "make amends" for her extremism. The closing words are also optimistic, a statement of intent to keep writing. But the fragment remains as she left it that day, a uniquely revealing memento.

The Death
of
Napoleon.

How should one envision this subject? With a great pomp of words or
with simplicity? That depends on the idea that one has of Napoleon, or
rather the idea of him that one is capable of having. The great orators
and the great writers, who know their politicians, and who, having minds
in some way on a level with that of Napoleon, can understand and
appreciate his legislative and military acts, may well celebrate his death
with those solemn and pompous phrases that characterize the funeral ora-
tion; but the ordinary person, without distinguished talent, is incapable
of following the flight of imperial eagles; he prefers to walk by the side
of the young Corsican, the soldier of fortune, who, for him, is always
the Corsican and soldier of fortune, even when the helmet and the uni-
form are concealed by a crown and regal robes. Notwithstanding, does
this ordinary person have the right to express his feelings on the life or
the death of Bonaparte? Does he know how to judge them? Yes; however
insignificant he may be, he has the right to form an opinion and even to
express it: neither king nor emperor has authority to silence the inner
                                                at times
voice that ^ every man hears speaking in his heart and that approves or
condemns, not only his own actions, but the actions of those around him.
Thus one cannot deprive mediocrity of the right to judge genius, but it
does not follow that her judgment will always be sound. The distinctive
quality of mediocrity is moderation, a quality precious but cold; more
often the result of a mild temperament, a happy balance of faculties, a
gift of nature and God, than of great self-imposed efforts. Consequently,
whatever the moralists may say, she is scarcely better suited to help us
form a correct judgment of the actions of extraordinary men than is

La Mort

de

Napoléon.

Comment doit-on envisager ce sujet? avec grande pompe de paroles ou

avec simplicité? C'est selon l'idée qu'on a de Napoleon ou plutôt l'idée

qu'on est capable d'en avoir. Les grands orateurs et les grands écrivains,

qui se connaissent en politiques, et qui, ayant l'esprit en quelque sorte au

niveau de celui de Napoléon, peuvent comprendre et appécier ses actes

militaires et legislatifs, peuvent bien célébrer sa mort dans ces périodes

solonnelles et pompeuses qui caractérisent l'oraison funébre; mais le

simple particulier, sans talent distingué, est incapable de suivre le vol des

aigles impériales; il aime mieux marcher à cote du jeune Corse, soldat

de fortune, qui, pour lui est toujours Corse et soldat de fortune, même

quand le casque et l'uniforme sont masqués par une couronne et des

robes de roi. Cependant ce simple particulier, a-t-il le droit d'exprimer

ses sentiments sur la vie ou la mort de Bonaparte? sait il en juger? Oui;

quelque insignifiant qu'il soit il a le droit de former une opinion et même

de l'exprimer: ni roi, ni empereur n'a autorité de faire taire cette voix

            parfois

intérieure que^ tout homme entend parler dans son coeur et qui approuve

ou condamne, non seulement ses propres actions, mais les actions de

ceux qui l'entourent. Ainsi on ne peut pas ôter à la médiocrité son droit

de juger le génie, mais il n'en suit pas que son jugement soit toujours

juste. La médiocrité a pour qualité distinctive la modération, qualité

précieuse mais froide, le résultat plutôt d'un doux tempérament, d'un

heureux équilibre des facultés, don de la nature et de Dieu, que de

grands efforts faits sur elle-même. Par conséquent, quoi que disent les

moralistes elle n'est guère plus propre à nous aider à former un jugement

correct sur les actions et les hommes extraordinaires, que ne l'est la

Prevention or Enthusiasm. Mediocrity can see the faults of Genius — its imprudence, its temerity, its ambition — but she is too cold, too limited, too egotistical to understand its struggles, its suffering, its sacrifices; she is envious too, and so its very virtues appear to her under a false and tarnished light. Let her then approach with respect the tomb hollowed out of the rock of St. Helena and, while refusing to bow down in adoration before a god of flesh and clay, preserving her independent though inferior dignity of being, let her take care not to cast a single word of insult at the sepulchre, empty now, but consecrated in the past by Napoleon's remains.

Napoleon was born in Corsica and died on St. Helena; between the two islands there is but a vast continent and the immense ocean. He was born a notary's son and died a captive; between the two states there is but the career of a triumphant soldier, but a hundred fields of battle, but a throne, a sea of blood, and a Golgotha. Truly his life is a rainbow; the two extreme ends touch the earth, the intervening arc spans the skies. Still, over Napoleon in his cradle a mother watched; in his childhood he had brothers and sisters; later, he had a wife who loved him very much; but Napoleon on his deathbed is alone, without mother, brother, sister, wife, or child. Let us run quickly through his exploits and then contemplate the abandonment of his final hour. There he is — exiled and captive — bound to an arid rock. He has committed the crime of Prometheus, and he undergoes his punishment. Prometheus wanted to make himself God and Creator, and he stole the fire of heaven to give life to the body he had formed; Bonaparte too wanted to create, not a man but an empire, and he tore the life from entire nations to give an existence, a soul, some reality, to his vast work. Jupiter, indignant at the impiety of Prometheus, bound him to a peak in the Caucasus; Europe, drained by the rapacity of Napoleon, lashed him to an isolated rock in the Atlantic. There perhaps he suffered all that they endure who, distant from home-

Prévention ou l'Enthousiasme. La Médiocrité peut voir les défauts du Génie, son imprudence, sa témerité, son ambition, mais elle est trop froide, trop bornée, trop égoiste pour connaître ses luttes, ses souffrances, ses sacrifices; aussi elle est envieuse, et ses vertus même lui paraissent sous un jour faux et terne. Qu'elle s'approche donc avec respect du tombeau creusé dans le rocher de Ste Hélène et tout en refusant de se courber en adoration devant un Dieu de chair et de boue, en conservant sa dignité d'être independant quoique inférieur qu'elle se garde bien de jeter un seul mot d'insulte sur ce sépulcre, vide maintenant, mais consacré autrefois par les restes de Napoleon.

Napoleon naquit en Corse et mourut en Ste Hélène; entre les deux îles il n'y a qu'un vaste continent et l'océan immense; il naquit fils d'un notaire et mourut captif; entre les deux états il n'y a qu'une carrière de soldat triomphant, que cent champs de bataille, qu'un trône, une mer de sang et une Golgothe. Vraiment sa vie c'est l'arc-en-ciel; les deux points extremes touchent la terre, la ligne courbe intermédiaire mesure les cieux. Cependant, sur Napoleon dans son berceau une mère veillait, dans son enfance il avait des frères et des soeurs, plus tard il avait une femme qui l'aimait beaucoup, mais Napoleon sur son lit de mort, est seul, sans mère, frère, soeur, femme ou enfant. Parcourons rapidement ses exploits et alors contemplons l'abandonnement de sa dernière heure. Il est là — exilé et captif — lié a un rocher aride. Il a commis le crime de Promethée et il subit sa peine; Promethée voulut se faire Dieu et Créateur et il vola le feu du ciel pour animer le corps qu'il avait formé; Bonaparte a aussi voulu créer, pas un homme mais un empire et il a arraché la vie à des nations entières pour donner une existence, une âme, de la réalité à sa vaste oeuvre. Jupiter, indigné de l'impiété de Promethée, l'attacha à une cime du Caucase —: l'Europe épuisée de la rapacité de Bonaparte l'a lié sur un roc isolé de l'Atlantique: La peutêtre il subit tout ce qu'éprouvent ceux, — qui, éloignés de patrie et de famille,

60 land and family, deprived of the affection of their kind, know the soul's
hunger and thirst; and is there a hunger more biting, a thirst more
burning? Even when a stranger's hand would offer a little help, it must
be rejected; for it is charity, not affection, which extends that hand; it is
a sweet illusion offered through pity, but one must not let oneself be
65 deceived by it, because contempt is the brother of charity, and charity
herself, however good, is quite cold. But to speak thus, is it not to
attribute to Napoleon a weakness that he never knew? Is it not to show
an utter incapacity to understand the spirit of that great man? The distinctive mark of Napoleon's genius, was it not his power to be wholly
70 self-sufficient? When did he allow himself to be enchained by a link of
affection? Other conquerors have sometimes hesitated in their course to
glory, halted by an obstacle of love or friendship, held back by a
woman's hand, recalled by a friend's voice; never he. He had no need,
like Ulysses, to tie himself to the mast nor to stop his ears with wax; he
75 did not dread the Sirens' song, he disdained it. He made himself a man
of marble and iron, the better to execute his grand projects. Napoleon
believed himself a whole nation in one body. The brothers, the sisters,
the wife, the child that Bonaparte the Corsican would have allowed himself — not to love, that would be saying too much, but to consider as men
80 and women — appeared to the eyes of Napoleon, the mighty Frenchman,
but as instruments, of which he made use so long as they contributed to
advancing his designs and which he cast aside when they could no
longer be useful to him. Let us not permit ourselves, then, to approach
the Corsican's grave with a feeling of pity or to stain the rock that
85 covers his remains with tears. Let it not be said that the hand which
separated him from his wife and his child was the hand of a tyrant; no!
It was a hand like his own, a hand strong but not bloodstained. He who
extended that hand knew well how to read Napoleon; he was his equal,
not his superior (there has never been one on earth), but his noble peer.

privé de l'affection de leurs semblables, connaissent la soif et la faim de

l'âme; et y a-t-il faim plus mordante, soif plus brulante? Quand même

une main étrangére voudrait offrir un peu de secours, il faut la repousser;

car, c'est la charité, ce n'est pas l'affection qui tend cette main c'est une

douce illusion qu'on offre par pitié, mais par laquelle il ne faut pas se

laisser tromper, car le mépris est frère de la charité, et la charité elle

même quoique bonne est bien froide. Mais parler ainsi, n'est-ce pas

attribuer à Napoleon une faiblesse qu'il ne connaissait pas? N'est-ce pas

montrer une incapacité totale de comprendre l'esprit de ce grand homme?

La marque distinctive du génie de Napoléon n'était-ce pas son pouvoir

de suffire entièrement à lui-même? Quand s'est il laissé enchainer par

un lien d'affection? D'autres conquérants ont quelquefois hésité dans

leur carrière de gloire, arrêtés par un obstacle d'amour ou d'amitié,

retenus par une main de femme, rappelés par une voix d'amie — lui

jamais — Il n'avait pas besoin comme Ulysse de se lier au mât ni de se

boucher les oreilles de cire, il ne redoutait pas le chant des Sirenes il le

dédaignait; il se fit homme de marbre et de fer pour mieux executer ses

grands projets. Napoleon se croyait tout un peuple dans un corps; les

frères, les soeurs, la femme, l'enfant que Bonaparte le Corse se serait

permis — pas d'aimer, ce serait trop dire, mais de considérer comme des

hommes et des femmes, ne paraissaient aux yeux de Napoléon, le puis-

sant Français, que comme des instruments, dont il se servit tant qu'ils

contribuaient à avancer ses desseins et qu'il jeta de côté quand ils ne

pouvaient plus lui être utiles. Qu'on ne se permet donc pas de s'appro-

cher du sépulcre du Corse avec un sentiment de pitié, ou de souiller la

pierre, qui couvre ses restes, des larmes Qu'on ne dise pas que la main

qui la sépara de sa femme et de son enfant était une main de tyran, non!

c'était une main pareille à la sienne, une main forte mais pas sanglante;

celui qui tendit cette main savait bien deviner Bonaparte, c'était son égal,

pas son supérieur, il n'y en a jamais été sur la terre, mais son noble

"Marie-Louise is not Napoleon's wife," says the only victor whom defeat did not know how to humble, nor victory elate. "It is France that he has wed, it is France that he loves, and it is from France that I divorce and separate him because out of their union was born the destruction of Europe!" Some weak and treacherous voices cried out around the man who thus pronounced sentence: "It is an abuse of your privilege as a conquerer; it is grinding the vanquished underfoot. Let England open her arms and take her enemy to her breast." England would perhaps have hearkened to that advice, because in every country there are imbecilic souls who let themselves be seduced by flattery and who fear reproach. But there came a man who did not know what fear was; who loved his homeland better than his own reputation; who, neither frightened by threats nor seduced by praises, presented himself before the national council and, intrepidly lifting his brow pure and bold, said, "Let Treason be silent! For it is treason that counsels you to temporize with Bonaparte. *I* know the nature of all those wars from which Europe still bleeds, like a victim pierced by the sacrificer's knife; I am resolved to shatter the blade that has dealt such deadly blows. We must banish Napoleon Bonaparte. Do not take fright at a word so harsh. I have no magnanimity, have I? It's all the same to me if you say so. My mission here is not to make myself a reputation as a perfect hero; it is to seek a cure for that exhausted, wounded Europe whose real interests you neglect in dreaming about your good name You are weak, but I will help you. Send Bonaparte to the isle of St. Helena. Do not hesitate, do not reflect, do not seek another place; it is the only one, I tell you; I have thought for you, and there is his destination. As for Napoleon, the man and soldier, I do not hold anything against him; he is a royal lion before whom you are only jackals; as for Napoleon the emperor, him I will eradicate!" The man who spoke thus has always known how to keep his promise, in fact he did eradicate the power of Napoleon.

paire. "Marie-Louise n'est pas la femme de Napoleon" dit le seul vainquer

que la défaite n'a pas su humilier, ni la victoire, enorgueillir "C'est la

France qu'il a epousée, c'est la France qu'il aime et c'est de la France

que je le divorce et que je le sépare car de leur union enfantait la

perdition de l'Europe!" De voix faibles et traîtresses s'ecrièrent autour

de celui qui prononça ainsi sentence "C'est abuser de votre droit comme

conquérant, c'est fouler aux pieds le vaincu; que l'Angleterre ouvre ses

bras et qu'elle reçoive son ennemi dans son sein." L'Angleterre aurait

peutêtre écouté ce conseil, car en tout pays il y a des âmes imbéciles qui

se laissent séduire par la flatterie et qui craignent le réproche. Mais un

homme s'est trouvé qui ne savait pas ce que c'était que la crainte; qui

aimait sa patrie mieux que sa propre renommée, qui ni effrayé par les

menaces, ni séduit par les louanges, s'est presenté devant le conseil

national et levant intrépidement son front pur et hardi, a dit, "Que la

trahison se taise! car c'est la trahison qui vous conseille de temporiser

avec Bonaparte. Moi, je sais ce que sont que toutes ces guerres dont

l'Europe saigne encore, comme une victime percée du couteau du sacrifi-

cateur: je ^suis resolu de briser la lame qui a frappé des coups si funestes.

Il faut bannir Napoleon Bonaparte. Ne vous effrayez pas d'un mot si dur

— Je n'ai pas de magnanimité — n'est-ce pas? Cela m'est bien égal si

vous dites cela; ma mission ici, ce n'est pas de me faire une reputation

de héro parfait, c'est de chercher une guérison pour cette Europe blessée

et épuisée dont vous négligez les vrais intérêts pour songer à votre

renommée Vous êtes faibles, mais je vous aiderai. Envoyez Bonaparte

à l'île de Ste Hélène; n'hesitez, ne réfléchissez pas, ne cherchez pas un

autre endroit; c'est le seul je vous dis, j'ai pensé pour vous, et c'est là

sa destination — Quant à Napoleon, homme et soldat, je ne lui en veux

pas, c'est un lion royal auprès de qui vous n'étes que des chacals, quant

à Napoleon empereur, je l'extirperai!" Celui qui parla ainsi a toujours

su garder sa promesse, en effet il extirpa le pouvoir de Napoleon. J'ai

120 I have said that this man is the peer of Napoleon; in genius, yes. In rectitude of character, in loftiness of aim, he is neither equal nor superior; he is of another species. Napoleon Bonaparte prized his reputation and greatly loved celebrity; Arthur Wellesley cares neither for one nor the other. Public opinion had a great value for Napoleon; for Wellington, 125 public opinion is a notion, a nothing that the breath of his mighty will blows away, like a soap bubble. Napoleon flattered the people and sought applause; Wellington treats them brusquely. If his own conscience approves, that is enough; all other praise burdens him. In revenge, the people, who adored Bonaparte, have often been irritated at 130 Wellington's arrogance and showed their hatred by gnashing their teeth and howling like wild beasts. Then the proud Coriolanus raised his Roman head, crossed his sinewy arms, and held himself erect upon his threshold, as if awaiting the attack. Alone and fearless he thus braved a whole crowd in a furor; before long, the people recognized their superior 135 rior and, ashamed of their rebellion, came to lick the feet of the master; but the haughty Satrap scorns their homage as much as their hatred and, in the streets of London, before his ducal palace of Apsley, he has no fear of spurning it with disdain. Despite that pride he is modest; he avoids eulogy; he rejects panegyric; never does he speak of ˄himself, his own exploits 140 and never does he suffer anyone else to mention them to him. His character equals in grandeur and surpasses in truthfulness that of every other hero, ancient or modern. The glory of Napoleon grew in a night, like Jonah's vine, and within a night, it withered. The glory of Wellington is like one of the ancient oaks that shade the mansion of his 145 fathers on the banks of the Shannon. It grows slowly; it needs time not only to spread its large branches but to sink deep roots, roots that will twist themselves around the solid foundations of the island whose Savior and Defender he has been.

dit que cet homme est le paire de Napoleon: en génie, oui; en droiture 120

de caractére, en élevation de but il n'est ni égal ni supérieur, il est d'une

autre espéce. Napoleon Bonaparte tenait à sa réputation et aimait

beaucoup la célébrité, Arthur Wellesley ne se soucie ni de l'une ni de

l'autre. L'opinion publique avait une grande valeur pour Napoleon; pour

Wellington l'opinion publique est un idée, un rien que le souffle de sa 125

puissante volonté fait disparaître, comme une bulle de savon. Napoleon

flattait le peuple et cherchait les applaudissements; Wellington le

brusque; si sa propre conscience l'approuve c'est assez, toute autre

louange l'obsède. En revanche, le peuple, qui adorait Bonaparte, s'est

souvent irrité contre la morgue de Wellington et a temoigné sa haine avec 130

des grincements de dents et des hurlements de bête fauve; alors le fier

Coriolane a levé sa tête romaine, croisé ses bras nerveux et s'est tenu

debout sur son seuil, comme pour attendre l'attaque. Seul et sans crainte

il a bravé ainsi toute une foule en fureur, bientôt le peuple a reconnu son

supérieur et, honteux de sa rebellion, est venu lécher les pieds du maître, 135

mais le hautain Satrape méprise son hommage autant que sa haine et dans

les rues de Londres, devant son palais ducal d'Apsley, il n'a pas craint

de le repousser avec dédain. Malgré cette fierté il est modeste; il se

ses propres exploits
soustrait d'éloge, il rejette le panégyrique, jamais il ne parle de lui, et

jamais il ne souffre qu'un autre lui en parle: son caractère égale en 140

grandeur et surpasse en vérité celui de tout autre héro ancien ou mod-

erne. La gloire de Napoleon croit[ra?] dans une nuit comme la vigne de

Jonah, et dans une nuit elle fut flétrie. La gloire de Wellington est

comme un des anciens chènes qui ombragent le château de ses pères sur

les rives du Shannon; elle croit lentement, il lui faut du temps pas 145

seulement de pousser des larges branches mais d'enfoncer des profondes

racines des racines qui s'entortilleront avec les fondements solides de

l'île dont il a été le Sauveur et le Défenseur

A century more and perhaps England will know the worth of her
150   hero; a century more and all Europe will know how much Wellington
deserves its recognition.

————

Encore un siècle et l'Angleterre connaitra peutêtre la valeur de son héro; encore un siècle et l'Europe entière saura combien Wellington a droit à sa reconnaissance.

The Death

of

Napoleon.

treat

5   How should one envision this subject? With (a grèat) pomp of (woŕds)

or with simplicity? That depends on the idea that one has of Napoleon, or

Let

Politicians
are men.

rather the idea of him that one is capable of having. The great orators

let those whose

and the great writers, who know their politici̶a̶n̶s̶, ̶a̶n̶d̶ ̶w̶h̶o̶,̶ ̶h̶a̶v̶i̶n̶g̶

Politics is
a science.

the genius

minds, in some way on a level with that of Napoleon, can understand and

10   appreciate his legislative and military acts, m̶a̶y̶ ̶w̶e̶l̶l̶ celebrate his death

in

w̶i̶t̶h̶ thòse solemn and pompous phrases that characterize the funeral ora-

mortal   *must renounce*

tion; but the ordinary <u>person</u>, without distinguished talent, <u>is incapable</u>

and be content

o̶f̶ following the flight of imperial eagles; h̶e̶ ̶p̶r̶e̶f̶e̶r̶s̶ to walk by the side

of

of the young Corsican,ˇ the soldier of fortune, who for him is always the

the crown has replaced   *has*

15   Corsican and soldier of fortune, even whenˇthe helmet and the uniformˇ

disappeared   *the*   *the emperor's cloak.*   *But*   *an*

<u>are conceal</u>ed by à crown and ⌈regal⌉ robes /. N̶o̶t̶w̶i̶t̶h̶s̶t̶a̶n̶d̶i̶n̶g̶,̶ does this

then   *formulate his opinion*

ordinary person have the right to express his feelingsˇon the life or the

Can he set himself up as

death of Bonaparte? D̶o̶e̶s̶ ̶h̶e̶ ̶k̶n̶o̶w̶ ̶h̶o̶w̶ ̶t̶o̶ judge t̶h̶e̶m̶? Yes; however

a man   *his own*

very good

insignificant he may be, he has the right to form an opinion and even to

state

20   e̶x̶p̶r̶e̶s̶s̶ it: neither king nor emperor has *the* authority to silence the inner

at times

voice that ˆevery man hears speaking in his heart and that approves or

of others

condemns, not only his own actions, but the actions o̶f̶ ̶t̶h̶o̶s̶e̶ <u>around</u> him.

question

Thus one cannot <u>depri</u>ve mediocrity of the right to judge genius, but it

What ordinarily

does not follow that her judgment will always be sound. ⌊ˇThe distinctive

distinguishes   *i̶n̶a̶d̶e̶q̶u̶a̶t̶e̶ ̶a̶n̶d̶*

25   <u>quality</u>⌋ of mediocrity is moderation, a quality precious but cold; m̶o̶r̶e̶

which is less

o̶f̶t̶e̶n̶ thè result of a mild temperament, a happy balance of faculties, a

rather

gift of nature and God, than of great self-imposed efforts. Consequently,

and   *without sufficient scope*

whatever the moralists may say, she is scarcely better suitedˇ to help

sanely   *e them*[?]

us f̶o̶r̶m̶ ̶a̶ <u>correct</u> judgm̶e̶n̶t̶ ̶o̶f̶ the acti̶o̶n̶s̶ of extraordinary men than is

La Mort

de

Napoléon.

traiter
Comment doit-on envisager ce sujet? avec (grande) pompe (de paroles)   5

ou avec simplicité? C'est selon l'idée qu'on a de Napoleon ou plutôt
                                                        Que
l'idée qu'on est capable d'en avoir. ˇ Les grands orateurs et les grands   *Les politiques*
                                    que ceux dont   *sont des hommes.*
écrivains, qui se connaissent en politique, ~~et qui, ayant~~ l'esprit en
                            u génie   *peut*   *La politique est*
quelque sorte au niveau de celui de Napoléon, ~~peuvent~~ comprendre et   *une science./*
                                                                        nt
apprécier ses actes militaires et legislatifs, ~~peuvent bien~~ célébrer sa mort   10
       en
~~dans~~ ces périodes solonnelles et pompeuses qui caractérisent l'oraison
                            mortel   *doit renoncer à*
funébre; mais le simple particulier, sans talent distingué, est incapable ~~de~~
                                            et se contenter de
suivre le vol des aigles impériales; ~~il aime mieux~~ marcher à côté du jeune
           du
Corse,ˇ soldat de fortune, qui, pour lui est toujours Corse et soldat de
                la couronne a remplacé   que   a disparu   la
fortune, même quand ˇle casque et ˇl'uniforme sont masqués par une   15
               le manteau   l'empereur   Mais un   donc
couronne et des robes de ⌈roi⌉. ~~Cependant~~ ce simple particulier, a-t-il
                        de formuler son opinion
le droit d'exprimer ses sentiments ˇ sur la vie ou la mort de Bonaparte?
peut-il s'eriger   *un homme*
~~sait-il~~ en juger? Oui; quelque insignifiant qu'il soit il a le droit de
se   *la dire*
former une opinion et même de l'~~exprimer~~: ni roi, ni empereur n'a *l* au- | ***tr. bon***
                            parfois
torité de faire taire cette voix intérieure que ^ tout homme entend parler   20

dans son coeur et qui approuve ou condamne, non seulement ses propres
                            d'autrui
actions, mais les actions ~~de ceux~~ qui l'entourent. Ainsi on ne peut pas
contester   *ne s'*
ôter à la médiocrité son droit de juger le génie, mais il n'en suit pas que
               Ce qui distingue d'ordinaire   x   c'est
son jugement soit toujours juste. ˇLa médiocrité a ⌊pour qualité distinctive⌋
                        insuffisante et   *qui est moins*
la modération, qualité précieuse mais froide, le résultat ~~plutôt~~ d'un doux   25

tempérament, d'un heureux équilibre des facultés, don de la nature et de
       plutôt
Dieu, que de grands efforts faits sur elle-même. Par conséquent, quoi
                                        ˙ *et sans portée suffisante*
que disent les moralistes, elle n'est guère plus propre à nous aider à
pour les[?]   *r   sainement   es   d*
~~former un~~ jugement correct ~~sur~~ les ~~actions~~ et les hommes extraordinaires,

Prevention or Enthusiasm. | ~~Mediocrity~~ can see the faults of Genius, its
*[Prevention] has a false eye and sees everything darkly; Enthusiasm sees larger than
life; Mediocrity is too [?] myopic. — she [can] discover*
imprudence, its temerity, its ambition — but she is too cold, too limited,
appreciate them. — the
too egotistical to understand its struggles, its suffering, its sacrifices; she

is envious too, and so its very virtues appear to her under a false and

tarnished light. Let her then approach with respect the tomb hollowed

out of the rock of St. Helena and, while refusing to bow down in adora-

tion before a god of flesh and clay, preserving her independent though

inferior dignity of being, let her take care not to cast a single word of

very g

insult at the sepulchre, empty now, but consecrated in the past by

Napoleon's remains.

at
Napoleon was born in Corsica and died on St. Helena; between the
and burning desert
two islands there is but a vast ~~continent~~ and the immense ocean. He was
*very good/
opposition
remarkably
fine./*
an ordinary gentleman's   an emperor but without crown and in irons
born ~~a notary's~~ son and died ~~a captive~~/; between the two states ~~there is~~
his cradle and his tomb, what is there? —
~~but~~ the career of a triumphant soldier, but ~~a hundred~~ fields of battle, but
then a prison [his coffin?]   whose
a throne, a sea of blood, ~~and a Golgotha. Truly~~ his life is a rainbow; the

two extreme ends touch the earth, the intervening arc spans the skies.
his father's house
Still, over Napoleon in his cradle a mother watched; in ~~his childhood~~ he
in his palace   to love him; courtiers to fawn
had brothers and sisters; later, he had a wife ~~who~~ loved him very much;
on him;
but Napoleon on his deathbed is alone, without mother, brother, sister,
Others have recounted and will recount
wife, or child. ~~Let us run quickly through his exploi~~ts ~~and~~ then contem-

plate the abandonment of his final hour. There he is — exiled and captive
enchained on   new
— bound to an arid rock. He ~~has committed the crime of~~ Prometheus, and
the chastisement of his pride   be
he undergoes his punishment. Prometheus wanted to ~~make himself~~ God
made away with
and Creator, and he stole the fire of heaven to give life to the body he

had formed; Bonaparte too wanted to create, not a man but an empire,
for that

and he tore the life from entire nations to give an existence, a soul, ~~some~~
gigantic
~~reality,~~ to his ~~vast~~ work. Jupiter, indignant at the impiety of Prome-
affixed   the   providence, to punish
theus, bound him to ~~a~~ peak in the Caucasus; Europe, ~~drained by~~ the
the Corsican chained
rapacity of Bonaparte, lashed him to an isolated rock in the Atlantic.

There perhaps he suffered all that they endure who, distant from home-

que ne l'est la Prévention ou l'Enthousiasme: | ~~La Médiocrité~~ peut v<u>o</u>ir   30
[La Prévention] a l'oeil faux et voit tout en noir; l'Enthousiasme voit plus
grand que nature; la Médiocrité est ~~trop~~ [?] miope. — elle [peut] découvrir
les défauts du Génie, s*es* imprudence*s*, sa témérité, son ambition, mais
en apprécier. — les
elle est trop froide, trop bornée, trop égoiste pour <u>connaître</u> ses luttes,

ses souffrances, ses sacrifices; aussi elle est envieuse, et ses vertus mêm<u>e</u>

lui paraissent sous un jour faux et terne.   Qu'elle s'approche donc avec

respect du tombeau creusé dans le rocher de Ste Hélène et tout en re-   35

fusant de se courber en adoration devant un Dieu de chair et de boue, en

conservant sa dignité d'être, indépendant quoique inférieur, qu'elle se   *tr b*

garde bien de jeter un seul mot d'insulte sur ce sépulcre, vide main-

tenant, mais consacré autrefois par les restes de Napoléon.

à
    Napoleon naquit en Corse et mourut <del>e</del>n Ste Hélène; entre les deux   # 〰 40
et brûlant désert
îles il n'y a qu'un vaste ~~continent~~ et l'océan immense; il naquit fils d'un   *tr bon/*
simple gentilhomme   empereur mais sans couronne et dans les fers   *opposition*
~~notaire~~ et mourut ~~captif~~/; entre les deux états ~~il n'y a que~~ une carrière   *remarquablement*
'un   des   son berceau et sa tombe qu'y a-t-il? — la↑   *belle./*
d<u>e</u> soldat triomphant, que cent champs de bataille, qu'un trône, une mer
    puis une prison [son cercueil?]   ~~dont~~
de sang ~~et une Golgotha~~. ~~Vraiment~~ sa vie c'est l'arc-en-ciel; les deux

points extremes touchent la terre, la ligne courbe intermédiaire mesure   45

les cieux.   Cependant, sur Napoleon dans son berceau une mère veillait,
    la maison de son père   *dans son palais eut*
dans s~~on enfance~~ il avait des frères et des soeurs, plus tard il avait une
~~(2)~~   *pr. l'aimer; ~~des courtisans pr. l'aduler~~*
femme ~~qui~~ l'<u>aim</u>ait beaucoup, mais Napoleon sur son lit de mort, est seul,
D'autres ont dit et diront
sans mère, frère, soeur, femme ou enfant.   ~~Parcourons rapidement ses~~
~~(1)~~
~~exploit~~s ~~et~~ <u>alor</u>s contemplons l'abandonnement de sa dernière heure.   Il   50
    enchaîné sur
est là — exilé et captif — ~~lié à~~ un rocher aride.   Il ~~a commis le crime de~~
nouveau   en   le châtiment de son orgueil   être
Promethée et il subit sa peine; Promethée voulut ~~se faire~~ Dieu et Créa-
    déroba
teur et il v~~o~~la le feu du ciel pour animer le corps qu'il avait formé;
    non   *~~pr. cela~~*
Bonaparte a aussi voulu créer, pas un homme mais un empire et il a ar-
un[?]
raché la vie à des nations entières pour donner une existence, une âme,   55
    gigantesque
~~de la réalité~~ à sa ~~vaste~~ oeuvre. Jupiter, indigné de l'impiété de Promethée,
le scella   la   providence pr punir   u
l'attacha à ~~une~~ cime du Caucase —: la Europe épuisée de la rapacité de
Corse   enchaîné
Bonaparte l'a lié sur un roc isolé de l'Atlantique: La peutêtre il subit
    la   la
tout ce qu'éprouvent ceux,— qui, éloignés de patrie et de famille, privé de

60 land and family, deprived of the affection of their kind, ~~know~~ *to* the soul's

hunger and thirst; | and is there a hunger more biting, a thirst more burn-

vulture
of
Prometheus

ing? [Even when a stranger's hand would offer a little help, it must be

rejected; for it is charity, not affection, which extends that hand; it is a

sweet illusion offered through pity, but one must not let oneself be

65 deceived by it, because contempt is the brother of charity, and charity

herself, however good, is quite cold. But to speak thus, is it not to

human

attribute to Napoleon a ˇweakness that he never knew? Is it not to show

an utter incapacity to understand the spirit of that great man? The dis-

tinctive mark of Napoleon's genius, was it not his power to be wholly

in his life

70 self-sufficient? Whenˇdid he allow himself to be enchained by a link of

affection? Other conquerors have ~~sometimes~~ hesitated in their course to

glory, halted by an obstacle of love or friendship, held back by a

woman's hand, recalled by a friend's voice; never he. He had no need,

of the ship

like Ulysses, to tie himself to the mastˇ nor to stop his ears with wax;

75 he did not dread the Sirens' song, he disdained it. He made himself ~~a~~

~~man~~ of marble and iron, the better to execute his grand projects. Napoleon
   not a man but the embodiment of a nation ~~embod~~ *His*   *his*
believed himselfˇa whole nation ~~in one body~~. | The brothers, the sisters
his   *Josephine and his imperial offspring*
the wifeˇ, ~~the child that~~ Bonaparte the Corsican ~~would have allowed him-~~
    ~~[?] that he had~~ *them*
~~self - not~~ to love*d*, that would be saying too much, ~~but to consider as men~~
          the man in him was dead, and the emperor considered them
80 ~~and wo~~men — appeared to the eyes of Napoleon, the mighty Frenchman,ˇ

but as instruments, of which he made use so long as they con~~tributed to~~
   were useful
~~advancing his designs and~~which he cast aside when they ~~could no~~
ceased to be
~~longer be~~ useful ~~to him~~. | Let us not permit ourselves, then, to approach
         with tears
the Corsican's grave with a feeling of pity or to stainˇ the rock that
   his soul would scorn all that.   *It has been said, I know,*
85 covers his remains, ~~with tears~~ ~~Let it not be said~~ that the hand which

separated him from his wife and his child was the hand of a tyrant; no!
        er   *This hand*
It was a hand like his own, a hand strongˇ but not bloodstained. ~~He who~~
was that of a man who had known   *that man was*   *in genius,*
~~extended~~ that ~~hand~~ ~~knew~~ well how to read Napoleon; ~~he~~ was his equal,
        Napoleon   *had*
not his superior (~~there has~~ never ~~been~~ one on earth), ~~but his noble peer~~.

sont en proie
l'affection de leurs semblables, ~~connaissent à~~ la soif et la faim de l'âme; | 60

et y a-t-il faim plus mordante, soif plus brulante?[Quand même une main

étrangère voudrait offrir un peu de secours, il faut la repousser; car,   *vautour*
                                                                                            de
c'est la charité, ce n'est pas l'affection qui tend cette main c'est une   *Prométhée*

douce illusion qu'on offre par pitié, mais par laquelle il ne faut pas se

laisser tromper,[car le mépris est frère de la charité, et la charité elle   65

même quoique bonne est bien froide. Mais parler ainsi, n'est-ce pas at-
                                    humaine
tribuer à Napoleon une ˇfaiblesse qu'il ne connaissait pas? N'est-ce pas

montrer une incapacité totale de comprendre l'esprit de ce grand homme?

La marque distinctive du génie de Napoléon n'était-ce pas son pouvoir
se   *dans sa vie*
de suffire entièrement à lui-même? Quand ˇs'est il laissé enchainer par   70

un lien d'affection? D'autres conquérants ont ~~quelquefois~~ hésité dans

leur carrière de gloire, arrêtés par un obstacle d'amour ou d'amitié,
                                                       la
retenus par une main de femme, rappelés par ~~une~~ voix d'*une* amie — lui
                eut   *du navire*
jamais — Il n'avait pas besoin comme Ulysse de se lier au mâtˇ ni de se
            avec de la
boucher les oreilles dé cire, il ne redoutait pas le chant des Sirènes il le   75

dédaignait; il se fit ~~homme~~ de marbre et de fer pour mieux executer ses
                    pas un homme mais l'incarnation d'un peuple ~~incarne~~
grands projets. Napoleon se croyaitˇ tòut un peuple ~~dans un corps~~ | ; ~~s~~es
                            Joséphine et son rejeton imperial
frères, ~~s~~es soeurs, ~~s~~a femmeˇ, ~~l'enfant que~~ Bonaparte le Corse ~~se serait~~
~~mo[?] les a-t-il~~   *s*
~~permis~~ — pas d'aimér, ce serait trop dire, ~~mais de considérer comme des~~
            était mort en lui, et l'empereur ne les considerait
*l'*homme~~s et des f~~emmes, ne paraissaient aux yeux de | Napoléon, le puis-   80

sant Français,ˇ que comme des instruments, dont il se servit tant qu'ils
        furent utiles
contri~~buaient à avancer ses desseins et~~ qu'il jeta de côté quand ils ne
cessèrent de l'être
~~pouvaient plus lui être~~ utiles| . Qu'on ne se permette donc pas de s'ap-
                                            de larmes
procher du sépulcre du Corse avec un sentiment de pitié, ou de souillerˇ
                            pas des   *on a   t je le sais*
la pierre, qui couvre ses restes| ~~de larmes~~ ~~Qu'on ne~~ dise pàs que la   85
        a son âme repudierait tout cela.]
main qui la sépara de sa femme et de son enfant était une main de
                                                plus
tyran, non! c'était une main pareille à la sienne, une mainˇ forte mais
non   *cette main était celle d'un homme qui avait*
pas sanglante; ~~celui qui ten~~dit cette ~~main savait~~ bien *su* deviner Bona-
cet homme était   en génie, non   *Napoléon*
parte, c'était son égal, ~~pas~~ son supérieur, ~~il n'y~~ en a jamais été sur la

                                          had said that man ~~that stoic hero~~
90   "Marie-Louise is not Napoleon's wife," ~~says the only victor~~ whom
                  had   been able   *that*
            defeat did not know how to humble, nor victory elate. "It is France ~~that~~
            Napoleon
            ~~he~~ has wed, it is France that he loves, and it is from France that I divorce
                                          begets
            and separate him because ~~out of~~ their union ~~was born~~ the destruction of
                        The [voice] of weaklings or traitresses   protested
            Europe!" ~~Some~~ weak and treacherous voices ~~cried out~~ around the man
                        against ~~the~~ that   *victory's*
95   ~~who thus pronounced~~ sentence: "It is an abuse of ~~your~~ privilege ~~as a~~

            ~~conquere~~r; it is grinding the vanquished underfoot. Let England open
                        [receive] her disarmed   as a guest
            her arms and take ~~her~~ enemy ~~to her breast~~." England would perhaps

            have hearkened to that advice, because in every country there are
            soft & timorous   soon   or frightened by
            ~~imbecile~~ souls ~~who let themselves be~~ seduced by flattery ~~and who fear~~
                                          ~~knows not~~ never knew   is
100   reproach. But there came a man who did not know what fear was; who
                                                                    impassive
            loved his homeland better than his own reputation; who, neither fright-
                        to   impervious to   he   s
            ened by ~~threats~~ nor seduced by ~~praises~~, presented himself before the
            [council] of the nation   he dared to say:
            ~~national~~ council and, intrepidly lifting his brow pure and bold, ~~said~~, "Let

            Treason be silent! For it is treason that counsels you to temporize with

105   Bonaparte. *I* know the nature of ~~all~~ those wars from which Europe still
                        under   butcher's   am want
            bleeds, like a victim ~~pierced by~~ the sacrificer's knife; I ^ ~~resolved~~ to
                        the arm   finish with
            shatter t~~he blade~~ that has dealt such deadly blows. We must banish

            Napoleon Bonaparte. Do not take fright at a word so harsh. I have no
                        so be it   what they   of me
            magnanimity, ~~have I~~? It's all the same to me ~~if you~~ say ~~so~~. My mission
                                          magnanimous,   to
110   ~~here~~ is not to make myself a reputation as a perfect hero; it is to seek a
                        Europe, which is dying, drained of resources & blood, and
            cure ~~for that exhausted, wounded Europe~~ whose real interests you neglect
                        an act[?] a   reputation for clemency
            in dreaming about your good name / You are weak, but I will help you.
                                                      over what ~~good the~~
            Send Bonaparte to ~~the isle of~~ St. Helena. Do not hesitate, ~~do not~~ reflect
            isle [?]   suitab[?]   reflected
            ~~and~~ ~~do not~~ seek another place; it is the only one, I tell you; I have thought
                        he must be and nowhere else.
115   for you, and there is ~~his destination~~. As for Napoleon, the man and sol-

            dier, I do not hold anything against him; he is a royal lion before whom
                        but   as   Napoleon, that's different
            you are only jackals; ~~as for~~ Napoleon the emperor, him I will eradicate!"

            The man who spoke thus has always known how to keep his promise, ~~in~~
            this one like all the others
            ~~fact, he did eradicate the power of Napoleon~~ | .

terre, ~~mais son noble paire~~. "Marie-Louise n'est pas la femme de Napo-
    avait dit cet ~~ee héros stoïque~~   *[a]vait pu*
leon" ~~dit le seul~~ vainqu*er* que la défaite n'a pas ~~su~~ humilier, ni la vic-
    homme]   *que Napoléon*
toire, enorgueillir "C'est la France ~~qu'il~~ a epousée, c'est la France qu'il

aime et c'est de la France que je le divorce et que je le sépare car ~~de~~ leur
    e   *La*   *des*   *ou des*
union enfant~~ait~~ la perdition de l'Europe!" ~~De~~ voix faibles et traîtresses
    protesterent   *contre ~~la~~ cette*   *u*
~~s'eerièrent~~ autour de celui ~~qui prononça ainsi~~ sentence "C'est abuser d~~e~~
    de la victoire
~~votre~~ droit ~~comme conqué~~rant, c'est fouler aux pieds le vaincu; que
    comme hôte son   *désarmé*
l'Angleterre ouvre ses bras et qu'elle reçoive ~~son~~ ennemi ~~dans son sein~~."

L'Angleterre aurait peutêtre écouté ce conseil, car en tout pays il y a des
    molles & timorées bientôt   *t*   *ou effrayées par*
âmes ~~imbéciles qui se laiss~~ent séduit*es* par la flatterie ~~et qui craign~~ent
    n'a jamais su ~~sait~~   *st*
le réproche. Mais un homme s'est trouvé qui ne savait pas ce que c'é~~tait~~
    a
que la crainte; qui aim~~à~~it sa patrie mieux que sa propre renommée, qui
    impassible au⌐   *inaccessible aux*   *il se*
ni effrayé par les menaces, ni ~~séduit~~ par les louanges, ~~s'est~~ présenté de-
    de la nation
vant le conseil nation~~al~~ et levant intrépidement son front pur et hardi, ~~a~~
    il osa dire:
~~dit~~, "Que la trahison se taise! car c'est la trahison qui vous conseille de

temporiser avec Bonaparte. Moi, je sais ce que sont ~~que toutes~~ ces guerres
    sous le
dont l'Europe saigne encore, comme une victime ~~pereée du~~ couteau du
    boucher   ~~suis veu~~*x*   *l'arme*
sacrificateur: je^ res~~o~~lu de briser ~~la~~ ~~lame~~ qui a frappé des coups si
    en finir avec
funestes. Il faut ba~~n~~nir Napoleon Bonaparte. Ne vous effrayez pas d'un
    soit
mot si dur — Je n'ai pas de magnanimité — ~~n'est-ce pas~~? Cel~~a~~/ m'est bien
    qu'on   *se de moi*
égal ~~si vous~~ dit~~es~~ cela;/ ma mission ~~ici, ce~~ n'est pas de me faire une
    magnanime   *a*   *l'Europe qui*
reputation de héro*s* parfa~~i~~t, c'est de chercher u~~ne~~ guéri~~rson pour cette~~
    meurt épuisée de ressources & de sang et
/Europe ~~blessée et épuisée~~˘ dont vous négligez les vrais intérêts pour
    une ~~un ae~~[?] de clemence
songer à v~~o~~tre renommée / Vous êtes faibles, mais je vous aiderai. En-
    pas à quoi ~~bon la isle~~[?]
voyez Bonaparte à ~~l'île de~~ Ste Hélène; n'hesitez, ~~ne~~ réfléchi~~rssez pas, etne~~
    conv[?]   *réfléchi,*
cherchez pas un autre endroit; c'est le seul je vous dis, j'ai pen~~s~~é pour
    qu'il doit être et pas ailleurs. —
vous, ~~et~~ c'est là ~~sa destination~~ — Quant à Napoléon, homme et soldat, je

ne lui en veux pas, c'est un lion royal auprès de qui vous n'étes que des
    mais Napoléon   *c'est autre chose*
chacals, quan~~t~~ à Napoleon empereur,˘ je l'~~extirp~~erai!" Celui qui parla
    celle-ci comme toutes les autres
ainsi a toujours su garder sa promesse, ~~en effet il extirpa le pouvoir de~~

equal   *For*

120   I have said that this man is the ~~peer~~ of Napoleon; in genius, yes. In

strength of character, for fpr

rectitude ~~of character~~, in loftiness of ~~aim~~, he is neither equal nor supe-

to him   *was avid for*

rior˘; he is of another species. Napoleon Bonaparte ~~prized his~~ reputation

was b[?] for popularity glory

and ~~greatly loved~~ celebrity; Arthur Wellesley cares neither for one nor

Popularity was a thing of   in   's eyes

the other. Public opinion ~~had a~~ great value for Napoleon; for Wellington,

rumor

125   public opinion is a notion, a nothing that the breath of his mighty will

Wellington treats them brusquely;

blows away, like a soap bubble. Napoleon flattered the people and

the one their   the other cares only for

sought applause; ~~Wellington treats them brusquely~~. If his ~~own~~ con-

when it   despite

science ~~approves, that is enough~~; all other praise burdens him. ~~In~~

Also   those   [but] got angry,   rebelled against

~~revenge~~, the people, who adored Bonaparte, have ~~often been irritated at~~

and when they were ing   growling

130   Wellington's arrogance ~~and~~ showed their hatred by gnashing ~~their teeth~~

at which he   modern

and howling like wild beasts., ~~Then~~ the proud Coriolanus raised his

he   alone

Roman head, crossed his sinewy arms, and ~~held himself erect~~ upon his

he   ed   he braved the outbreak; and when[?] the

threshold, ~~as if~~ awaiting the attack; ~~Alone and fearless he thus braved~~

flood of people died away, powerless, a few paces from him, ~~and~~ then when the

a ~~whole~~ crowd in a furor; before ~~long~~, the ~~people recognized their supe-~~

mob   its

135   ~~rior and~~, ashamed of their rebellion, came to lick the feet of the master,

the   patrician   ed   of today   of yesterday

but the haughty Satrap scorns ~~their~~ homage as much as ~~their~~ hatred˘and,

displayed his contempt   and right up to

in the streets of London, before his ducal palace of Apsley, he ~~has no~~

does not preclude in him a rare   y

~~fear~~ of ~~spurning~~ it ~~with dis~~dain. ~~Despite~~ that pride ˘he is modest;

everywhere   his own exploits

he avoids eulogy; he rejects panegyric; never does he speak of himself,

140   and never does he suffer anyone to mention them to him. His character

of the world

equals in grandeur and surpasses in truthfulness that of every other hero˘,

ancient or modern. The glory of Napoleon grew in a night, like Jonah's

sufficed⌐ to shrivel it

vine, and within a night, it withered. The glory of Wellington is like one

the   old

of the ancient oaks that shade the mansion of his fathers on the banks

The oak

145   of the Shannon. It grows slowly; it needs time not only to spread its

toward the sky   into the earth those   entangle

large branches˘but to sink˘deep roots, roots that will twist themselves

in   of the soil of the island, and then the tree, steadfast as

~~around~~ the solid foundations of ~~the island~~ whose Savior and Defender he

the rock, braves the ~~effort~~ both the weather's ills and ~~tempests'~~ the winds' and

has been.

tempests' efforts.

l'égal
Napoleon |. J'ai dit que cet homme est le paire de Napoleon: en génie,

comme trempe de caractère, comme comme   ne lui est
oui; en droiture de caratére, en élévation de but il n'est'ni égal ni supé-

était avide de la
rieur, il est d'une autre espéce. Napoleon Bonaparte tenait à sa réputa-

était b[?]   de popularité gloire
tion et aimait beaucoup la célébrité, Arthur Wellesley ne se soucie ni de

la popularité était chose de   aux yeux
l'une ni de l'autre. L'opinion publique avait une grande valeur pour

rumeur
Napoleon; pour Wellington l'opinion publique est un idée, un rien que

le souffle de sa puissante volonté fait disparaître:, comme une bulle de

Wellington le brusque; l'un
savon. Napoleon flattait le peuple et cherchait ses applaudissements;

l'autre ne se soucie que de   quand elle
Wellington le brusque[?]; si sa propre conscience |l'approuve c'est assez,
malgré   Aussi   ce

s'irritait s'insurgeait
toute autre louange l'obsède. En revanche, le peuple, qui adorait Bona-

et quand il   ait
parte, s'est souvent irrité contre la morgue de Wellington et a temoigné

par   [gr]ognements   a qui il
sa haine avec des grincements de dents et des hurlements de bête fauve;

moderne   ait   il se croisait
alors le fier Coriolane à levé sa tête romaine, croisé ses bras nerveux et

seul   il   ait   il bravait
s'est tenu debout sur son seuil, comme pour attendre l'attaque; Seul et

l'émeute; et lorsque[?] le flot populaire venait mourir impuissant à quelques pas
sans crainte il a bravé ainsi toute une foule en fureur, bientôt le peuple

de lui, puis et quand la foule   se   venait
a reconnu son supérieur et, honteux de sa rebellion, est venu lécher les

le   patricien   ait   d'aujourd'hui
pieds du maître, mais le hautain Satrape méprise son l hommage autant

d'hier ·étalait son dédain   et jusque
que sa haine et dans les rues de Londres, devant son palais ducal d'Ap-

n'exclut pas chez lui
sley, il n'a pas craint de le repousser avec dédain. Malgré cette fierté

une rare   ie partout   à
il est modeste; il se soustrait à l'éloge, il rejette le panégyrique, jamais

ses propres exploits
il ne parle de^lui, et jamais il ne souffre qu'un autre lui en parle: son

caractère égale en grandeur et surpasse en vérité celui de tout autre

du monde   ût   en
héros, ancien ou moderne. La gloire de Napoleon croit[ra?] dans une

suffit   pour la dessécher
nuit, comme la vigne de Jonah, et il dans d'une nuit elle fut flétrie. La

les vieux
gloire de Wellington est comme un des anciens chènes qui ombragent le

le chêne
château de ses pères sur les rives du Shannon; elle croit lentement, il lui

non   pour   vers le ciel   pour
faut du temps pas seulement de pousser des larges branches mais d'en-

dans le sol   s'enchevêtrent dans
foncer des profondes racines, des racines qui s'entortilleront avec les

du sol de l'île et lorsque l'arbre, inébranlable comme le roc,
fondements solides de l'île dont il a été le Sauveur et le Défenseur

brave l'effort et la faux du temps et l'effort des tempêtes des vents et des tempêtes

A century more and perhaps England will know the worth of her
150   hero; a century more and all Europe will know how much Wellington
deserves its recognition.

========

Encore un siècle et l'Angleterre connaitra peutêtre la valeur de son héros ¦ encore un siècle et l'Europe entière saura combien Wellington a droit à sa reconnaissance. 150

———

On the Death of Napoleon.

. . . . Napoleon was born in Corsica and died at St. Helena.
Between those two islands, nothing but a vast and burning desert and the
boundless ocean. He was born the son of a simple gentleman, & died an
emperor, but uncrowned & in irons.   Between his cradle and his tomb,
what was there? The career of a self-made soldier, fields of battle, a sea
of blood, a throne, then blood again and fetters. His life is a rainbow;
the two extreme ends touch the earth, the luminous arc spans the skies.
Over Napoleon's cradle, a mother watched; in his father's house he had
brothers and sisters; later, in his palace, he had a wife who loved him,
a . . . But on his deathbed, Napoleon was alone: no more mother, nor
brother, nor sister, nor wife, nor child! . . . Others have recounted &
will recount his exploits; me, I pause to contemplate the abandonment of
his final hour.

There he is, exiled and captive, chained upon a rock. A new
Prometheus, he suffers the chastisement of his pride. Prometheus had
wanted to be God and Creator; he stole the fire of Heaven to give life to
the body he had formed. As for Bonaparte, he had wanted to create, not
a man, but an empire; and to give an existence, a soul, to his gigantic
work, he did not hesitate to tear the life from entire nations. Jupiter,
indignant at the impiety of Prometheus, nailed him alive to a peak in the
Caucasus. Thus, to punish the ~~rapacity~~ rapacious ambition of Bonaparte, Providence chained
him, until death should follow, to an isolated rock in the Atlantic.
Perhaps there he too felt, gnawing at his flank, those insatiable vultures
of whom the fable speaks; perhaps he suffered too that thirst of the heart,
that hunger of the soul, which ~~torment~~ torture the exile, far from his
country and his homeland!

But to speak thus, is it not to attribute gratuitously to Napoleon

Sur la mort de Napoléon.

. . . . Napoléon naquit en Corse et mourut à Ste. Hélène. —
Entre ces deux îles, rien qu'un vaste et brûlant désert et l'océan immense. — Il naquit fils d'un simple gentilhomme, & mourut empereur,   5
mais sans couronne & dans les fers. — Entre son berceau et sa tombe,
qu'y a-t-il? — la carrière d'un soldat parvenu; des champs de bataille, une
mer de sang, un trône, puis du sang encore et des fers. — Sa vie, c'est
l'arc en ciel; les deux points extrêmes touchent la terre; la comble
lumineuse mesure les cieux. — Sur Napoléon au berceau, une mère veil-   10
lait; dans la maison paternelle il avait des frères et des soeurs; plus tard,
dans son palais, il eut une femme qui l'aimait, un . . Mais sur son lit de
mort, Napoléon est seul: plus de mère, ni de frère, ni de soeur ni de
femme, ni d'enfant!! . . . D'autres ont dit & rediront ses exploits — moi,
je m'arrete à contempler l'abandonnement de sa dernière heure. —   15

   Il est là, exilé et captif, enchaîné sur un écueil. — Nouveau
Promethée il subit le châtiment de son orgueil — Promethée avait voulu
être Dieu et Créateur; il déroba le feu du Ciel pour animer le corps qu'il
                                         il
avait formé — Et lui, Bonaparte, ˇ a voulu créer, non pas un homme mais
un Empire, et pour donner une existence, une âme, à son oeuvre gigan-   20
tesque, il n'a pas hésité à arracher la vie à des nations entières; — Jupiter
indigné de l'impiété de Promethée le riva vivant à la cime du Caucase —
                             l'ambition
Ainsi, pour punir la rapacèté de Bonaparte, la Providence l'a enchaîné
jusqu'a ce que mort s'en suivîs, sur un roc isolé de l'Atlantique. Peut-
être là aussi a-t-il senti, lui fouillant le flanc, ces insatiables vautours   25
                                      aussi
dont parle la fable, peutêtre a-t-il souffertˇ cette soif du coeur, cette faim
de l'âme qui tourmentent torturent l'exilé, loin de sa famille, et de sa
patrie!

   Mais parler ainsi n'est-ce pas attribuer gratuitement à Napoléon

a human weakness that he never experienced? For when did he allow himself to be enchained by a link of affection? No doubt other conquerors have hesitated in their course to glory, halted by an obstacle of love or friendship, held back by a woman's hand, recalled by a friend's voice; never he! He had no need, like Ulysses, to tie himself to the mast of the ship, nor to stop his ears with wax. He did not dread the Sirens' singing. He disdained it; he made himself marble and iron, to execute his grand projects. Napoleon did not regard himself as a man, but as the incarnation of a people. He did not love; he considered his friends and relations but as instruments, which he valued so long as they were useful, and which he cast aside when they ceased to be. Let us not permit ourselves, then, to approach the Corsican's Sepulchre with a feeling of pity, or to stain with tears the rock that covers his remains; his soul would scorn all that. It has been said, I know, that it was a cruel hand that separated him from his wife and his child. No; it was a hand that, like his own, trembled not, either from passion or from fear; it was the hand of a man, cool and convinced, who had known how to read Napoleon. And here is what he said, that man whom defeat could not humble, nor victory elate: "Marie-Louise is not Napoleon's wife. It is France that Napoleon has wed; it is France that he loves; their union begets the destruction of Europe; that is the divorce I insist on; that's the union which must be shattered."

The voices of weaklings & traitors protested against that sentence: "It is abusing the privilege of victory! It is grinding the vanquished underfoot! Let England show herself clement; let her open her arms to receive her disarmed enemy as her guest." England would perhaps have hearkened to that advice, because everywhere & always there are weak and timorous souls, soon seduced by flattery or frightened by reproach. But Providence let a man be found who had never known what fear was, who loved his homeland better than his reputation; impassive before

une humaine faiblesse qu'il n'éprouva jamais? Quand donc s'est-il laissé enchaîner par un lien d'affection —? Sans doute d'autres conquérants, ont hésité dans leur carrière de gloire, arrêtés par un obstacle d'amour ou d'amitié, retenus par la main d'une femme, rappelés par la voix d'un ami — lui, jamais! — Il n'eut pas besoin comme Ulysse, de se lier au mât du navire, ni de se boucher les oreilles avec de la cire: Il ne redoutait pas le chant des Sÿrènes — Il le dédaignait; il se fit marbre et fer, pour exécuter ses grands projets. — Napoléon ne se regardait pas comme un homme, mais comme l'incarnation d'un peuple. — Il n'aimait pas; il ne considérait ses amis et ses proches que comme des instruments, auxquels il tint, tant qu'ils furent utiles, et qu'il jeta de côté, quand ils cessèrent de l'être. — Qu'on ne se permette donc pas d'approcher du Sépulchre de Corse, avec un sentiment de pitié, ou de souiller de larmes la pierre qui couvre ses restes, son âme répudierait tout cela. — On a dit, je le sais, qu'elle fut cruelle, la main qui le sépara de sa femme et de son enfant. — Non, c'était une main qui, comme la sienne, ne trembla ni de passion ni de crainte, c'était la main d'un homme froid, convaincu, qui avait su deviner Bonaparte: et voici ce que disait cet homme que la défaite n'a pu humilier, ni la victoire, enorgueillir: «Marie Louise n'est pas la femme de Napoléon. — c'est la France que Napoléon a épousée; c'est la France qu'il aime; leur union enfante la perte de l'Europe; voilà le divorce que je veux; voilà l'union qu'il faut briser. —"

La voix des timides & des traîtres protesta contre cette sentence: «c'est abuser du droit de la victoire! — c'est fouler aux pieds le vaincu! — Que l'Angleterre se montre clémente; qu'elle ouvre ses bras pour recevoir comme hôte, son ennemi désarmé." — L'Angleterre aurait peutêtre écouté ce conseil, car partout & toujours il y a des âmes faibles et timorées, bientôt séduites par la flatterie, ou effrayées par le reproche. — Mais la Providence permit qu'un homme se trouvât qui n'a jamais su ce que c'est que la crainte; qui aima sa patrie plus que sa renommée;

60 threats, inaccessible to praise, he presented himself before the council of the nation, and, raising his calm and lofty brow, he dared to say, "Let treason be silent! For it is treason that counsels you to temporize with Bonaparte. *I* know the nature of those wars from which Europe still

65 bleeds, like a victim under the butcher's knife; I want to shatter the arm that discharged such deadly blows. We must finish with Napoleon Bonaparte. You take fright wrongly at a word so harsh. I have no magnanimity, it's said. So be it! What matter to me, what they say about me? I am not here to make myself a reputation as a magnanimous hero, but

70 to heal, if a cure is possible, the Europe that is dying, drained of resources and blood, the Europe whose real interests you neglect, preoccupied as you are with an empty reputation for clemency. You are weak. Very well! I've come to help you. Send Bonaparte to St. Helena! Do not hesitate, do not seek another place; it's the only one

75 suitable. I'm telling you, I have reflected for you; there he must be, and nowhere else. As for Napoleon, the man, the soldier, I have nothing against him; he is a Royal Lion, before whom you are only jackals. But Napoleon the emperor, that's different; I will eradicate him from the soil of Europe." And the man who spoke thus has always known how to keep his promise, that one, like all the others.

80 I have said, and I repeat, that man is the equal of Napoleon for Genius; for strength of character, for rectitude, for loftiness of thought and aim, he is of a wholly different species. Napoleon Bonaparte was avid for reputation and Glory; Arthur Wellesley cares neither for the one nor the other. Public opinion, popularity, were things of great worth, in

85 Napoleon's eyes; for Wellington, public opinion is a notion, a nothing that the breath of his inflexible will blows away, like a soap bubble. Napoleon flattered the people; Wellington treats them brusquely. The one sought their applause; the other cares only for the testimony of his conscience. When it approves, that is enough; all other praise burdens

impassible devant les menaces, inaccessible aux louanges, il se présenta 60

devant le conseil de la nation, et levant son front tranquille et haut, il osa

dire: .Que la trahison se taise — car c'est trahir que de conseiller de

temporiser avec Bonaparte — Moi je sais ce que sont ces guerres dont

l'Europe saigne encore, comme une victime sous le couteau du boucher.

— Je veux briser l'arme qui a porté des coups si funestes - Il faut en finir 65

avec Napoléon Bonaparte. — Vous vous effrayez à tort d'un mot si dur

— Je n'ai pas de magnanimité dit-on.! — Soit! que m'importe ce qu'on dit

de moi: — Je n'ai pas ici, à me faire une réputation de héros magnanime,

mais à guérir, si la cure est possible, l'Europe qui se meurt, épuisée de

ressources et de sang, l'Europe dont vous négligez les vrais intérêts, 70

préoccupés que vous êtes d'une vaine renommée de clémence. — Vous

êtes faibles. Eh bien! je viens vous aider: — Envoyez Bonaparte à Ste

Hélène! — n'hésitez pas, ne cherchez pas un autre endroit; c'est le seul

convenable. — Je vous le dis, j'ai réfléchi pour vous; c'est là qu'il doit

être et non pas ailleurs. — Quant à Napoléon, homme, soldat, je n'ai rien 75

contre lui; c'est un Lion Royal, auprès de qui, vous n'êtes que des

chacals — Mais Napoléon empereur, c'est autre chose, je l'extirperai du

sol de l'Europe.— . Et celui qui parla ainsi a toujours su garder sa pro-

messe, celle-là, comme toutes les autres. — Je l'ai dit, et je le répète, cet

homme est l'égal de Napoléon par la Génie; comme trempe de caractère, 80

comme droiture, comme élévation de pensée et de but, il est d'une tout

autre espèce: Napoléon Bonaparte était avide de renommée et de Gloire;

Arthur Wellesley ne se soucie ni de l'une, ni de l'autre; — l'opinion

publique la popularité, étaient choses de grande valeur, aux yeux de

Napoléon; pour Wellington l'opinion publique est une rumeur, un rien 85

que le souffle de son inflexible volonté fait disparaître, comme un bulle

de savon. — Napoléon flattait le peuple; Wellington le brusque; l'un

cherchait les applaudissements, l'autre ne se soucie que du témoignage

de sa conscience. — Quand elle approuve, c'est assez; tout autre louange

him. Thus the people, who adored Bonaparte, got angry, rebelled against Wellington's arrogance. At times they showed their anger and hatred by growling, by howling like wild beasts; and then, with the impassivity of a Roman senator, the modern Coriolanus deflected the furious crowd with a look. He folded his sinewy arms across his broad
chest, and alone, erect upon his threshold, he awaited, he braved the storm of people whose squalls died away a few paces from him. & when the mob, ashamed of its rebellion, came to lick the feet of the master, the haughty patrician scorned the homage of today, as he had the hatred of yesterday, and in the streets of London and right before his ducal palace
of Apsley, he repulsed the clumsy eagerness of the enthusiastic masses with a manner full of cold disdain. That pride nonetheless does not preclude in him a rare modesty; everywhere he avoids eulogy, he escapes from panegyric. Never does he speak of his exploits, and never does he suffer anyone else to mention them in his presence. His character equals
in grandeur and surpasses in truthfulness that of every other hero, ancient or modern. The glory of Napoleon grew in a night, like Josiah's vine, and a day sufficed to shrivel it. The glory of Wellington is like one of the old oaks that shade the mansion of his fathers, on the banks of the Shannon. The oak grows slowly; it needs time to spread its gnarled
branches toward the sky, and to sink ~~deeply~~ into the soil those deep roots that will entangle themselves in the solid foundations of the land. But then, the centuries'-old tree, steadfast as the rock where it has its base, will brave both the weather's ills and the winds' & tempests' efforts. It will take perhaps a century for England to know the worth of her hero.
In a century, all Europe will know how much Wellington deserves its recognition.

l'obsède. — Aussi ce peuple, qui adorait Bonaparte, s'irritait, s'insurgeait   90
contre la morgue de Wellington; parfois il lui témoigna sa colère et sa
haine par des grognements, par des hurlements de bêtes fauves; et alors,
avec une impassibilité de sénateur Romain, le moderne Coriolan torsait
du regard l'émeute furieuse; il croisait ses bras nerveux sur sa large
poitrine, et seul, debout sur son seuil, il attendait, il bravait cette tempête   95
populaire dont les flots venaient mourir à quelques pas de lui. — & quand
la foule honteuse de sa rébellion, venait lécher les pieds du maître, le
hautain patricien méprisait l'hommage d'aujourd'hui, comme la haine
d'hier, et dans les rues de Londres et jusque devant son palais ducal
d'Apsley, il repoussait d'un genre plein de froid dedain, l'incommode   100
empressement du peuple enthousiaste — Cette fierté néanmoins n'excluait
pas en lui, une rare modestie; partout il se soustrait à l'éloge, se dérobe
au panégyrique; jamais il ne parle de ses exploits, et jamais il ne souffre
qu'un autre que lui en parle en sa présence. — Son caractère égale en
grandeur et surpasse en vérité celui de tout autre héros ancien ou   105
moderne. — La gloire de Napoléon crût en une nuit, comme la vigne de
Josiah, et il suffit d'un jour pour la flétrir; la gloire de Wellington est
comme les vieux chênes qui ombragent le château de ses pères, sur les
rives du Shannon; le chêne croît lentement, il lui faut du temps pour
pousser vers le ciel ses branches noueuses, et pour enfoncer ~~profondé-~~   110
~~ment~~ dans le sol, ces racines profondes qui s'enchevêtrent dans les
fondements solides de la terre, mais alors, l'arbre séculaire, inébranlable
comme le roc où il a sa base, brave & la faux du temps et l'effort des
vents & des tempêtes — Il faudra peutêtre un siècle à l'Angleterre pour
qu'elle connaisse la valeur de son héros. — Dans un siècle, l'Europe   115
entière saura combien Wellington a de droit à sa reconnaissance.

Comments

One morning [in 1850] I brought her the first page of the chapter on the Peninsular War [Wellington's campaign] in my Introductory History, and said, "Tell me if this will do for a beginning, &c." I read the page or two to her as we stood before the fire, and she looked up at me and stole her hand into mine, and, to my amazement, the tears were running down her cheeks. She said, "Oh! I do thank you! Oh! we are of one mind! Oh! I thank you for this justice to the man!"

—Harriet Martineau[1]

I used to think, as I sat looking at M. Paul, while he was knitting his brow or protruding his lip over some exercise of mine, which had not as many faults as he wished (for he liked me to commit faults: a knot of blunders was sweet to him as a cluster of nuts), that he had points of resemblance to Napoleon Bonaparte. I think so still.

—Lucy Snowe, *Villette*[2]

I will now copy out another [devoir], written nearly a year [after "Peter the Hermit"], during which the progress made appears to me very great.

—Elizabeth Gaskell[3]

"Progress" is not the word all readers would apply to "The Death of Napoleon." Its subject reevokes Charlotte's worship of Wellington, the hero of her earliest plays and stories and the counterpart to Branwell's chief man, Bonaparte. Its structure too hints that she moved backward, not forward, forgetting Heger's lessons about keeping to the point whenever feeling carried her away. Even the French does not display the "ease and grace of style" that Gaskell claims it had gained.[4]

But Gaskell was misled by the version Heger mailed her, a "copy" he had massively revised. She reproduced this text as "On the Name of Napoleon" because she misread *mort* as *nom,* an error that her third edition rectifies. But she never discovered the extent of his rewriting; perhaps she only glanced at the original in Brussels, a draft thick with Heger's alterations. That version came to Haworth in 1954, a gift from his descendants to the Brontë Society, which published it soon after with his markings stripped away and accompanied by Margaret Lane's translation.[5]

Publication in two versions, however incomplete, marks this devoir as unusually accessible to scholars. Still, it has remained an uncommunicative witness, its riddles unexplored, its content largely unexamined,[6] and its role in her development unclear. With the reproduction of more complete transcripts, perhaps we can get at its hidden testimony and reassess the progress it inscribes.

The first puzzle is its date. Gaskell, seeing 1843 on Heger's copy, assumed that Charlotte wrote it in her second term abroad; but since she herself wrote only "May 31st," the year could be another reconstruction. In 1842 Heger gave both sisters a lesson on Hugo's "Sur Mirabeau," after which Emily wrote her portrait of Harold and Charlotte her portrait of Peter. "Napoleon" also responds to Hugo's essay, in more detail than either of the others. Then there is the gracelessness of Charlotte's French in the draft shorn of Heger's corrections. (Unlike Lane's eloquent, enhancing translation, mine retains the awkward patches, so as to bring out changes between versions and communicate to non-French speakers the extent of Charlotte's struggles with the language.)

But more persuasive factors corroborate the date that Heger and Gaskell assign. Charlotte is reaching for sophisticated rhetoric, trying to execute comparisons and tonal shifts that would have been beyond her range the first year. Fifteen weeks after coming to the pensionnat, she could have launched her devoir with a novice's questions, but she could not have sustained it through twelve pages or composed the rainbow metaphor and Wellington's speeches. Hints for those speeches may have come from Heger's lesson and his dictée "Mirabeau on the Tribune," but a glance at that text (after Emily's "Harold" in this volume) makes immediate imitation seem unlikely. "The Death of Napoleon" does owe a debt to Hugo, but to passages that Charlotte either read outside of class or heard Heger analyze later.

For example, in the second part of "Mirabeau," Hugo personifies mediocrity and denounces its treatment of great men: "Mediocrity would be greatly annoyed by the man of talent, if the man of genius were not there; but the man of genius is there, and so she supports the man of talent and makes use of him against the master. . . . Mediocrity is in favor of him who annoys her the least and resembles her the most."[7] He concludes part 4 by calling Mirabeau "the god of a nation divorced from its king."[8] He refers in many places to the people, who adored Mirabeau as Charlotte's people adored Bonaparte, and he portrays Mirabeau within the French Assembly as she portrays the duke before Parliament. He classifies Mirabeau and Bonaparte as "men of revolution," in contrast to the "men of progress" who patiently till the soil and cultivate its fruits,[9] a trope that may prefigure Charlotte's oaks. In addition, there are analogous details—a list of relationships turned sour,[10] lion imagery—and similar attempts, near the end of both essays, to anticipate the judgments of the future.

Why would Charlotte have reverted to "Mirabeau" a year after Heger gave his lesson? Perhaps the essay made a lasting impression.[11] Or, if Heger recycled his material, perhaps she attended his lecture a second time and then wrote a devoir that would demonstrate the distance she had come since writing "Peter the Hermit." Perhaps she was rereading her notebooks of the year before or returning to the texts that Heger had consulted, in an effort to regain the old sense of closeness and the pleasure of following his lead.

That March she had translated Auguste Barbier's poem about Napoleon, "L'Idole," into English. It too could have stimulated thoughts of her own idol, the man who ended Bonaparte's career. Barbier's poem depicts a brutal Corsican who rides his "young mare," France, so ruthlessly, pressing her on "with his vigorous thigh," that she dies in action, bringing him down with her.[12] As Enid Duthie says, "It conforms to another of the archetypal patterns of Charlotte's art, that of the victim, in this case a willing one, who is finally driven to the breaking-point."[13] Charlotte herself had not yet reached the breaking point, but she was on her way.

Throughout this period, her letters home allude to her increasing loneliness. ". . . I never exchange a word with any other man than Monsieur Heger and seldom indeed with him," she wrote to Emily. ". . . I rarely speak to Monsieur now, for not being a pupil I have little or nothing to do with him," she wrote to Branwell. The tasks she set herself could not replace the assignments that had filled her hours in 1842; now she passed her evenings alone in the dormitory, where she recurred "fanatically" to Angria, "the world below."[14]

Bonaparte and Wellington spanned her worlds. Arthur Wellesley, the first duke of Wellington (1769–1852), had been Patrick Brontë's hero while he was still at Cambridge, and when his four children began their games and stories (*The Young Men's Plays, The Islanders, The Glass Town Saga*) the duke was chief citizen and ruler.[15] They drew information from their father's books and magazines, which probably included a life of Wellington and certainly included one of Bonaparte by Walter Scott,[16] whose novels Charlotte also read avidly. At thirteen, when the games had been in progress for three years, she could have rattled off the details of her favorite's biography: family members, residences, campaigns, statesmanship, appearance, conduct, character. Napoleon's role had diminished by then, but she and Branwell brought him back sporadically.[17] He makes a last, posthumous appearance in her final story, not as the formidable soldier of the early tales, but as the emperor romanticized by her protagonist, Caroline Vernon.[18]

The real Napoleon died on May 5, 1821. On May 5, 1840, his death again became topical when Louis Philippe, the king of France, applied to Britain to exhume Napoleon's remains and rebury them in Paris. The project was carried out later that year, and the body reinterred in Les Invalides. Charlotte's allusion to the "sepulchre, empty now" acknowledges the still-recent transfer. These events were literally brought home to the pensionnat when Heger's friend and colleague, Joachim-Joseph Lebel, received a fragment of the coffin from Napoleon's nephew, whose secretary he had once been. He passed it on to Heger, who gave it to Charlotte on August 4, 1843.[19]

In any case, Napoleon would not have seemed remote to schoolgirls living ten miles away from Waterloo.[20] For most, he remained an unparalleled commander, an emperor even in defeat. They would hardly have shared an Englishwoman's reverence for the man who had him put away. According to Louise de Bassompierre, who took classes with Charlotte in 1842, "one day there was a little altercation . . . on the subject of the Emperor Napoleon; the students reproached Miss Charlotte with the conduct of England toward the Emperor, and seemed to hold her responsible for it; I remember that I calmed the most excited by saying that Miss Brontë had nothing to do with it and that they had better drop the subject."[21] In class she was outnumbered or else too timid to vindicate her hero's decision. But her devoir counters such reproaches in the passage on the "imbecilic souls" who favor leniency.

These circumstantial clues facilitate conjecture on her motives for writing the essay. Heger may or may not have set the assignment. As she says, she was no longer officially his student, but her contract entitled her to literature lessons, and if she chose to follow the instructions he gave others or to seek his guidance on a topic of her own, she could claim his attention in good conscience. She had to do something to offset her feelings of isolation, homesickness, remoteness from her teacher, and confinement in an alien culture. To write rational prose about Napoleon and Wellington was healthier than plunging into fantasy.[22] Even though her medium, the devoir, was a humble one, she was in control once she picked up her pen—and what she created, Heger would read.

But in both versions of "The Death of Napoleon," control and response are problematic. Charlotte seems to have begun with a framework. She establishes her context through a formal introduction, the kind she had attempted in "Peter the Hermit," although here, instead of cataloging men who changed the world, she considers perspectives for assessing one such man. Having brought her readers to Napoleon's tomb, she returns to his life through her rainbow image and a series of comparisons and contrasts. The culminating contrast of Bonaparte with Wellington leads back to the topic her opening anticipates, the judgment of a great man's life. In outline, then, the essay has a balanced structure, built around Napoleon's death. But as soon as the hand of Wellington emerges, the body of the Corsican recedes. Even in the introduction, personal digressions intrude on her alleged theme and subject.

Earlier, in speaking of her attitude toward genius, I mentioned the references to Madame Heger half-concealed in her critique of mediocrity.[23] Hugo's attack on mediocrity in "Mirabeau" provides a literary model for that passage, but Charlotte's is a much more personal animus against a creature envious, cold, and callous. Her feelings surface again in the section on Prometheus, where the hungry soul must reject a stranger's help because "charity, not affection . . . extends that hand; it is a sweet illusion offered through pity" (63–64). Even the duke's speech contributes to the drama her subconscious is constructing. Wellington, the Englishman of valor and integrity, announces that "Marie-Louise is not Napoleon's wife" and insists on divorcing and separating him from a union that threatens all of Europe. Again, she has a precedent in Hugo, but if Lucy's words on Paul have any basis in her author's life, Charlotte is not speaking only about Bonaparte. Her devoir makes Napoleon into two people: the young and fiery Corsican, a lion among jackals, and the heartlessly tyrannical emperor. Its narrator locates himself beside the young soldier and sets the duke to banishing the tyrant.

To this subtext, Heger is oblivious. He does not perceive the barb in her assault on mediocrity, although before he cuts the introduction altogether he deletes her claim that nature, rather than effort, produces a mild disposition. He also attributes mediocrity's limits to short-sightedness rather than to coldness, elaborating Charlotte's statement in a threefold analogy on vision.[24] He reacts to the suffering soul's rejection of charity by striking the passage cleanly from her text, with a businesslike "vulture of Prometheus" in the margin to recall her to the legend she cited. Hunger and thirst carry over to his version, but as tortures of the (masculine) exile. He also retains the passage on divorce, which in context does not seem unduly personal.

Cumulatively, Heger's cuts eradicate digression and keep the devoir focused on Napoleon and Wellington. Emotion remains, but it goes public. Charlotte's vision and arguments also survive, though in a style she lacked the expertise to adopt and might not have chosen, even if she could have. Heger reshapes sentence after sentence, usually not because of faults she has committed, but because he wants to improve her style and enhance the essay's literary qualities. So Prometheus cannot be "bound" to the peak, he must be "affixed" there as seals are set on documents, or "nailed alive"—more literally, "riveted." And Wellington's hand cannot remain "strong but not bloodstained"; it must be a hand that "trembled not, either from passion or from fear." The version Heger mailed to Gaskell is the product of three layers of revision: a first in pencil, a second in ink, and a third in the transfer to fresh paper. The third deletes his excesses as well as Charlotte's and makes the whole essay more dramatic. There, the duke speaks and acts with the authority that she would have wanted him to have. But Heger's changes also overlay her voice with his; they remold her wax and set his stamp in it.

Margaret Lane assumes that "M. Heger's pride as a teacher tempted him to improve [the devoir] vastly before he let Mrs. Gaskell copy it."[25] But much of the improving had been done before she got to Brussels. Why did Charlotte Brontë accept and even welcome alterations that so ruthlessly appropriate her text? Lucy Snowe's parenthetical aside suggests one answer: whether or not Heger "liked [her] to commit faults," she believed that correction gave him pleasure. Writing was her means of communicating with him; his words on her page satisfied her hunger. If, in return, she could believe she fed his appetite, then despite the unilateral nature of his changes, the exercise would have been collaborative.

A further reason is suggested by the final text and Lebel's present to Charlotte. Heger read model compositions on Prize Day, an event that took place in late summer. His version, like the one of Emily's "Harold," seems made to be spoken aloud. Charlotte's classmates may have challenged her exalted views of Wellington, but gathered with their families and other Brussels residents, they would have heard his merits proclaimed by a professor who was locally famous as an orator. And Heger was not only an eloquent speaker; he encouraged views that differed from his own. ("Very good," he wrote next to her statement on each person's right to form and express an opinion.) However despotically he managed her prose, he left her judgments intact, here as elsewhere.

Those judgments are often adolescent and more than slightly inconsistent. She says genius, by its nature, is imprudent and tormented, but one of her geniuses never behaves rashly and the other is incapable of suffering. She claims that a cool, balanced nature limits Mediocrity and then extols the cool and balanced Wellington. In him, an arrogant self-confidence is laudable; in Bonaparte, it is inhuman and exploitive. Consistency, however, is not what Charlotte aims for, in this most political of her devoirs.

Two days before, she had confided to Emily, "I fancy [M. Heger] has taken to considering me as a person to be let alone."[26] Blocked by Madame Heger in her efforts to get through to him, she sought to reconnect through her writing. Her success can be gauged by the attention he lavished on "The Death of Napoleon." It is a writer's exercise, not a love story. Still, the dense rescripting, the lines that slash her sentences, the words that overlay hers and extend across her spaces, can be read as signs of care that transcend duty. Heger may have cared most for his vision of a student's text, but she cared most about her master's notice.

In this way, as in others, the text encodes relationships, dialogues with voices from her past and her present that would influence her future life and fiction.

The Death of Moses

—————

Moses was one hundred twenty years old, his mission was accomplished, he saw Israel encamped at the borders of the Promised Land, and there remained but two things for him to do, to bless the people and to die. He summoned the people, and he said to them, "I see before me the river Jordan which God has forbidden me to cross; hence it is here that we must part. You must enter into Canaan to conquer nations greater and more powerful than you; as for me, I remain here to die." Then he reminded them of the history of the forty years that they had wandered in the desert. He enumerated their sins, their suffering, the blessings and the retributions of their God., ànd ôrdïnàrÿ làngüàgè After Moses, law-giver and leader, had spoken, Moses prophet and chosen of God began to speak, and ordinary language no longer sufficing to express the thoughts that stirred his soul, he launched into the figurative language of poetry, that noble biblical poetry which takes its fire from the eastern sun and its inspiration from Jehova himself. That night the Lord spoke unto Moses, saying, "Get thee up into Mount Nebo to behold Canaan, that fertile land which I have given unto the Israelites, and die on that mountain as Aaron thy brother died on Mount Hor."

The morrow having come, Moses summons the twelve tribes one by one and gives to each his blessing, a blessing that recalls to us the one Jacob gave to the patriarchs; both flowed from lips touched by the blazing coal of the altar.

And now it is evening; the sun approaches the horizon; its fiery disk casts ruby rays upon the plains of Moab. On those plains the Hebrew tribes are encamped, but at this hour the camp is empty; only some camels and some dromedaries graze, each near the tent of its master.

La Mort de Moïse

=====

Moïse avait cent-vingt ans, sa besogne était accomplie, il voyait Israël
campé sur les bords de la Terre promise et il ne lui restait que deux
choses à faire, à bénir le peuple et à mourir. Il appela le peuple et il leur   5
dit "Je vois devant moi le fleuve Jourdain que Dieu m'a defendu de
traverser; ainsi, c'est ici que nous devons nous séparer; vous devez
entrer dans Canaan pour vaincre des nations plus grandes, plus puissantes
que vous, moi, je reste ici pour mourir." Puis il leur rappela l'histoire
des quarante ans qu'ils avaient erré dans le desert; il énuméra leurs   10
péchés, leurs souffrances, les bontés et les vengeances de leur Dieu.,
et\le langage ordinaire Après que Moïse, législateur et chef, avait parlé,
Moïse prophète et élu de Dieu prit la parole et le langage ordinaire ne lui
suffisant plus pour exprimer les pensées dont son âme était agitée, il
s'élança dans le langage figuré de la poésie, de cette belle poésie biblique   15
qui emprunte son feu du soleil de l'orient et son inspiration de Jehova
même. Cette nuit le Seigneur parla à Moïse et lui dit "Monte sur le mont
Nébo pour voir Canaan, cette terre fertile que j'ai donnée aux Israëlites,
et meurs sur cette montagne comme ton frère Aaron est mort sur mont
Hor".   20

Le lendemain arrivé, Moïse appelle une à une les douze tribus et
donne à chacune sa bénédiction, bénédiction qui nous rappelle celle de
Jacob aux patriarches; toutes deux coulaient des lèvres touchées du
charbon ardent de l'autel.

Et maintenant c'est le soir, le soleil s'approche de l'horizon, son   25
disque en feu jette sur les plaines de Moab des reflets de rubis: sur ces
plaines les tribus hébreues se sont campées, mais à cette heure le camp
est solitaire; quelques chameaux et quelques dromadaires seuls broutent

The tabernacle itself is abandoned. It rises, majestic and vast, amid the white pavilions; but neither Levite nor priest remains. The fire dies on the altar and the ark of the covenant has for its sole guardian the carved cherub who covers it with his wings. A poor leper wanders around the sacred place, not daring to enter it and ready to flee at the first sound that announces the return of the people.

Where then are those people? Let us cross that desert plain, whence the sound of Hebrew trumpets and cymbals has driven the gazelle and the zebra. Let us approach that mountain, the most prominent in all the chain whose blue peaks bound the eastern horizon. What black shadow encircles its base? Is it a grove of olive trees or cedars? Let us come even closer. It is a vast crowd, a whole nation reunited, five hundred thousand persons, not counting women and children. It is the congregation of the Israelites, warriors and priests and women. What event do they await? On what object do they all fix their gaze? The warriors have removed their helmets, the priests their mitres, and the women their veils, and all raise their heads toward^ Nebo. Over that summit hovers a cloud, the only one darkening that sapphire sky; a reddish cloud, charged with lightning; a column of vapor that seems ready to turn into a column of fire. It is the mystic cloud that veils Jehova, the holy symbol that has guided Israel across the desert. This evening it crowns Mount Nebo as the flame crowns the altar. One would say that solemn rites are to be celebrated, that a great sacrifice is in preparation. Where then is the victim? A man ascends the mountainside, alone and enveloped in a cloak. He is an old man; one can see his bald brow and his white hair gleaming in the sunlight. But is it really merely a ray of sunlight, that glory which blazes from afar like a star on his temples? Cover your eyes; bow your head. That glory is the reflection of divinity. That man is Moses!

l'herbe, chacun près de la tente de son maître. Le tabernacle même est
abandonné; il s'élève majestueux et vaste au milieu des pavillons blancs
mais ni lévite ni prêtre n'y reste, le feu s'éteigne sur l'autel et l'arche a
pour tout gardien, le cherubin sculpté qui la couvre de ses ailes. Un
pauvre lépreux rôde autour du lieu consacré, n'osant pas y entrer, et prêt
à s'enfuir au premier bruit qui annoncera le retour du peuple.

Où est donc ce peuple? Traversons cette plaine déserte, d'où le son
des trompettes et des cymbales hébreues a chassé la gazelle et le zèbre,
approchons nous de cette montagne, la plus saillante de toute la chaîne
dont les cimes bleues bornent l'horizon de l'orient. Quelle ombre noire
en ceint la base? Est-ce un bois d'oliviers ou de cèdres? Approchons
nous de plus près; c'est une vaste foule, toute une nation réunie, cinq
cent milles hommes, sans compter les femmes et les enfants; c'est la con-
grégation des Israëlites, guerriers et prêtres et femmes Quel événément
attend-t-on?. Sur quel objet tous les regards sont-ils fixés?. Les guerriers
ont oté leurs casques, les prêtres leurs mitres et les femmes leurs voiles
                        le sommet de
et tous lèvent la tête vers^ Nébo.; Sur ce sommet plane un nuage, le seul
qui obscurcit ce ciel de saphir; un nuage rougeâtre, chargé d'éclairs; une
colonne de vapeur qui semble prête à se transformer en une colonne de
feu. C'est la nue mystique qui voile Jehova, le saint symbole qui a guidé
Israël à travers le desert; ce soir il couronne Mont Nébo comme la
flamme couronne l'autel; on dirait que des rites solennels vont se célébrer, qu'un grand sacrifice se prépare, où donc est la victime? Un
homme gravit la côte de la montagne, seul et enveloppé d'un manteau;
c'est un vieillard, on voit reluire au soleil son front chauve et ses
cheveux blancs: mais est-ce bien un rayon de soleil, cette gloire qui de
loin brille comme une étoile sur ses tempes? Couvrez vous les yeux,
baissez la tête, cette gloire, c'est le reflet de la divinité; cet homme, c'est
Moïse!

[*When you are
writing, place
your argument
first in cool,
60 prosaic
language; but
when you have
thrown the
reins on the
neck of your
imagination, do
not pull her
up to reason.*]

Before following him we must pause a moment to answer certain questions, with which Reason, incredulous and cold, comes to trouble us.

Must we regard the narratives contained in the history of the Jews as a kind of parable, showing truth through the veil of Fiction, or should we rather take them in their literal sense? When the Bible says, "God spoke to Moses as a man speaks to his friend, face to face," should we under-stand that Moses, a creature of dust, found himself in the actual presence

65
of that infinite and incomprehensible Spirit who has created all, or only that, as a religious and devout man, he enjoyed an intimate communion of the soul with God?

When the sacred historian shows us the law delivered on Mount Sinai, amid the burning fire, the thick cloud, the darkness of the tempest,

70
does he mean that such a spectacle really occurred in the deserts of Arabia, or does he, through essentially oriental imagery, wish thus to express the severity of the legislative code that the exigencies of the time and the rebellious nature of the people demanded?

Finally, everything one reads about the death of Moses in the last

75
chapters of Deuteronomy: is it the naked truth, or truth beneath the mask of Allegory? Useless questions, doubts that Reason proposes because she feels incapable of grasping the mysteries of Revelation. If man had only Reason for a guide, he would never get to heaven. Pride encumbers his wings; it is a weight that keeps him from rising. Fortunately, Faith

80
comes to his aid, an angel of humble mien but lofty flight, a seraph whose soaring flight attains the seventh heaven and the very throne of the Eternal. Seen through the eyes of Reason, the wonders of the old Testament offer a mythology that is harsh, obscure, incredible. But as soon as Faith leans over the volume, as soon as she lifts her lamp above

85
the shadowy page, all becomes clear. Who believes in God and His creative power will readily believe in the literal truth of the miraculous history of the Jews. Violation of the laws of Nature gives him no

Avant de le suivre il faut nous arrêter un instant pour répondre à de certaines questions, dont la Raison, incrédule et froide, vient nous troubler.

"Devons nous regarder les narrations contenues dans l'histoire des Juifs comme une espèce de paraboles, montrant la vérité à travers le voile de la Fiction, ou bien, devons nous les prendre dans leur sens litéral? Quand la Bible dit, que "Dieu parla à Moïse comme un homme parle à son ami, face à face," devons nous entendre que, Moïse, être de poussière, se trouva dans la presence actuelle de cet Esprit infini et incomprehensible qui a tout créé, ou seulement que comme homme religieux et dévot, il jouissait d'une communion intime de l'âme avec Dieu?

Quand l'historien saint nous montre la loi livrée sur mont Sinaï, au milieu du feu brulant, de la nuée épaisse, de l'obscurité de la tempête, veut-il dire qu'un tel spectacle s'est réellement presenté dans les deserts de l'Arabie, ou veut-il, par des images essentiellement orientales, exprimer ainsi la sévérité du code législatif que demandaient les exigences du temps et la nature rebelle du peuple?

Enfin, tout ce qu'on lit sur la mort de Moïse dans les derniers chapitres de Deutéronome, est-ce la verité nue, ou la verité sous le masque de l'Allégorie? Questions inutiles, doutes que la Raison propose parcequ'elle se sent incapable de comprendre les mystères de la Révélation; si l'homme n'avait qu'elle pour guide, il n'atteindrait jamais au ciel; l'orgueil embarrasse ses ailes, c'est un poids qui l'empèche de monter. Heureusement la Foi lui vient en aide, ange au regard humble mais au vol élevé, seraphin, dont l'essor parvient au septième ciel et au trône de l'Éternel même. Vues des yeux de la Raison, les merveilles de l'ancien Testament presentent une mythologie sévère, obscure, incroyable; mais aussitôt que la Foi se penche sur le volume, aussitôt qu'elle lève sa lampe sur la page ténébreuse, tout devient clair. Qui croit en Dieu et dans sa fonction créatrice, croira facilement en la vérité litérale de l'histoire miraculeuse des Juifs; la violation des lois de la Nature

difficulty. He tells himself, "He who created Nature and ordained her laws can easily modify them, change them, destroy them according to His will." Let us then follow Moses as he ascends Mount Nebo, and let neither doubt nor scruple any longer halt our steps.

He has gained the summit; he has lost sight of the multitude. A total solitude, an absolute silence, surround him. The dark crests of the cedars slope at his feet; a pure blue sky is above his head. Before him appears the sacred cloud, motionless and alone, from time to time discharging electric exhalations that disappear without a sound. The prophet awaits; Nature too awaits.

Why do the trees, so deeply rooted, quiver like bulrushes^reeds shaken by the wind? Why is Pisgah rocked from its peak to its foundation? One sees, one hears nothing, neither storm, nor tempest, nor even the light evening breeze. Suddenly the cloud catches fire, it bursts into flame. At once the calm returns; in the silence a voice speaks.

"Look to the South, to the lands of Gilead and of Manasseh, to Jericho the city of palm trees, as far as the farthest sea. This is the land that I have promised to give unto Abraham and his posterity after him. I have shown it to thee but thou shalt not enter in." The voice falls silent. Moses lifts up his head, which he has hidden in the dust, and looks^turns to the South.

It is the moment when the sun sets. Its last rays shine with a brilliance both gentle and resplendent, spreading rose and vermilion lights all around. Those magic lights tint the vast plain that unfolds at the foot of Pisgah, a fertile plain, watered by the tides of a river, shaded by thick forests, whose long alleys extend into that sea of verdure like promontories into the ocean. Vast herds inhabit those savannas. Here and there a majestic bull, a bull of Bashan, rests beneath a tall lone tree. In the distance rise the fortified walls of a city. The domes, the towers, and the terraces and columns of an immense palace, built of white

n'offre pour lui aucune difficulté: il se dit: "Celui qui créa la Nature, et

qui en régla les lois, peut bien les modifier, les changer les annéantir

selon sa volonté." Suivons donc Moïse lorsqu'il gravit Mont Nebo et que

ni doute ni scrupule n'arrête plus nos pas.

Il a gagné le sommet, il a perdu de vue la multitude; une solitude

entière, un silence absolu l'entoure: Les crêtes noires des cèdres s'in-

clinent à ses pieds, un ciel pur et bleu est au-dessus de sa tête; devant lui

parait le nuage consacré, immobile et seul, laissant échapper de temps en

temps des exhalaisons électriques qui disparaissent sans bruit. Le

prophète attend, la Nature attend aussi.

Pourquoi les arbres, si profondement enracinés, frissonent-ils comme
roseaux
des joncs qu'un vent secoue? Pourquoi Pisgah est-il ébranlé depuis sa

cime jusqu'à sa base? On ne voit, on n'entend rien, ni orage, ni tem-

pête, ni même la légère brise du soir. Soudain la nue s'allume, elle

éclate en flamme, aussitôt le calme revient, dans le silence une voix

parle.

"Regarde vers le Sud, vers les contrées de Gilead et de Manasseh,

vers Jericho la ville de palmiers, jusqu'à la mer lointaine. C'est la terre

que j'ai promis de donner à Abraham et à sa postérité après lui: je te l'ai

montrée mais tu n'y entreras pas." La voix se tait; Moïse lève son front,
se tourne
qu'il a caché dans la poussière et regarde vers le Sud.

C'est le moment où le soleil se couche; ses derniers rayons brillent

d'un éclat, à la fois doux et resplendissant, repandant partout des clairs

roses et vermeils; ces clairs magiques teignent la vaste plaine qui se

déroule aux pieds de Pisgah, plaine fertile, arrosée par les ondes d'un

fleuve, ombrée de forêts touffues dont les longues allées s'avancent dans

cette mer de verdure comme des promontoires dans l'océan. De grands

troupeaux peuplent ces savanes; par ci, par là un taureau majestueux, un

taureau de Bashan se repose sous un grand arbre isolé: de loin s'élèvent

les murs fortifiés d'une ville; des domes, des tours et les terrasses et les

marble, take form against an azure sky, the whole enclosed in a garland of gardens and palm trees. Nearer, one sees on the plain a few tents and

120 [here, a reminder about the necessity of preserving a certain veri- similitude]

a fountain also shaded by palm trees. Maidens draw water from it. They are dressed in Asiatic costumes, and pearls gleam on their arms and^their on swarthy necks and in their black hair.

A tranquil scene, but profaned by the hideous image of an idol. The fountain and grove of palms are consecrated to Moloch. There he rears
125 his monstrous head, and the maidens, leaving the spring, bend the knee before his altar.

Moses has seen all: the rich countryside, the superb city, the idolatrous worship. He has felt the joy of the Hebrew who beholds his people's inheritance, the triumph of the leader whose efforts are crowned
130 with success, and the bitter regrets of the man condemned to die at the moment when life offers him the greatest charm. An instant suffices for the birth and extinction of all these feelings, for a new impression, quite otherwise powerful, has come to take possession of his soul.

Standing on Pisgah, his eye scans the plain of Jericho and plumbs the
135 valley of Zoar. That eye lights up; one sees by its sudden flash that something other than a fair landscape has presented itself to his view. There below, arising in the hollow of the valley, extending across the surface of the plain, the phantoms of the Future reveal themselves to the prophet's eyes. The Future parts the clouds in which it likes to wrap its
140 realm of shades and lets a ray of the Present pierce its obscure mysteries. The races, the centuries, the dynasties pass in review at his feet. He who has led Israel, slave redeemed, through the desert sees it established in the longed-for Canaan. He sees its prosperity under the shepherd-king, its glory under the superb Solomon. Rehoboam comes, hatchet in hand,
145 and splits in two the trunk of the tree of Jacob. Ahijah, Baasha, and the perverse Ahab follow. Jezebel, painted and bejeweled, pollutes the earth with her vices. The chariot of Jehu, son of Zimri, approaches with the

colonnes d'un immense palais, bâti en marbre blanc, se dessinent contre

un ciel d'azur, le tout encadré en une guirlande de jardins et de palmiers.

Plus près, on voit dans la plaine quelques tentes et une fontaine ombrée

aussi de palmiers; des jeunes filles y puisent de l'eau; elles sont vêtues

en costumes asiatiques et des perles brillent sur leurs bras et ^sur leurs cous

bruns et dans leurs cheveux noirs.

Scène tranquille mais profanée de l'image hideuse d'une idole; la

fontaine et le bocage de palmiers sont consacrés à Moloch; il y lève sa

tête monstrueuse et les jeunes filles, en quittant la source, fléchent le

genou devant son autel.

Moïse a tout vu, la campagne riche, la ville superbe, le culte

idolâtre; il a ressenti la joie de l'Hebreu qui voit l'heritage de son

peuple, la triomphe du chef dont les efforts sont couronnés de succès, les

regrets amers de l'homme, condamné a mourir au moment où la vie lui

offre le plus de charmes. Un instant suffit pour la naissance et l'extinc-

tion de tous ces sentiments, car une nouvelle impression toute autrement

puissante est venue s'emparer de son âme.

Debout sur Pisgah, son oeil parcourt la plaine de Jericho et plonge

dans la vallée de Zoar: cet oeil s'allume, on voit à son étincelle subite

qu'autre chose qu'un beau paysage s'est offert à ses regards. Là-bas,

s'élevant dans le creux du vallon, s'étendant sur la surface de la plaine

les fantômes de l'Avenir se révèlent aux yeux du prophète; le Futur

écarte les nuages dont il aime à entourer son empire de ténèbres et laisse

pénètrer d'un rayon du Présent ses mystères obscures. Les races, les

siècles les dynasties passent en revue à ses pieds; lui qui a conduit Israël,

esclave racheté à travers le desert, le voit établi dans son Canaan tant

désiré; il voit sa prosperité sous le roi-berger, sa gloire sous le superbe

Salomon: Rheoboam vient la hâche à la main et fend en deux parties le

trone de l'arbre de Jacob, Aliyah, Baasha, et le pervers Ahab succèdent;

Jézabel fardée et parée, souille la terre de ses vices; le char de Jehu fils

sound of thunder, and its wheels crush the house of Ahab. Next appears the haughty Athaliah, her garments dyed in royal blood. Then comes a long dynasty of weak and evil kings. Jerusalem and Samaria are bent beneath the weight of their own sins. A solitary voice is heard in the streets, threatening calamity and ruin. It is the voice of Isaiah, and his predictions are not long in coming to pass that ruin is not long in coming. The era of captivity arrives. The virgin of Zion, torn from the fatherland, is led captive into Babylon. There she is, stripped of crown and scepter, sitting sorrowfully beneath the willows of the Euphrates. The days of suffering being accomplished, the poor exile returns. Jerusalem is reborn from its ruins. Once again the vine and the olive tree flourish in Judea. Yet scarcely has she tasted tranquillity when she throws down the refreshing cup and thirsts after the intoxicating wine of luxury and of idolatry. She brings about her banishment again, and again she shakes off the yoke of slavery and returns, worn and exhausted, to the banks of her beloved Jordan.

Tracing the decadence of Zion from generation to generation, Moses comes at last to her ruin. The scepter of supremacy has passed from Asia to Europe. The diadem of the universal empire adorns the brow of Italy. Rome — become queen of the world, yet ever as greedy of conquest as when, a young Amazon, full of ardor and ambition, she followed Romulus in his barbaric wars and possessed no goods beyond her bow and her quiver, no territory beyond a field whose extent was measured by a bull's hide cut in strips — Rome rises an instant from her throne, founded on the seven hills, and extending her arm over the Adriatic and Aegean, crushes the palm of Judea, already in collapse from a thousand storms.

Whence comes the ecstasy that, at this terrible crisis, lights up the face of Moses? He clasps his hands, he raises his eyes, and a transport unutterable beams from his brow. The revelation has changed. He has seen, passing across the sky and halting at a fixed point, a mysterious

de Zimri approche avec bruit de tonnerre et les roues en écrasent la

maison d'Ahab. Ensuite parait l'orgueilleuse Athalie, ses vêtements teints

de sang royal; puis vient une longue dynastie de rois faibles et malfais- 150

ants. Jerusalem et Samaria sont courbées sous le poids de leurs propres

péchés: une voix solitaire se fait entendre dans les rues, menaçant mal-

ses prédictions ne tardent pas à s'accomplir

heur et ruine C'est la voix d'Isaïe et cette ruine ne tarde pas à venir

L'époque de la captivité arrive: la vierge de Zion, arrachée à sa patrie,

est menée captive à Babylone, et la voilà, depouillée de couronne et de 155

sceptre, tristement assise sous les saules de l'Euphrate. Les jours de

souffrances étant accomplis, la pauvre exilée revient; Jerusalem renait de

ses ruines; la vigne et l'olivier fleurissent encore en Judée. Cependant,

à peine à t-elle goûté la tranquillité qu'elle rejette la coupe rafraîchissante

d'

et s'altère du vin enivrant du luxe et de idolâtrie; elle se fait bannir de 160

nouveau et de nouveau elle secoue le joug de l'esclavage et revient

flétrie, epuisée sur les rives de son Jourdain chéri.

Traçant de génération en génération la décadence de Zion Moïse

arrive enfin à sa ruine. Le sceptre de la suprématie a passé de l'Asie en

Europe; le diademe de l'empire universel orne le front de l'Italie. Rome, 165

devenue reine du monde, mais toujours aussi avare de conquête que

lorsque, jeune Amazone, pleine de fougue et d'ambition, elle suivait

Romulus dans ses guerres barbares et ne possédait d'autre bien que son

arc et son carquois, d'autre territoire qu'un champ dont l'étendue était

mesurée par une peau de taureau coupée en tranches Rome se leve un in- 170

stant de son trône, basé sur sept montagnes, et étendant le bras sur là

Adriatique et l'Ægean, écrase le palmier de Judée, déjà affaissé par mille

tempêtes. D'où vient l'extase qui, à cette crise terrible, se éclate sur la

figure de Moïse?, il joigne les mains, il lève les yeux et un transport

indicible rayonne sur son front. La révélation s'est changée; il a vu 175

passer à travers le ciel et s'arrêter à un point fixe, une étoile mysté-

rieuse; le ciel s'est entreouvert et une vision glorieuse s'est revelée: des

star. The heavens have opened up, and a glorious vision is revealed. White and winged forms have surrounded him. Celestial voices have

180 heralded great joy for all the world. And after those angels have withdrawn from him into the clouds, he has seen, between the stars and the earth, the form of a woman holding a child in her arms. His soul has recognized the Messiah. He murmurs the words of Simeon: "Lord, now lettest thy servant depart in peace, for mine eyes have seen thy salvation,

185 which thou hast prepared to be presented to all people, to be the light to lighten all nations, and the glory of thy people Israel."

In that rapture the soul broke free from the body. Moses exists no longer ceased to live.

formes blanches et ailées lui ont entouré; des voix celestes lui ont annoncé une grande joie pour toute la terre, et après que les anges se sont retirés d'avec lui dans les nues, il a vu, entre les astres et la terre, une forme de femme, tenant dans ses bras un enfant. Son âme a reconnu le Messie, il murmure les paroles de Simeon "Seigneur tu laisses maintenant aller ton serviteur en paix, car mes yeux ont vu ton salut que tu as préparé pour être presenté à tous les peuples, pour être la lumière qui doit éclairer toutes les nations, et la gloire de ton peuple d'Israël"

Dans cet élan l'âme s'est echappée du corps, Moïse n'existe plus a cessé de vivre

[Notes on The Death of Moses]

form of arrayed in pure and holy beauty
A woman is there ~~between~~ in heaven and earth
appears

It remains always between him and heaven

A woman holding a child in her arms

appears between heaven and the earth — vaporous

Her gaze says clouds form her vestments and her veil — her

I am the descen- a celestial beauty adorns her countenance, her aspect

dant and poster- ~~eal~~ beauty is the ideal beauty — calm serious

ity of David lofty — in the eyes of the child one reads the

the bright star God within —

of the morning

Moses prays — he is quite pale — his time has come and

~~death is at his side — all power deserts him —~~ he

drop~~s to the earth~~ the agonies of death and the transports
are in combat in his heart
of paradise ~~are in~~ contend in him — night falls —
the shadows   shadows
darkness encircle Mount Nebo ~~a darkness~~ that no

human eye can penetrate —even in thought we have no
to seek there   to try to dispel them
not   further —

And after the angel[s] have withdrawn from him
into heaven   moon
A~~nd~~ he has seen between the ~~heaven~~ and the earth

a form of a woman holding a child in her arms
~~the prophet~~
his soul recognized   more
~~He recognizes~~   the Messiah — life has nothing

he murmurs the words of Simeon

~~to offer him and he renders up his soul in saying~~

As saint
~~as~~ Simeon

[Notes sur La Mort de Moïse]

forme de révêtue d'une beauté sainte et pure

. Une femme est là ~~entre~~ en le ciel et la terre
parait

Il reste toujours entre lui et le ciel

Une femme tenant dans ses bras un enfant

parait entre le ciel et la terre — des nuages   5

Son regard dit   vaporeux forme ses vêtemens et son voile — sa

Je suis le réjeton   une beauté celeste pare son front, son aspect est

et le posterité   ~~eal~~ beauté est la beauté idéale — calme sérieuse

de David   élevée — dans les yeux de l'enfant on lit le

l'étoile brillante   Dieu intérieur —   10

du matin

Moise prie — il est tout pâle — son heure arrive et

~~la mort est à son côtes — toute force l'abandonne~~ — il

s'etend ~~par terre~~ les agonies de la mort et les transports
sont en lutte dans son coeur

de paradis ~~sont en~~ luttent en lui — la nuit tombe —
des ténèbres   ténèbres
l'obscurité entourent mont Nébo ~~obscurité~~ que nul oeil   15

humain ne peut pénétrer — même en idée nous n'avons
y chercher   essayer de les écarter
pas à   plus loin —

Et après que les ange se sont retirés de avec lui
dans le ciel   lune
Et il a vu entre le ~~ciel~~ et la terre une forme

de femme tenant dans ses bras un enfant   20
~~le prophète~~
son ame a reconnu   plus
~~Il reconnait~~   le Messie — la vie n'a rien de

il murmure les paroles de Simeon

~~à lui offrir et il rend l'âme en disant~~

Comme le saint
~~comme~~ Simeon

25 "Lord, now lettest thy servant depart in

peace — for mine eyes have seen thy salvation

which thou hast prepared to be presented to all people

to be the light to lighten all nations

and the glory of thy people Israel"

   in that   the soul
   in a rapture i̶t̶ broke free from the body — Moses

30

   no l̶o̶n̶g̶e̶r̶ ̶e̶x̶i̶s̶t̶s̶   is dead

"Seigneur, tu laisses maintenant aller ton serviteur en   25

paix — car mes yeux ont vu ton salut

que tu as préparé pour être présenté à tous les peuples

pour être la lumière qui doit éclairer toutes les nations

et la gloire de ton peuple d'Israël

  dans cet   l'âme
d'un élan   ~~elle~~ s'est echappée du corps — Moïse   30

   n'~~existe pl~~us est mort

Comments

If we turn to the Sacred Volume, where shall we find a legislator or an historian, who, for brevity and perspicuity, pathos and elegant sublimity, can bear a comparison with Moses?

—Patrick Brontë, "The Signs of the Times . . ." (1835)[1]

In the choice of subjects left to her selection, she frequently took characters and scenes from the Old Testament, with which all her writings show that she was especially familiar. The picturesqueness and colour (if I may so express it), the grandeur and breadth of its narrations, impressed her deeply. To use M. Héger's expression, "Elle était nourrie de la Bible." After he had read De la Vigne's poem on Joan of Arc, she chose the "Vision and Death of Moses on Mount Nebo" to write about; and, in looking over this *devoir*, I was much struck with one or two of M. Héger's remarks. . . .

—Elizabeth Gaskell[2]

Gaskell's words appear to explain this essay's origin and context: Heger read, Charlotte reacted, and a devoir on Moses resulted. Its point of departure is the patriarch's last hours, as recounted at the end of Deuteronomy.[3] It then sweeps panoramically through Israel's history, developing richly detailed tableaus and drawing on four more books of scripture: Psalms, I and II Kings, and Luke.

But the manuscript itself does not fully corroborate Gaskell's account of its sources. "The Death of Moses" has little in common with the two poems Heger could have read his students, "The Life of Joan of Arc" and "The Death of Joan of Arc," by Casimir Delavigne; both are militant elegies written to revive French nationalism.[4] Its analogies to Alfred de Vigny's poem "Moïse" appear much stronger.[5] And the version Gaskell saw in 1856 is not the one that stayed in the Heger family archives. Heger showed her "Vision and Death of Moses on Mount Nebo," a devoir that he had corrected. The draft that survives has a less descriptive title and bears no trace of Heger's intervention. It also has a small strip torn away from the year, so that dating becomes another issue.

Almost certainly, though, it dates from 1843. The polish of its prose, its length, and its complexity all mark it as a second-year devoir.[6] It is probably also a follow-up copy, made after Heger had seen the original and kept along with the corrected version in his files of student exercises.[7] Why he chose to retain two copies is a riddle that can no longer be answered; presumably at some point he gave one away, as he gave Gaskell "Peter the Hermit." Because the marked version has vanished, however, his remarks survive only through her statements. (I reproduce them in the English translation at lines 58 and 120.)

The issue of its sources requires more research into the French texts Charlotte could have drawn on and her motives for writing about Moses. Her reliance on the Bible was a constant in her life abroad, but if the poem that Heger read was not remotely biblical, why did it inspire this major effort? Does internal evidence in either Delavigne poem support Heger's claim that she drew on it?

Superficially, the links seem tenuous. "The Death of Joan of Arc" is an anti-English diatribe. The narrator wallows in the details of Joan's martyrdom, excoriates Bedford and his soldiers for inciting it, and upbraids the French for acquiescing. Even English priests, he claims, calumniated God's word in ordering the saintly virgin burnt at the stake. "The Life of Joan of Arc" is only slightly less harsh. It opens by comparing swollen flood-waters, which threaten in their pride to engulf the universe, with the English forces that threaten to engulf France, until Joan of Arc drives them back. To Charlotte, who, as Heger said, was nurtured on the Bible, this reference could have brought to mind the parting of the Red Sea, when Moses led the Hebrews out of Egypt.[8] Delavigne's later reference to the God "who delivered our oppressed tribes / From the weight of a heavy yoke" may also have reminded her of Moses.[9] But here, it is a shepherdess who halts the enemy and rallies the French around their sovereign: "Une femme paraît; une vierge, un héros. / Elle arrache son maître aux langueurs du repos ("A woman appears; a virgin, a hero. / She wrests her master from the languor of repose).[10] These lines suggest several points of contact.

In Charlotte's notes for the ending of her devoir, the only rough notes for any devoir that are extant, she too creates the image of a "woman" who "appears": the Virgin holding in her arms the infant Jesus. Although this revelation cannot save the dying Moses, it exalts the final moments of his life. More broadly, the religious tenor of the rough notes suggests that Charlotte meant to rework the death of Moses so that it would culminate in a Christian vision and associate salvation with a woman. The patriarch remains at the center of her devoir, but she introduces two crucial new figures, Mary and the angel Faith, feminine in French, who rescues man when doubt and logic tempt him. Plainly, she sees nothing inconsistent about championing the literal truth of the Bible and giving her Moses a New Testament epiphany, couched in St. Simeon's words. (Her practice here accords with her lifelong penchant for adapting scripture to a personal mythology. Fourteen years later, she would have Jane Eyre envision another saving "Mother" who appears in the heavens and strengthens Jane's resolve to flee from Rochester.)[11]

Charlotte's other readings in French poetry may also have informed her choice of subject. In *The Genius of Christianity,* a source for at least one earlier devoir, Chateaubriand argues that writers should look to the Bible for their inspiration. The French Romantic poets who turned to scripture made Moses a popular topic.[12] Vigny and Lamartine both represent the spectacle of his climb and his encounter with the cloud of smoke and fire. Although no proof exists that Charlotte knew their poems, she and Heger analyzed Lamartine's fourth Harmony, and if she continued to read through the series, she would have found Moses in the ninth, "Jehovah or the Idea of God."[13] Her reading of Vigny is even more conjectural, yet his name is close enough to Delavigne's to hint that Heger's memory conflated them.[14] Like her, Vigny portrays the view from Nebo's summit in sweeping, though not detailed, perspective. His Moses, however, has grown weary of his mission; "sad and alone in [his] glory," he asks God for the final sleep of death.[15]

If Charlotte's text does date from 1843, it was written at a time when she was urging herself to give up on Brussels and go home. In twenty days the school would close for summer vacation. She saw little of Heger as it was, and probably only in public rooms and corridors, since Madame had cut off closer contact. Apparently she no longer took private lessons, so she would have to have been in his classes in order to hear him read. If he lectured on either Joan of Arc poem, he would have had to deal with its anti-English sentiment, reminding Charlotte once again that she was an outsider at the pensionnat. ("[I]t is curious how these clowns of Labassecour secretly hate England," Lucy Snowe observes when Paul Emanuel's anti-English diatribe evokes the class's "vindictive delight.")[16]

But "The Death of Moses" is not defensive. It is Charlotte's strongest affirmation of her religious faith and, indirectly, of her faith in the creative vision of the artist. On both topics, Heger's comments are revealing. According to Gaskell, he chides Charlotte for digressing to question the literal truth of scripture. With a rhetorician's logic, he warns her against breaking the momentum once she warms to her subject. But for Charlotte, the conflict between faith and reason would always be too pressing to sideline. If the Bible could be construed as allegory, what would happen to belief? If her own common sense prevailed over feeling, how could she justify remaining at the pensionnat? This copy of the devoir does not delete the passage to which Heger objected. Charlotte pretty clearly made the decision that it belonged where it was.

Heger's other objection, according to Gaskell, concerns the need for verisimilitude: "Moses might from his elevation see mountains and plains, groups of maidens and herds of cattle, but could hardly perceive the details of dress, or the ornaments of the head."[17] But again, Heger argues on the grounds of reason, whereas Charlotte is writing from faith. If Moses can stand at the top of Mount Nebo, seeing into Canaan and then into the future, why can he not also observe the smallest details, and why should she refrain from creating the images that bring his vision into focus? As Duthie says, after setting up the scriptural context she structures her devoir as a triptych: Moses climbing as the crowds watch, Moses gazing from the summit, and Moses looking ahead to the messiah.[18] In each panel, as in the introduction, details vivify the picture: the ray at his temples, the pearls against the maidens' skin, the hatchet that splits the tree of Jacob. Those details connect this text with others that she wrote[19] and with French Romantic historiography, which also sought to animate the past by making it picturesque and personal.

Charlotte intended to show her professor what she, an English Protestant, knew about the Bible. Yet despite her manifold references to scripture, this is less an exercise in scholarship than in imaginative writing, even myth making. Back in 1841 she had envisioned Brussels as her own "promised land."[20] That dream had crumbled. But if Brussels now threatened to become her wilderness, she could nonetheless survive by keeping faith in her religion and in her own creative powers.

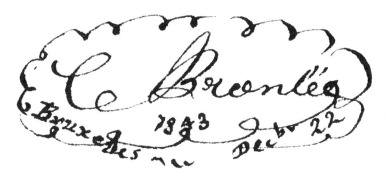

The medallion Charlotte Brontë drew at the end of her revision of "Athens
Saved by Poetry," a copy probably made for Heger. The Pierpont Morgan
Library.

Athens

Saved by Poetry

The long Peloponnesian War had come to an end; for the Spartans it was

exalta.

5 the climax of triumph and of exultation. The Lacedaemonian general,

⌊*not Fr*[?] *ed*

relaxing the reins of discipline, was allowing his soldiers to taste the

license of victory, and the evening of the third day after the fall of

difference   *one*   *into*

⌡[*with*]*in* Athens ˇsaw the camp of austere Spartans transformed in a scene of

⌊ *into*

disorderly debauch. Lysander himself, the cold, the crafty, the ambitious

Lysander

10 ˆseemed to yield to the influence of the moment; he invited the chiefs of

under

the army to a banquet in his tent; he ordered his helots to serve a rude

but abundant repast, like the one that Achilles prepared for Ulysses and

his companions, when he himself did the cooking with "his inaccessible

hands." A whole roast lamb, half an ox, th and some coarse loaves that

This

15 *beginning* the helots presented in baskets, formed the dressings of the banquet.

is perhaps

a little   Around the table sat, or rather reclined, the guests, twelve in number, on

lacking in

nobility   couches covered with carpets, a luxury that the Spartans had borrowed

G   from the Athenians and the Athenians from the Persians. Lysander

carved up the meat with his dagger and distributed large portions to his

20 guests. At first the meal was passed in silence; the twelve men of war,

boorish and stiff, ate with the voracity and taciturnity of twelve

famished

wolves.

   At length, their raging hunger appeased, the general rapped on his

buckler, whereupon the slaves removed the remains of the feast, a few

25 bones and a few crusts of bread, and then they carried in great vases

filled with the wine of Samos and Chios. Lysander arose, poured out a

libation in honor of the gods, and then filled the captains' cups; each one

drank, still in silence. Before long came a change; the good Athenian

wine began to animate those forms of bronze; the creases in their stern

Athènes

sauvée par la Poësie

La longue guerre du Péloponèse venait d'être achevée c'était pour les

du *exalta.*

Spartiates la crise de triomphe et d'exultation. Le général lacédémonien,   5

p.f.

relâchant les rênes de la discipline, permettait à ses soldats de goûter la

licence de la victoire et le soir du troisième jour après la chûte d'Athènes

on *en*   *différence ⌠ dans*

vit le camp des austères Spartiates transformé dans une scène de   *⌡ en*

débauche desordonnée. Lysandre lui-même, le froid, le rusé, l'ambitieux

Lysandre

semblait céder à l'influence du moment; il invita les chefs de l'armée   10

sous

à un banquet dans sa tente il fit servir par ses ilotes un repas rude mais

abondant pareil à celui que prépara Achille pour Ulysse et ses compag-

nons, quand lui-même faisait la cuisine avec "ses mains inaccessibles".

Un agneau rôti entier, la moitié d'un boeuf, qu et des gros pains que les   *Ce commence-*

ilotes presentaient en paniers, formaient les apprêts du festin; autour de   *ment manque* 15

                                                                 peutêtre un

la table étaient assis, ou plutôt couchés, les convives, au nombre de   *peu de*

                                                                  noblesse

douze, sur les lits couverts de tapis, objet de luxe que les Spartiates

avaient emprunté aux Athéniens et les Athéniens aux Perses. Lysandre   *B*

partageait la viande avec sa dague et distribuait de grandes portions à ses

hôtes; d'abord le repas se passait en silence, les douze hommes de   20

guerre, rudes et rigides mangeaitent avec la voracité et la taciturnité de

affamés

douze loups. Enfin, la rage de la faim étant apaisée, le général frappa

sur son bouclier, aussitôt les esclaves ôtèrent les restes du régal,

quelques os et quelques croûtes de pain, et ensuite ils apportèrent de

grands vases, remplis du vin de Samos et de Chios. Lysandre se leva,   25

versa une libation en l'honneur des dieux et puis remplit les coupes des

capitaines; chacun but, toujours en silence. Bientôt il s'opéra un

changement, le bon vin athénien commençait à animer ces formes de

bronze, les rides se déplièrent sur leurs fronts sévères, leurs langues se

30

brows unfurrowed, their tongues were loosened, and they *finally* spoke. At first

it was in axioms curt and dry; each one believed himself a Lycurgus.

Then, *as they grew* growing still warmer, the glory of the fatherland became the sub-

ject of their talk; they boasted of Lacadaemon's triumphs. Lysander en-

couraged the enjoyment of his officers, but while pouring drinks for the

35 *good*
why?

others, he himself observed a most exemplary moderation. He too felt

much disposed to revel in the triumph of Spartan arms, but he wished to

do everything coolly, and after the custom of cold, egoistic men he took

a mean pleasure in amusing himself at the expense of his companions.

As the night advanced, the gaiety *was becoming* became more boisterous; Lysander,

40

despite his forced *calculated* temperance, had drunk enough to make him slightly

relinquish his absolute dominion over himself. Arrogance and insolence

began to glitter in his gaze, ordinarily veiled, and when he spoke of the

conquered Athenians, it was no longer with that false and politic modera-

tion which he habitually *had* feigned but to heap insults and invectives upon

45

them. His subalterns seconded him warmly, and before long the Lacedae-

importance
of the tense

monian chiefs had *swore* sworn the utter ruin of Athens; they had vowed to raze

its buildings, slit the throats of its inhabitants, and shred *root out* the foundations

with the plow.

"Yes!" cried Lysander: "She will perish, this old enemy of our Lace-

by-
50 *to. -[?]*

daemon, and this very evening I will have her elegy sung *by* to one of her

sons. "Epialte!" he said to a helot, "go find the imbecile of a poet we

took prisoner last night. If he resists (for these simpletons are always

hotheads), drag him here by his chains. And let a lyre be brought; I want

to put his talent to the test." Epialte disappeared; the officers applauded

55

the speech of their chief and drank in deep drafts to his glory.

The orgies *y* were precisely at their *as* peak of revelry when the *its* slave

returned leading the poet. A burst of laughter greeted him; the

captive saluted and stopped at the entrance to the tent; his eyes seemed

vry. good

to be dazzled by the light of the lamps and the glare of steel breast-

enfin
dénouèrent et ils parlèrent. C'était d'abord des axiomes brefs et secs, 30
ue   comme on   it
chacun se croyait un Lycurge, puis, s'échauffant davantage, la gloire de

la patrie devint le sujet de leurs discours, ils vantèrent les triomphes de

Lacédémone — Lysandre encourageait l'enjouement de ses officiers, mais

tout en versant à boire aux autres, il observait lui-même une modération   *bon.*
                                                                                 pourquoi?
fort exemplaire; lui aussi se sentait très disposé à jouir du triomphe des   35

armes spartiates mais il voulait tout faire à froid et d'après la coutume

des hommes froids et égoistes il prenait un plaisir méchant à s'amuser

aux dépens de ses compagnons
                                             enait
À mesure que la nuit avançait la gaieté devint plus bruyante:
                                calculée
Lysandre, malgré sa tempérance forcée, avait assez bu pour le faire   40

relâcher un peu son empire absolu sur lui-même; l'arrogance et l'inso-

lence commençaient à étinceller dans son regard, ordinairement voilé, et

lorsqu'il parlait des Athéniens vaincus ce n'était plus avec cette modé-
                               avait
ration fausse et politique, qu'il feignait d'habitude, mais en les comblant

d'injures et d'invectives; ses subalternes le secondèrent vivement et bien-   45
                            jurèrent
tôt les chefs lacédémoniens avaient juré la ruine entière d'Athènes, ils   *valeur du temps*

avaient fait serment d'en raser les bâtiments; d'en égorger les habitants,
                labourer
d'en déchirer les fondements avec la charrue.

"Oui!" s'écria Lysandre: "Elle périra, cette vieille ennemie de notre
                                          par   *par-*
Lacédémone, et ce soir même je ferai chanter son élégie à un de ses fils.   *à. -[?]*   50

Epialte!" dit il à un ilote "va chercher l'imbécile de poète qu'on a pris

prisonnier hier soir. S'il resiste, (car ces nigauds ont toujours la tête

montée) traine le ici par ses chaines, et qu'on apporte une lyre, je veux

faire l'essai de son talent" Epialte disparut: les officiers applaudirent
                                 rent
aux discours de leurs chef et buverent à longs traits à sa gloire   55
            t   *son*
Les' orgies étaient justement à leur plus haut degré de jouissance
                                                                    it
quand l'esclave rentra conduisant le poète, un éclat de rire l'accueilla;

le captif salua et s'arrêta à l'entrée de la tente, il paraissait avoir les yeux

éblouis de la lumière des lampes et de l'éclat des cuirasses en acier et des   *tr. bon*

plates and the draperies of scarlet. "Come, then," cried Lysander,

"what art thou afraid of? Thou'rt like an owl gone astray at high noon."

"The dungeon was darker than I thought," said the poet to himself.

Then he advanced slowly without answering Lysander — and began to

arrange the folds of his garment, which the helot's hands had slightly

rumpled. This done, he crossed his arms beneath his cloak and waited

quietly, without saying a word. He was a true Athenian, elegant,

gracious; an Athenian who had been brought up in the groves of the

Academy, who had fed on the philosophy of Plato and Socrates, on the

poetry of Sophocles and Euripides. Despite his rather slight stature and

his somewhat effeminate features, there was in his noble attitude and

classic contours something indefinably superior that raised him far above

those Spartans, big as giants and strong as bulls. Still, at that moment

the Spartans, inspired by the generous wine of Samos, did not at all

perceive that superiority; on the contrary, they all believed themselves

poor choice

to be demigods and looked on the poet as a worm. *objon*[?]

"Slave!" said Lysander, "Dost know why I have summoned thee?"

"I know not, oh noble Lysander!" replied the captive, with as much

politeness as brevity; the expression of his eye added, "I suspect that it's

a drunkard's fancy."

"It's to make thee sing, and since folk in thy profession must always

have a fine subject to inspire them, I will give thee one: 'The Sack of

Suppose that

Athens.' tomorrow that insolent town will be destroyed from top to

bottom. Invoke then the Muses, and like a second Homer, sing a second

Troy. Go to it!"

The poet played with his chains, which he wore as if they had been

the most superb ornaments of gold and gems. "I don't know how to

sing," he said nonchalantly.

"Ah! thou is too modest. Courage! If thou singest false, thou wilt

pay for it with a few strokes of the lash. Give him the lyre, Epialte."

draperies èn écarlate*s*. "Arrive donc;" cria Lysandre "qu'est-ce que tu

crains? tu es comme un hibou qui s'est égaré en plein midi.

"Le cachot était plus noir que je ne pensais" dit la poète en luimême,

puis il avança lentement sans répondre à Lysandre — et se mit à arranger

les plis de son vêtement que les mains de l'ilote avaient un peu froissé.

Ceci fait, il croisa les bras au dessous de son manteau et attendàit

tranquillement sans mot dire. C'était un vrai Athénien élégant, gracieux;

un Athénien qui avait été élevé dans les bocages de l'Académie, qui

s'était nourri de la philosophie de Platon et de Socrate, de la poësie de

Sophocle et d'Euripide. Malgré sa taille un peu petite et ses traits un peu

effeminés, il y avait dans ses poses nobles, et dans ses contours clas-

siques un je ne sais quoi de supérieur qui l'élévait de loin au dessus de

ces Spartiates, grands comme des géants et forts comme des taureaux.

Cependant dans ce moment les Spartiates, inspirés par le vin généreux de

Samos, ne'apercevaient pas du tout de cette supériorité, au contraire ils

se croyaient tous de demi-dieux et regardaient le poète comme un ver.

"Esclave!" dit Lysandre "Sais-tu pourquoi je t'ai fait appeler?"

"Je l'ignore ô noble Lysandre!" répondit le captif avec autant de

politesse que de brièveté; l'expression de son oeil ajouta — "je crois que

c'est un tour d'ivrogne"

"C'est pour te faire chanter et puisque aux gens de ton métier il faut

toujours un beau sujet pour les inspirer, je vais t'en donner un. Le Sac

d'Athènes. *Suppose que* demain cette ville insolente sera détruite de fond en comble:

invoque donc les Muses et, second Homère, chante une seconde Troie —

allez"

Le poète jouait avec ses chaînes qu'il portait comme si elles avaient

été les plus superbes ornements en or et pierreries — "Je ne sais pas

chanter" dit-il nonchalamment.

"Ah! tu est trop modeste; courage! si tu chantes faux tu en seras quitte

pour quelques coups de fouet, donne-lui la lyre Épialte."

Marginal annotations:

60 *bon*

habitude d'homme accoutumé à parler en public. **B.** 65

70

tr B

mauvais choix *objon*[?] 75

80 **B**

85 *obj.*[?]

They gave him a lyre. He took it and put it down. "I insist on

obedience. Sing, slave!"

"Slave?" murmured the Athenian.

"Slave and dog!" retorted Lysander.

The poet slowly raised his head; brushed the locks from his pale and

lofty brow; fixed the Lacedaemonian with an eye in which there burned

the flame of a pure, free, noble soul; and said calmly:

I have chains
  ^

"I am a man in the power of a wild beast. Thou hast teeth,ᴧ tiger,

tear me apart."

Two lances were propped against the seat where Lysander sat. He

seized one of them and hurled it with force, but his hand trembled from

drunkenness, and he missed his mark. The lance, instead of piercing the

vry. good
Detail
remarkably !
apt.

        cut br~~e~~ak   *that secured* ~~raised~~ *the*

poet, did but s̶e̶v̶e̶r̶ a cord serving to attach a flap of the tent; the flap fell

and through a great opening a new scene came into view:

Night, with its deep sky made vivid by the trembling fires of the

stars; a vast plain silvered by the moon. Far off, Mount Hymettus

bearing Athens like a crown
crowned by the city of Athens, the superb white columns of the Parthe-

silvered with
non gleaming in the moon's rays like veritable pearls of the diadem.

            u
Lastly, the Illysės, whose waves reflected that luminous sky, that classic

mountain, and the glorious brow of Diana.

The poet turned away from the burning interior of the tent, where the

red hangings, the dazzling lamps, the purple wine, and the warriors'

inflamed faces conveyed the reverse of that other world, so calm, so

quiet, that stretched beyond it. A moment more, and he was on his

knees; hands clasped, he seemed to invoke the Lares of the city

threatened with ruin. Before long he arose; he took up the lyre he had

put on the ground. "Orpheus," said he, "knew how to move mountains

            by
and tame wild beasts ~~from~~ the sounds of his lyre; may I not also find in

poetry and music a charm powerful enough to soften these hyena hearts

over the fate of my unhappy homeland?" He let his fingers stray amongst

On lui présenta une lyre — il la prit et la posa par terre. "Je pretend<u>d</u>   90

qu'on m'obéisse, chante esclave!"

"Esclave?" murmura l'Athénien.

"Esclave et chien!" repartit Lysandre

Le poète leva lentement la tête, écarta ses cheveux de son front large
          obj.[?]
et pâle, f<u>i</u>xa le Lacédémonien d'un oeil où brulait la flamme d'une âme   95

pure libre, noble et dit avec calme:

"Je suis un homme au pouvoir d'une bête féroce, tu as des dents,^   *j'ai des chaînes*
                                                                            ^
tigre, déchire moi."

Deux lances étaient appuyées contre le siège où était assis Lysandre,

il en prit une et la jeta avec force, mais sa main tremblait d'ivresse et il   100
                                                              couper cas<s>s</s>er
manqua son coup — la lance, au lieu de percer le poète, ne fit que <s>servir</s>
          qui retenait <s>soulevé</s> *le*   *tr. bon*
un cordon servant à attacher un rideau de la tente, le rideau tomba et à   *Détail*
                                                                          remarquablemt !
travers une grande ouverture se révèla une nouvelle scène   *heureux.*

La Nuit avec son ciel profond, vivifié des feux tremblants des étoiles;
                                                  portant Athènes
une vaste plaine argentée par la lune— de loin Mont Hymette couronné   105
comme une couronne
de la ville d'Athènes, les superbes colonnes blanches du Parthénon
argentées   aux
reluisant dans les rayons lunaires comme les véritables perles du dia-
                              u
dême; enfin l'Illiss<u>e</u>s, dont les flots répetaient ce ciel lumineux, cette

montagne classique, et le front glorieux de Diane.

Le poète se détourna de l'intérieur brulant de la tente, où les   110

draperies rouges, les lampes éblouissantes, le vin pourpre, les visages

enflammés des guerriers donnaient le revers de cet autre monde si calme

si tranquille qui s'étendait en dehors.— Encore un moment, et il s'était

mis à genoux; les mains jointes il semblait invoquer les Lares de la ville

menacée de ruine. Bientôt il se leva, il ramassa la lyre qu'il avait posée   115

par terre; "Orphée" dit-il "savait émouvoir les montagnes et apprivoiser
                        par les
les bêtes féroces <u>des</u> sons de sa lyre, ne puis-je pas aussi trouver dans la

poësie et la musique un charme assez puissant pour attendrir ces coeurs

d'hyène sur le sort de ma malheureuse patrie?" Il laissa errer ses doigts

the strings of the instrument and drew from it sad and gentle sounds; those sounds, at first random, soon took form and became a very plaintive air, such as Aegean islanders sing. He stopped; a profound silence had already replaced the tumult of the debauch; from afar one heard the murmur of the waves of the Illysés, and the rustle of a light breeze caressing the reeds and olive trees that shade its banks. This rustle, this

125

vry G

murmur inspired the poet; he listened to them with lowered head. Memories of his childhood came back to him, the dreams that had soothed him on his mother's knees. He recalled the ancient legends that constituted the mythology of Greece, legends terrible and sad: the royal

130

race of Pelops, hounded always by a dark destiny; the fate of the king of kings returning victorious from ten years of war in a distant land to perish on his dishonored hearth; Clytemnestra stained by her husband's blood, Orestes exiled, and Electra slave and orphan. These memories served as his subject; he picked up his lyre — he sang.

—————

135

vG

The steeds of the Sun, wearied by their long journey, plunge into the ocean; the waves engulf them; disappearing, they leave traces of fire on the sea and in the sky; but day blends with twilight and the sea grows dim; the glory of the heavens passes.

Then comes Night, calm and grave; a single planet glitters on her

140 *vry. G. —*

pensive brow. She passes over the cities, leaving silence and slumber in her wake. She passes over the mountaintops, setting out her sentinels, the stars, to keep watch while men sleep. She passes over the sea and leaves the solitary sailor the star that must guide his bark. She passes over the barren desert and gives to the stork and the pelican the sign to

145

vG

seek their nests. She descends upon Argos; all sleep; the lamps are out. She enters an ancient forest, dark and deep, and there she stops; it is her cherished abode.

Night veils her brow and bows her head. A pine, an old oak, a black

parmi les cordes de l'instrument et en tira des sons doux et tristes; ces 120

sons, d'abord interrompus, s'arrang^rèaient bientôt et devinrent un air très

plaintif, tel que chantent les habitants des îles de l'Egée. Il s'arrêta un

silence profond avait déjà remplacé le tumulte de la débauche, on enten-

dit de loin le murmure des ondes de l'Iliss^ues et le souffle d'une légère

brise caressant les roseaux et les oliviers qui en ombragent les bords. Ce 125

souffle, ce murmure servit d'inspiration au poète, il les écouta la tête   *tr B*

baissée; les souvenirs de son enfance revinrent dans son esprit, les rêves

qui l'avaient bercé sur les genoux de sa mère. Il se rappela les anciennes

legendes qui constituaient la mythologie de la Grèce; legendes terribles

et tristes; la race royale des Pélopides poursuivie toujours par un noir 130
                                                                après
destin, le sort du roi des rois revenant vainqueur dè dix ans de guerre
                                    dans ses
dans un pays lointain pour périr sur son foyers déshonorés Clytemnestre

tachée du sang de son époux, Oreste exilé et Electre esclave et orpheline.
                                                        et
Ces souvenirs lui servirent de sujet il reprit sa lyre — il chanta

<hr>

Les coursiers du Soleil, fatigués de leur longue carrière, plongent dans 135

l'océan; les ondes les engloutissent; en disparaissant ils laissent des traces   *tB*

de feu sur la mer et dans le ciel; mais le jour se confond avec le

crépuscule et la mer pâlit, la gloire du ciel se passe.

Puis vient la Nuit calme et sérieuse, une seule planète scintille sur

son front pensif. Elle passe par les villes, laissant le silence et le   *tr. B. —* 140

sommeil sur ses pas; Elle passe sur les sommets des montagnes, plaçant

ses sentinelles les étoiles, qu'elle fait veiller tandis que les hommes

dorment. Elle passe par la mer et laisse au marin solitaire l'astre qui

doit guider sa barque. Elle passe par le desert inhabité et donne à la

cigogne et au pélican le signal de chercher leurs nids. Elle descend sur 145

Argos, tout dort, les lampes sont éteintes; elle entre dans un antique forêt   *tB*

profonde, sombre et elle s'y arrête, c'est son séjour chéri.

La Nuit voile son front et penche sa tête; un pin, un vieux chêne, un

cedar entwine their branches around her. Obscurity surrounds her;

silence accompanies her. Neither man nor beast exists in that region of

shadows; even at high noon no hunter dares enter there, for the rumor

runs that this forest is peopled by rustic phantoms: amid the gnarled

branches of the trees leer grotesque Satyrs, and where the foliage is thick

and the moss is soft rest monstrous Fauns. Dryads also prowl about

155
those long alleys, and the Oreads go down to them from the mountains

of Epidaurus.

Who speaks? Whence comes that voice which suddenly breaks the

silence? So far from any town, so far from human habitation, who

wanders here? What mortal? what woman? for listen! it is a woman who

160
speaks.

"Oh Agamemnon! Agamemnon!"

moans
Night trembles, frightened by that doleful cry; the forest rḛs̰o̰ṵn̰d̰s̰

with it.

"Agamemnon — my father! They have driven me from thy grave;

165
they have torn from my hands the urn that contains thy ashes. They

revile me, they threaten me when I weep for thee! I have fled the pre-

cincts of my tyrants; I have sought these solitudes to weep alone. Alone,

do I say? No, the Fury follows me. She is ever on Electra's traces."

serves as a doleful
The voice stops; the rustling of the wind and leaves ma̰k̰ḛs̰ ̰t̰h̰ḛ ̰r̰ḛf̰r̰a̰ḭn̰
accompaniment to
170
of her cry. But Electra knows not how to quell the agonies that torment

her; again she invokes Agamemnon, she returns to her dark memories.

"My noble father! I see him again as he was the day he left for

Troy; that fatal city, tomb of Greek warriors, tomb of Iphigenia! Then

I was but six years old and already I loved my father so! I was playing

175
by a fountain, that fountain in the courtyard of our palace; I was tossing

in some flowers I had gathered that morning in the plain. My mother

called me. 'Thy father is leaving,' she said. 'He is going to a distant

country, to fight against the Trojans and reclaim that fair Helen whom

noir cèdre entrelacent leurs branches autour d'elle; l'obscurité l'environne, le silence l'accompagne. Ni homme, ni bête n'existent dans cette région de tenèbres; même en plein midi nul chasseur n'ose y pénètrer car le bruit court que cette forêt est peuplée de fantômes agrestes: parmi les branches noueuses des arbres grimacent de grotesques Satyres et, où la feuillage est épaisses et la mousse molle reposent des Faunes monstrueux; aussi les Dryades rodent dans ces longues allées et les Oréades y descendent des montagnes d'Épidaure.

Qui parle? D'où vient cette voix qui rompe subitement le silence? Si loin des villes, si loin des habitations humaines qui erre ici? Quel mortel? quelle femme? car, écoutez! c'est une femme qui parle:

"Ô Agamemnon! Agamemnon!"

La Nuit tressaille, effrayée de ce cri lugubre, la forêt en retentit. *gémit*

"Agamemnon — mon père! on m'a chassée de ton tombeau, on a arraché à mes mains l'urne qui renferme tes cendres — on m'insulte, on me menace quand je pleure pour toi! J'ai fui la demeure de mes tyrans j'ai cherché ces solitudes pour pleurer seule. Seule dis-je? non, l'Eumenide me suit; — elle est toujours sur les pas d'Electre."

La voix s'arrête, le bruissement du vent et des feuilles fait le refrain *sert d'accompagnemt* de ses plaintes. *lugubre à* Mais Electre ne sait pas contenir les angoisses qui la travaillent; encore elle invoque Agamemnon, elle revient à ses noirs souvenirs.

"Mon noble père! Je le vois encore comme il était le jour qu'il partit pour Troie; cette ville funeste, tombeau des guerriers grecs, tombeau d'Iphigénie! Alors je n'avais que six ans et déjà j'aimais tant mon père! Je jouais près d'une fontaine, cette fontaine dans la cour de notre palais; j'y jetais des fleurs que j'avais cueillies le matin dans la plaine: ma mère m'appela: "Ton père va partir" dit-elle: "Il va dans un pays lointain, combattre les Troyens et racheter cette belle Hélène que Paris a enlevée à Ménélaus; viens lui dire adieu "

Paris took away from Menelaus. Come bid him farewell.'

"I ran; on the threshold of the palace I met my father. He was clad all in steel; a black plume shaded his helmet; he bent down and took me in his arms, and I pressed my cheek against his leathern breastplate. My heart was heavy⌣ _depressed_; I was sad to see my father leave. He was my sole support; my mother had never loved me, for I had neither the beauty of Iphigenia nor the majesty of Orestes. He left us, promising to return soon. Alas! how many long years passed before he saw his homeland again! The very day of his departure I planted the shoot of a vine near the fountain; before his return, the fountain was draped in it, as in a green veil. At last he returned; I still remember the day _the eve_ of his arrival, when his whole kingdom glowed with signal fires. From mountain to mountain ran those heralds of flame, announcing the king of kings returning victorious to his people. He came back radiant, the laurel on his brow, the victor's garland entwined with the sovereign's diadem. Argos trembled with joy, and I,⌣ _poor_ Electra, thought the merciful gods had put an end to my sufferings. I had found my father again! Exquisite happiness, scarcely tasted, when the cup ran over with blood! Clytemnestra appears at the door of the palace; she awaits her spouse; on seeing him, she opens her arms and smiles at him, but she is all pale, like a grinning death's-head.

"Who then sits at Agamemnon's side in the triumphal chariot? It is a woman wearing a veil. How mute and motionless she stays in the midst of the joyous tumult; she resembles the mysterious image of <u>Sais</u>, the goddess of truth. Agamemnon alights; he clasps his spouse to his loyal heart. In that moment a cry, a harrowing cry, is heard; there is the veiled statue, standing in the chariot; the veil is rent _drawn aside,_ and all Argos recognizes Cassandra, princess, prophetess, and slave! Oh I see her still, her ghost appears before my eyes in the shadows of this forest! White, stiff, petrified, as if her veins were filled with ice in place of blood; all

"Je courus, sur le seuil du palais je rencontrai mon père; il était tout

vêtu d'acier, un panache noir ombrageait son casque; il se pencha et me 180

i

prit dans ses bras, et j'appuya ma joue contre sa poitrine couverte d'une

déprimé

cuirasse. J'avais le coeur gros, j'étais triste de voir partir mon père, il

était mon seul soutien, ma mère ne m'avait jamais aimée car je n'avais *moi,*

ni la beauté d'Iphigénie ni la majesté d'Oreste. Il nous quitta en promet-

tant de revenir bientôt: helas! que de longues années s'écoulèrent avant 185

qu'il revit sa patrie! Le jour même de son départ je plantai un rejeton de *B*

vigne près de la fontaine, avant son retour la fontaine en était drapée

la veille

comme d'un voile vert. Enfin il revint, je me rappelle encore le jour de

aux

son arrivée quand tout son royaume brillait du feu des fanals; de mon-

tagne en montagne couraient ces hérauts de flamme, annonçant le roi des 190

rois qui revenait vainqueur à son peuple. Il revint radieux, le laurier au

front, la guirlande du conquérant entrelacée avec le diadême du souve-

pauvre

rain. Argos tressaillit de joie et moi, Electre, je crus que les dieux

miséricordieux avaient mis fin à mes souffrances, j'avais retrouvé mon

père! bonheur exquis, à peine gouté, quand la coupe deborda de sang! 195

Clytemnestre apparait à la porte du palais, elle attend son époux, elle

ouvre les bras en le voyant, et elle lui sourit mais elle est tout pale, c'est

comme un mort qui rit.

Qui donc est assis à côté d'Agamemnon dans le char triomphal?

C'est une femme portant un voile; comme elle reste muette et immobile 200

au milieu du tumulte joyeux, elle ressemble à l'image mystérieuse de

Sais, la déesse de la vérité. Agamemnon descend, il serre son épouse

contre son coeur loyal. Dans ce moment on entend un cri, un cri dé-

écarté

chirant; la statue voilée est là, debout sur le char; le voile est déchiré et

tout Argos reconnait Cassandre, princesse, prophétesse et esclave! Oh 205

je la vois encore, son spectre se révèle à mes yeux dans les ténèbres de

cette forêt! blanche, raide, petrifiée, comme si ses veines étaient

remplies de glace en place de sang; toute échevelée, ses tresses défaites,

disheveled, her locks in disarray, streaming at the mercy of the wind; her
white shoulders gleaming beneath her wild hair, like the moon through
clouds. And her great dark eyes — what fire shone in them! what flash
of inspiration! They were not a woman's eyes, they were a god's — or
a demon's — I know not which; both are terrible when they glitter
beneath a brow of flesh. Apollo showed himself in the orbs of his
prophetess and fixed on the king his supernatural gaze. 'Woe! woe!' she
cried. 'Woe betide the lion who seeks the she-wolf's lair!' And she
spewed forth curses whose horror made Argos quake, but none gave
them either credence or attention.

"Then she suddenly became a woman again; she fell to her knees and
piteously murmured: 'Agamemnon, hear me; thou hast saved me from
the hands of fierce Ajax; I would save thee too.' Atrides turned to her;
the tenderness of a great soul softened his stern features: 'Poor maiden!'
said he, 'ever prey to this dreadful delirium'; and he took her hand.
Cassandra wept; her forces were spent; she could no longer struggle
against her destiny. She bowed her head and brushed the hand of
Agamemnon with her lips, murmuring gently, 'My king, my master, at
last it is done. I resign myself to all, for I know that thy lot will be
mine; the same axe that fells the oak will break the reed.' And that night
saw the death of Agamemnon and Cassandra, the triumph of Aegisthus
and Clytemnestra."

*   *   *   *   *   *   *   *

Here the poet, breathless, paused to breathe. He glanced around the tent
to gauge the effect his verses had produced. Oh horror! Lysander, his
captains, and his helots slept, lying on their couches or on the ground,
were all fast asleep. Here was the explanation for the respectful silence
that, until now, had encouraged him to continue, and that he had thought
to be the sign of fixed attention, of overwhelming emotion. Oh shame!
Oh indignity! His Athenian soul rebelled against an insensitivity so

flottant au gré des vents, ses épaules blanches reluisant sous ses cheveux épars, comme la lune à travers des nuages: et ses grands yeux noirs — quel feu y brillait! quelle étincelle d'inspiration! Ce n'étaient pas des yeux de femme, c'étaient des yeux de dieu — ou de demon — je ne sais pas lesquels, tous deux sont terribles quand ils brillent sous un front de chair. Apollon se révèla dans les prunelles de sa prophétesse et fixa sur le roi son regard surnaturel. "Malheur! malheur!" s'écria-t-elle. "Malheur au lion qui cherche l'antre de la louve!" et elle versa des malédictions dont la terreur fit trembler Argos, mais personne n'y ajoutait ni croyance ni attention.

Puis elle redevint subitement femme, elle tomba à genoux et murmura piteusement: "Agamemnon écoute moi, tu m'as sauvée des mains du féroce Ajax, je voudrais te sauver aussi" Atride se tourna vers elle, la tendresse d'une grande âme adoucit ses traits sévères: "Pauvre jeune fille!" dit-il "toujours en proie à ce délire funeste" et il lui prit la main. Cassandre pleura, ses forces étaient épuisées, elle ne pouvait plus lutter contre son destin; elle pencha la tête et effleura de ses lèvres la main d'Agamemnon en murmurant doucement "Mon roi, mon maître, enfin c'est fini, je me resigne à tout car je sais que ton sort sera le mien; la même hâche qui abattra le chène, brisera le roseau." Et cette nuit vit la mort d'Agamemnon et de Cassandre, le triomphe d'Égisthe et de Clytemnestre"

*　　*　　*　　*　　*　　*　　*　　*

Ici le poète, hors d'haleine, s'arrêta pour respirer, il jeta un coup d'oeil autour de la tente pour s'assurer de l'effet qu'avaient produit ses vers. Ô horreur! Lysandre, ses capitaines et ses îlotes ~~dorma~~ couchés sur leurs lits ou par terre dormaient tous d'un profond sommeil. Voici donc l'explication du silence þ respectueux, qui, jusqu'à présent l'avait encouragé à continuer et qu'il avait cru l'indice d'une attention fixe, d'une émotion <u>accablante</u>: ô honte! ô indignité! son âme athénienne se révolta contre une insensibilité si brutale. Cependant, après la première effer-

brutal. Still, after the first effervescence of his rage, he told himself that it would be too absurd to get annoyed at the stupidity of a dozen barbarians, and laughing softly at them and at himself, he seized the opportunity to leave the tent and return to Athens, which he reached in perfect safety.

The next morning, on awakening, Lysander seemed to have entirely forgotten the poet and his project of vengeance. First he asked earnestly for a cup of fresh water; then he complained of having a very bad headache (and he softly cursed the vintages of Samos); next, getting up, he went straight to the Illisse and took a bath in those limpid waves where Diana had been so well mirrored the night^ before. On returning, he set about framing a treaty with the Athenians, interrupting himself from time to time to remark that the names of Agamemnon, Electra, etc., were continually ringing in his ears, and that he knew not whence this came, since he had never in his life bothered about those persons.

Anyhow, be that as it may, Athens escaped the sacking and carnage with which she had been threatened. Perhaps the wine of Samos had somewhat helped to bring about her safety, but the lyre and Electra had also worked as a strong enough opiate to justify the words given in title to the beginning of this history, i.e., Athens Saved by Poetry.

———

The Subject was taken seriously, at the outset and above all in the middle.

The author, frightened toward the end of the heights to which he thought himself raised, began to laugh at himself, out of uncertainty about how to make a dignified descent and to have the laughers on his side.

The author makes a mistake.

One should not make fun of one's reader.

Example, see Alfred de Musset.

vescence de sa colère, il se dit que ce serait trop ridicule de se fâcher de la stupidité d'une douzaine de barbares, et riant tout bas d'eux et de luimême, il profita de l'occasion de quitter la tente et de retourner à Athènes; il y arriva en toute sureté.

Le lendemain, en s'eveillant, Lysandre paraissait avoir entièrement oublié et le poète et son projet de vengeance. D'abord il demanda, avec instances, une tasse d'eau fraîche, puis il se plaignit d'avoir très fort mal à la tête (et il maudissait tout bas les vendanges de Samos) ensuite se levant, il alla tout droit à l'Ilisse et prit un bain dans ces ondes limpides où Diane s'était si bien mirée le soir^précédent. En revenant il se mit à fabriquer un traité avec les Athéniens s'interrompant de temps en temps pour remarquer que les noms d'Agamemnon, d'Electre, &c. lui bourdonnaient continuellement aux oreilles, et qu'il ne savait pas d'où çela venait puisque, jamais de sa vie il ne s'était inquiété de ces personages là.

Enfin, quoiqu'il en soit, Athènes echappa au sac et au carnage dont on luil' avait menacée; peutêtre le vin de Samos avait-il aidé un peu en effectuant son salut mais aussi la lyre et Electre avaient opéré en opiate assez forte pour justifier les mot mis en titre au commencement de cette histoire i.e. Athènes sauvée par la Poësie.

———

le Sujet a été pris au sérieux, au début et surtout au milieu — .

l'auteur effrayé vers la fin de la hauteur à laquelle il se croyait élevé, s'est mis à rire de lui-même, par embarras de descendre dignement et pr. avoir les rieurs à son côté.

l'auteur a un tort.

on ne doit pas se moquer de son lecteur.

Exemple voir Alfred de Musset.

Comments

Charlotte Brontë endured a long September without classes or Constantine Heger. This assignment, the first of the new school year, must have come as a deliverance and challenge. "Athens Saved by Poetry" is her most ambitious devoir. The manuscript runs to twenty pages and is only the first of two versions. The other is a seventeen-page variant headed "Devoir de Style pour M: Heger." It too has been corrected by pupil and master, though Heger's second-round notations are much lighter and no final comment appears.[1] Following its last words, Charlotte added the medallion reproduced here as figure 8.

Getting at the devoir's origins and context might seem difficult because of its complexity, but they can be plausibly conjectured. Enid Duthie has identified its most important sources, the Brontë juvenilia suggest further precedents, and Charlotte herself provides fictionalized clues to its basis and production in *Villette*.

In the novel's thirty-fifth chapter, "Fraternity," Lucy Snowe refers to a devoir of hers which has so impressed Paul Emanuel's colleagues that they accuse him of having written it and forged her name. Protesting that it is clearly novice work, she starts to explain how she composed it: "The subject was classical. When M. Paul dictated the trait on which the essay was to turn, I heard it for the first time; the matter was new to me, and I had no material for its treatment. But I got books, read up the facts, laboriously constructed a skeleton out of the dry bones of the real, and then clothed them, and tried to breathe into them life, and in this last aim I had pleasure."[2] To what extent do Lucy's methods imitate Charlotte's? The answer seems to be: pretty closely.

"Athens Saved by Poetry" is Charlotte's only devoir on a classical subject. As Duthie says, it is based on an episode recounted in Plutarch's *Life of Lysander.* When, at the conclusion of the Peloponnesian War, Lysander tried to change the Athenians' form of government, they so bitterly opposed him that the Spartans and their allies considered more extreme retribution. One proposal was to sell them into slavery; another to raze Athens to the ground. But afterward, at a banquet for the leaders, "a certain Phocian sang the first chorus in the 'Electra' of Euripides"; it moved the listeners to such compassion that they gave up the idea of razing a city so renowned, which had bred such great poets.[3]

This episode may not seem to qualify as the "trait" on which an essay would turn. But in French, "trait" also connotes "outline," and Heger customarily dictated outlines that his students were expected to develop.[4] (His other term for instructions was *matière,* which in Lucy's account becomes "matter.") If he did dictate a version of the incident, he may not have gone directly to Plutarch. A colleague at the Athénée Royal, M. Baron, narrates it in the introduction to a volume of Delavigne poems that he had edited.[5] Heger knew Delavigne's *Messéniennes*— he told Gaskell that one of them inspired "The Death of Moses"[6]—and though there is no proof that he used Baron's edition, the text a fellow teacher had prepared for classroom use would presumably have come to his attention. It would also have been typical of Heger to indicate where his students should elaborate: for instance, in describing the banquet. Still, the initiative to write a devoir so intricate could only have been Charlotte's.

Lucy says the topic was new to her; a brief, uncelebrated passage from Plutarch must have been just as new to Charlotte. The Brontë sisters grew up on the Bible, not the classics, although they had some access to the major works: Chapman's and Pope's *Iliad* were both at Ponden House, and Patrick Brontë had in his collection an authoritative classical dictionary.[7] But Branwell would have been her most direct source. He studied Greek and Latin with their father—at ten, he was reading Homer and Virgil—and, since the siblings collaborated closely, Charlotte got at least a taste of his lessons. At fourteen she wrote "The Violet," a poem that refers to Homer, Sophocles, Euripides, and Aeschylus;[8] she also started writing about Zenobia Ellrington, a "female blue-stocking" who read Greek in the original.[9] Her reading of Byron too would have given her indirect access to Greek myth and history, together with precedents for weaving such allusions into her own creative work.[10]

With this background, she might have struck Heger as knowing much more than she did. Lucy reports that Paul Emanuel chronically suspected her of knowing Greek and Latin: "The privileges of a 'classical education,' it was insinuated, had been mine; on flowers of Hymettus I had revelled; a golden store, hived in memory, now silently sustained my efforts, and privily nurtured my wits."[11] Whether or not Heger shared Paul's misconception, this assignment must have revived Charlotte's longing for the classical training she lacked. Instead, she had the books in Heger's library. At minimum, she would have needed Plutarch (unless Heger lectured on Lysander's character); *The Iliad,* books 9 and 20, for her banquet scene; a classical dictionary or encyclopedia; a source on Electra and the House of Atreus; and a source, perhaps the *Agamemnon,*[12] for Cassandra's speeches. She probably could have found them all at the pensionnat, although, as a previous editor points out, she could only have taken her quotation on Achilles' "inaccessible hands" from Chapman's Homer.[13] Perhaps it stayed with her because of its strangeness. If not, she could have borrowed a copy of Chapman in Brussels (the local English bookshop was owned by a man who seems to have taught English classes at the school),[14] or she could have read it in the three-month interval between her trips abroad. During that time, she almost certainly read translations of Schiller's poems in *Blackwood's,* among them "The Veiled Image at Sais."[15]

Lucy's account of her methods gives no clue to the books Charlotte may have consulted. But it does confirm her reliance on sources and her struggle to compensate for scholarly deficiencies: "With me it was a difficult and anxious time till my facts were found, selected, and properly jointed; nor could I rest from research and effort till I was satisfied of correct anatomy; the strength of my inward repugnance to the idea of flaw or falsity sometimes enabled me to shun egregious blunders; but the knowledge was not there in my head, ready and mellow; it had not been sown in Spring, grown in Summer, harvested in Autumn, and garnered through Winter; whatever I wanted I must go out and gather fresh; glean of wild herbs my lap full, and shred them green into the pot."[16] Here too *Villette* seems autobiographical. Charlotte would have worried about getting the details right and fashioning parts so stylistically divergent into members of one body of text. Her technique was to link them, not only by the plot line, but through a common pattern of narration. "Athens" develops as a series of dramatic tableaus, each of which moves from a description of the setting to a human confrontation, with dialogue: first there is the banquet, next the vision of the city, then the poet's evocation of Night's journey and the forest, Electra's recollections (which form an inner series), and the poet's rude discovery and its aftermath. Working out a form so complex must have sparked anxiety, especially since Heger had long since pointed out her tendency to stray from her subject.

As revealing as the summary Lucy gives of her methods are the metaphors in which they are figured. Charlotte first portrays Lucy as a kind of schoolroom Frankenstein who labors to assemble, clothe, and animate "dry bones" because she lacks the storehouse of organic knowledge that a life spent studying classics would have given her. But dried, stored knowledge may conversely lack the flavor of herbs freshly gathered and dishes improvised to satisfy immediate hunger. Countering the image of the monster and its maker is that of the woman skilled in homelier arts who takes pleasure in creating what she can. But this image too is implicitly refuted, by Lucy's report of men's responses: Paul has shown off her devoir to two professors who take it "for the work of a ripe scholar."[17] Lucy may protest that it is "not remarkable,"[18] but Charlotte makes it crucial to the text, an absent presence that attests to Lucy's powers as a writer.

"Athens Saved by Poetry" is not ripe work, if the gauge is Charlotte's later fiction. Its melodramatic and romantic sensibility links it to her juvenilia, rather than her novels. So do its Electra and Cassandra, whose sorrows seem less Attic than Gothic or Victorian. (There is no precedent in any Greek source for the six-year-old who tosses her flowers in the fountain and runs to papa for a kiss.) Its supercharged prose further controverts her efforts to sustain a tone in keeping with its classical subject. Anglicisms still creep into her French, along with little errors in grammar. And yet her achievement is remarkable.

Charlotte was not by disposition a scholar; she had picked up her knowledge of Greece piecemeal. Nonetheless the essay seems authentic in its details: historic, geographic, tragic, mythic. It is also a deliberate exercise in style, or styles, since she keeps shifting mood and voices. A plain-speaking narrator launches the essay; that voice is succeeded by the eloquent poet's and then by the suffering Electra's; when the original narrator resumes, the genre shifts into satire. The sentence structure too is exceptionally varied, as if she were trying to strike all the chords that a lofty composition could sustain. Dialogue gives her scope for further permutations. It dramatizes conflict, individualizes sorrow, helps to mark the rank and gender of the speakers.

Within each section she keeps the tone consistent, never dropping the mask to make a personal appeal, as she does in "Napoleon" and "Moses." Still, she writes this devoir for an audience of one man, and certainly she knows what will please him. Heger does not react like Lucy's Paul Emanuel, who "never once praised, or even mentioned, in [her] hearing . . . [the devoir] which [she] had deemed forgotten."[19] Until the final section he commends her work repeatedly, clustering his praises in two areas: details of behavior that illuminate character and descriptions that make scenery sublime. As usual, he calls her attention to faulty French and heightens the drama of her phrasing, but in his marginal comments he is less a chiding teacher than a man who appreciates her talent and her efforts and lets her know where her text needs strengthening.

His final comment complicates these messages. He does not approve of the sudden deflation that the poet's discovery inaugurates. As a classics teacher, he wants unity; he may also have a typically French distaste for mixing literary genres. Yet after his first sentence, he directs his criticism to the writer rather than the devoir. By speaking of "the author" in the masculine third person, he distances his words from any intimacy with her. Then he implicitly erodes that distance by telling her he understands her motives. *Author*, to a woman yearning to become one, would be a further proof of his regard. Backhanded as a compliment, it might still suggest to her that *she* was a subject he took seriously.

There are signs throughout this devoir of a novelist's way of working: the emphasis on story, the attempts to portray character, the care she takes with dialogue and episode. A writer's eye is evident as well in the nuances, like the hurled lance that opens both the tent flap and the next scene. As Lucy Snowe suggests, breathing life into dry bones was the ultimate aim of Charlotte's efforts. And, to some extent, she would have measured her achievement by the comments she received from her professor.

But if she had continued to subscribe to Heger's standards, she would never have become a major writer. His responses reveal a histrionic sensibility, compatible with hers as she outgrew her juvenilia but at odds with the temper of her novels. The section he attacks does represent a sharp drop from the heights of Electra's lament. It is also more predictive of Charlotte's later fiction than any other section of "Athens." Her poet—gifted, cultivated, honorable, captive—has to cope in a world of barbarians. For his safety, his illusions must be punctured; he rages, recovers, and then escapes. Athens survives as well, whatever the causes, and the body of the text is not harmed by the humor that restores a more modest realism.

Almost certainly, the mood of this section is connected to Charlotte's own disenchantment. As Duthie says, it "betrays her growing sense of frustration in an uncongenial milieu."[20] But even if her discontent motivates the ending, it is inappropriate only by criteria that dictate a uniformly high tone. Charlotte's novels break such rules continually.

Perhaps it is Heger who "makes a mistake" in his assessment of the author's problem. She is not too flustered to make a "dignified descent," although she may feel awkward about writing a conclusion that her master is likely to criticize. Significantly, though she has the chance to change the ending—in her second draft she could have cut or revised it—it stays almost exactly as it was.

The medallion at the very end of that copy is dated December 22 (see fig. 7). Perhaps she prepared it as a Christmas offering. By then, she must have known that she would soon leave Brussels, probably never to return. But whether or not she wanted Heger to keep it, both copies seem to have gone with her to Haworth, since she still had them at her death.[21]

Letter

From a Poor Painter to a Great
Lord. /

Milord:

I could begin this letter in the form of an apology but, from what I
know of your character, I think you would prefer a simple account of
facts to a thousand banal excuses. My purpose in writing to you is to
solicit your patronage; I address myself to you rather than another

G   because, rich and powerful as you are, I know that your riches and your
power are the least of your qualities. If you possessed only your vast

Indeed[?]

lands and your title of Baron, I would al̮ways render you due respect, but
that respect, like the circumstances that exacted it, would be something
superficial and venal; if you were to order my works, I would sell them
to you, as one sells furniture or fabric, but to a rich imbecile I would not
accord a grain of genuine attachment, an atom of distinterested devotion.
Perhaps I would even rebel against an authority whose only basis was
superiority of rank; I feel that it would be like throwing a lighted torch
into a powder keg to expose myself to the caprice and insolence of a
patron without heart and without intelligence. As for you, milord, you

in

are my equal in intellect and my superior in virtue and experience, so I
will render you homage from the heart, pure and real, in which self-
interest counts for nothing.

Before giving me the help that I solicit, you have the right to demand
precise details about my situation and my character. I am going to tell
you who I am, what my position is, and why I have embraced it.

I am, Milord, a twenty-five year old man who has chosen to become
a painter, who has just completed his studies in Rome, who arrives in

Lettre

d'un pauvre Peintre à un grand
Seigneur. /

Milord: 5

Je pourrais commencer cette lettre en forme d'apologie mais, d'après
ce que je connais de votre caractère, je pense que vous aimeriez un
simple détail de faits mieux que mille excuses banales. Mon but en vous
écrivant, c'est de solliciter votre patronage; je m'adresse à vous plutôt
qu'à un autre, parceque, tout riche et puissant que vous êtes, je sais que   *B*   10
vos richesses et votre pouvoir sont les moindres de vos qualités. Si vous
                                                            Certes[?]
ne possédiez que vos vastes terres et votre titre de Baron, je vous
rendrais toujours hommage mais, cet hommage serait, comme les cir-
constances qui l'exigeaient, une chose extérieure et vénale: si vous
commandiez de mes oeuvres |, je vous en vendrais, comme on vend des   15
meubles ou des étoffes, mais à un riche imbécile je n'accorderais pas un
grain d'attachement réel, un atome de dévouement désintéressé. Peut-
être même me revolterais-je contre une autorité dont le seul fondement
serait un superiorité de rang: je sens que ce serait jeter une torche
allumée dans un magasin de poudre que de m'exposer aux caprices et aux   20
insolences d'un patron sans coeur et sans tête. | Quant à vous milord,
                                                    en
vous êtes mon égal en intellect et mon supérieur en vertu et expérience |,
je vous rendrai donc l'hommage du coeur, pur et réel, où l'intérêt n'est
pour rien.

Avant de m'accorder les secours que je sollicite vous avez le droit de   25
demander des détails minutieux sur ma position et mon caractère: Je vais
vous dire qui je suis, quel est mon état et pourquoi je l'ai embrassé.

Je suis, Milord, un homme de vingt-cinq ans qui s'est fait peintre par
gout, qui vient d'achever ses études à Rome, qui arrive dans ce pays sans

this country without acquaintances and without family, and who has no
other fortune than his palette, his paintbrushes, his craftsmanship, and
the love of his art. Such is my position; I know how hazardous, how
suspect, even how contemptible it is in the eyes of certain people who
regard as shameful everything that is perilous and uncertain. Why then
have I chosen a career whose dangers I know so well? What right have
I to hope to succeed where so many others have succumbed? Milord,
I shall answer those questions, and frankly. I entered upon this career
because I believed that it was my vocation; I hope to succeed in it
because I sense in myself the courage to persevere despite all the
obstacles I may encounter. These are not the words of a braggart who
thinks himself brave because he has never been put to the test; I know
what misfortune is; I have suffered it in its harshest forms. The four
years that I spent in Italy were not exclusively devoted to the study of the
arts; I had also to take my degree in the school of Adversity, and if I did
not sink under the severity of its discipline, it is because the love of my
art was in me a passion that rekindled the fire in my veins when cold and
hunger had frozen them. "But," you would say, "the love of your art
is nothing if you do not have the talent necessary to attain excellence in
it." Milord, I believe I have talent. Do not be indignant at my
presumption or accuse me of conceit; I do not know that feeble feeling,
the child of vanity; but I know well another feeling, Respect for myself,
a feeling born of independence and integrity. Milord, I believe I have
Genius.

That declaration shocks you, you find it arrogant; I find it very
simple. Doesn't everyone agree that no artist can succeed without
genius? Then would it not be imbecility to dedicate oneself to the arts
without being sure one has that indispensable quality? But how to
acquire that assurance? Can one not be mistaken about it? Man is so

connaissances et sans parents et qui n'a d'autre fortune que sa palette, ses _B_ 30
pinceaux, son savoir et l'amour de son art | . Telle est ma position; je
sais combien elle est hasardeuse, combien elle est suspecte, combien
même elle est méprisable aux yeux de certaines gens qui regarde comme
honteux tout ce qui est périlleux et incertain. Pourquoi donc ai-je choisi
une carrière dont je connais si bien les dangers? Quel droit ai-je 35
d'espérer réussir où tant d'autres ont succombé? Milord | je vais ré-
pondre à ces questions et franchement. Je suis entré dans cette carrière
parceque j'ai cru que c'était ma vocation: j'espère y réussir parceque je _B_
me sens le courage de persévérer malgré tous les obstacles que je puisse
y rencontrer. Ce que je dis là | n'est pas le discours d'un vaniteux qui se 40
croit courageux parcequ'il n'a jamais été mis à l'épreuve, je sais ce que _B_
c'est que le malheur; je l'ai essuyé sous ses plus rudes formes. Les
quatre ans que j'ai passés en Italie n'ont pas été exclusivement consacrés
à l'étude des arts; j'ai dû aussi prendre mes dégrés dans l'école de
l'Adversité, et si je n'ai pas succombé sous la sévérité de sa discipline, 45
c'est parceque l'amour de mon art était en moi une passion dont la _B_
flamme réchauffait mes veines quand le froid et la faim les avaient
glacées. "Mais," diriez-vous "l'amour de votre art n'est rien si vous
n'avez pas le talent nécessaire pour y atteindre de l'excellence." Milord,
je crois avoir du talent. Ne vous indignez pas de ma présomption, ne 50
m'accusez pas d'amour-propre, je ne connais pas ce sentiment faible,
enfant de la vanité; mais je connais bien un autre sentiment, le Respect
pour moi-même, sentiment né de l'independance et de l'intégrité. _⁄_
Milord, je crois avoir du Génie.

Cette déclaration vous choque; vous la trouvez arrogante moi, je la 55
trouve tout simple. N'est-il pas convenu de tout le monde que sans génie
nul artiste ne peut réussir? Donc ne serait ce pas de l'imbécilité que de
se vouer aux arts sans s'assurer qu'on a cette qualité si indispensable?
Mais comment acquérir cette assurance? ne peut-on pas s'y tromper?

inclined to flatter himself. I know only one sure method. One must live in the world, compare oneself with others, submit oneself to the test of experience, pass through its furnace, ten times fiercer than Nebuchadnezzar's, and if one emerges from it without being transmuted into the

very G ordinary lead of society, it is because one's soul contains a few grains of that pure gold which is called Genius. Milord, I lived for a long time with others without any thought of comparing myself with them; throughout my early youth the difference that existed between myself and most of the people around me was, for me, an embarrassing enigma that I did not know how to resolve. I believed myself inferior to everyone, and it grieved me. I believed it my duty to follow the example set by the

most
majority of my acquaintances, an example sanctioned by the approbation of legitimate and prudent mediocrity, yet all the while I felt myself incapable of feeling and acting as they felt and acted. Say one of my comrades performed some feat and he was applauded; I imitated him and I was scolded. People found me always clumsy, always boring. There was always excess in what I did; I was either too wrought up or too cast down; without meaning to, I showed everything that passed in my heart, and sometimes storms were passing through it. In vain I tried to imitate

G the gentle gaiety, the serene and even temper, that I saw in the faces of my companions and found so worthy of admiration; all my efforts were useless. I could not restrain the ebb and flow of blood in my arteries, and that ebb and flow left its mark upon my physiognomy and upon my harsh and unengaging features; I cried in secret. Finally, a day came (I was eighteen) when I opened my eyes and glimpsed a heaven in my own soul. Suddenly I realized that I had a force within that could serve as a substitute for that noble calm which I had so much admired: | I discovered that the heart holds certain things called feelings; I felt that those feelings were alive and deep within my nature, and that they were soon to make me both slave and master of all that pleases, animates, touches us in this

l'homme est si porté à se flatter. Je ne connais q'une méthode bien sûre   60
— Il faut vivre dans le monde, se comparer avec les autres, se soumettre
à l'épreuve de l'expérience, passer par sa fournaise, dix foix plus ardente
que celle de Nebuchadnezzar et si on en sort sans être transmué dans
le plomb ordinaire de la société, c'est qu'on a dans son esprit quelques   *tr B*
grains de cet or pur qu'on appelle le génie- | Milord, j'ai vécu long-   65
temps avec les autres, sans avoir la pensée de me comparer avec eux:
pendant toute ma première jeunesse la différence qui existait entre moi
et la plupart des personnes qui m'entouraient, était pour moi une énigme
embarrassante que je ne savais pas résoudre je me croyais inférieur à
tous et je m'en chagrinais Je croyais de mon devoir de suivre l'exemple   70
que me donnait la majorité des mes connaissances, exemple sanctionné
par l'approbation de la médiocrité prudente et légitime et cependant je me
sentais incapable de sentir et d'agir comme sentait et agissait cette
majorité. Tel de mes camarades fit une action et il était applaudi, moi
je l'imitai et j'étais grondé; on me trouvait toujours maladroit, toujours   75
ennyeux. Il y avait toujours de la superfluité en ce que je faisais; j'étais
ou trop ému ou trop abattu; sans vouloir je laissais voir tout ce qui se
passait dans mon coeur et il y passait quelquefois des orages: en vain
j'essayais d'imiter la douce gaieté, l'humeur sereine et égale que je   *B*
voyais sur les figures de mes compagnons et que je trouvais si digne   80
d'admiration; tous mes efforts étaient inutiles; je ne pouvais pas mettre
un frein au flux et reflux du sang dans mes artères et ce flux et reflux se
marquaient toujours sur ma physionomie et sur mes traits durs et peu
attrayants; je pleurais en secret. Enfin, un jour arriva (j'avais dix-huit
ans) quand j'ouvris les yeux et entrevis un ciel dans mon propre âme.   85
Tout à coup je m'aperçus que j'avais une force intérieure qui pourrais
me servir de substitut pour ce noble calme que j'avais tant admiré: | je
découvris que le coeur contient certaines choses qu'on appelle les sentiments je sentis que ces sentiments étaient vifs et profonds dans ma

glorious Creation; slave, because I was subjugated by it to the point of prostration, master because I knew how to draw inexpressible delight from it at will. I had loved society, and society had coldly rejected me; now I loved Nature, and she sweetly unveiled her face to me and let me

G imbibe the calm of happiness in the contemplation of her divine features. I thought I no longer needed mankind; I had found friends in the desert and in the forest. The simplest things gave me genuine pleasure. It took no more than an old oak with a mossy trunk, with twisted branches, than a bubbling spring bordered with wild flowers, than the ivy-covered ruins of a tower bristling with brambles and thorns, to throw me into the most

G exquisite transports of the soul. I became a painter and a dreamer.

At twenty-one my dreams dissipated. I do not know what voice it was that cried in my ear, "Rouse yourself! leave your world of phantoms, enter the real world, look for Work, confront Experience, struggle and conquer!" I arose, I wrenched myself away from that solitude, those dreams that I loved, I left my country and went abroad.

When I disembarked on the shores of Italy a light seemed to fall upon my future; I saw it full of uncertainty but also full of hope. It stretched before me like a large and uncultivated field. I knew that wheat was not sprouting in it yet, but already I was dreaming of the harvest. I lacked neither courage nor fortitude; immediately I set to work. Sometimes, it is true, despair overwhelmed me for an instant, ^for when I saw the works of the great masters of my art I felt myself only too contemptible; but the fever of emulation came to drive away that momentary prostration and ^in from that deep consciousness of inferiority, I derived new energy for work; there was born in me a fixed resolution: "I will do all, suffer all, in order to win all." And so I suffered much in Florence, in Venice, and in Rome, and in those places I won what I wished to possess: an intimate

nature | et que bientôt ils allaient me rendre à la fois esclave et seigneur   90

de tout ce qui plait, qui anime, qui touche dans cette belle Création;

esclave, parceque j'en était subjugué jusqu'à la prostration, | seigneur

parceque je savais en tirer à volonté des délices inexprimables — J'avais

aimé la société et la société m'avait froidement repoussé, | maintenant

j'aimais la Nature, et elle me dévoila son front avec douceur et me laissa   *B*   95

puiser le calme du bonheur dans la contemplation de ses divins traits. Je

croyais n'avoir plus besoin de l'homme; j'avais trouvé des amis dans le

desert et dans la forêt — les choses les plus simples me rendaient des

jouissances réelles — il ne fallait qu'un vieux chêne au tronc mousseux,

aux branches tordues, qu'une source d'eau vivante bordée de fleurs   100

sauvages, qu'une tourelle en ruines drapée de lierre, herissée de ronces   *B*

et d'epines, pour jeter les plus doux transports dans mon âme. Je devin<u>t</u>ˢ

peintre et rêveur.

   À vingt et un ans mes rêves se dissipèrent — je ne sais pas quelle

voix me cria à l'oreille — "Eveille-toi! quitte ton monde de fantômes,   105

entre dans le monde réel — cherche le Travail, confronte l'Ex<u>péri</u>ence

lutte et sois vainqueur!" Je me levai, je m'arrachai à cette solitude, à

ces rêves que j'aimais, je quittai mon pays et je passai chez l'étranger.

   Quand je débarquai sur les côtes de l'Italie une <u>lumière</u> semblait

tomber sur mon avenir; je le vis plein d'incertitude mais aussi p<u>l</u>ein^[?]   110

d'espérance. Il s'étendait devant moi comme un champ large et inculte

— je savais que le blé n'y germait pas encore et déjà je rêvais la moisson.

Je ne manquais ni˄ courage ni˄ for<u>titu</u>de, aussitôt je me mis à travailler,

quelquefois il est vrai le désespoir m'accablait un instant˄quand je voyais

les oeuvres des grands maîtres de mon art je me <u>sentis trop</u> méprisable;   115

mais la fièvre de l'emulation vint chasser cet abattement momentané et

<u>de</u> cette conscience profonde d'infériorité, je puisais de nouvelles forces

pour le travail — il naquit en moi une resolution fixe — "je veux tout

faire, tout souffrir pour tout gagner " Aussi j'ai beaucoup souffert à

knowledge of all the technical mysteries of Painting, a taste cultivated in accord with the rules of art. As for natural genius, neither Titian nor Raphael nor Michelangelo would have known how to give me that which comes from God alone; the little I have, I possess from my Creator, and within my soul I carefully guard that one drop of the river of life which Mercy has poured out to sweeten so much bitterness: I believe I make good use of it in employing it to add something to the pure pleasures of my fellow men.

Milord, it is to put myself in a position to exercise that faculty that I entreat your help; I could begin my career alone, but then I would still have to work for many years in obscurity and indigence. I know that in the long run true merit always triumphs, but if power does not offer a helping hand, the day of success can be a long time in coming. Sometimes, indeed, death precedes victory, and what is the good of throwing laurels on a grave?

Milord, excuse me if this letter seems long to you. I did not think to count the lines; I thought only of speaking to you sincerely.

Milord, I am

Your obedient servant,

George Howard

Florence à Venise et à Rome et j'y ai gagné ce que je désirais posséder; 120
une connaissance intime de tous les mystères mécaniques de la Peinture,
un gout cultivé selon les règles de l'art. Quant au génie naturel, ni
Titian ni Raffaelle ni Michel-Ange n'aurait su me donner ce qui vient de
Dieu seul; le peu que j'ai, je le tiens de mon Créateur et je garde
précieusement dans mon âme cette seule goutte de la rivière de la vie que 125
la Miséricorde y a versée pour adoucir tant de fiel: je crois en faire bon
usage en l'employant pour ajouter quelquechose aux plaisirs purs de mes
semblables.

Milord c'est pour me mettre en état d'exercer cette faculté que je
réclame votre aide; je pourrais commencer ma carrière seul, mais alors, 130
je dois encore travailler plusieurs années dans l'obscurité et dans la
misère. Je sais qu'à la longue le vrai mérite triomphe toujours, mais, si
le pouvoir ne lui tend pas la main le jour de succès peut tarder longtemps
à venir. Quelquefois même la mort dévance la victoire, et à quoi bon
jeter des lauriers sur un tombeau? 135

Milord pardon si cette lettre vous parait longue — je n'ai pas pensé
à compter les lignes, j'ai pensé seulement à vous parler sincèrement.

Milord je suis

Votre serviteur obéissant

George Howard

Comments[1]

This is apparently the last of Charlotte's devoirs, aside from her revision of "Athens." She wrote it shortly after she had tried to quit the pensionnat and Heger had talked her out of leaving.[2] That it represents an urgent bid for his attention, as Lyndall Gordon claims, is more than likely.[3] But whatever her hope of reviving their dialogue, his lightly penciled comments suggest no reciprocity beyond a professional concern with her French and acquiescence in her painter's lofty sentiments. Nonetheless, the devoir provides substantial clues to Charlotte's uses of her Brussels experience and to her growth as a writer.

The first clue is implicit in the title, which establishes a context that recurs throughout her fiction: the relationship between a dependent and a man with power, a young impoverished person and a master. This struggling artist ostensibly writes to solicit the aid of a patron. However, of the manuscript's eleven pages, little more than two address the "Great Lord" directly, and even in those passages, the writer primarily defends his own position and attitude. He dispenses with the customary pleas and apologies; he praises the baron as an intellectual equal and as a man whose superior virtues he is qualified and ready to appreciate. As for his benefactor's rank and riches, he regards them with the self-possession, verging on defiance, that later marks Jane Eyre and William Crimsworth. (The artist's statement, "Respect for myself, a feeling born of independence and integrity," anticipates Jane's response to temptation, "The more solitary, the more friendless, the more unsustained I am, the more I will respect myself.")[4]

In his confident stance, there may also be echoes of the letters Branwell wrote to the editor of *Blackwell's* when, at eighteen, he attempted to contribute: "Now, sir, to you I appear writing with conceited assurance but *I am not*; for I know myself so far as to believe in my own originality. . . . In letters previous to this I have perhaps spoken too openly respecting the extent of my powers. But I did so because I determined to say what I believed."[5] But even if the tone of those letters came back to Charlotte, Branwell is no model for her artist. This painter understands what he must go through to succeed. He is already marked as a survivor.

As the letter progresses, it increasingly reveals the pervasive concerns of Charlotte's fiction. The narrator has long been accustomed to emotional and physical privation. He has always been conscious of his difference from others, though in childhood he found that difference baffling. Self-centered in his suffering, yet gifted and perceptive, he tries to hide his feelings and conform to his society, until he comes to appreciate the value of a singular and independent spirit.

Yet there are also indications that the fictional author differs from the woman who created him. Charlotte Brontë, like her painter, was torn by conflicting moods. But she conscientiously resisted the desire to become "both slave and master of all that pleases, animates, touches us in this glorious Creation. . . ." That she struggled to govern her unruly impulses is evident from her actual letters. "I have some qualities that make me very miserable," she wrote to Ellen Nussey in 1836, "some feelings that you can have no participation in—that few very few people in the world can at all understand I don't pride myself on these peculiarities, I strive to conceal and suppress them as much as I can. But they burst out sometimes and then . . . I hate myself for days afterwards."[6] As a writer too she attempted to avoid the extremes that fascinate her painter. If in her fantasies she still recurred to Angria, she did not forget her earlier promise to quit its "burning clime" for cooler regions.[7]

Nonetheless her style, like her subject, is Romantic, recalling the stories in her Angrian cycle rather than the work of her maturity. In fact, the surname of her author, "Howard," is the pseudonym for Haworth in "My Angria and the Angrians," a manuscript of 1834.[8] The themes too derive from a Romantic sensibility: the primacy of feeling, the youth alone and set apart, the solace Nature offers, the exquisite charm of ruins. Heger's frequent "G's" (for "Good") reward that sensibility, which Charlotte would have counted on his sharing. But she also knew where to set its limits. There is no Romantic challenge to religious orthodoxy and certainly no hint of sexual license. This painter wants to create a "pure" art that will benefit his fellow creatures.

In this, and above all in his attitude toward genius, he reflects the lessons Charlotte learned in Brussels. His program implicitly follows the advice that Heger gave her in "The Fall of the Leaves." Possessing some "few grains of that pure gold . . . called Genius," he dedicates himself not only to refining them but also to developing his skills and tastes through study, as Charlotte herself sought to do. Before she went abroad, she had told Henry Nussey, ". . . I am now twenty-four approaching twenty-five. . . . At this age it is time that the imagination should be pruned and trimmed—that the judgment should be cultivated—and a *few* at least, of the countless illusions of early youth should be cleared away."[9] Life in the pensionnat had certainly helped to clear away some subsequent illusions. "—I am tired of being amongst foreigners it is a dreary life—especially as there is only one person in this house worthy of being liked," she confessed three days before she wrote this devoir.[10]

It takes little genius to deduce the parallels between the real and fictional relationship. As George Howard seeks to move the "Great Lord" by exposing his feelings, his hopes, and his character, so Charlotte Brontë seeks to move Heger by implying her sufferings as a foreigner and outcast, as well as her unshakable resolve. She did not succeed in re-creating the terms or the tone of their earlier relations, and of course such re-creation was impossible. But by channeling her aspirations into this assignment she exerts control over desire and privation, a control that she would strengthen as a novelist.

Appendix
List of Manuscript Locations

L'Amour Filial Filial Love (EB)
  BPM, Bonnell Collection 130

Anne Askew: Imitation Anne Askew: Imitation (CB)
  Huntington Library, HM 2560

Athènes sauvée par la Poësie Athens Saved by Poetry (October) (CB)
  BPM, Bonnell Collection 120

Athènes sauvée par la Poësie Athens Saved by Poetry (December) (CB)
  Pierpont Morgan Library, Bonnell Collection

Le But de la Vie The Aim of Life (CB)
  New York Public Library, Berg Collection

Le Chat The Cat (EB)
  New York Public Library, Berg Collection

La Chenille The Caterpillar (CB)
  Heger Family

La Chute des Feuilles The Fall of the Leaves (CB)
  Heger Family (photocopy in BPM)

Dictées of La Pauvre Fille The Poor Girl; *Prière du Soir à bord d'u[n]*
vaisseau Evening Prayer on Board a Ship; *Eudore* Eudorus; *Mirabeau*
à la Tribune Mirabeau on the Tribune; *Prise de Jerusalem par les*
croisés Capture of Jerusalem by the Crusaders; and *La chute des*

Feuilles The Fall of the Leaves (CB)
> BPM, Bonnell Collection 115 (this notebook contains twenty-one dictées; for a complete listing, see Alexander, *Bibliography,* 182)

Imitation: Portrait de Pierre L'Hermite Imitation: Portrait of Peter the Hermit (CB-Heger)
> John Rylands University Library, Manchester, JRULM.Eng.ms.EL fB 91/26

L'Immensité de Dieu The Immensity of God (CB)
> University of Leeds, Brotherton Collection

La jeune Fille malade The Sick Young Girl (CB)
> Princeton University, Parrish Collection

La Justice humaine Human Justice (CB)
> BPM, Bonnell Collection 121

Lettre (Ma chère Jane) Letter (My dear Jane) (CB)
> BPM, Bonnell Collection 122

Lettre (Ma chère Maman) Letter (My Dear Mama) (EB)
> Heger Family

Lettre (Madame) Letter (Madam) (EB)
> BPM

Lettre d'invitation à un Ecclésiastique Letter of Invitation to an Ecclesiastic (CB)
> John Rylands University Library, Manchester, JRULM.Eng.ms.400

Lettre d'un frère à un frère Letter from one brother to another (EB)
> Harry Ransom Humanities Research Center, University of Texas, Austin

Lettre d'un pauvre Peintre à un grand Seigneur Letter from a Poor Painter to a Great Lord (CB)
> New York Public Library, Berg Collection

La Mort de Moïse The Death of Moses (CB)
> Heger Family

La Mort de Napoléon The Death of Napoleon (CB)
> BPM 20

Notes sur la Mort de Moïse Notes on the Death of Moses (CB)
> BPM, Bonnell Collection 124(3)

Sur la mort de Napoléon On the Death of Napoleon (CB)
> John Rylands University Library, Manchester, JRULM.Eng.ms. fB 91/27

Le Nid The Nest (CB)
   Berg Collection, New York Public Library

Le Palais de la Mort The Palace of Death (EB)
   BPM 106

Le Palais de la Mort The Palace of Death (CB)
   BPM 21

Le Papillon The Butterfly (EB)
   Berg Collection, New York Public Library

Plaidoyer pour les chats Plea for Cats; *Les deux chiens* The Two Dogs
(CB fragments in a notebook entitled "Devoir")
   Brotherton Collection, University of Leeds

Portrait: Harold la veille de la Bataille de Hastings Portrait: Harold on
the Eve of the Battle of Hastings (EB-Heger)
   John Rylands University Library, Manchester, JRULM.Eng.ms.EL
   fB 91/28

Portrait: Le Roi Harold avant la Bataille de Hastings Portrait: King
Harold before the Battle of Hastings (EB)
   BPM, Bonnell Collection 129

Portrait: Pierre l'Hermite Portrait: Peter the Hermit (CB)
   British Library, Ashley MS 2444

La Prière du Soir dans un camp Evening Prayer in a Camp (CB)
   Princeton University, Parrish Collection

Le Siège d'Oudenarde The Siege of Oudenarde (EB)
   Swarthmore College, Friends Historical Society

Le siège d'Oudenarde The Siege of Oudenarde (CB)
   Swarthmore College, Friends Historical Society

Sacrifice d'une veuve Indienne Sacrifice of an Indian Widow (CB)
   BPM 19

Two of Charlotte's devoirs can no longer be located: "Lettre d'un Missionaire, Sierra-Leone, Afrique" and "L'Ingratitude." C. W. Hatfield cites them in "The Early Manuscripts of Charlotte Brontë: A Bibliography (*BST* 6 [1924]: 234), and Gaskell talks about the first: "Touched as Charlotte was by the letter of St. Ignatius [of Antioch, to the Roman Christians] . . ., she claimed equal self-devotion, and from as high a motive, for some of the missionaries of the English Church sent out to toil and to perish on the poisonous African coast, and wrote as an 'imitation' 'Lettre d'un Missionaire, Sierra-Leone, Afrique' (11.239)." There is also an exercise by Charlotte in German—a letter, "Meine liebe Freundinn"—in the Berg Collection, New York Public Library. It is reprinted in *Lets.* 322–23.

Notes

Textual Notes explain allusions in the devoirs and provide cross-references to other Brontë sources. Editorial Notes refer to features of the manuscripts that require explanation or could not be transcribed. Textual Notes are keyed to line numbers in the English text; Editorial Notes to numbers in the French text. In the Textual Notes, where the numbering on facing pages differs, the French line number(s) follow the English in parentheses; when only the French text is under discussion, the line number is followed by an *F.* In the Editorial Notes, on the rare occasions when an English line is referenced, the number is followed by an *E.* All references to and quotations from CB's letters, unless otherwise noted, are from *Lets.,* but without the signs of deletion and addition that Margaret Smith includes. All references to Gaskell, unless otherwise noted, are to vol. 1. Unless another translator is credited, all translations are mine.

Abbreviations and Editions of Sources Commonly Cited
All biblical references are to the King James Version.

BPM   The Brontë Parsonage Museum
BLFC   Brontë family, *The Brontës: Their Lives, Friendships, and Correspondence,* ed. Thomas J. Wise and John Alexander Symington, 4 vols., Shakespeare Head edition (Oxford: Basil Blackwell, 1932)

BST	*Transactions of the Brontë Society*
CBEW	Charlotte Brontë, *An Edition of The Early Writings of Charlotte Brontë,* ed. Christine Alexander, vol. 1, *1826–1832* (Oxford: Basil Blackwell, 1987); vol. 2, pt. 1, *1833–1834,* and pt. 2, *1834–1835* (1991)
EW	Christine Alexander. *The Early Writings of Charlotte Brontë* (Oxford: Basil Blackwell, 1983)
CB Poems	Charlotte Brontë, *The Poems of Charlotte Brontë: A New Text and Commentary,* ed. Victor A. Neufeldt (New York: Garland, 1985)
DNB	*Dictionary of National Biography.* Oxford: Oxford UP, 1917
EB Poems	Emily Jane Brontë. *The Complete Poems,* ed. Janet Gezari (Harmondsworth, U.K.: Penguin, 1992)
5 Novs.	Charlotte Brontë, *Five Novelettes,* ed. Winifred Gérin (London: Folio Press, 1971)
Gaskell	Elizabeth Gaskell, *The Life of Charlotte Brontë,* ed. Alan Shelston (Harmondsworth, U.K.: Penguin, 1975). Cited by chapter and page.
Gérin CB	Winifred Gérin, *Charlotte Brontë: The Evolution of Genius* (Oxford: Oxford UP, 1967)
Gérin EB	Winifred Gérin, *Emily Brontë* (Oxford: Oxford UP, 1972)
JE	Charlotte Brontë, *Jane Eyre,* ed. Jane Jack and Margaret Smith (Oxford: Clarendon, 1969)
JE Norton	Charlotte Brontë, *Jane Eyre*, 2d ed., ed. Richard J. Dunn, Norton Critical Editions (New York: Norton, 1987)
Lets.	Charlotte Brontë, *The Letters of Charlotte Brontë, with a Selection of Letters by Family and Friends,* ed. Margaret Smith, vol. 1, *1829–1847* (Oxford: Clarendon, 1995)
Misc.	Charlotte and Patrick Brontë, *The Miscellaneous and Unpublished Writings of Charlotte and Patrick Branwell Brontë,* ed. Thomas J. Wise and John Alexander Symington, 2 vols., Shakespeare Head edition (Oxford: Basil Blackwell, 1936 and 1938)
WH	Emily Brontë, *Wuthering Heights,* ed. Hilda Marsden and Ian Jack (Oxford: Clarendon, 1976)
WH Norton	Emily Brontë, *Wuthering Heights*, 3d ed., ed. William M. Sale, Jr., and Richard J. Dunn, Norton Critical Editions (New York: Norton, 1990)

Editions of the Brontës' Novels Used in This Book

CHARLOTTE BRONTË

Jane Eyre, ed. Jane Jack and Margaret Smith (Oxford: Clarendon, 1969)
Jane Eyre, 2d ed., ed. Richard J. Dunn, Norton Critical Editions (New York: Norton, 1987). Cited as *JE* Norton.

The Professor, ed. Margaret Smith and Herbert Rosengarten (Oxford: Clarendon, 1987). Cited by chapter and page.

Shirley, ed. Herbert Rosengarten and Margaret Smith (Oxford: Clarendon, 1979)

Villette, ed. Herbert Rosengarten and Margaret Smith (Oxford: Clarendon, 1984). Cited by chapter and page.

EMILY BRONTË

Wuthering Heights, ed. Hilda Marsden and Ian Jack (Oxford: Clarendon, 1976). Cited as *WH.*

Wuthering Heights, 3d ed., ed. William M. Sale, Jr., and Richard J. Dunn, Norton Critical Editions (New York: Norton, 1990). Cited as *WH* Norton.

Preface

1. Gaskell, 11.225.

2. Janet Harper, a later student at the pensionnat, reports that Heger "had quantities of Charlotte's and Emily's French exercises," one of which he gave to her (463). He also gave some to Marion Douglas, which were "upon no account to get into print"; see Weir, "New Brontë Material Comes to Light," 250–51; and "The Hegers and a Yorkshire Family," 32.

3. The most complete account of Thomas J. Wise's notorious dispersal of Brontë manuscripts appears in *CB Poems,* xxii–xxvii; see also Winnifrith, 15–18. Because the devoirs had less market value, they escaped massive mutilation, though I have found some signs of tampering.

4. This count is based on my inspection of devoirs listed in Alexander, *A Bibliography of the Manuscripts of Charlotte Brontë,* 179–91; and Rosenbaum and White, pt. 1, 75–77, 104–5.

5. Records of previous publication can be found in the bibliographies listed in n. 4, above. Studies of several devoirs by CB include Duthie, *Foreign Vision,* ch. 2 and passim; Lonoff, "Charlotte Brontë's Belgian Essays," 387–409; and the analytic survey of the Brussels period appearing in chs. 14 and 15 of Barker. Lyndall Gordon alludes to the last two devoirs, 109–13. Augustin-Lewis Wells provides a French perspective, 86–99, but his claims are not always accurate. Studies of single devoirs include Macdonald, "The Brontës at Brussels," 277–91, which describes Heger's classes and includes translated parts of "La Chute des Feuilles"; Spielmann, "An Early Essay by Charlotte Brontë," 236–46, which reviews Heger's methods and briefly remarks on his corrections of "La Chute des Feuilles"; Dessner, 213–18, which provides scholarly and critical analysis of "Le Nid" and also discusses Heger's methods; and Lonoff, "On the Struggles," 373–82, which considers "Lettre d'un pauvre Peintre . . ." from a critical and biographical perspective.

EB's devoirs and experience in Brussels have been surveyed or considered by Benvenuto, 75–84; Chitham, 144–48; Davies, 46–52, 104–9, 182–83, and 248–51; Duthie (see citation above); Gérin *EB,* 124–26 and appendix A; Hewish, 61–71; Lane, "The Mysterious Genius," 139–51; Musselwhite, ch. 4; Ratchford, introduction and notes to E. Brontë, *Five Essays Written in French;* and Spark, in Spark and Stanford, 56–65. On "Le Palais de la Mort," see Lane, "The Palace of Death," 803–4 and Maxwell, 139–40. On "Le Papillon," see Homans, 141–43; Miller, ch. 4; and Willson, 22–25. On "Lettre (Ma chère Maman)," see Homans, 149–150 and Wells, 92–94. On connections between her devoirs and her drawing, see Alexander and Sellars, 117, 123, 125–27.

6. Gérin alludes to three devoirs in her chapter on EB in Brussels, but only to make the point that EB's "philosophical reflections" would have been anomalous there (*EB,* 126).

7. A few early scholars acknowledge Heger's contributions. In her prefaces to *The Life and Works of The Sisters Brontë,* Mary A. Ward refers in several places to the crucial influence of Heger's classes and French Romanticism. Clement K. Shorter calls Brussels "the turning-point of Charlotte's career" and adds that "M. Héger kindled her intellectual impulses" (71). Esther Alice Chadwick claims, "Of the four children of Patrick Brontë, all of whom became authors, the only two who have left enduring literature are Charlotte and Emily, the two sisters who went to the Rue d'Isabelle and received the guidance and help of the Belgian professor . . ." ("A Gift," 861). But these early estimates did not lead to close examination of the devoirs. Wise and Symington must have seen some but discount them as literary texts: "During the Brussels experiences (1842–1843) Charlotte would seem to have put all literary effort on one side" (*BLFC* 1:81). Gérin writes in 1971—the year in which she published five of EB's devoirs— "From 1840 to 1844, there are no preserved manuscripts to attest to any literary activity" (*5 Novs.,* 19); John Maynard analyzes CB's feelings for Heger and the insights she expresses in her letters and poems, but he too ignores the devoirs as a source of psychological and literary development.

Introduction

1. See Ratchford, *The Brontës' Web of Childhood,* ch. 26. As Alexander says, these claims are "extravagant" (*EW,* 4), but she herself links the juvenilia to the novels (see *EW,* ch. 28 through conclusion), challenging Winnifrith's earlier suggestion that such inferences are best left alone (17–18). See also Gérin's introduction, *5 Novs.,* 21–22; and Maynard, ch. 3 and 72–73.

2. The now-standard account is in Gérin *CB,* chs. 14, 15, and appendix A. For later and more psychoanalytic readings, see Moglen, 66–78; Maynard, 18–26; and Fraser, 182–95.

3. Alexander, *Bibliography,* xviii.

4. A note in the school's admissions register suggests her intellectual position then and probably beyond: "Altogether clever of her age but knows nothing systematically" (Barker, 129).

5. See the list of readings she recommended to Ellen Nussey, *Lets.*, 130–31; Alexander on early influences, *EW,* 18–24; and Barker, 145–50.

6. See "The Enfant," *CBEW* 1:34–36. Duthie speculates that CB became attracted to French when Branwell began to be taught Greek and Latin: "Charlotte must have admired and perhaps envied her brother's newly acquired classical knowledge. It may well have awakened in her the ambition to excel in her turn in a modern language" (*Foreign Vision,* 6).

7. See Duthie, "Charlotte Brontë's Translation," 347–51.

8. The prize was a New Testament in French, inscribed to her by the Misses Wooler on December 14, 1831 (Barker, 174).

9. Nussey, 62. Hester Chapone's *Letters on the Improvement of the Mind,* a book on which Miss Wooler based her curriculum, firmly recommends the study of French, which "cannot be dispensed with in the education of a gentlewoman" (136). CB entered Roe Head with her own copy of Tocquot's *New and Easy Guide to the Pronunciation and Spelling of French* (Barker, 174).

10. See, for example, the installments of "A Frenchman's Journal" in the *Second Series of the Young Men's Magazines* (*CBEW* 1); *Lets.*, 118–19; and "Caroline Vernon" (*5 Novs.*, 319–24).

11. See *Lets.*, 165–71; and C. W. Hatfield, "Charlotte Brontë and Hartley Coleridge, 1840," *BST* 10 (1940): 15–16.

12. "*[Le] seul maître que j'ai jamais eu*" (*Lets.*, 356).

13. Gaskell reports that at Roe Head School CB had to read Hugo Blair's *Lectures on Rhetoric and Belles Lettres* (6.133 and 576 n. 10). Later, as a teacher there, she apparently corrected themes and exercises by her students (see "Well, here I am at Roe Head," Pierpont Morgan Library MS, ed. Christine Alexander, reprinted in *JE* Norton, 410; previously published in *Misc.* 2:123). But there is no record of what she read in Blair's book and no allusion in the extant correspondence to essays she herself may have written.

14. Dessner, 215. Wemyss Reid was the earliest critic to say that her Belgian experience was crucial, but he refers more to its emotional than to its intellectual effects (58). Shorter makes the most extravagant claim: "Charlotte Brontë, despite her genius, could not, one may believe, have 'arrived' had she not met M. Héger. She went to Brussels full of the crude ambitions, the semi-literary impulses that are so common on the fringe of the writing world. She left Brussels a woman of genuine cultivation, of educated tastes, armed with just the equipment that was to enable her to write . . ." (72).

15. *Lets.*, 262–63.

16. *Lets.*, 272. CB's allusion, five days later, to "the subject we both have considerably at heart" (273) also hints that she was working to sell EB on Brussels.

17. *Lets.*, 407–8.

18. E. and A. Brontë, *The Poems of Emily Jane Brontë and Anne*

Brontë, xxii–xxiii; extract in "Extract from the Prefatory Note to "Selections from Poems by Ellis Bell," *WH,* 446.

19. *Lets.,* 268 (CB to Aunt Branwell).

20. *EB Poems* lists three poems from this period, the first completed in Brussels and the second two completed in Haworth: "H.A. and A.S.: 'In the same place, when Nature wore,'" May 17, 1842 (138–39); "Written in Aspin Castle: 'How do I love on summer nights,'" August 20, 1842–February 6, 1843 (139–42); and "Self-Interrogation: 'The evening passes fast away,'" October 23, 1842–February 6, 1843 (23–24). See also Gezari's notes, 268–69 and 236.

21. *EB Poems,* 23, lines 5–8 and 24, line 40. See also Hewish, 70.

22. According to Alexander and Sellars, "her progress in drawing is evident in the two surviving works made while she was in Brussels" (116); for more on her increasing skill and Heger's influence, see 116–21.

23. *BLFC* 1:281 (Heger's letter to Patrick Brontë, as translated); see *Lets.,* 300 and 299, for the French. This often-published letter is not in Heger's handwriting; its scribe remains unidentified.

24. The Hegers' family histories, the details of their meeting, and the founding of the Pensionnat Heger are described in Gaskell, ch. 11; Gérin *CB,* ch. 13; Fraser, ch. 9; and other books.

25. Gaskell, 11.224. Gérin adds that the Brontës were charged the regular fee for boarders—650 francs, or 26 pounds—but the fees for extras were waived (Gérin *CB,* 195).

26. *BLFC* 1:281, as translated; see *Lets.,* 300 and 298, for the French.

27. *BLFC* 1:280, as translated; see *Lets.,* 300 and 298, for the French.

28. "Ce talent . . . avait pour principe un don précieux, une sorte de magnétisme intellectuel à l'aide duquel le professeur s'introduisait dans l'esprit de l'élève, excitant sa curiosité, la tenant incessamment en éveil . . ." (*L'Indépendance belge,* May 9, 1896; quoted in French in Chadwick, *Footsteps,* 220–21).

29. "Le nombre des enfants qui fréquentent les écoles, en Belgique, est d'*un* sur *onze* habitants" (Chadwick, "A Gift," 851). See also Gaskell, 11.229. The letter Gaskell quotes, "by a French lady resident in Brussels," does not indicate when Heger undertook his philanthropic work. But Lucy Snowe's account of M. Paul in *Villette* suggests that Heger gave some time to Catholic charity while CB was in Belgium.

30. Chadwick, *Footsteps,* 215.

31. *The Secret of Charlotte Brontë,* 217–18.

32. Gaskell, 11.231.

33. Gaskell, 11.239.

34. BPM, Bonnell 115. Heger may also have dictated extracts in a manuscript now in the Brotherton Collection, but these cannot be positively attributed, because CB gives no information on their sources and the pages have been torn from a notebook.

35. Gaskell, 11.233; and *Lets.,* 285.

36. Macdonald claims he taught them by the system he generally followed in his upper-level literary composition classes. Her description of that system accords with Gaskell's: "He would read aloud some eloquent, pathetic, or amusing passage from a classical French author. He would then analyse this passage, and signalise its beauties or criticise its defects. Afterwards he would either himself suggest, or allow his pupils to select, a subject for composition, attuned to the same key . . .; but of a sufficiently different character to make anything resembling unintelligent imitation impossible" ("The Brontës at Brussels," 283).

37. Gaskell, 11.234. Heger's great-grandson Paul Pechère, describes Heger's attitude similarly; see "A Plaque Is Unveiled in Brussels . . .," *BST* 17 (1980): 372–74. Macdonald too corroborates this account; see n. 36, above.

38. *Lets.,* 283–84.

39. See Chadwick, *Footsteps,* 257; Macdonald, *Secret,* 188; and Harper, 462–63.

40. *Lets.,* 284.

41. Harper, 463.

42. Louise de Bassompierre, quoted in "Two Brussels School-fellows," 26. The text in *BST* is corrupt, however, so I have translated directly from the letter, which is in the Brotherton Collection, Leeds.

43. On the tensions in CB's relations with both EB and Anne, see Angeline Goreau's persuasive introduction to Anne's *Agnes Grey,* 13–36. See also Muriel Spark on CB as the manager of her sisters' reputations, in Spark and Stanford, 56.

44. *Lets.,* 284–85 (or Gaskell, 11.232–33).

45. *BLFC* 2:189.

46. Gaskell, 11.231.

47. Heger, 10–11.

48. "Editor's Preface," *WH,* 443.

49. Gaskell, 11.230–31.

50. Gaskell, 11.234. She took this phrase directly from the letter that Heger mailed her with two devoirs he had copied.

51. *Secret,* 175. Confirmation of Heger's penchant for maxims is provided in one of his letters to another student; see Weir, "New Brontë Material," 385.

52. "Esprit de Sagesse, conduisez-nous: / Esprit de Vérité, enseignez-nous: / Esprit de Charité, vivifiez-nous: / Esprit de Prudence, préservez-nous: / Esprit de Force, défendez-nous: / Esprit de Justice, éclairez-nous: / Esprit Consolateur, apaisez-nous" (quoted in Macdonald, *Secret,* 219). She adds that she reconfirmed her memories by writing to Heger's daughter Louise.

53. Ibid., 220.

54. *BLFC* 1:92 (or Gaskell, 576 n. 9), quoting Mary Taylor's letter of January 18, 1856.

55. Macdonald, *Secret*, 220. She connects it to a phrase of Voltaire's: "J'admets tous les genres, hors le genre ennuyeux."

56. Of the dictées transcribed in CB's notebook (BPM, Bonnell 115), two, by Bossuet and Massillon, are from the seventeenth century; two, by Buffon and Barthélemy, are eighteenth century; three, by Soumet, Millevoye, and Frayssinous, are by early nineteenth-century authors; one is by the nineteenth-century Romantic historian Michaud; and the rest are by Romantic writers—Chateaubriand, Hugo, Lamartine, Nodier—who were still alive and producing. See also Duthie, *Foreign Vision*, 25–26.

57. *Secret*, 220–21.

58. "Je vois tout à travers le ver[r]e coloré de la comparaison," amended to "Comme vous savez bien j'ai la mauvaise habitude de tout voir [à travers . . .]. Duthie also comments on this connection (*Foreign Vision*, 60).

59. Chapter head, *EW*, 234.

60. "Well, here I am at Roe Head," *JE* Norton, 411; previously published in *Misc.* 2:123.

61. Ibid., 410.

62. *Lets.*, 260.

63. *CBEW* 1:323, 2.1:124.

64. "The Bridal," *CBEW* 1:343.

65. "Caroline Vernon" (1839), *5 Novs.*, 355.

66. *CB Poems*, 165.

67. From devoirs 21 and 24, respectively.

68. *Secret*, 221.

69. As a young man working in Paris, "The only pleasures [Heger] could allow himself were to go to the Comédie Française as a paid *claquer* and to study declamation in this manner at second hand" (Gérin *CB*, 193). As has often been noted, his passion for the theater influenced his teaching.

70. Harper, 462.

71. Gaskell, 11.233.

72. See chs. 5–6. But the Moore brothers, both part-Belgian, seem to have more in common with Heger than with Branwell.

73. Louise de Bassompierre was one student who recalled his reading of their devoirs; she thought EB's were better (Chadwick, *Footsteps*, 228; see also 257). Macdonald interviewed a Mlle. C., a student in CB's English class, who recalls, "it gave offense that Monsieur Heger frequently read aloud her devoirs as an example to others" because she "was considered too old to be put on equal terms" with them ("The Brontës at Brussels," 286).

74. "Biographical Notice," *WH*, 436.

75. Gaskell 2:1.307.

76. Macdonald, *Secret*, 221.

77. Gaskell 2:13.509.

78. Macdonald, *Secret*, 221.

79. On the characteristics of her adult style, see Peters. A study of the links between that style and CB's devoirs remains to be done.

80. Recalled by Laetitia Wheelwright (Chadwick, *Footsteps*, 226). Also see the obituary notice of Fanny Wheelwright, *Hastings and St. Leonards Observer*, March 22, 1913, reproduced in Gérin *CB*, 207.

81. "The Brontës at Brussels," 283.

82. See *Lets.*, 284–85 (or Gaskell, 11.232–33). CB does not use the word "barbarisme" in this letter, which describes Heger's response to a translation, but she says that her use of an English word "nearly plucks the eyes out of his head when he sees it."

83. Devoirs 20 and 21, respectively.

84. Devoir 25.

85. Alexander also states that in correcting CB's devoirs, he "censured her tendency to redundancy and digression" (*EW*, 245).

86. Devoir 28.

87. Devoir 11 (July 31 version).

88. Dessner, 215.

89. "Bien écrire, c'est tout à la fois bien penser, bien sentir, et bien rendre; c'est avoir en même temps de l'esprit, de l'âme et du gout" (*Discours*, 23–24).

90. CB transcribed a dictée, "The Horse," from Buffon's *Natural History* (BPM, Bonnell 115, 38–39). More important, Heger's advice is often analogous to Buffon's and possibly derives from it. Compare them on rules and genius or on the combination of genius and culture that leads to "true eloquence"; see Buffon, *Discours*, 23, 11, and Heger's "observation" on "The Fall of the Leaves."

91. "An Early Essay," 237.

92. See "At first I did attention give" and "I gave, at first, Attention close," *CB Poems*, 274–75 and 333–36.

93. "[A] M'elle Charlotte Brontë, son maitre [*sic*] et ami C. Heger" (inscription on the wrapper of the first of two Prize Day speeches that Heger gave to CB, as reported in an auction notice preserved on the back flyleaf of *Villette*, vol. 3, Special Collections, Margaret Clapp Library, Wellesley College).

94. As reported to me by Heger's great-great-grandson François Fierens, November 1990.

95. Weir, "New Brontë Material," 256–57. The recipient of this undated letter, Meta Mossman, attended the school in the 1880s. See also Madame Heger's letter to Katie Douglas Mossman (253) and Barker's quotations from an unpublished letter by a Mr. Westwood, whose wife's cousin had been at the pensionnat: "He made much of her, & drew her out, & petted her, & won her love" but with "no such fore-gone intention" and "no illicit affection. . . . He was a worshipper of intellect & he worshipped Charlotte Brontë thus far & no further" (419).

96. Gaskell, 11.230.

97. Devoir 12.

98. Harper, 463. Macdonald gives a more prosaic motive: "it was

amongst the traditions of the school that [he] had kept [the] most promising compositions since the commencement of his Professorship, and had already specimens of the style of several generations of his pupils" ("The Brontës at Brussels," 284).

99. "At first I did attention give . . .," *CB Poems,* 274.

100. See Gaskell, 11.324, and the Comments on devoir 10.

101. Duthie, *Foreign Vision,* 7.

102. On the dating of this manuscript, see the Comments to devoir 25.

103. *Lets.,* 317.

104. Ibid.

105. Compare the letter CB wrote to W. S. Williams six years later, after the deaths of EB and Anne: "The faculty of imagination lifted me when I was sinking, three months ago; its active exercise has kept my head above water since; its results cheer me now, for I feel they have enabled me to give pleasure to others [through *Shirley*]. I am thankful to God, who gave me the faculty; and it is for me a part of my religion to defend this gift and to profit by its possession" (*BLFC* 3:24).

106. Beer, 6.

107. See Sue Lonoff, "An Unpublished Memoir by Paul Heger," *BST* 20 (1992): 344–45. Irene Tayler argues that Emanuel also incorporates aspects of James Taylor, an "irritable and despotic little man" who worked for George Smith, impressed CB with his talent, and apparently fell in love with her (203 ff.).

108. *Lets.,* 284 (or Gaskell, 11.232).

109. *Villette,* 28.474.

110. Devoir 9, dictée, lines 25–26.

111. "Imperialist Nostalgia and *Wuthering Heights,*" in *Wuthering Heights,* ed. Linda Peterson (Boston: Bedford, 1992), 440.

112. O! pourquoi n'ai-je pas de mère?
> Pourquoi ne suis-je pas semblable au jeune oiseau
> Dont le nid se balance aux branches de l'ormeau?
>> Rien ne m'appartient sur la terre,
>> Je n'eus pas même de berceau,
> Et je suis un enfant trouvé sur une pierre
>> Devant l'église du hameau.
> (Soumet, "La Pauvre Fille," second verse)

This is the first dictée in BPM, Bonnell 115; the third, "Morning Prayer" ("La Prière du matin") is also sentimental.

113. From "He saw my heart's woe discovered my soul's anguish" (1847), *CB Poems,* 340.

114. *Shirley,* 78 (ch. 5, mod. eds.).

115. On her attitudes toward gender in Brussels, see Lonoff, "Charlotte Brontë's Belgian Essays," 401–4.

116. Weir, "New Brontë Material," 256.

117. Rough draft in possession of François Fierens.

118. *Villette*, 19.287–88.

119. Zoë Heger also had the physical attractions that CB felt she lacked. Macdonald's interview with a student who had taken CB's English class in 1843 drives the contrast home: "At this period, Mlle C. recollects Madame Héger to have been a very pretty woman, and very careful of her personal appearance. . . . Charlotte Brontë's personal appearance was extremely insignificant and even displeasing; and she dressed badly" ("The Brontës at Brussels," 287).

120. "Le cours d'instruction, basé sur la Religion" (*Lets.* 1:252; Chadwick, *Footsteps*, 191).

121. ". . . M. Héger est profondement et ouvertement religieux" (unnamed correspondent in Gaskell, 11.229).

122. Fraser (172 n. 12) credits this account to Duthie, *Foreign Vision*, and Wroot. I have seen it in neither source, but it has come down through Heger's family.

123. See Rabion. CB used the 1841 edition, almost certainly with the same undated title page.

124. The clerical writers are Massillon, a preacher; Father de Fraysinnous; Bossuet, a prelate and sacred writer; and Father Barthélemy. The notebook (BPM, Bonnell 115) is usually listed as having twenty-one entries, but the fifth is a longer version of the second ("Prière du Soir au bord d'un Vaisseau").

125. *Indépendence Belge,* March 9, 1896, quoted in French in Chadwick, *Footsteps*, 220.

126. See *Lets.,* 290 (or Gaskell, 11.240–41); and *Villette* 36.609–12. Paul's declaration of tolerance ends a sequence in which Lucy resists attempts at conversion; though CB writes his words, they accord with other witnesses' accounts of Heger's attitude.

127. *Lets.,* 284 (or Gaskell, 11.232).

128. Gaskell, 11.239.

129. Writing before Alexander's editions, Winnifrith claims that there is "little religion" in CB's early writings (30). Alexander's work refutes that assumption; see *EW,* 18 and "Recent Research," 21.

130. "Elle était nourrie de la Bible" (Gaskell, 11.238).

131. "The New Creation," in Wesley 2:508–9.

132. See Miller, ch. 4; and Comments on "The Butterfly" in this volume.

133. *Vanity Fair*—and *Jane Eyre," Quarterly Review* 84 (December 1848): 173; reprinted in *JE* Norton, 442.

134. *Lets.,* 289 (or Gaskell, 11.240).

135. Hugo, "Moïse sur le Nil" (from *Odes*), in Rabion, 335–38; Lamartine, "Harmonie VIII [Livre Deuxième]. Jehova ou l'Idée de Dieu," in *Harmonies,* 362–63; Chateaubriand, *Moïse: Tragédie en cinq actes en vers* (Paris: Minard, 1983); and Vigny, "Moïse," in *Poèmes,* 11–15.

136. See Comments on devoir 26.

137. Devoir 3.

138. Patrick Brontë shared this conviction that the beauties of nature reveal their Creator; according to Barker, he passed that belief on to his children (59).

139. *Villette*, 31.531–32.

140. *The Professor*, 18.148.

141. Musselwhite, 88–89.

142. Musselwhite draws selectively on Lacan's theory of the child's initiation into the "Symbolic Order"; see 81 and 84.

143. Musselwhite, 94–95.

144. Ibid., 93.

145. Musselwhite, 97. See Gaskell, 11.234 and 239.

146. Musselwhite, 105.

147. See Chronology, n. 10.

148. See "Bibliographical Notice," *WH*, 435–36. This count includes a number of fragments. The poem that CB presumably came across is "The Prisoner (A Fragment)," *EB Poems*, 14–16.

149. "Biographical Notice," *WH*, 437.

150. See n. 18, above.

151. Gaskell, 2:1.307.

152. Davies, 50. See also her discussion of German influences on EB, 49–51.

153. U. C. Knoepflmacher says the source was first cited by a French critic, Montégut, in 1857 (228). Marsden and Jack identify Romer Wilson's *All Alone: The Life and Private History of Emily Jane Brontë* (London: Chatto and Windus, 1928) as the first book to cite this source, adding that EB could have known the story from an essay on Hoffman by Scott (*WH*, 418). MacKay's account is more scholarly; see "Irish Heaths and German Cliffs: A Study of the Foreign Sources of *Wuthering Heights*," *Brigham Young University Studies* 7 (autumn 1965): 28–39. Wells points up numerous parallels between *Wuthering Heights* and another Hoffman story, *The Brigands* (157–66).

154. Gérin *EB*, 145.

155. From "The Poems and Ballads of Schiller. No. I." *Blackwood's* 52 (September 1842): "The Diver, a Ballad" ("Le Plongeur"), 287–90 and "The Knight of Toggenburg" ("Le Chevalier de Taggenburg"), 291–93; from "No. II" (October 1842): "The Alp Hunter" ("Le Chasseur des Alpes"), 446–47 and "The Maiden's Lament" ("La Plainte de la jeune fille"), 447; from "No. IV" (December 1842): "The Indian's Death Song" ("Chant funébre pour l'Indien mort"), 765. CB's translations are in two exercise books, British Library, Ashley MS 160 and BPM, Bonnell 117. In devoir 27, she also alludes to a Schiller poem, "The Veiled Image at Sais," translated in "No. III" of the *Blackwood's* series (November 1842).

156. *JE*, 507 (ch. 34, mod. eds.).

157. See Comments on that devoir.

158. *WH*, 364 (ch. 31, mod. eds.).

159. Spielmann, "The Inner History," 601.

160. Spielmann provides a full account of her motives (ibid., 600–602); the letters themselves, with his translation, are printed in *BLFC* 2:9–14, 17–19, 21–23, and 67–71.

161. *BLFC* 2:12; see also *Lets.,* 357–58 and 355, for the French.

162. *BLFC* 2:23–24; see also *Lets.,* 379 and 378, for the French. Cf. devoir 13.

163. *BLFC* 2:69–70; see also *Lets.,* 435–36 and 433–34, for the French.

164. "J'entends par style, le procédé propre à chaque écrivain, non-seulement pour exprimer, mais pour trouver et disposer ses idées. Le style dépend donc, non pas de la nature du sujet, mais du tempérament, du coeur, de l'esprit, du goût de l'écrivain, le tout forcément modifié par l'influence du siècle et du pays. Voilà le véritable sense du mot de Buffon: le style est l'homme. Le style est ce que l'on nomme, dans les arts, *la manière, le faire,* ce qui donne au peintre et au sculpteur son cachet, ce qui le distingue des autres et constitue son originalité. . . . La première ambition de l'écrivain doit être d'avoir ainsi un style à soi" (A. Baron, *Du Style [extrait d'un ouvrage inédit sur la composition littéraire],* Académie Royale de Belgique, extract from vol. 14, no. 4, of the bulletins, n.d.).

165. See *Charlotte Brontë,* passim. Peters's analysis of *The Professor* (32–34) suggests that CB's style there was still in transition from her pre-Brussels writing.

166. See Margaret Smith's analysis of the manuscript revisions and her comments on textual revisions in her introductions to the Clarendon editions.

167. Joseph Geer, who transcribed a discarded manuscript titled *John Henry* by modern editors, cites the problems posed by "the occurrence of a great many alterations and additions." He adds that they "seem to have been made at the same time that the manuscript was being produced" ("An Unpublished Manuscript by Charlotte Brontë," *BST* 15 [1966]: 21).

168. *Shirley,* 437–38 (ch. 22, mod. eds.).

169. Gaskell, 2:1.307. The other reliable account of CB's procedures, Martineau's comments on the writing of *Jane Eyre,* suggests that she still relied on inspiration but combined it with more reflective methods: "She wrote in little square paper books, held close to her eyes, and (the first copy) in pencil. On she went, writing incessantly for three weeks; by which time she had carried her heroine away from Thornfield, and was herself in a fever, which compelled her to pause. The rest was written with less vehemence, and more anxious care" ("Death of Currer Bell," *Daily News* [London], April 6, 1855, 5, reprinted in *The Brontës: The Critical Heritage,* ed. Miriam Allott [London: Routledge and Kegan Paul, 1974], 303–4).

170. Smith, 192.

171. *BLFC* 3:20.

172. Ibid. 3:21.

173. CB may have taken the title from "Scène des Femmes savantes," an

extract from Molière's *Les Femmes savantes* reprinted in Rabion. In the same chapter of *Shirley* (558–59; ch. 27, mod. eds.), she alludes to several poems in that anthology.

174. "Son ardeur s'est changée en force, ou plutôt, puisque cette force était en quelque façon dans cette ardeur, elle s'est réglée. Remarquez: elle n'est pas détruite elle se règle" (BPM, Bonnell 115). Two other pieces that CB read in Brussels consider the issue of freedom and control through the example of a horse: "Le Cheval," by Buffon, transcribed in the same notebook, and "L'Idole," by Barbier, which she translated with the title "Napoleon" (*CB Poems*, 355–56).

175. *BLFC* 2:201.

176. See *Villette*, ch. 35, and Comments on "Human Justice."

177. *The Professor*, 16.136–37.

178. *JE*, 152–55 (ch. 13, mod. eds.).

179. *Shirley*, 552 (ch. 27, mod. eds.).

Chronology

My dating of the devoirs and cahiers is based on examination of the manuscripts or, where they have disappeared, on Alexander's bibliography. Wherever the dating is provisional, I explain it in the Comments on the devoir.

1. Only one of the exercise books is dated (April 1), and according to the BPM records, it is not the first.

2. See Alexander and Sellars, 258–59; one of the drawings, "Watermill," is inscribed "A token of affection and respect to Madame Heger from one of her pupils."

3. On this exhibit, see Charlier, 386–90.

4. So described by CB in a letter of late June 1843 to Ellen Nussey; Mme Heger's letter has not survived.

5. Letter to Ellen Nussey, October 14, 1846, *Lets.*, 503.

6. Barker gives the date of this letter as ca. June 1843, adding that *BLFC* dates it incorrectly (917 n. 49); *Lets.* also places it at this time.

7. Cited in Mildred Christian, "A Census of Brontë Manuscripts in the United States (Part One)," *Nineteenth-Century Fiction* 2 (December 1949): 197.

8. See Higuchi, 273–83.

9. See Barker, 917 n. 46.

10. "A Miss Emily Bro[n]të témoignage de sincère affection" (Special Collections, Margaret Clapp Library, Wellesley College). The last numeral of the year is oddly written, which may be why Barker gives the date as 1842 (910); however, the speech was written and printed in 1843.

11. On Mary Taylor's repeated attempts to get Charlotte out of Brussels, see Gaskell, 589 n. 15.

12. Charlier, 389–90.

13. "Veuillez me faire le plaisir d'accepter cette petite boîte en souvenir de moi" (*Lets.*, 377).

14. *Les Fleurs de la poésie française depuis le commencement du XVIe siècle jusqu'à nos jours,* edited by Rabion; see Gérin *CB*, 254–55, and *Shirley,* 755 n.

15. Alexander and Sellars, 264.

1. Sacrifice of an Indian Widow / Sacrifice d'une veuve Indienne (CB)

TEXTUAL NOTES

7. Golunde is a misspelling of Golcunda, an ancient city of southeast India famous for its diamonds. CB also alludes to it in "An Interesting Passage in the Lives of Some Eminent Men . . ." (1830): "As I fried with heat under an African summer's sun, I continued casting up my eyes to a zenith more intensely brilliantly blue than the most flawless sapphire that ever sparkled in Golconda" (*CBEW* 1:171).

21. William Cavendish, Lord Bentinck (1774–1839) was governor-general of India. On December 4, 1829, he abolished suttee in law, though not fully in practice (see Comments). In her two juvenilia accounts of the origins of "The Islanders' Play" (March 12 and June 30, 1829), CB says that Bentinck was Anne's "chief man" (*CBEW* 1:7, 22). Christine Alexander identifies this Bentinck as the M.P. Lord George (1:7), but the children could have known about both public men.

40–42 (41–43). Details of the widow's costume will be echoed in "The Death of Moses": "pearls gleam on their arms and on their brown necks" (lines 122–23).

47 (48). One *toise* (an ancient French measure) is 1,949 meters in length; forty *toises* equal about fifty miles. Presumably CB did not intend to place the burial so far from the sea.

63. My translation may obscure a possible Biblical allusion to Matt. 26.41. Compare St. John Rivers's note to Jane Eyre and her response when he presses her to sacrifice herself as a missionary with him in India:

"[W]atch and pray that you enter not into temptation: the spirit, I trust, is willing, but the flesh, I see, is weak. I shall pray for you hourly—Yours, St. John."

"My Spirit," I answered mentally, "is willing to do what is right; and my flesh, I hope, is strong enough to accomplish the will of Heaven, when once that will is distinctly known to me. At any rate, it shall be strong enough to search. . . ." (*JE*, 538; ch. 36, mod. eds.)

EDITORIAL NOTES

Heger makes light grammatical corrections but leaves a number of errors unnoted and offers no substantive comments. CB herself corrects several of the words he underlines. Her ink color and line width change from p. 2 to p. 3 of the manuscript. Darker ink and thinner strokes appear on p. 3. The ink and stroke used first resume in the middle of p. 4 and continue until the end of the devoir.

1. No umlaut on *Bronte.*
2. *Sacrifice* in CB's double-line print.
3. Subtitle in small print.
4. Long archaic first *s* in misspelled *richeses; L'Inde Anglaise* in left margin.
20. The word *barbare* added to p. 2 in p. 3 ink.
21. Ink change begins with *les.*
22. H's *pr* > CB's *à,* and CB corrects again above; H's accent on *résistait.*
24. H's accent on *préparatifs;* CB writes *cette* first, then erases *tte* to form *ce.*
41. First ink resumes after *blanche.*
43. CB corrects *exprima* by adding *it;* H's accent on *résignation.*
51. CB corrects accent on *sèches.*
64. CB corrects *crut* to *crus.*
65. CB adds accent to *e,* deletes last two letters of *épaisses.*
68. H adds light *s* to *flamme;* CB > *s* and converts comma to a colon.
72. CB starts to write *Du,* converts to *Au.*

COMMENTS

1. "The Spell, An Extravaganza," *CBEW* 2.2:193. The idea of such a sacrifice may also have come from Byron's *Sardanapalus,* in which the Greek slave Myrrha elects to die on the hero-king's pyre. CB alludes to this poem in "The Scrap Book," *CBEW* 2.2:365. Alexander also notes an indirect allusion to suttee earlier in that tale (343).

2. *JE,* 343–44 (ch. 24, mod. eds.).

3. Gaskell, 11.238. When Gaskell interviewed Heger in 1856, he cited this poem in connection with "The Death of Moses," but his memory was not always reliable.

4. "[Elle m]ontre aux Anglais son bras à demi-consumé. / Pourquoi reculer d'épouvante, / Anglais? son bras est désarmé. / La flamme l'environne, et sa voix expirante / Murmure encore ("She shows the English her half-consumed arm. / Why recoil in horror, / Englishmen? her arm is disarmed. / The flame surrounds it, and her expiring voice / Still murmurs . . ." (Delavigne, 27).

5. Since *sati* is now the accepted term, I use it rather than *suttee.*

6. [Georgy Croly], "Burning of Indian Widows," *Blackwood's* 23 (February 1828): 161–62.

7. Juliet Barker alerted me to this possible source. She also cites "a reference in Patrick [Brontë]'s letter to the *Leeds Mercury* of 16 March 1844 to widow burning being a matter rather less urgent than the number of accidental deaths in fires in [England]" (letter to the author, February 4, 1992). Twenty years earlier, the matter seemed more urgent; Patrick was an inaugural member of the Church Missionary Association founded at Bradford in 1813 (60).

8. See the Textual Notes for lines 7 and 21.

9. Anonymous editorial comment in the Baptist Missionary Society quarterly, *The Friend of India* 7 (1824): 284. This volume contains reports of four completed satis and one prevented case.

10. *DNB* 2:295.

11. Mani, 396. Men were not the sole observers, however; I have read two accounts by women who presumably accompanied their husbands.

12. The word *sati* derives from the Hindu word for "saint." Widows by their death were said to guarantee themselves and their spouses access to heaven.

13. Bertha, the Creole from the other Indies, nearly succeeds in burning Rochester alive when she leaps to her own death at Thornfield. St. John, in urging Jane to go with him to India, hurries her toward death in a stifling climate, an end "almost equivalent to committing suicide" (*JE,* 528 [ch. 35, mod. eds.]). His sister Diana endorses Jane's resistance, agreeing that she should not "be grilled alive in Calcutta" (530). On these and other linked allusions—more broadly, on the novel's colonialist discourse—see Gayatri Chakravorty Spivak, "Three Women's Texts and a Critique of Imperialism," in *Race, Writing, and Difference,* ed. Henry Louis Gates (Chicago: U of P Press, 1986), 262–80; May Ellis Gibson, "The Seraglio or Suttee: Brontë's *Jane Eyre," Postscript* 4 (1987): 1–8; Laura E. Donaldson, "The Miranda Complex: Colonialism and the Question of Feminist Reading," *Diacritics* 18 (fall 1988): 65–77; Susan L. Meyer, "Colonialism and the Figurative Strategy of *Jane Eyre," Victorian Studies* 32 (winter 1990): 247–68; and Jenny Sharpe, "Colonialism, Gender, and Resistance: The Racial Identity of Female Agency in *Jane Eyre,"* in *Allegories of Empire: The Figure of Woman in the Colonial Text* (Minneapolis: U of Minnesota Press, 1993).

2. The Sick Young Girl / La jeune Fille malade, with dictée The Poor Girl / La Pauvre Fille (CB)

TEXTUAL NOTES (DEVOIR)

My translation is indebted to Jean P. Inebit's ("Four Essays," 98–99).

10–11, 15. Possible allusion to the song from *Cymbelline* 2.3: "Hark! hark! the lark at heaven's gate sings, / And Phoebus 'gins arise, / His steeds to water at those springs / On chaliced flowers that lies. . . ."

29–30. H's marginal comment refers to a poem, "*La jeune captive,"* by André Chénier (1762–94). For more on the analogies, see Comments.

32. Luke 8.41–42 and 8.49–56.

EDITORIAL NOTES (DEVOIR)

2. *La jeune Fille* in CB's double-line print.

3. The word *malade* smaller and single-line but larger than devoir script.

5. The word *pour* w.u.?; Heger's *m'* runs diagonally down to CB's line.

9. H's circumflex on *bâti.*

10. Illegible H addition crossed out above line.

14. H's accents *déploie.* His figure in margin.

18. Archaic first *s* in *tendresse.*

23. H's period; some kind of slash above *puis.*

24. The phrase *la vie de* w.u.?

28. A faint erasure and the formation of *étaient* suggest that CB started to write another form of *être.*

33. CB's *s* is under the *z* of *exaucez* (she forgot to change *ton*).

36. H writes and crosses out something over *mais*.

37. CB's final words, *dans ses regards,* are centered on the last line in MS.

TEXTUAL NOTES (DICTÉE)

This is the first dictée in CB's notebook (BPM, Bonnell 115). Its unidentified author is Alexandre Soumet (1788–1845). The last verse that appears in CB's transcript does not appear in any published edition I have seen, including the anthology that Heger gave CB, and differs from the others metrically. Heger may have made the addition (he certainly altered other published texts), but there is no proof that he did so.

EDITORIAL NOTES (DICTÉE)

1. Title large, in CB's devoir script.

20. The little cross indicates a missing line (*Je ne partage . . .*) added below (line 26).

25. Elongated first *s* in *caresses*.

26. Added line in CB's rough-draft script.

46. Traces of revision around *mourait* (to correct tense?).

COMMENTS

1. *Lets.,* 283–84.

2. Soumet (1788–1845) wrote *Clytemnestre, Saül, Jeanne d'Arc, Elizabeth de France,* and other plays. When he was in Paris between 1825 and 1829, Heger may have seen Soumet's tragedies.

3. Stone, 1131.

4. Several forms of circumstantial evidence suggest this possibility: CB's allusion here to "La Jeune Captive"; Heger's reference to Delavigne's "Joan of Arc" in his conversation with Gaskell; the appearance of several such poems—Chénier's, Soumet's, and Guttinguer's "L'Enfant malade"— in a book Heger later gave to CB and probably used himself as a source, Rabion's *Fleurs de la Poésie Française;* and Heger's practice of "synthetical teaching," reading several texts that had a common theme or topic in order to compare and contrast them. Heger's taste for such poetry is also suggested by the French translation CB made the following year of Schiller's "Des Mädchens Klage"; see *CB Poems,* 365 and 490.

5. "Quoi que l'heure présente ait de trouble et d'ennui, / Je ne veux point mourir encore" (lines 5–6, translation in Robertson, 6). Chénier's captive, a victim of the French Revolution, also speaks of waking at dawn, although "From peaceful sleep / Peaceful [she] wake[s]" (Robertson, 19–20). Heger may have read both lyrics to his students, pointing out comparisons and contrasts. He used this method with other texts; see Comments on devoirs 10 and 11.

6. Luke 8.41–42, 49–56.

7. Quoted in Textual Notes (lines 10–11, 15). In 1826 Schubert set the song to music for the piano, so the Brontës could have heard as well as read it. The English composer Thomas Chilcot (d. 1766) also set the song to music, for the harpsichord.

8. "J'ai les ailes de l'espérance: / Echappée aux réseaux de l'oiseleur cruel, / Plus vive, plus heureuse, aux campagnes du ciel / Philomèle chante et s'élance ("La Jeune Captive," lines 15–18, in Delvaille, 362–63; translation in Robertson, 6).

9. *Lets.* 266.

10. Duthie, *Foreign Vision,* 26. She also notes that Soumet's isolated heroine anticipates Brontë's fictional protagonists, who are "not only lonely but singularly alone in the world" (26).

11. *Lets.* 1:260. See also the untitled poem "I gave, at first, Attention close," *CB Poems,* 333.

12. Millevoye did not write a "Jeune Malade," but he did write a poem about a dying youth that CB greatly admired; see devoir 23, dictée.

13. *Shirley,* 78 and 106 (chs. 5 and 6, mod. eds.).

3. Evening Prayer in a Camp / La Prière du Soir dans un camp, with dictée Evening Prayer on Board a Ship / Prière du Soir à bord d'u[n] vaisseau (CB)

TEXTUAL NOTES (DEVOIR)

Whatever Heger's comments may suggest about CB's French, her vocabulary is varied and generally well used, and her style is literary rather than oral, which suggests that she already has some conception of good style. According to my Belgian assistant, most French speakers would find her style acceptable, though rough as an imitation of Chateaubriand.

12. "ruby": a word CB characteristically uses to describe a sunset. Compare "We wove a web in childhood" (*CB Poems,* 165): "The light of an Italian sky / Where clouds of sunset lingering lie / Is not more ruby red."

16–17. Heger's vertical lines appear to strike out the phrase "and it seemed to me to attest to the influence of religion," perhaps because CB interrupts an objective description to give her opinion. But she does it to imitate Chateaubriand.

18. "banks of the Nile" could be an echo from the juvenilia; the children's African kingdom included the Nile.

19. Abercrombie: Sir Ralph Abercromby led a campaign against the French in Alexandria in 1801, backed by two troops of Highlanders; see Comments.

23F. Again, Heger may be curbing CB's subjectivity in replacing "de notre Seigneur" ("of our Lord") with the more impersonal "du Seigneur" ("of the Lord"). But "la prière du Seigneur" is also a technically correct phrase for the Lord's Prayer.

33. Ishmael: Abraham's son by Hagar; see also Comments, n. 17.

39. Golgotha: site of the crucifixion; see also Comments, n. 16.

EDITORIAL NOTES (DEVOIR)
MS corrected in pen and pencil.

2. *La Prière du Soir* in CB's double-line print.

3. The phrase *dans un camp* in single-line version of double-line print, smaller than devoir script.

4. H's accent (ink) on *désert;* his comma (ink) after *chaleur; à peine* (ink) is in left margin in MS, directly preceding *alors.*

5. The word *longue* w.u. in pencil and struck out diagonally in ink.

6. H's arching line in ink surrounds *bande,* w.u. in pencil.

8. The letter *e* d.u. in pencil; *présageait* w.u. in pencil.

9. The word *et* crossed out in ink.

11. Underlining in ink.

12. Crossout in ink.

13. H's accent on *était* and *désert* in pencil.

15. The *u* of *peut* underlined three times in pencil.

16. Vertical line begins at *et* and runs down to end of *influence* in the next line.

17. Vertical line through *religion* runs down through *temple* in the next line.

18. The words *loin des* w.u. in pencil.

19. Triple line under *ait* in pencil.

23. H's accent on *dévotion,* and his comma after *qui* in ink.

24. H's comma in ink after *étranger.*

25. H's comma in ink after *chrétien.*

27–28. The phrase *symbole . . . adorateurs* w.u. in pencil; revision above line in ink with indecipherable pencil beneath.

30. The *ait* added to *changé* extends below the line; strikeout of *avait* in ink.

32. H's *payens*(?) under his *mobiles* in pencil.

36. The letter *y* underlined three times in pencil; other corrections in ink.

39. Probably H's dash in ink.

40. H's comments in ink over illegible pencil; H's *et ce* above line, then CB's *que,* followed by H's faint *je* in pencil and *ne peux* in ink above; H > *peindre* and continues to next line. Carets added to aid comprehension.

TEXTUAL NOTES (DICTÉE)

Heger dictated two paragraphs from *La Génie du Christianisme,* vol. 1, part 1, book 5, chapter 12. CB's notebook (BPM, Bonnell 115) contains two copies of the dictée (the second and the fifth entries). The second entry has been lightly corrected and ends with paragraph two; the fifth is uncorrected and complete. On the variations from the published versions, see the Editorial Notes to the dictée.

EDITORIAL NOTES (DICTÉE)

To determine the extent of Heger's alterations, I checked the dictée against four versions that would have been available in Brussels: the first edition, *Génie du Christianisme* (Paris: Migneret, 1802), 1:225–26; *Génie du Christianisme; ou, Beautés de la réligion Chrétienne,* 2d ed. (Paris: Migneret, 1803), 1:214–15; *Génie du Christianisme; ou, Beautés de la réligion Chrétienne* (Lyon: Balanche, 1804), 2:95–97; and *Oeuvres complètes de Chateaubriand,* vol. 11, *Génie du Christianisme, Tome I* (Paris: Ladvocat, 1826), 255–56. There are some variations among them, but much larger variations between the published versions as a group and the dictée. To indicate the extent of Heger's changes and additions, I have shaded them in the typescript. Note that "pv" means "printed version."

1. *Prière du Soir* in CB's double-line print.

2. The phrase *à bord d'u vaisseau* [*sic*] in smaller single-line print.

3. *S* is lowercase in all pvs.

4. The phrase *vagues étincelantes* is *flots* in all pvs.

5. All pvs read *navire, au milieu.*

6. No paragraph and *le balancement* is plural in all pvs.

7–8. *Quelques nuages* directly follows *horizon* in all pvs.

10. All pvs read *vers le.*

11. All pvs read *brillante* instead of *chargée.*

12. All pvs reads *pilier.*

14. Sentence ends with a period in all pvs.

16–17. All pvs read *d'un voix rauque leur simple cantique,* and *Notre-Dame-de-Bon-Secours* is in italics, capped as here but variously hyphenated.

19–21. The words *ocean, mère,* and *douleur* u.c. in all pvs.

22. No paragraph in all pvs, which omit the first part of the line, beginning *La conscience.*

23. *Infini* l.c. and *nos* (for *ces*) in all pvs.

24. In two editions *endormies* is *muettes;* all pvs then go to *la* or *La nuit.*

28. The word *prière* is plural in all pvs.

30. All pvs read *dans'l'orient.*

31. Early pvs read *à la faible voix;* 1826 ed. reads *à la voix.*

32. All pvs read *sentir.*

COMMENTS

1. "[D]e toutes les religions qui ont jamais existé la religion chrétienne est la plus poétique, la plus humaine, la plus favorable à la liberté, aux arts et aux lettres" (*Oeuvres complètes* 11:21).

2. "[D]eux perspectives de la nature, l'une marine et l'autre terrestre" (*Oeuvres complètes* 11:252).

3. The dictée covers paragraphs 6–7 of part I, book 5, chapter 12.

4. See the Editorial Notes on the dictée for more detailed comparisons.

5. P. Brontë, 363. I have reproduced the spelling but not the spacing. For Branwell's other references to Chateaubriand, see ibid., pp. 15, 17, 19, 25, 26, and 364.

6. The 1812 edition of an English translation of Chateaubriand's *Travels in Greece, Palestine, Egypt, and Barbary* is item 1,273 of the catalog of books contained in the library of Ponden House sold at auction by William Weatherhead (Keighley), Saturday, November 4, 1899. On the Brontës' use of the Ponden House library, see Gérin, *Branwell Brontë,* 42–44.

7. On the Brontës' use of *Blackwood's,* see Gérin, *Branwell Brontë,* 28–29.

8. [Archibald Alison], "Chateaubriand. No. I. Itinéraire," *Blackwood's* 31 (March 1832): 553–65; and "Chateaubriand. No. II. Genie de Christianisme," *Blackwood's* 32 (August 1832): 217–33.

9. See her May 1942 letter to Ellen Nussey, Chronology, or *Lets.* 284–85.

10. "[L]es ruines nous montrent la fragilité de l'existence humaine, nous enseignent la précarité des nations, nous révèlent la fuit irrémédiable du temps" (Favre, 9).

11. For example, "Dieu même est le grand secret de la nature; la divinité était voilée en Egypte, et le sphinx s'asseyait sur le seuil de ses temples" (*Oeuvres complètes* 11:30; "God himself is the great secret of nature; divinity was veiled in Egypt and the sphinx sat at the threshold of its temples").

12. "If any lesson is taught by [a tomb], why should we complain that a king resolved to render that lesson perpetual? Majestic monuments constitute an essential part of the glory of every human society. Unless we maintain that it is a matter of indifference whether a nation leaves behind it a name or no name in history, we cannot condemn those structures which extend the memory of a people beyond its own existence, and make it contemporary with the future generations that fix their residence in its forsaken fields" (Chateaubriand, *Travels,* 207).

13. Branwell's alter ego, Young Soult, is allegedly the son of Marshall Soult, who led the French against the duke of Wellington. Soult also led the French against John Moore (1771–1809), commander of the English forces before Wellington and another favorite of Branwell's. Moore had been Abercromby's protégé; in the campaign that CB alludes to here, he was in charge of a division.

14. *CBEW* 2.2:196.

15. See Fortescue, 149–54; and *DNB* 1:46.

16. Golgotha, literally the place of a skull, is the site where Jesus was crucified. See Matt. 27.33, Mark 15.22, John 19.17–18.

17. See Gen. 16, 21.8–21, 25.12–18.

18. *Villette,* 36.611.

4. The Nest / Le Nid (CB)

TEXTUAL NOTES

34–35 (37). On the possible connection of these lines to Chateaubriand's *Génie,* see Comments. The idea of nature as a volume goes back further and was common in the eighteenth century.

39 (41). In making "cloud" plural and changing "the" to "a," Heger generalizes CB's reference to Moses' encounters with God; see also her devoir "The Death of Moses" (68–70).

41 (43). Heger questions "traces" because in French it then had the sense of an animal's traces or tracks.

44 (46). I have translated *bornes* as "bounds" because that is the word most commonly used with "seas" in this context in the King James Bible. CB uses the word *bourn* in *Jane Eyre,* but in the singular, and to connote "destination."

EDITORIAL NOTES (CORRECTED VERSION)
Heger has corrected this manuscript in pencil and in ink, sometimes retracing the pencil with ink.

2. *Le Nid* in CB's double-line print.
3. The *r* of *certaine* has something under it; corrected by CB.

5. The word *prèmiere* is uncorrected by H and may end with a minuscule *s*.

8. H's *empourprer* > something illegible in pencil.

9. Tear in page after *bourgeon* abridges the *s*.

12. The words *dont il* crossed out in pencil, w.u. in ink. H > the first *e* in *guetter* with his own *e*.

13. H's hyphen in *vert-tendre*.

15. H corrects the *t* in *entrevit* on line in ink and above line in pencil; the *e* of *pures* is crossed out twice.

16. H pencils *agita ses ailes* and then > *ses ailes* with *agita* in ink.

17. H's colons.

18. Diagonals in pencil, underlining in ink; H > penciled words in ink.

20. H's colon and exclamation point.

21. H's *l* above line > his *c*, changing *this* to *the*.

22. H's comma.

24. After *craintive* H inserts two dots diagonally before CB's period.

26. The *s* of *des* struck out twice; *à la*(?) may > *la; toutes* > *de*, striking it out incorrectly.

29. H's colon.

30. H's colon; *étroite* in ink and pencil.

32. The word *de* crossed out in pencil, underlined and replaced in ink.

33. The *es* of *cessé* d.u.; H's accent in ink; his additional *s* and vertical line in pencil; he > CB's comma with a colon.

37. The underline of *li* in *rempli* and vertical line in pencil.

38. Page is torn; word missing is almost certainly *volume*.

41. H converts CB's comma to a semicolon.

42. H's semicolon and (second) comma.

43. H's accent on *délicats*.

44. H corrects accent of *Hébreux*.

46. H's period and vertical line in pencil.

COMMENTS

1. *JE*, 87 (end ch. 8, mod eds.). Jane has just been "allowed to commence French and drawing" at Lowood. Alexander links her naive vision of success to CB's own "illusory delight [in] her early artistic productions" (Alexander and Sellars, 58).

2. "Existence de dieu prouvée par les merveilles de la nature" (*Oeuvres complètes,* vol. 11, bk. 5).

3. *Lets.,* 284–85.

4. Dessner, 214.

5. "Une admirable Providence se fait remarquer dans les nids des oiseaux. On ne peut contempler, sans être attendri, cette bonté divine qui donne l'industrie au foible, et la prévoyance à l'insouciant" (*Oeuvres complètes* 11:214). The English translation, by Archibald Alison, is from *Blackwood's* 32 (August 1832): 229.

6. "Le temps a rongé les fastes des rois de Memphis, sur leurs pyramides funèbres; et il n'a pu effacer une seule lettre de l'histoire que l'ibis égyptien porte gravée sur la coquille de son oeuf" (*Oeuvres complètes* 11:217). (Chateaubriand uses the word *fastes,* here and elsewhere, to denote ancient

registers or annals.) In *Villette,* Lucy Snowe sees in the park, at the festival, "the image of a white ibis, fixed on a column . . . an avenue, at the close of which was couched a sphynx . . ." (38.656).

5. The Immensity of God / L'Immensité de Dieu (CB)

TEXTUAL NOTES

Neither the date nor CB's customary signature appears on this devoir, which was taken from a notebook and rebound (see Comments, n. 1). The absence of comments and the number of errors further suggest that she did not turn in this copy. But though her French is far from perfect, she has evidently studied and thought about style.

8. "luminaries" is a word that CB uses in the juvenilia. See, for instance, "A Leaf from an Unopened Volume," *CBEW* 2.1:328.
10–11. Possibly a reference to *Paradise Lost,* 4.605–9:
> . . . now glow'd the Firmament
> With living Saphirs: *Hesperus* that led
> The starrie Host, rode brightest, till the Moon
> Rising in clouded Majestie, at length
> Apparent Queen unvaild her peerless light,
> And o're the dark her Silver Mantle threw.

17–19. A very close paraphrase of Pss. 8.3–4.
37. Christiaan Huygens (1629–95): Dutch astronomer, physicist, and mathematician; originator of the theory of light waves.

EDITORIAL NOTES

Paragraphs have not been indented. In manuscript, the breaks are defined by spaces between the conclusion of a sentence and the next line.

1. *L'Immensité de Dieu* in larger roman print with elaborate capitals.
18. CB started to write the masculine plural *agencés,* then amended it to the feminine plural.
30. CB seems to have changed *telle* to *toute.*
34. CB deletes the words with a waved line; the last words deleted are illegible.

COMMENTS

1. *JE,* 414 (ch. 24, mod. eds.).
2. Thomas J. Wise formerly owned and probably cut up the notebook; see Preface, n. 3. This devoir is now bound with a translation of "Coronach" that Neufeldt thinks was probably done in 1843 (*CB Poems,* 490). The allusion to Psalm 8 may also hint at a later date, since after EB returned to Haworth, CB mailed her a copy of *Les Psaumes de David mis en vers français,* dated "Juillet 3" on the flyleaf; see Bemelmans, 294–95. On the other hand, the devoir's mood is so optimistic and the text so responsive to Heger's advice that it seems more like the texts from her first spring. Its brevity too suggests the earlier date.
3. "The Infinite in the Heavens," lines 10, 65, 140, 148, 151. I quote

longer extracts in French to suggest their style and tenor:

> Je m'assieds en silence, et laisse ma pensée
> Flotter comme une mer où la lune est bercée.
>
> . . . .
>
> Mais dans la voûte même où s'élèvent mes yeux,
> Que de mondes nouveaux, que de soleils sans nombre . . .
>
> . . . .
>
> Chaque tache de lait qui blanchit l'horizon,
> Chaque teinte du ciel qui n'a pas même un nom,
> Sont autant de soleils, rois d'autant de systèmes,
> Qui, de seconds soleils se couronnant eux-mêmes,
> Guident, en gravitant dans ces immensités,
> Cent planètes brûlant de leurs feux empruntés . . .
>
> . . . .
>
> Atome, il se mesure à l'infini des cieux,
> Et que, de ta grandeur soupçonnant le prodige,
> Son regard s'éblouit, et qu'il se dit: Que suis-je?
> Oh! que suis-je Seigneur! . . . ("L'Infini dans les cieux," lines 9–10,

64–65, 135–40, 148–51, *Harmonies,* 107–12).

4. "Je conçus . . . la pensée d'écrire au hasard . . . quelques cantiques modernes, comme ceux que David avait écrit avec ses larmes" (from Lamartine's comments on his first Harmony, "Invocation," in the subscribers' edition to his *Works* [1849–1850]; quoted in Benichou, *Le Sacre de l'écrivain,* 188).

5. The description in Milton that matches hers most closely is from *Paradise Lost,* 4.605–9: ". . . now glow'd the Firmament / With living Saphirs: *Hesperus* that led / The starrie Host, rode brightest, till the Moon / Rising in clouded Majestie, at length / Apparent Queen unvaild her peerless light, / And o're the dark her Silver Mantle threw." Chateaubriand makes a number of allusions to Milton in *The Genius of Christianity,* and Heger could have cited some in class. But CB had been reading and memorizing Milton since her childhood; a copy of *Paradise Lost* (Edinburgh: Robertson and Gillies, 1797) with her signature is in the library at Haworth.

6. See the Textual Notes for line 37.

7. One of CB's exercise books (BPM, Bonnell 119) bears the title "Cahier d'*Arithmétique*"; CB lists her professor as Heger. See Alexander, *Bibliography,* 185.

8. "Quand on pense que le télescope d'Herschell a compté déjà plus de cinq millions d'étoiles; que chacune de ces étoiles est un monde plus grand et plus important que ce globe de la terre; que ces cinq millions de mondes ne sont que les bords de cette création; que, si nous parvenions sur le plus éloigné, nous apercevrions de là d'autres abîmes d'espace infini comblés d'autres mondes incalculables, et que ce voyage durerait des myriades de

siècles, sans que nous pussions atteindre jamais les limites entre le néant et Dieu . . ." (*Harmonies,* 115).

9. "Et je m'estime moins qu'un de ces grains de sable; / Car ce sable roulé par les flots inconstants, / S'il a moins d'étendue, hélas! a plus de temps / Il remplira toujours son vide dans l'espace . . . ("And I count myself less than one of those grains of sand; / Because if that sand rolled by the inconstant waves / Has less extent, alas! it has more time, / It will always fill its gap in space . . ."; "L'Infini dans les cieux," lines 155–58, *Harmonies,* 112; see also line 130).

10. "C'est une souffle affaibli des bardes d'Israël, / Un ëcho dans mon sein" (from "Première harmonie. Invocation," *Oeuvres,* 102). Chateaubriand's *Genius* urges poets to consult the Old Testament as well as the New.

11. See *Shirley,* 546 (ch. 27, mod. eds.).

12. ". . . Un golfe de la mer, d'îles entrecoupé, / Des blancs reflets du ciel par la lune frappé, / Comme un vaste miroir brisé sur la poussière, / Réfléchit dans l'obscur des fragments de lumière / (. . . A gulf of the sea, flecked with isles, / White reflections of the sky struck by the moon, / As a vast mirror shattered in the dust / Reflects in darkness fragments of light"; "L'Infini dans les cieux," lines 35–38, *Harmonies,* 108). In *Shirley,* CB writes, "All its lights and tints looked like the 'reflets' of white, or violet, or pale green gems" (644 [ch. 32, mod. eds.]).

13. On August 15, 1843, before his Prize Day speech.

14. "Ainsi chaque pas, dans la voie scientifique, est un pas vers Dieu; ainsi plus on remonte le grand fleuve de la science, mieux on voit que la source en est au ciel" ("Discours" of 1834, reprinted in Chadwick, "A Gift," 856).

6. The Cat / Le Chat (EB), with two fragments, Plea for Cats / Plaidoyer pour les chats and The Two Dogs / Les deux chiens (CB)

TEXTUAL NOTES ("THE CAT")
My translation is indebted to Lorine White Nagel's (*Five Essays,* 9–10; rpt., "Three Essays," 338–39).

3. The Brontës apparently had a cat at this time. When it died on March 4, 1844, CB wrote, "Emily is sorry" (*Lets.,* 344).

23 (24). Timon: legendary misanthrope of Athens (5th cent. B.C.) and the subject of Shakespeare's *Timon of Athens.*

24–25 (25–26). In CB's *The Professor,* Frances Evans Henri comments on the school's "Romish" inhabitants: "they all think it lawful to tell lies, they all call it politeness to profess friendship where they feel hatred" (17.145).

38–39 (40–42). Compare Nellie Dean's description of Edgar Linton in *Wuthering Heights*: "The soft thing . . . possessed the power to depart, as much as a cat possesses the power to leave a mouse half killed, or a bird half eaten—" (89 [ch. 8, mod. eds.]).

47–48 (50–51). "the great ancestor": Adam.

EDITORIAL NOTES ("THE CAT")
EB rules a double-lined left margin but does not underline her name and the date.

2. *Le Chat* is in EB's normal devoir hand but larger and to the left of center. The double underline is also left of center, starting at the end of *Le* and continuing half an inch beyond *Chat*.

8. The *ph* of *physiques* may > something illegible.

23. The word *duvet* seems to have been *chevet* (partly erased).

38. The word *sanglant* looks like *sangtant* because EB has crossed the *l*, probably by mistake.

47–52. The text becomes increasingly contracted as EB approaches the bottom of the page. The last two lines are crammed below the final line that she ruled, and *Paradis* barely fits.

EDITORIAL NOTES (FRAGMENTS)
These excerpts are from pp. 8–10 of a manuscript entitled *Devoir*. Both titles are in CB's normal devoir hand.

16. CB changes l.c. *p* to capital in *Pataud*.

17. CB's *r* > a *z* she erases in *détailler*.

COMMENTS
1. EB's word choice in this devoir provides some circumstantial support for CB's claim. As my Belgian assistant, Sabine Mourlon-Beernaert, points out, "elle est bornée" (11), "il est venu à bout" (23–24), "A peu près" (31), "assurément" (51), and other expressions are characteristic of oral discourse, rather than literary language.

2. The entries are consecutive and appear on pp. 8–10 of a notebook in the Brotherton Collection.

3. See the *matière* for devoirs 21 and 22 and the Comments on devoirs 7 and 8. Also compare William Crimsworth's statement: "One day, I gave as a devoir [a] trite little anecdote . . . to be related with amplifications" (*The Professor*, 16.132).

4. As Gaskell says, "the fierce, wild intractability of its nature was what often recommended [an animal] to Emily" (12.268). See that section also for descriptions of EB's conduct with Keeper and for connections to *Shirley*.

5. *The Professor*, 12.103. "[E]spièglerie" ("The Two Dogs," line 24) also reemerges in that novel, where Pelet refers to one of Crimsworth's difficult students as "une jolie espiègle" (11.95).

6. Hewish, 63.

7. Both Branwell sisters had converted to the Church of England but, like Patrick, they remained well disposed to Wesleyan Methodists. On the importance of Wesleyan and other Evangelical beliefs to EB's writings, see Miller, ch. 4, and the Introduction to this volume, lxi. As Adrian Desmond

points out, ideas about animal creation and the fall had important implications for antivivisectionists and for the medical schools of the early nineteenth century (*The Politics of Evolution* [Chicago: U of Chicago P, 1989], 183–84).

8. Suggested by Hewish, 63.

9. BPM, Bonnell 115, sixteenth entry.

10. Buffon, *Natural History* 4:49–51.

7/8. The Siege of Oudenarde / Le Siège d'Oudenarde (CB and EB versions)

EDITORIAL NOTES (DEVOIR 7)

2. Title in same script as body of text.

10. EB has an acute accent on *fidéles* but also seems to have tried to correct it.

23. EB starts to write something other than *tournait,* converts it.

26. EB starts to write *reculé,* converts to *reculait.*

29. The *g* of *grands* is struck out diagonally, the rest of the word horizontally.

EDITORIAL NOTES (DEVOIR 8)

CB strikes out words with a horizontal line or with tidy little diagonals through each letter; these last sometimes resemble waves when a word or phrase runs on. The manuscript revisions are unusually heavy, suggesting that this may be a preliminary copy from which she prepared a finished version for Heger.

2. Title same size and script as body of text.

3. The first *de* is lightly crossed out in the MS, but the lines are long and smeared, as if erased; the word should not be deleted.

9. Something indecipherable under the *ve* of *brave.*

10. CB seems to have ended *tous* with an *s,* changed it to a *t,* and then struck the *t* and restored the *s.*

24. *L > l* in *Lalaing;* second *l* seems altered too.

25. CB starts to write *le,* shifts to *l'* before *avertit.*

39. Accent on *envoyèrent* looks more acute than grave, but CB obviously meant the latter.

42. CB starts to write *Lalaig,* converts *g* to *n* and adds a *g.*

COMMENTS

1. They are listed in Rosenbaum and White but not in Alexander's bibliography, and the Friends Library at Swarthmore could only report that they were part of the Jenkins Collection. My research so far reveals no tie between that Jenkins and Evan Jenkins, the British chaplain in Brussels whose wife first wrote the Brontës about the Pensionnat Heger.

2. The schedule, now in the possession of François Fierens, reads as follows: "Histoire / Histoire sainte.—Quelques notices sur les grands hommes de l'antiquité et sur ceux qui ont illustré la Belgique."

3. As the *Biographie Nationale* observes, "In that epoch of incessant warfare, Simon de Lalaing had ample means to satisfy the bellicose tastes of a knight-at-arms. He traversed the history of his era, fighting almost everywhere" (11:127).

4. Barante, 92; the *Biographie Nationale* cites twenty lancers and two hundred archers.

5. On its importance, see Hayden White in Hollier, 635–36.

6. Barante, 93.

7. This episode is detailed in *Oeuvres de George Chastellain publiées par . . . Lettenhove: Chronique 1430–1431, 1452–1453* (Brussels: Heussner, 1863), 2:231–2, which reproduces a much earlier chronicle.

8. "Le sire de Lalaing avait laissé en Hainaut deux jeunes enfants. Les Gantois cherchèrent deux enfants de même taille et à peu près de même apparence, les amenèrent devant le rempart, et crièrent de loin au capitaine et à sa femme, qui était là apportant des pierres sur la muraille, que dans une course en Hainaut ils venaient de saisir leurs enfants, et qu'ils allaient les mettre à mort si la ville n'était pas rendue. Ils comptaient sur la tendresse de la mère et la faiblesse du chevalier. Mais le sire de Lalaing fit amener des coulevrines à cet endroit même, et ordonna qu'on tirât encore plus fort" (Barante, 93).

9. "Périsse tout, hormis l'honneur!" (*Biographie Nationale* 11:129).

10. Gaskell, 11.230.

11. Sabine Mourlon-Beernaert, typed comments.

12. As Barker points out, though, the allusions differ in their emphasis and stance toward Lalaing's courage. Where CB praises a noble individual, EB contrasts Lalaing with men who "are more often motivated to self-sacrifice by brute, unthinking courage than by a deliberate denial of the heart's best feelings" (388).

13. *Encyclopaedia Britannica*, 11th ed.

9. Anne Askew: Imitation / Anne Askew: Imitation, with dictée Eudorus / Eudore

TEXTUAL NOTES (DEVOIR)
The only sign of intervention in this copy is the added "of Eudorus" (3). But if Heger had read the rest of the manuscript, he would have responded to the frequent grammar errors, so this may be a draft that CB kept in her notebook, turning in a copy now lost.

3. "of Eudorus": an allusion to Chateaubriand's *Martyrs* and the dictée reproduced after the devoir.

4. Mary Tudor (1516–58), also called "Bloody Mary," reigned as queen of England and Ireland from 1553 to 1558.

8. "in her cell": the real Anne Askew was imprisoned in Newgate. On the day of the episode that CB describes, she was removed to "the sign of the Crown," where three people, including the bishop of London, prevailed on her to recant. When she refused, she was sent to the Tower of London and "let down into a dungeon" to be racked (Foxe 5:547).

10–13. On the imagery, compare CB's poem of February 1, 1830, "A wretch in prison by Murry":

O! that the glad stars through my dungeon bars
Would shed their lustre clear
That the solemn moon would lighten the gloom
Which reigns in silence here
O for some fair light to illume this night
With a swift & silver glance
Through these grates to play, with a pearly ray
And lightly here to dance . . . (*CB Poems,* 27).

13. "the young captive": perhaps an allusion to the poem "La jeune captive," by André Chénier (1762–94). Six weeks earlier, Heger had written these words in the margin of CB's devoir "The Sick Young Girl."

16. Garden of Gethsemane: the place where Jesus went with Peter and the sons of Zebedee the night he was betrayed by Judas. My translation follows Matt. 26.39. See also Mark 14.36 and Luke 22.42.

29 (30). "rack" is underlined because it is in English; presumably, CB did not know the French equivalent.

33–34. Stephen Gardiner (1490?-1555): bishop of Winchester (1530–50) under Henry VIII and Edward VI until he was tried and imprisoned in the Tower; lord chancellor of England (1553–55) under Queen Mary; a noted scholar and advocate of conservative policy through the early Reformation.

50 (49). An allusion to the Crucifixion. See Matt. 27.46 and Mark 15.34–35.

51 (50). Thomas Cranmer (1489–1556): first archbishop of Canterbury in the reformed Church of England (1533–54) and a leading innovator in its reconstruction. He and Gardiner were bitter enemies. After Gardiner's ascension to power under Mary, Cranmer was imprisoned, stripped of his offices, and forced to defect from Protestantism. He was still condemned to death at the stake. At the burning, he disavowed his false recantation and thrust his right hand (which had signed the documents) into the fire to be consumed (a precedent for Rochester?).

61–62 (61). "beds of roses" is a phrase in Marlowe's "The Passionate Shepherd to His Love" (1599), echoed in Shakespeare's *Merry Wives of Windsor* (song, 2.1).

62–63 (61–62). Compare this passage from the Brontë children's "Tales of the Islanders," June 1, 1829: "These cells are dark, vaulted, arched and so far down in the earth that the loudest shreik [*sic*] could not be heard by any inhabitant of the upper world and in these as well as the dungeons the most unjust torturing might go on without any fear of detection . . ." (*CBEW* 1:24).

78–81. CB closely paraphrases Matt. 10.33 and 10.28 but substitutes "Gehenna" for "hell" and "take the life from" for "kill"; with these exceptions, the translation follows the Scripture.

81. Gehenna: biblical Hebrew word for hell.

I have seen this devoir only in photocopy and may therefore have missed faint signs of changes.

1. Mark resembling ∝ follows CB's name.

2. *Anne Askew* in CB's double-line print.

3. *Imitation* in small single-line print. Heger(?) has added *de Eudore.*

33. CB seems to have changed ending of *entra* (from *entre*?).

36. CB may have punctuation after *dit* or she may have started to write *dis* followed by three points.

59. One MS page ends with the word *seule,* and the next begins with it; the duplication has been edited out.

67. Punctuation after *religion* is very faint, perhaps not a comma.

70. The article *le* erased before *ciel* and *l* erased before *enfer* (the apostrophe remains visible in MS).

TEXTUAL NOTES (DICTÉE)

"Eudorus" is an extract from *Les Martyrs,* the Christian epic that Chateaubriand published in 1809. (The English version printed here is from *The Martyrs,* translated by O. W. Wight; it concludes chapter 22.) It is set in the reigns of Diocletian (284–305) and his son-in-law Galerius (305–11), the era of the final conflict between Christianity and Roman paganism. Its hero is Eudorus, a Greco-Roman warrior from a Christian family, who has lapsed from the faith, gone through years of adventuring, and returned to the fold with quenchless fervor. By chance, he encounters the beautiful and cultured Cymodoce, who is lost. She serves as priestess in the temple of her father, Demodocus, the last of Homer's descendants (Demodocus had put her there to protect her from Hierocles, a Sophist, the powerful proconsul of Achaia, and Eudorus's inveterate enemy). Predictably, the priestess becomes a Christian convert and Eudorus's fiancee. The epic ends with the proclamation of Christianity as the faith of the Empire, but not before the martyred pair are clawed to death by tigers, after marrying on their knees in the arena.

The critics did not treat *Les Martyrs* kindly. (Sainte-Beuve preferred the story of Eudorus's checkered past, which occupies seven of the twenty-four chapters, to anything about his present virtues.) They pounced on Chateaubriand's anachronisms, pointed out errors in his facts, and lambasted his theology. Nonetheless, the book went through numerous editions. When Wight did his translation in 1859, revising an incomplete translation of 1812, he claimed that it was still read extensively.

EDITORIAL NOTE (DICTÉE)

23. Heger omitted the phrase that follows "Cymodocée aux lieux infâmes!" (22): "Cymodocée dans les bras d'Hiéroclès!"

COMMENTS

1. The documents were published first in Germany by John Bale (1546) and circulated back into England. John Foxe reproduced them with addi-

tions in his *Actes and Monuments* (Basle, 1559; English version, 1563). Further documentation from the Tudor period is provided in John Strype's *Ecclesiastical Memorials* (1721).

2. Letter to Ellen Nussey, May 1842, reprinted in *Lets.,* 284.

3. As Chateaubriand explains, "J'ai tâché de tracer mon tableau de manière qu'il pût être transporté sur la toile sans confusion, sans désordre, et sans changer une seule des attitudes: le peuple romain à genoux; les soldats présentant les aigles; les vieux évêques assis, la tête couverte d'un pan de leur robe; Eudore debout, soutenu par les centurions, et laissant tomber la coupe au moment où il prononce ce mot: 'Je suis chrétien!'; la diversité des costumes; l'agape servie sous le vestibule de la prison, etc.: tout cela pourroit peut-être s'animer sous le pinceau d'un plus grand peintre que moi" ("I have tried to trace my tableau in such a manner that it could be transferred to the canvas without confusion, without disorder, and without changing any of the poses: the Roman populace on its knees; the soldiers presenting the eagles; the old bishops seated, their heads covered with a flap of their robes; Eudorus standing, held up by the centurians, and letting the cup fall the moment he pronounces the phrase, 'I am a Christian!'; the diversity of the costumes; the agape served within the vestibule of the prison, etc.: all that, perhaps, could take on life through the brush of a greater painter than I"; "Remarques," *Les Martyrs,* 541–42).

4. Saints Jerome and Augustine live out of their eras, Huns and Goths are similarly moved through time and space, and historical events change location. Chateaubriand freely conceded the anachronisms, arguing that the changes were in the epic's—and the reader's—best interests. See his preface to *Les Martyrs* (*The Martyrs,* xxvi–xxviii); his "Accueil de la critique," *Oeuvres romanesques,* 27; and the Textual Notes on devoir 9, dictée.

5. See Mavor, 20.2:52–53. He spells the name "Ascue," which suggests that he was not CB's source.

6. *Lets.,* 130.

7. On the complexities of Askew's responses, see Lonoff, "Charlotte Brontë's Belgian Essays," 402.

8. Foxe 5:551.

9. Foxe does not mention the ballad. It is quoted in *Writings of Edward the Sixth . . . Anne Askew. . . ,* vol. 3 of the British Reformers series (London: Religious Tract Society, 1831), 33–35.

10. Foxe 5:541.

11. See *The Novel and the Police* (Berkeley: U of California Press, 1988), 168. Miller cites Gilbert and Gubar as the critics who drew attention to this "historical configuration" (in their *Madwoman in the Attic*).

12. See Comments on devoir 2. The image of the moon seen through bars could echo Chateaubriand's description of the sunset. See devoir 3, dictée, lines 3–5.

13. For examples of Askew's biblical rejoinders, see Foxe 5:540–41.

14. Alexander says that she "drew comfort from the stories of early Christians," citing St. John the Divine and St. Stephen (*EW,* 241–42).

10. Portrait: King Harold before the Battle of Hastings / Portrait: Le Roi Harold avant la Bataille de Hastings (EB), Portrait: Harold on the Eve of the Battle of Hastings / Portrait: Harold la veille de la Bataille de Hastings (H), with dictée Mirabeau on the Tribune / Mirabeau à la Tribune (CB)

TEXTUAL NOTES (EB'S DEVOIR)

Harold (ca. 1022–66) was king of the English when they were defeated by the Normans. Appointed to the kingship by the dying King Edward early in 1066, he inherited a kingdom beset by challengers from two sides. He was able to overcome his brother Tostig, who had formed an alliance with Harold Hardrada of Norway, but William of Normandy and his troops arrived just two days after that victory. On October 14, on a hill about six miles inland from Hastings, Harold met William's attack. He had mustered troops from southern and eastern England, primarily infantry and special guards. His men repelled repeated assaults throughout the day, but at nightfall, Harold was mortally wounded. His death on the field marked the beginning of the Norman Conquest.

The battle and its consequences were and are familiar to all English schoolchildren. See *Encyclopaedia Britannica,* 11th ed.

EDITORIAL NOTES (EB'S DEVOIR)

See Comments on the appearance and condition of this four-page manuscript. Because the writing has faded on pp. 1 and 4, it cannot always be deciphered. Heger's corrections are in pen and in pencil. The pen layer seems to be earlier, but precedence may vary and is hard to determine.

2. *Portrait* in EB's normal script but slightly enlarged.

4. H writes *ces hommes* twice, in ink and in pencil. Other corrections above line are in pencil and continue below line in ink. I have added a connecting sign for clarity.

7. The *é*'s are crossed out in pencil, *loin* added in ink.

8–10. *B* in left margin in ink.

11–14. H's underlining in pencil, words in ink except for *abaissant* in pencil with the *t* reinforced in ink; faint *de* in pencil, possibly deleted, over EB's *bas; compagne . . . quand* crossed out in ink.

17. Both *à*'s in ink; first crossout in ink, second in pencil.

18. The word *pâle* in ink.

18–19. Underlining in pencil; three vertical lines in ink delete *son . . . inébranlable; intrépidité inébranlable* may be w.u.

20–21. On one round of revision, H circles $+$ . . . *de* (here bracketed) and corrects the phrase. In the ink layer, he appears to delete it and link Harold to the previous paragraph. All further corrections are in ink.

23. H's corrections are in pencil except crossout of *sa* and one slash in *lui.* EB's *L* > *s* in *La* or vice versa; H strikes out the word and presumably the phrase (through *car*); character before *transorme* may not be an *f.*

24–25. The word *végétant* below the line in MS. H's line descends from *son,* loops under and around *tranquille,* and ascends above *sur un.* It and w.u. are in pencil. My caret is added to suggest H's intent, though he may want EB to retain *tranquille.* The phrase *il eut été* is in left margin in MS, preceding *un.*

26. Crossout in pencil.

27–28. Crossout of *le* in ink; all underlining in pencil. H adds a line to connect his *d'agir* with *et de;* my broken line indicates the link; H's intervening *et* is redundant.

29. The letters *embr* underlined in ink and pencil; other corrections pencil.

30–32. All corrections in pencil. H converts EB's comma to semicolon after *vices.* H's *sa* and *qu'un* > other illegible corrections; *couronne* is above ~~roy~~.

34. *Mais* in left margin, preceding EB's new paragraph, which is not indented.

35. The notation *tB* is in the left margin, slightly below line, in ink.

36. Crossouts are in pencil.

37. H's semicolon > EB's dash; his comma after *Harold;* crossout running into 38 in pencil.

38–39. Crossouts from *les* to *peuple* are in ink.

39–41. H's corrections are originally in ink, then amended in pencil; crossouts and underlining are in pencil. Words I have reproduced in the margin were written in ink and crossed out in pencil above *son Créateur* in the MS; at the location marked by a bracketed question mark there is a notation similar to an oversized ampersand.

41–47. Corrections are in pencil; there are additional corrections in 45–46, but they are too faint to decipher.

50. H's *N > C; que* very small.

EDITORIAL NOTES (HEGER'S VERSION)
When Heger makes corrections that affect his meaning, I include them in the transcript. He also crosses out and overwrites words, but because his French is not in question, that editing is not noted.

TEXTUAL NOTES (DICTÉE)
In this dictée, Heger conflates two extracts from Hugo's seven-part essay. The first is from part 3, beginning with sentence 6 of paragraph 2 and continuing to the end of the paragraph. The other is from part 6 (not paragraph 6, as he wrote Gaskell) and runs from paragraph 10 through paragraph 12, sentence 10. The shift, signaled in the text with an asterisk, occurs at the end of line 14. Otherwise Heger remains faithful to the published text, only changing one phrase (see Comments, n. 21) and omitting a Latin phrase, *cuncta supercilio moventis,* that follows the allusion to Jupiter (45, 44F). CB's dictée is accurate too, aside from punctuation and a few misspelled or misheard words. The placement of her commas suggests where Heger paused and what he emphasized in speaking.

In translating the dictée and the French in the comments, I have drawn on but substantially revised an anonymous English translation in Hugo, *Things Seen,* 348, 361–62.

EDITORIAL NOTES (DICTÉE)
1. *Mirabeau* is in CB's double-line print.
2. The phrase *à la Tribune* is in small single-line print.
9. The word *amoncelé* should be *amonceler.*

18. The word *courant* comes at the end of a line, and a necessary comma is missing there.

27. The word *les* should be *des.*

31. *Oh!* begins a new paragraph in Hugo's text.

34. In Hugo, *la production extérieure.*

37. CB starts to write *brisque,* changes it to *brusque.*

42. A dot over the first *e* of *chevelure* may be a spot on the manuscript or a misspelling (*chivelure*).

44. After *Jupiter,* Hugo adds *cuncta supercilio moventis.*

47. The word *moment* should be plural.

49. *Victor Hugo* is in CB's proper-noun print.

COMMENTS

1. For details on Harold's brief kingship, see the Textual Notes.

2. "Rosina" (September 1, 1841) alludes to King Julius Brenzaida's death "beneath this palace dome— / True hearts on every side" (*EB Poems*, 136). See also "Why ask to know the date—the clime," her last surviving poem (184–85).

3. Gaskell, 11.234.

4. "[D]ans ma leçon je me bornais à ce qui concerne *Mirabeau orateur,* c'est à dire au paragraphe VI.—C'est après l'analyse de ce morceau, considéré surtout du point de vue du fond, de la disposition, de ce qu'on pourrais appeler *la charpente,* qu'ont été faits les deux portraits ci-joints" (May 22, 1856, letter, John Rylands Library, Manchester; Gaskell's version [11.234] omits the reference to the paragraph). Heger's letter identifies Hugo's essay as a well-known ("*fort étendu*") article published in 1834 and entitled "Literature et philosophie mêlées." Actually, "Sur Mirabeau" is one of several articles gathered in that volume.

5. All three manuscripts—"Peter," "Napoleon," and "Harold"—together with Heger's covering letter and a fourth manuscript of "extracts" from CB's letters to him are in a collection of Gaskell's papers at the John Rylands Library. Only "Peter" is in CB's handwriting, on paper that she ruled, with Heger's corrections. The rest are in the same hand (which I take to be Heger's), and they are consistent in paper, ink, and format.

6. Gaskell, 11.238.

7. Possibly he interchanged pen and pencil; the manuscript layering is not fully consistent; see Editorial Notes of this devoir.

8. Gaskell, 11.234.

9. See n. 4.

10. "Sur Mirabeau," pt. 2, 198. David E. Musselwhite first called attention to this passage, which he incorrectly cites as the "set piece" Heger read to the Brontës (99). But Musselwhite did not know about CB's dictée, and since this is paragraph 6 of part 2 (Heger says he drew on paragraph 6), his confusion is understandable.

11. Heger read Carlyle's portrait of Cromwell to the Brontës; it had

recently appeared in *On Heroes, Hero-Worship, and the Heroic in History.* See Gaskell, 11.239 and Comments on devoir 11.

12. "Sur Mirabeau" repeatedly makes the point that Mirabeau died just in time. "His was a sovereign and sublime head. '91 crowned it. '93 would have cut it off" (pt. 3, 203).

13. EB's conception of potentiality resembles Keats's, although there is no proof that she read him.

14. For example, "il avait enfin pu extravaser dans la société tous ses bouillonnements intérieurs si longtemps comprimés dans la famille" ("he had at last been able to pour out into society all the ebullience so long repressed within his family"; pt. 2, 198).

15. Gaskell, 11.233.

16. The Gaskell copy has not been previously published. Dorothy H. Cornish's translation of the Haworth version came out in 1947 (98); it makes no reference to Heger's corrections or to Cornish's own editing choices. In 1971 Gérin published a French version (*EB*, 267–68). She attempts to include some of the corrections but admits that the manuscript is "in very poor condition" and misreads quite a few lines.

17. Hewish, 66. He does not admire the portrait, which he says "lacks the bite of 'The Cat'" and "shows a stereotyped hero freed from the falsities of the court to face the ultimate reality of death" (ibid.).

18. Spark and Stanford, 63.

19. Musselwhite, 97.

20. See ibid., 97–100.

21. It does not, however, appear in Hugo's essay; Hugo speaks of *la production extérieure* (pt. 6, 211).

11. Portrait: Peter the Hermit / Portrait: Pierre l'Ermite, Imitation: Portrait of Peter the Hermit / Imitation: Portrait de Pierre l'Hermite, with dictée The Capture of Jerusalem by the Crusaders / Prise de Jerusalem par les croisés (CB)

TEXTUAL NOTES (PORTRAIT)

2–10. On correspondences between this passage and Carlyle's *On Heroes, Hero-Worship, and the Heroic in History,* see Comments.

6. Alexander (the Great), 356–323 B.C.: Macedonian king who conquered Greece, the Persian Empire, and Egypt. Attila (406?-453): king of the Huns, who invaded Europe.

8. Oliver Cromwell (1599–1658): Calvinist leader of the English Revolution that overthrew Charles II; he became lord protector of the Commonwealth.

9. Robespierre (1758–94): a leader of the French Revolution, eventually guillotined.

16. Picardy: a province of northwestern France; Peter is said to have been born in Amiens, its capital.

18. Saladin: Salah-al-Din Yusuf ibn-Ayyub (1138?-93), sultan of Egypt

and Syria who conquered Jerusalem and was defeated in the Third Crusade. Saracens: common European term for Muslims at the time of the Crusades.

22. Samson: biblical strong man, often alluded to by CB; on his breaking of knots, see Judg. 15.9–15.

32F. "comparais": Heger's marginal comment may direct CB to compare the two "ne" constructions marked by the symbol ⧧.

33–34. "the broad road . . .": a paraphrase of Matt. 7.13–14.

47. "imprint of Divinity": when Moses came down from Sinai after receiving the Lord's commandments, "the skin of his face shone." See Exod. 34.29–35.

61 ff. (63). CB seems to be portraying a scene that allegedly occurred on the day before the capture of Jerusalem during the First Crusade, given by Michaud as July 14, 1099.

70–75 (71–76). Compare these lines with CB's description of the biblical Holy Land in "The Death of Moses," 111–19.

81 (83–84). Godfrey of Bouillon (d. 1100): a knight and leader of the First Crusade who became advocate of the Holy Sepulchre after the capture of Jerusalem. Tancred: a knight who led the Normans in the First Crusade and became prince of Galilee after the capture of Jerusalem.

93 (95). "mantle of the prophet Elijah": see 1 Kings 13 and cf. 2 Kings 2.8.

95–97 (96–98). "holy sepulchre": where Jesus was buried. The great aim of the First Crusade was to redeem it and Jerusalem from the "infidels." Silver crescent: symbol of the Muslims. Oriflamme: orange-red flag of the Abbey of St. Denis, used as standard by early French kings. Red Cross: cross of St. George and national emblem of England.

101 (102–3). Moses delivered the Israelites from Egyptian slavery; his successor, Joshua, led them into Canaan, the promised land.

EDITORIAL NOTES (PORTRAIT)
The manuscript of this version, now at the British Library, was formerly owned by Thomas J. Wise. (On its provenance, see Comments, n. 2.) Wise notoriously altered Brontë manuscripts, and this one bears signs of tampering; Heger's marks have been erased from the pages wherever they could be gotten at. My assistant and I did what we could to decipher the traces, but some of the fainter signs escaped us.

The following words, which have also been erased, appear on the back of the last page, upside down and in another handwriting: "Mons Heger ne fait pas bien de ne pas céder à ses élèves ce qui leur a [ont?] couté tant de travail" ("M. Heger does wrong not to yield to his students what has cost them so much work").

2. *Portrait* in CB's double-line print.

3. *Pierre l'Ermite* in same style but single-line, followed by a period and a further mark, perhaps a flourish.

4. Before *être*, CB changes *d'* to *à*.

5. CB changes *morals* to *moraux*.

6. H's comma after *conquérant*.

7. Small addition to *passe*, perhaps the start of a canceled *s*.

8. H's comma after *révolutionnaire*.

12. Diphthong of *coeur* very contracted, resembling *cour*.

17. Above line, H > plural endings of CB's *les leurs* to make them singular.

18. H converts CB's *de les* either to *de ses* or *des;* see further revision in next "Pierre" draft.

20. The marginal symbol ⧺ is to the left of the crossed out words in MS; H's words may have been erased.

24–27. H adds an arcing line in left margin; something above it is erased.

31. The symbol ⧺ may signal a construction similar to the one in line 20.

32. The word *atteindre* is struck out with one diagonal.

35. H's *le* is in margin, directly preceding *casque*.

37 ff. Dots and diagonals in the left margin may indicate lines with grammatical errors, but erasure has removed any comments that may have accompanied them.

38. H converts CB's comma to a semicolon.

39. H's above line *la* may > *de* before *rigueur*.

42–43. The *f* of H's *fut* runs down into CB's *était*, as if to delete it.

45. H's accent on *Génie; f* of H's *fit* runs down into CB's *faisait*, as if to delete it.

54. There is an indecipherable notation in left margin; *infidelles* [*sic*] may be crossed out rather than underlined.

59. The word *petit* slopes below the line in the MS.

60. H's comma after *enthousiasme*.

62. Very faint *tr* on line in margin preceding *une nation*.

63–64. H appears to be deleting these lines only, but in fact lines 63–85 and further words drop out of the second draft.

66. The *o* in *occident* may be u.c.

72. CB has corrected *t* of *sainte*, originally an *e*.

73. CB's erased *ep* precedes *ancienne*.

76. *Jerusalem* in CB's proper-noun print; she erases *tte* following *ce*.

77. *Temple* in CB's proper-noun print.

83–84. *Godfroi* and *Tancréde* in CB's proper-noun print.

89. CB's strikeout.

91. The word *levés* may have an accent on the first *e*.

95. A letter (*p*?) before *prophète* has been erased.

EDITORIAL NOTES (IMITATION)

CB incorporates most of the revisions that Heger indicated in her first draft, which she wrote more than five weeks earlier. He seems even more attentive to this version than to the last; he makes more analytic comments in the margins and attends more closely to details.

2. *Imitation* in large double-line, slightly back-sloping letters closer to cursive than print, with a Gothic *I*.

3. Subtitle in very small letters and in CB's proper-noun print.

4. First comma H's, second CB's.

6. H's accent on *conquérant*.

7. H's comma after *ouragan*.

8. H's comma after *quelquefois;* his accent on *révolutionnaire*.

9. Words above line here are in margin in MS, crossing CB's border to precede *vices*.

11. CB starts to add *e* to *Mahomèt* and then curtails it; H canceled the *e* in draft 1.

17. H's accent on *inquiéter*.

18. CB deletes *s* of *des;* compare H's correction in draft 1, line 18.

26. A comma after *âme* may be missing because the word runs into the binding.

29. H's accent on *avidément.*

37. H strikes out CB's *et* and her above-the-line addition.

47. H adds an apostrophe to create *l'apôtre.*

49. In *il fallait* CB begins an *f* after the first *i* and then converts it to an *l.*

61. H alters verb tense on *exerçait.*

64. H draws a line to connect *là* to *multitude* in line 65.

65–67. H's diagonals run left and right (/ \ ) in MS to cut the rest of the paragraph.

69. H's semicolon after *Elijah;* he adds *Pierre* in the margin, directly preceding *lit.*

72. H's accent on *à.*

73. H has a connecting sign, replaced here by a caret.

74. H's dash after *soldats;* his comma after ~~matin.~~

75. H's line after *promis* may signal the need for punctuation; CB's crossout of *promesse.*

76. H's comma.

TEXTUAL NOTES (DICTÉE)

The extract begins with paragraph 4 of Charlotte's dictée. The earlier paragraphs cover the time of the Christians' entry (3 P.M. on Good Friday) and the terrible carnage the Crusaders inflicted: they massacred the Saracens in the streets of Jerusalem, in their houses, and even in the mosque where they fled for asylum.

My translation is revised from W. Robson, *History of the Crusades* 1:227.

EDITORIAL NOTES (DICTÉE)

CB's dictée varies in a few words from published versions of this passage. The variants, excluding punctuation, are recorded below (pv = printed version).

1–2. Title and subtitle in CB's single-line, proper-noun script.

4. Pv reads *s'arrêter au tableau.*

8. The phrase *dérober aux Sarrasins* is *dérober à la recherche des Sarrasins* in pv.

11. Pv reads *fidèles.*

12. Pv reads *chrétiens.*

14. The phrase *le cenobite pieux* is *le généreux cénobite* in pv.

22. *Michaut* [sic] in smaller print.

COMMENTS

1. In addition to "On the Death of Napoleon," which she reproduces from Heger's copy, she reports seeing "Vision and Death of Moses on Mount Nebo" and "Letter, from a Missionary, Sierra Leone, Africa"; "The Caterpillar" and "The Fall of the Leaves," which she does not mention, are still in the Heger family.

2. After CB's death, the devoirs she brought back went to Arthur Bell Nicholls, her widower. Though Nicholls lent Gaskell a "bundle" of manuscripts, Gaskell's comments make it clear that she was unaware of the June 23 draft. Nicholls later sold what he had to Wise and Clement K. Shorter. Though much of that collection was dispersed, the bookplate inside the folder of this devoir, "Thomas James Wise / His Book," reveals that Wise retained it in his private (Ashley) library.

3. Gaskell, 11.234. See also Comments on devoir 10.

4. Gaskell, 11.238–39. She is defining Heger's "synthetical teaching," his method of exposing students to the views of different writers on the same subject, Cromwell in this case.

5. Macdonald, "The Brontës at Brussels," quoting interviews with two former pensionnat students. Madame G. also called CB "sickly looking." Mlle C. "recollect[ed] Madame Héger to have been a very pretty woman, and very careful of her personal appearance," whereas "Charlotte Brontë's personal appearance was extremely insignificant and even displeasing; and she dressed badly" (287).

6. "[S]ans fortune et sans renommée" (Michaud, *Histoire des croisades,* 90); "[il] n'avait d'autre puissance que la force de son caractère et de son génie" (ibid., 89). The first volume of Michaud's massive work came out in 1808. By 1841, two years after his death, his *History of the Crusades* was in its sixth edition. Michaud aimed for scholarly accuracy as well as a lively account of events, and his many footnotes indicate his sources; he was, however, all inclusive rather than discriminating.

7. *Encyclopaedia Britannica,* 11th ed., s.v. "Peter the Hermit." See also Hagenmeyer.

8. See *Histoire des Croisades,* 89–90 (*History of the Crusades* 1:40–41).

9. Gaskell, 11.243. See also Lucy Snowe's account of such lectures in *Villette,* 13.162–63.

10. On Martin's influence, see Alexander and Sellars, 20–21. CB may also have seen an illustrated volume of Michaud.

11. News of the lectures was widespread enough to reach John Ruskin in Geneva; on the responses, see Michael K. Goldberg's introduction to *On Heroes,* xxix, lxii ff. The book itself may also have been stocked in an English bookstore in Brussels.

12. "Sur Mirabeau," 193, 195.

13. "Advice," devoir 4.

14. Gaskell, 11.234.

15. Michaud, *Histoire des croisades,* 427; *The History of the Crusades,* 215.

16. The deletion may have been more strongly indicated, but since erasures have been made throughout this manuscript, only these markings are visible.

17. *CB Poems,* 274.

12/13. Letter (Madam) / Lettre (Madame) (EB) and Letter of invitation to a Clergyman / Lettre d'invitation à un Ecclésiastique (CB)

EDITORIAL NOTES (DEVOIR 12)

The off-center placement of *Lettre* and *Réponse* and their positions in respect to the double lines imitate the spacing of EB's manuscript. I have normalized the paragraph indentations.

1. A small square of the page (with *Emil* and the top half of *y*) has been ripped away; on the reverse side (line 8) the word after *une* is missing because of the tear.

26. The phrase *de mon travail* added in left margin.

EDITORIAL NOTES (DEVOIR 13)

1. 1842 is added below date, perhaps later and not by CB.
2. *Lettre* in CB's double-line print.
3. The subtitle is printed and much smaller than the title.
17. The letter *q* after *précieux* has been erased but remains visible.
20. A second *t* in *tout* converted to *s*.
30. CB has added *e* (feminine ending) to *un*.

COMMENTS

1. *Lets.,* 300 (298, for the French) and 301 nn. 6, 7; see also Gérin *EB,* 130–34.

2. J. J. Green, "The Brontë-Wheelwright Friendship," *Friends Quarterly Examiner* (November 1915), reprinted in Gérin *EB,* 130.

3. Chitham additionally observes, "The tone of the letter is almost rude, and we must wonder how M. Heger felt about it. He could surely not overlook the unfriendly rebuke given by the music teacher, and nor should we. For pupil, substitute the naive guest, Lockwood; for scornful teacher, substitute Heathcliff . . ." (146).

4. She had been invited to attend lectures on Galvanism. Her letter concludes, "so that, everything considered it is perhaps as well that circumstances have deprived us of this pleasure" (May 11, 1831, in *Lets.,* 109–10).

14. Letter (My dear Mama) / Lettre (Ma chère Maman) (CB)

TEXTUAL NOTES

My translation often parallels Phyllis Bentley's ("More Brontë Devoirs," 384) because EB's French has such obvious English equivalents that it leaves the translator few options.

EDITORIAL NOTES

Some of Heger's underlines wave slightly, but the difference between them and his straight underlining is hard to ascertain and so is not noted, except in line 6.

4. H's *trop* > his *bien.*
5. EB has erasure under *aie.*
11. H's colon after EB's comma.
14. H's comma after *jouent.*
16. H's comma after *nous.*
19. H makes EB's comma into a semicolon.
20. H draws a line below and past *j'ai à* to *vous.*

COMMENTS

1. "If the girl is in quarantine, nineteenth-century experience and literary convention make it likely that she is dying; suppressing her reproaches against the mother, the girl instead identifies with her, with fatal results. . . ." Homan's reading of this devoir also stresses the speaker's am-

bivalence toward the absent mother, the "mixture of yearning and repressed anger" (150).

2. CB's "Biographical Notice" of 1850 (quoted in the Introduction, xxv–xxvi) makes a point of EB's homesickness.

3. For example, Ratchford assumes that A.G.A.'s infant daughter dies and cites both a poem and an earlier fragment on the theme of "a young girl in prison" (*Gondal's Queen,* 120–24, 168).

4. Tayler finds different links between this letter and *Wuthering Heights:* "[T]he dramatic situation—illness in isolation and cure by reunion—is familiar indeed. The first is echoed in Catherine's 'frightful isolation' among the Lintons. . . , the second in the reintegration that Catherine and Heathcliff seek beyond death" (98–99).

15. Filial Love / L'Amour Filial (EB)

TEXTUAL NOTES

3. EB invokes the Fifth Commandment, Exod. 20.12 and Deut. 5.16; see also Comments, n. 3.

10–12 (11–13). Compare Chateaubriand on the instincts of animals: "La poule si timide, par exemple, devient aussi courageuse qu'un aigle quand il faut défendre ses poussins" (*Oeuvres complètes* 11:206; "The timorous hen, for example, becomes as courageous as an eagle when she must defend her chicks"). Heger had read the Brontës other excerpts from this section.

15 (16). "voice of thunder": a reference to God speaking to Moses on Mount Sinai, which quaked in the storm and was covered with a cloud of fire.

19 (20). EB implicitly reverses the movement of Gen. 1.2–4 from chaos to order and darkness to light.

31–34 (34–36). Perhaps a reversal of Rom. 8.33–34; see Comments.

EDITORIAL NOTES

2. *L* and *A* of title double-line print.

26. EB starts to write *pens* at the end of a line, runs out of space, adds *é* on next line, then cancels *é* and rewrites *pensé* above.

28. EB inserts *leur* and the apostrophe for *n'a* without canceling the *e.*

30. The *f* of *infatigable* > something indecipherable.

33. The word *s'éveillera* was originally in the present tense, with *ra* added, running into the comma.

COMMENTS

1. Last stanza of the untitled poem "Shed no tear o'er that tomb," July 26, 1839 (*EB Poems,* 109). Chitham was the first to observe the connection between the tone of this poem and the devoir's (147).

2. According to MacDonald, Heger insisted that his students rewrite their devoirs after he had marked them, incorporating "the improvements suggested" ("The Brontës at Brussels," 283).

3. Exod. 20.12. An alternate version appears in Deut. 5.16: "Honour thy father and thy mother, as the Lord thy God hath commanded thee; that thy

days may be prolonged, and that it may go well with thee, in the land which the Lord thy God giveth thee."

4. Winnifrith, 37–40. He rejects Gérin's suggestion that their exposure to Calvinist tenets came through Maria Branwell.

5. Calvin, 136.

6. Rom. 8.33–34.

7. See Gen. 1.1–4 and 1.26–27.

8. *EB Poems,* 97–98, lines 15, 22–23, 53.

9. *EB Poems,* 256.

16. Letter from one brother to another / Lettre d'un frère à un frère (EB)

TEXTUAL NOTES

3. I take the English title from Lorine White Nagel's translation (*Five Essays,* 15; rpt., "Three Essays," 339–40). In other respects, our versions often differ because she translates Heger's revisions as if they were EB's words.

22. CB uses the "bark" trope in *The Professor:* "At that hour my bark hung on the topmost curl of a wave of fate, and I knew not on what shoal the onward rush of the billow might hurl it" (23.213).

EDITORIAL NOTES

2. Although H indicates that he will designate errors with a double underline and words to be changed with a wavy underline, his practice does not always correspond to this intention.

7. The word *écoulées* may > something illegible.

8. *séparation* w.u.?

9. H's *en* > his *pour.*

15–16. A diagonal slash begins after *joui* and runs down through *possesseur;* presumably H wanted the phrase to conclude with *joui.*

19. H's circumflex in *goûter.*

20. The word *cette* is below the line in MS, directly beneath *la.*

24. EB started to write *se*(?) under *s'étaient;* the *us* of H's *voulus* > *ais.*

27. H's semicolon.

28. EB crosses out *a,* substituting *entre.*

29. H's semicolon.

38. EB crosses out *naissait* and adds *nut* to change the verb to *connut.* H seems to be reducing her phrase to *me le témoigna par des caresses.*

39. H's circumflex in *vôtre.*

40–41. I have adjusted the spacing to fit H's phrase above the lines; he has *fait taire* above *la place* and adds a curved line to show that it belongs before *la nature.*

42. H's semicolon.

43. H's apostrophe; EB's crossout of *heureux.*

43–46. H's name is horizontal in left margin, facing away from text.

45. H's circumflex in *fâcher.*

47. The word *viens* is above the line in the MS because EB ran out of space.

COMMENTS

1. "Lines" (*EB Poems,* 97); dated April 28, 1839. Several Gondal poems from this period appear to deal with themes of absence and longing, and of return cut off either by death or criminality. See, for example, the untitled

poem of January 12, 1839: "To a silent home thy foot may come / And years may follow of toilsome pain; / But yet I swear by that Burning Tear / The loved shall meet on its hearth again" (*EB Poems*, 94).

2. *WH*, 194 (ch. 15, mod. eds.).

3. See *EW*, 42–43.

4. See ibid., ch. 29; and *CBEW* 2.2:150.

5. Alexander outlines the story (*EW*, 220); it appears in facsimile in *Misc.* 1:327.

6. *Misc.* 2:390.

7. EB, *Five Essays*, 15 n.

8. See *EB Poems*, 95 and 255–56.

9. *Gondal's Queen*, 177; *EB Poems*, 184. These lines come from an untitled Gondal manuscript dated September 14, 1846; see also Ratchford's note on p. 174.

10. *EB Poems*, 9–11 and 230; see also *The Complete Poems of Emily Jane Brontë*, 218–19.

17/18. The Butterfly / Le Papillon (EB) and The Caterpillar / La Chenille (CB)

TEXTUAL NOTES (DEVOIR 17)

My translation is indebted to Lorine White Nagel's (*Five Essays*, 17–19; rpt., "Three Essays," 340–41).

On the mood of this devoir and some of its imagery, compare EB's "A Day Dream" (*EB Poems*, 17–19; dated March 5, 1844). Several critics have also pointed out that *Wuthering Heights* ends with a vision of the moths that flutter around the three graves.

37–38. As Homans has noted, EB's image recalls Gen. 3.14–15: "crushing under foot the caterpillar, which she calls a reptile, she bruises the head of the serpent" (143).

43F. *voute* [*sic*] *azurée*: common French Romantic phrase for the sky.

52ff. Gezari compares this conclusion and its rejection of eternal damnation to the convictions EB expresses in two untitled poems of 1840; see *EB Poems*, 121–24, 263.

EDITORIAL NOTES (DEVOIR 17)

2. *Devoir* is on a separate page in special double-line letters.

3. *Le Papillon* is in regular print.

29. The word *récriai* extends into the right margin, and *je* extends beyond the left margin of the next line.

31. The word *tourment* runs off the page, so EB may have meant to include the final *e*.

33. The second *de* was inserted and extends over the line marking the left margin.

48. The words *ton* and *tu verras* were respectively *votre* and *vous verriez*, which have been erased.

49. The word *de* ends the page and is repeated on the next page, clearly a mistake.

My translation is indebted to Phyllis Bentley's ("More Brontë Devoirs," 362–64), though I have kept this version more literal than hers to catch the remaining stiffness in CB's French.

12–13. Compare Pss. 8.5

25–35. The English "it" removes the possible gender implications of CB's parable: *la chenille,* the ugly worm, is feminine; *l'insecte* and *le papillon* are masculine.

44–46 (45–48). Possibly a reference to Sir Isaac Newton, who was widely known to have made this comparison; for example, Mary Shelley alludes to it in *Frankenstein.* Patrick Brontë cites Newton (though not this episode) in his poem "On Halley's Comet in 1835."

60F. Compare "La Mort de Napoléon," first draft, line 36.

63–69. Throughout this passage CB closely follows 1 Cor. 15.42–44, 52, 54. I therefore use the words of the Bible but retain her "animal" (64) instead of the biblical "natural."

2. *Devoir* is on a cover page in double-line print with a Gothic *D.*

3. *La Chenille* is in double-line print.

COMMENTS

1. *Lets.,* 289.

2. See devoirs 10/11 and 12/13.

3. See devoirs 7/8 and 21/22.

4. See Benvenuto, 78; Willson, 22–25; and Miller, ch. 4.

5. From "A Day Dream," *EB Poems,* 18.

6. "Resolution and Independence" and *The Excursion* have both been cited in connection with EB's poetry; see *EB Poems,* 241, 257, 264, etc. Further English precedents for both devoirs have been suggested—in Shakespeare (*Lear*), Keats, Blake, Benjamin Constant, the Methodists James Hervey and John Wesley, and, of course, the King James Bible. See, respectively, Benvenuto, 78–79; Hewish, 66; and Miller, 193.

7. "[I]t is difficult to see how the sudden appearance of the butterfly . . . is an adequate answer to the universe of cruelty already evoked, in which pain and beauty exist side by side" (Hewish, 66–67).

8. Like the others on this list, Bernardin de Saint-Pierre sought to prove God's existence through the wonders of nature. He claimed that metamorphosis challenged Locke's theory that there were no innate ideas: at each stage, the insect must have been thinking, for it could not have reacted from experience. See *Oeuvres* 3:15–16.

9. *The System of Natural History . . . Carefully Abridged,* trans. CON [*sic*] (Edinburgh: J. Ruthven, 1800), 2:87.

10. "Là, près des ruches des abeilles, / Arachné tisse ses merveilles, / Le serpent siffle, et la fourmi / Guide â des conquêtes de sables / Ses multi-

tudes innombrables / Qu'écrase un lézard endormi!" ("Neuvième Harmonie. Suite de Jéhovah. Le Chêne," *Harmonies,* 133).

11. *Genius,* 136; emphasis mine. See also *Oeuvres complètes* 11:185. Duthie was the first to cite the connection between Chateaubriand and these devoirs (*Foreign Vision,* 215 n. 29).

12. The project of natural theology was to show how creation manifests "the Power, Wisdom, and Goodness of God." These words appear in the notice to all the volumes in the *Bridgewater Treatises,* the major early Victorian source of instruction on this movement. *Naturphilosophie,* in Philip F. Rehbock's words, is a "strain of scientific thought deriving from Kantian idealism" (17) that attracted many eighteenth- and nineteenth-century German philosophers. Goethe was its leading proponent in the biological sciences. EB's allusion to an "embryo" (line 46) may reflect a theory of the natural philosophers. For further information and a list of their premises, see Rehbock, 18–19, 20–21.

13. Davies also makes the point that EB "accept[ed] none of the brainwashing about Nature's benignity which was her Wordsworthian inheritance" (108).

14. Miller, 164–65. He quotes and comments on a sermon he titles "The Great Deliverance," however, it is given in Wesley's *Works* as "The General Deliverance."

15. Wesley 2:443–45.

16. Ibid., 446–47.

17. See Winnifrith, ch. 3 passim. Lane notes that this essay, "remote though it may be from the conventional Methodist-tinged Church of England in which she was brought up, nevertheless fits firmly within the Christian framework" (*Purely for Pleasure,* 145). A further connection may be Robert Southey, the poet laureate to whom CB wrote for advice about her writing. In 1820 Southey published in two volumes his *Life of Wesley; and the Rise and Progress of Methodism.* Though it is not on record as a book the Brontës owned, they may have had access to it elsewhere.

18. "The New Birth," *Works* 2:192, paraphrasing Eph. 1.18.

19. Homans, 142. This conclusion is part of a reading of "The Butterfly" that differs substantially from mine.

20. A possible exception is her poem "A Day Dream," briefly quoted in the text. There, the speaker's mood is transformed by "little glittering spirits" that sing of mortal suffering as the necessary prelude to "universal joy" (*EB Poems,* 18–19).

21. As Duthie says, "In style, form and rhythm [this devoir] is much superior to anything she had yet written in French" (*Foreign Vision,* 29).

22. See his marginal comments on devoirs 11 and 26.

23. See his comments on devoir 4.

24. "Le thème est banal, mais l'expression est riche, souple et poétique" (Wells, 90). He claims that only the "religious tone" ("la tonalité religieuse

dont elle enveloppe son sujet") gives it away as an essay by a non-native speaker.

19. The Aim of Life / Le But de la Vie (CB)

EDITORIAL NOTES

1. Underlining conspicuously extends beyond the name and date.
2. The title is in elaborate letters (see fig. 5).
12. The word *scintillaient* is in the margin preceding *les premières*.
33. The word *manque* almost runs off the end of the page, and no period follows.

COMMENTS

1. See the entries in the Chronology for May 29, June 5, August 6, and September 2, 1843.
2. All published sources spell the name "Sarah Ann," but since the child herself added the final *e,* I have retained it.
3. The Wheelwrights' account of the date differ. Chadwick, who spoke to one of the Misses Wheelwrights (she does not indicate which) says that the parents traveled after Julia Wheelwright's death from typhoid that September (*Footsteps,* 228–29); according to Frances Wheelwright, however, her parents took a "summer holiday" ("Two Brussels School-fellows," 28). Wise and Symington place the trip in May 1843 (*BLFC* 1:289), but their accounts are often unreliable. Smith reports that they went to the pensionnat "daily throughout the vacation for various lessons" (*Lets.,* 301 n. 7).
4. Because the children all disliked EB, who made the three youngest take piano lessons during recess, CB only started to visit them regularly after EB left Brussels. Sources on the Wheelwrights include J. J. Green, "The Brontë-Wheelwright Friendship," *Friends Quarterly Examiner* (November 1915); "Two Brussels School-fellows," 27–29; Chadwick, *Footsteps,* 225–29; and Gérin *CB,* 207.
5. Gaskell, 11.261; and *Lets.,* 334 (without "the").
6. I am grateful to Sabine Mourlon-Beernaert for alerting me to this point.
7. On its derivation, see Editorial Method.
8. See the Chronology entry for August 15, 1843; he also gave her an anthology, *Les Fleurs de la poésie française.*
9. In *Villette,* Lucy refers to the striking of St. Jean Baptiste's clock. See, for instance, 12.153.
10. *5 Novs.,* 199.
11. All three sisters paced the sitting room as they discussed work in progress; see Gaskell, 2.1:307. Her character Frances Henri also paces (*The Professor,* 19.167 and 23.214).
12. On the dialogic aspects of this devoir, see Lonoff, "Charlotte Brontë's Belgian Essays" 389–91.
13. Chapone, 54–55. Fraser says that Miss Wooler's "regime of studies" was based on this book (73).

20. Human Justice / La Justice humaine (CB)

TEXTUAL NOTE

56. Pharisees: members of an ancient Hebrew sect, referred to by Jesus, who were known for hypocritical self-righteousness and arrogance in their adherence to religious law; also, people who resemble them.

EDITORIAL NOTES
On the layers of correction in the manuscript, see the Comments.

2. The title is in CB's double-line script.

4. CB crosses out *gens,* presumably after H underlines it.

5. CB crosses out *est melé,* presumably after H underlines it.

6. CB's correction, *ions,* runs diagonally below line; H's accent on *législateurs;* CB crosses out *leurs,* which has w.u. and double line below.

7. CB crosses out *dictums,* presumably after H underlines it.

9–10. H's commas.

10–11. CB crosses out *la chose . . . administre.*

12. CB crosses out *Prenons . . . un,* changes *d'un homme accusé* to the plural, then crosses out the whole phrase.

13. CB crosses out *la conviction,* corrects accent on second *e* of *précède.*

14. CB crosses out *imposition.*

17. Three lines under *avec;* H's accent on *misérables; obj*(?) in pencil in left margin.

18–19. H's underlining in pencil overwritten with ink; penciled line is double, ink w.u. is single, with a dip under *vite;* H's accent on *développer; objon* in ink in left margin.

22. The word *des* underlined four times; possibly H suggests that CB reverse *vicieux* and *malheureux.* The *à* in left margin seems to precede the indecipherable words below it.

23. Above the line, CB's dot may represent a comma; H strikes out *pas.*

26–27. W.u. under *les pièges* and *de la loi* connected by a fainter circular line running under *trompeurs;* comma after *trompeurs* deleted; *arts* w.u. in ink and pencil. CB inserts *que . . . ignorant* below the line (bottom of MS pp. 2–3); my arrow indicates its place in the sentence.

28. H crosses out *son.*

29. Above line, H misspells *arraché.*

32. H's accent on first *e* in *épithètes.*

33. Four lines under *est; de fange* w.u. in pencil overwritten with ink; *jetée* w.u., with an additional triple line under the *ée.*

36. H's accents on first *e* of *réalité* and on *cède.*

42. Three lines under *était.*

43. Four lines under *le;* CB's *a > e.*

47. In MS *qui* appears in margin to left of *conseille;* double line strikes out *dit-il.*

50. Three lines under *le;* CB's *a > e.*

51. CB crosses out *qu'il est lepre.*

56. H's accent on *désespoir.*

57. The phrase *se charger* w.u. in pencil, *d'une partie* in ink. In MS *partie?* ends the line, concluding the devoir, but in response to H's question, CB adds *du fardeau* on the next, preceding her centered double line.

COMMENTS

1. *Villette,* 35.582–83.

2. *Villette,* 35.583. Margaret Smith infers that volume 3, which CB mailed to Smith, Elder on November 20, was "well under way by 3 November" (xxxii). This episode comes midway through the volume, in chapter 35, "Fraternity."

3. *Villette,* 35.582.

4. BPM, Bonnell 115. These two dictées follow the one by Michaud that CB used in writing "Peter the Hermit," so she must have transcribed them toward the end of the spring term or at the beginning of the fall. Duthie identifies them, respectively, as excerpts from *Sermons pour la Carême,* book 4, and *Défense du Christianisme,* discours 3 (*Foreign Vision,* 232).

5. Macdonald's description of his methods ("The Brontës at Brussels," 283) is summarized in Introduction.

6. On the signs of correction that could not be reproduced in typescript, see Editorial Notes.

7. The manuscript is part of the Bonnell bequest to the Brontë Parsonage Museum. Wise, who got his devoirs from Nicholls after CB's death, sold the Bonnells their collection. One possible sign that she returned to this devoir is a word scribbled sideways on page 4 of the manuscript, which could be "adieu." However, this identification is uncertain, and I cannot judge its provenance from the ink.

8. *Villette,* 35.579.

9. "Mrs. Sweeny's soothing syrup" refers back to Lucy's first night at the pensionnat, when she and Mme Beck discover the Irish nursery-governess passed out beside her bottle (*Villette,* 8.93).

10. Matthew Arnold set the theme in an 1853 letter: "Why is *Villette* disagreeable? Because the writer's mind contains nothing but hunger, rebellion, and rage . . ." (quoted in Allott, 93). Important twentieth-century feminist responses include Millett, 140–47; Gilbert and Gubar, 399–440; and Auerbach, 97–113.

21/22. The Palace of Death / Le Palais de la Mort (CB and EB versions)
TEXTUAL NOTES (DEVOIR 21)

14–15. "young sphere . . . launched in space": compare the combination of religion and astronomy in "The Immensity of God."

17. "noble savage": an allusion to Rousseau, with whose work CB was to some extent familiar; Heger and his colleagues were skeptical of Rousseau's educational theories.

18 (19). Methuselah: biblical patriarch who allegedly lived 969 years (Gen. 5.21–28).

19. Enoch, Abraham, Jacob: biblical patriarchs. Abraham was progenitor of the Hebrews; Jacob was his son. There are several Enochs; one was the son of Cain (Gen. 4.17), another the father of Methuselah.

20. Mesopotamia: literally, country among the rivers; ancient land between the Tigris and Euphrates, north and east of Palestine.

36 (37). By Dan, which she crossed out, CB might have meant the Don, a
river of southern Russia; she substitutes the Neva, a northern Russian river.

55 (56). "faithful laborer in these fields": perhaps an ironic allusion to
Jesus' parable of the laborers in the vineyard, Matt. 20.

68 (70). Amazon: CB's interest in these legendary warrior women also
emerges in "The Death of Moses," where she personifies early Rome as "a
young Amazon, full of ardor and ambition" (line 167). She alludes to the
Amazon Penthesilia in a letter of 1850 (*BLFC* 3:187) and in *Villette* (30.505).

69 (71). Thalestris: queen of an Amazon nation on the Black Sea in the
time of Alexander the Great, most famously described by Diodorus. For
further information, see Comments.

89 ff. Compare the words of St. John Rivers, resisting his love for Rosa-
mond Oliver: "I rested my temples on the breast of temptation, and put my
neck voluntarily under her yoke of flowers; I tasted her cup. The pillow was
burning: there is an asp in the garland . . ." (*JE,* 476 [ch. 32, mod. eds.]).

96–97 (100). There may be an echo here of "Médisance" ("Slander"), a
dictée by Massillon that CB copied: "[C]'est une source pleine d'un venin
mortel; tout ce qui en part est infecté, et infecte tout ce qui l'environne; ses
louanges même sont empoisonnées . . . ses gestes, ses mouvements, ses regards, tout à son poison, et le répand à sa manière . . ." ([Slander] is a
source full of mortal venom; all that emanates from it is infected, and it in-
fects all that surrounds it; its very praises are poisonous . . . its gestures, its
motions, its looks, all [have] their poison and spread it in their own way . . .).

EDITORIAL NOTES (DEVOIR 21)
The title and the "*Matière*" take up the first page of the manuscript. The devoir begins on the second page (typescript line 11). H makes distinctions between wavy and
straight underlines, but some of his notations under verb forms are ambiguous.

2. Title in CB's double-line print.
3. *M* of *Matière* in CB's double-line print.
11. H's commas.
12. The phrase *parler de* may be w.u.
13. Indecipherable notation, crossed out, below *pensée bonne* in left margin.
16. In MS *obj^{on}* in left margin.
17. H's diagonal line after *époque.*
18–19. All punctuation H's.
20. H's circumflex; his accent on *Mésopotamie.*
21. H's ~~de temps à~~ is directly above his correction (to the plural) of *du pâturage.*
23. CB probably started to write *appelé* but changed it to an infinitive.
25. H's comma after *qui.*
26. H's accent on *deserts;* his comma following.
28. H converts CB's *la* to *là* and adds a comma, altering the syntax; my addition
above line to indicate the change.
31. In margin, here and elsewhere, indecipherable signs (an abbreviation?) follow
cherchez le sens de ce mot.

33. H's comma.

35. Four lines under *y*.

37. CB's deletion of *Dan;* H's accent on *Neva.*

40. Three lines under *m* in *columnes.*

41. Wavy semicircular line around *taillis.*

42. The word *froids* w.u.?

43. Underlining of *teinte* is slashed by a perpendicular line below second *t;* see Comments.

44. Three lines under *les* and *garde.*

54. H's deletion of *mais.*

56. H's comma; H strikes out *fidèle;* CB has erased *t* under *c* of *ces.*

57. H's comma.

59. H's comma.

60. H's comma after *l'amitié.*

61. Comma after *amour* and semicolon both H's.

63. CB's strikeout of *gliss;* more indecipherable marks in margin following *mot.*

65. H corrects CB's accent on *laissèrent.*

75. Indecipherable marks in margin after *mot.*

78. H's comma.

79. Question mark after *pieds* may be H's; line canceling *après* curves up over word.

82. H's comma after *sourit;* his *le* > CB's *les;* his *la* > her *lant* in *semblant.*

83. Three lines under *sa.*

85. H's comma after *vives.*

87. CB deletes *joie.*

88. More symbols in margin following following *cherchez.*

89. H's accent on *désordre.*

93. H's accent on *Intempérance.*

94. H's accent on *réclame.*

95. CB converts *rivaux* to *rivales; sacrifiée* may have a last, crossed-out letter trailing down.

96. H's *en* is in left margin, next to *cent.*

97–98. *Mort* in both lines is slightly w.u.; H probably objected to the repetition.

101. The *or* of *mortel* d.u. above w.u., and the word is surrounded by ⊓.

TEXTUAL NOTES (DEVOIR 22)

Margaret Lane has done a graceful and literary translation of this devoir ("French Essays," 281–85); mine attempts to stick more closely to EB's less-than-polished French.

22 ff. "the bones that lay strewn . . .": Lane comments that EB's essay has a "medieval flavour" not found in her poems and cites this passage as "belong[ing] more to the fifteenth century than to the nineteenth" (*Purely for Pleasure,* 148).

25, 27–29. EB's list recalls four of the Seven Deadly Sins: Anger, Envy, Sloth, and Covetousness.

EDITORIAL NOTES (DEVOIR 22)

As in CB's devoir, the "*Matière*" fills the first page of the manuscript, the devoir beginning on the second page (typescript line 10). H underscores with moderately wavy lines but does not seem to create a deliberate distinction between straight and waved underlining. All corrections from line 62 on are in pencil; those before are in ink. EB's capitalization of *La* before *Mort* is inconsistent, and sometimes her *l* appears to be midway between upper and lower case.

    2. *Matière* in large print. Title small, as if squeezed in as an afterthought. H repeats *Matière*, beginning the word in the left margin.

    10. The title appears to the left of center.

    21. The word *côtés* may be *côtes*.

    24. H strikes out *i* of *hidieusement.*

    29. *Avarice* > something indecipherable.

    30. The *r* of *obtinrent* > something indecipherable.

    32. An *l* > *L*(?) before *Ambition;* the top of the *F* in *Fanatisme* extends as if she were beginning a *T.*

    55. The word *je* precedes *serai* in the margin.

    60. The word deleted below *bannières* may be *lumières; du* may > *au.*

    62. First two letters of *Famine* > something indecipherable.

    73. H strikes out the *e* of *tarde.*

    87. *M* may be *m,* here and in line 89.

COMMENTS

    1. It is not clear whether they got these instructions in class or in a private lesson. As *The Professor* and *Villette* suggest, the dictée is a standard classroom exercise; CB kept at least one notebook of such extracts to be analyzed or imitated later. These devoirs, in contrast (and like "The Siege of Oudenarde"), follow a much stricter outline. Perhaps Heger gave such dictées to the class at large, or perhaps he saved them for pupils who could benefit from more controlled writing.

    2. Aside from minor changes in paragraphing and punctuation, they differ only in the following: lines 4–5: "ministre était" (CB); "ministre était alors" (EB); line 5: "la mort eut tant" (CB); "la Mort avait tant" (EB); lines 7–8: "parait" (CB); "paraissait" (EB). The ellipses may indicate that Heger broke off or that he added untranscribed explanations. That both sisters set Ambition first, allude to Civilization, and give Intemperance a feverish complexion hint at supplementary instructions or collaboration between them.

    3. "Four Essays," 96–98.

    4. "The Palace of Death," 803–4. In this article, Lane mentions that CB's "Death of Napoleon" exists in two versions, but apparently she remains unaware of CB's "Palace of Death."

    5. Margaret Lane, "The Palace of Death" (Letter), *The Listener* 52 (November 18, 1954): 865; on the same page, Frederick G. Richford suggests a further precedent in Caxton's translation of *Geoffroi de la Tour;* see Maxwell for discussion.

    6. In "French Essays," 281–84, with French and English on facing pages but without the comments from *The Listener.* A note explains that the "introductory section . . . has been freely translated by the Editor."

    7. Maxwell, 139. He did not know of the "Matière" preceding CB's essay,

but the "Matière" before EB's and the many points in common between the two texts persuaded him that both developed from an outline and topic that Heger had dictated.

8. Duthie cites a pertinent passage from Buffon's *History of Animals*: "Intemperance alone destroys and wastes more men than all of human nature's other plagues combined" ("L'intempérance détruit et fait languir plus d'hommes, elle seule, que tous les autres fléaux de la nature humaine réunis"; Duthie, *Foreign Vision*, 216 n. 44). But though Buffon is a source for earlier assignments, no proof exists that Heger mentioned this passage.

9. For example, at about this time she drafted these stanzas:

Time stands before the door of Death,
    Upbraiding bitterly;
And Conscience, with exhaustless breath,
    Pours black reproach on me:

And though I think that Conscience lies,
    And Time should Fate condemn;
Still, weak Repentance clouds my eyes,
    And makes me yield to them! ("Self-Interrogation," *EB Poems*, 23)

10. Gérin notes that Gothic fiction (by Mary Shelley, Scott, Hoffman, and others) was reviewed or serialized in the issues of *Blackwood's* that the Brontë children read and reread (*EB*, 213–19).

11. See, for example, "A Brace of . . . . Characters" (*CBEW* 2.2:328, 331). Duthie also detects a similarity between Ambition's "Gothic train of 'gloomy phantoms'" and "the Genii in the early Angrian tales" (*Foreign Vision*, 33).

12. See *JE*, 215–16 (ch. 17, mod. eds.).

13. On CB's knowledge of the classics, see the Comments on devoir 27.

14. Diodorus Siculus (1st cent. B.C.) wrote the first surviving account of this Amazon. Four centuries later, the Roman Quintus Curtius provided a description close to CB's: "the fold of the robe, which [the Amazons] gather in a knot, does not reach below the knee." Although I have taken this quotation from a modern source (Kleinbaum, 20), I have seen late-eighteenth-century translations into English and French, with illustrations. Auerbach makes the additional point that "Amazons bob up repeatedly in Victorian writing" (78–79; see also 3–4).

15. Listed in Heger's roster for the school year 1842–43.

16. "La forme qu'elle cachait . . . était une squelette!" (British Library, Ashley MS 160). This is one of Wise's manuscripts, and because he cut the pages from CB's notebook and bound them, its date cannot be ascertained.

17. "Il est dans le Ciel une puissance divine, compagne assidue de la religion et de la vertu. . . . Quoique ses yeux soient couverts d'un bandeau, ses regards pénètrent l'avenir; quelquefois elle tient des fleurs naissantes dans sa main; quelquefois une coupe pleine d'une liqueur enchanteresse, rien n'approche du charme de sa voix, de la grâce de son sourire; plus on avance

vers le tombeau plus elle se montre pure et brillante aux mortels consolés; la Foi et la Charité lui disent—ma soeur—elle se nomme . . . . l'Espérance" (BPM, Bonnell 115, 28–29). An earlier version, with light corrections and points subtracted in the margins for mistakes, is on p. 22 of a notebook ("Exercises sur les Participes") now in the Stark Collection, Harry Ransom Humanities Research Center.

18. There may also be a connection between this devoir and another dictée from the same notebook, "La Médisance" ("Slander"); see Textual Notes for lines 96–97 (100).

19. Gaskell, 11.230.

20. See Comments on devoir 5, especially n. 11.

23. The Fall of the Leaves / La Chute des Feuilles (CB), with dictée The Fall of the Leaves / La chute des Feuilles (CB)

TEXTUAL NOTES (DEVOIR)

My translation is indebted to Phyllis Bentley's ("More Brontë Devoirs," 376–83). M. H. Spielmann's transcript of the French text ("An Early Essay by Charlotte Brontë," 239–46) was also useful in deciphering Heger's comments.

3F. "La chute des Feuilles": elegy written by Charles-Hubert Millevoye (1784–1816). For further information on the poem and the poet, see Comments and the Textual Notes on the dictée.

4–9. This paragraph is unusually stiff, as if CB were trying for a scholarly effect.

12. Possibly an echo of the "pearl of great price" (Matt. 13.46).

27–28. "German student who believed . . .": possibly an allusion to Frankenstein, a Genevese who went to Ingolstadt to study medicine. He became obsessed with alchemy, a topic CB raises in line 61. (I am grateful to Janet Gezari for this suggestion.)

51–52. "Is that the methods all great poets follow?" This question and CB's approach to it are consistent with Shelley's views in the *Defense of Poetry*: "Poetry is not like reasoning, a power to be exerted according to the determination of the will. . . . I appeal to the great poets of the present day, whether it be not an error to assert that the finest passages of poetry are produced by labour and study." Written in 1821, the essay was first published in 1840.

53. "Souls made of fire and children of the Sun?": from Edward Young, *The Revenge* (1721), act 2, scene 5. Young later wrote *Conjectures on Original Composition* (1759).

99. Heger seems to be suggesting that Virgil fashioned the story of Aeneas into a great epic, that Moliere refined the raw comedies of Plautus, and that Buffon in his Natural History developed the work of his collaborator Daubenton.

113F, 142F, 143F. Heger uses *poëte* and *poësie* rather than the more standard *poète* and *poésie;* in his period, those terms suggested works in verse of an exalted scale or sweep.

121F. *livre*: a unit of weight measurement, a little less than half a kilogram and therefore close to one pound.

135. Demosthenes: great Greek orator and leader, 4th cent. B.C., who reputedly overcame a stammer by declaiming with pebbles in his mouth and speaking over the waves.

EDITORIAL NOTES (DEVOIR)
CB capitalized the title of the poem inconsistently. I have standardized it in English and added quotation marks where she omits them.

2. In the manuscript *Devoir / de style* occupies two lines on the first page, with the text beginning on the second; *Devoir* is larger in CB's devoir (italic) script, *de style* smaller in upright letters.

3. Title in CB's normal devoir hand, single line.

27–28. CB erases something between *croyait* and *apprendre* and adds the infinitive ending to *apprendre.*

33. CB starts to write *qui,* converts it to *qu'il.*

34. My sign added below *soit,* linking that word to H's *pourquoi* below the line, to show what he questions.

37. H suggests reversing the numbered clauses.

45. Last letters of *obscur* unclear; could be *obj^{on.}*

53. Quoted English line in CB's proper-noun print.

81. *La chute des feuilles* in CB's proper-noun print.

90. CB erased *-at,* the original ending of *cherche,* and apparently inserted a final *e* before the erasure.

91–96. H's *excellent* is perpendicular to the text.

99. H adds *en barres* below his line, sloping down toward CB's.

103. H's accent in *présence.*

106. *La chute des feuilles* in CB's proper-noun print.

107. CB's *sa* > her *ses.*

109. H uses a kind of caret rather than a diagonal.

114. H's ~~inconte~~ > something illegible.

115. H's second *en* is above the line.

131. The phrase *de tout* > something illegible, possibly *c'est.*

138. In MS *qu'un* > *pas.*

144. A faint *l* precedes *en* (no apostrophe); *savourez* > something illegible.

134–40. Marginal comments perpendicular to text.

TEXTUAL NOTES (DICTÉE)
Millevoye may have written this elegy as early as 1809 (see Comments). It first became known to the public in 1812, when it won the prestigious Jeux Floraux. Subsequently, Millevoye kept revising it. According to his biographer, Pierre Ladoué, it exists in at least five variants:

—the version that won the Jeux Floraux; though the manuscript is lost, a draft has been preserved in the records of the Academy of Toulouse for 1811

—the version in his first collected elegies (1812)

—versions in two subsequent collections (both 1815)

—the posthumous edition of his *Oeuvres complètes* (1822).

This information is collated from the appendix and bk. 1, ch. 3, of Ladoué.

A "Nouvelle édition" of the *Oeuvres complètes* was published in Brussels in 1823. Like its predecessor, it includes three variants: the official version (1822); the second of the 1815 versions; and the first published version (1812).

CB's dictée suggests that Heger read the class a transcript of the manuscript version (1811). That one does not appear in the collected editions, though it must have appeared in periodicals. He departs from it in two places, however; line 10 appears only in the 1822 official version, and lines 23–26 of the dictée follow the 1812 version. Perhaps he had access to an unrecorded variant; more probably, he did a bit of editing. In any case, his taste accords with Sainte-Beuve's, who also preferred the first draft. See his introduction to Millevoye, 7; see also Charles Nodier's editorial note to *Oeuvres complètes de Millevoye* (Paris: Ladvocat, 1822), 1:179.

CB's transcription appears to be accurate, aside from punctuation errors. For example, in line 5 the comma should follow *Triste,* rather than *mourant,* and in line 23 an exclamation point should follow *meurs.* The one vocabulary error is *me prédit* (10); it should be *a prédit.*

There are two nineteenth-century translations. John Bowring did the first in 1823; however, as Sainte-Beuve has pointed out, he translated the poem from Russian, not French, and was under the impression that "Milonov" had written it. For the record, I quote his first stanza: "Th' autumnal winds had stripp'd the field / Of all its foliage, all its green; / The winter's harbinger had still'd / That soul of song which cheer'd the scene" ("The Fall of the Leaf," *Specimens of the Russian Poets* [London: Whittaker, 1823], 2:223). A second translation appeared in a book edited by Henry Wadsworth Longfellow, *The Poets and Poetry of Europe* (Philadelphia: Carey and Hart, 1845). Though closer to Millevoye's text than Bowring's, it too takes liberties: "Autumn had stripped the grove, and strewed / The vale with leafy carpet o'er, / Shorn of its mystery the wood, / And Philomel bade sing no more . . ." (484). I have therefore done a modern version that tries to suggest (though not to duplicate) the shifts in meter of the French original and give its sense as literally as possible.

COMMENTS

1. It is positioned between dictées on which she based two devoirs submitted in June 1842: "Eudorus" (fourth entry; see devoir 9) and "Mirabeau on the Tribune" (eighth entry; see devoirs 10 and 11).

2. *Lets.,* 312.

3. CB dated one translation (from Belmontet) "Fevrier, 1843," another (from Barbier) "Mars 1843," and a notebook of translations from German into English "April 25th 1843." The remainder are undated, cut from their

original notebook(s) and rebound by Thomas Wise. Neufeldt dates those texts from this period (*CB Poems,* 490) and I agree with his assessment.

4. Sir Walter Scott, *The Lady of the Lake,* canto 3, pt. 16 (Philadelphia: Edward Earle, 1810), 94.

5. *CB Poems,* 364; *séches sic.*

6. "La perle du recueil, la pièce dont tous se souviennent" (Millevoye, 7).

7. On these questions, see the section "Genius" in the Introduction.

8. Preface to *Lyrical Ballads* (1800), reprinted in *The Complete Poetical Works of Wordsworth* (Boston: Houghton Mifflin, 1932), 791, 794.

9. Devoir 4 (corrected version), lines 47–52.

10. On the successive revisions, see the Textual Notes on the dictée. There is no way to prove what Heger knew about the context of the poem and Millevoye's theories. But if he had read any edition of the poet's work, he would have seen the essay, a brief biography, and at least one variant of "La Chute des Feuilles."

11. "Millevoye avait été invité a dîner, le jour de la foire de saint Séverin, à Crécy, chez un magistrat retraité. Le poète partit le matin pour faire une promenade dans la forêt. Les convives l'attendirent vainement. Il ne rentra que le soir. Le lendemain des paysans racontèrent qu'ils l'avaient vu seul et faisant des gestes. Quelques jours après Millevoye lisait la *Chute des feuilles*" (reported by Henri Potez—who heard it from a M. Coache of Abbeville, who heard it from his grandmother—in *L'Elegie en France,* 433–34). Potez expresses his own skepticism about the story.

12. "Même en chantant le bonheur, elle peut conserver la teinte de tristesse qui lui est propre. Ce mélange d'impressions opposées ajoute à son effet. Elle se plaît surtout au souvenir de ce qui n'est plus. . . . Il n'est point pour elle d'objet inanimé; pour elle les ruines sont vivantes, la solitude est peuplée, et la tombe a cessé d'être muette" ("Sur l'élégie," *Oeuvres,* 33–34).

13. Information drawn from Porter, 30–31.

24. Letter (My Dear Jane) / Lettre (Ma chère Jane) (CB)

TEXTUAL NOTES

67 (71). "desert of heath": *bruyère* may also have been the word that CB found closest to "moor."

68–70 (72–74). In "Isidore," chapter 9 of *Villette,* Lucy alludes to the "marsh-phlegm" of the Labessecourians (113). CB's description of the Belgians in her May 1 letter to Branwell (reproduced in Comments) is similar.

71–72 (75–76). "The Violet," a poem CB wrote at age fourteen, includes the lines, "Not e'en the eagles royal wing / Waves in the sky" (*CB Poems,* 65).

81 (85). Glen Morven: literally, "great glen," or dale. Glen More is in Perthshire on the south side of Schiehallion.

82 (86). Ben Nevis: mountain in the Grampians (Scotland), the highest

elevation in Great Britain. Shihallion (properly, Schiehallion): mountain in Perthshire; see Comments, n. 10. In *The Spell* CB alludes to Ben Carnach, Glen Avon, and Loch Sunart (*CBEW* 2.2:215); she also alludes to them in "A Brace of . . . . Characters" (*CBEW* 2.2:327, 329, 330).

EDITORIAL NOTES
The five-page manuscript is written in CB's rough-draft hand, the script she uses to compose her notes for "The Death of Moses." The first paragraph is fully indented; the others vary in degree of indentation. For ease of reading, I have normalized them. All corrections are hers; her additions are made in the left margin.

5. CB adds a small unaccented *e* to change *trouvé* from a participle to the present tense but does not delete the accented *e;* the second *e* slopes down.

30. The *'a* above the line is not crossed out but is clearly included in the deletion; there is an accent mark resembling a grave above *trouve* and an *s*(?) above the second *ne.*

36. CB starts to accent *répousser,* cancels accent.

40. The *ap* added to *parait* is in smaller letters; *un* in margin, preceding *oiseau.*

50–54. The marginal comment is probably meant to replace the canceled *dit l'oiseau . . . vigne* on lines 52–53; ~~saut~~ is below *se balançant.*

58. CB deletes this passage but misses the *pe* of *tape, je,* and *singe;* her line passes under, not through, *évanouis.*

66. Indecipherable marks below the line, resembling parentheses.

70–71. In MS, a single diagonal extends from *qui* through *dans un* and presumably the end of the paragraph.

80. The word *nous* may be crossed out; *conduit* in large letters slopes down to the line.

COMMENTS
1. *Lets.,* 317.

2. Four of the five pages have a margin penciled in; the last does not.

3. *EW,* 175. Alexander identifies the entry as the fragment that begins "My Compliments to the weather. . . ."

4. BPM, Bonnell 98(6), quoted and paraphrased in *EW,* 175.

5. See *EW,* 171 and 175 (MS of June 28, 1838, BPM, Bonnell 114).

6. *5 Novs.,* 206.

7. Ibid., 209.

8. Ibid., 210. Alexander correctly warns against the "mistake" of reading CB's life into her manuscripts (*EW,* 186) but then points out the many similarities between this character and her author: "Like Charlotte, Elizabeth Hastings paints landscapes, is proud of her knowledge of French and takes a great deal of interest in politics . . ." (187). She also paces like CB and reflects the same concerns about her social insignificance and plainness.

9. See, for example, Lord Ravenswood's description to Mina Laury of living together in his castle in the Highlands ("The Spell," ch. 7, in *CBEW* 2.1:215).

10. Schiehallion, for example, is cited in Scott's *Waverly* (ch. 18 n) and in *Rob Roy* (ch. 23). The mountain also "acquired great celebrity" from having been chosen by a Greenwich astronomer for an experiment to ascertain

"the Newtonian principle of gravitation" (*The Gazetteer of Scotland* [Dundee: Chalmers, 1803]).

11. The sketch follows page 5 of the manuscript. But unlike the paper on which "My dear Jane" is written, the paper on which the sketch appears is hand-ruled. The difference suggests that the sketch may not have been drawn to accompany this fragment; this may be another case of Wise's tampering with manuscripts to make them more salable.

12. See, for instance, Eddie Flintoff, *In the Steps of the Brontës* (Newbury, Berkshire: Countryside, 1993), 136.

13. *Lets.,* 289.

14. Ibid., 317.

15. Ibid., 329.

25. The Death of Napoleon / La Mort de Napoléon (CB) and On the Death of Napoleon / Sur la mort de Napoléon (H)

TEXTUAL NOTES (CORRECTED VERSION)

My translation is indebted to Margaret Lane's ("French Essays," 274–81) but differs for reasons explained in Comments.

38. "sepulchre, empty now": Napoleon's body had been exhumed and returned to France for reburial; also see Comments.

40. Napoleon was born in 1769 and died in 1821.

44. Golgotha: site of the Crucifixion; CB also alludes to it in "Evening Prayer in a Camp" (line 39).

51 ff. "crime of Prometheus": in Greek mythology, the Titan who stole fire from Olympus to give it to mankind. CB alludes to this episode in "The Spell. An Extravaganza" (June 21, 1834): "And thou, too, our young Jupiter; denounce vengeance, hurl thy thunderbolts, bind Prometheus to the rock, transfix him with barbed lightnings, and get the insatiable vulture to gnaw the irradicable liver!" (*CBEW* 2.2:221). The trope was also common among French Romantic poets; consider the lines in Hugo's poem "Mazeppa" on "le grand vautour fauve / Qui fouille au flanc des morts. . . ."

60–61. "the soul's hunger and thirst": in his August 15, 1843, Prize Day speech Heger refers to "l'émulation" as "cette soif ardente de l'âme, cet insatiable appétit vers les choses meilleures" (11). In revising CB's devoir, he retains her phrase but moves it to a new position; compare "Sur la mort de Napoléon," lines 26–27.

74–75. Ulysses: reference to an episode in the *Odyssey,* book 12.

89 ff. "his noble peer": Arthur Wellesley, first duke of Wellington (1769–1852); conquerer of Napoleon at Waterloo, 1815; prime minister of England, 1828–30; CB's and Patrick Brontë's hero.

95 ff. "It is an abuse of your privilege . . .": Louise de Bassompierre recalls a classroom "altercation" on this subject; see Comments and n. 21 there.

123 ff. On Wellington's disregard for public opinion, CB echoes his own

statements: "I (who have more reason than any other public man of the present day to complain of libels of this description) never take the smallest notice of them; and have never authorized any contradiction to be given ..." (response to the press of January 7, 1811, *Maxims and Opinions...*, ed. George Henry Francis [London: Henry Colburn, 1845], 109, as cited by Kirshner, 1).

128 ff. "In revenge, the people ...": as Kirshner points out (1), Brontë's Shirley echoes this passage: "England has howled savagely against this man, uncle; and she will one day roar exultingly over him. He has been unscared by the howl, and he will be unelated by the shout" (*Shirley*, 630; ch. 32, mod. eds.). Shirley also refers to Wellington as "the present idol of my soul" (629).

131. "the proud Coriolanus": Roman patrician, subject of a Shakespeare play, notoriously arrogant toward the plebians he was willing to rescue from starving.

136. Satrap: in ancient Persia, governor of a province.

137. "ducal palace of Apsley": as Duthie points out (*Foreign Vision*, 44), this allusion is anachronistic. Wellington bought Apsley House from his brother, the marquis of Wellesley, in 1816, when his popularity was at a high. He confronted hostile mobs most famously during the first Reform Bill agitation of 1831–32. One nineteenth-century biographer comments, "How he escaped with his life, passing daily as he did through crowds of persons inflamed to the highest pitch of fury against him, it is not easy to say" (Brialmont 3:417).

142–43. Jonah's vine: biblical allusion to Jonah 4.6–11. Compare Lucy Snow's allusion to Jonah's gourd (*Villette*, 6.64). In his version, Heger mistranscribes the name as Josiah.

144–45. "banks of the Shannon": Patrick Brontë and his children took pride in Wellington's Irish roots.

146 ff. "[the oak] grows slowly": in revising this passage for his version, Heger probably plays on La Fontaine's famous fable "Le Chêne et le roseau" ("The Oak and the Reed"). Compare his phrase "brave & la faux du temps et l'effort des vents & des tempêtes" (113–14) with La Fontaine's "Brave l'effort de la tempête." The fable appears in the anthology Heger gave CB, *Les Fleurs de la poésie française* (Rabion, 52–53).

149. "a century more ...": again, a suggestion of the uneven course of Wellington's reputation in his lifetime.

EDITORIAL NOTES (CORRECTED VERSION)
This is the most cluttered of the devoir manuscripts; it is not possible to reproduce the full range of Heger's markings and the size of his letters, which range from extra large to miniature. His notations are in ink and in pencil. As usual, words inked in the MS appear in bold, and penciled words appear in regular type; all other markings are in ink unless noted here as being in pencil.

2–4. The title is in large letters, normal devoir script. The accent on *Napoléon* is double-lined.

8. The *s* is deleted in pencil.

12. The word *particulier* may be w.u.

13. H's accents on *côté.*

16. In MS *le manteau* appears below *des robes; donc* in left margin possibly follows *particulier* but is adjacent to H's *le manteau.*

18. The locution *sait-il* is a *Belgicisme; un homme* is below the line, with a connecting diagonal.

19. The phrase *la dire* is below the line; H's *l* is elongated.

22. The phrase *qui l'entourent* may be w.u.

23. H begins something over the crossed-out *n* but cancels it.

24. The word *qualité* is partly underlined in pencil; an ink line loops around *pour qualité distinctive.*

25. The crossouts of *le* and *plutôt* are in pencil.

25–29. My arrows track the sentence H rewrites after crossouts: *froide et sans portée suffisante pour les*[?] *juger. . . .*

27. The word *plutôt* appears in the left margin, next to *que;* the underlining is in pencil.

29. A semicircular line extends over *et,* further suggesting its deletion; *correct* w.u. in pencil.

30–31. H's revision spans three lines, above and below CB's; in MS a penciled line shows where the insert goes; in this book, a caret and *[La Prévention]* clarify the sequence, which begins ~~ne voit qu'en face de la réalité; l'Enthousiasme voit plus que la~~ (not reproduced). H's *Médiocrité > Moderation;* the *d* of *découvrir >* something illegible; *elle* is below and to the left of CB's *peut; découvrir* is above her *voir.*

31. Something > *trop,* canceling it out; the illegible word that follows is struck out; H's *ses >* CB's *son.*

33. The final *e* of *même* is underlined in pencil, with the underscore extending beyond the letter.

35. Here and in line 40, CB writes S^{te.}

37. H's commas after *d'être* and *inférieur* and his accent on *indépendant* are all in pencil.

40. H's ⧺ notation and wavy line in left margin of MS may suggest that the next draft should begin here.

41–43. H's marginal comment runs perpendicular to the text in the MS.

42. My arrows; in MS *son . . . tombe* is directly below *les deux états, qu'y a-t-il* is above *a qu'une,* and *—la* is above *carrière.*

44. H's *a > e* in *Golgotha,* in pencil.

47. The phrase *dans son palais* has a line rather than a caret below it.

48. Something illegible is crossed out above *femme; aimait* is underlined and crossed out in pencil.

49–50. Crossouts in pencil, including *(1);* corrections in ink.

51. The phrase *lié a* is crossed out in pencil with a v-shaped symbol; a line below *enchainé* links it to *lié.*

52. Crossout of *sa* in pencil; H's *le > la* in pencil.

53. H's *déroba > vola* and trails down.

57. The word *punir* is in the left margin of the MS, preceding *de la rapacité.*

58. The word *enchaîné,* which trails down, partly > *lié.*

60–65. Margin comment is perpendicular to text.

61. H's bracket in pencil.

67. Small additional line runs down from *pas* to *grand.*

73. H's tiny *une* runs below line.

75. H's accent on *Sirènes.*

77. A line arcs up above *tout* to indicate placement of H's phrase; his ~~incarne~~ is below *d'un peuple* and probably modified CB's *peuple;* the line after *corps* is in pencil.

77–78. H's *s's > l's* in *ses, ses, sa.*

79. H's ~~mo~~[?] in pencil below *les a-t-il.*

80–81. H makes CB's *hommes* singular and adds *l'* to attach it to his own phrase, which he then transposes; I could not exactly reproduce this sequence in the English version.

83. Vertical line after *utiles* and line under original *t* of *permet* in pencil.

84. H's *de larmes* may > something illegible.

85. H's ~~pas~~ > *de,* which he also crosses out; his ~~des~~ below line.

86. The phrase *son âme . . . cela* is written above this line but clearly follows *restes.*

88. The word *su* trails down below the line.

89. The phrase *en génie* trails down below the line; *B* in pencil under *N* of *Napoléon.*

90. The word *paire* is partly struck out in ink and partly underlined in pencil, perhaps w.u.

91. The word *vainquer* [*sic*] is underlined in pencil; *pas su* is a *Belgicisme.*

92. H adds a more substantial comma to CB's small one after *victoire.*

95–96. H's *cette* > his *la;* his *u > e* in *du* and extends the line to *votre* to delete it.

97. H's *son* is in the left margin, preceding *ennemi.*

99. The phrase *molles &* is in the left margin; *timorées* continues into page, above *imbéciles;* H's *tes > re* of *seduire.*

100. H originally writes *sait* above underlined *savait* (both in pencil) and then overwrites it with *n'a jamais su.*

101. The word *aimait* is crossed out in pencil; *a* above is in pencil and ink.

107. H's *veux* > CB's *suis* above the line; the end of *x* descends diagonally to strike out *resolu.*

109. H probably meant to delete *la* from *cela.*

111. A line after ~~cette~~ indicates where *l'Europe* belongs.

114. S^te in MS; H's *r* breaks into *réfléchissez;* his *et* extends to strike out *pas* and *ne.*

115. Indecipherable word, beginning *conv* becomes *convenable* in H's draft.

120. Vertical line after *Napoleon* in pencil.

121. One of H's *comme*s is superfluous; line from *e* of third *comme* descends to strike out *en;* his *ne lui* > something illegible.

123. H's *gloire* > his *popularité* and may be capitalized.

126. Both the semicolon and comma appear to be H's.

127. H's *s > l* of *les.*

128. H's *malgré* starts on line and runs down; it may be struck out; his line around *l'approuve* curves. The sense of his corrections is not wholly clear.

130. H's *a qui il > et a;* he strikes it out and writes *et quand il* above.

132. H's *l > s* of *ses.*

133–35. H writes and then strikes out *le flot populaire* between *il bravait* and *l'emeute* (not shown in printed text); *lorsque*(?) is above *et le flot; impuissant* > something illegible; *puis* is above *lui, et* and a line from the *s* extends downward to strike out *et; foule > peuple.*

137. H's *l > s* of *sa.*

138. My ⌋ indicates where H's phrase belongs.

140. CB strikes out *lui* and adds words above line.

142. H's comma.

143. CB seems to have begun writing *Josiah* and then corrects *si* to get *Jonah;* in H's draft for Gaskell, he incorrectly writes *Josiah.*

144E. My line added to show placement of *sufficed.*

146. End of H's *non* drops down to strike out CB's *pas.*

147. H's *ces* > CB's *des;* H's comma.

148. H's *du sol* > CB's *l'île* and is then crossed out; H adds *inébranlable* above his phrase, indicating placement with a caret.

EDITORIAL NOTES (HEGER'S VERSION)

When Heger makes corrections that affect his meaning, I include them in the transcript. He also crosses out and overwrites words, but because his French is not in question, that editing is not noted here.

COMMENTS

1. This quotation appears in Gaskell 2:9.610 n. Gaskell also quotes Patrick Brontë's observation, "When mere children, as soon as they could read and write, Charlotte and her brother and sisters, used to invent and act little plays of their own, in which the Duke of Wellington my Daughter Charlotte's Hero, was sure to come off, the conquering hero . . ." (vol. 1, ch. 3; quoted here from the manuscript version in Barker, 109).

2. *Villette,* 30.503.

3. Gaskell, 12.255.

4. Gaskell, 11.238.

5. "French Essays," 274–81. The first page of the manuscript is also reproduced there in photocopy.

6. For previous comments on this devoir, see Duthie, *Foreign Vision,* 42–45; Lonoff, "Charlotte Brontë's Belgian Essays," 395–97; Kirshner, 1–2; and Barker, 416–17.

7. Adapted from Hugo, "Mirabeau," 342–43 ("La médiocrité serait bien importunée par l'homme de talent si l'homme de génie n'était pas là; mais l'homme de génie est là, elle soutient l'homme de talent et se sert de lui contre le maître. . . . La médiocrité est pour celui qui la gêne le moins et qui lui ressemble le plus," Hugo, "Sur Mirabeau," 199).

8. "Mirabeau," 355 ("le dieu d'une nation en divorce avec son roi," Hugo, "Sur Mirabeau," 207).

9. "Mirabeau," 373–74. The full passage in French reads ". . . le parti de l'avenir se divise en deux classes: les hommes de révolution, les hommes de progrès. Ce sont les hommes de révolution qui déchirent la vieille terre politique. . . . Aux hommes de progrès appartiennent la lente et laborieuse culture des principes . . . le travail au jour le jour, l'arrosement de la jeune plant, l'engrais du sol, la récolte pour tous" ("Sur Mirabeau," 218–19).

10. "Ainsi, père, mère, femme, son précepteur, son colonel, la magistrature, la noblesse, le roi, c'est-à-dire tout ce qui entoure et côtoie l'existence d'un homme dans l'ordre légitime et naturel, tout est pour lui traverse, obstacle, occasion de chute et de contusion . . ." ("Sur Mirabeau," 207; "Thus,

father, mother, wife, his tutor, his colonel, the magistracy, the noblesse, the king, that is to say, all that surrounds and skirts the existence of a man in the legitimate and natural order, [all is] for him a cross, an obstacle, [an occasion of tumble and contusion]. . .," "Mirabeau," 355). See these texts for numerous other parallels.

11. Her response remained strong long after Brussels: "The fact is that this great Mirabeau was a mixture of divinity and dirt; that there was no divinity whatever in his errors . . .; that they ruined him, brought down his genius to the kennel . . .; that they cut him off in his prime, obviated all his aims, and struck him dead in the hour when France most needed him" (letter to W. S. Williams, June 22, 1848, in *BLFC* 2:224–25).

12. "Napoleon" (CB's title), lines 5 and 50 (*CB Poems,* 355–356; see also the variants, 488–489).

13. Duthie, *Foreign Vision,* 40; see also 39.

14. *Lets.,* 317.

15. Alexander gives a useful overview of this subject; see *EW,* 24–28 ff.

16. Scott's *Life of Napoleon Buonaparte* was published in nine volumes, in 1827. CB refers to it in "First Volume of Tales of the Islanders June 30 1829" (*CBEW* 1:28); see also *CBEW* 1:88–90.

17. Napoleon and Marie Louise figure in "The Green Dwarf," a story she wrote at seventeen; see *CBEW* 2.1:139–42. (Clement Shorter printed the fragment in which they appear as "Napoleon and the Spectre.") In Branwell's "The Pirate," also from 1833, Napoleon threatens an invasion (*Misc.* 1:174). Zamorna's later (1835) banishment to Ascension Isle echoes Napoleon's to St. Helena, as Duthie has pointed out (*Foreign Vision,* 11).

18. On "Caroline Vernon" and Napoleon, see *EW,* 196–97; the text is in *Five Novelettes.*

19. See Seaward, 185–88. Gérin points out that Lebel was the model for Pelet in *The Professor* (*CB,* 314–15).

20. As an Anglican resident in Brussels, CB would have had a weekly reminder of Napoleon's presence there: he had given the Protestant community the Chapel Royal, where she and EB went for Sunday services.

21. "[U]n jour même il y eut une petite altercation entr'elles au sujet de l'Empereur Napoléon: les élèves reprochurent à Miss Charlotte la conduite de l'Angleterre envers l'Empereur, et semblaient lui en endosser à elle-même la responsabilité: je me souviens que je rappelai les plus excitées au calme en leur disant que Miss Brontë n'y était pour rien et qu'il valait mieux abandonner ce sujet . . ." (letter of March 1913, printed in "Two Brussels School-fellows, 26–27). She infers that Brontë's gratitude was later expressed in her use of the name "de Bassompierre" in *Villette.*

22. CB's choice, though probably unconscious at the time, might be the basis for chapter 31 of *Jane Eyre,* in which Jane contrasts her healthy life as village schoolmistress with fantasies of life in France as Rochester's mistress.

23. Introduction, liii–liv.

24. Heger heavily reworked his own comparison, but space does not permit full disclosure in the typescript; see Editorial Notes for further details.

25. "The Palace of Death," 803.

26. *Lets.*, 320.

26. The Death of Moses / La Mort de Moïse and Notes on the Death of Moses / Notes sur La Mort de Moïse (CB)

TEXTUAL NOTES (DEVOIR)

My translation is indebted to Phyllis Bentley's ("More Brontë Devoirs," 366–75). The account of Moses' death in the devoir is based on Deut. 32.48–52 and 34.1–5.

2. This title is a variant of the one Gaskell cites (11.238); see Comments.

3. Moses' age is given in Deut. 31.2 and 34.7.

3–4. CB facetiously begins "My Angria and the Angrians" (1834) with a vision of the Children of Israel going into exodus (*CBEW* 2.2:240).

14–17. Deut. 32.1–43, sometimes titled "The Song of Moses," is written as poetry; so is Deut. 33.2–29, "Moses Blesses the Tribes of Israel."

17–20. The quotation adopts the phrasing of Deut. 32.49–50.

23. In Deut. 33.4–25 Moses recalls Jacob's blessing of the tribes; Jacob's version of the blessing is in Gen. 49.

26. "ruby rays"/"reflets des rubis": in *Shirley,* CB considers the difficulties of rendering *reflets* in English (644; ch. 33, mod. eds.).

58–64. Heger's marginal comment, as quoted and translated by Gaskell (11.238), does not appear in this draft of the devoir, though clearly it would come at this point; see Comments.

61. The veil is an image often used by the Romantics; CB's allusion to Sais in "Athens Saved by Poetry" (202) comes from a Schiller poem about the veiled goddess of truth.

62–63 (63–64). "When the Bible says . . .": see Deut. 5.4.

68–70. "When the sacred historian . . .": see Deut. 5.22, and compare "The Nest," 37–42 (39–44).

80–81. The seraph allusion may anticipate a passage in "The First Blue-Stocking," the devoir CB inserts into *Shirley.* Eva, seeking "Guidance—help—comfort" is aided by "that Seraph, on earth named Genius" (551–52; ch. 28, mod. eds.); see also the seraph allusion in *Villette,* 22.350.

103–106. "Look to the South . . .": much of CB's phrasing parallels Deut. 34.1–4.

111–14. Duthie (*Foreign Vision,* 217 n. 43) points out the correspondence of this passage to one in Chateaubriand's *Atala;* René leads Atala "[aux pieds] des coteaux qui formaient des golfes de verdure en avançant leurs promontoires dans la savane" ("to the foot of slopes that formed gulfs of verdure advancing their promontories into the savannah"). It also recalls a passage from CB's "A Leaf from an Unopened Volume" (1834) in which

Lord Charles Wellesley gazes down on "a noble expanse of green sunny slopes stretching on further than the eye could follow like a magnificent sea of verdure, dotted here and there by trees which, for their colossal and sublime magnitude, might be compared to islands. Groups of deer reposed under the groves of foliage which each gigantic son of the forest lifted into that profoundly tranquil atmosphere of evening. Hills long and low bounded the distance; to the right hand appeared a far-off glittering sweep of the Calabar, followed all along its banks by the domes and pillars of Adrianopolis, but dimly seen through the golden haze flung over them by the declining sun" (*CBEW* 2.1:328).

115. Deut. 32.14 alludes to the goats and rams of Bashan; see also Psalms 22.12. This image also appears in a BPM manuscript, probably part of CB's Roe Head Journal, ca. October 1836: "Wiggins [Branwell] might indeed talk of scriblomania if he were to see me just now, encompassed by the bulls (query calves of Bashan), all wondering why I write with my eyes shut, staring, gaping" (*JE* Norton, 416).

120–22. Gaskell paraphrases Heger's remarks (12.238), which she saw on the draft no longer extant; I quote them further in Comments. The description in *Jane Eyre* of Blanche Ingram playing Rebekah recalls this passage: "She, too was attired in Oriental fashion . . . her beautifully-moulded arms bare, one of them upraised in the act of supporting a pitcher, poised gracefully on her head. Both her cast of form and feature, her complexion and her general air, suggested the idea of some Israelitish princess of the patriarchal days . . ." (28.161).

124. Moloch, or Molech: a god of the Ammonites, linked to the practice of child sacrifice.

143 (144). "shepherd-king": David, the father of Solomon.

144. Rehoboam: the son who succeeded Solomon and antagonized the people of Israel. All the tribes except Judah rebelled and made Jereboam their king; see 1 Kings 12.

145. "splits in two the trunk": CB's image of a split tree here may anticipate the chestnut that splits on the night of Jane Eyre's betrothal to Rochester (end ch. 23).

145–47. Throughout this section, CB chooses characters and episodes from 1 Kings. Ahijah was the father of King Baasha of Israel (15.27, 33). Baasha was succeeded by Elah, Zimri, Omri, and then Ahab. Ahab married Jezebel and introduced the worship of her god, the Phoenician Baal, into Israel.

147–49. On Jehu and Athaliah, see 2 Kings 9–11. Jehu killed Ahaziah, son of Athaliah and king of Judah. Athaliah then destroyed all the king's sons, except for one who was secretly rescued, and seized the throne herself; she too was slain. CB seems also to have known Racine's 1691 tragedy *Athalie,* since Shirley Keelder implores Henry Moore to recite "Le Songe d'Athalie" ("Athalie's Dream") from it (*Shirley,* 458; ch. 28, mod. eds.).

152. Isaiah: Hebrew prophet, purported author of the biblical book of that name.

153. The era of captivity: the expulsion of the Jews to Babylon by Nebuchadnezzar II and the period of their exile there (6th cent. B.C.).

156. Euphrates: river of southwestern Asia.

169–70. "no territory beyond a field . . .": CB confuses the legend of the founding of Rome with that of Carthage, whose citadel, or *bursa,* was measured in this way; see Livy, *The History of Rome,* bk. 34, sec. 62.12.

172. "[Rome] crushes the palm of Judea": on this point, the devoir is anachronistic. In 65 B.C. Jerusalem was captured by Pompey and a few years after by Herod the Great with the aid of the Romans; but its "crushing," first by Titus and then by Julianus Severus, took place after Jesus' death.

179. "Celestial voices . . .": see Luke 2.10.

183–86. "the words of Simeon . . .": Simeon, a "just and devout" man, saw the infant Jesus before dying. CB makes a few modifications in the biblical account. For example, she skips "according to thy word" after "peace" and changes "the Gentiles" to "all the nations." By and large, however, she follows Luke 2.29–32.

EDITORIAL NOTES (DEVOIR)
CB made several erasures in this draft; not all could be reconstructed.

1. The last digit of the date is torn off.
2. The title is in CB's double-line print.
3. Erasure under *voyait.*
4. Erasure at end of *restait.*
8–9. Diagonal line in pencil that seems accidental runs from *nations* to *rappela.*
17. An erased *s* may conclude *Monte.*
45. CB alters.
54. Pencil line descends from colon after *blancs;* reason unclear.
63. The word *litéral* is spelled with one *t* (the English way) rather than two.
72. An *e* under *i* in *sévérité; de* erased between *que* and *demandaient.*
125. The *u* erased from *à[u].*
126. An *e* > *a* in *les.*
132. The *r* in *offre* > something illegible, possibly an accent; beneath *c* in *extinction* CB seems to have begun a *t.*
170. Possibly a dash after *Rome.*
172. CB does not erase *a* in converting *la* to *l'.*

TEXTUAL NOTES (NOTES)
These untitled and unsigned notes evidently accompany "The Death of Moses" and suggest CB's ideas for its ending.

25–29. CB paraphrases Luke 2.30–32, on which I have drawn for the translation.

COMMENTS
1. Quoted in Lock and Dixon, 351.
2. Gaskell, 11.238.

3. The account of his last hours is given in a dozen verses, Deut. 32.48–52 and 34.1–7; she also refers to his song and his blessings. See Textual Notes for further details.

4. They are, respectively, the fourth and fifth of Delavigne's *Messéniennes,* a title that alludes to the misfortunes of Messina in its wars with Sparta, as elegized by Tyrtius. Delavigne intended to develop analogies between the past and present.

5. Wells claims that it is "manifestly inspired" by Vigny's *Moïse* (90); however, he provides no evidence.

6. Gaskell discusses this devoir in her chapter on 1842 but without recording its date. Duthie, Alexander, and Wells assign 1843 to it, as does my Belgian assistant.

7. CB seems to have taken back to Haworth only the rough notes for the ending.

8. This episode becomes the basis for an argument between Robert Moore and Helstone in *Shirley,* 46–47 (ch. 3, mod. eds.).

9. "C'est lui qui délivra nos tribus opprimées / Sous le poids d'un joug rigoureux. . . ." These lines closely follow a question that might also have made an impression on CB: "Qui t'inspira de quitter ton vieux père, / De préférer aux baisers de ta mère, / L'horreur des camps, le carnage et la mort?" ("Who inspired you to leave your old father, / To prefer to the kisses of your mother, / The horror of the camps, carnage and death?"; Delavigne, 21).

10. Delavigne, 44.

11. *JE,* 407 (ch. 27, mod. eds.).

12. Chateaubriand, Lamartine, de Vigny, and Chateaubriand himself wrote of Moses; see Introduction, lxii.

13. Lamartine shows Moses climbing Sinai, not Nebo, but the spectacle is similar: "Un homme, un homme seul, gravit tes flancs qui grondent: / En vain tes mille échos tonnent et se répondent, / Ses regards assurés ne se détournent pas! / Tout un people éperdu le regarde d'en bas; / Jusqu'aux lieux où ta cime et le ciel se confondent, / Il monte, et la tempête enveloppe ses pas! ("A man, a lone man mounts your groaning flanks: / In vain your thousand echoes thunder and reply, / His firm gaze does not turn aside! / A whole bewildered people regards him from below; / To the place where your peak and the sky merge, / He ascends, and the tempest envelops his steps"; *Harmonies,* 137 [the poem is listed as Harmony 8, series 2, in a text that Heger could have used in his classes: Lamartine, *Oeuvres* [Brussels: Société Belge, 1841], 130–31).

14. Gaskell kept a careful record of Heger's statements, aside from minor lapses in French. If she says he cited "De la Vigne's . . . Joan of Arc," then he did not cite Vigny's "Moses." But he also told Gaskell during their interview that CB based "Peter the Hermit" on one dictée, whereas CB's notebook reveals another source for it. In this case too, she may have been responding to more than one text she had read.

15. "Laissez-moi m'endormir du sommeil de la terre," lines 70, 90, 106; "triste et seul dans ma gloire," line 98 (*Poèmes,* 11–13).

16. *Villette,* 29.493.

17. Gaskell, 11.238.

18. Duthie also traces sources for CB's "landscape painting" and pictorial vision; see *Foreign Vision,* 46–47.

19. See the Textual Notes on lines 111–14 and 145; oriental imagery and costume descriptions also recur throughout her juvenilia.

20. *Lets.,* 274.

27. Athens Saved by Poetry / Athènes sauvée par la Poësie (CB)

TEXTUAL NOTES (ORIGINAL)

My translation is indebted to Dorothy L. Cornish's ("Four Essays," 90–96).

4. Peloponnesian War(s): fought between Sparta (Lacedaemon) and Athens, 431–404 B.C. Lysander brought them to a close.

9. Lysander: Spartan leader and naval commander, d. 395 B.C.

12–13 ff. CB conflates two passages in *The Iliad.* The first is from book 9, a description of the banquet prepared by Achilles and his friend Patroclus for Ulysses and other leaders. The second is from the conclusion of book 20, a description of Achilles in battle: "Thus to be magnified, / His most inaccessible hands in human blood he dyed" (*The Iliads of Homer,* trans. George Chapman [London: Charles Knight, 1843], 1:201–2 and 2:166). Heger underlines the phrase to question it, and she deletes it from her revised version.

26 (25). Samos and Chios: both islands were famous for their wines and fertile soil, and both were allies of Athens.

31. Lycurgus: legendary leader and lawgiver who reformed the constitution of Sparta, 7th cent. B.C.(?).

51. Epialte seems to be an invented name.

67–68. "groves of the Academy": The Academy was the garden near Athens in which Plato taught (ca. 387 B.C.), and in which his followers continued to meet for nine centuries.

75. "worm": Byron often uses this term; see, for example, "Manfred," line 125.

105–9. Illysus (or Illysos): the stream that emanates from Mount Hymettus, in central Greece. Brow of Diana: the moon (Diana, or Artemis, Apollo's twin, is the goddess associated with it).

116. Orpheus: mythical poet and supreme musician, from Thrace.

130 ff. Race of Pelops: in Greek myth, Pelops was the son of Tantalus. The Peloponnesus (the peninsular region of continental Greece) is named for him, and tragedies about his descendants, who were cursed because Pelops failed to pay a bet, are among the most famous in Greek literature. His sons are Atreus and Thystes (who added a further curse to his brother's house). Atreus is the father of Agamemnon and Menelaus, also called

Atreides (sons of Atreus). Menelaus married Helen. Agamemnon married her half-sister, Clytemnestra; their children are Orestes, Iphigenia, and Electra.

153–55. Satyrs: lesser deities of Greek mythology, goat-eared and lustful. Fauns: playful deities, half-man, half-goat, not so sexual as satyrs. Dryads: tree nymphs. Oreads: mountain nymphs.

156. Epidaurus: city in the Peloponnesus; also cited in the dictée "The Fall of the Leaves" (line 13).

168 (166). Fury: Greek goddess of vengeance, almost always used in the plural, since there are three; euphemistically called the Eumenides, literally the "well-minded ones."

194 (193). Argos: Greece.

200 ff. Triumphal chariot: the allusion to the chariot, the cries of woe, and the later curse that uses animal imagery probably come from Aeschylus' *Agamemnon* (see Comments, n. 12). Cassandra, a daughter of Priam and Hecuba, rulers of Troy, was given the gift of prophecy by Apollo, who fell in love with her; when she rejected his love, he additionally decreed that her prophecies would never be believed.

202. Sais: a city of ancient Egypt. Schiller wrote a poem, "The Veiled Image at Sais," about "a young man who, in search of the Truth, lifts the veil from a giant statue in an Egyptian temple, and is struck dead" (*Villette,* 749 n). A translation of the poem by Bulwer-Lytton appeared in *Blackwood's* in October 1842, the month before their aunt's death brought the Brontës home. In *Villette* Lucy calls this goddess a "Titaness amongst dieties" (39.674).

207–11 (207–10). CB's description of Cassandra recalls one of Zenobia Ellrington in "The Bridal," a story of 1832 (*CBEW* 1:343; quoted in the Introduction, p. xxxvii).

221. Ajax: not the son of Telamon, but of Oïleus, also known as Little or Lesser Ajax (*Iliad*). During the sack of Troy, Cassandra fled to the temple of Athena, where he found her and dragged her off. Agamemnon saved her by declaring that Ajax had impiously raped her in the temple and taken her as his own prize. The *Aeneid* and the *Odyssey* are sources for this myth.

228. "axe that fells the oak will break the reed": possibly a reference to the La Fontaine fable, "Le Chêne et le roseau"; see the textual note to lines 146 ff of devoir 25.

264. Alfred de Musset: French poet and dramatist, 1810–57.

EDITORIAL NOTES (ORIGINAL)

Throughout the text, CB transcribes names in her proper-noun print. Names so treated (with line numbers) include: Péloponèse (4), Athènes (7, 241), Achille (12), Ulysse (12), Lysandre (18, 25, 33, 40, 49, 60, 63, 77, 99, 242), Samos (25, 245), Chios (25), Lycurge (31), Lacédémone (33), Epialte/Épialte (51, 54, 89), Platon (68), Socrate (68), Sophocle (69), Euripide (69), Le Sac d'Athènes (81–82), Hymette (105), Parthénon (106), Illise (108, 246), Diane (109, 247), Lares (114), Orphée (116), Egée (122), Grèce (129), Pélopides (130), Clytemnestre (132, 196, 229), Oreste (133,

184), Electre (133, 166, 168, 193, 249), Argos (146, 193, 205, 217), Satyres (153), Faunes (154), Dryades (155), Oréades (155), Épidaure (156), Troie (172), Iphigénie (173, 184), Hélène (177), Paris (177), Ménélaus (178), Agamemnon (199, 202, 229, 249), Sais (202), Cassandre (205, 224, 229), Apollon (214), Ajax (221), Atride (221), Égisthe (229), Athènes sauvée par la Poësie (256).

2–3. *Athènes* in CB's normal devoir hand, enlarged; smaller subtitle.

5. The comment *p.f.* (*pas français?*) below *exultation.*

6. H uses three slashes to strike out ending of *permettait;* his circumflex on *goûter.*

8. Below H's inserted *on* is an indecipherable notation.

14. H's marginal comment is perpendicular and applies to the entire section.

15. The verb *apprêter* means "to prepare," as a dress, a hide, or a meal; the noun applies to the finishing of the first two, but not to the third, which is why H underlines it.

19. In the space between *por* and *tions* CB seems to have started writing *i.*

22. H's *affamés* below CB's line.

31. H's accent on *s'échauffant.*

34. H's comma.

46. H's accents on *entière* and *Athènes.* (CB's dot on the *i* of *entière* slants to accent the *e,* but H adds an accent anyway.)

50. Illegible abbreviation after *à.* - in margin.

51–52. H objects to the repetition of *pris prisonnier.*

55. CB's strikeout of the *s* of *leurs;* H inserts three lines under *buverent.*

56. H's *t* hooks around and deletes last three letters of *étaient.*

57. CB's crossout of *ca;* H's second line under *accueilla* snakes down.

60E. Sign added to show the effect in English of H's correction: "draperies in scarlet" to "scarlet draperies."

75. The word *ver* w.u.? The comment *obj^{on}* is within the text, below and to the right of *mauvais choix.*

82. H begins something illegible in margin.

83–84. CB's closing quotation mark is over dash; she then writes *allez* with another closing mark, suggesting that it was an afterthought.

85. H's circumflex on *chaînes.*

88. Three lines under *est.*

90. Four lines under *d* of *pretend.*

95. Three lines under *fixa.*

101. H's *couper* is above CB's *casser,* which he strikes out.

121. H's accent, changing *arrangeaint* to *s'arrangèrent.*

124. The letters *us > e* in *Ilisse* and run below line.

136. H's *tB* diagonal to text.

140. H's *tr. B.* diagonal, extending past line 141.

141. CB's *E >* her *e* in *Elle.*

150. CB's crossout of *nt* in *existent.*

154. CB's crossout of final *s* in *épaisses.*

168. H begins and strikes out something before *lugubre.*

182. H starts to write something over *déprimé;* his caret extends into CB's line.

191. CB's *son peuple > sa patrie,* almost hiding it.

193. H's caret for *pauvre* extends into CB's line.

196. H starts to write something above *du palais,* cancels it.

236. The word *accablante* w.u.?

In the text revised in December, CB makes a number of small changes, some in response to Heger's comments, but many more to alter punctuation. I have not reproduced that draft because the changes are rarely substantive. Instead I list the variants below, keying the line numbers to the numbers in the printed draft. All corrections are hers unless otherwise noted; those that Heger instigated are marked "[H]." Wherever "H again . . ." appears, she has not made the correction he suggested. The proper nouns formerly in special lettering are in her regular devoir hand.

1. CB omits her name. In its place is *Devoir de Style pour M: Heger.* The date is the same but not underlined.

5. The word *du > de* [H]; after *crise,* the line reads *du triomphe: le général lacedemonien; et d'exultation* is deleted.

6. Comma deleted; *permit > permettait* [H]; circumflex on *goûter* [H].

7. The word *chûte* missing circumflex.

8. The word *austères* deleted; *en* replaces *dans* [H].

9. Hyphen omitted from *lui-même.*

10. *Lysandre,* precedes *semblait* [H].

11. The word *sous* replaces *dans* [H]; it is w.u. [H]; comma after *tente;* circumflex on *ilôtes; grossier* replaces *rude.*

12. Comma after *abondant;* accent omitted from *prépara;* CB begins and deletes *Uly* before *Achille.*

13. Semicolon after *compagnons; quand . . . inaccessibles* deleted [H].

14. The word *un* l.c.; comma deleted after *boeuf;* ~~qu~~ and *s* of *des* deleted [H]: *d'un boeuf et de gros pains.*

15. CB does not change *apprêts; festin* w.u. [H]; comma replaces semicolon after it.

16. Commas deleted before and after *ou plutôt couchés.*

17. The word *objets* replaces *objet.*

18. The word *empruntés* replaces *emprunté.*

19. *B* in margin [H]; *portions* is unchanged and w.u. [H].

20. The word *passa* replaces *passait* [H], with final *a* underlined [H].

21. Comma after *guerre* deleted.

22. H again adds *affamés* after *loups; lacédémonien* added after *général.*

23. Accents omitted from *ôtèrent* and *régal.*

24. Comma deleted after *pain.*

25. *Chio* replaces *Chios* [H].

27. Semicolon deleted after *capitaines; Chacun* captitalized; semicolon after *silence; bientôt* l.c.

28. Semicolon after *changement.*

29. The word *déplièrent* spelled correctly [H].

30. H again adds *enfin* with caret after *parlèrent.*

31. *Lycurgue* replaces *Lycurge* [H]; H again adds *comme on,* preceded by comma that CB has omitted; *s'échauffait* replaces *s'échauffant* [H].

33. Period after *Lacédémone;* comma after *mais.*

34. Comma after *autres* [H]; hyphen omitted from *lui-même.*

36. Comma before *d'après* [H].

37. Comma after *égoistes* [H]; *mechant plaisir* replaces *plaisir méchant.*

39. The word *gaiété* has two accents; *devenait* replaces *devint* [H], with ending w.u. [H].

40. The word *calculée* replaces *forcée* [H]; *lui* replaces *le* [H].

41. First accent deleted from *rélâcher; son empire absolu* remains and is w.u. [H]; hyphen omitted from *lui-même.*

43. Comma added after *vaincus.*

44. Comma after *politique* deleted; *feignait* underlined [H] because CB has not added *avait.*

46. The word *jurèrent* replaces *avaient juré* [H].

47. The word *firent* replaces *avaient fait; bâtiments* is above the line, replacing crossed-out *fondements;* comma replaces semicolon after it; comma after *habitants* deleted.

48. The word *labourer* replaces *déchirer* [H].

49. Colon deleted.

50. Exclamation point replaces comma after *Lacédémone; par* replaces *à* [H].

51. *Epialte"! s'écriat-il à un ilôte: "Va* replaces *Epialte!" dit il à un ilote "va.*

51–52. H again underlines the unchanged *pris prisonnier.*

52. Accent added to *résiste.*

52–3. Parentheses deleted by CB restored [H].

53. Circumflex added to *chaînes;* dash replaces comma after *lyre.*

54. New paragraph begins with *Epialte.*

55. The word *leur* no longer has canceled *s; burent* replaces *buverent* [H]; no new paragraph after *gloire.*

56. *Les orgies étaient* becomes singular [H]; *son* replaces *leur* [H].

57. Comma after *rentra;* semicolon replaces comma after *poète; l'accueillit* replaces *l'accueilla* [H].

59. The word *de* replaces *des* before *lampes.*

60. The word *écarlates* replaces *en écarlate* [H]; semicolon deleted; closing quotation mark omitted after *donc;* added [H]; her exclamation point follows it; *q* of *qu'* u.c.

61. Comma added after *hibou;* CB deletes *qui s'est;* restored above line [H]; CB omits period, adds closing quotation.

63. Dash deleted.

64. CB changes *de l'ilote* to *des ilôtes;* corrected to *de l'ilôte* [H]; one *s* deleted from *froissé.*

65. The word *attendit* replaces *attendait* [H].

66. Comma added after *tranquillement;* new paragraph after *dire;* comma added after *Athénien.*

68. The word *poèsie* replaces *poësie.*

69. *Malgré* changed to *Malgrè* [H].

70. Comma after *nobles* deleted.

71. Comma added after *classiques; un* deleted.

73. Commas added after *Cependant* and *moment;* comma deleted after *Spartiates.*

74. Comma deleted after *Samos; ne s'apercevaient* replaces *n'apercevaient* [H].

75. The word *chien* replaces *ver* [H].

77. Opening quotation mark omitted; closing quotation mark precedes exclamation point.

78. Dash deleted.

80. Commas added after *chanter* and *métier; puisqu'aux* replaces *puisque aux.*

81. Comma added after *un.*

81–82. Title in special lettering.

82. *Demain* capitalized; CB does not add H's *Suppose que.*

83. Comma deleted after *et; Troïe* replaces *Troie.*

84. Exclamation point after *allez.*

85–86. Entire sentence (*Le poète . . . pierreries—*) deleted; paragraph begins *Je ne sais. . . .*

87. The phrase *dit le poète* replaces *dit-il;* period omitted.

88. Comma replaces semicolon after *modeste.*

89. Colon replaces comma after *fouet;* period after *Épialte* omitted.

90. No accent on *présenta;* semicolon replaces dash after *lyre; s* [H] and accent added to *prétends.*

91. Colon replaces comma after *obéisse;* closing quotation mark omitted after *esclave!*

92. Exclamation point replaces question mark after *esclave.*

93. Period added after *Lysandre.*

95. The word *fixa* remains as it was; *Lacédémonien* l.c.; *brula le feu* replaces *brulait la flamme.*

96. Comma added after *pure.*

97–98. No paragraph; after *féroce,* sentence continues: *j'ai des chaînes, tu as des dents, tigre déchire moi!* [H].

101. Semicolon replaces dash; commas deleted after *lance* and *poète; couper* replaces *casser* [H].

102. The phrase *cordon qui teneait le* replaces *cordon servant à attacher un.*

103. Accents omitted from *révèla;* period added after *scène.*

104. CB omits accent on *étoiles;* added [H].

105. Dash replaces semicolon after *lune;* comma added after *Hymette.*

105–6. The phrase *portant Athènes comme une couronne* replaces *couronné de la ville d'Athènes* [H]; comma after *Parthénon.*

107. Comma added after *lunaires.*

108. *Illisus* replaces *Illise* [H]; *répétaient* replaces *répetaient.*

109. H again underlines *classique;* comma after it deleted.

112. The phrase *offraient un contraste frappant avec cet* replaces *donnaient le revers de cet,* which H underlined; comma added after *calme.*

113. Dash deleted after *dehors.*

114. Comma added after *ville.*

116. Colon replaces semicolon after *terre.*

117. The words *par les* replace *des* [H].

118. The word *dans* added before *la musique* and comma after.

121. The word *arrangèrent* replaces *arrangeaient* [H]; *devint* replaces *devinrent.*

122. Comma added after *arrêta.*

124. *Illisus* replaces *Ilisse* [H].

127. Comma replaces semicolon after *baissée.*

130. Accent omitted from *Pélopides;* comma after it.

131. The word *après* replaces *de* [H].

132. Comma added after *lointain; dans ses foyers déshonorés* replaces *sur son foyer déshonoré* [H]; comma follows.

134. The word *et* replaces dash [H].

140. The word *pensif* deleted.

142. Comma deleted after *étoiles;* no space between *tandis que.*

150. Comma deleted after *homme.*

153. Comma added after *arbres;* comma deleted after *et;* accent omitted on *où;* added [H].

154. The word *épaisse* singular.

158. Comma added after *humaines.*

159. Period replaces colon after *parle.*

160. Closing quotation mark omitted.

161. The word *gémit* replaces *retentit* [H].

162. Dash after *Agamemnon* and comma after *tombeau* deleted.

163. The word *contient* replaces *renferme;* comma replaces dash after *cendres.*

164. Comma added after *tyrans.*

166. Semicolon after *suit* [H].

167–68. The phrase *sert d'accompagnement lugubre à* replaces *fait le refrain de* [H].

170. Period omitted after *souvenirs.*

172. Comma replaces semicolon after *Troie; cette* deleted.

174. CB deletes comma and *cette fontaine* so the line reads *près d'une fontaine dans la cour.*

180. Instead of *casque; il,* the text reads *casque. Il.*

181. Comma after *bras* deleted; *appuyai* replaces *appuya* [H].

182. The words *de larmes* added after *gros* (H had suggested *déprimé*).

183. Comma added after *aimée; car* deleted and *moi* added between commas after *avais* [H].

186. Accent omitted from *départ,* comma added after.

189. The word *fanaux* replaces *fanal* [H].

192. The word *roi* written and crossed out before *souverain.*

193. CB does not add H's *pauvre.*

195. Accent added to *déborda.*

197. Circumflex added to *pâle.*

200. Comma added after *femme.*

206. Exclamation point replaces comma after *encore.*

210. CB writes *sous* and deletes it, replacing it with *à travers;* semicolon replaces colon; exclamation point replaces dash.

219. No new paragraph.

220. CB starts to write *écoutez,* crosses out *z.*

225. Comma replaces semicolon after *destin.*

227. Comma added after *tout;* no punctuation after *mien.*

228. The word *brisera* written and crossed out before *chène; abattra* written above it.

230. Instead of *respirer, il,* the text reads *respirer. Il.*

231. The word *avait* replaces *avaient.*

232. Circumflex moved to *o* in *ilôtes;* comma after.

234. No accent on *présent.*

236. Period added after *accablante;* first *ô* u.c.; *son* capitalized.

240. Comma deleted after *luimême; pour* replaces *de* before *quitter.*

241. No period after *sureté.*

243. Comma deleted after *demanda.*

244. Comma deleted after *instances;* semicolon replaces comma after *fraîche;* comma added after *puis.*

244–45. The phrase *d'un fort mal de* replaces *d'avoir très fort mal à la.*

245. Comma added after *ensuite.*

246. *Ilissus* replaces *Ilisse.*

247. Comma added after *revenant.*

248. Comma added after *Athéniens.*

249. CB added *de Clytemnestre,* after *d'Electre,.*

250. The word *lui* added after *çela;* comma added after *venait.*

252. No paragraph; accent added to *échappa.*

254. Commas added before and after *mais aussi.*

254–55. H again underlines *en opiate assez forte;* dash added after it.

255. Final *s* added to *mot.*

256. Title centered on two added lines: *Athènes sauvée par la / Poèsie.*

COMMENTS

1. A list of all the variants in the second version appears above, 446–50.

2. *Villette,* 35.580–81.

3. *The Life of Lysander,* in Plutarch 4:273. See also Duthie, *Foreign Vision,* 50.

4. See, for example, devoirs 21 and 22.

5. "De la vie et des ouvrages de Callinus et de Tyrtée," introductory essay in Delavigne, xxxiv.

6. Gaskell, 11.238.

7. J. Lemprière, *Bibliotheca Classica; or, A Classical Dictionary, Containing a Full Account of All the Proper Names Mentioned in Ancient Authors* (London, 1797), is still at the BPM; the children scribbled in it. See *EW,* 295 n. 36.

8. *CB Poems,* 64–69. As Barker says, "Her stories and poems . . . are peppered with casual references to Scipio Africanus, Socrates, Ovid, Virgil's *Eclogues* and Herodotus and it is clear from their context that she knew more about them than simply their brief entries in her father's Lemprière's *Bibliotheca Classica*" (166).

9. On Lady Zenobia, see *CBEW* 1:286 n. 2 and 301 n. 5.

10. For instance, at the end of "Mazeppa," a tale teller discovers that his audience (the king) has been asleep for an hour.

11. *Villette,* 30.511.

12. Of the two most famous sources for Cassandra, Aeschylus' *Agamemnon* and Euripedes' *Trojan Women,* the first seems far more likely to have been CB's prototype. In the *Agamemnon,* the chariot and references to animals are prominent features; in the *Trojan Women,* the prophesies do not match up, and Cassandra speaks about becoming Agamemnon's mistress and murderer.

13. It comes from *The Iliad,* book 20, though only Chapman renders it this way. According to the *BST* editor's note, "The Greek epithet is hard to translate with an exact brief equivalent. The word means that those hands are not to be fastened or touched, because they are irresistible. 'Inaccessible' does not convey the right meaning to the general reader. 'Invincible' is nearer the mark if a one-word translation is insisted on. CB must have realized the strangeness of the Homeric epithet she used, but depended on an acclaimed authority" ("Four Essays," 90).

14. Gérin *CB,* 195.

15. "Poems and Ballads of Schiller. No. II," *Blackwood's* 52 (October 1842): 448–49. See also the Textual Note to line 202 and Introduction, lxviii.

16. *Villette,* 35.581.

17. Ibid.

18. Ibid., 35.579.

19. Ibid.

20. Duthie, *Foreign Vision,* 54.

21. Both versions come from the collection of Henry H. Bonnell, who purchased them at auctions of Nicholls's manuscripts in 1914 and 1916. Nicholls owned the devoirs by inheritance from CB; they did not come to him from Belgium.

28. Letter from a Poor Painter to a Great Lord / Lettre d'un pauvre Peintre à un grand Seigneur (CB)

TEXTUAL NOTES

At fourteen CB wrote "The Swiss Artist," a two-part serial for her *Blackwood's Young Men's Magazine.* Alexandre de Valence, its nine-year-old protagonist, is discovered in his humble alpine hut by the comte de Lausanne, who becomes his patron and takes him to Paris and Italy. Ten years later, "wealthy and far-famed," Alexandre returns to his "venerable parents." He has undergone no hardships but he has improved his genius by examining "in detail" the work of famous masters. The links between the devoir and the serial seem tenuous, but see *CBEW* 1:92–94 and 115–17.

60 (63). Nebuchadnezzar's furnace: Nebuchadnezzar II (605–562 B.C.) was the king of Babylon who destroyed Jerusalem and began the Babylonian captivity of the Jews (which CB refers to in "The Death of Moses," lines 154–55). He cast Shadrach, Meshach, and Abednego into his fiery furnace because they refused to worship his golden idol, but their God kept them safe within the flames (Daniel 3).

87–89 (90–93). In EB's "Plead for Me" (dated 1844 in manuscript), the speaker refers to the "God of visions" as "My slave, my comrade, and my king" and then explains each term (*EB Poems,* 22–23). I am grateful to Janet Gezari for this reference.

117–18 (123). Titian, Raphael, and Michelangelo are all included in the list that CB wrote at thirteen "of painters whose works I wish to see" (Gaskell 5.117–18).

130 (135). "laurels on a grave" and other details of this section may anticipate a poem that CB wrote three years later, "I gave, at first, Attention close." The speaker, Jane, wins the prize in a school competition, a laurel wreath bestowed by her master. Nonetheless, she says, "The hour of triumph was to me / The hour of sorrow sore; / A day hence I must cross the sea, / Ne'er to recross it more" (*CB Poems,* 335–36).

EDITORIAL NOTES
Several words have slightly wavy underlining.

2–4. *Lettre* in CB's double-line print; subtitle in smaller print; H's period and slash after *Seigneur.*

6. The word *cette* > something (*ce l?*).

10. H's commas after *autre* and *êtes.*

15. H's line indicates the need for a comma, which he adds.

28. H's commas before and after *Milord.*

29. *Rome* in CB's proper-noun print.

54. H's mark in the left margin is indecipherable.

63. *Nebuchadnezzar* in CB's proper-noun print.

66. H's comma after *autres.*

84. Large space between *secret.* and *Enfin.*

110. H writes something illegible—perhaps *ai*—over *plein.*

120. *Florence, Venise,* and *Rome* in CB's proper-noun print.

123. *Titian, Raffaelle,* and *Michel-Ange* in CB's proper-noun print; *su* is a *Belgicisme* and should be *pu.*

140. *George Howard* in CB's proper-noun print.

COMMENTS

1. These comments draw on my earlier article, "On the Struggles of Poor and Unknown Artist."

2. *Lets.,* 334 (October 13, 1843).

3. Gordon describes it as her "last and most dramatic effort to bare her soul to Monsieur"—and to invite him to promote her potential (111–113).

4. *JE,* 424 (ch. 27, mod. eds.).

5. *BLFC* 1:134 (December [7] 1835). The letters of solicitation that Branwell wrote at twenty-two and twenty-three to Hartley Coleridge are much humbler; see *BLFC* 1:204–5, 210–11.

6. *Lets.,* 153. Four years later, she wrote of Ellen's placid, cheerful temperament, "this is better than the ardent nature that changes twenty times a day" (219).

7. *Misc.* 2:404.

8. *CBEW* 2.2:248.

9. *Lets.,* 245.

10. *Lets.,* 335 n. 7.

Bibliography

Alexander, Christine. *A Bibliography of the Manuscripts of Charlotte Brontë*. Westport, Conn.: The Brontë Society, in association with Meckler Publishing, 1982.

———. *The Early Writings of Charlotte Brontë*. Oxford: Basil Blackwell, 1983.

———. "Recent Research on Charlotte Brontë's Juvenilia." *BST* 18 (1981): 15–24.

Alexander, Christine, and Jane Sellars. *The Art of the Brontës*. Cambridge: Cambridge UP, 1995.

Allen, James Smith. *Popular French Romanticism: Authors, Readers, and Books in the Nineteenth Century*. Syracuse: Syracuse UP, 1981.

Allott, Miriam, ed. *Charlotte Brontë. Jane Eyre and Villette: A Casebook*. London: Macmillan, 1973.

Auerbach, Nina. *Communities of Women: An Idea in Fiction*. Cambridge: Harvard UP, 1978.

Ballard, George. *Memoirs of Several Ladies of Great Britain*. Ed. Ruth Perry. Detroit: Wayne State UP, 1985.

Barante, Guillaume de. *Histoire des ducs de Bourgogne de la maison de Valois, 1364–1477*. Vol. 2. Brussels: Adolph Wahlen, 1838.

Barker, Juliet R. V. *The Brontës*. London: Weidenfeld and Nicolson, 1994.

Beer, Patricia. *Reader, I Married Him*. London: Macmillan, 1974.

Bellessort, André. *Dix-huitième siècle et romantisme*. Paris: Fayard, 1941.

Bemelmans, Joseph. "A Charlotte Brontë Manuscript." *Notes and Queries* 228 (August 1983): 294–95.

Bénichou, Paul. *Le Sacre de l'écrivain (1750–1830)*. Paris: Corti, 1973.

———. *Le Temps des prophètes*. Paris: Gallimard, 1977.

Bentley, Phyllis. *The Brontës and Their World*. New York: Viking, 1969.

Benvenuto, Richard. *Emily Brontë*. Boston: Twayne, 1982.

Bernardin de Saint-Pierre, Jacques-Henri. *Oeuvres complètes*. Vols. 3–10, *Etudes de la nature; Harmonies de la nature*. Paris: Dupont, 1826.

Biographie Nationale: L'Adadémie Royale des Science, des Lettres et des Beaux-Arts de Belgique. Brussels: Bruylant-Christophe, 1890–91.

Blackwood's Edinburgh Magazine. Vols. 1–52. 1824–1842.

Brialmont, Henri. *History of the Life of Arthur Duke of Wellington*. Trans. and rev. by G. R. Gleig. Vol. 3. London: Longman, Green, Longman, and Roberts, 1860.

Brontë, Anne. *Agnes Grey*. Intro. Angeline Goreau. London: Penguin, 1988.

Brontë, Charlotte. *An Edition of The Early Writings of Charlotte Brontë*. Ed. Christine Alexander. Vol. 1, *1826–1832*. Oxford: Basil Blackwell, 1987. Vol. 2, pt. 1, *1833–1834;* pt. 2, *1834–1835*. 1991.

———. [Exercise book] "Cahier d' *of English Translations*." Pierpont Morgan Library, Bonnell Collection.

———. [Exercise book] "Cahier d' *of German Translations*." BPM, 117.

———. [Exercise book] "Devoir." University of Leeds, Brotherton Library, Brotherton Collection.

———. [Exercise book] "Traduction." British Library, Ashley MS 160.

———. [Exercise book: transcriptions of poems and prose extracts.] BPM, Bonnell 115.

———. "Exercices sur les participes." University of Texas at Austin, Humanities Research Center, Stark Collection.

———. *Five Novelettes*. Ed. Winifred Gérin. London: Folio, 1971.

———. *Jane Eyre*. Ed. Jane Jack and Margaret Smith. Oxford: Clarendon, 1969.

———. *Jane Eyre*. 2d ed. Ed. Richard J. Dunn. Norton Critical Editions. New York: Norton, 1987.

———. *The Letters of Charlotte Brontë, with a Selection of Letters by Family and Friends*. Margaret Smith, ed. Vol. 1, *1829–1847*. Oxford: Clarendon, 1995.

———. *The Poems of Charlotte Brontë: A New Text and Commentary*. Ed. Victor A. Neufeldt. New York: Garland, 1985.

———. *The Professor*. Ed. Margaret Smith and Herbert Rosengarten. Oxford: Clarendon, 1987.

———. *Shirley*. Ed. Herbert Rosengarten and Margaret Smith. Oxford: Clarendon, 1979.

———. *Villette*. Ed. Herbert Rosengarten and Margaret Smith. Oxford: Clarendon, 1984.

Brontë, Charlotte, and Patrick Brontë. *The Miscellaneous and Unpublished Writings of Charlotte and Patrick Branwell Brontë.* Ed. Thomas J. Wise and John Alexander Symington. 2 vols. Shakespeare Head edition. Oxford: Basil Blackwell, 1936 and 1938.

Brontë, Emily Jane. *The Complete Poems.* Ed. Janet Gezari. Harmondsworth, U.K.: Penguin, 1992.

———. *The Complete Poems of Emily Jane Brontë.* Ed. C. W. Hatfield. New York: Columbia UP, 1941.

———. *Five Essays Written in French.* Intro. and notes by Fannie E. Ratchford. Trans. Lorine White Nagel. Austin: U of Texas P, 1948.

———. *Wuthering Heights.* Ed. Hilda Marsden and Ian Jack. Oxford: Clarendon, 1976.

———. *Wuthering Heights.* 3d ed. Ed. William M. Sale, Jr., and Richard J. Dunn. Norton Critical Editions. New York: Norton, 1990.

Brontë, Emily Jane, and Anne Brontë. *The Poems of Emily Jane Brontë and Anne Brontë.* Ed. Thomas J. Wise and John Alexander Symington. Oxford: Basil Blackwell, 1934.

Brontë family. *The Brontës: Their Lives, Friendships, and Correspondence.* Ed. Thomas J. Wise and John Alexander Symington. 4 vols. Shakespeare Head edition. Oxford: Basil Blackwell, 1932.

Brontë, Patrick Branwell. *The Poems of Patrick Branwell Brontë.* Ed. Victor A. Neufeldt. New York: Garland, 1990.

Buffon, Georges Louis Leclerc de. *Discours sur le style.* 1753. Reprint, Paris: Librairie Hachette, 1875.

———. *Natural History, General and Particular, by the Count de Buffon.* 2d ed. Trans. William Smellie. Vol. 4. London: Strahan and Cadell, 1785.

———. *Oeuvres complètes.* Vol. 18, *Histoire naturelle: Mammifères*, vol. 3. Paris: Verdière et Ladrange, 1824.

Calvin, John. *John Calvin's Sermons on the Ten Commandments.* Ed. and trans. Benjamin W. Farley. Grand Rapids: Baker Books, 1980.

Carlyle, Thomas. *On Heroes, Hero-Worship, and the Heroic in History.* Intro. Michael K. Goldberg. Berkeley: U of Calif. P, 1993.

Chadwick, Esther Alice. "A Gift from M. le Professeur Constantin Heger to Charlotte Brontë." *The Nineteenth Century and After* 81 (April 1917): 846–61.

———. *In the Footsteps of the Brontës.* London: Pitman, 1914.

Chapone, Hester. *Letters on the Improvement of the Mind.* London: John Sharpe, 1822.

Charlier, Gustave. "Brussels Life in 'Villette.'" *BST* 12 (1955): 386–90.

Chateaubriand, François-René de. *The Beauties of Christianity.* Trans. Frederic Shoberl. Philadelphia: M. Carey, 1815.

———. *The Genius of Christianity; or, The Spirit and Beauty of the Christian Religion.* Trans. Charles I. White. Baltimore: John Murphy, 1856.

———. *Les Martyrs; ou, Le Triomphe de la religion chrétienne.* Paris: Garnier Frères, 18(?).

———. *The Martyrs.* Trans. O. W. Wight. New York: Derby and Jackson, 1859.

———. *Oeuvres complètes.* Vols. 11–14, *Génie du Christianisme.* Paris: Ladvocat, 1826.

———. *Oeuvres romanesques et voyages.* Ed. Maurice Regard. Paris: Gallimard, 1969.

———. *Travels in Greece, Palestine, Egypt, and Barbary.* Trans. Frederick Shoberl. Vol. 2. London: Henry Colburn, 1812.

Chitham, Edward. *A Life of Emily Brontë.* Oxford: Basil Blackwell, 1987.

Cornish, Dorothy H. "The Brontës' Study of French." *BST* 11 (1947): 97–100.

Crump, Rebecca W. *Charlotte and Emily Brontë: A Reference Guide.* 3 vols. Boston: Hall, 1982–86.

Davies, Stevie. *Emily Brontë: Heretic.* London: Women's Press, 1994.

Delavigne, Casimir. *Oeuvres complètes. Poésies diverses,* vol. 3. Intro. M. Baron. Brussels: J. P. Meline, 1832.

Delvaille, Bernard, ed. *Mille et cent ans de poésie française.* Paris: Robert Laffont, 1991.

Depage, Henri. "Les Origines du Pensionnat Heger." *Edelweiss* (magazine), June 1956: 10–13.

des Essarts, Emmanuel. "Les Romantiques oubliés: Alexandre Soumet." *Revue bleue,* 4th ser., 16 (September 7, 1901): 305–10.

Descotes, Maurice. *La Légende de Napoléon et les écrivains français du XIXe siècle.* Paris: Minard, 1976

Dessner, Lawrence J. "Charlotte Brontë's 'Le Nid,' an Unpublished Manuscript." *BST* 16 (1973): 213–18.

Dictionary of National Biography. Oxford: Oxford UP, 1917.

Duthie, Enid. "Charlotte Brontë's Translation: The First Canto of Voltaire's "Henriade.'" *BST* 13 (1959): 347–51.

———. *The Foreign Vision of Charlotte Brontë.* London: Macmillan, 1975.

Favre, Yves-Alain. *La Poésie romantique en toutes lettres.* Paris: Bordas, 1989.

Florian, Jean-Pierre. *Fables.* 3d ed. Paris: Lemarié, 1793.

Fortescue, John. *Six British Soldiers.* London: Williams and Norgate, 1928.

"Four Essays by Charlotte Brontë: The Authentic Fire in Exercises at Brussels." Trans. Dorothy Cornish and Jean P. Inebit. *BST* 12 (1952): 88–99.

Foxe, John. *The Acts and Monuments.* 4th ed. Vol. 5. London: Religious Tract Society, n.d.

Fraser, Rebecca. *The Brontës: Charlotte Brontë and Her Family.* New York: Crown, 1988.

"French Essays by Charlotte and Emily: Charlotte on 'The Death of Napoleon'; Emily on 'The Palace of Death.'" Trans. Margaret Lane. *BST* 12 (1954): 272–85.

Gaskell, Elizabeth. *The Life of Charlotte Brontë.* Ed. Alan Shelston. Harmondsworth, U.K.: Penguin 1975.

———. *The Life of Charlotte Brontë.* Intro. Clement K. Shorter. Haworth edition. New York: Harper, 1902.

Gérin, Winifred. *Branwell Brontë.* London: Thomas Nelson, 1961.

———. *Charlotte Brontë: The Evolution of Genius.* Oxford: Oxford UP, 1967.

———. *Emily Brontë.* Oxford: Oxford UP, 1972.

Gilbert, Sandra M., and Susan Gubar. *The Madwoman in the Attic: The Woman Writer and the Nineteenth-Century Imagination.* New Haven: Yale UP, 1979.

Gordon, Lyndall. *Charlotte Brontë: A Passionate Life.* London: Chatto and Windus, 1994.

Hagenmeyer, Henri. *Le Vrai et Le Faux Pierre l'Hermite: Analyse critique.* Trans. Furcy Raynaud. Paris: Librairie de la Société Bibliographique, 1883.

Harper, Janet. "Charlotte Brontë's Héger Family and Their School." *Blackwood's* 191 (April 1912): 461–69.

Heger, Constantin. *Discours prononcé à la distribution des prix . . . de l'Athénée Royal de Bruxelles, Le 15 août 1843.* Pamphlet, Bibliothèque Royale Albert Ier.

Hewish, John. *Emily Brontë: A Critical and Biographical Study.* London: Macmillan, 1969.

Higuchi, Akiko. "Concert at the Fete in *Villette.*" *BST* 20 (1992): 273–83.

Hollier, Denis, ed. *A New History of French Literature.* Cambridge: Harvard UP, 1989.

Homans, Margaret. *Women Writers and Poetic Identity: Dorothy Wordsworth, Emily Brontë, and Emily Dickinson.* Princeton: Princeton UP, 1980.

Houghton, Walter. *The Victorian Frame of Mind, 1830–1870.* New Haven: Yale UP, 1957.

Hugo, Victor. "Mirabeau." In *Things Seen (Choses Vues): Essays.* Boston: Estes and Lauriat, n.d. (ca. 1890).

———. "Sur Mirabeau." In *Oeuvres complètes.* Vol. 5, *Littérature et philosophie mêlées. . . .* Paris: Club français du livre, 1967.

Hunt, Herbert J. *The Epic in Nineteenth-Century France.* Oxford: Basil Blackwell, 1941.

Kirshner, Ralph. "The Duke of Wellington in the Writings of Charlotte Brontë." *Brontë Newsletter,* no. 2 (1983): 1–2.

Kleinbaum, Abby Wettan. *The War Against the Amazons.* New York: McGraw-Hill, 1983.

Knoepflmacher, U. C. *Wuthering Heights: A Study.* Athens: Ohio UP, 1993.

Ladoué, Pierre. *Un Précurseur du romantisme: Millevoye (1782–1816). Essai d'histoire littéraire.* Paris: Librairie académique Perrin, 1912.

Lamartine, Alphonse de. *Harmonies poétiques et religieuses.* Paris: Hachette, 1897.

———. *Oeuvres poétiques complètes.* Paris: Gallimard, 1963.

Lane, Margaret. "The Mysterious Genius of Emily Brontë." In *Purely for Pleasure.* London: Hamish Hamilton, 1966.

———. "The Palace of Death." *The Listener* 52 (November 11, 1954): 803–4.

Lindner, Cynthia A. *Romantic Imagery in the Novels of Charlotte Brontë.* London: Macmillan, 1978.

Lock, John, and Canon W. T. Dixon. *A Man of Sorrow: The Life, Letters and Times of the Rev. Patrick Brontë, 1777–1861.* London: Nelson, 1965.

Lonoff, Sue. "Charlotte Brontë's Belgian Essays: The Discourse of Empowerment." *Victorian Studies* 32 (spring 1989): 387–409.

———. "On the Struggles of a Poor and Unknown Artist." *BST* 18 (1985): 373–82.

Macdonald, Frederika. "The Brontës at Brussels." *Women at Home* 2 (1894): 277–91.

———. "Charlotte Brontë's Professor." *Cornhill Magazine,* n.s., 35 (October 1913): 519–33.

———. *The Secret of Charlotte Brontë Followed by Some Reminiscences of the Real Monsieur and Madame Heger.* London: T. C. and E. C. Jack, 1914.

Mani, Lata. "Cultural Theory, Colonial Texts: Reading Eyewitness Accounts of Widow Burning." In *Cultural Studies,* ed. Lawrence Grossberg, Cary Nelson, and Paula A. Treichler. New York: Routledge, 1992.

Mavor, William. *Universal History.* 25 vols. New York: Samuel Stansbury, 1804.

Maxwell, J. C. "Emily Brontë's 'The Palace of Death.'" *BST* 15 (1967): 139–40.

Maynard, John. *Charlotte Brontë and Sexuality.* Cambridge: Cambridge UP, 1984.

Michaud, Joseph-François. *Histoire des croisades.* 3 vols. Vol. 1, *L'Histoire de la première croisade.* 4th ed. Paris: Aimé André, 1825.

———. *The History of the Crusades.* Trans. W. Robson. New York: Armstrong, 1884(?).

Miller, J. Hillis. *The Disappearance of God.* Cambridge: Harvard UP, Belknap, 1975.

Millett, Kate. *Sexual Politics.* New York: Dell, 1969.

Millevoye, Charles-Hubert. *Oeuvres de Millevoye.* Intro. Charles-Augustin Sainte-Beuve. Paris: Garnier, 1874.

Moglen, Helene. *Charlotte Brontë: The Self Conceived.* New York: Norton, 1976.

"More Brontë Devoirs: Charlotte on 'La Chenille' and 'La Mort de Moïse'; M. Heger's Comments on 'La Chute des Feuilles.'" Trans. Phyllis Bentley. *BST* 12 (1955): 361–85.

Musselwhite, David E. *Partings Welded Together: Politics and Desire in the Nineteenth-Century English Novel.* London: Methuen, 1987.

Myer, Valerie Grosvenor. *Charlotte Brontë: Truculent Spirit.* Critical Case Studies. London: Vision, 1987.

Nussey, Ellen. "Reminiscences of Charlotte Brontë." *Scribner's Monthly,* May 1871. Reprint, *BST* 2 (1899): 58–83.

Pellissier, Georges. *The Literary Movement in France During the Nineteenth Century.* Trans. Anne Garrison Brinton. New York: Putnam's, 1897.

Peters, Margot. *Charlotte Brontë: Style in the Novel.* Madison: U of Wisconsin P, 1973.

Plutarch. *Plutarch's Lives.* Trans. Bernadotte Perrin. Vol. 4. Loeb Classical Library. London: Heinemann, 1916.

Porter, Laurence M. *The Renaissance of the Lyric in French Romanticism: Elegy, "Poëme" and Ode.* Lexington, Ky.: French Forum, 1978.

Potez, Henri. *L'Elégie en France avant le romantisme.* Paris: Calmann Lévy, 1897.

Rabion, ed. *Les Fleurs de la poésie française depuis le commencement du XVIᵉ siècle jusqu'à nos jours.* 8th ed. Tours: Alfred Mame, 1865.

Ratchford, Fannie E. *The Brontës' Web of Childhood.* New York: Columbia UP, 1941.

———. *Gondal's Queen.* Austin: U of Texas P, 1955.

Rehbock, Philip F. *The Philosophical Naturalists: Themes in Early Nineteenth-Century British Biology.* Madison: U of Wisconsin P, 1983.

Reid, T. Wemyss. *Charlotte Brontë: A Monograph.* London: Macmillan, 1877.

Robertson, William John. *A Century of French Verse.* London: A. D. Innes, 1895.

Rosenbaum, Barbara, and Pamela White, comps. *Index of English Literary Manuscripts.* Vol. 4, *1800–1900.* London: Mansell, 1982.

Sabatier, Robert. *Histoire de la poésie francaise.* Vol. 5, book 1, *La Poésie du dix-neuvième siècle: Les romantismes.* Paris: Albin Michel, 1977.

Sadoff, Diane. *Monsters of Affection: Dickens, Eliot, and Brontë on Fatherhood.* Baltimore: Johns Hopkins UP, 1982.

Scott, David. *Pictorialist Poetics: Poetry and the Visual Arts in Nineteenth-Century France.* Cambridge: Cambridge UP, 1988.

Seaward, Mark R. D. "Charlotte Brontë's Napoleonic Relic." *BST* 17 (1978): 185–88.

Shorter, Clement K. *Charlotte Brontë and Her Sisters.* New York: Scribner's, 1905.

Smith, Margaret. "The Manuscripts of Charlotte Brontë's Novels." *BST* 18 (1983): 189–205.

Spark, Muriel, and Derek Stanford. *Emily Brontë: Her Life and Work.* New York: Coward-McCann, 1966.

Spielmann, Marion H. "An Early Essay by Charlotte Brontë." *BST* 6 (1924): 236–46.

———. "The Inner History of the Brontë-Heger Letters." *Fortnightly Review* 111 (April 1919): 599–605.

Stevens, Joan, ed. *Mary Taylor: Friend of Charlotte Brontë. Letters from New Zealand and Elsewhere.* Auckland, N.Z., and Oxford: Auckland UP/Oxford UP, 1972.

Stone, Samuel Irving. "Rachel and Soumet's *Jeanne d'Arc. PMLA* 47 (December 1932): 1130–49.

Tayler, Irene. *Holy Ghosts: The Male Muses of Emily and Charlotte Brontë.* New York: Columbia UP, 1990.

"Three Essays by Emily Bronte." Trans. Lorine White Nagel. *BST* 11 (1950): 337–41.

"Two Brussels School-fellows of the Brontës." *BST* 5 (1919): 25–29.

Vericour, L. Raymond de. *Modern French Literature.* Rev. by William Staughton Chase. Boston: Gould, Kendall, and Lincoln, 1848.

Vigny, Alfred de. *Poèmes.* Brussels: Hauman, 1834.

Ward, Mary A. Prefaces. *The Life and Works of The Sisters Brontë.* The Haworth edition. London: Smith, Elder, 1899–1903.

Ware, Jno. N. "Bernardin de Saint-Pierre and Charlotte Brontë." *Modern Language Notes* 40 (June 1925): 381–82.

Weir, Edith M. "The Hegers and a Yorkshire Family." *BST* 14 (1963): 32.

———. "New Brontë Material Comes to Light . . . Letters from the Hegers," trans. Janet Ironside. *BST* 11 (1949): 249–61.

Wells, Augustin-Louis. *Les Soeurs Brontë et l'etranger.* Paris: Rodstein, 1937.

Wesley, John. *The Works of John Wesley.* Ed. Albert C. Outler. Nashville: Abingdon, 1985.

Willson, Jo Anne. " 'The Butterfly' and *Wuthering Heights*: A Mystic's Eschatology." *Victorian Newsletter*, no. 33 (spring 1968): 22–25.

Winnifrith, Tom. *The Brontës and Their Background: Romance and Reality.* London: Macmillan, 1973.

Writings of Edward the Sixth . . . Anne Askew. . . . Vol. 3. British Reformers Series. London: Religious Tract Society, 1831.

Wroot, Herbert E. *Persons and Places of the Brontë Novels.* 1906. Reprint, New York: Burt Franklin, 1970.

Index

Entries for the English and French versions are indexed under the English word; where the French word or title substantially differs, it follows the English.

agery, xxxv–xxxvii; version of King Harold essay, 104–107; version of Napoleon essay, 294–301; on writing, 256. *See also* Gaskell, Elizabeth.

Heger, Louise, lxix

Heger, Marie Pauline, 233

Heger, Madame: *see* Heger, Zoë Parent

Heger, Paul, lvi

Heger, Zoë Parent (wife of Constantin Heger), xxii, xxviii, liii, lv, lix, lxiv, lxix

Helen (of Troy), 344–345

Helstone, Caroline (*Shirley*), xxxix, lviii, 22

Henri, Frances Evans (*The Professor*), lxiv, lxxiv–lxxv

"Henry Hastings," 267–268

Henry VIII, 92

Hero(es), xxxi, xxxv, xlv, l, liv, 114, 115, 135, 136–137, 278–279, 290–291, 300–301, 303; and slave, xlviii–xlix, 98–99, 102–103, 106–107

Heroines, lxii, lxxv

Hewish, John, 65, 116, 188

Hierocles, lvi, 86–87

Hindu, 10; Hindustan/Indoustan, 2–3, 11

Hoffman, E.T.A.: "Das Majorat"/"The Entail," lxviii

Homans, Margaret, 154, 191

Homer, xxxi, 257, 338–339, 354

Howard, George, 366, 370

Hugo, Victor, l, lvii, lxii, 110–111, 112–113, 255; "Mirabeau on the Tribune," xxix, xxxviii, 108–111, 114–117, 134, 136, 137, 138, 304, 307; "Sur Mirabeau," lxv, 303

Human justice: essay, "La Justice humaine," 204–215; in *Villette*, xxxvii, lxxiv, lxxv

Huygens, Christiaan, xxxi, 50–51, 53

Hymettus (Mount), 340–341

Iliad, 234, 353, 354

Illyssus river, 340–341, 342–343

"Immensity of God, The,"/"L'Immensité de Dieu," xxxi, xliv, 48–55

Intemperance personified, 216–217, 222–223, 224–225, 230–231, 233, 234, 235

Iphigenia, 344–345

Ishmael: descendants of, 26–27, 35

"Islanders, The," 172, 305

Israel, 310–311, 312–313, 318–319, 326–327, 328

Jacob, 216–217, 318–319, 332; Jacob's ladder, 264–265

Jairus, 14–15

Jane (in CB fragment): *see* "Letter. My dear Jane"

Jane Eyre (CB), lxii, lxviii, lxxi, lxxv, 8, 11, 44, 202, 234, 266, 330, 369

Jehu, 318–319

Jericho, 316–317, 318–319

Jerusalem, 91, 122–123, 124–125, 130–131, 132–133, 320–321

Jesus, 14–15, 80–81, 330

Jezebel, 318–319

Joan of Arc, 9, 77, 328, 329–330, 331

Jonah's vine, xlix, 278–279, 290–291; Josiah's vine (Heger), 300–301

Jordan river, 122–123, 310–311, 320–321

Joshua, 124–125, 130–131

Judea, 320–321

Jupiter, 110–111, 272–273, 284–285, 294–295

Juvenilia, xiv, 33–34, 54; of CB, xxi, lviii, lxxi, 8, 9, 90, 202, 234, 266, 269, 354, 357; of EB, xxvi; and fables, 233; habits of, xlv; imagery in, xxxvii; parodies in, xxxviii; sexual imbalance in, lxxv; as source of devoirs, lxviii, 352, 355; use of French in, xxiii; women of, 92, 93. *See also* Angrian saga; Gondal saga

"King Harold before the Battle of Hastings"/"Le Roi Harold avant la Bataille de Hastings," xxxiii, xlviii, lxi, lxv, 96–103, 112–117, 134, 136, 137, 187, 303, 304; Heger's version, xlviii–xlix, 104–107, 308; dictée for, 108–111

Lalaing, Madame, 72–73, 78, 79

Lalaing, Simon de, 68–75, 77, 78–79

Lamartine, Alphonse de, lxiv, lvii, lxii, 42, 188, 255, 330; *Harmonies poétiques et religieuses (Poetic and religious harmonies)*, 46, 52, 53, 54, 236, 330

Lane, Margaret, 232, 233, 303, 308

Lawyer(s), 204–205, 208–209, 215

Lebanon, 122–123

Lebel, Joachim-Joseph, 305, 308

"Letter of Invitation to a Clergyman"/"Lettre d'invitation à un Ecclésiastique," xxix, 144–149

"Letter. Madam"/"Lettre. Madame," xxix, xlvii, 140–143, 148–149

"Letter. My dear Jane"/"Lettre. Ma chère Jane," xxx, xxxvi, 260–269

"Letter. My dear Mama"/"Lettre. Ma chère Maman," xxxi, lxv, 150–155, 160